Brief Contents

BLANK

Essentials of
Services
Marketing

Christopher Lovelock
Jochen Wirtz
Patricia Chew

Prentice Hall

Singapore   London   New York   Toronto   Sydney   Tokyo   Madrid
Mexico City   Munich   Paris   Capetown   Hong Kong   Montreal

Published in 2009 by
Prentice Hall
Pearson Education South Asia Pte Ltd
23/25 First Lok Yang Road, Jurong
Singapore 629733

Pearson Education offices in Asia: *Bangkok, Beijing, Hong Kong, Jakarta, Kuala Lumpur, Manila, New Delhi, Seoul, Singapore, Taipei, Tokyo*

Printed in Singapore

4   3   2   1
12 11 10 09

ISBN 13   978-981-06-7995-8
ISBN 10   981-06-7995-5

Prentice Hall
is an imprint of

www.pearsoned-asia.com

With gratitude and in loving memory of Christopher Lovelock,
One of the guiding lights of services marketing.

Our co-author, mentor and friend,
And above all, an inspiration.

Jochen Wirtz
Patricia Chew

BLANK

This photo was taken on 25 January 2008, a month before Christopher's sudden demise, when the authors met to work on this book

As a team, Christopher Lovelock, Jochen Wirtz and Patricia Chew provide a blend of skills and experience that is ideally suitable for writing an authoritative, yet engaging and reader-friendly services marketing text. This book marks Christopher's and Jochen's third collaboration on a Services Marketing textbook, and is Patricia's first project as a co-author with them.

The late **Christopher Lovelock** was one of the pioneers of services marketing. He consulted and gave seminars and workshops for managers around the world, with a particular focus on strategic planning in services and managing the customer experience.

Professor Lovelock's distinguished academic career has included 11 years on the faculty of the Harvard Business School and two years as a visiting professor at IMD in Switzerland. He has also held faculty appointments at Berkeley, Stanford, and the Sloan School at MIT, as well as visiting professorships at INSEAD in France and The University of Queensland in Australia.

Author or co-author of over 60 articles, more than 100 teaching cases, and 26 books, Dr Lovelock has seen his work translated into twelve languages. He served on the editorial review boards of the International Journal of Service Industry Management, Journal of Service Research, Service Industries Journal, Cornell Hotel and Restaurant Administration Quarterly, and Marketing Management, and was also an ad hoc reviewer for the Journal of Marketing.

Widely acknowledged as a thought leader in services, Christopher Lovelock had been honored by the American Marketing Association's prestigious Award for Career Contributions in the Services Discipline. In 2005, his article with Evert Gummesson, "Whither Services Marketing? In Search of a New Paradigm and Fresh Perspectives," won the American Marketing Association's Best Services Article Award and was a finalist for the IBM award for the best article in the Journal of Service Research. Earlier, he received a best article award from the Journal of Marketing. Recognized many times for excellence in case writing, he had twice won top honors in the Business Week "European Case of the Year" Award.

Jochen Wirtz holds a PhD in services marketing from the London Business School. He is a tenured Associate Professor at the National University of Singapore, where he teaches services marketing in executive, MBA, and undergraduate programs. He is also the director of the dual degree UCLA - NUS Executive MBA Program and an Associate Fellow at the Saïd Business School, University of Oxford.

Dr Wirtz has published widely on services marketing in over 70 academic articles, including the Harvard Business Review, Journal of Consumer Psychology, Journal of Retailing, Journal of Service Research, Journal of Services Marketing, and Journal of the Academy of Marketing Science. He has also published over 80 conference papers, 50 book chapters and 10 books, which includes his collaboration with Dr Lovelock in writing one of the world's leading services marketing text books, Services Marketing: People, Technology, Strategy, Sixth edition (Prentice Hall, 2007).

Dr Wirtz serves on the editorial review boards of 11 academic journals, including the Journal of Service Management, Journal of Service Research, and Cornell Hospitality Quarterly, and he is also an ad hoc reviewer for the Journal of Consumer Research and Journal of Marketing. Dr Wirtz chaired the American Marketing Association's biennial Service Research Conference in Singapore. In recognition of his excellence in research and teaching, Dr Wirtz received 16 awards, including the prestigious, university-wide "Outstanding Educator Award" at the National University of Singapore.

Dr Wirtz has been an active Management Consultant, working with international consulting firms, including Accenture, Arthur D, Little, and KPMG, and major service firms in the areas of strategy, business development and customer feedback systems. Originally from Germany, Dr. Wirtz spent seven years in London before moving to Asia.

Dr Patricia Chew holds a PhD in services marketing from the National University of Singapore. She is Head of Marketing at SIM University in Singapore where she oversees the design and curriculum development for all marketing courses, and appoints and manages the faculty. Dr Chew teaches Services Marketing at SIM University and also at the National University of Singapore in MBA and BBA programs.

Dr Chew's research focuses on services marketing, where she has published several articles and conference papers, particularly on incentivized referrals and word-of-mouth. One of her articles on incentivized word-of-mouth won the 'Emerald Literati Club Award for Excellence' for the 'Most Outstanding Paper' of the year in the International Journal of Service Industry Management.

Dr Chew has consulted on services marketing-related project for companies like LG Capital, National Library Board in Singapore, SK Telecoms and Singapore Pools.

About the Contributors of the Cases

T. F. Cawsey has recently retired and was a Professor at the School of Business & Economics, Wilfrid Laurier University, Canada.

Kah Hin Chai is Assistant Professor of Industrial Systems Engineering at the National University of Singapore, Singapore.

Robert J. Fisher is Professor at Alberta School of Business, University of Alberta, Canada.

Lorelle Frazer is Professor at Griffith University, Australia.

Roger Hallowell is managing partner, The Center for Executive Development, and former Professor at Harvard Business School, USA.

Loizos Heracleous is a Professor of Strategy and Organization, University of Warwick, UK.

James L. Heskett is Baker Foundation Professor at Harvard Business School, USA.

Robert Johnston is Professor, Warwick Business School, UK.

Mukta Kamplikar is Senior Practice Consultant at the Tata Management Training Centre, Pune, India.

Sheryl E. Kimes is the Singapore Tourism Board Distinguished Professor in Asian Hospitality Management at the School of Hotel Administration, Cornell University.

Jill Klein is Associate Professor of Marketing, INSEAD, France.

Ken Mark is a full-time case writer at the Richard Ivey School of Business, University of Western Ontario. He graduated in 1998 from the HBA program at Ivey.

Gordon H. G. McDougall is Professor at the School of Business & Economics, Wilfrid Laurier University, Canada.

Indranil Sen was a Research and Planning Manager at DHL Asia Pacific.

Sanjay Singh was an MBA student at NUS Business School, National University of Singapore, Singapore.

Lauren Wright is Professor of Marketing, California State College, Chicago, USA.

BLANK

Contents

XIV

BLANK

Preface

Services dominate the expanding world economy as never before, and nothing stands still. Technology continues to evolve in dramatic ways. Established industries and their often famous and old companies decline and may even disappear as new business models and industries emerge. Competitive activity is fierce, with firms often using new strategies and tactics to respond to changing customer needs, expectations and behaviors. Clearly, the skills in marketing services have never been more important. This book has been written in response to the global transformation of our economies to services.

As the field of services marketing grows, there is a need for business schools to equip their students with a services marketing text that is reader-friendly and easy to understand. This book aims to meet that need. It takes a strongly managerial perspective, yet is rooted in solid academic research. It is presented in an easily comprehensible way suitable for both practitioners and students alike. Practical management applications are reinforced by many examples within the 15 chapters. This is complemented by 20 outstanding classroom-tested cases.

This book has been designed to complement the materials found in traditional marketing principles texts. The book offers a carefully designed "toolbox" for service managers, teaching students how different concepts and frameworks can best be used to examine and resolve the varied challenges faced by executives and managers in different service industries.

For what types of courses can this book be used?

This text is suitable for courses directed at undergraduate and polytechnic students. Essentials in Services Marketing places marketing issues within a broader general management context. The book will appeal to students heading for a career in the service sector, whether at the executive or management level.

Whatever the job is in the services industry, a person has to understand the close ties that link the marketing, operations and human resources functions in service firms. With that perspective in mind, we have designed the book so that instructors can make selective use of chapters and cases to teach courses of different lengths and formats in either services marketing or services management.

The table on pages xxviii and xxix links the cases to the chapters in the book.

What are the book's distinguished features?

Key features of this highly readable book include:

▶ Strong managerial focus supported by the latest academic research. It not only helps service marketers to understand customer needs and behavior, but also to use these insights to develop strategies for competing effectively in the marketplace.

▶ Full-color learning aids. This is at the time of printing, the only full-color Services Marketing textbook. The well-designed graphics engage students with lively illustrations to make salient points come alive.

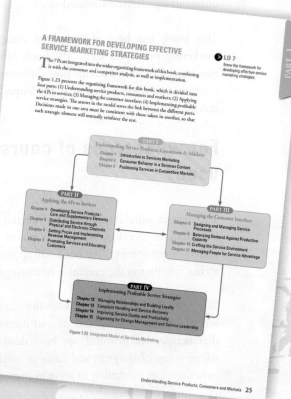

The text is organized around an integrated framework students immediately can relate to. It allows students to progressively follow topics, in a sequenced manner.

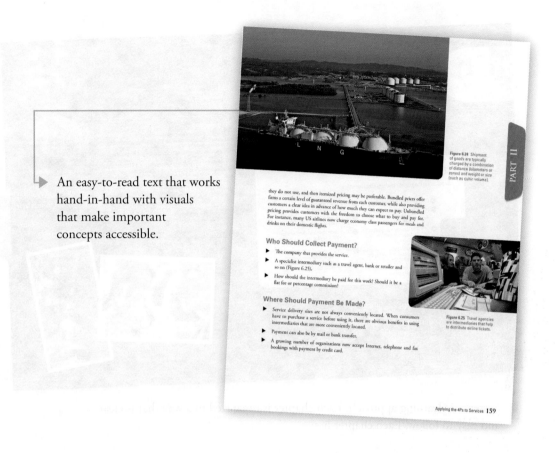

An easy-to-read text that works hand-in-hand with visuals that make important concepts accessible.

they do not use, and then itemized pricing may be preferable. Bundled prices offer firms a certain level of guaranteed revenue from each customer, while also providing customers a clear idea in advance of how much they can expect to pay. Unbundled pricing provides customers with the freedom to choose what to buy and pay for. For instance, many US airlines now charge economy class passengers for meals and drinks on their domestic flights.

Who Should Collect Payment?

► The company that provides the service.

► A specialist intermediary such as a travel agent, bank or retailer and so on (Figure 6.25).

► How should the intermediary be paid for this work? Should it be a flat fee or percentage commission?

Where Should Payment Be Made?

► Service delivery sites are not always conveniently located. When consumers have to purchase a service before using it, there are obvious benefits in using intermediaries that are more conveniently located.

► Payment can also be by mail or bank transfer.

► A growing number of organizations now accept Internet, telephone and fax bookings with payment by credit card.

Figure 6.24 Shipment of goods are typically charged by a combination of distance (kilometers or zones) and weight or size (such as cubic volume).

Figure 6.25 Travel agencies are intermediaries that help to distribute airline tickets.

Applying the 4Ps to Services 159

PART II

► Inclusion of carefully selected American, European and Asian cases to accompany the text chapters. This offers an international perspective.

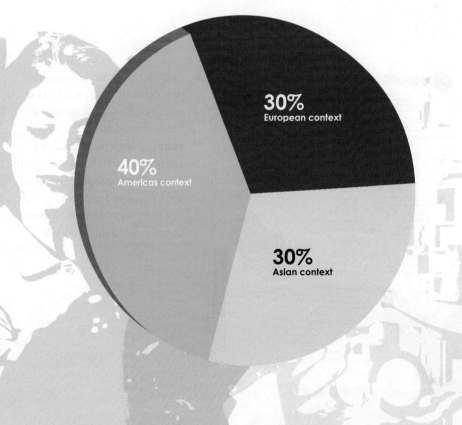

30% European context

40% Americas context

30% Asian context

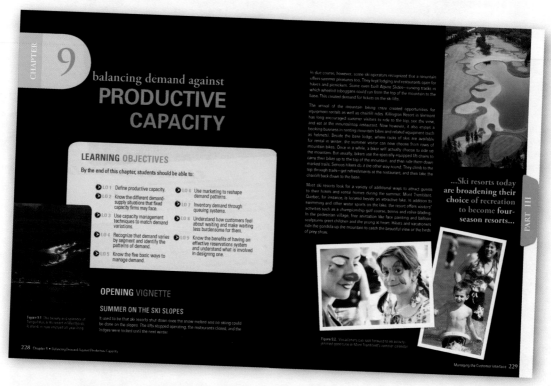

Systematic learning approach. Each chapter is organized in a way that is clear and easy to follow. Each chapter has:

- An opening vignette, which introduces the concepts taught in the chapter
- Learning markers that flag chapter milestones where content related to learning objectives are discussed
- Interesting examples to link theory to practice

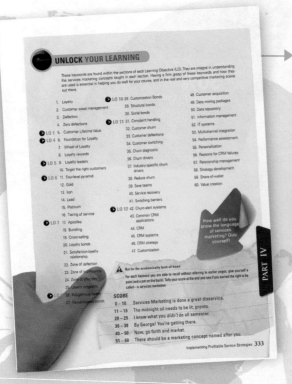

Important terms, are tagged as key words to assist students in internalizing the language of services marketing. Every learning objective contains a number of such keywords. At the close of each chapter, students are invited to test their recognition and grasp of these terms—questionnaire style

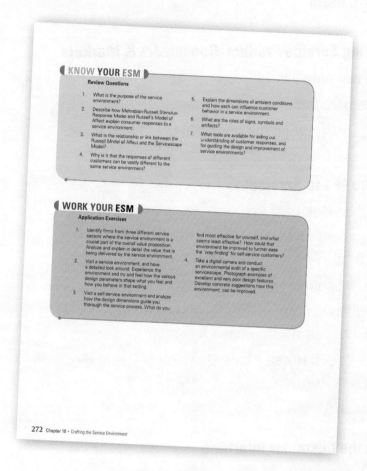

▶ *Know Your ESM* asks pointed questions designed to consolidate understanding of key concepts through discussion and study

▶ *Work Your ESM* extends understanding beyond the question-and-answer format through scenarios that exercise and apply the concepts learnt

This table shows the case contexts and links each cases to the chapters in the book.

Cases	Primary Chapters
Part I: Understanding Service Product, Consumers & Markets	
Case 1: Sullivan Ford Auto World	1
Case 2: Four Customers in Search of Solutions	2
Case 3: Banyan Tree: Branding the Intangible	3, 4
Part II: Applying the 4Ps to Services	
Case 4: Ginger: Smart Basics™	4
Case 5: Managing Word-of-Mouth: The Referral Incentive Program that Backfired	5
Case 6: Capital One: Launching a Mass Media Campaign	5
Case 7: Revenue Management of Gondola: Maintaining the Balance Between Tradition and Revenue	6
Case 8: The Accra Beach Hotel: Block Booking of Capacity During a Peak Period	6
Case 9: Aussie Pooch Mobile	7
Part III: Managing the Customer interface	
Case 10: Biometrics Meets Services	8
Case 11: Shouldice Hospital Limited (Abridged)	8, 9, 10
Case 12: Red Lobster	11
Case 13: Menton Bank	11
Part IV: Implementing Profitable Service Strategies	
Case 14: Dr. Mahalee Goes to London	12
Case 15: GoodLife Fitness Clubs	12
Case 16: Customer Asset Management at DHL in Asia	12
Case 17: The Complaint Letter	13
Case 18: The Accellion Service Guarantee	13
Case 19: Using Technology to Revolutionize the Library Experience of Singaporean Readers	14
Case 20: Dr Beckett's Dental Office	All chapters

Secondary Chapters	Continent	Country	Industry
2, 10	Americas	United States	Automobile Servicing
13	Europe	Germany	Telecommunication
5	Asia/Middle East/ Americas	-	Resort/Hospitality
5, 7, 8, 11, 14	Asia	India	Hotel/Hospitality
-	Asia	Vietnam	Insurance
-	Americas	Canada	Banking
-	Europe	Italy	Tourism
9	Americas	Barbados	Resort/Hospitality
-	Australia	Australia	Pet Grooming
-	Global	-	Multi-industry
11, 14	Americas	Canada/United States	Medical
-	Americas	United States	Food & Berevage
-	Americas	United States	Banking
8	Europe	United Kingdom	Banking
-	Americas	Canada	Health & Fitness
-	Asia	-	Logistics
-	Europe	United Kingdom	Hotel/Hospitality
-	Global	-	Information Technology
-	Asia	Singapore	Library
4, 5, 8, 10, 11, 14	Americas	United States	Medical

What aids are available for instructors?

We have developed pedagogical aids to help instructors develop and teach courses built around this book and to create stimulating learning experiences for students both in and out of the classroom.

Teaching Aids within the Text

▶ An opening vignette highlights key issues discussed in the chapter.

▶ Learning objectives and milestone markers for these when a section provides material that meet these learning objectives.

▶ Boxed inserts throughout the chapters that often lend themselves to in-class discussion.

▶ Interesting graphics, photographs, and reproductions of advertisements enhance student learning, provide opportunities for discussion and add visual appeal.

▶ Keywords that help to reinforce important terms and concepts.

▶ Chapter summaries that meet each chapter's learning objectives.

▶ Review Questions and Application Exercises are located at the end of each chapter

Pedagogical Materials Available from the Publisher

▶ Detailed course design and teaching hints, plus sample course outlines.

▶ Chapter-by-chapter teaching suggestions plus discussion of learning objectives and sample responses to study questions and exercises.

▶ A description of 16 suggested student exercises and five comprehensive projects (designed for either individual or team work).

▶ Detailed teaching notes for each case, including teaching objectives, suggested study questions, in-depth analysis of each question, and helpful hints on teaching strategy designed to aid student learning, create stimulating class discussions, and help instructors create end-of-class wrap-ups and "takeaways."

▶ A note that offers advice to students on case preparation and written analysis of cases.

▶ A test bank for use in quizzes and exams.

▶ More than 400 PowerPoint slides, linked to each chapter and featuring both "word" slides and graphics. All sides have been designed to be clear, comprehensible and easily readable.

Acknowledgements

Over the years, many colleagues in both the academic and business worlds have provided us with valued insights into the management and marketing of services through their publications, in conference or seminar discussions, and stimulating individual conversations. We have benefited enormously from in-class and after-class discussions with our students and executive program participants.

We are much indebted to those researchers and teachers who helped to pioneer the study of services marketing and management, and from whose work we continue to draw inspiration. Among them are John Bateson of SHL Group; Leonard Berry of Texas A&M University; Mary Jo Bitner and Stephen Brown of Arizona State University; Richard Chase of the University of Southern California; Pierre Eiglier of Université d'Aix-Marseille III; Raymond Fisk of the Texas State University; Christian Grönroos of the Swedish School of Economics in Finland; Stephen Grove of Clemson University, Evert Gummesson of Stockholm University; James Heskett and Earl Sasser of Harvard University, and Benjamin Schneider of the University of Maryland. We salute, too, the contributions of the late Eric Langeard and Daryl Wyckoff.

A particular acknowledgment is due to five individuals who have made exceptional contributions to the field, not only in their role as researchers and teachers but also as journal editors, in which capacity they facilitated publication of many of the important articles cited in this book. They are Bo Edvardsson, University of Karlstad and Editor, International Journal of Service Industry Research (IJSIM); Robert Johnston, University of Warwick and Founding Editor of IJSIM; Jos Lemmink, Maastricht University and former Editor, IJSIM; A. "Parsu" Parasuraman, University of Miami and Editor, Journal of Service Research (JSR), and Roland Rust of the University of Maryland, Editor, Journal of Marketing and Founding Editor, JSR.

Although it is impossible to mention everyone who has influenced our thinking, we particularly want to express our appreciation to the following: Tor Andreassen, Norwegian School of Management; David Bowen of Thunderbird Graduate School of Management, John Deighton, Theodore Levitt, and Leonard Schlesinger, all currently or formerly at Harvard Business School; Loizos Heracleous of University of Warwick; Douglas Hoffmann of Colorado State University; Sheryl Kimes of Cornell University; Jean-Claude Larréché of INSEAD; David Maister of Maister Associates; Anna Mattila of Pennsylvania State University; Anat Rafaeli of Technion-Israeli Institute of Technology, Frederick Reichheld of Bain & Co; Bernd Stauss of Katholische Universität Eichstät; Charles Weinberg of the University of British Columbia; Lauren Wright of California State University, Chicago; George Yip of London Business School; and Valarie Zeithaml of the University of North Carolina.

We have also gained important insights from our co-authors on international adaptations of Services Marketing, and are grateful for the friendship and collaboration of Guillermo D'Andrea of Universidad Austral, Argentina; Harvir S. Bansal of Wilfrid Laurier University; Luis Huete of IESE, Spain; Laura Iacovone of University of Milan and Bocconi University; Keh Hean Tat of Peking University, China; Denis Lapert of INT-Management, France; Barbara Lewis of Manchester School of Management, UK; Lu Xiongwen of Fudan University, China; Jayanta Chatterjee of Indian Institute of Technolgy at Kanpur, India, Javier Reynoso of Tec de Monterrey, Mexico; Paul Patterson of the University of New South Wales, Australia; Sandra Vandermerwe of Imperial College, London, UK; and Rhett Walker of LaTrobe University, Australia.

It takes more than authors to create a book and its supplements. Warm thanks are due to the editing and production team who worked hard to transform our manuscript into a handsome published text. Our gratitude goes to the Pearson South Asian team led by Joy Tan, Regional Publishing Director. The editorial ensemble also includes Ivan Lee, Publishing Manager; Monica Gupta, Acquisitions Editor; Regina Lim, Editorial Administrator; Lo Hwei Shan, Editor; and Jeremy Wong, Editor.

Finally, we would like to thank you, our reader for your interest in this exciting and fast evolving field of services marketing. If you have interesting research, cases or other materials such as advertisements, photos, cartoons, anecdotes that would look good in the next edition of this book, or any other feedback, please do e-mail us at jochen@nus.edu.sg. We would love to hear from you!

CHRISTOPHER LOVELOCK
JOCHEN WIRTZ
PATRICIA CHEW

Essentials of
Services Marketing

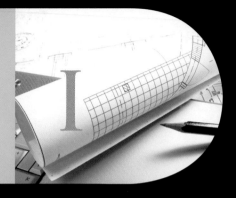

THE *ESM*
FRAMEWORK

Understanding Service Products, Consumers and Markets

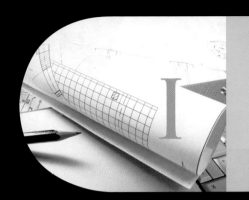

PART I lays the building blocks for studying services and learning how one can become an effective marketer. It consists of the following three chapters:

Chapter 1 Introduction to Services Marketing

Highlights the important of services in our economies. We also define the nature of services and how they create value for customers without transfer of ownership. The chapter highlights some distinctive challenges involved in services marketing and introduces the 7 Ps of services marketing. These are woven into an integrated model of services marketing that forms the basis for each of the four parts in this book. The framework is shown in the figure on the facing page, and it will accompany us throughout the book.

Chapter 2 Consumer Behavior in a Services Context

Provides a foundation for understanding consumer needs and behavior in both high-contact and low-contact services. The chapter is organized around the three-stage model of service consumption that explores how customers search for and evaluate alternative services, make purchase decisions, experience and respond to service encounters, and finally, evaluate service performance.

Chapter 3 Positioning Services in Competitive Markets

Discusses how a value proposition should be positioned in a way that creates competitive advantage for the firm. The chapter shows how firms can segment a service market, position their value proposition and finally focus on attracting their target segment.

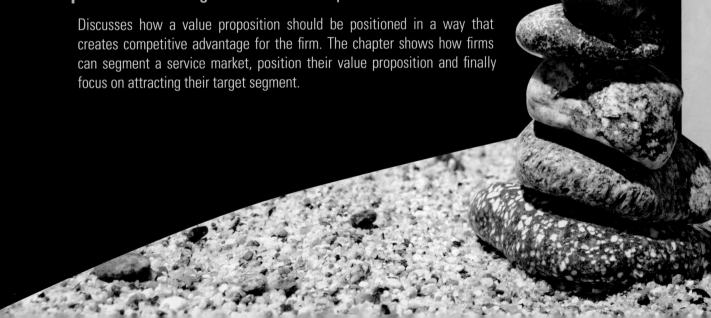

introduction to
SERVICES
MARKETING

LEARNING OBJECTIVES

By the end of this chapter, students should be able to:

LO 1 Understand how services contribute to a country's economy.

LO 2 Identify the powerful forces that are transforming service markets.

LO 3 Define services using the non-ownership service framework and understand how non-ownership affects services marketing strategies.

LO 4 Identify the four broad categories of services.

LO 5 Identify the characteristics of services and the distinctive marketing challenges they pose.

LO 6 Understand the components of the expanded services marketing mix (the 7 Ps of services marketing).

LO 7 Know the framework for developing effective service marketing strategies.

OPENING VIGNETTE[1]

Every summer, millions of people travel across borders to visit foreign lands, looking for adventure or exotic experiences that will provide them with a welcome break from their daily routines. Today, a growing number of travelers combine their vacation with health treatment.

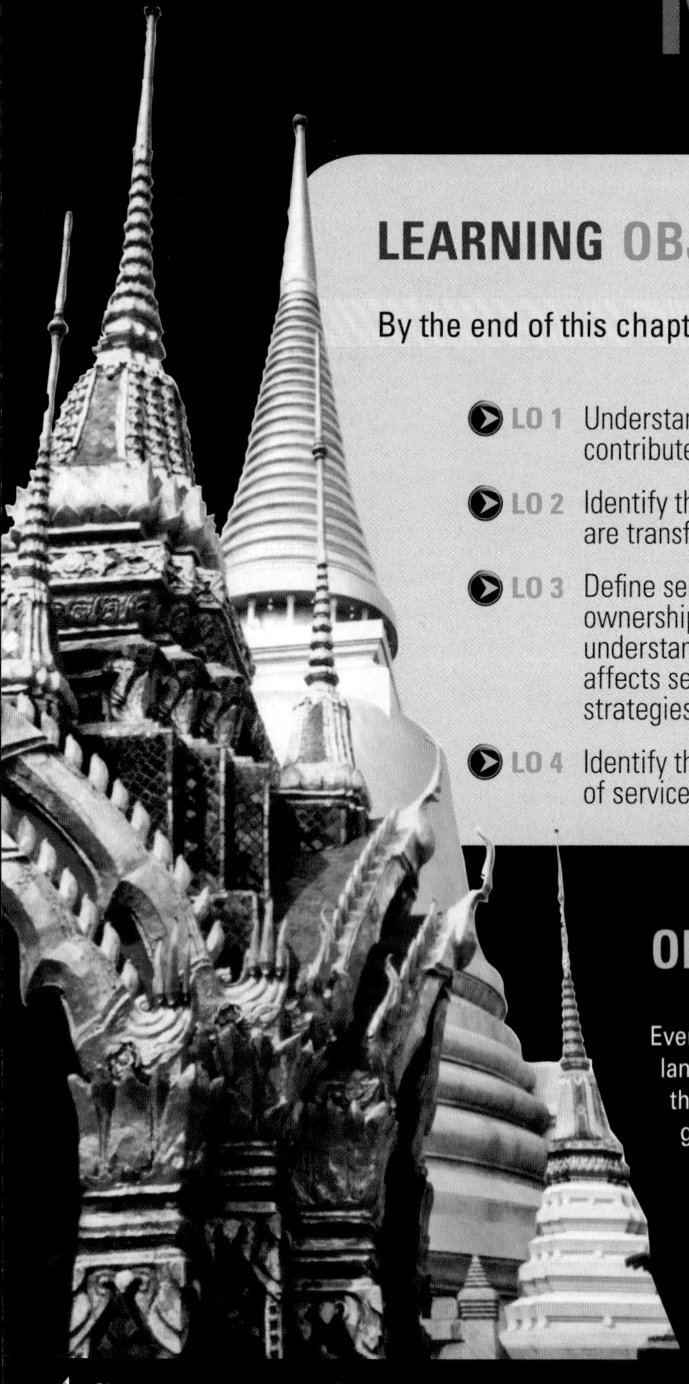

Figure 1.1 Thailand, famous for its temples, resorts and beaches, is now a booming destination for medical tourists as well.

Thailand, famous for its temples, resorts and beaches, is now a booming destination for medical tourists as well. Bumrungrad Hospital, Thailand's premier hospital is located in Bangkok. Bumrungrad in the Thai language means "care for the people." It has state-of-the art technology, first class medical care and accommodation comparable to any five-star hotel. This hospital is like a United Nations and boasts of having more foreign patients than any other hospital in the world. Its 900 physicians have been trained at the best Thai and international medical schools, and many have had international working experience, too. It is considered the No. 1 international hospital in the world, but its services are priced at about one-eighth of charges in the United States.

In 1997, as a result of the Southeast Asian economic crisis, Bumrungrad had to change its strategy to draw in foreign patients in order to survive the crisis. To do that, Bumrungrad had to market itself aggressively as a hospital that meets all international standards. It obtained ISO certification for all its departments and systems in 1997. In 1999, it became the first hospital in the world to receive ISO certification as a Comprehensive Tertiary Acute Medical Center. Bumrungrad also participated in road shows, and set up 17 representative offices around the world to create awareness and promote its services. It has tie-ups with airlines and foreign healthcare companies. In 2001, it realized the potential of the Muslim market and launched a successful advertising campaign in Arabic newspapers. In mid-2003, it upgraded its website in such a manner that foreign patients could make travel arrangements, and purchase tour packages. Many of the facilities at the hospital could also be viewed online. Today, it has more than one million patients a year and almost 430,000 are foreign patients from 190 different countries.

...Bumrungrad reinvented its business model...

Figure 1.2 Bumrungrad has grown beyond a typical brick-and-mortar health institution.

LO 1

Understand how services contribute to a country's economy.

WHY STUDY SERVICES?

Here's a paradox. While we live in a service-driven world, many business schools still teach marketing from a manufacturing perspective. If you have previously taken a marketing course, it is very likely that you learned more about marketing consumer goods than about marketing services. Fortunately, there is a growing group of enthusiastic scholars, consultants and teachers, including the authors of this book, who have chosen to focus on services marketing. Together, they build on the extensive research that has been conducted in this field over the past three decades. In fact, a recent article in Harvard Business Review suggests that service science should be a field of study in itself.[2] You can be confident that this book will provide you with information, insights and skills that are highly relevant in today's business environment.

Services Dominate the Economy in Most Nations

The size of the service sector is increasing in almost all countries around the world—a trend that applies to both developed and emerging countries. In the opening story, Thailand has a growing service sector based on medical tourism. Fig 1.3 shows the contribution of the service sector to the Gross Domestic Product (GDP) globally.

Figure 1.4 breaks this down further into a selection of countries. When you examine Figure 1.4 more closely, you can see that services usually account for between three-fifths and four-fifths of GDP in developed nations.

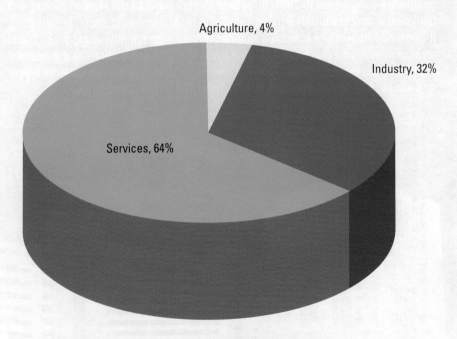

Figure 1.3 Contribution of services industries to GDP globally, 2007.

SOURCE

The World Factbook 2007, Central Intelligence Agency, https://www.cia.gov/library/publications/the-world-factbook/fields/2012.html, accessed January 2008.

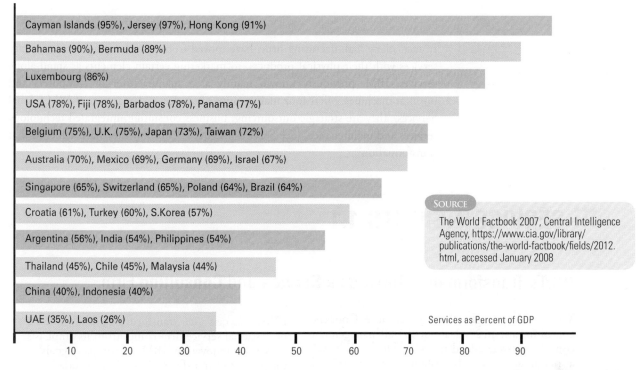

Cayman Islands (95%), Jersey (97%), Hong Kong (91%)

Bahamas (90%), Bermuda (89%)

Luxembourg (86%)

USA (78%), Fiji (78%), Barbados (78%), Panama (77%)

Belgium (75%), U.K. (75%), Japan (73%), Taiwan (72%)

Australia (70%), Mexico (69%), Germany (69%), Israel (67%)

Singapore (65%), Switzerland (65%), Poland (64%), Brazil (64%)

Croatia (61%), Turkey (60%), S.Korea (57%)

Argentina (56%), India (54%), Philippines (54%)

Thailand (45%), Chile (45%), Malaysia (44%)

China (40%), Indonesia (40%)

UAE (35%), Laos (26%)

Services as Percent of GDP

10   20   30   40   50   60   70   80   90

SOURCE

The World Factbook 2007, Central Intelligence Agency, https://www.cia.gov/library/publications/the-world-factbook/fields/2012.html, accessed January 2008

Figure 1.4 Estimated size of service sector in selected countries as a percentage of Gross Domestic Product.

Which is the world's most service-dominated economy? Probably, it is the Cayman Islands (95 percent)—a group of small, British-administered islands in the western Caribbean, famous for both tourism and offshore financial and insurance services. Panama's strong showing (78 percent) reflects the fact that the Panama Canal (Figure 1.5) is widely used by both cruise ships and freight vessels. These ships are supported by container ports services, flagship registry, repairs, provisioning, refueling and insurance.

Financial services and tourism have also been booming. Close to the other extreme is Laos, where the service sector contributes only 26 percent to its GDP. Eighty percent of its workforce is in the agriculture sector, and agriculture contributes 50 percent to the GDP of Laos. China also has a large agricultural sector and booming manufacturing and construction industries. However, China is experiencing rapid economic growth, which is stimulating demand for business and consumer services. In future, services will account for a larger percentage of China's GDP than the current 40 percent.

Figure 1.5 The Panama Canal forms the backbone of Panama's service economy.

Most New Jobs are Generated by Services

Since the service sector is growing so rapidly around the world, in virtually all developed countries, new job creation comes from services. New services are being introduced all the time.

Service jobs do not just refer to relatively lowly paid frontline jobs such as in restaurants or call centers. Many new service jobs are well-paid positions that require good educational qualifications. A lot of the growth in services is in the industrial services.[3] Some of the fastest growth is in knowledge-based industries like professional and business services, education, and health care.[4]

In fact, many manufacturing firms have moved from just bundling supplementary services with their physical products, to marketing certain elements as stand-alone services. IBM, previously known mainly as a manufacturer of computers and business machines, offers four main groups of services today as part of IBM Global Services. They are strategic outsourcing, business consulting, integrated technology services and maintenance. (See Service Insights 1.1 on how they have achieved that transformation[5]).

::: SERVICE INSIGHTS 1.1

IBM's Transformation Towards a Service and Consulting Firm

When IBM bought Price waterhouse Coopers' consulting arm in 2002, about 30,000 management consultants were added to its workforce. This was a major step towards becoming a professional services firm. By 2007, its Global Services division constituted 54.8 percent of group revenues, or $54.2 billion of $98.9 billion.

IBM has always been known as an equipment manufacturer. However, the computer industry was changing and IBM's margins were eroding. IBM therefore turned its attention to selling "solutions" rather than products. It helps customers to bundle and customize solutions of hardware, software and services. Later, IBM added high-margin business consulting, combining its technology products and research with business-minded consultants.

IBM's success in transforming itself into a professional service firm comes from its emphasis on service innovation. IBM set company goals in the process of transformation. They included:

- Expanding its services portfolio through service innovation.
- Deepening the relationship with its client by helping clients provide more value to their customers.
- Reducing support costs through web-enabled transactions and electronically delivered products.
- Using new relationship management technology to understand its customers better.
- Improving availability of products.

The keys to IBM's successful transformation were:

- Executive focus on business and cultural change.
- Listening to customers.
- Establishing the needed capabilities using internal and external resources.
- Allowing a tolerance for risk.

That is why services now account for over 50 percent of the company's revenue and an even higher share of the profits.

SOURCE

K. Subramanian, "The Transformation of IBM," *The Hindu*, 24 July 2006, http://www.hindu.com/2006/07/24/stories/2006072400291600.htm; Kevin Custis and Allan Henderson, "Hiding in Plain Sight: Service Innovation, a New Priority for Chief Executive," white paper of IBM Global Business Services, IBM Institute for Business Value, IBM, 2006; http://www.ibm.com/investor, accessed January 2008.

POWERFUL FORCES ARE TRANSFORMING SERVICE MARKETS

⊙ LO 2

Identify the powerful forces that are transforming service markets.

What are the factors affecting the trend of rapid service growth? Government policies, social change, business trends, advances in information technology and globalization are among the powerful forces that are transforming today's service markets (Figure 1.6).

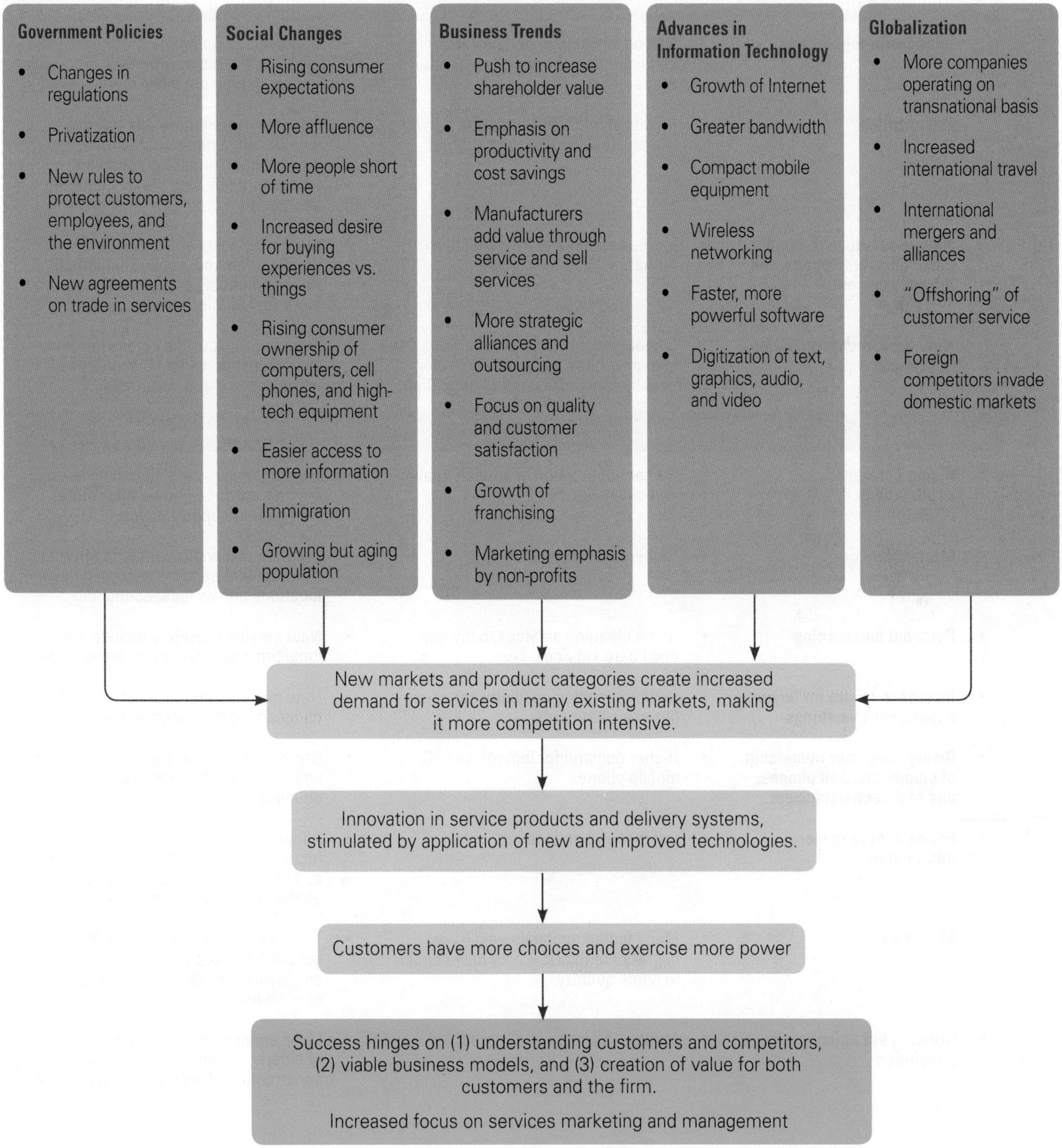

Government Policies	Social Changes	Business Trends	Advances in Information Technology	Globalization
• Changes in regulations	• Rising consumer expectations	• Push to increase shareholder value	• Growth of Internet	• More companies operating on transnational basis
• Privatization	• More affluence	• Emphasis on productivity and cost savings	• Greater bandwidth	• Increased international travel
• New rules to protect customers, employees, and the environment	• More people short of time	• Manufacturers add value through service and sell services	• Compact mobile equipment	• International mergers and alliances
• New agreements on trade in services	• Increased desire for buying experiences vs. things	• More strategic alliances and outsourcing	• Wireless networking	• "Offshoring" of customer service
	• Rising consumer ownership of computers, cell phones, and high-tech equipment	• Focus on quality and customer satisfaction	• Faster, more powerful software	• Foreign competitors invade domestic markets
	• Easier access to more information	• Growth of franchising	• Digitization of text, graphics, audio, and video	
	• Immigration	• Marketing emphasis by non-profits		
	• Growing but aging population			

New markets and product categories create increased demand for services in many existing markets, making it more competition intensive.

Innovation in service products and delivery systems, stimulated by application of new and improved technologies.

Customers have more choices and exercise more power

Success hinges on (1) understanding customers and competitors, (2) viable business models, and (3) creation of value for both customers and the firm.

Increased focus on services marketing and management

Figure 1.6 Factors stimulating the transformation of the service economy.

Table 1.1 shows specific examples of each of these forces and its impact on the service economy. Collectively, these forces are reshaping demand, supply, the competitive landscape and even the way customers buy and use services. Advancements in information technology allow much service work to be carried out far from where customers are located.

Table 1.1 Specific examples of forces that transform and impact the service economy.

Government Policies	Example	Impact on Service Economy
• **Changes in regulations**	• Ban on smoking in restaurants, and limitation of transfats in food preparation	• Improved customer comfort and health measures in restaurants will encourage people to dine out more often.
• **Privatization**	• Privatization of infrastructure services like utilities and transportation	• Potential retrenchment of existing suppliers in a more competitive environment, but job creation and investments by new players entering the market
• **New regulations to protect customers, employees, and the environment**	• Increased taxes to aviation industry for harmful gas emission	• Increased costs of air travel may dampen demand; policy stimulates development of jet engines that are more fuel efficient and less polluting
• **New agreements on trade in services**	• Companies from foreign countries can take over basic services like water, health, transportation and education	• Transfer of expertise across borders. New investments result in improved infrastructure and better quality

Social Changes	Example	Impact on Service Economy
• **Rising consumer expectations**	• Higher expectation of service quality and convenience	• Training of service staff to deliver good service; extended hours offer more part-time job opportunities
• **More affluence**	• Higher spending on tourism	• Creation of a wider variety of offerings; development of new services in new locations boosts local economies
• **Personal outsourcing**	• Home cleaning services, baby and child care services	• New service providers include both local firms and national/regional chains
• **Increased desire for buying experiences vs. things**	• Higher spending on luxury services like spa treatments	• New players emerge; existing health clubs and resort hotels add spas
• **Rising consumer ownership of computers, cell phones, and high tech equipment**	• Higher demand for laptops and 3G mobile phones	• Greater need for designers, engineers and marketers for these types of equipment
• **Easier access to more information**	• Internet and podcasting	• Allows firms to build closer, more focused relationships with customers and new opportunities to reach them on the move in real time
• **Migration**	• Many Indian nationals who have migrated to the USA now move back to home country	• Transfers talent to home country but may create a vacuum in the employment market of developed economies
• **Growing but aging population**	• Matured European countries	• More services catering to the needs of elderly, including health care and, construction of retirement communities

Business Trends	Example	Impact on Service Economy
• Push to increase shareholder value	• Shareholders pressure company boards to deliver higher returns	• Search for new revenue sources such as additional fees, higher prices, adoption of revenue management strategies, plus cuts in customer service to reduce costs
• Emphasis on productivity and cost savings	• Move to self-service technologies	• Rethink service delivery system, invest in new technologies that replace employees
• Manufacturers add value through service and sell services	• IBM's consulting and IT services for financial markets	• Competition with service providers from other industries, such as traditional management consulting firms
• More strategic alliances	• Airlines form alliances such as Star Alliance and Oneworld	• Routes are rationalized to avoid duplications, schedules and ticketing are coordinated; marketing is leveraged and operating efficiency improved
• Focus on quality and customer satisfaction	• Hotels and motels at all levels define standards more tightly and seek to meet them consistently	• Training programs to equip service staff with necessary skills; investment in modernization of existing facilities and construction of new ones offering better amenities
• Growth of franchising	• Fast food chains expand around the world	• Challenge of maintaining consistent service standards worldwide while adapting to local food preferences and cultures
• Marketing emphasis by nonprofits	• Museums seek to expand audiences and generate more frequent repeat visits	• Fund raising for improved facilities; addition of new revenue generating services like restaurants and facilities rental

Advances in Information Technology	Example	Impact on Service Economy
• Growth of Internet	• Information at the fingertips of the customers, making them more knowledgeable and informed	• Creation of new services that gather the various sources of information and repackage them to provide value to customers
• Greater bandwidth	• Allows for delivery of sophisticated and interactive educational content	• Service delivery processes need to be redesigned
• Compact mobile equipment	• 3G mobile phones that integrate many high tech functions	• Advanced marketing and maintenance services needed
• Wireless networking	• Public libraries, cafes, and hotels provide this service (free or at a price) to attract customers	• More brick and mortar service firms are expected to provide similar benefits to stay competitive
• Faster, more powerful software	• Customized software development by software consulting firms like Infosys	• Increase in training software engineers to develop packaged services instead of piece meal services
• Digitization of text, graphics, audio, and video	• Online download service providers	• Need for service providers to invest in maintaining a secure and credible website and guarantee virus-free files for download

Globalization	Example	Impact on Service Economy
• **More companies operating on transnational basis**	• MNCs such as banks and "Big 4" accounting firms have numerous operations around the world	• Increase in the scope of service that can be provided; training of staff in local markets to upgrade skills, capabilities, and service standards
• **Increased international travel**	• More services offered to more places; new travel options for business and pleasure	• More services provided by airlines, ferries and cruise ships, coach tours, international trains, leading to greater competition
• **International mergers and alliances**	• Merger between international airlines (e.g. KLM and Air France), banks, insurance companies, etc.	• Greater market leverage and operational efficiency but consolidation may lead to job losses
• **"Offshoring" of customer service**	• Call center operations relocated to India, Philippines, etc.	• Investment in technology and infrastructure stimulates local economies, raises living standards, and attracts related industries
• **Foreign competitors invade domestic markets**	• International banks such as HSBC and ING do business in the USA	• Build branch network by purchasing one or more regional banks; invest heavily in new and improved branches and in electronic delivery channels

A study by the international consulting firm McKinsey & Co. estimated that 11 percent of service jobs around the world could be carried out remotely (Figure 1.7).

In practice however, McKinsey estimates that only 1 percent of all service employment in the developed countries is being "offshored" in 2008.[6]

"We found someone overseas who can drink coffee and talk about sports all day for a fraction of what we're paying you."

Figure 1.7 Services today can be outsourced to cheaper destinations at the drop of a hat—so keep your job and (and hat on) by remaining productive.

 LO 3
Define services using the non-ownership service framework and understand how non-ownership affects services marketing strategies.

WHAT ARE SERVICES?

Thus far, we have been discussing the growth of the service sector and factors that are transforming this sector. But what exactly is a *service*?

Services Offer Benefits Without Ownership

When you stay in a hotel room during your overseas trip, you pay for it, but do not own it. When you are treated by your physician, you do not have ownership of the doctor. Service businesses do not normally transfer ownership of their products to customers. Instead, we can say that services represent a form of rental. Customers pay for the temporary right to use an object, hire the labor and expertise of personnel, or obtain access to facilities and networks.[7] What customers value and are willing to pay for are desired experiences and solutions. The word rent here is a general term we use to describe a payment made for use of something or access to facilities or networks (usually for a defined period of time), instead of buying it outright (which is not even possible in many instances).

We can identify five broad categories within the non-ownership framework:

▶ **Rented goods services**. These services allow customers to obtain the temporary right to use a physical object that they prefer not to own. Examples include:

  o Boats
  o Fancy dress costumes
  o Construction and excavation equipment

▶ **Defined space and place rentals**. This is when customers obtain the use of a certain portion of a larger space in a building, vehicle or area. They usually share this space with other customers. Examples of this kind of rental include:

  o Seat in an aircraft
  o Suite in an office building
  o Storage container in a warehouse

▶ **Labor and expertise rentals**. Here, other people are hired to perform work that customers either cannot or choose not to do themselves. Some of these include:

  o House cleaning
  o Car repair
  o Management consulting

▶ **Access to shared physical environments**. Customers rent the right to share the use of the environments. The locations may be indoors or outdoors, or a combination of both. Examples include:

  o Theme parks (Figure 1.8)
  o Trade shows
  o Toll roads

▶ **Systems and networks: access and usage**. Customers rent the right to participate in a specified network. Service providers use a variety of terms for access and use, depending on customer needs. Examples include:

  o Telecommunications
  o Utilities
  o Banking

Figure 1.8 Customers rent the right to use theme park facilities.

In many instances, two or more of these categories may be combined. For example, when you take a taxi, you are hiring the driver (labor) and a vehicle (space). The distinction between ownership and non-ownership affects the nature of marketing tasks and strategy. Service Insights 1.2 highlights six important marketing implications of renting versus owning.

::: SERVICE INSIGHTS 1.2

Six Marketing Implications of Renting Versus Owning

1 *There is a market for renting durable goods instead of selling them.* Often, when a need is temporary, it makes more sense to rent than to own the product that meets that need. Even for longer term use, there may be financial advantages in making rental/lease payments instead of capital investments. Therefore, marketers can add further value through services such as delivery and pickup, cleaning, insurance and maintenance. They can even supply trained personnel to operate rented equipment.

2 *Renting portions of a larger physical entity can form the basis for services.* Renting "my apartment" or "our office suite" signals the right to exclusive but temporary use of a unit within a larger building. Customers benefit from economies of scale by sharing a large facility with many users, while enjoying various degrees of separation and privacy.

3 *Customers need to be more closely engaged with service suppliers.* When buyers own something, they can use it in almost any way they like. In services however, rental means that service providers require some control over how customers use equipment and facilities. Customers must cooperate by learning and obeying the "rules."

4 *Time plays a central role in most services.* A key marketing challenge for service providers is to ensure that the objects, facilities or labor that

they offer, are rented out as fully as possible over time. They also need to ensure that the rates charged will maximize returns by being adjusted to reflect varying levels of demand by different market segments. In that way, value can be created through higher revenues and profits. Since, many customers are time sensitive, service providers must improve the speed of delivery and convenience of service schedules, minimize waiting times and be sensitive to how people value and perceive time differently.

5 *Customer choice criteria may differ between rentals and outright purchases.* For example, the choice of criteria for renting a car while on vacation in Hawaii is quite different from those for purchasing a car back home. Instead of worrying about physical characteristics such as color, upholstery and number of cup holders, customers will focus on the ease of making reservations, the rental location and hours, the attitudes and performance of service personnel, the cleanliness and maintenance of vehicles, and so forth.

6 *Services offer opportunities for resource sharing.* In a world where many resources are believed to be finite, rental instead of ownership may be the best way to avoid waste (Figure 1.9).

SOURCE

Adapted from Lovelock, C.& Event, G. (2004). Whither services marketing? In search of a paradigm and fresh perspectives. *Journal of Service Research*, 7 (August), pp. 20-41.

Figure 1.9 Shopping malls are usually shared spaces rented by many tenants.

FOUR BROAD CATEGORIES OF SERVICES

LO 4

Identify the four broad categories of services.

Even if we accept that services do not transfer ownership, there are still major differences among services. These differences have important marketing implications. In services, people, physical objects, and data can be processed. The nature of the processing can be tangible or intangible. Tangible actions are performed on people's bodies or to their physical possessions. Intangible actions are performed on people's minds or to their intangible assets. This gives rise to the classification of services into four broad categories. They are people-processing, possession-processing, mental stimulus processing and information processing (Figure 1.10) with important marketing implications.[8]

Nature of the Service Act	Who or What is the Direct Recipient of the Service?	
	People	Possessions
Tangible Actions	**People-processing** (services directed at people's bodies): • Barbers • Health care	**Possession-processing** (services directed at physical possessions): • Refueling • Disposal / recycling
Intangible Actions	**Mental stimulus processing** (services directed at people's mind): • Education • Advertising / PR	**Information processing** (services directed at intangible assets): • Accounting • Banking

Figure 1.10 Four broad categories of services.

People processing

These are services that are directed at the people themselves. They include being transported, fed or made more beautiful (Figure 1.11). Implications of people processing services include:

▶ Customers have to be present in the physical location (service factory). This requires planning about the location of the service operation.

▶ Active cooperation of the customer is needed in the service delivery process.

▶ Need for managers to think about the process and output from the customer's point of view. Apart from financial costs, non-financial costs like time, mental and physical effort, and even fear and pain need to be taken into account.

Possession Processing

Customers may ask service organizations to provide treatment for some of their physical possessions. These physical possessions could include a house that is attacked by insects, dirty laundry (Figure 1.12), or a malfunctioning elevator for instance. The implications of such services are:

▶ There is no simultaneous production and consumption.

▶ Customer involvement tends to be limited to just dropping off or picking up the item (Figure 1.13).

Figure 1.11 A lady customer getting her hair washed and later styled in a salon, to look beautiful for a night out.

Figure 1.12 A laundry service is a possession-processing service.

Figure 1.13 Customer involvement is limited to dropping off the car for maintenance.

Mental Stimulus Processing

These services touch people's minds and have the power to shape attitudes and influence behavior. These services include education, news and information, professional advice and certain religious activities. The core content of services in this category is information-based. Hence, it (whether music, voice, or visual images) can be converted to digital bits or analog signals and recorded (Figure 1.14). There are some implications that arise from these kinds of services:

▶ The customers do not have to be physically present in the service factory. They only need to be able to take in the information when it is being presented.

▶ Since the customers are in a position where they depend on the service provider, there is a potential for them to be given information that is untrue. Therefore, the service provider must maintain strong ethical standards.

▶ Services in this category can be "inventoried" for consumption at a later date, or even consumed repeatedly.

Figure 1.14 Orchestral concerts provide mental stimulation and pleasure.

Information processing

Information is the most intangible form of service output. However, it can be transformed into more permanent and tangible forms like letters, reports, books, CD-ROMs, or DVDs. Some of the services that are most highly dependent on the effective collection and processing of information are financial and professional services like accounting (Figure 1.15), law, marketing research, management consulting and medical diagnosis.

Figure 1.15 An accountant helps an elderly couple sort out their tax filing.

It is sometimes difficult to tell the difference between information processing and mental stimulus processing services. For example, if a stock broker performs an analysis of a client's brokerage transactions, it seems like information processing. However, when the results of the analysis are used to make a recommendation about the most appropriate type of investment strategy for the future, it would seem like mental stimulus processing. Therefore, for simplicity, mental stimulus processing services and information processing services are sometimes termed information-based services.

Definitions of Service

Clearly, services cover a huge assortment of different and often complex activities across the four broad categories we just discussed, which makes them difficult to define. Early definitions of services contrasted them against goods. One example is the definition that services are acts, deeds or performances. Goods on the other hand, were defined as devices, materials, objects or things. In these early definitions, intangibility and perishability were the two most universally-cited characteristics that critically distinguished services from goods.

The Product–Service Continuum

We now recognize that intangibility can consist of both mental and physical dimensions. Mental intangibility is that which cannot be easily visualized and understood, while physical intangibility is that which cannot be touched or experienced by the other senses.[9] A useful way to distinguish between goods and services is to place them on a continuum, ranging from tangible-dominant to intangible-dominant (see Figure 1.16 for a hypothesized scale presenting an array of examples).[10]

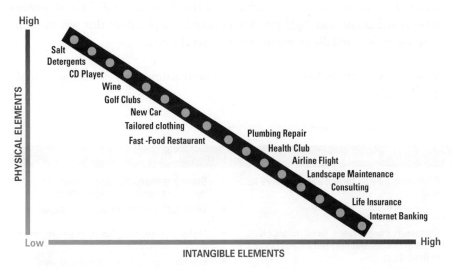

Salt
Detergents
CD Player
Wine
Golf Clubs
New Car
Tailored clothing
Fast -Food Restaurant
Plumbing Repair
Health Club
Airline Flight
Landscape Maintenance
Consulting
Life Insurance
Internet Banking

PHYSICAL ELEMENTS — High / Low
INTANGIBLE ELEMENTS — Low / High

Figure 1.16 Distinguishing between goods and services using the product-service continuum.

SOURCE

Adapted from Lynn Shostack.

Although economists, starting with Adam Smith in 1776, have long maintained that services are perishable and cannot be stored, many service performances are, in fact, designed to create durable value for their recipients (your own education being a case in point). As we noted earlier, rather than continuing to focus on the difference between goods and services, Christopher Lovelock and Evert Gummesson recently advanced a more valid distinction between ownership and non-ownership (see Definition of Services) as ways of obtaining desired benefits and solutions in the marketplace.[11] When buying a service, customers rarely acquire ownership of the elements that create value for them (food in restaurants and spare parts needed for repairs are among the exceptions). This new way of thinking is reflected in the definition of services presented below.

DEFINITION OF SERVICES

Services are economic activities offered by one party to another. Often, time-based performances are used to bring about desired results in recipients themselves or in objects or other assets for which purchasers have responsibility. In exchange for their money, time and effort, customers expect to obtain value from access to goods, labor, professional skills, facilities, networks and systems. However, they do not normally take ownership of any of the physical elements involved.[12]

LO 5

Identify the characteristics of services and the distinctive marketing challenges they pose.

SERVICES POSE DISTINCTIVE MARKETING CHALLENGES

Since services are different from goods, are the marketing concepts and practices that were developed for manufacturing companies directly transferable to service organizations? The answer is often "no." When customers rent something rather than own it, their expectations and decision criteria are different. Thus, marketing management tasks in the service sector tend to differ from those in the manufacturing sector in several important ways. Table 1.2 lists eight common differences between services and goods, and highlights key managerial implications that will form the basis for analysis and discussion in this and later chapters.

However, while the differences are useful generalizations, they *do not apply equally to all services.*

Table 1.2 Marketing implications of eight common differences between services and goods.

Difference	Implications	Marketing-Related Topics
Most service products cannot be inventoried	• Customers may be turned away or have to wait	• Smooth demand through promotions, dynamic pricing, and reservations • Work with operations to adjust capacity
Intangible elements usually dominate value creation	• Customers cannot taste, smell, or touch these elements and may not be able to see or hear them • Harder to evaluate service and distinguish from competitors	• Make services tangible through emphasis on physical clues • Employ concrete metaphors and vivid images in advertising, branding
Services are often difficult to visualize and understand	• Customers perceive greater risk and uncertainty	• Educate customers to make good choices, explain what to look for, document performance, offer guarantees
Customers may be involved in co-production	• Customers interact with provider's equipment, facilities, and systems • Poor task execution by customers may hurt productivity, spoil service experience, curtail benefits	• Develop user-friendly equipment, facilities, and systems • Train customers to perform effectively; provide customer support
People may be part of the service experience	• Appearance, attitude and behavior of service personnel and other customers can shape the experience and affect satisfaction	• Recruit, train, and reward employees to reinforce the planned service concept • Target the right customers at the right times, shape their behavior
Operational inputs and outputs tend to vary more widely	• Harder to maintain consistency, reliability, and service quality or to lower costs through higher productivity • Difficult to shield customers from results of service failures	• Set quality standards based on customer expectations; redesign product elements for simplicity and failure-proofing • Institute good service recovery procedures • Automate customer-provider interactions; perform work while customers are absent
The time factor often assumes great importance	• Customers see time as a scarce resource to be spent wisely; dislike wasting time waiting, want service at times that are convenient	• Find ways to compete on speed of delivery, minimize burden of waiting, offer extended service hours
Distribution may take place through non-physical channels	• Information-based services can be delivered through electronic channels such as the Internet or voice telecommunications, but core products involving physical activities or products cannot	• Seek to create user-friendly, secure web sites and free access by telephone • Ensure that all information-based service elements can be downloaded from site

Most Service Products Cannot be Inventoried

Most services involve actions and performances. They are temporary and perishable. Thus, they cannot be stored away as inventory for future use. (Exceptions are found among those service activities that can be recorded for later use in electronic or printed form, such as a video of a concert or a lecture.) When there is no demand, unused capacity is wasted. During the periods when demand exceeds supply, customers may be disappointed if they are turned away. A key task for service marketers, is therefore to find ways of smoothing demand levels to match available capacity.

Intangible Elements Usually Dominate Value Creation

It is often the intangible elements such as processes, Internet-based transactions and the expertise and attitudes of service personnel that create the most value in service performances. When customers cannot taste, smell, touch, see or hear these elements, it may be more difficult for them to assess these important service features before purchase. Marketers often employ physical images and metaphors to highlight service benefits and demonstrate the firm's competencies. These physical clues and strong brand associations help to make services more "tangible"[13] (see Figure 1.17).

Figure 1.17 Insurance services are intangible, but Nationwide illustrates their reliability with a dash of creative advertising.

Figure 1.18 Vivid images can facilitate visualization of the service offering.

Services are Often Difficult to Visualize and Understand

Many services can be described as "mentally intangible." This means that it is difficult for customers to visualize the experience in advance of purchase and to understand what they will be getting. Pictures of the actual service offering can help make it easier for customers to know what to expect (see Figure 1.18).

This situation can make service purchases seem risky. Service marketers can reduce perceived risk for customers by educating them on what to expect both during and after service delivery, documenting performance, explaining what was done and why, offering guarantees, and by emphasizing the firm's credentials and experiences.

The remaining key differences listed in Table 1.2 are elaborated on in the expanded services marketing mix.

● **LO 6**

Understand the components
of the expanded services
marketing mix.

EXPANDED MARKETING MIX FOR SERVICES

From Table 1.2, it is evident that the nature of services poses distinct marketing challenges. Hence, the 4 Ps of goods marketing are not adequate to deal with the issues arising from marketing services and have to be extended. In this book, we revisit the traditional 4 Ps (i.e. *product, place, price and promotion*) of the marketing mix and focus on service-specific issues. Furthermore, the traditional marketing mix does not cover managing the customer interface. We therefore discuss the three additional service-specific 3 Ps of *process, physical environment* and *people*. Together, we refer to them as the *7 Ps of services marketing*.

The Traditional Marketing Mix of 4 Ps
Applied to Services

Product Elements. Service products lie at the heart of a firm's marketing strategy. If a product is poorly designed, while the remaining Ps are well executed, they still would not create value for the customer. Planning the marketing mix begins with creating a service concept that offers value. Service products consist of a core product and supplementary service elements. The core product responds to the customer's primary need, while the supplementary elements are mutually reinforcing value-added enhancements.

Place and Time. Service distribution may take place through non-physical channels (see Table 1.2). Manufacturers require physical distribution channels to move their products from the factory to customers, either directly or through wholesale and retail intermediaries. Some service businesses are able to use electronic channels to deliver all (or at least some) of their service elements. Today's banks offer customers a choice of distribution channels, including visiting a branch, using a network of ATMs, doing business by telephone, or conducting banking transactions over the Internet. Many information-based services can be delivered almost instantaneously to any location in the world that has Internet access. To deliver service elements to customers, decisions need to be made on where and when, as well as the methods and channels used. Firms can also deliver directly to end users, or through intermediaries, such as retail outlets that receive a fee or commission.

The time factor often assumes great importance (see Table 1.2). Many services are delivered in real time while customers are physically present. As a result, speed and convenience of place and time have become important determinants of effective service delivery. Increasingly, busy customers expect service to be available when it suits them, rather than when it suits the supplier. Nowadays, more and more services are available 24/7 (Figure 1.19). A key concern for many customers is how much time elapses between making a request for service and receiving the finished output. Successful service marketers understand customers' time constraints and priorities. They collaborate with operations managers to find new ways to compete on speed. They also strive to minimize customer waiting times and seek to make waiting itself less burdensome (for further reading, see Chapter 8: Designing and Managing Service Processes and Chapter 9: Balancing Demand Against Productive Capacity).

Figure 1.19 Time is the essence—service providers must be swift and smart in their customer interactions.

Price and Other User Outlays. This component must be addressed from both the firm's perspective, as well as the customer's perspective. For firms, the pricing strategy determines income generation. This income is used to offset the cost of providing the service, and to create profits. From the customer's perspective, price is a key part of the costs they must incur to obtain the wanted benefits. To calculate whether a particular service is "worth it," customers go beyond looking at money, to assessing whether it is worth their time and effort (Figure 1.20). Service marketers therefore, need to take into account customers' non-monetary costs when setting prices. Another important topic for pricing of services is revenue management that focuses on maximizing the revenue that can be generated from available capacity at any given time.

Promotion and Education. What should we tell customers and prospects about our services? No marketing program can succeed without effective communications. This component plays three vital roles: It provides needed information and advice, persuades the target customers of the merits of a brand or service product, and encourages customers to take action at specific times.

Customers may be involved in co-production (see Table 1.2). Some services require customers to participate actively in creating the service product. This is often described as co-production. You're expected to co-operate with service personnel in settings such as hair salons, hotels, quick-service restaurants, libraries and even doing some of the work yourself rather than being waited on. In fact, service scholars argue that customers often function as partial employees.[14] Since, customers are co-producers and contribute to how others experience service performances, proactive marketers try to shape customers' roles and manage their behaviour. Therefore, in services marketing, much communication is educational in nature to teach customers how to effectively move through a service process.

Figure 1.20 Money is not the sole consideration when measuring the worth of a service.

The Extended Services Marketing Mix for Managing the Customer Interface

Process. Smart managers know that for services, *how* a firm does things is as important as what it does. This is particularly so if the product is a rather ordinary one that is also offered by many competitors. Thus, creating and delivering product elements require design and implementation of effective processes. Customers are often actively involved in the processes as co-producers. Thus, the impact of badly designed processes can become very dissatisfying, both for staff and customers alike.

Operational inputs and outputs tend to vary more widely (see Table 1.2) and make customer service process management a challenge. When a service is delivered face-to-face, you have probably noticed that the quality and nature of service execution often varies among employees, between the same employee and different customers, and even from one time of the day to another. Attitudes, transactional speed and quality of performance can vary widely. These factors can make it difficult for service organizations to improve productivity, control quality and ensure reliable delivery.

As a former packaged goods marketer once observed after moving to a new position at Holiday Inn:

> We can't control the quality of our product as well as a Procter and Gamble control engineer on a production line can…When you buy a box of Tide, you can reasonably be 99 and 44/100ths percent sure that this stuff will work to get your clothes clean. When you buy a Holiday Inn room, you're sure at some lesser percentage that it will work to give you a good night's sleep without any hassle, or people banging on the walls and all the bad things that can happen in a hotel.[15]

Nevertheless, the best service firms have made significant progress in reducing variability by adopting standardized procedures, implementing rigorous management of service quality, training employees more carefully, and automating tasks previously performed by human beings. They also make sure that employees are well trained in service recovery procedures in case things do go wrong.

Figure 1.21 Hospitality is shown through employees wearing smart outfits and a ready smile.

Furthermore, firms have much to gain from helping customers to become more competent and productive when using services, especially self-services. This means that service marketers should work with specialists from different departments to develop customer service processes and related websites, equipment, facilities and systems that are user friendly.

Finally, part of process design and management is also managing the "flow" of customers through service processes, which therefore also requires managing both capacity and demand. Both, customers waiting and idle capacity are bad news and effective services marketing aims to avoid such situations.

Physical Environment. The appearance of visible cues such as buildings, landscapes, vehicles, interior furnishing, equipment, staff members' uniforms, signs and printed materials, together with the use of colors, smells and sounds, all provide tangible evidence of a firm's image and service quality. Service firms need to manage physical evidence carefully, because it can have a profound impact on customers' impressions.

People. People may be part of the service experience (see Table 1.2). You must have noticed many times how the difference between one service supplier and another lies in the attitudes and skills of their employees. Well-managed firms devote special care to selecting, training and motivating those people who will be responsible for serving customers directly. When you encounter other customers at a service facility, you know that they, too, can affect your satisfaction. How they are dressed, how many are present, who they are and how they behave can all serve to reinforce or negate the image that a firm is trying to project and the experience it is trying to create (Figure 1.21).

A FRAMEWORK FOR DEVELOPING EFFECTIVE SERVICE MARKETING STRATEGIES

 LO 7
Know the framework for developing effective service marketing strategies.

The 7 Ps are integrated into the wider organizing framework of this book, combining it with the consumer and competitor analysis, as well as implementation.

Figure 1.22 presents the organizing framework for this book, which is divided into four parts: (1) Understanding service products, consumers and markets; (2) Applying the 4 Ps to services; (3) Managing the customer interface; (4) Implementing profitable service strategies. The arrows in the model stress the link between the different parts. Decisions made in one area must be consistent with those taken in another, so that each strategic element will mutually reinforce the rest.

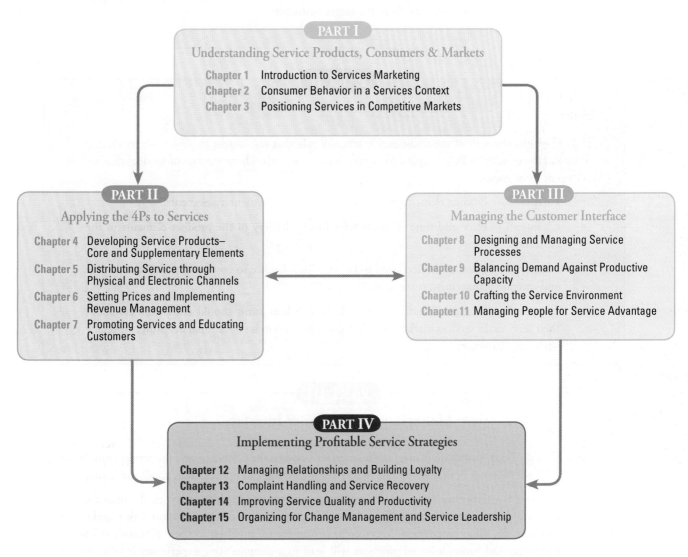

Figure 1.22 Integrated Model of Services Marketing.

The key contents of the four parts of this book are:

PART I

Understanding Service Products, Consumers & Markets

Part I of the book lays the building blocks for studying services and learning how one can become an effective services marketer.

- Chapter 1 – defines services and how we can create value without transfer of ownership.

- Chapter 2 – provides a foundation for understanding consumer needs and behavior. A three-stage model of service consumption is used to explore how customers make decisions, respond to service encounters and evaluate service performance.

- Chapter 3 – Positioning the value proposition against that of competitors is necessary to ensure commercial viability. The position must be so distinctive and defensible that the firm can attract a sufficient volume of business from the target customers.

PART II

Applying the 4Ps to Services

Part II revisits the 4 Ps of the traditional marketing mix that was taught in your basic marketing course. However, the 4 Ps are expanded to take into account the characteristics of services that are different from goods.

- Chapter 4 – Product elements such as the core and supplementary elements.

- Chapter 5 – Place and time elements refer to the delivery of the product elements to the customers.

- Chapter 6 – Prices of services need to be set with reference to costs, competition and value and revenue management considerations.

- Chapter 7 – Promotion and education deals with how firms should tell customers about their services. In services marketing, much communication is educational in nature, especially with new customers.

PART III

Managing the Customer Interface

Part III of the book focuses on managing the interface between the customers and the service firm. It covers the additional 3 Ps that are unique to services marketing and not found in goods marketing.

- Chapter 8 – Processes create and deliver the product elements. It begins with the design of effective delivery processes, specifying how the operating and delivery systems link together to create the value proposition. Very often, customers are involved in these processes as co-producers and badly designed processes will lead to a disappointing experience. It will also make it difficult for front-line staff to do their jobs well.

- Chapter 9 – This chapter is still related to process management and focuses on managing the widely fluctuating demand and balancing that against available productive capacity. Well managed demand and capacity leads to smooth processes with less waiting time for customers. Marketing strategies for managing demand involve smoothing demand fluctuations and inventorying demand through reservation systems and formalized queuing. Understanding customer motivations in different segments is one of the keys to successful demand management.

- **Chapter 10** – Physical environment is very often what creates the first impression on customers. This is also known as the servicescape, which needs to be engineered to create the right impression and facilitate effective service process delivery.

- **Chapter 11** – People play a very important role in services marketing. Many services require direct interaction between customers and contact personnel. The nature of these interactions strongly influences customers' perception of service quality. Hence, service firms devote a significant amount of effort to recruiting, training and motivating employees.

PART IV

Implementing Profitable Service Strategies

Part IV focuses on four key implementation issues, each of which is discussed in the following chapters:

- **Chapter 12** – Achieving profitability requires creating relationships with customers from the right segments and then finding ways to build and reinforce their loyalty through the Wheel of Loyalty. Loyalty bonds are created to deepen the relationships with customers, but firms also have to reduce customer churn/defections. The chapter closes with a discussion of Customer Relationship Management (CRM) systems.

- **Chapter 13** – A loyal customer base is often built from effective complaint handling and service recovery. The chapter discusses consumer complaining behavior and principles of effective service recovery systems. Service guarantees are discussed as a powerful way of institutionalizing effective service recovery and as an effective marketing tool signaling high quality service.

- **Chapter 14** – Productivity and quality are both necessary and related to financial success in services. Chapter 14 covers service quality, diagnosing quality shortfalls using the Gap Model, and strategies to close quality gaps. Customer feedback systems are introduced as an effective tool for systematically listening to and learning from customers. Productivity is introduced as closely related to quality, and it is emphasized that in today's competitive markets, firms need to simultaneously improve both quality and productivity—not one at the expense of the other. Various productivity improvement strategies are discussed, including total quality management, ISO 9000 Certification, Malcolm-Baldrige Model, and Six Sigma applied to service operations.

- **Chapter 15** – Finally, to remain competitive and forward-looking, a firm must organize for change management. For this, it needs a top management that propels the firm to be a service leader in its industry. We use the service profit chain as an integrative model to demonstrate the strategic linkages involved in running a successful service organization. Implementing the service profit chain requires integration of the three key functions of marketing, operations, and human resources. We discuss how to move a service organization to higher levels of performance in each functional area. Finally, the chapter discusses the role of leadership in both evolutionary and turnaround environments, and in creating and maintaining a climate for service.

CHAPTER SUMMARY

LO 1 ▶ Services represent an important and growing contribution to most economies in the world. As economies develop, services form the largest part of the GDP of those economies. Globally, most new jobs are generated in the service sector.

LO 2 ▶ There are many forces that are transforming our economies and making them more services heavy such as government policies, social changes, business trends, advances in information technology and globalization. Their impact on the service economy ranges from the creation of new services, and increasing competition to new measures to protect consumers.

LO 3 ▶ What exactly is a service? The key distinguishing feature of services is that it is a form of rental rather than ownership. Service customers obtain the rights to use a physical object or space, hire the labor and expertise of personnel, or pay for access to shared physical environments, facilities and networks. Services are performances that bring about the desired results for the customer.

LO 4 ▶ How can services be classified? There are four broad categories of services. They are people-processing, possession-processing, mental stimulus processing and information processing. Mental stimulus processing and information processing can be combined into what is called information-based services. Each of these has important implications for marketing.

LO 5 ▶ Services also have unique characteristics that make them different from products. These characteristics again have important implications for marketing. These distinct characteristics are:

o Most service products cannot be inventoried

o Intangible elements usually dominate value creation

o Services are often difficult to visualize and understand

o Customers may be involved in co-production

o People may be part of the service experience

o Operational inputs and outputs tend to vary more widely

o Time factor often assumes great importance

o Distribution may take place through non-physical channels

LO 6 ▶ Due to the unique characteristics of services, the traditional marketing mix of the 4 Ps needs to be amended. The 4 Ps are: (1) Product elements, (2) Place and time, (3) Price and other user outlays, (4) Promotion and education. Some important amendments are:

o Product elements include more than the core elements. It also includes supplementary elements

o Promotion is also viewed as a form of communication and education, rather than just advertising and promotions

In addition, services management requires three additional Ps covering the management of the customer interface. The three additional Ps of services marketing are:

o Process design (including managing demand and capacity)

o Physical environment, and

o People

LO 7 ▶ A framework for successful implementation of a sound services marketing strategy forms the underlying structure of this book. This framework consists of the following four interlinked parts:

o Part I begins with the need for service firms to understand their business, customers and markets.

o Part II shows us how to apply the traditional 4 Ps to services marketing.

o Part III covers the 3 Ps of extended services marketing mix and provides an understanding of how to manage the customer interface.

o Part IV shows how to implement profitable service strategies and discusses how to achieve profitability by creating relationships with customers using the Wheel of Loyalty, and how to build a foundation for loyalty through effective complaint handling and service recovery. This part also focuses on the need for both productivity and quality to ensure financial success.

UNLOCK YOUR LEARNING

These keywords are found within the sections of each Learning Objective (LO). They are integral in understanding the services marketing concepts taught in each section. Having a firm grasp of these keywords and how they are used is essential in helping you do well for your course, and in the real and very competitive marketing scene out there.

LO 1
1. Service science
2. Service dominated economy
3. Supplementary services

LO 2
4. Advances in information technology
5. Business trends
6. Globalization
7. Government policies
8. Social change

LO 3
9. Rent
10. Resource sharing
11. Ownership
12. Non-ownership

LO 4
13. Acts
14. Deeds
15. Durable value
16. Mental intangibility
17. Performances
18. Physical intangibility
19. Product service continuum
20. Tangible-dominant

21. Intangible-dominant

LO 6
22. Convenience
23. 7Ps
24. People
25. Physical environment
26. Physical evidence
27. Place and time
28. Price and other outlays
29. Process
30. Promotion and education
31. Product

LO 7
32. Competition
33. Complaining behavior
34. Costs
35. Customer interface
36. Customer relationship management
37. Demand
38. Human resources
39. Integration
40. ISO 9000 Certification
41. Malcolm-Baldrige Model

42. Marketing
43. Operations
44. Quality gaps
45. Service capacity
46. Service guarantees
47. Service profit chain
48. Service recovery
49. Service strategies
50. Six Sigma
51. Total quality management
52. Value proposition
53. Wheel of Loyalty

How well do you know the language of services marketing? Quiz yourself!

 Not for the academically faint-of-heart

For each keyword you are able to recall without referring to earlier pages, give yourself a point (and a pat on the back). Tally your score at the end and see if you earned the right to be called—a *services marketeer.*

SCORE

01 – 10	Services Marketing is done a great disservice.
11 – 20	The midnight oil needs to be lit, pronto.
21 – 30	I know what you *didn't* do all semester.
31 – 40	By George! You're getting there.
41 – 50	Now, go forth and market.
51 – 53	There should be a marketing concept named after you.

Review Questions

1. What are the main reasons for the growing share of the service sector in the major economies of the world?

2. What are the five powerful forces transforming the service landscape and what impact do they have on the service economy?

3. "A service is rented rather than owned." Explain what the statement means and use examples to support your explanation.

4. Describe the four broad categories of services, and provide examples for each of them.

5. What types of services do you think are (a) most affected and (b) least affected by the problem of variable inputs and outputs? Why?

6. Why is time important in services?

7. "The 4 Ps are all a marketing manager needs to create a marketing strategy for a service business." Prepare a response that argues the contrary and justify your conclusions.

8. What are the elements in the framework for developing effective service marketing strategies?

❮ WORK YOUR ESM ❯

Application Exercises

1. Visit the websites of the following national statistical bureaus: U. S. Bureau of Economic Analysis (www.bea.gov); Statistics Canada (www.statcan.ca); Eurostat (http://europa. eu.int/en/comm/eurostat/); Central Bureau of Statistics (Indonesia) (www.bps.go.id); Japanese Statistics Bureau (www.stat. go.jp); Statistics South Africa (www.statssa. gov.za); National Statistical Office Thailand (web.nso.go.th); and the respective website for your home country if it is not covered here. In each instance, obtain data on the latest trends in services as (a) percentage of GDP; (b) the percentage of employment accounted for by services; (c) breakdowns of these two statistics by type of industry; and (d) service exports and imports. Looking at these trends, what are your main conclusions for the main sectors of these economies, and within services, for specific service sectors?

2. Legal and accounting firms now advertise their services in many countries. Search for a few advertisements and review the following: What do these firms do to cope with the intangibility of their services? What could they do better? How do they deal with consumer quality and risk perceptions, and how could they improve that aspect of their marketing?

3. Give examples of how the Internet and telecommunications technologies (e.g. Interactive Voice Response Systems [IVRs] and mobile commerce [M-commerce]) have changed some of the services that you use.

4. Choose a service company with which you are familiar and show how each of the seven elements (7 Ps) of services marketing applies to a specific service product.

ENDNOTES

1   http://www.bumrungrad.com/; http://www.
    bumrungrad.com/overseas-medical-care/About-
    Us/Factsheet.aspx; http://www.cbsnews.com/
    stories/2005/04/21/60minutes/printable689998.
    html, accessed in February 2008

2. Chesbrough, H. (2005). Towards a new science
    for services," *Harvard Business Review*,
    (February), pp. 43-44.

3. Weissenberger-Eibl, M. & Koch, D.J. (2007).
    Importance of industrial services and service
    innovations. *Journal of Management and
    Organization*, 13, pp. 88-101.

4. The great jobs switch. *The Economist*, (October
    1, 2005), 11, p. 14.

5. http://www.ibm.com/investor/1q07/
    1q07earnings.phtml; http://www.ibm.com/
    investor/2q07/2q07earnings.phtml; http://www-
    03.ibm.com/press/us/en/pressrelease/22463.
    wss, accessed January 2008.

6. Farrell, D., Laboissiere, M.A., & Rosenfeld, J.
    (2005). Sizing the emerging global labor market.
    The McKinsey Quarterly, 3, pp. 93-103.

7. Lovelock, C.H. & Gummesson, E. (2004).
    Whither services marketing? In search of a new
    paradigm and fresh perspectives. J*ournal of
    Service Research*, 7(August), pp. 20-41

8. These classifications are derived from
    Christopher H. Lovelock. (1983). Classifying
    services to gain strategic marketing insights.
    Journal of Marketing, 47(Summer), pp. 9-20.

9. Bateson, J.E.G. (1979). Why we need service
    marketing. In Conceptual and Theoretical
    Developments in Marketing. Ferrell, O.C.,
    Brown, S.W., & Lamb Jr., C.W. eds. Chicago:
    American Marketing Association, pp. 131-146.

10. Shostack, G.L. (1977). Breaking free from
    product marketing. *Journal of Marketing*,
    41(April), pp. 73-80.

11. Lovelock, C.H., & and Gummesson, E. Whither
    services marketing? *Op. Cit.*

12. Adapted from a definition by Christopher
    Lovelock (identified anonymously as Expert 6,
    Table II, p. 112). In Edvardsson, B., Gustafsson,
    A. & Roos, I. (2005). Service portraits in service
    research: A critical review. *International Journal
    of Service Industry Management*, 16(1), pp.
    107-121.

13. George, W.R. & Berry, L.L. (1981). Guidelines
    for the advertising of services. *Business
    Horizons*, (July-August); Mittal, B. & Baker, J.
    (2002). Advertising strategies for hospitality
    services. *Cornell Hotel and Restaurant
    Administration Quarterly*, 43(April), pp. 51-63.

14. Mills, P.K. & Moberg, D.J. (1982). Perspectives
    on the technology of service operations.
    Academy of Managemnet Review 7(3), pp.
    467-78; An-Tien Hsieh, Chang-Hua Yen, and
    Ko-Chien Chin. (2004). Participative customers
    as partial employees and service provider
    workload. *International Journal of Service
    Industry Management*,15(2), pp. 187-200.

15. Knisely, G. (1979). Greater marketing emphasis
    by Holiday Inns breaks mold, *Advertising Age*,
    (January 15).

2

consumer behavior in a
SERVICES CONTEXT

LEARNING OBJECTIVES

By the end of this chapter, students should be able to:

LO 1 Understand the three-stage model of service consumption.

LO 2 Learn how consumers evaluate and choose between alternative service offerings and why they have difficulty making those evaluations.

LO 3 Know the perceived risks that customers face in purchasing services and the strategies firms can use to reduce these perceived risks.

LO 4 Understand how customers form expectations and the components of these expectations.

LO 5 Know how reducing or increasing the level of customers' contact with a service organization affects the nature of their service experiences.

LO 6 Be familiar with the servuction model and understand the interactions that together create the service experience.

LO 7 Obtain insights from viewing service delivery as a form of theater.

LO 8 Know how role and script theory contribute to a better understanding of service experiences.

LO 9 Know how customers evaluate services and what determines their satisfaction.

Figure 2.1 New York University is the gateway to bigger and better things for students like Susan Lee.

OPENING VIGNETTE[1]

SUSAN LEE, SERVICE CUSTOMER

Susan Lee, a final-year business student, had breakfast and then logged onto the Internet to check the local weather forecast. It predicted rain, so she grabbed an umbrella before leaving the apartment. On the way to the bus stop, she dropped a letter in a mailbox. The bus arrived on schedule. It was the usual driver, who recognized her and gave a cheerful greeting as she showed her commuter pass.

Arriving at her destination, Susan left the bus and walked to the College of Business. Joining a crowd of other students, she found a seat in the large lecture theater where her marketing class was held. The professor was a very dynamic individual who believed in having an active dialog with the students. Susan made several contributions to the discussion and felt that she learned a lot from listening to others' analyses and opinions.

Susan and her friends had lunch at the recently renovated Student Union. It was a well-lit and colorfully decorated new food court, featuring a variety of small kiosks. There were both local suppliers and brand-name fast food chains, which offered choices of sandwiches, as well as health foods and a variety of desserts. Although she had wanted a sandwich, there was a long queue of customers at the sandwich shop. Thus, Susan joined her friends at Burger King and then splurged on a café latte at the adjacent Have-a-Java coffee stand. The food court was unusually crowded that day, perhaps because of the rain pouring down outside. When they finally found a table, they had to clear away the dirty trays. "Lazy slobs!" commented her friend Mark, referring to the previous customers.

After lunch, Susan stopped at the cash machine, inserted her bank card, and withdrew some money. When she remembered that she had a job interview at the end of the week, she telephoned her hairdresser and counted herself lucky to be able to make an appointment for later. This was because of a cancellation by another client. When she left the Student Union, it was still raining.

Susan looked forward to her visit to the hairdresser. The store, which had a bright, trendy décor, was staffed by friendly hairdressers. Unfortunately, the cutter was running late and Susan had to wait for 20 minutes. She used that time to review a human resources course. Some of the other waiting customers were reading magazines provided by the store. Eventually, it was time for a shampoo, after which the cutter proposed a slightly different cut. Susan agreed, although she drew the line at the suggestion to lighten her hair colour as she had never done it before and was unsure how it would look. She did not want to take the risk. She sat very still, watching the process in the mirror and turning her head when requested. She was very pleased with the result and complimented the cutter on her work. Then she tipped the cutter and paid at the reception desk.

The rain had stopped and the sun was shining as Susan left the store. On the way home she stopped by the cleaners to pick up some clothes. The store was rather gloomy, smelled of cleaning solvents, and the walls badly needed repainting. She was annoyed to find that although her silk blouse was ready as promised, the suit that she needed for the interview was not. The assistant, who had dirty fingernails, mumbled an apology in an insincere tone. Although the store was convenient and the quality of work was quite good, Susan considered the employees unfriendly and not very helpful and was unhappy with their service. However, she had no choice but to use them as there were no other dry cleaners around.

Back at her apartment building, she opened the mailbox in the lobby. Her mail included a bill from her insurance company. However, it required no action since payment was deducted automatically from her bank account. She was about to discard the junk mail when she noticed a flyer promoting a new dry-cleaning store, which included a discount coupon. She decided to try the new firm and pocketed the coupon.

Since it was her turn to cook dinner, she looked in the kitchen to see what food was available. Susan sighed when she realized that there was nothing much. Maybe she would make a salad and call for delivery of a large pizza.

...Customers today are subjected to many service choices...

Figure 2.2 Food for thought—Susan is just another customer facing a large selection of services out there.

LO 1
Understand the three-stage model of service consumption.

CUSTOMER DECISION MAKING: THE THREE-STAGE MODEL OF SERVICE CONSUMPTION

The story of Susan Lee depicts consumer behavior in a variety of situations and stages. Service consumption can be divided into three main stages: the pre-purchase, service encounter and post-purchase stages. Figure 2.3 shows that each stage consists of two or more steps. During the pre-purchase stage, the four steps are awareness of need, information search, evaluation of alternatives and making a decision to purchase. During the service encounter stage, the customer initiates and experiences and consumes the service. During the post-purchase stage, evaluation of the service performance occurs, and this determines future intentions such as wanting to buy again from the same service firm and recommending the service to friends. As can be seen on the left hand side of the diagram, the nature of the steps varies, depending on whether they are high-contact (high degree of interaction between service personnel and customer) or low-contact (little, if any face-to-face contact between service personnel and customer) services. On the right-hand side of the diagram, one can find the key concepts discussed in this chapter. The rest of the chapter will be organized around the three stages and the key concepts.

Figure 2.3 The three-stage model of service consumption.

High-Contact Services	Low-Contact Services	Steps	Key Concepts
		1. Pre-purchase Stage	
Can visit physical sites, observe (+ low-contact options)	Surf web, phone calls, visit library	Awareness of Need Information search • Clarify needs • Explore solutions	*Need arousal*
		• Identify alternative service products and suppliers	*Evoked set*
		Evaluation of alternatives (solutions and suppliers)	*Search, experience, and credence attributes*
		• Review supplier information (e.g. advertising, brochures, websites etc.)	
		• Review information from third parties (e.g. published reviews, ratings, comments on web, blogs, complaints to public agencies, satisfaction ratings, awards)	*Perceived risk*
Can visit in person and observe (possibly test) facilities equipments, operation in action; meet personnel, see customers (+ remote options)	Primarily remote contact (web sites, blogs, phone, e-mail, publications, etc)	• Discuss options with service personnel • Get advice and feedback from third party advisors, other customers	*Formation of expectation* *- desired service level* *- predicted service level* *- adequate service level* *- zone of tolerance*
		Make decision on service purchase	
		2. Service Encounter Stage	
At physical site (or remote reservation)	Remote	Request service from chosen supplier or initiate self-service (payment may be upfront or billed later)	*Moments of truth* *Service encounters* *Servuction system* *Role and script theories* *Theater as metaphor*
At physical site *only*	Remote	Service delivery by personnel or self-service	
		3. Post-purchase Stage	
		Evalution of service performance	*Confirmation/ disconfirmation of expectations*
		Future intentions	*Dissatisfaction, satisfaction and delight*

PRE-PURCHASE STAGE

The pre-purchase stage begins with *need awareness* and continues through information search and evaluation of alternatives, to a decision on whether to buy a particular service.

Need Awareness

When a person or organization decides to buy or use a service, it is triggered by an underlying need or *need arousal*. The awareness of a need will drive information search and evaluation of alternatives before a decision is reached. Needs may be triggered by:

▶ People's unconscious minds (e.g. personal identity and aspirations)

▶ Physical conditions (e.g. chronic back pain; e.g. Susan Lee's hunger need drove her to Burger King finally)

▶ External sources (e.g. marketing activities) (Figure 2.4).

When people recognize a need, they are more likely to be motivated to take action to resolve it. In the story of Susan Lee, her need for the services of a hairdresser was triggered by her remembering that she had a job interview at the end of the week. She wanted to look her best for the interview. In developed economies, consumers now have a greater need to spend on more elaborate vacations, entertainment and other service experiences. This shift in consumer behavior and attitudes provides opportunities for those services that understand and meet changing needs. For example, some service providers have taken advantage of the increased interest in extreme sports by offering services such as guided mountain climbs, paragliding, white-water rafting trips and mountain biking adventures (see Figure 2.5). The idea of service experiences also extend to business and industrial situations. A good example of this is modern trade shows, where exhibitors set out to engage customers' interest through interactive presentations and entertainment.[2]

Information Search

Once a need has been recognized, customers are motivated to search for solutions. Several alternatives may come to mind and these form the *evoked set*, which is the set of possible products or brands that a customer may consider in the decision process. For Susan Lee, the first choice in her evoked set was a sandwich shop but due to the queue, she chose the second choice in her evoked set, Burger

Reserve a car that's made for the environment.

Figure 2.4 Hertz targets the environment-conscious segment so they recognize the need for an eco-friendly car

Figure 2.5 As extreme sports enthusiasts increase worldwide, more service providers offer rough-and-tumble activities like white water rafting.

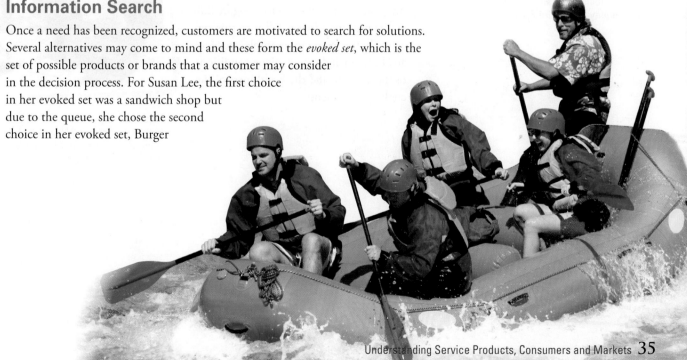

King. The *evoked set* can be derived from past experience or external sources such as advertising, retail displays, news stores and recommendations from service personnel, friends and family. Once there is an evoked set, the different alternatives need to be evaluated before a final choice can be made.

Evaluation of Alternatives

Service Attributes

When faced with several alternatives, customers need to compare and evaluate the different service offerings. Many services however, are difficult to evaluate before purchase. This is because of the nature of service attributes. Many goods and some services are high in *search attributes*. More complex goods and most services are high in *experience attributes* and some services are high in *credence attributes*.

▶ Search attributes are tangible characteristics that customers evaluate before purchase. Style, color, texture, taste and sound are examples of such features. Search attributes are found in many service environments. For example, you can assess some attributes before you visit a particular restaurant, including the type of food, the location and availability of parking.

▶ Experience attributes are those that cannot be evaluated before purchase. Customers must "experience" the service to know what they are getting. Vacations (Figure 2.6), live entertainment performances and sporting events fall into this category. In a restaurant for example, you will not know how much you like the food, the service provided by the waiter, and the atmosphere in the restaurant on that particular evening until you have consumed the service.

▶ Credence attributes are characteristics that customers find hard to evaluate even after consumption. These often relate to the benefits actually delivered. Counseling, surgery, legal advice (Figure 2.7), financial investment, planning services (Figure 2.8) and consulting services fall into this category. In the restaurant example, credence attributes include the hygiene conditions of the kitchen, and the healthiness of the cooking ingredients.

Figure 2.6 Holiday-makers experiencing first hand, the grandeur and beauty of Niagara Falls.

Figure 2.7 Legal services are high in credence attributes and require customers to trust in the expertise of their lawyers.

Copyright 2002 by Randy Glasbergen.
www.glasbergen.com

Investments and Financial Services

GLASBERGEN

"I have 30,000 fish saved for my retirement. I'd like to roll them over into something that doesn't stink to high heaven!"

Figure 2.8 Financial services are high in credence attributes.

When evaluating competing services, customers try and assess the likely performance of each service on those dimensions (or service attributes) that are important to them and choose the one that is seen to best meet their needs. It is therefore important for service firms to be able to deliver and communicate superior performance on attributes that matter to their target customers. For services with high credence qualities and high customer involvement, firms should focus on what the key service dimensions are, and provide tangible information about service performance outcomes to attract customers. When customers have low involvement with those services, firms should focus on more emotional appeals, and the service experience to attract the customers.[3]

Perceived risk

Since services have more experience and credence attributes, they are harder to evaluate before purchase, and first-time users especially are likely to face greater uncertainty about whether they will like the service. Susan Lee had not tried coloring her hair before. Hence, when the hairdresser suggested that she lighten her hair color, she was worried and declined. This uncertainty increases customers' *perceived risk*. Think about how you felt the first time you had to make decisions about choosing an unfamiliar service, especially one with important consequences. The risk perception increases with the increasing possibility of negative consequences. Table 2.1 outlines seven categories of perceived risks.

 LO 3

Know the perceived risks that customers face in purchasing services and the strategies firms can use to reduce these perceived risks.

Table 2.1 Perceived risks in purchasing and using services.

Type of Risk	Examples of Customer Concerns
Functional (unsatisfactory performance outcomes)	• Will this training course give me the skills I need to get a better job? • Will this credit card be accepted wherever and whenever I want to make a purchase? • Will the dry cleaner be able to remove the stains from this jacket?
Financial (monetary loss, unexpected costs)	• Will I lose money if I make the investment recommended by my stockbroker? • Could my identity be stolen if I make this purchase on the Internet? • Will I incur a lot of unanticipated expenses if I go on this vacation? • Will repairing my car cost more than the original estimate?
Temporal (wasting time, consequences of delays)	• Will I have to wait in line before entering the exhibition? • Will service at this restaurant be so slow that I will be late for my afternoon meeting? • Will the renovations to our bathroom be completed before our friends come to stay with us?
Physical (personal injury or damage to possessions)	• Will I get hurt if I go skiing at this resort? • Will the contents of this package get damaged in the mail? • Will I fall sick if I travel abroad on vacation?
Psychological (personal fears and emotions)	• How can I be sure that this aircraft will not crash? • Will the consultant make me feel stupid? • Will the doctor's diagnosis upset me?
Social (how others think and react)	• What will my friends think of me if they learnt that I stayed at this cheap motel? • Will my relatives approve of the restaurant I have chosen for the family reunion dinner? • Willl my business colleagues disapprove of my selection of an unknown law firm?
Sensory (unwanted effects on any of the five senses)	• Will I get a view of the parking lot rather than the beach from my restaurant table? • Will the hotel bed be uncomfortable? • Will I be kept awake by noise from the guests in the room next door? • Will my room smell of stale cigarette smoke? • Will the coffee at breakfast taste disgusting?

Figure 2.9 Winning awards is a tangible cue for service excellence.

People typically feel uncomfortable with perceived risks during the pre-purchase stage and use a variety of methods to reduce them, including:

▶ Seeking information from respected personal sources such as family, friends or peers.

▶ Using the Internet to compare service offerings and search for independent reviews and ratings.

▶ Relying on a firm that has a good reputation.

▶ Looking for guarantees and warranties.

▶ Visiting service facilities or trying aspects of the service before purchasing. They examine tangible cues or physical evidence such as the feel and look of the service setting or awards won by the firm or its employees (Figure 2.9).

▶ Asking knowledgeable employees about competing services.

Customers are risk averse, and everything else being equal, they will choose the service with the lower risk perception. Therefore, firms need to proactively work to reduce customer risk perceptions. Suitable strategies vary according to the nature of the service, and may include all or some of the following:

▶ Free trial. This is suitable for services with high experience attributes (see Figure 2.10).

▶ Advertising. This provides consumers with an interpretation and value of any particular product or service. For example, Credit Cards are a means of payment; a piece of plastic that gives consumers greater mobility and security over cash – only the card is tangible. Advertising helps communicate the benefits, usage

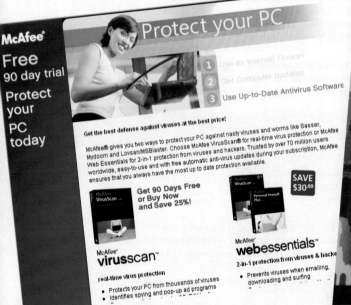

Figure 2.10 McAfee offers free trial software to attract prospective customers.

Figure 2.11 In airports, MasterCard communicates to arriving travellers that the world is their oyster with MasterCard.

Figure 2.12 Zurich shows customers what they can do for them.

occasions and / or instances of how the consumer can enjoy the tangible product, thus stimulating awareness, interest and preference of the product. The example in Figure 2.11 illustrates how MasterCard is the Card of choice, and can be used while visiting cities such as Rome, Italy. Insurance companies might also find it hard to communicate what they are selling and Zurich helps customers to understand what they do in a very interesting advertisement (Figure 2.12).

▶ Displaying credentials. Many professionals such as doctors, architects and lawyers use this. They can also showcase past successes (Figure 2.13).

▶ Using *evidence management*, an organized approach where customers are presented with coherent evidence of the company. This includes the appearance of furnishings, equipment and facilities; and employees' dress and behavior.[4] For example, the bright and trendy decor at the hairdressing salon that Susan Lee visited may have helped her to choose this particular salon at her first visit and now probably also contributed to her feeling satisfied in the end, even though she had to wait for 20 minutes for her cutter (Figure 2.14).

Figure 2.13 This doctor displays his accreditations to communicate his credentials.

▶ Offering guarantees. These include money-back guarantees and performance warranties.

▶ Encouraging prospective customers to visit the service facilities in advance of purchase.

▶ Giving customers access to online information about the status of an order or procedure. Many logistic companies use this, for example FedEx, DHL and UPS.

Figure 2.14 A chic and classy hairdressing salon projects positive evidence management.

When companies manage the risk perceptions of their customers well, customers' uncertainty is reduced, which increases the chance of being the service provider chosen. Another way to increase the chance of providing customers with an enhanced service experience is to manage their expectations.

LO 4

Understand how customers form expectations and the components of these expectations.

Service Expectations

Customers assess attributes and risks related to a service offering. In the process, they develop expectations about how the service they choose will perform. Expectations can be very firm if they are related to attributes that were important in the choice process. For example, if a customer paid a premium of $350 for a direct flight rather than one that has a stopover to save four hours on a journey, then the customer will not take it lightly if there is a six-hour flight delay. A customer will also have high expectations if he paid a premium for high quality service, and will be deeply disappointed when the service fails to deliver. We will discuss expectations again as part of the post-purchase satisfaction process. Here, we will now focus on the formation and types of expectations.

Expectations are formed during the search and decision making process. They can be situation specific. For example, if it is a peak period, expectations of service delivery timing will be lower than when it is a non-peak period. Expectations also change over time. They can be influenced by factors controlled by the service provider, such as advertising, pricing, new technologies or service innovation. Social trends, like increased access through the Internet can also change expectations. For example, health care consumers are now better informed and often want to participate more in decisions relating to medical treatment. Service Insights 2.1 describes a new assertiveness among parents of children with serious illnesses.

What are the components of customer expectations? Figure 2.15 shows the factors that influence the different levels of customer expectations.[5]

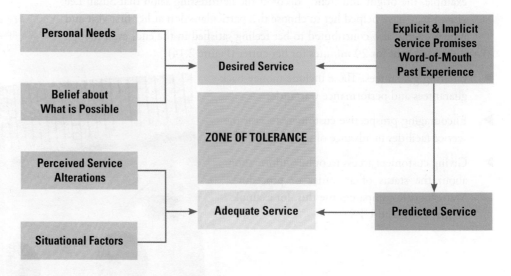

Figure 2.15 Factors influencing customer expectations of service.

::: SERVICE INSIGHTS 2.1

Parents Seek Involvement in Medical Decision Affecting their Children

Many parents want to participate actively in decisions relating to their children's medical treatment. Thanks in part to in-depth media coverage of medical advances and health-related issues, as well as the educational efforts of consumer advocates, parents are better informed and more assertive than in previous generations. They are no longer willing simply to accept the recommendations of medical specialists. In particular, parents whose child has been born with congenital defects or has developed a life-threatening illness are often willing to invest immense amounts of time and energy to learn everything they can about their child's condition. Some have even founded non-profit organizations centered on a specific disease to bring together other families facing the same problems and to help raise money for research and treatment.

The Internet has made it much easier to access health care information and research findings. A study by the Texas-based Heart Center of 160 parents who had Internet access and children with cardiac problems found that 58 percent obtained information related to their child's diagnosis. Four out of five users searching for cardiology-related information stated that locating the information was easy; of those, half could name a favorite cardiology web site. Almost all felt that the information was helpful in understanding their child's condition. The study reported that six parents even created interactive personal web sites related specifically to their child's congenital heart defect.[6]

Commenting on the phenomenon of highly informed parents, Norman J. Siegel, MD, former chair of pediatrics at Yale New Haven Children's Hospital, observed:

> It's a different practice today. The old days of "trust me, I'm going to take care of this" are completely gone, I see many patients who come in carrying a folder with printouts from the Internet and they want to know why Dr. So-and-So wrote this. They go to chat rooms, too. They want to know about the disease process, if it's chronic. Some parents are almost as well informed as a young medical student or house officer.

Dr. Siegel said he welcomed the trend and enjoyed the discussions but admitted that some physicians found it hard to adapt.

SOURCE

Lovelock, C. & Gregory (2003), *New Haven*, CT: Yale School of Management, (case).

The factors are:

▶ **Desired service**. "Wished for" level of service. Customers hope that they will get service based on their personal needs and what they think is possible. Desired service could also be influenced by explicit and implicit promises made by service providers, word of mouth, and past experience. However, it may not always be possible to have the "wished for" level of service and most customers are realistic. Hence, they also have a minimum level of expectation, called adequate service and predicted service level.

▶ **Adequate service**. The minimum level of service that customers will accept, without being dissatisfied.

▶ **Predicted service**. This is the level of service that the customers actually anticipate receiving. Predicted service can also be affected by service provider promises, word of mouth and past experiences (see Figure 2.16). The level of predicted service that customers anticipate affects how they define *adequate service* on that occasion. If good service is predicted, the level of adequate service will be higher, than if poorer service is predicted.

Figure 2.16 This advertisment creates high expectations for Singapore Airline Suites in its new A380 Airbus aircraft.

▶ **Zone of tolerance**. The extent to which customers are willing to accept variation in service delivery. It is difficult to achieve consistent delivery by all employees in the same company. Even for the same employee, it is not easy to deliver consistent service from one time of the day to another or from one day to another. This is the range of service within which customers do not pay particular attention to service performance. If the zone of tolerance is relatively narrow, like in a study of guests at four-star, five-star and resort hotels in Northern Cyprus (located in the Eastern Mediterranean),[7] it is important to pay attention to the quality of service delivery. Susan Lee's zone of tolerance for the dry cleaner was high, as she did not have any other alternatives to choose from at that time. However, for food, her zone of tolerance for waiting was low as she had many other alternatives to choose from.

Purchase Decision

When consumers have evaluated possible alternatives, including comparing the performance of important attributes of competing service offerings, the perceived risk associated with each offering, and developed their desired, adequate and predicted service level expectations, they will now select the option they like best. Sometimes, the purchase decision process can be quite simple. This is especially so if the perceived risks are low and the alternatives are clear. In many instances however, purchase decisions involve trade-offs. Price is often the key factor. For example, is it worth paying for a better seat in a theater so that you can be located closer to the performers? (Figure 2.17)

Some decisions are more complex and may involve a number of trade-offs. For example, when choosing an airline, convenience of schedules, reliability, seat comfort, attentiveness of cabin crew and availability of meals may vary among the carriers. Once the decision has been made, the consumer is ready to move to the service encounter stage.

Figure 2.17 Consumers have to evaluate whether paying top dollar for better seats is worth the price.

SERVICE ENCOUNTER STAGE

A *service encounter* is a period of time when the customer interacts with a service provider. We use a number of models and frameworks to better understand consumers' behavior during the service encounter when they consume and experience the service. The "moments of truth" metaphor shows the importance of effectively managing touch points, and the high/low contact service model helps to understand the extent and nature of touch points. The third concept, the servuction model, focuses on the various types of interactions that a firm offering high contact services has to manage well. Finally, the theater metaphor communicates effectively how one can look at "staging" service performances to create the experience customers desire.

Service Encounters are "Moments of Truth"

Richard Normann borrowed the metaphor "*moment of truth*" from bullfighting to show the importance of contact points with customers:

> [W]e could say that the perceived quality is realized at the moment of truth, when the service provider and the service customer confront one another in the arena. At that moment they are very much on their own. . . It is the skill, the motivation, and the tools employed by the firm's representative and the expectations and behaviour of the client which together will create the service delivery process.[8] (Figure 2.18)

Figure 2.18 The service provider is the matador that skillfully manages the service encounter.

Jan Carlzon, the former chief executive of Scandinavian Airlines System, used the "moment-of-truth" metaphor as a reference point for transforming SAS from an operations-driven business into a customer-driven airline. Carlzon made the following comments about his airline:

Last year, each of our 10 million customers came into contact with approximately five SAS employees, and this contact lasted an average of 15 seconds each time. Thus, SAS is "created" 50 million times a year, 15 seconds at a time. These 50 million "moments of truth" are the moments that ultimately determine whether SAS will succeed or fail as a company. They are the moments when we must prove to our customers that SAS is their best alternative.[9]

Each service firm faces similar challenges in defining and managing the moments of truth that its customers will encounter (Figure 2.19).

 LO 5

Know how reducing or increasing the level of customers' contact with a service organization affects the nature of their service experiences.

Service Encounters Range from High-Contact to Low-Contact

Services involve different levels of contact with the service operation. Some of these encounters can be very brief and may consist of a few steps, like if a customer calls a customer contact center. Others may extend over a longer time frame and involve multiple interactions of varying degrees of complexity. For example, a visit to a theme park might last all day.

Figure 2.19 Discussing the house blueprints with the contractor is a moment of truth.

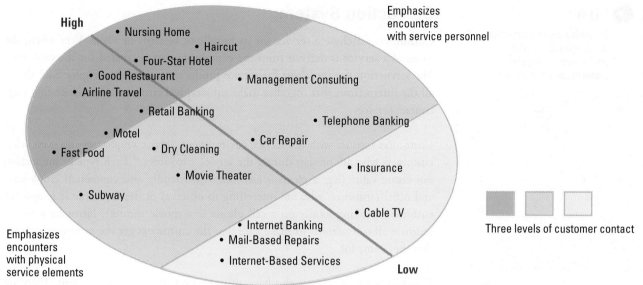

Figure 2.20 Levels of customer contact with service organizations.

In Figure 2.20, we group services into three levels of customer contact. These represent the extent of interaction with service personnel, physical service elements or both. We recognize that the level of customer contact covers a spectrum. However, it is useful to examine the differences between organizations at the high and low ends.

▶ High-contact: Customers and service organizations are interacting throughout the service delivery. When the customers visit the service facility, they enter the "factory." When viewed this way, it means that a motel is a lodging factory, a hospital is a health treatment factory and an airline is a transportation factory. During the service delivery process, customers are exposed to many physical clues about the organization. These are the exterior and interior of its buildings, the equipment and furnishings, the appearance and behavior of service personnel, and even other customers. For Susan Lee, the clues at the dry cleaners, such as the gloomy interior, the walls that need repainting etc., all added to her experience of a bad service.

▶ Low-Contact: There is very little, if any face-to-face contact between customers and the service organization. Contact is at arm's length through electronic or physical distribution channels (see Figure 2.21). In fact, this is a fast-growing trend in today's world where convenience plays an important part in customer choice. Many high-contact services are transformed into low-contact services when customers serve themselves. Susan Lee used the ATM machine to withdraw cash rather than visit a bank as it was more convenient. For example, customers can conduct more of their banking transactions by mail, telephone and the Internet. As highlighted in Figure 2.20, some service industries offer customers a choice of delivery systems that feature different levels of contact.

Figure 2.21 Today's technology means that services can be conducted at arm's length through electronic or physical distribution channels.

LO 6

Be familiar with the servuction model and understand the interactions that together create the service experience.

Servuction System

Consumers purchase a service for its bundle of benefits or value. Very often, the value of a service is derived from the experience that is created for the customer. The servuction system (short for service production system) in Figure 2.22 shows all the interactions that together make up a typical customer experience in a high contact service.

Customers interact with the service environment, service employees and even other customers who are present during the service encounter.[10] Each type of interaction can create value (e.g. a pleasant environment, friendly and competent employees, and other customers who are interesting to observe) or destroy value (e.g. another customer speaking loudly on a cell phone in a movie theater). Firms have to co-ordinate all interactions to make sure that the customers get the service experience that they came for.

Different levels of contact also have an impact on the servuction system. There are many more interactions, or moments of truth, that have to be managed in a high-contact service. The servuction system consists of a technical core which is invisible to the customer, and the service delivery system.

▶ Service operations system: The technical core where inputs are processed and the elements of the service product are created. This technical core is typically in the back-stage and invisible to the customer. Like in a theatrical play, the visible components can be termed "front stage," while the invisible components can

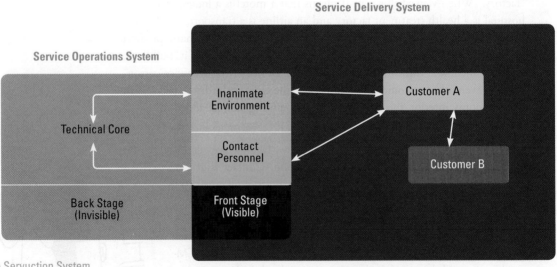

Figure 2.22 The Servuction System.

SOURCE

Adapted from Pierre Eiglier and Eric Langeard, Services as Systems: Marketing Implications, in Pierre Eiglier, Eric Langeard, Christopher H. Lovelock, John E. G. Bateson and Robert F. Young, *Marketing Consumer Services: New Insights*. Cambridge, MA: Marketing Science Institute, Report #77-115, November 1977.

be termed "backstage."[11] The front stage relates to the actors (service personnel) and the backstage relates to the stage set (physical facilities, equipment and other tangibles). What goes on backstage is usually not of interest to customers. However, if what goes on backstage affects the quality of the front stage activities, customers will notice. For example, if a spa customer finds that they have been billed for services that they did not receive, they are likely to be upset. The proportion of the overall service operation that is visible to the customers depends on the level of contact. High-contact services involve the physical person of the customer. Therefore, the visible component of the service operations element tends to be more substantial. Low-contact services usually have most of the service operations system backstage, and this could be remotely located (Figure 2.23).

▶ Service delivery system: Where the final "assembly" takes place and the product is delivered to the customer. This subsystem includes the visible part of the service operations system—buildings, equipment and personnel—and possibly other customers. Using the theater analogy, a high-contact service is like a live theater. Customers in low-contact services normally do not see the "factory," where the work is performed. For example, a credit card customer may never have to visit a physical bank. They only talk to the service provider on the phone if there is a problem, and there is very little left of the "theater" performance.

Figure 2.23 Back office operations are typically not seen by the customer.

▶ Other contact points: These consist of all points of contact with the customer. Examples include, advertising communications, sales calls, billing, market research surveys, web site, random exposures to facilities and vehicles, and word of mouth.

Theater as Metaphor: An Integrative Perspective

The theater is a good metaphor for services and their creation through the servuction system. This is because service delivery consists of a series of events that customers experience as a *performance*.[12] This metaphor is particularly useful for high-contact service providers such as physicians, educators, and for businesses that serve many people at the same time. Examples of such businesses are professional sports, hospitals and entertainment (Figure 2.24).

▶ **LO 7**
Obtain insights from viewing service delivery as a form of theater.

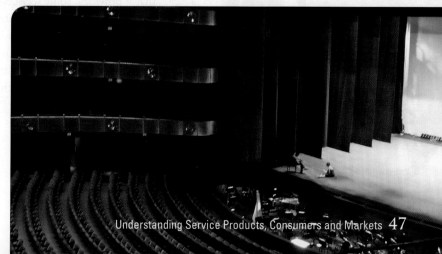

Figure 2.24 When service facilities and personnel are all in place — the stage is set for a memorable service performance for the customer.

► Service facilities: This is the stage on which the drama unfolds. Sometimes, there may be a need to change the sets from one act to another. For example, when airline passengers move from the check-in stations to the boarding lounge, the physical environment is different. Some stages have minimal "props," like in bed and breakfast motels for instance. In contrast, other stages have more elaborate "props," like resort hotels that have elaborate architecture, interior design and landscaping.

► Personnel: The front stage personnel are like the members of a cast, playing roles as *actors* in a drama. The actor in this case, the assistant at the dry cleaners store in our Susan Lee story, did not play her role well. She was unfriendly and unhelpful. The backstage personnel are the support production team in the play. In such cases, front stage personnel are expected to wear special costumes when on stage (such as those plain and light colored gowns worn by hospital staff, the fanciful uniforms worn by hotel doormen or the basic uniforms worn by UPS drivers) (Figure 2.25).

LO 8

Know how role and script theory contribute to a better understanding of service experiences.

The actors in a theater need to know what roles they are playing and need to be familiar with the script. Similarly, in service encounters, knowledge of role and script theories can help organizations to understand, design and manage both employee and customer behaviors during service encounters.

► Roles: A *role* can be defined as "a set of behavior patterns learned through experience and communication, to be performed by an individual in a certain social interaction in order to attain maximum effectiveness in goal accomplishment."[13] Roles have also been defined as expectations of society, which guide behavior in a specific setting or context.[14] In service encounters, both employees and customers have their roles to play. If either party is uncomfortable in the role, or if they do not act according to their roles, it will affect the satisfaction and productivity of both parties. Service firms should proactively define, communicate and train their employees in their roles to achieve performance that yields high customer satisfaction.

► Scripts: Like a movie script, a service script specifies the sequences of behavior that employees and customers are expected to follow during service delivery. Employees receive formal training. Customers learn scripts through experience, education and communication with others. Any deviations from the known script may frustrate both customers and employees, and lead to dissatisfaction. If a company decides to change a service script (for example, by using technology to transform a high-contact service into a low-contact one), service personnel and customers need to be educated about the new approach and the benefits that it provides. Some services are tightly scripted (like flight attendants' scripts for economy class). This reduces variability and ensures uniform quality. On the other hand, some scripts may be more flexible (like flight attendants' scripts for first class). This allows for customization. Figure 2.26 shows a script for teeth cleaning and a simple dental examination. It involves three parties, namely the patient, the receptionist and the dental hygienist. Each has a specific role to play and a script to follow.

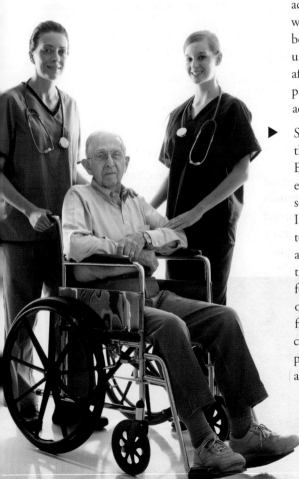

Figure 2.25 Health-care providers are easily recognizable in their nursing gowns.

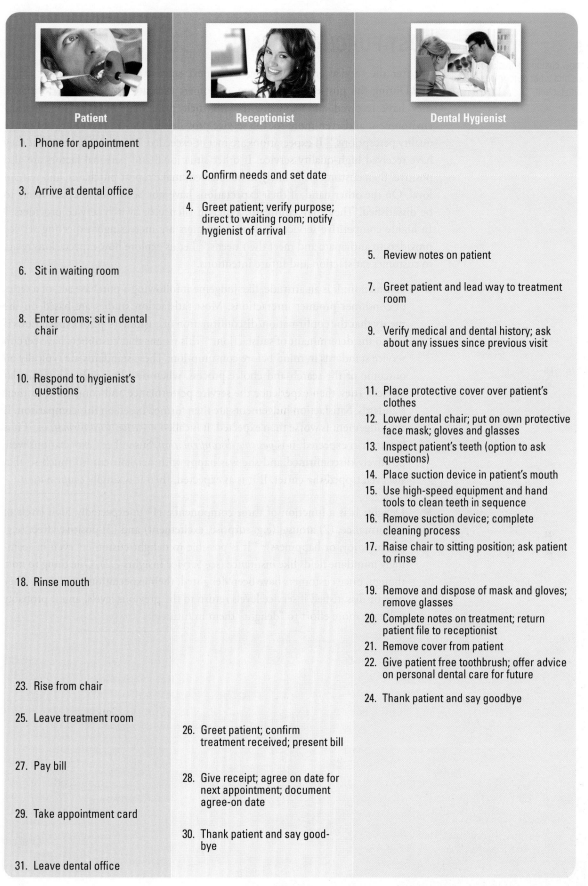

Patient	Receptionist	Dental Hygienist
1. Phone for appointment		
	2. Confirm needs and set date	
3. Arrive at dental office		
	4. Greet patient; verify purpose; direct to waiting room; notify hygienist of arrival	
		5. Review notes on patient
6. Sit in waiting room		
		7. Greet patient and lead way to treatment room
8. Enter rooms; sit in dental chair		
		9. Verify medical and dental history; ask about any issues since previous visit
10. Respond to hygienist's questions		
		11. Place protective cover over patient's clothes
		12. Lower dental chair; put on own protective face mask; gloves and glasses
		13. Inspect patient's teeth (option to ask questions)
		14. Place suction device in patient's mouth
		15. Use high-speed equipment and hand tools to clean teeth in sequence
		16. Remove suction device; complete cleaning process
		17. Raise chair to sitting position; ask patient to rinse
18. Rinse mouth		
		19. Remove and dispose of mask and gloves; remove glasses
		20. Complete notes on treatment; return patient file to receptionist
		21. Remove cover from patient
		22. Give patient free toothbrush; offer advice on personal dental care for future
23. Rise from chair		24. Thank patient and say goodbye
25. Leave treatment room		
	26. Greet patient; confirm treatment received; present bill	
27. Pay bill		
	28. Give receipt; agree on date for next appointment; document agree-on date	
29. Take appointment card		
	30. Thank patient and say good-bye	
31. Leave dental office		

Figure 2.26 Script for teeth cleaning and simple dental examination.

LO 9

Know how customers evaluate services and what determines their satisfaction.

POST-PURCHASE STAGE

After the service encounter stage, the next stage is the post-encounter stage. During the post-encounter stage, customers evaluate the service performance they have received and compare it with their prior expectations. The physical environment and even more so, the service provided by service personnel, influence quality perceptions.[15] If expectations are met or exceeded, customers believe that they have received high-quality service. If other situational and personal factors are also positive, then customers are likely to be satisfied, make repeat purchases, and remain loyal. On the other hand, if their expectations have not been met, they are likely to be dissatisfied. They may complain, suffer in silence or switch service providers.[16] In highly competitive service markets, customers are increasingly expecting service providers to anticipate and meet their needs.[17] Let us explore how expectations relate to customer satisfaction and future intentions.

▶ Satisfaction: It is an attitude, like judgement following a purchase act, or a series of consumer product interactions. Most satisfaction studies are based on the theory that the confirmation/disconfirmation of customers' prior expectations is key to the determinant of satisfaction.[18] This means that customers have certain service standards in mind before consumption. These standards are typically an outcome of the search and choice process, when deciding to buy a particular service. They then experience the service performance and compare it to their standards. Satisfaction judgements are then formed based on this comparison. If the judgement is worse than expected, it is called *negative disconfirmation*. If it is better than expected, it is *positive disconfirmation*. Susan Lee's expectations were positively disconfirmed and she was happy with her hair cut, so much so that she even tipped the cutter. If it is as expected, then it is simply *confirmation*.

▶ Delight: It is a function of three components: (1) unexpectedly high levels of performance, (2) arousal (e.g. surprise, excitement) and (3) positive affect (e.g. pleasure, joy, or happiness).[19] It is possible to delight customers even in seemingly mundane fields like insurance (see Service Insights 2.2). One thing to note though, once customers have been delighted, their expectations are raised. They may be dissatisfied if service levels return to the previous levels, and it probably will take more effort to "delight" them in future.[20]

::: SERVICE INSIGHTS 2.2

Progressive Casualty Insurance Co. prides itself on providing extraordinary customer service—and its accomplishments in the area of claims processing are particulary impressive. To lower its costs and simultaneously improve customer satisfaction and retention, the company introduced its Immediate Response service, offering customers 24/7 access to claims handling. Adjusters work out of mobile claims vans rather than offices, and Progressive has a target of 9 hours for an adjuster to inspect a damaged vehicle. In many instances, claims representatives actually arrive at the scene of an accident while the evidence is still fresh. Consider the following scenario. The crash site in Tampa, Florida, is chaotic and tense. Two cars are damaged, and although the passengers are not bleeding, they are shaken up and scared. Lance Edgy, a senior claim representative for Progressive, arrives on the scene just minutes after the collision. He calms the victims and advises them on medical care, repair shops, police reports, and legal procedures. Edgy invites William McAllister, Progressive's policy holder, into an air-conditioned van equipped with comfortable chairs, a desk, and two cell phones. Even before the tow trucks have cleared away the wreckage, Edgy is able to offer his client a settlement for the market value of his totaled Mercury. McAllister, who did not appear to have been at fault in this accident, later stated in amazement: "This is great—someone coming right out here and taking charge. I didn't expect it at all."

The shortened time cycle has advantages for Progressive, too. Costs are reduced, there's less likelihood that lawyers will become involved when settlement offers are made promptly, and it is easier to prevent fraud. Progressive continues to find new ways to delight its customers. Its web site, www.progressive.com, has been consistently rated as the top among Internet-based insurance carriers by Gomez.com (an Internet quality measurement firm), which places a priority on a site's educational, purchasing, and servicing capabilities. Progressive has also been cited for pleasantly surprising its customers with consumer-friendly innovations and extraordinary customer service.

SOURCE

Henkoff, R. (1994, June 27). Service is Everybody's Business. *Fortune*, p. 50; Hammer, M. (2004) Deep change: How operational innovation can transform your company. *Harvard Business Review* 82 (April), pp. 84–95; www.progressive.com, accessed June, 2008.

CHAPTER SUMMARY

LO 1 ▶ Service consumption can be divided into three stages consisting of the pre-purchase stage, service encounter stage and post-purchase stage.

▶ The pre-purchase stage consists of the following four steps: (1) awareness of need, (2) information search, (3) evaluation of alternative solutions and suppliers and (4) making a decision. The following theories help us to better understand consumer behavior in this stage:

LO 2 / 3 o People often have difficulty in evaluating services because they tend to have much experience and credence attributes. As a result, there is a greater sense of uncertainty and higher perceived risk. Perceived risks can be monetary and non-monetary, such as psychological and social risks.

o Customers do not like to take risks, and firms therefore should employ risk reduction strategies such as offering free trials, guarantees, displaying credentials and providing information via their websites.

LO 4 o Apart from the need to manage perceived risks, firms also have to manage customer expectations that are formed prior to the service encounter stage. What are the components of customer expectations? The components of service expectations include desired and adequate service levels, as well as predicted service levels. Between the desired and adequate service levels is the zone of tolerance, within which customers are willing to accept variation in service levels. Expectations form the basis later for customer satisfaction evaluation in the post-purchase stage.

▶ The next stage is the service encounter stage where the customer initiates, experiences and consumes the service. A number of models can help us to better understand customer behavior during this stage.

LO 5 o First, we distinguish high- and low-contact services. In high-contact services, there is an increased level of customer contact with the service organization. In low-contact services, customers may interact more with web sites and equipment, such as ATMs or call centers. Firms that offer high contact services have to be mindful of the impact of the physical environment and the presence of other customers on their target customers. The behavior of the service personnel can also have a great impact on the service experience. For firms offering low contact services the focus will be on the maintenance of the equipment, and also the design and maintenance of the web site for instance.

LO 6 o Second, we use the servuction model to understand the interactions a customer experiences when consuming a service. The servuction model shows all the interactions that together make up a typical customer experience in a high contact service. Customers interact with the service environment, service employees and even other customers who are present during the service encounter. Each type of interaction can create value (e.g. a pleasant environment, friendly and competent employees, and other customers who are interesting to observe) or destroy value (e.g. another customer speaking loudly on a cell phone in a movie theater). Firms have to orchestrate all interactions to create the service experience customers came to it for.

o In addition to the service delivery system discussed above, the servuction system also includes the service operations system. The service operations system encompasses what is backstage and invisible to the customers. Value is created from the interactions in the front stage, but what goes on in the service operations system backstage can affect the service quality of front stage activities. Therefore, firms also have to co-ordinate the backstage activities well even though they are invisible to the customers.

LO 7 / 8 o Finally, service delivery can be viewed as a form of theater. Therefore, firms can view their services as 'staging' a performance with props and actors. The props are the service facilities and equipment. The actors are the service personnel and customers. Each of the actors needs to understand their roles and scripts so that the service is carried out effectively. Firms can also make use of the role and script theories to design and manage both employee and customer behaviors during service encounters.

LO 9 ▶ The post-purchase stage is where customers evaluate the service performance, and where they form intentions to buy again from this firm or make recommendations to friends.

o During the post-purchase stage, evaluation of a service performance takes place. There may be confirmation or disconfirmation of an expectation. Positive disconfirmation leads to satisfaction, while negative disconfirmation leads to dissatisfaction.

o When there is positive disconfirmation coupled with pleasure and surprise, customer delight occurs.

UNLOCK YOUR LEARNING

These keywords are found within the sections of each Learning Objective (LO). They are integral in understanding the services marketing concepts taught in each section. Having a firm grasp of these keywords and how they are used is essential in helping you do well for your course, and in the real and very competitive marketing scene out there.

LO 1
1. Evaluation of alternatives
2. Evoked set
3. Pre-purchase stage
4. Post-purchase stage
5. Service encounter stage
6. Information search
7. Need awareness
8. Need arousal

LO 2
9. Credence attributes
10. Search attributes

LO 3
11. Experience attributes
12. Service attributes

LO 4
13. Adequate service
14. Desired service
15. Predicted service

16. Purchase decision
17. Service encounter
18. Service expectations
19. Zone of tolerance
20. Moment of truth

LO 5
21. High contact
22. Low contact

LO 6
23. Backstage
24. Factory
25. Front stage
26. Other contact points
27. Servuction system
28. Service operations system
29. Service delivery system

LO 7
30. Actors

31. Performance
32. Service facilities
33. Theatre

LO 8
34. Roles
35. Scripts

LO 9
36. Satisfaction
37. Confirmation
38. Delight
39. Negative disconfirmation
40. Positive disconfirmation

How well do you know the language of services marketing? Quiz yourself!

⚠ **Not for the academically faint-of-heart**

For each keyword you are able to recall without referring to earlier pages, give yourself a point (and a pat on the back). Tally your score at the end and see if you earned the right to be called—a *services marketeer.*

SCORE

0 – 8	Services Marketing is done a great disservice.
9 – 16	The midnight oil needs to be lit, pronto.
17 – 24	I know what you *didn't* do all semester.
25 – 31	A close shave with success.
32 – 39	Now, go forth and market.
39 – 40	There should be a marketing concept named after you.

Review Questions

1. Explain the three-stage model of service consumption.

2. Describe search, experience and credence attributes and give examples of each.

3. Explain why services tend to be harder for customers to evaluate than goods.

4. Why does consumer perception of risk constitute an important aspect in selecting, purchasing and using services? How can firms reduce consumer risk perceptions?

5. How are customers' expectations formed? Explain the difference between desired service and adequate service with reference to a service experience you have had recently.

6. What are "moments of truth"?

7. What are the elements in the servuction system? How does each of the parts contribute to the customer experience as a whole?

8. How do the concepts of role theory, script theory and theatrical perspective help to provide insights into consumer behaviour during the service encounter?

9. Describe the relationship between customer expectations and customer satisfaction.

Application Exercises

1. Select three services, one high in search attributes, one high in experience attributes, and one high in credence attributes. Specify what product characteristics make them easy or difficult for consumers to evaluate. Suggest specific strategies that marketers can adopt in each case to facilitate evaluation and reduce perceived risk.

2. Develop a simple questionnaire designed to measure the key components of customer expectations (i.e. desired, adequate; and predicted service and the zone of tolerance). Conduct 10 interviews with target customers on a service of your choice to understand the structure of their expectations. Develop recommendations for firms offering this service based on your findings.

3. What are the backstage elements of (a) a car repair facility, (b) an airline, (c) a university, and (d) a consulting firm? Under what circumstances would it be appropriate or even desirable to allow customers to see some of these backstage elements, and how would you do it?

4. Visit the facilities of two competing service firms in the same industry (e.g. two banks, restaurants or gas stations) that you believe have different approaches to service. Compare and contrast their approaches using suitable frameworks from this chapter.

5. Apply the script and role theory to a common service of your choice. What insights can you give that would be useful for management?

6. Describe a low-contact service encounter each via email and via phone; and a high-contact, face-to-face encounter that you have had recently. How satisfied were you with each of the encounters? What were the key drivers of your overall satisfaction with these encounters? In each instance, what could the service provider have done to improve the situation?

7. Describe an unsatisfactory encounter that you have experienced with (a) a high-contact service and (b) a low-contact self-service operation. In each instance, what could the service provider have done to improve the situation?

ENDNOTES

1 Adapted from *Principles of Services Marketing and Management*, 2nd edition, Lovelock and Wright.

2 Pin, B. J. & Gilmore, J. H. (1998). Welcome to the experience economy. *Harvard Business Review*, 76 (July-August), pp. 97–108.

3 Prenshaw, P. J., Kovar, S. E., & Burke, K. G. (2006). The impact of involvement on satisfaction for new, nontraditional, credence-based service offerings. *Journal of Services Marketing*, 20(7), pp. 439–452.

4 Berry, L. L. & Bendapudi, N. (2003). Clueing in customers. *Harvard Business Review*, 81(February), pp. 100–107.

5 Zeithaml, V. A., Berry L. L., & Parasuraman, A. (1996). The behavioral consequences of service quality. *Journal of Marketing*, 60(April), pp. 31–46; Teas R. K. & DeCarlo, T. E. (2004). An examination and extension of the zone-of-tolerance model: A comparison to performance-based models on perceived quality. *Journal of Service Research*, 6(3), pp. 272–286.

6 Ikemba, C.M.etal. (2002). Internet use in families with children requiring cardiac surgery for congenital heart disease. *Pediatrics*, 109 (3), pp. 419 - 422

7 Nadiri, H. & Hussain, K. (2005). Diagnosing the zone of tolerance for hotel services. *Managing Service Quality,* 15(5), pp. 259–277.

8 Normann, R. (1978). Moments of truth. *Swedish study*; Normann, R. (1991). *Service management: Strategy and leadership in service businesses* (2nd ed., pp. 16-17). Chichester: John Wiley & Sons.

9 Carlzon, J. (1987). *Moments of truth* (p. 3). Cambridge, MA: Ballinger Publishing Co.

10 Eiglier, P & Langeard, E. (1997). Services as systems: Marketing Implications. In P. Eiglier, E. Langeard, C. H. Lovelock, J. E. G. Bateson, & R. F. Young (Eds.), *Marketing consumer services: New insights,* Report #77-115, November, (pp.83-103). Cambridge, MA: Marketing Science Institute; Langeard, E., Bateson, J. E., Lovelock, C. H., & Eiglier, P. (1981). *Services marketing: New insights from consumers and managers,* Report #81-104, August (p. 1). Cambridge, MA: Marketing Science Institute.

11 Grove, S. J., Fisk, R. P., & John, J. (2000). Services as Theater: Guidelines and Implications. In T. A. Schwartz & D. Iacobucci (Eds.), *Handbook of services marketing and management* (pp. 21–36). Thousand Oaks, CA: Sage Publications.

12 Grove, S. J., Fisk R. P., & John, J. (2003). Services as theater. *(op. cit.);* Baron, S., Harris, K., & Harris, R. (2003). Retail theater: The 'Intended Effect' of the performance. *Journal of Service Research*, 4(May), pp. 316–332; Harris, R., Harris, K., & Baron, S. (2003). Theatrical service experiences, Harris, K., & Baron, S. (2003). Theatrical service experiences: Dramatic script development with employees. *International Journal of Service Industry Management*, 14(2), pp. 184–199.

13 Grove S. J. & Fisk, R. P. (1983). The dramaturgy of services exchange: An analytical framework for services marketing. In L. L. Berry, G. L. Shostack, & G. D. Upah (Eds.), *Emerging perspectives on services marketing* (pp. 45–49). Chicago: American Marketing Association.

14 Solomon, M. R., Suprenant, C., Czepiel, J. A., & Gutman, E. G. (1985). A role theory perspective on dyadic interactions: The service encounter. *Journal of Marketing*, 49(Winter), pp. 99–111.

15 Wall E. A. & Berry, L. L. (2007). The combined effects of the physical environment and employee behavior on customer perception of restaurant service quality. *Cornell Hotel and Restaurant Administration Quarterly*, 48(1), pp. 59–69.

16 Ganesh, J., Arnold M. J., & Reynolds, K. E. (2000). Understanding the customer base of service providers: An examination of the differences between switchers and slayers. *Journal of Marketing*, 64(3), pp. 65–87.

17 Karmarkar, U. (2004). Will you survive the service revolution? *Harvard Business Review*, 82 (June), pp. 101–108.

18 Oliver, R. L. (200). Customer Satisfaction with Service. In T. A. Schwartz & D. Iacobucci (Eds.), *Handbook of service marketing and management* (pp. 247–254). Thousand Oaks, CA: Sage Publications; Wirtz J. & Mattila, A. S. (2001). Exploring the role of alternative perceived performance measures and needs-congruency in the consumer satisfaction process. *Journal of Consumer Psychology*, 11(3), pp. 181–192.

19 Oliver, R. L., Rust, R. T., & Varki, S. (1997). Customer delight: foundations, findings, and managerial insight. *Journal of Retailing*, 73(Fall), pp. 311–336.

20 Rust R. T. & Oliver, R. L. (2000). Should we delight the customer? *Journal of the Academy of Marketing Science,* 28(1), pp. 86–94.

3 positioning
SERVICES in COMPETITIVE MARKETS

LEARNING OBJECTIVES

By the end of this chapter, students should be able to:

LO 1 Know the four focus strategies to achieve competitive advantage.

LO 2 Understand how to identify and select the target segment.

LO 3 Tell the difference between important and determinant attributes for consumer choice and positioning services.

LO 4 Understand how to use service levels for positioning services.

LO 5 Know the four principles of effective positioning.

LO 6 Know the six questions for developing an effective positioning strategy.

LO 7 Understand how to develop an effective positioning strategy using market, internal, and competitor analysis.

LO 8 Demonstrate how positioning maps help to analyze competitive positioning.

OPENING VIGNETTE[1]

POSITIONING A CHAIN OF CHILDCARE CENTERS AWAY FROM THE COMPETITION

Roger Brown and Linda Mason met at business school, following previous experience as management consultants. After graduation, they operated programs for refugee children in Cambodia and then ran a 'Save the Children' relief program in East Africa. When they returned to the United States in 1986 they saw a need for child care centers that would provide care, educational environments and give parents confidence in their children's well-being.

Through research, they discovered an industry that had many weaknesses. There were no barriers to entry, profit margins were low, the industry was labor intensive, there were low economies of scale, there was no clear brand differentiation, and there was a lack of regulation in the industry. Brown and Mason developed a service concept that would allow them to turn these industry weaknesses into strengths for their own company, Bright Horizons (BH). Instead of marketing their services directly to parents—a one-customer-at-a-time sale—BH formed partnerships with companies seeking to offer an on-site day care center for employees with small children. The advantages included:

- A powerful, low-cost marketing channel.

- A partner/customer who supplied the funds to build and equip the center; and would therefore want to help BH to achieve its goal of delivering high-quality care.

- Benefits for parents, who would be attracted to a BH center (rather than competing alternatives) because of its nearness to their own workplace, thus lowering traveling time and offering greater peace of mind.

BH offered a high pay and benefits package to attract the best staff, so that they could provide quality service, one aspect that was lacking in the other providers. Since traditional approaches to childcare either did not have a proper teaching plan or had strict, cookie-cutter lesson plans, BH developed a flexible teaching plan. It was called "World at Their Fingertips," and had a course outline, but gave teachers control over daily lesson plans.

The company sought accreditation for its centers from the National Association for the Education of Young Children (NAEYC) and actively promoted this. BH's emphasis on quality meant that it could meet or exceed the highest local/state government licensing standards. As a result, lack of regulation became an opportunity, not a threat for BH and it gives a source of competitive advantage.

With the support and help from its clients, which include many hi-tech firms, BH has developed innovative technologies such as streaming video of its classrooms to the parents' desktop computers, digitally scanned or photographed artwork, electronic posting of menus, calendars, and student assessments, as well as online student assessment capabilities. All these serve to differentiate the BH and help it to stay ahead of the competition.

BH sees labor as a competitive advantage. It seeks to recruit and retain the best people. It has been named by *Fortune* magazine for the ninth time as among the "100 Best Companies to Work for" in the United States in 2008. In the United Kingdom, BH has been recognized as one of the 2007 Financial Times 50 Best Workplaces by the Great Place to Work Institute, UK. By mid 2007, BH had 18,000 employees worldwide, and was operating more than 500 centers in the United States, Canada, and Europe for over 400 of the world's leading employers, including corporations, hospitals, universities, and government offices. Clients want to hire BH as a partner because they know they can trust the staff.

A raft of integrated and involved service solutions sets BH apart from the competition...

ACHIEVE COMPETITIVE ADVANTAGE THROUGH FOCUS

In an industry with low barriers to entry and a lot of competition, BH managed to find a niche position and differentiate itself from competition. They linked up with employers instead of individual parents, emphasized on service quality, and used accreditation as a selling point. As competition increases in the service sector, service organizations must find ways to stand out from competitors. Brand positioning can help to create awareness, generate interest and desire among prospective customers, and increase adoption of products and services. Senior marketing executives have come to realize that for brands to stand out, they must be carefully created, marketed and positioned. What this means is that managers need to think carefully about all aspects of the service package. In addition, they need to emphasize competitive advantage on those attributes that will be valued by customers in their target segment(s). Competitive advantage can be achieved through focus, which we will discuss next.

⊘ LO 1

Know the four focus strategies to achieve competitive advantage.

Four Focus Strategies

To focus means that firms should not try to appeal to all potential buyers in a market. Customers have varied needs, purchasing behavior, and consumption patterns. Retirees for example, have very different financial needs from people in other stages of life. Firms can focus on retirees as a segment (Figure 3.1). Often, customers are also geographically widely spread. Different service firms also have different abilities to serve different types of customers. Hence, rather than trying to compete in an entire market, each company needs to focus its efforts on those customers it can serve best. In marketing terms, *focus* means providing a relatively narrow product mix for a particular market segment. Nearly all successful service firms apply this concept. They have identified the important elements in their service operations and concentrated their resources on them.

Figure 3.1 Some firms focus on providing financial solutions to retirees as a segment.

The extent of a company's focus can be described along two dimensions—market focus and service focus.[2] *Market focus* is the extent to which a firm serves few or many markets, while *service focus* describes the extent to which a firm offers few or many services. These two dimensions define the four basic focus strategies shown in Figure 3.2.

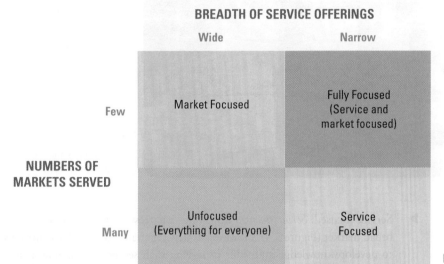

BREADTH OF SERVICE OFFERINGS

	Wide	Narrow
Few	Market Focused	Fully Focused (Service and market focused)
Many	Unfocused (Everything for everyone)	Service Focused

NUMBERS OF MARKETS SERVED

Figure 3.2 Basic focus strategies for services.

SOURCE

Johnston, R. (1996). Achieving focus in service organizations. *The Service Industries Journal*, 16 (January), pp.10–20.

▶ Fully focused: A *fully focused* organization provides a limited range of services (perhaps just a single core product) to a narrow and specific market segment (Figure 3.3). There are both opportunities and risks to such a strategy. If a firm has recognized expertise in a well-defined area, it may provide protection against would-be competitors, and then the firm can charge high prices. The biggest risk is that the market may be too small to get the volume of business needed for financial success. Other risks include the danger that demand for the service may decrease because of alternative products, or that purchasers in the chosen segment may be affected by an economic downturn.

▶ Market focused: A *market focused* company concentrates on a narrow market segment, but has a wide range of services. Before choosing a market focused strategy, managers need to be sure that their firms have the operational capability to do an excellent job of delivering each of the different services selected. They also need to understand customer purchasing practices and preferences. Service Insights 3.1 features the example of Rentokil Initial, a provider of business-to-business services. Rentokil has profited from the growing trend in outsourcing of services related to facilities maintenance which has enabled it to develop a large range of services for its clients.

Figure 3.3 Firms providing luxurious limousine airport services focus on serving business executives and high net-worth individuals.

Figure 3.4 Warehousing service firms provide logistics solutions for broad markets.

▶ Service focused: *Service focused* firms offer a narrow range of services to a fairly broad market (Figure 3.4). However, as new segments are added, the firm needs to develop knowledge and skills in serving each segment. This may require a broader sales effort and greater investment in marketing communication.

▶ Unfocused: Finally, many service providers fall into the *unfocused* category, because they try to serve broad markets and provide a wide range of services. The danger with this strategy is that unfocused firms often are "jack of all trades and master of none."

It is recommended that firms have some sort of focus, whether on market segments or on services. Firms should not use the unfocused strategy as this will only dilute their efforts and cause them to spread their resources too thin when they try to do many things at the same time.

MARKET SEGMENTATION FORMS THE BASIS FOR FOCUSED STRATEGIES

Segmentation is one of the most important concepts in marketing. Since different service firms have different abilities to serve different types of customers, each firm should segment their market. The firm should then identify those parts, or segments of the market that it can serve best.

LO 2
Understand how to identify and select the target segment.

Identifying and Selecting Target Segments

A *market segment* is one where a group of buyers share common characteristics, needs, purchasing behaviors, or consumption patterns. Buyers grouped into the same segment should be as similar as possible. Between segments however, they should be as dissimilar as possible. A *target segment* is one that a firm has selected, from among those in the broader market, and defined on the basis of several variables. For

SERVICE INSIGHTS 3.1

Positioning A Brand Across Multiple Services At Rentokil Initial

With revenue for the first quarter of 2007 at £521.5 million, Rentokil Initial is one of the world's largest business support services companies. The company has about 70,000 employees in over 40 countries where the 'Rentokil' and 'Initial' brands have come to represent innovation, deep expertise and consistent quality of service. It has grown and changed very much from its origins as a manufacturer of rat poison and a pesticide for killing wood-destroying beetles. When the firm realized that it could make more money by providing a service to kill rodents than by selling products that customers themselves would use to target these pests, it shifted to pest control and extermination services.

Through growth within the firm and buying over other companies, Rentokil Initial has developed an wide range of products that includes testing and safety services, security, parcels delivery, interior plants landscaping (including sale or rental of tropical plants), specialized cleaning services, pest control, rental and cleaning of uniforms, clinical waste collection and disposal, personnel services, and a washroom solutions service. The firm sees its core competence as "the ability to carry out high-quality services on other people's premises through well-recruited, well-trained, and motivated staff."

Promoting use of additional services to existing customers is an important part of the firm's strategy. Initial Integrated Services offers clients full integration of services. Clients purchase sector-specific solutions that deliver multiple services but features just "one invoice, one account manager, one helpdesk, one contract and one motivated service team."

According to former chief executive, Sir Clive Thomson:

> Our objective has been to create a virtuous circle. We provide a quality service in

industrial and commercial activities under the same brand-name, so that a customer satisfied with one Rentokil Initial Service is potentially a satisfied customer for another… Although it was considered somewhat odd at the time, one of the reasons we moved into [providing and maintaining] tropical plants [for building interiors] was in fact to put the brand in front of decision makers. Our service people maintaining the plants go in through the front door and are visible to the customer. This contrasts with pest control where no one really notices unless we fail… The brand stands for honesty, reliability, consistency, integrity and technical leadership.

Investment in Research and Development (R&D) ensures constant improvement in its many service lines. For example, the company has built a most intelligent mousetrap called the RADAR. It attracts rats and mice into a sealable chamber and kills them humanely by injecting carbon dioxide. Using Rentokil's unique "pestconnect" technology, the trap causes e-mails to be sent to the customer and the local branch when a rodent is caught. A Rentokil technician receives a text message identifying which unit has been activated at which customer's premises, and its precise location. Now technicians can promptly remove dead animals and better control future infestation.

Rentokil Initial's success lies in its ability to position each of its many business and commercial services in terms of the company's core brand values, which include providing superior standards of customer care and using the most technically advanced services and products. The brand image is strengthened through physical evidence in terms of distinctive uniforms, vehicle color schemes, and use of the corporate logo.

SOURCE

Thompson, C. (1997). "Rentokil Initial: Building a Strong Corporate Brand for Growth and Diversity," In F. Gilmore (Ed.) *Brand Warriors* (pp. 123-124). London: HarperCollinsBusiness; TXT Technology 4 Pest Control, press release, Dec 6, 2005. Available: www.rentokil-initial.com, Accessed February 2008. .

example, Contiki Holidays is a worldwide leader in vacations for those in the 18–35 years age group (Figure 3.5). Their holiday packages are aimed at the fun loving youth group. To cater to different lifestyles and budget needs, Contiki further segmented its packages to include "Getaway" for the independent travelers, "Contiki Resorts" for those who seek rest and relaxation, and "Superior" and "Budget" tours for travelers who want a packed program and yet travel according to their budget needs.

Figure 3.5 Contiki targets the young and fun loving travelers.

Some market segments provide better sales and profits opportunities than others. But firms must also look at whether they can match or exceed competing offerings directed at the same segment. Sometimes, research will show that certain market segments are "underserved." This means that their needs are not well met by existing suppliers. Such markets are often surprisingly large.

In many emerging market economies, there are huge numbers of consumers whose incomes are too small to attract the interest of service businesses that are used to focusing on the needs of wealthier customers. Collectively, however, small wage earners are a very big market and may offer even greater potential for the future as many of them move upwards toward middle class status. For example, it is very different to position services targeted at customers at the bottom of the pyramid (Figure 3.6). They are the low-income group. When Smart Communications Inc. wanted to target the low-income people in Philippines, they looked at Proctor and Gamble for ideas on how to keep product prices low. They found that there are micropacks for items such as shampoo, soaps, and food at a low-ticket price. Therefore, when Smart Communications Ltd. launched its mobile service to the low-income group, they offered prepaid pricing plans with airtime in small packages, with prices in small denominations that started from as low as US$0.50. This strategy was a resounding success and within ten months, revenues exceeded $2 million a day.[3]

Figure 3.6 A community-based savings bank in Battambang, Cambodia, offers microfinancing to a range of lower-income clients that includes consumers and the self-employed.

SERVICE ATTRIBUTES AND LEVELS

Once a target segment has been selected, firms need to provide their market with the right service concept. How can a firm develop the right service concept for a particular target segment? Research is often needed to see what attributes of a given service are important to specific market segments. However, it is dangerous to over-generalize. The importance of attributes may differ for the same individual according to:

▶ The purpose of using the service.

▶ Who makes the decision.

▶ The timing of use (time of day/week/season).

▶ Whether the individual is using the service alone or with a group.

▶ Who is in the group.

Think about what determines your choice when choosing a restaurant for lunch (1) on vacation with friends or family, (2) meeting with a potential business client, and (3) going for a quick meal with a co-worker. Given a reasonable selection of alternatives, it is unlikely that you would choose the same type of restaurant in each instance, let alone the same one. It is possible too, that if you left the decision to another person in the party, he or she would end up with a different choice.

Important versus Determinant Attributes

Consumers usually make their choices between alternative service offerings based on the perceived differences between them. However, the attributes that differentiate competing services are not always the most important ones. For example, "safety" may be considered a very important attribute in the choice of an airline, but it is not the attribute that buyers base their final decision on because typically all airlines the buyer considers are likely to be perceived as performing equally well on

safety. Therefore, *determinant attributes* (i.e. those that actually determine buyers' choices between competing alternatives) are often not on the top of the list of service characteristics that are important for making buying decisions. Rather, consumers focus on attributes that are different between competing alternatives. For example, convenience of departure and arrival times (Figure 3.7), availability of frequent flyer miles, quality of food and drinks on board might be examples of determinant characteristics for business travelers

LO 3

Tell the difference between important and determinant attributes for consumer choice and positioning services.

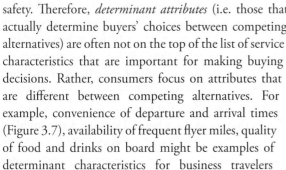

Figure 3.7 Convenient departure times are determinant attributes for business travelers.

Figure 3.8 With an army of 54,000 dedicated professionals, over 8 million square meters of warehouse space, and an extensive global network spanning 190 countries, CEVA Logistics satisfies the condition of reach as a determinant attribute of choice.

when selecting an airline. In contrast, for budget-conscious holiday-makers, price is often a determinant attribute. For a logistics firm, clients with global operations are likely to look at reach as a determinant attribute. Hence, a company that is able to deliver to far and remote places will be used over one that cannot (Figure 3.8).

● LO 4

Understand how to use service levels for positioning services.

Establishing Service Levels

While we need to understand the difference between important and determinant attributes, creating a positioning strategy requires more than just identifying those attributes. Decisions must be made on the level of performance to offer on each attribute. Some service attributes are easily quantified, while others are qualitative. Price, for instance, is a quantitative measure. Punctuality of transport services can be expressed in terms of the percentage of trains, buses, or flights arriving within a specified number of minutes from the scheduled time. Both of these measures are easy to understand and therefore quantifiable. On the other hand, characteristics such as the quality of personal service, or a hotel's degree of luxury are more qualitative and therefore subject to individual interpretation. For instance, if customers say they value physical comfort, what does that mean for a hotel? Does it refer to ambient conditions, such as temperature and absence of noise? Or does it refer to visible, tangible elements, such as the bed? In practice, both ambient conditions and tangible elements must be addressed.

Customers can often be segmented according to their willingness to give up some level of service for a lower price. Price-insensitive customers are willing to pay a relatively high price to obtain high levels of service on each of the attributes that are important to them. In contrast, price-sensitive customers will look for an inexpensive service that offers relatively low levels of performance on many key attributes (see Service Insights 3.2). However, there may still be attributes like safety, on which they are not willing to forego.

::: **SERVICE** INSIGHTS 3.2

Capsule Hotels

Capsule hotels consist of small rooms almost the size of large cupboards. Some of these cupboard-like rooms cost only about US$18 a night. The main benefits of these hotels are convenience and price. They started in space-constrained Japan in the 1980s but did not take off in other parts of the world until recently. Now, capsule hotel chains have been launched in many countries and include Pod Hotel in New York, Yotel in London, citizen M and Qbic in Amsterdam, and StayOrange.com Hotel in Kuala Lumpur, Malaysia

These new chains have also modified their service offering, differentiating themselves from the early capsule hotels in Japan. For example, the Yotel group offers different classes of rooms which they call cabins. This concept was derived from the capsule hotels of Japan and the first class cabins in British Airways' planes. In the premium room for example, the double bed can be converted into a couch at the touch of a button, there are tables to accommodate hand luggage, a luxury bathroom,

a study desk that unfolds and has all the techno points available, including free Internet access, a flat-screen TV system, and 24-hour in cabin service. The cost of that premium room at the London Heathrow Airport is £80 a night, and the cost for a standard room per day is only £55, a fraction of the typical price for a hotel room in London.

Yotel and Qbic have aggressive growth plans, and we can expect capsule hotels to become a mainstream choice for travelers in the future!

SOURCES

Capsule Hotel: Thinking Small. *The Economist*, 17 November 2007. http://www.stayorange.com/; www.yotel.com; http://www.thepodhotel.com/index.html; http://en.wikipedia.org/wiki/Capsule_hotel accessed in February 2008;" Yotel Capsule Hotel at Heathrow Airport Terminal 4. http://edition.cnn.com/2007/BUSINESS/10/02/latest.news/index.html.

POSITIONING DISTINGUISHES A BRAND FROM ITS COMPETITORS

▶ **LO 5**
Know the four principles of effective positioning.

Once we have segmented the market, and understood determinant attributes and related service levels, we need to see how best we can position our service in a competitive market. Competitive positioning strategy is based on establishing and maintaining a unique place in the market for an organization and/or its individual product offerings. Effective positioning is based on four principles[4]:

1. A company must establish a position in the minds of its target customers.

2. The position should have one simple and consistent message.

3. The position must set a company apart from its competitors (Figure 3.9).

4. A company cannot be all things to all people—it must focus its efforts.

"In hindsight, I'd say my first mistake was letting my competitors advertise on my website."

Figure 3.9 For powerful positioning, a firm needs to set itself apart from its competitors.

These principles apply to any type of firm that competes for customers. Firms must understand the principles of positioning in order to develop an effective competitive position. Grant Thornton, the fifth largest firm in the industry, has successfully positioned itself as offering easy access to partners and having "a passion for the business of accounting" (Figure 3.10). The concept of positioning forces service managers to analyze their firm's existing offerings and provide specific answers to the following six questions for developing an effective positioning strategy:

◉ LO 6

Know the six questions for developing an effective positioning strategy.

1. What does our firm currently stand for in the minds of current and potential customers?

2. What customers do we serve now, and which ones would we like to target in the future?

3. What is the value proposition for each of our current service products, and what market segments is each one targeted at?

4. How does each of our service products differ from those of our competitors'?

5. How well do customers in the chosen target segments perceive our service products as meeting their needs?

6. What changes do we need to make to our service products in order to strengthen our competitive position within our target segment(s)?

One of the challenges in developing a positioning strategy is to avoid the trap of investing too heavily in points of difference that can easily be copied. As researchers Kevin Keller, Brian Sternthal, and Alice Tybout noted that "Positioning needs to

Figure 3.10 The ardent accountant with the dangling rose in mouth and come-hither eyes amusingly conveys Grant Thornton's passion for what they can do for their clients.

keep competitors out, not draw them in."[5] When Roger Brown and Linda Mason, the founders of the BH chain of child-care centers featured in the beginning of this chapter, were developing their service concept and business model, they took a long, hard look at the industry.[6] Discovering that for-profit child-care companies had adopted low-cost strategies, the Browns selected a different approach that competitors would find very difficult to copy.

DEVELOPING AN EFFECTIVE POSITIONING STRATEGY

LO 7
Understand how to develop an effective positioning strategy using market, internal, and competitor analysis.

After we understand the importance of focus and the principles of positioning, let us discuss how to develop a positioning strategy. Positioning involves decisions on attributes that are important to customers. To improve a product's appeal to a specific target segment, it may be necessary to reduce its price, to change the times and locations when it is available, or to change the forms of delivery that are offered. Market internal and competitor analysis is needed to develop an effective positioning strategy, which we will discuss next.

Market, Internal, and Competitor Analyses

Positioning links market analysis and competitor analysis to internal corporate analysis. From these three, a position statement can be developed that allows the service organization to answer our six questions for developing an effective positioning strategy. Figure 3.11 identifies the basic steps involved in identifying a suitable market position and developing a strategy to reach it.

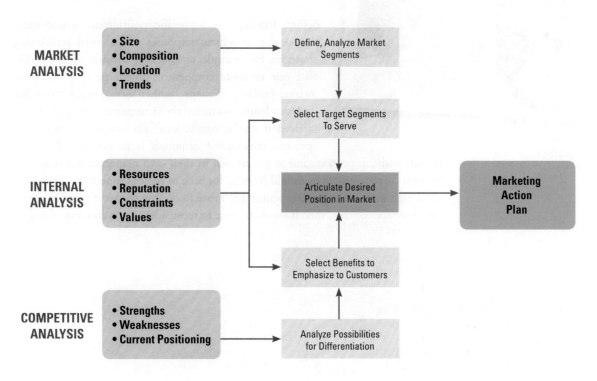

Figure 3.11 Developing a market positioning strategy.

Market Analysis

The focus is on the overall level and trend of demand, and the geographic location of this demand. Is demand increasing or decreasing for the benefits offered by this type of service? Are there regional or international variations in the level of demand? Are there other ways of segmenting the market? The size and potential of different market segments should also be looked into. Research may be needed to gain a better understanding not only of customer needs and preferences within each of the different segments, but also of how each perceives the competition.

Internal Corporate Analysis

The objective is to identify the organization's resources (financial, human labor and know-how, and physical assets), limitations, its goals (profitability, growth, professional preferences, etc.), and how its values shape the way it does business. Using insights from this analysis, management should be able to select a limited number of target market segments which can be served with either new or existing services.

Competitor Analysis

Analysis of competitors helps firms to understand the strengths and weaknesses competitors have (Figure 3.12). This may in turn suggest opportunities for differentiation. Relating these insights back to the internal corporate analysis should suggest what might be possible opportunities for differentiation and competitive advantage. This will help managers to decide which benefits should be emphasized to which target segments. This analysis should consider both direct and indirect competition.

Figure 3.12 Executives conducting competitive analysis.

Before deciding on a specific positioning, management should also anticipate responses to potential positioning strategies. For example, one needs to consider the possibility that one or more competitors might go after the same market position. Perhaps another service organization has independently conducted the same positioning analysis and arrived at similar conclusions? The best way to anticipate possible competitive responses is to identify all current or potential competitors, and to put oneself in their own management's shoes. An internal corporate analysis should be done for each of these competitors.[7] If chances seem high that a stronger competitor will move to occupy the same position with a better service concept, then it would be wise to reconsider the positioning strategy.

Companies that try to compete in a space where there is already intense competition would end up in a "bloody" fight that stains the ocean red, because a strategy of matching and beating rivals tends to emphasize the same basic dimensions of competition. The way out is to use the "blue ocean" strategy, looking for a market space that makes the competition irrelevant[8] (Figure 3.13). The challenge is to create a new market space that competitors will not be able to match. James Heskett frames the issue nicely:

> The most successful service firms separate themselves from "the pack" to achieve a distinctive position in relation to their competition. They differentiate themselves. by altering typical characteristics of their respective industries to their competitive advantage.[9]

Position statement

The outcome of the three forms of analysis is a statement that states the desired position of the organization in the marketplace. With this understanding, marketers can now develop a specific plan of action.

Figure 3.13 Cirque du Soleil reimagines the circus show with its dazzling brand of ballet and theater.

Such a positioning analysis and its implementation have to be done periodically as positions usually change over time. They change in response to changing market structures, technology, competitive activity, and the evolution of the firm itself. Typically, repositioning includes adding or removing services and target segments. Some companies decreased their offerings and stopped certain lines of business in order to be more focused. Others expanded their offerings to increase sales to existing customers and attract new ones. For example, supermarkets and other retailers have added banking services, while online providers are adding new and innovative services such as Google Earth and YouTube in Google's case.

USING POSITIONING MAPS TO ANALYZE COMPETITIVE POSITIONING

LO 8

Demonstrate how positioning maps help to analyze competitive positioning.

Positioning maps are great tools to visualize competitive positioning, to map developments over time, and to develop scenarios of potential competitor responses. Developing a positioning "map"—a task sometimes referred to as perceptual mapping—is a useful way of showing consumers' perceptions of alternative products graphically. A map usually has two attributes, although three-dimensional models can be used to portray three of these attributes. When more than three dimensions are needed to describe product performance in a given market, then a series of separate charts need to be drawn.

An Example of Applying Positioning Maps to the Hotel Industry

The hotel business is highly competitive, especially during seasons when the supply of rooms exceeds demand. Within each class of hotels, customers visiting a large city may find that they have several options to choose from. Some customers may choose the degree of luxury and comfort, some may choose attributes such as location, safety, cleanliness, and special rewards programs for frequent guests (Figure 3.14).

Let us look at an example of how to apply positioning maps, based on a real-world situation. Managers of the Palace, a successful four-star hotel, developed a positioning map of their own and competing hotels. This helped them to develop a better understanding of future threats to their current market position, in a large city that we will call Belleville.

Located on the edge of the financial district, the Palace was an elegant old hotel that had been renovated to a great extent and modernized a few years earlier. Its competitors included eight 4-star establishments, and the Grand, one of the city's oldest hotels, which had a 5-star rating. The Palace has been very profitable in recent years, and has an above average occupancy rate. For many months of the year, it was sold out on weekdays. This shows that it was popular with business travelers. These business travelers were very attractive to the hotel, because of their willingness to pay a higher room rate than tourists or conference delegates. However, the general manager and his staff saw problems ahead. Planning permission had recently been granted for four large new hotels in the city, and the Grand had just started a major renovation and expansion project, which included construction of a new wing. There was a risk that customers might see the Palace as falling behind.

To understand better the nature of the competitive threat, the hotel's management team worked with a consultant to prepare charts that displayed the Palace's position in the business traveler market both before and after the entrance of new competition. Four attributes were selected for study: room price, level of personal service, level of physical luxury, and location.

Figure 3.14 A luxury hotel like Dubai's Burj Al Arab is favorably positioned along many determinant attributes, including level of personal service, level of physical extravagance, and location.

Data Sources

Management did not conduct new consumer research. Instead, they got their customer perception data from various sources:

▶ Published information.

▶ Data from past surveys.

▶ Reports from travel agents and knowledgeable hotel staff members who mixed frequently with customers.

Information on competing hotels was not difficult to obtain, since the locations were known. Information was obtained through following ways:

▶ Visiting and evaluated physical structures.

▶ Sales staff kept themselves informed on pricing policies and discounts.

▶ For service level, they used the ratio of rooms per employee, easily calculated from the published number of rooms and employment data provided to the city authorities.

▶ Data from surveys of travel agents conducted by the Palace provided additional insights on the quality of personal service at each competitor.

Measures

Scales were then created for each attribute:

▶ Price was simple. The average price charged to business travelers for a standard single room at each hotel was already quantified.

▶ The room per employee ratio was the basis for a service level scale, with low ratios being equated with high service. This scale was then changed slightly because of what was known about the quality of service actually delivered by each major competitor.

▶ Level of physical luxury was more subjective. The management team identified the hotel that members agreed was the most luxurious (the Grand) and then the four-star hotel that they viewed as having the least luxurious physical facilities (the Airport Plaza). All other 4-star hotels were then rated on this attribute relative to these two benchmarks.

▶ Location was defined using the stock exchange building in the heart of the financial district as a reference point. Past research had shown that majority of the Palace's business guests were visiting destinations in this area. The competitive set of ten hotels lay within a four-mile, fan-shaped radius, extending from the exchange through the city's main retail area (where the convention center was also located) to the inner suburbs and the nearby airport.

Two positioning maps were created to portray the existing competitive situation. The first (Figure 3.15) showed the ten hotels on the dimensions of price and service level; the second (Figure 3.16) displayed them on location and degree of physical luxury.

Findings

Some findings were intuitive, but others provided valuable insights.

▶ A quick glance at Figure 3.15 shows a clear correlation between the attributes of price and service. Hotels offering higher levels of service are relatively more expensive. The shaded bar running from the upper left to the lower right highlights this relationship.

▶ Further analysis shows that there appear to be three groups of hotels within what is already an upscale market category. At the top end, the 4-star Regency is close to the 5-star Grand. In the middle, the Palace is grouped with four other hotels, and at the lower end, there is another group of three hotels.

▶ One surprising insight from this map is that the Palace appears to be charging quite a lot more (on a relative basis) than its service level would seem to justify. Since its occupancy rate is very high, guests are evidently willing to pay the going rate.

▶ In Figure 3.16, we see how the Palace is positioned relative to the competition on location and degree of luxury. We would not expect these two variables to be related and they do not appear to be so.

▶ A key insight here is that the Palace occupies a relatively empty portion of the map. It is the only hotel in the financial district. This probably explains its ability to charge more than its service level (or degree of physical luxury) would seem to justify.

▶ There are two groups of hotels in the vicinity of the shopping district and convention center (Figure 3.17). They are a relatively luxurious group of three, led by the Grand, and a second group of two offering a moderate level of luxury.

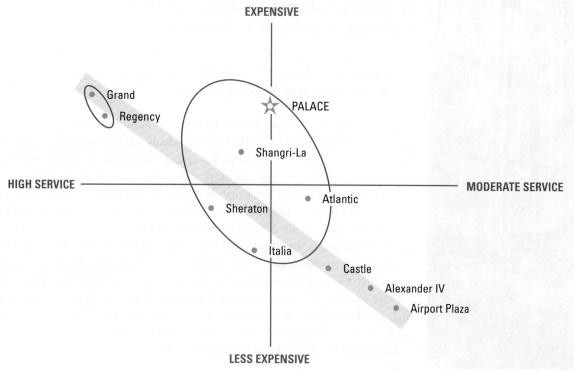

Figure 3.15 Positioning map of Belleville's principal business hotels: Service Level versus Price Level.

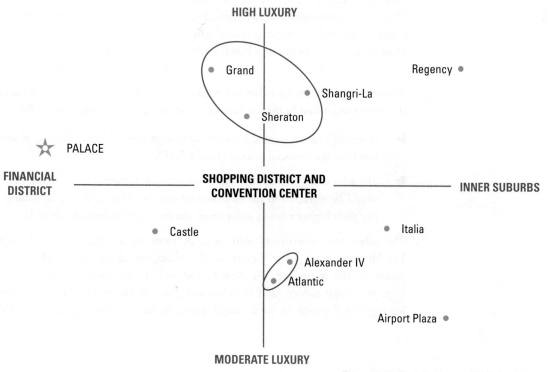

Figure 3.16 Positioning map of Belleville's principal business hotels: Location versus Physical Luxury.

Figure 3.17 The kaleidoscopic glass panes of the Montreal Convention Center is a huge draw for hoteliers and other services providers.

Mapping Future Scenarios to Identify Potential Competitive Responses

What about the future? The Palace's management team next wanted to anticipate the positions of the four new hotels being constructed in Belleville, as well as the probable repositioning of the Grand (see Figures 3.18 and 3.19).

Pricing was easy to estimate. New hotels use a formula for setting posted room prices (the prices typically charged to individuals staying on a week-night in high season). This price is linked to the average construction cost per room at the rate of one dollar per night for every thousand dollars of construction costs. For example, a 200-room hotel that costs $80 million to build would have an average room cost of $400,000. This would mean that they need to set a price of $400 per room night. Using this formula, Palace managers concluded that the four new hotels would have to charge quite a lot more than the Grand or Regency. This would establish what marketers call a *price-umbrella* above existing price levels. Competitors will then have the choice of raising their own prices. To account for their high prices, the new hotels would have to offer customers very high standards of service and luxury. At the same time, the New Grand would need to raise its own prices to recover the costs of renovation, new construction, and enhanced service offerings (see Figure 3.18).

In terms of location, the construction sites were already known. Two would be in the financial district, and two near the convention center, which was itself under expansion. Press releases distributed by the Grand had already declared its management's intentions. After renovation, the "New Grand" would not only be larger, but also more luxurious, and would include many new service features. Three of the newcomers would be linked to international chains and their strategies could be guessed by studying recent hotels opened in other cities by these same chains. Two of the brand new hotels planned to seek 5-star status.

Assuming no changes by either the Palace or other existing hotels, the impact of the new competition in the market was clearly a significant threat to the Palace.

▶ It would lose its unique location advantage and in future be one of three hotels in the financial district (Figure 3.19).

▶ The sales staff believed that the existing business customers of many Palaces would be attracted to the Continental and the Mandarin and be willing to pay their higher rates in order to obtain the superior benefits offered.

The other two newcomers were seen as more of a threat to the Shangri-La, Sheraton, and New Grand in the shopping district/convention center group. In the meantime, the New Grand and the newcomers would create a high price/high service (and high luxury) group at the top end of the market, leaving the Regency in what might prove to be a unique space of its own.

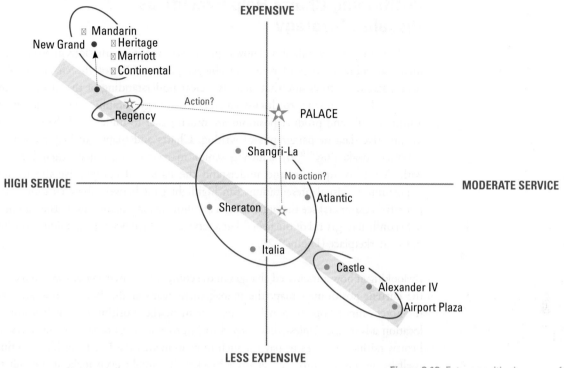

Figure 3.18 Future positioning map of Belleville's business hotels: Service Level versus Price Level.

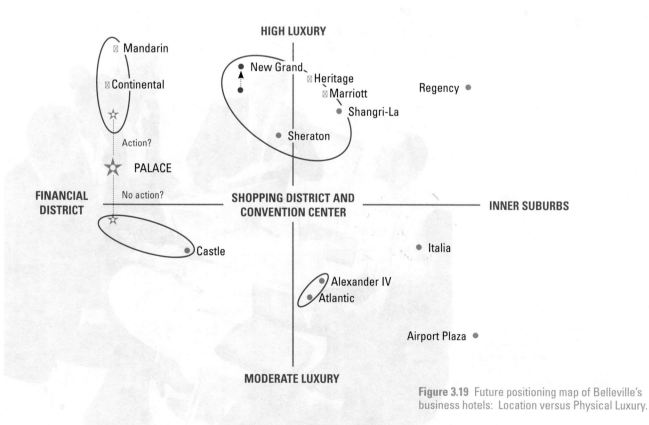

Figure 3.19 Future positioning map of Belleville's business hotels: Location versus Physical Luxury.

Positioning Charts Help Executives Visualize Strategy

The Palace Hotel example shows how capturing competitive situations in positioning maps can allow us to understand the bigger picture. One of the challenges that strategists face is to ensure that there is a clear understanding of the firm's current situation before moving to discuss changes in strategy. Graphic representations of a firm's profile and product positions are much easier to understand than tables of quantitative data or paragraphs of writing. Charts and maps can help to achieve a "visual awakening."[10] By allowing senior managers to compare their business with that of competitors and understand the nature of competitive threats and opportunities, visual presentations can highlight gaps between how customers (or potential customers) see the organization and how management sees it. This can thus help confirm or get rid of the belief that a service or a firm occupies a unique position in the marketplace (Figure 3.20).

By looking at how anticipated changes in the competitive environment would redraw the current positioning map, the management team at the Palace could see that the hotel cannot hope to remain in its current market position once it had lost its location advantage. Unless they moved to improve its level of service and physical luxury, raising its prices to pay for such improvements, the hotel was likely to find itself being pushed into a lower price bracket that might even make it difficult to maintain current standards of service and physical upkeep.

Figure 3.20 Placing the relevant actors and players on a positioning chart helps identify what approaches or strategies will be most effective for the different positions.

LO 1 ▶ In any competitive industry, firms need to focus to achieve competitive advantage. There are three focused strategies that can be used to achieve competitive advantage. They are (1) fully focused, (2) service focused, and (3) market focused. There is a fourth, the unfocused strategy. However, it is not advisable for firms to choose an unfocused strategy as this will mean that they spread themselves too thin to remain competitive.

LO 2 ▶ Marketing segmentation forms the basis for the three focused strategies. In marketing segmentation, firms should identify and select target segments that it can serve best.

LO 3 ▶ When determining the attributes that are important to its target segments, there is a need to understand the difference between important and determinant attributes in consumer choice decisions.

o   An attribute may be important to the consumer, but that may not be important for buying decisions (e.g. safety is important, but all airlines a traveler considers are seen as safe). If that is the case, such an attribute should not be used as a basis for segmentation.

o   Determinant attributes are attributes that consumers focus on when comparing alternative services and can be used for product positioning.

LO 4 ▶ Once the important and determinant attributes are understood, management should decide what service level the firm can achieve for each of the attributes. Service levels are often used to segment customers according to their willingness to trade off price and service level across a broad variety of attributes.

LO 7 ▶ With the understanding of service attributes and levels, firms can develop their market positioning strategy. To do that, they need to conduct market, internal and competitor analyses. The outcome of these analyses is the position statement. Positioning changes and does not stay still. It needs to develop and change according to changes in competitive responses and consumer trends.

LO 8 ▶ One important tool to help firms develop their positioning strategy are positioning maps. They provide a visual way of summarizing research data and display how different firms are perceived as performing relative to each other on determinant attributes. When combined with information on the preferences of different segments, including the level of demand that might be anticipated from such segments, positioning maps help to identify opportunities for creating new services or repositioning existing ones to take advantage of unserved market needs.

UNLOCK YOUR LEARNING

These keywords are found within the sections of each Learning Objective (LO). They are integral in understanding the services marketing concepts taught in each section. Having a firm grasp of these keywords and how they are used is essential in helping you do well for your course, and in the real and very competitive marketing scene out there.

LO 1
1. Competitive advantage
2. Focus
3. Market focus
4. Service focus
5. Focus strategies
6. Fully focused
7. Unfocused
8. Market segmentation
9. Segmentation

LO 2
10. Market segment
11. Target segment

LO 3
12. Determinant attributes

LO 4
13. Positioning strategy

LO 5
14. Positioning
15. Principle of positioning

LO 7
16. Competitor analysis
17. Internal corporate analysis
18. Market analysis

19. Positioning Analysis
20. Position statement
21. Repositioning

LO 8
22. Perceptual mapping
23. Positioning "map"
24. "Visual awakening"

How well do you know the language of services marketing? Quiz yourself!

 Not for the academically faint-of-heart

For each keyword you are able to recall without referring to earlier pages, give yourself a point (and a pat on the back). Tally your score at the end and see if you earned the right to be called—a *services marketeer.*

SCORE

0 – 3   Services Marketing is done a great disservice.

4 – 8   The midnight oil needs to be lit, pronto.

9 – 12   I know what you *didn't* do all semester.

13 – 16 A close shave with success.

17 – 20 Now, go forth and market.

21 – 24 There should be a marketing concept named after you.

Review Questions

1. Why should firms focus their efforts? Describe the basic focus strategies, and give examples of how these work.

2. Why is market segmentation important to service firms?

3. How do you identify and select target market segments?

4. What is the difference between important and determinant attributes in consumer choice decisions? How can research help you to understand which is which?

5. How are service levels of determinant attributes related to positioning services?

6. What are the four principles of effective positioning?

7. What are the six questions for developing an effective positioning strategy?

8. Describe what is meant by positioning strategy and how do the marketing concepts of market, internal and competitive analysis relate to it?

9. How can positioning maps help managers better understand and respond to competition?

WORK YOUR ESM

Application Exercises

1. Travel agencies are losing business to online bookings offered to passengers by airline web sites. Identify some possible focus options open to travel agencies wishing to develop new lines of business that would make up for the loss of airline ticket sales.

2. Provide two examples of service firms that use service levels (other than airlines, hotels, and car rentals) to differentiate their products. Explain the determinant attributes and their service levels that are used to differentiate the positioning of one service from another?

3. Choose an industry that you are familiar with (such as cell phone service, credit cards, or an online music store) and create a perceptual map showing the positions of the different competitors in the industry. Use attributes that you think consumers use to make decisions.

4. Imagine that you have been hired to give advice to Palace Hotel. Consider the options facing the hotel based on the four attributes in the positioning charts (Figures 3.15 and 3.16). What actions do you recommend the Palace take? Explain your recommendations.

ENDNOTES

1. Brown, R. (2001). How we built a strong company in a weak industry, *Harvard Business Review*, 79(February), 51–57. Retrieved March 2008 from http://www.brighthorizons.com.html.

2. Johnston, R. (1996). Achieving focus in service organizations. *The Service Industries Journal*, 16(January), 10–20.

3. Anderson, J., & Markides, C. (2007). Strategic innovation at the base of the pyramid. *MIT Sloan Management Review*, Fall, 40(1), 83–88.

4. Trout, J. (1997). The new positioning: *The latest on the World's #1 business strategy*, NY: McGraw-Hill.

5. Keller, K. L., Sternthal, B., & Tybout, A. (2002). Three questions you need to ask about your brand. *Harvard Business Review*, 80(September), 84.

6. Brown, R. (2001). *Op. Cit.*

7. For a detailed approach see, Porter, M. E., (1980). A framework for competitor analysis. *Competitive Strategy* (pp. 47-74). New York: The Free Press.

8. Kim W. C., & Mauborgne, R. (2005). *Blue ocean strategy: How to create uncontested market space and make competition irrelevant*. Boston: Harvard Business School Press.

9. Heskett, J. L. (1984). *Managing in the service economy* (p. 45). Boston: Harvard Business School Press.

10. Kim W. C., & Mauborgne, R. (2002). Charting your company's future. *Harvard Business Review*, 80(June), 77–83.

BLANK

THE *ESM*
FRAMEWORK

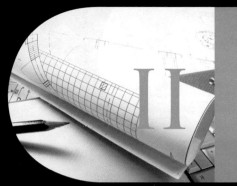

Applying the 4Ps to Services

PART II revisits the 4Ps of the traditional marketing mix. However, the 4Ps are expanded to take into account the characteristics of services that are different from goods. It consists of the following four chapters:

Chapter 4 Developing Service Products: Core and Supplementary Elements

Discusses the meaningful service concept that includes both the core and supplementary elements. The supplementary elements both facilitate and enhance the core service offering.

Chapter 5 Distributing Service through Physical and Electronic Channels

Examines the time and place elements. Manufacturers usually require physical distribution channels to move their products. Some service businesses however, are able to use electronic channels to deliver all (or at least some) of their service elements. Especially for the services delivered in real time with customers physically present, speed and convenience of place and time have become important determinants of effective service delivery.

Chapter 6 Setting Prices and Implementing Revenue Management

Provides an understanding of pricing from both the firm and customer's point of view. For firms, the pricing strategy determines income generation. Service firms need to implement revenue management to maximize the revenue that can be generated from available capacity at any given time. From the customer's perspective, price is a key part of the costs they must incur to obtain the wanted benefits. The cost to the customer includes non-monetary costs.

Chapter 7 Promoting Services and Educating Customers

Deals with how firms should tell their customers about their services through promotion and education. In services marketing, much communication is educational in nature, especially with new customers. Since customers are co-producers and contribute to how others experience service performances, much communication in services marketing is educational in nature to teach customers how to effectively move through a service process.

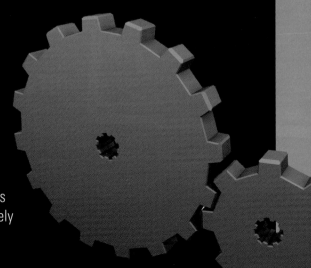

LEARNING OBJECTIVES

By the end of this chapter, students should be able:

LO 1 Define what a service product is.

LO 2 Know how to design a service concept.

LO 3 Describe the flower of service and know how the facilitating and enhancing supplementary services relate to the core product.

LO 4 Know how service firms use different branding strategies for their product lines.

LO 5 List the categories of new service development, ranging from simple style changes to major innovations.

LO 6 Be familiar with the factors needed to achieve success in developing new services.

Figure 4.1 Starbucks is a familiar brand that even has traditional tea consumers drinking out of its cups.

OPENING VIGNETTE[1]

As you walk along the street, the aroma drifts through the air and attracts you. It is drawing you toward the store with the green sign that has now become a common sight. You enter Starbucks, the place where you can sit down and enjoy a great cup of coffee in a comfortable settee or on a chair. You can also surf the Internet on the free wireless broadband service that is available in many of the Starbucks outlets around the world. Starbucks is a place that you would associate with coffee, before anything else.

As a service innovation, Starbucks has been transforming itself into a place for entertainment. It wants to extend the pop culture. It does that through Hear Music Starbucks. Customers can buy from an extensive selection of hand-selected and compiled physical CDs in the Starbucks Hear Music Coffeehouses. Alternatively, they can burn personalized CDs from a digital inventory of more than a million sound tracks, including new recordings that can only be found in some Starbucks outlets. Debut albums of some new musicians are actually launched and available only exclusively at Starbucks outlets. Starbucks also sells movie DVDs and books from emerging as well as established authors. It has tied up with Apple's iTunes Wi-Fi Music Store to allow music playing at selected Starbucks cafes, up to the last ten songs played, to be browsed, bought and downloaded wirelessly onto the iPhone or iPod. This music will sync back to the Mac or PC the next time it is connected. Soon, we will no longer associate Starbucks with just mocha. Rather, we will see it as a place to relax and feel at home. Starbucks is a company that has developed new service innovations with great success. However, it cannot rest on its laurels as competition is intense. It has to continue to reinvent itself to maintain its edge in the industry.

> **...One of the trendsetters of lifestyle services, Starbucks has popularized the coffeehouse as contemporary and chic...**

COMMERCIAL TRAVEL COMES TO SPACE

It's expensive, but it's worth it.

"They seem to be popping up EVERYWHERE these days."

SERVICE PRODUCT

What do we mean by a service "product"? A service product consists of two components, the core product and supplementary services. The core product is based on the core set of benefits and solutions delivered to customers. These are usually defined with reference to a particular industry like healthcare or transportation. For example, in healthcare, the core product may be the restoration of the body back to an optimum condition. Surrounding the core product is a variety of service-related activities called *supplementary services*. Supplementary services augment the core product by facilitating its use and enhancing its value and appeal. The supplementary services often play an important role in differentiating and positioning the core product against competing services.

DESIGNING A SERVICE PRODUCT

How should one go about designing a service concept? Experienced marketers know that they need to look at the entire service performance in a holistic manner. The firm needs to determine specific aspects that it plans to compete on. In order to do that, the value proposition needs to combine three components: (1) core product, (2) supplementary services, and (3) delivery processes. The delivery processes are those that are used to deliver both the core product and supplementary services. The design of the service offering must address the following issues:

▶ How the different service components are delivered to the customer.

▶ The nature of the customer's role in those processes.

▶ How long delivery lasts.

▶ The recommended level and style of service to be offered.

There are four categories of services introduced in Chapter 1—people processing, possessing processing, mental stimulus processing, and information processing. Each of these has a different impact on operational procedures, the degree of customer contact with service personnel and facilities, and requirements for supplementary services. People processing services usually have more supplementary elements. This is because the customer must go to the service factory and spend time there during service delivery (Figure 4.2).

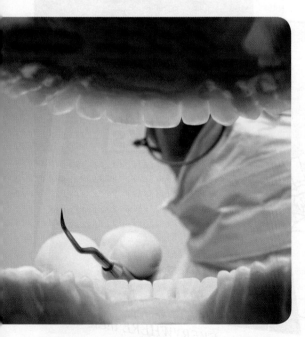

Figure 4.2 Dental patients need to go to the clinic to receive treatment.

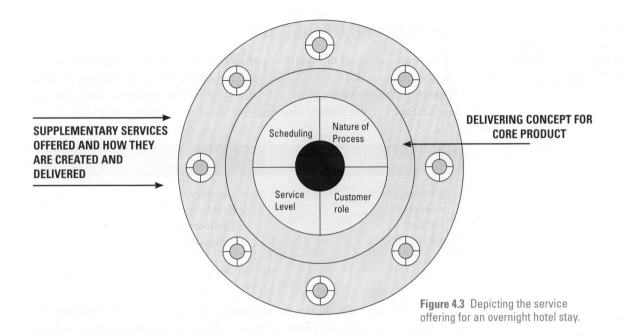

SUPPLEMENTARY SERVICES
OFFERED AND HOW THEY
ARE CREATED AND
DELIVERED

DELIVERING CONCEPT FOR
CORE PRODUCT

Scheduling

Nature of
Process

Service
Level

Customer
role

Figure 4.3 Depicting the service offering for an overnight hotel stay.

The integration of the core product, supplementary services, and delivery processes is captured in Figure 4.3. The figure shows the components of the service offering for an overnight stay at a luxury hotel. The core product is an overnight rental of a bedroom. The delivery processes surrounding this core product are:

▶ Nature of the process—people processing in this instance.

▶ Customer's role—what customers are expected to do for themselves; what the hotel will do for them, such as making the bed, supplying bathroom towels, and cleaning the room.

▶ Scheduling—how long the room may be used before another payment becomes due.

▶ Service level—what level and style of service.

Surrounding the core product is a variety of supplementary services. These range from reservations to meals and in-room service elements. Delivery processes must be specified for each of these elements. The more expensive the hotel is, the higher the level of service is required of each element. For example, very important guests might be received at the airport and transported to the hotel in a limousine. Check-in arrangements can be done on the way to the hotel. By the time the guests arrive at the hotel, they are ready to be escorted to their rooms, where a butler is on hand to serve them. Specific design in terms of customer service processes, which is called service blueprinting, is discussed in Chapter 8, Designing and Managing Service Processes.

LO 3

Describe the flower of service and know how the facilitating and enhancing supplementary services relate to the core product.

THE FLOWER OF SERVICE[2]

There are two kinds of supplementary services. *Facilitating supplementary services* are either needed for service delivery, or help in the use of the core product. *Enhancing supplementary services* add extra value for the customer. These different supplementary services can be classified into one of the following eight clusters.

Facilitating Services	Enhancing Services
o Information	o Consultation
o Order-taking	o Hospitality
o Billing	o Safekeeping
o Payment	o Exceptions

In Figure 4.4, the eight clusters are displayed as petals surrounding the center of a flower, hence we call it the *Flower of Service*. The petals are arranged in a clockwise sequence depending on how they are likely to be encountered by customers. However, the sequence may sometimes vary. For instance, payment may have to be made before service is delivered rather than afterwards. In a well-designed and well-managed service organization, the petals and core are fresh and well-formed. A service that is badly designed or poorly delivered is a like a flower with missing or dried petals. Even if the core is perfect, the flower looks unattractive. Think about one of your negative experiences as a service customer. When you were dissatisfied with a particular purchase, was it the core that was at fault, or was it a problem with one or more of the petals?

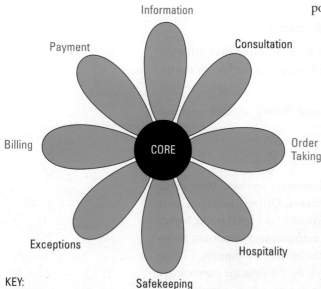

Figure 4.4 The Flower of Service: Core product surrounded by cluster of supplementary services.

KEY:
Facilitating elements
Enhancing elements

A company's market positioning strategy helps to decide which supplementary services should be included (see Chapter 3). If a company's strategy is to add benefits to increase customers' perceptions of quality, then more supplementary services are required. For example, airlines such as Emirates, the award-winning Dubai-based airline, may offer supplementary service like goodie bags to soothe hyperactive children. There is also in-flight entertainment such as cartoons and games that can keep the children occupied for hours. This will help to reduce the stress faced by parents traveling with young children. If the strategy is to compete on low prices, then fewer supplementary services are required.

FACILITATING SUPPLEMENTARY SERVICES

Information

To obtain full value from any good or service, customers need relevant information (Figure 4.5). New customers and prospects are especially hungry for information. Information may sometimes be required by law. These include conditions of sale and use, warnings, reminders, and notification of changes. Customers also appreciate advice on how to get the most value from a service and how to avoid problems. Companies should make sure that the information they provide is both timely and accurate. If not, it is likely to make customers feel irritated or cause them inconvenience.

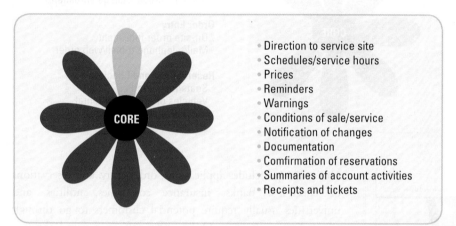

- Direction to service site
- Schedules/service hours
- Prices
- Reminders
- Warnings
- Conditions of sale/service
- Notification of changes
- Documentation
- Comfirmation of reservations
- Summaries of account activities
- Receipts and tickets

Figure 4.5 Examples of information.

Traditional ways of providing information to customers include using front-line employees, printed notices, brochures, and instruction books. Information can also be provided through videos or software-driven tutorials, touch-screen video displays, or through company web sites. The types of information range from train and airline schedules, to assistance in locating specific retail outlets, to information on the services of professional firms. Many business logistics companies offer shippers the opportunity to track the movements of their packages, which have been assigned a unique identification number (Figure 4.6). For example, Amazon.com provides online customers with a reference number and they can track the goods that they have bought, and know when to expect the goods.

Figure 4.6 Shipments can be tracked around the world with their identity code.

Order-Taking

Once customers are ready to buy, the company accepts applications, orders, and reservations (Figure 4.7). The process of order-taking should be polite, fast, and accurate so that customers do not waste time and endure unnecessary mental or physical effort. Technology can be used to make order-taking easier and faster for both customers and suppliers.

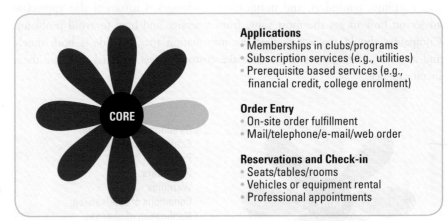

Applications
- Memberships in clubs/programs
- Subscription services (e.g., utilities)
- Prerequisite based services (e.g., financial credit, college enrolment)

Order Entry
- On-site order fulfillment
- Mail/telephone/e-mail/web order

Reservations and Check-in
- Seats/tables/rooms
- Vehicles or equipment rental
- Professional appointments

Figure 4.7 Examples of order-taking elements.

Figure 4.8 OpenTable takes dining reservations to a whole new level by allowing diners to bypass the traditional call-and-hope reservation experience with a mere click.

Order-taking includes applications, order entry, and reservations or check-ins. Banks, insurance companies, utilities, and universities usually require potential customers to go through an application process. Order entry can be received through a variety of sources such as through sales personnel, phone, and e-mail or online (Figure 4.8). Airlines now make use of ticketless systems, based on telephone or web site reservations. Customers receive a confirmation number when they make reservations and need to only show identification at the airport to claim their seats and receive a boarding pass. Northwest Airlines promotes order-taking online.

Billing

Billing is common to almost all services (unless the service is provided free of charge). Customers usually expect bills to be clear. Inaccurate, illegible, or incomplete bills risk disappointing customers who may, up to that point, have been quite satisfied with their experience. If customers are already dissatisfied, the billing mistake may make them even angrier. Billing should also be timely, because it encourages people to make payment faster. Procedures range from verbal statements to a machine-displayed price, and from handwritten invoices to elaborate monthly statements of account activity and fees (Figure 4.9). Perhaps the simplest approach is self-billing. This is when the customer adds up the amount of an order and authorizes a card payment or writes a check. In such instances, billing and payment are combined into a single act, although the seller may still need to check for accuracy.

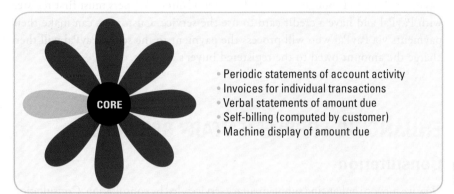

- Periodic statements of account activity
- Invoices for individual transactions
- Verbal statements of amount due
- Self-billing (computed by customer)
- Machine display of amount due

Figure 4.9 Examples of billing elements.

Busy customers dislike being kept waiting for a bill to be prepared. There are different ways in which bills can be presented to customers in a faster way. Hotels and rental car firms now have express check-outs. Many hotels may push bills under guestroom doors on the morning of departure showing charges to date. Others offer customers the choice of seeing their bills beforehand on the TV monitors in their rooms. Some car rental companies have an express check-out procedure. An agent meets customers as they return their cars. After they have checked the mileage and fuel gauge readings, the bill is printed on the spot using a portable wireless terminal.

Payment

In most cases, a bill requires the customer to take action on payment. One exception is the bank statement which shows details of charges that have already been deducted from the customer's account. Increasingly, customers expect it to be easy and convenient to make payment, including using credit, when they make purchases in their own countries, and while traveling abroad.

A variety of options exist for customers to make payment (Figure 4.10). For self-service payment systems, one may make payment by inserting coins, banknotes, tokens or cards into machines. Good maintenance of the equipment is important.

Self-Service
- Insert card, cash or token into machine
- Electronic funds transfer
- Mail a check
- Enter credit card number online

Direct to Payee or Intermediary
- Cash handling or change giving
- Check handling
- Credit/charge/debit card handling
- Coupon redemption

Automatic Deduction from Financial Deposits
- Automated systems (e.g., machine-readable tickets that operate entry gate)
- Human systems (e.g., toll collectors)

Figure 4.10 Examples of payment elements.

If the equipment breaks down, it can destroy the purpose of such a system. Most payment still takes the form of cash or credit cards. However, more and more shopping is being done online. PayPal offers a fuss-free and secure way to make payments for goods bought over the Internet. Online shoppers must first register with PayPal and have a credit card to use the service. Customers can make their payments via PayPal who will process the payment to the seller. PayPal will then charge the amount owed to the registered buyer's account.

ENHANCING SUPPLEMENTARY SERVICES

Consultation

Now we move to enhancing supplementary services, led by consultation. Consultation involves a dialog to probe customer requirements and then develop a solution that is suited to the needs of the customer. Figure 4.11 provides examples of several supplementary services in the consultation category.

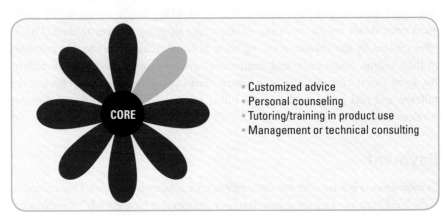

- Customized advice
- Personal counseling
- Tutoring/training in product use
- Management or technical consulting

Figure 4.11 Examples of consultation elements.

Figure 4.12 An auditor provides a human touch during the process of consultation.

At its simplest level, consultation consists of immediate advice from a knowledgeable service person in response to the request, "What do you suggest?" (For example, you might ask the person who cuts your hair for advice on different hairstyles and products). Finally, management and technical consulting for corporate customers include the "solution selling" associated with expensive industrial equipment and services. Effective consultation requires an understanding of each customer's current situation, before suggesting a suitable course of action. Good customer records can be a great help in this respect, particularly if relevant data can be retrieved easily from a remote terminal.

In an Internet environment, which encourages customers to engage in self-service applications and be more self-reliant, companies should not forget the personal touch of a "live" human being during the process of consultation (Figure 4.12). The human touch of a friendly customer-service officer will certainly be valued and remembered, and will go a long way for customers.

Counseling is another type of consultation that is less direct than consultation. It involves helping customers understand their situations better, so that they can come up with their "own" solutions and action programs. For example, diet centers such as Weight Watchers use counseling to help customers change behaviors so that weight loss can be sustained after the diet program has ended. Finally, advice, another form of consultation, can also be offered through tutorials, group training programs, and public demonstrations.

Hospitality

Hospitality-related services should, ideally, reflect pleasure at meeting new customers and greeting old ones when they return. Well-managed businesses try, at least in small ways, to ensure that their employees treat customers as guests. Courtesy and consideration for customers' needs apply to both face-to-face encounters and telephone interactions (Figure 4.13). Hospitality is an element that can be more clearly displayed in face-to-face encounters. In some cases, it starts (and ends) with an offer of transport to and from the service site on courtesy shuttle buses. If customers must wait outdoors before the service can be delivered, then a thoughtful service provider will offer weather protection. If customers have to wait indoors, then there can be a waiting area with seating and even entertainment (TV, newspapers or magazines) to pass the time. Recruiting employees who are naturally warm, welcoming, and considerate helps to create a hospitable atmosphere. Shoppers at Giordano, an international clothing retailer with markets in the Asia Pacific and the Middle East, are given a cheerful "Hello" and "Thank you" when they enter and leave the store, even if they did not buy anything.

The quality of the hospitality services offered by a firm can increase or decrease satisfaction with the core product. This is especially true for people-processing services where customers cannot easily leave the service facility. Private hospitals often seek to enhance their appeals by providing the level of room service that might be expected in a good hotel. This includes the provision of quality meals. Some airlines seek to differentiate themselves from their competitors with better meals and more attentive cabin crew and Singapore Airlines is well-recognized in both areas.[3]

Greeting
Food and beverages
Toilets and washrooms
Waiting facilities and amenities
- Lounges, waiting areas, seating
- Weather protection
- Magazines, entertainment, newspapers
Transport
Security

Figure 4.13 Examples of hospitality elements.

Cosmetic Surgeons' Offices **Turn Off Patients**

It appears that plastic surgeons could use some service marketing training along with their other courses in medical school. Two experts, Kate Altork and Douglas Dedo, who did a study of patients' reactions to doctors' offices found that many patients will cancel a surgery, change doctors, or refuse to consider future elective surgery if they feel uneasy in the doctor's office. The study results suggested that patients do not usually "doctor-jump" because they do not like the doctor, but because they do not like the environment in which the service occurred. The list of common patient dislikes includes: graphic posters of moles and skin cancers decorating office walls; uncomfortable plastic identification bracelets for patients; examining rooms with no windows or current reading material; bathrooms that are not clearly marked; and not enough wastebaskets and water coolers in the waiting room.

What do patients want? Most requests are surprisingly simple and involve simple comforts such as tissues, water coolers, telephones, plants, bowls of candy in the waiting room, and live flower arrangements in the lobby. Patients also want windows in the examining rooms and gowns that wrap around the entire body. They would like to sit on a real chair when they talk to a doctor instead of sitting on a stool or examining table. Finally, patients who have not yet gone for surgery prefer to be separated from patients who have had surgery because they feel uneasy sitting next to someone in the waiting room whose head is enclosed in bandages.

These study results suggest that cosmetic surgery patients would rather visit an office that looks more like a health spa than a hospital ward. By thinking like service marketers, savvy surgeons could use this information to create patient-friendly environments that will go well with, rather than go against, their technical expertise.

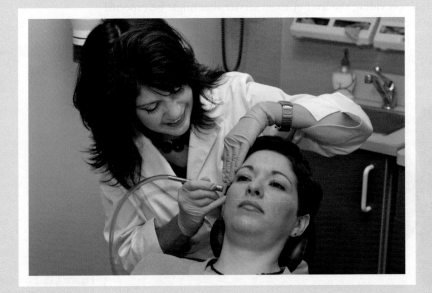

SOURCE

Bannon, L. (1997). Plastic surgeons are told to pay more attention to appearances. *Wall Street Journal*, March 15, p. B1.

Failures in hospitality can extend to the physical design of the areas where customers wait prior to receiving service. A survey found that unappealing offices and lack of comfort can drive away patients of cosmetic surgeons (Service Insights 4.1).

Safekeeping

While visiting a service site, customers often want their personal possessions to be "looked after." In fact, some customers may choose not to go to certain places that do not have safekeeping services like a safe and convenient car park. On-site safekeeping services includes coatrooms; baggage transport, handling and storage; safekeeping of valuables; and even child care and pet care (Figure 4.14).

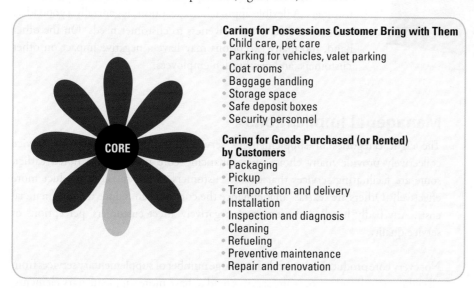

Caring for Possessions Customer Bring with Them
- Child care, pet care
- Parking for vehicles, valet parking
- Coat rooms
- Baggage handling
- Storage space
- Safe deposit boxes
- Security personnel

Caring for Goods Purchased (or Rented) by Customers
- Packaging
- Pickup
- Tranportation and delivery
- Installation
- Inspection and diagnosis
- Cleaning
- Refueling
- Preventive maintenance
- Repair and renovation

Figure 4.14 Examples of safekeeping elements.

Exceptions

Exceptions involve supplementary services that fall outside the normal service delivery. Exceptions include special requests, and problem solving (Figure 4.15).

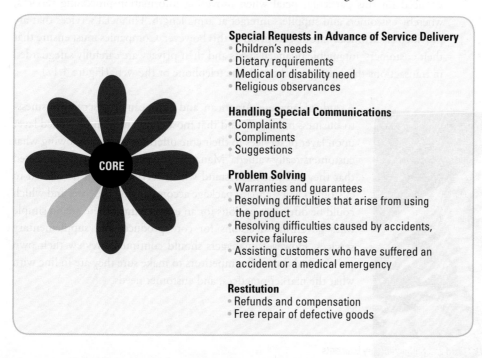

Special Requests in Advance of Service Delivery
- Children's needs
- Dietary requirements
- Medical or disability need
- Religious observances

Handling Special Communications
- Complaints
- Compliments
- Suggestions

Problem Solving
- Warranties and guarantees
- Resolving difficulties that arise from using the product
- Resolving difficulties caused by accidents, service failures
- Assisting customers who have suffered an accident or a medical emergency

Restitution
- Refunds and compensation
- Free repair of defective goods

Figure 4.15 Examples of exception elements.

Companies should anticipate exceptions and develop back-up plans and guidelines in advance. That way, employees will not appear helpless and surprised when customers ask for special assistance. Well-defined procedures make it easier for employees to respond promptly and effectively (Figure 4.16).

Managers need to keep an eye on the level of exception requests. Too many requests may indicate that standard procedures need to be changed. For example, if a dentist keeps receiving requests for more information about a particular dental procedure, then this may indicate that it is time to perhaps print some brochures that educate customers. A flexible approach to exceptions is generally a good idea, because it reflects responsiveness to customer needs. On the other hand, too many exceptions may have a negative impact on other customers, and overburden employees.

Figure 4.16 McDonald's well-established procedures lets employees respond smartly to customers' requests.

Managerial Implications

The eight categories of supplementary services forming the Flower of Service collectively provide many choices for enhancing core products. As noted earlier, some are facilitating services that enable customers to use the core product more effectively. Others are "extras" that enhance the core or even reduce its non-financial costs. Any badly handled element may negatively affect customers' perceptions of service quality.

Not every core product is surrounded by a large number of supplementary services from all eight petals. People-processing services tend to have more supplementary elements, especially hospitality, since they involve close (and often extended) interactions with customers. When customers do not visit the service factory, the need for hospitality may be limited to just letters and telecommunications. Possession-processing services sometimes place heavy burdens on safekeeping elements. However, there may be no need for this particular petal when providing information-processing services, whereby customers and suppliers interact at arm's length. Financial services that are provided electronically are an exception to this however. Companies must ensure that their customers' intangible financial assets and their privacy are carefully safeguarded in transactions that take place through the telephone or the web. (Figure 4.17).

Figure 4.17 Security features ensure that online transactions are safe.

A study of Japanese, American, and European firms serving business-to-business markets found that most companies simply added layer upon layer of services to their core offerings without knowing what customers really valued.[4] Managers surveyed in the study indicated that they did not understand which services should be offered to customers as a standard package accompanying the core, and which could be offered as options for an extra charge. There are no simple rules governing decisions for core products and supplementary services. However, managers should continually review their own policies and those of competitors to make sure they are in line with what the market practices, and customer needs.

BRANDING SERVICE PRODUCTS AND EXPERIENCES

 LO 4
Know how service firms use different branding strategies for their product lines.

In recent years, more and more service firms have started talking about their products. What is the difference between a service and a product? A *product* is a defined and consistent "bundle of output." One bundle of output can be differentiated from another bundle of output. Service providers can usually offer a "menu" of products, representing an assembly of carefully prescribed elements built around the core product. They may also bundle in certain value-added supplementary services. Let us look at some examples from hotels, a computer support service, and an international airline.

Product Lines and Brands

Most service firms offer a line of products rather than just a single product. As a result, they must choose among three broad alternatives: using a single brand to cover all products and services, a separate stand-alone brand for each offering, or some combination of these two extremes.[5] These alternatives are represented as a spectrum in Figure 4.18. The term *branded house* is used to describe a company like the Virgin Group, which applies its brand name to multiple offerings in often unrelated fields.[6] Next on this spectrum are what they term *sub-brands*. A sub-brand is one where the master brand is the main reference point, but the product itself has a distinctive name too. Singapore Airlines Raffles Class, the company's business class service, is an example. The next category of brands are *endorsed brands*, where the product brand is the main focus, but the corporate name is still featured (many hotel corporations

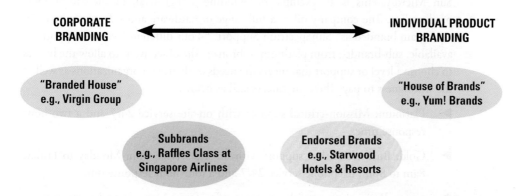

Figure 4.18 The spectrum of branding alternatives.

use this approach). At the far end of the spectrum is the *house of brands* strategy. Yum! Brands Inc. adopts the house of brands strategy, with more than 35,000 restaurants in 110 countries. While we may not have heard of Yum! Brands, many certainly are familiar with their restaurant brands—A & W, KFC, Pizza Hut, Taco Bell, and Long John's Silver. Each of these brands is actively promoted under their own brand name (Figure 4.19).

Hotel Branding

There are many hotel chains that have a global presence. Many of these chains offer a family of sub-brands/endorsed brands. For instance, Hilton Hotels Corporation has ten sub-brands, and the Accor Group has ten sub-brands. Marriott International has 15 brands including the wholly owned Ritz-Carlton chain. However, to protect its exclusive image, Ritz-Carlton is not normally identified for marketing purposes as part of the Marriott Group.

For a multibrand strategy to succeed, each brand must promise a different set of benefits targeted at a different customer segment. In some instances, segmentation is situation-based. The same individual may have different needs and willingness to pay under differing circumstances, like when traveling with family or traveling on business. A strategy of brand extension is aimed at encouraging customers to continue staying within the brand family and this may be encouraged through loyalty programs. A study of the brand-switching behavior of some 5,400 hotel customers found that brand extensions do seem to encourage customers to stay within the brand. However, brand extensions may be less effective in discouraging switching when the number of brands reaches four or more.[7]

Sun Microsystems Hardware and Software Support

Sun Microsystems is an example of branding a high-tech, business-to-business product line. The company offers a full range of hardware and software support in a program branded as "SunSpectrum Support."[8] Four different levels of support are available, sub-branded from platinum to bronze. The objective is to allow the buyers to choose a level of support that meets the needs of their own organizations as well as the willingness to pay. These are categorized as below:

▶ Platinum: Mission-critical support with on-site service 24/7 and a two-hour response time.

▶ Gold: Business critical support with on-site service from Monday to Friday, 8am to 8pm, telephone service 24/7 and a four-hour response time.

▶ Silver: Basic support with on-site service from Monday to Friday, 8am to 5pm, telephone service from Monday to Friday, 8am to 8pm, and a four-hour response time.

▶ Bronze: Self-support with phone service 8am to 5pm.

British Airways Sub-brands

British Airways (BA) is a good example of strong sub-branding in the airline industry. BA offers seven distinct air travel products. They are:

▶ First—deluxe service,

▶ Club World—intercontinental business class,

▶ World Traveller Plus—intercontinental premium economy class,

▶ World Traveller—intercontinental economy class,

▶ Club Europe—intra-European business class,

▶ Euro-Traveller—intra-European economy class, and

▶ UK Domestic—economy-class service between London and major British cities.

Each BA sub-brand represents a specific service concept and a set of clearly stated product specifications for pre-flight, in-flight, and on-arrival service elements.

Offering a Branded Experience

Branding can be used at both the company and product level by almost any service business. In a well-managed firm, the corporate brand is not only easily recognized, but it also has meaning for customers. The brand stands for a particular way of doing business. Applying distinctive brand names to individual products helps marketers to establish a mental picture of the service in customers' minds and to clarify the nature of the value proposition.

The Forum Corporation, a consulting firm, differentiates between (1) experience with high variation from customer to customer, (2) a branded experience that is similar across different firms, differentiated only by the brand name (ATMs are a good example), and (3) a "Branded Customer Experience" in which the customer's experience is shaped in a specific and meaningful ways.[9] (See Service Insights 4.2 for Forum's recommendations on how to achieve this.)

Don Shultz emphasizes that "The brand promise or value proposition is not a tag line, an icon, or a color or a graphic element, although all of these may contribute. It is, instead, the heart and soul of the brand...."[10] An important role for service marketers is to become brand champions, familiar with and responsible for shaping every aspect of the customer's experience. We can relate the notion of a branded service experience to the Flower of Service metaphor by emphasizing the need for consistency in the color and texture of each petal. Unfortunately, many service experiences remain much disorganized and create the impression of a flower stitched together with petals drawn from many different plants!

We will return to a discussion of branding in the context of marketing communications strategy in Chapter 7.

Moving Toward **The Branded Customer Experience**

Forum Corporation identifies six basic steps to develop and deliver the Branded Customer Experience:

1 Target profitable customers, employing behavior rather than demographic segmentation as behavior is a more accurate indicator of tastes and preferences.

2 Achieve a superior understanding about your targeted customers' value.

3 Create a brand promise—an expression of what target customers can expect from their experience with your organization—which is of value to customers, addresses a need, can be implemented, can be incorporated into standards, and provides focus for the organization and its employees.

4 Apply that understanding to provide a truly different customer experience.

5 Give employees the skills, tools, and supporting processes needed to deliver the customer experience that has been defined.

6 Make everyone a brand manager who is behind the brand and supports the brand.

7 Make promises that your processes can exceed.

8 Measure and monitor. Consistency of delivery is paramount.

SOURCE

"Forum Issues #17" Boston: The Forum Corporation, 1997; Wheeler, J., & Smith, S. (2003). "Loyalty by Design" Forum Corporation, 2003. Available: www.forum.com/publications, accessed March 2008.

NEW SERVICE DEVELOPMENT

Intense competition and rising customer expectations are having an impact on nearly all service industries. Thus, success lies not only in providing existing services well. Companies also need to create new approaches to services.

LO 5
List the categories of new service development, ranging from simple style changes to major innovations.

A Hierarchy of New Service Development Categories

Following are seven categories of new services that we can identify, ranging from simple style changes to major innovations. They are in increasing complexity:

▶ Style changes

▶ Service improvements

▶ Supplementary service innovations

▶ Process line extensions

- Product line extensions
- Major process innovations
- Major service innovations

1. *Style changes* are the simplest type of innovation, usually involving no changes in either processes or performance. However they are often highly visible, create excitement, and may serve to motivate employees. Examples include repainting retail branches and vehicles in new color schemes, designing new uniforms for service employees, introducing a new bank check design, or minor changes in service scripts for employees.

2. *Service improvements* are the most common type of innovation. They involve small changes in the performance of current products, including improvements to either the core product or to existing supplementary services. For example, students need to be physically present to attend lectures. Now, colleges have moved to taping lectures and these can now be viewed online, when the students are free. Hence, students now have a choice as to whether to attend lectures or not.

3. *Supplementary service innovations* take the form of adding new facilitating or enhancing service elements to an existing core service, or of significantly improving an existing supplementary service. Low-tech innovations for an existing service can be as simple as adding parking at a retail site, or agreeing to accept credit cards for payment. To enhance the existing core service, The Snap Printing group that operates in Australia, New Zealand, Ireland, and China, now provides a complete web-based service that allows customers to get advice, as well as customized printing requirements direct and online. Multiple improvements may have the effect of creating what customers perceive as an altogether new experience, even though it is built around the same core. Theme restaurants like the Rainforest Café enhance the core food service with new experiences (Figure 4.20). The cafés are designed to keep customers entertained with aquariums, live parrots, waterfalls, fiberglass monkeys, talking trees that spout environment-related information, and regularly timed thunderstorms, complete with lightning.[11]

Figure 4.20 Rainforest Café makes a supplementary service innovation by enhancing the core food service with the experience of being in a jungle.

4. *Process line extensions* are less innovative than process innovations. However, they often represent new ways of delivering existing products. The intention is either to offer more convenience and a different experience for existing customers, or to attract new customers who find the traditional approach unappealing. Most commonly, they involve adding a lower contact distribution channel to an existing high-contact channel, such as creating telephone-based or Internet-based banking service. Barnes and Noble, the leading bookstore chain in the United States, added a new Internet subsidiary, BarnesandNoble.com to help it compete against Amazon.com (Figure 4.21). Such dual-track approaches are sometimes referred to as "Clicks and Mortar." Creating self-service options to complement delivery by service employees is another form of process line extension.

Figure 4.21 Barnes and Noble extends their process line by offering an Internet-distribution channel, entering the age of the "Clicks and Mortar."

5. *Product line extensions* are additions to current product lines by existing firms. The first company in a market to offer such a product may be seen as an innovator. The others are merely followers, often acting to defend themselves. These new services may be targeted at existing customers to serve a broader variety of needs, or designed to attract new customers with different needs (or both). For example, many banks now sell insurance products in the hope of increasing the number of profitable relationships with existing customers.

6. *Major process innovations* consist of using new processes to deliver existing core products in new ways with additional benefits. For example, the University of Phoenix competes with other universities by delivering undergraduate and graduate degree programs in a non-traditional way. It has no permanent campus, but offers courses either online or at night in rented facilities. Its students get most of the benefits of a college degree in half the time and at a much lower price than other universities.[12] In recent years, the growth of the Internet has led to the creation of many service process innovations that exclude the use of traditional stores and save customers time and travel. Often, these models add new, timely, information-based benefits such as the opportunity to visit chat-rooms with fellow customers, and suggestions for additional products that match well with what has already been bought.

7. *Major service innovations* are new core products for markets that have not been previously defined. They usually include both new service characteristics and radical new processes. Examples include relatively recent web-based television services, and YouTube's video sharing web services (Figure 4.22).

Figure 4.22 YouTube allows users to easily embed any hosted videos on web pages or blogs, an innovation which found favor among social-networking websites.

As the above typology suggests, service innovation can occur at many different levels. However, not every type of service innovation has an impact on the features of the service product, and not all are experienced by the customers.

LO 6

Be familiar with the factors needed to achieve success in developing new services.

Achieving Success in Developing New Services

For a new product to be successful, the sound core product is necessary but not sufficient. It is the quality of the total service offering, and also the marketing support that goes with it that is important for success. Chris Storey and Christopher Easingwood emphasize that success is based on market knowledge: "Without an understanding of the marketplace, knowledge about customers, and knowledge about competitors, it is very unlikely that a new product will be a success."[13]

A study by Scott Edgett and Steven Parkinson focused on discriminating between successful and unsuccessful new financial services.[14] They found that the three factors contributing most to success were, in order of importance:

1. *Market synergy*—the new product fit well with the existing image of the firm, was better than competitors at meeting customers' known needs, and received strong support during and after the launch from the firm and its branches. In addition, the firm had a good understanding of its customers' purchase decision behavior.

2. *Organizational factors*—there was strong interfunctional cooperation and coordination. Development personnel were fully aware of why they were involved and of the importance of new products of the company.

3. *Market research factors*—detailed and properly designed market research studies were conducted early in the development process. There was a clear idea of the type of information to be obtained. A good definition of the product concept was developed before undertaking field surveys.

Another survey of financial service firms to determine what distinguished successful from unsuccessful products yielded similar findings.[15] In this instance, the key factors for success were synergy (the fit between the product and the firm in terms of needed expertise and resources being present) and internal marketing (the support given to staff before its launch to help them understand the new product and its underlying systems, plus details about direct competitors, and support). Yet another study found similar factors, that marketing synergy and human resource issues like meeting customer needs, and having a human resource strategy that links to the development of service processes are keys to success (Figure 4.23).[16]

Figure 4.23 When sound human resource strategy is wedded to vibrant marketing synergy, a successful product is born.

LO 1 ▶ A service product consists of two components, the core product and supplementary services. The core product is based on the core set of benefits and solutions delivered to customers. Supplementary services are those elements that facilitate and enhance the use of the core product.

Designing a service concept is a complicated task that requires an understanding of how the core and supplementary services should be combined, sequenced, delivered, and scheduled to create benefits that meet the needs of the target market segments.

LO 2 ▶ Different types of core products often share similar supplementary elements. The Flower of Service concept categorizes supplementary services into eight groups (each represented as a petal surrounding the core). The eight groups can be categorized as (1) facilitating and (2) enhancing supplementary services.

LO 3 ▶ Facilitating supplementary services are needed for service delivery or help in the use of the core product. They are:

o   Information

o   Order-taking

o   Billing, and

o   Payment.

Enhancing supplementary services add extra value for the customer and include:

o   Consultation

o   Hospitality

o   Safekeeping

o   Dealing with exceptions.

The use of a flower helps us to understand that all the supplementary elements must be performed well. A weakness in one element will spoil the overall impression.

LO 4 ▶ Many firms offer several service products with different performance attributes and brand each package with a distinctive name. They can use a variety of branding strategies such as branded house, sub-brands, endorsed brands, and house of brands. However, each of these different brands in the family should offer a meaningful benefit or this strategy is likely to be ineffective against competition.

LO 5 ▶ When competition is intense, firms can create new approaches to services in order to maintain a competitive edge. There is a hierarchy of new service development that has seven categories ranging from simple changes to major innovations. They are:

o   Style changes

o   Service improvements

o   Supplementary service innovations

o   Process line extensions

o   Product line extensions

o   Major process innovations, and

o   Major service innovations.

Major service innovations are relatively rare. More common is the use of new technologies, such as the Internet, to deliver existing services in new ways. In mature industries, where the core service can become a commodity, the search for competitive advantage often depends on creating new supplementary services or greatly improving performance on existing ones.

LO 6 ▶ The chances of success for a new service concept increase when it:

o   Fits well with the firm's expertise, resources and existing image,

o   Provides a superior advantage over competing services in terms of meeting customers' needs, and is

o   Well-supported by coordinated efforts between the different functional areas in a firm.

UNLOCK YOUR LEARNING

These keywords are found within the sections of each Learning Objective (LO). They are integral in understanding the services marketing concepts taught in each section. Having a firm grasp of these keywords and how they are used is essential in helping you do well for your course, and in the real and very competitive marketing scene out there.

LO 1
1. Core product
2. Service product
3. Supplementary services

LO 2
4. Delivery processes
5. People processing
6. Service concept

LO 3
7. Biling
8. Consultation
9. Enhancing supplementary services
10. Exceptions
11. Facilitating supplementary services

12. Flower of Service
13. Hospitality
14. Information
15. Order-taking
16. Payment
17. Safekeeping

LO 4
18. Branded house
19. Sub-brands
20. Endorsed brands
21. House of brands
22. Multi-brand strategy
23. Branding

24. Branded customer experience

LO 5
25. Categories of new services
26. Major process innovations
27. Major service innovations
28. Process line extensions
29. Product line extensions
30. Style changes
31. Service improvements
32. Supplementary service innovations

LO 6
33. Internal marketing
34. Market synergy

How well do you know the language of services marketing? Quiz yourself!

 Not for the academically faint-of-heart

For each keyword you are able to recall without referring to earlier pages, give yourself a point (and a pat on the back). Tally your score at the end and see if you earned the right to be called—a *services marketeer.*

SCORE

0 – 5   Services Marketing is done a great disservice.

6 – 11   The midnight oil needs to be lit, pronto.

12 – 18   I know what you *didn't* do all semester.

19 – 24   A close shave with success.

25 – 29   Now, go forth and market.

30 – 34   There should be a marketing concept named after you.

Review Questions

1. Define what is meant by core product and supplementary services. Can they be applied to goods as well as services? Explain your answer.

2. Explain the flower of service concept. What insights does this concept provide for service marketers?

3. Explain the distinction between enhancing and facilitating supplementary services. Give several examples of each, relative to services that you have used recently.

4. How is branding used in services marketing? What is the distinction between a corporate brand like Marriott and the names of its different inns and hotel chains?

5. What are the approaches that firms can take to create new services?

6. Why do new services often fail? What factors are associated with successful development of new services?

WORK YOUR **ESM**

Application Exercises

1. Select a service that you are familiar with and identify the core product and supplementary services. Identify a competitor's service and show how the competitor's core product and supplementary services differ from the one you had originally identified.

2. Select some branding examples from financial services such as specific types of retail bank accounts or insurance policies and define their characteristics. How meaningful are these brands likely to be to customers?

3. Using a firm that you are familiar with, analyze what opportunities it might have, to create line extensions for its current and/ or new markets. What impact might these extensions have on its present services?

PART II

• ENDNOTES

1   Horovitz, B. (2006). Starbucks aims beyond lattes to extend brand. *USA Today, 18 May 2006.* www.starbucks.com and www.hearmusic.com. Accessed March 2008.

2   Lovelock, C. H. (1992). Cultivating the Flower of Service: New ways of looking at core and supplementary services. In P. Eiglier, & E. Langeard (Eds.), *Marketing, Operations, and Human Resources: Insights into Services*, (pp. 296–316). Aix-en-Provence, France: IAE, Université d'Aix-Marseille III.

3   Heracleous, L., Wirtz, J., & Pangarkar, N. (2006). *Flying High: Cost Effective Service Excellence – Lessons from Singapore Airlines.* Singapore: McGraw Hill.

4   Anderson J. C., & Narus, J. A. (1995). Capturing the value of supplementary services. *Harvard Business Review*, 73(January–February), pp. 75–83.

5   Devlin, J. (2003). Brand architecture in services: The example of retail financial services. *Journal of Marketing Management*, 19, pp. 1043–1065.

6   Aaker D., & Joachimsthaler, E. (2000). The brand relationship spectrum: The key to the brand challenge, *California Management Review*, 42(4), pp. 8–23.

7   Jiang, W., Dev, C. S., & Rao, V. R. (2002). Brand extension and customer loyalty: Evidence from the lodging industry. *Cornell Hotel and Restaurant Administration Quarterly*, (August), pp. 5–16.

8   www.sun.com/service/support/sunspectrum, Accessed 2 February 2008.

9   Wheeler J., & Smith, S. (2003). *Managing the Customer Experience.* Upper Saddle River, NJ: Prentice Hall.

10 Shultz, D. E. (2001). Getting to the heart of the brand. *Marketing Management*, (Sep.– Oct.), pp. 8–9.

11 Rubel, C. New menu for restaurants: Talking trees and blackjack. *Marketing News*, (July), p.1. Available: http://www.rainforestcafe.com/, Accessed March 2008.

12 Traub, S. T.,& Drive-Thru U. (1997). *The New Yorker*, (October);. Macht, J. (1998). Virtual You. *Inc. Magazine*, (January), pp. 84–87. Available: http://www.phoenix.edu/about_us/about_us.aspx, Accessed March 2008.

13 Storey C. D., & Easingwood, C. J. (1998). The augmented service offering: A conceptualization and study of its impact on new service success. *Journal of Product Innovation Management*, 15, pp. 335–351.

14 Edgett S., & Parkinson, S. (1994). The development of new financial services: Identifying determinants of success and failure. *International Journal of Service Industry Management*, 5(4), pp. 24–38.

15 Storey C., & Easingwood, C. (1993). The impact of the new product development project on the success of financial services. *Service Industries Journal*, 13(3), pp. 40–54.

16 Ottenbacher, M., Gnoth, J., Jones, P. (2006). Identifying determinants of success in development of new high-contact services. *International Journal of Service Industry Management*, 17(4), pp. 344–363

BLANK

5

distributing SERVICE through PHYSICAL and ELECTRONIC CHANNELS

Figure 5.1 WIZZIT's cell phone banking services has revolutionized the South African banking scene.

LEARNING OBJECTIVES

By the end of this chapter, students should be able to:

▶ **LO 1** Understand the various manner of distribution for services.

▶ **LO 2** Be familiar with the place and time decisions of physical channels.

▶ **LO 3** Recognize the issues of delivering services through electronic channels.

▶ **LO 4** Understand the part played by intermediaries in distributing services.

▶ **LO 5** Understand the special challenges of distributing people-processing, possession-processing, and information-based services internationally.

OPENING VIGNETTE[1]

WIZZIT: REACHING OUT TO THE UNBANKED IN SOUTH AFRICA

Banks are very often associated with physical buildings and branches, as well as ATM networks. WIZZIT Payments (Pty) Ltd (WIZZIT) however, is a bank that does not distribute its services using the normal distribution channels.

It is a "virtual bank" as it has no branches. Instead, WIZZIT uses the cell phone as a distribution platform. In South Africa, there are 16 million unbanked people. Opening accounts at bank branches are inconvenient as they have to travel a long way. It is considered expensive for the rural folks. However, 35 percent of South Africa's unbanked already own cell phones.

To reach its customers, WIZZIT goes into the rural areas, set up gazebos, and shows the villagers how electronic money works and how they can benefit from it. They also use the "WIZZ Kids," who are young individuals from the lower income group. These WIZZ Kids teach potential customers about WIZZIT and earn a commission for each new customer they sign up.

To make their services appealing to the low-income people, WIZZIT does not have a minimum balance requirement, and does not charge fixed monthly fees. Payment is by transaction, depending on the transaction type. Customers can use their cell phones to make person-to-person payments, transfer money and make prepaid purchases for electricity and their cell phone subscriptions. Customers are also provided with a Maestro brand debit card that they can use to make purchases, get cash back at retail outlets, and withdraw money at any South African ATM. Since the start of the service in December 2004 to 2006, WIZZIT has already acquired more than 50,000 customers. People use WIZZIT because they find it is convenient, affordable, and secure.

...WIZZIT transcends the traditional banking model in South Africa...

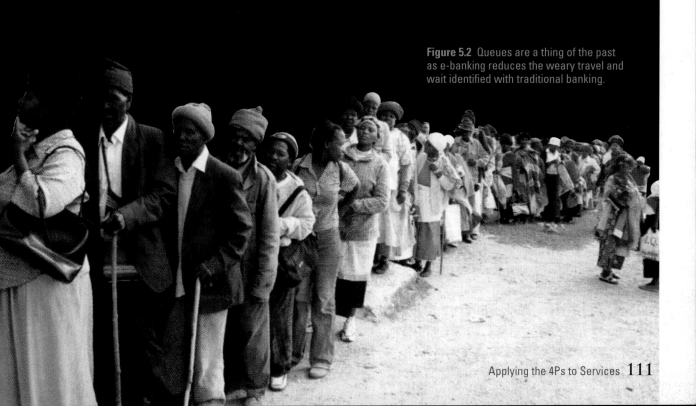

Figure 5.2 Queues are a thing of the past as e-banking reduces the weary travel and wait identified with traditional banking.

DISTRIBUTION IN A SERVICES CONTEXT

Distribution is usually associated with moving boxes to retailers and other channels for sale to end-users. In a service context, however, we often have nothing to move. Experiences, performance, and solutions are not being physically shipped and stored. In addition, more and more informational transactions are conducted via electronic and not physical channels. We will first discuss the options for service distribution and delivery.

⊙ **LO 1**

Understand the various manner of distribution for services.

DETERMINING THE TYPE OF CONTACT: OPTIONS FOR SERVICE DELIVERY

Several factors have an impact on distribution and delivery strategies for services. A key question is: Does the nature of the service or the firm's positioning strategy require customers to be in direct physical contact with its personnel, equipment, and facilities? (As we saw in Chapter 1, this is unavoidable for people-processing services, but for other categories, it may not be necessary.) If so, do customers have to visit the facilities of the service organization or will the service organization send personnel and equipment to the customers' own sites? Alternatively, can exchanges between provider and customer be completed at arm's length through the use of either telecommunications or electronic channels of distribution?

Distribution Options for Serving Customers

As shown in Table 5.1, there are six possible choices for a firm in terms of distribution sites. Should it expect customers to come to a company site? Or should service personnel go to visit customers at their own locations? Alternatively, can service be delivered at arm's length, without either side having to meet? For each of these three options, should the firm maintain just a single outlet or offer to serve customers through multiple outlets at different locations?

Type of Interaction between Customer and Service Organization	Availability of Service Outlets	
	Single Site	**Multiple Sites**
Customer goes to service organization	Theater Hair salon	Bus service Fast-food chain
Service organization comes to customer	House painting Mobile car wash	Mail delivery Banking branch network
Customer and service organization transact remotely (mail or electronic communications)	Credit card company Local TV station	Broadcast network Telephone company

Table 5.1 Six options for service delivery.

Customers Visit the Service Site.

When customers have to visit the service site, the following factors need to be considered.

▶ The convenience of service factory locations—Elaborate statistical analysis using retail gravity models is sometimes used to help firms make decisions on where to locate supermarkets or similar large stores, relative to the homes and workplaces of future customers.

▶ Operational hours—Many banks, for instance, are extending their opening hours to meet the needs of busy professionals who do not have time to take care of their banking needs during office hours.

Service Providers go to their Customers.

For some types of services, the service provider visits the customer (Figure 5.3). Compass Group, the largest food service organization in the United Kingdom and Ireland, provides catering and support services to over 7,000 locations. They must visit the customer's site, because the need is location specific. When should service providers go to their customers?

▶ Going to the customer's site is unavoidable whenever the object of the service is some immovable physical item, such as a tree to be pruned, installed machinery to be repaired, or a house that requires pest-control treatment.

▶ In remote areas like Alaska or Canada's Northwest Territory, service providers often fly to visit their customers, because the latter find it so difficult to travel. Australia is famous for its Royal Flying Doctor Service, in which physicians fly to make house calls at farms and sheep stations in the Outback.

▶ In general, service providers are more likely to visit corporate customers at their premises than to visit individuals in their homes, reflecting the larger volume associated with business-to-business transactions.

Figure 5.3 Compass Group caters to fine dining and other gastronomical experiences.

It is more expensive and time consuming for service personnel and their equipment to travel to the customer than for the customer to visit them. Thus, the trend has been toward requiring customers to go to the service provider instead (fewer doctors make house calls nowadays!). However, it may be profitable to serve individuals who are willing to pay a premium for the convenience of receiving personal visits. One young veterinary doctor has built her business around house calls to sick pets. Other consumer services of this kind include mobile car washing, office and in-home catering, and made-to-measure tailoring services for business people.

A growing service activity involves the rental of both equipment and labor for special occasions. It can also be for customers, especially businesses wishing to increase their capacity during busy periods. Service Insights 5.1 describes the business-to-business services of Aggreko, an international company that rents generating and cooling equipment around the world.

Service Transaction is conducted at Arm's Length.
Dealing with a service firm through arm's length transactions may mean that a customer never sees the service facilities and never meets the service personnel face-to-face. An important consequence is that the number of service encounters tends to be fewer. Those encounters that do take place with service personnel are more likely to be made through a call center or, even more remotely, by mail or e-mail.

::: SERVICE INSIGHTS 5.1

Power and Temperature Control for Rent

You probably think of electricity as coming from a distant power station and of air conditioning and heating as installed in fixed locations. So how would you deal with the following challenges?.

- Luciano Pavarotti, the famous tenor, is giving an open-air concert in Münster, Germany, and the organizers require an uninterruptible source of electrical power, that is independent of the local electricity supply, for the duration of the concert.

- A tropical cyclone has hit the small mining town of Pannawonica in Western Australia, destroying everything in its path, including power lines. Electrical power must be restored as soon as possible so that the town and its infrastructure can be rebuilt.

- In Amsterdam, organizers of the World Championship Indoor Windsurfing competition need to power 27 wind turbines that will be installed along the length of a huge indoor pool to create winds of 20–30 mph (32–48 km/h).

- A US Navy submarine needs a shore-based source of power when located in a remote Norwegian port.

- Sri Lanka has a great shortage of electricity-generating capability after water levels fall dangerously low at major hydroelectric dams due to insufficient monsoon rains two years in a row.

- Hotels in Florida need to be dried out following water damage in a hurricane.

- A large, power-generating plant in Oklahoma urgently seeks temporary capacity to replace one of its cooling towers, destroyed the previous day in a tornado.

These are all challenges faced and met by a company called Aggreko, which describes itself as "The World Leader in Temporary Utility Rental Solutions." Aggreko operates from more than 100 depots in 28 countries worldwide. It rents out a "fleet" of mobile electricity generators, oil-free air compressors, and temperature control devices ranging from water chillers and industrial air-conditioners to giant heaters and dehumidifiers.

Aggreko's customers are usually large companies and government agencies. Although much of its business comes from predicted needs, such as backup operations during planned factory maintenance or the filming of a James Bond movie, the firm is ready to help solve unexpected problems and emergencies.

Much of the firm's rental equipment is kept in soundproofed, box-like structures that can be shipped anywhere in the world to create the specific type and level of electrical power output or climate-control capability required by the customer. Consultation, installation, and ongoing technical support add value to the core service. Emphasis is placed on solving customer problems rather than just renting equipment. Some customers have a clear idea of their needs in advance. Others however, require advice on how to develop creative and cost effective solutions to what may be unique problems. Still others are desperate to restore power that has been lost due to an emergency. In the last mentioned instance, speed is very important since downtime can be extremely expensive and lives may depend on the promptness of Aggreko's response.

The company's web site declares: "Our customers are our focus:

> We listen to them,
>
> We learn about them,
>
> We embrace their challenges as our own,
>
> We know their issues,
>
> We anticipate their concerns, and
>
> We inspire them with exceptional service."

Delivering service requires Aggreko to ship its equipment to the customer's site. Following the Pannawonica cyclone, Aggreko's West Australian team swung into action, rapidly setting up some 30 generators ranging from 60–750kVA, plus cabling, refueling tankers, and other equipment. The generators were transported by four "road trains," each comprising a giant tractor unit pulling three 40-feet (13m) trailers. Technicians and additional equipment were flown in on two Hercules aircraft. The Aggreko technicians remained on site for six weeks, providing 24/7 service while the town was being rebuilt.

SOURCE

Aggreko's "International Magazine," 1997. Available: www.aggreko.com, Accessed February 2008. Source for photo: http://www.aggreko.com/about_aggreko/history.aspx, Accessed March 2008.

When there is infrequent contact with service personnel, the one call is a 'moment of truth,' and can have a great impact on how the customer sees the service firm. One of the things that customers dislike tremendously is to be kept waiting on the phone. It is thus very important to manage voice-to-voice waiting.[2]

What are examples of transactions via arm's length?

▶ Repair services for small pieces of equipment sometimes require customers to ship the product to a maintenance facility, where it will be serviced and then returned by mail (with the option of paying extra for express shipment). Many service providers tie up with integrated solutions logistics firms such as UPS or DHL. These firms can store and arrange for express delivery of spare parts for aircraft (B2B delivery). They can also pick up defective cell phones from customers' homes and return the repaired phone to the customer (B2C pick up and delivery).

© 2000 Randy Glasbergen.

"Thanks, but I'd rather get my financial advice off the Internet."

Figure 5.4 Financial advice can be delivered through the Internet.

Any information-based product can be delivered almost instantaneously through the Internet to almost any point in the globe (Figure 5.4). As a result, physical logistics services now find themselves competing with telecommunications services.

Channel Preferences Vary Among Consumers

The use of different channels to deliver the same service has different costs for a service organization. It also affects the service experience for the customer. Banking services, for instance, can be delivered remotely via computer and cell phone, a voice response system, a call center, and automatic teller machines. It can also be delivered face-to-face in a branch, or in the case of private banking, in a wealthy customer's home. Flowers can be bought from a florist and one can choose the flowers and consult on the arrangement face-to-face. Flowers can also be ordered online, with customers usually choosing one of the arrangements presented on the web site.

Recent research has explored how customers choose between personal, impersonal, and self-service channels, and has identified the following key drivers:[3]

Figure 5.5 Frequent travelers are familiar with the check-in service and are willing to use self check-in as an alternative.

▶ For complex and high perceived risk services, people tend to rely on personal channels. For example, customers are happy to apply for credit cards using remote channels, but prefer to talk to the service provider face-to-face when obtaining a mortgage.

▶ Individuals with higher confidence and knowledge about a service and/ or the channel are more likely to use impersonal and self-service channels (Figure 5.5).

▶ Customers who are more technology savvy (have a greater likelihood to accept and use new technology) will view service quality more positively when using self-service technologies.[4]

▶ Customers who look for the functional aspects of a transaction prefer more convenience. This often means the use of impersonal and self-service channels. Customers with social motives tend to use personal channels.

▶ Convenience is a key driver of channel choice for the majority of consumers. Service convenience means saving time and effort, rather than saving money. A customer's search for convenience is not just confined to the purchase of core products. It also extends to convenient times and places. People want easy access to supplementary services too, especially information, reservations, and problem solving.

Service providers have to be careful when channels are priced differently. Increasingly, customers are very smart and take advantage of price variations among channels and markets, a strategy known as arbitrage.[5] For example, customers can ask the expensive full-service broker for advice (and perhaps place a small order), and then conduct the bulk of their trades through the much lower-priced discount broker. Service providers need to develop effective strategies that will enable them to deliver value and capture it through the appropriate channel.

PLACE AND TIME DECISIONS

> **LO 2**
> Be familiar with the place and time decisions of physical channels.

How should service managers make decisions on the places where service is delivered and the times when it is available? The answer: Start by understanding customer needs and expectations, the activities of competitors, and the nature of the service operation. As we noted earlier, the distribution strategies used for some of the supplementary service elements may be different from those used to deliver the core product itself. For instance, as a customer, you are probably willing to go to a particular location at a specific time to attend a sporting or entertainment event. However, you are unlikely to want to travel to a location for making a reservation. In fact, you probably expect convenience when reserving a seat in advance. Hence, you may expect the reservations service to be open for longer hours, to offer booking and credit card payment by phone or the web (Figure 5.6), and to deliver tickets through postal or electronic channels.

Figure 5.6 Making online transactions such as reservations, with a credit card affords convenience.

Where Should Service Be Delivered in a Bricks-and-Mortar Context?

Deciding where to locate a service facility for customers is very different from considering the location of the backstage elements. For customers, convenience and preference are the deciding factors. For backstage elements, cost, productivity, and access to labor are often the main determinants. Firms should make it easy for people to access frequently purchased services facing active competition.[6] Examples include retail banks and quick service restaurants. However, customers may be willing to travel further from their homes or workplaces to reach specialty services (Figure 5.7).

Figure 5.7 People get upset when electronic distribution systems let them down.

SOURCE

Reprinted from Christopher Lovelock (1994). *Product Plus*, p 283. New York: McGraw Hill. Copyright© Christopher H. Lovelock 1994.

Locational Constraints

Although customer convenience is important, operational requirements may restrict the location of the services.

▶ Airports, for instance, are often inconveniently located relative to travelers' homes, offices, or destinations. Due to noise and environmental factors, finding suitable sites for the construction of new airports, or expansion of existing ones is a very difficult task. The only way to make airport access more convenient is to install fast rail links, such as San Francisco's BART service, London's Heathrow Express, or the futuristic 260mph (420km/h) service to Shanghai's new airport, the first in the world to use magnetic levitation technology (Figure 5.8).

Figure 5.8 Shanghai's futuristic Maglev train is a working marvel of technology.

▶ Terrain and climate can also impose location constraints. Ski resorts have to be in the mountains, and ocean beach resorts on the coast (Figure 5.9).

▶ The need for economies of scale is another operational issue that may restrict the choice of locations. Major hospitals offer many different healthcare services, even a medical school, at a single location. Customers requiring complex, in-patient treatment must go to the service factory, rather than be treated at home. However, an ambulance, or even a helicopter, can be sent to pick them up.

Ministores

An interesting innovation among multi-site service businesses involves creating numerous small service factories to maximize geographic coverage.

▶ Automated kiosks represent one approach. ATMs offer many of the functions of a bank branch within a small, self-service machine that can be located within stores, hospitals, colleges, airports, and office buildings.

▶ Another approach is the separation of the front and back stages of the operation. Taco Bell's K-Minus strategy, highly innovative at the time of its introduction, involves restaurants without kitchens.[7] Food preparation takes place in a central location. Then meals are shipped to restaurants and to other "points of access" such as mobile food-carts, where they can be reheated prior to serving.

▶ Increasingly, firms offering one type of service business are purchasing space from another provider in a complementary field. Examples include mini bank branches within supermarkets, and food outlets such as Dunkin Donuts and Subway sharing space with a quick service restaurant like Burger King.

Figure 5.9 The scenic Reñaca Resort, one of the most popular and developed beaches in Viña del Mar, Chile, is subjected to a location constraint.

Locating in Multi-Purpose Facilities.

The most obvious locations for consumer services are close to where customers live or work. Modern buildings are often designed to be multi-purpose. They not only have office or production space, there are also services like a bank (or at least an ATM), a restaurant, a hair salon, several stores, and maybe a health club. Some companies even include a children's day-care facility to make life easier for busy working parents. Interest is growing in locating retail and other services on transportation routes and in bus, rail, and air terminals.

▶ Most major oil companies have chains of small retail stores to complement the fuel pumps at their service stations. This offers customers the convenience of one-stop shopping for fuel, car supplies, food, and household products (Figure 5.10).

▶ Truckstops on major highways often include Laundromats, toilets, ATMs, Internet access, restaurants, and inexpensive hotels. This is in addition to a variety of vehicle maintenance and repair services for both trucks and cars.

When Should Service Be Delivered?

In the past, most retail and professional services in industrialized countries followed a traditional schedule of about 40–50 hours a week. The situation inconvenienced working people, who either had to shop during their lunch break or on Saturdays. Today, the situation has changed. For some highly responsive service operations, the standard has become "24/7" service—24 hours a day, seven days a week, around the world. (For an overview of the factors behind the move to extended hours, see Service Insights 5.2).

Figure 5.10 Gas station in Beijing with supermarket in the background.

DELIVERING SERVICES IN CYBERSPACE

As we look at the eight petals of the Flower of Service, we can see that no fewer than five supplementary services are information based (Figure 5.11). Information, consultation, order-taking, billing, and payment (e.g. via credit card) can all be transmitted electronically.

The distribution of information, consultation, and order taking (or reservations and ticket sales) has reached extremely sophisticated levels in some global service industries such as hotels, airlines, and car rental companies. A number of channels targeted at key customer segments are needed. For instance, Starwood Hotels & Resorts Worldwide—whose 871 hotels in approximately 100 countries include brands like Sheraton, Westin, Meridian, and St. Regis—has 35 Global Sales Offices (GSOs) around the world to manage customer relationships with key global accounts. They

⋮⋮⋮ SERVICE INSIGHTS 5.2

Factors that encourage Extended Operating Hours

At least five factors are driving the move toward extended operating hours and seven-day operations. This is becoming a global trend.

- *Economic pressure from consumers.* There are a growing number of two-income families and single wage earners who live alone. They need time outside normal working hours to shop and use other services. Once one store or firm in any given area extends its hours to meet the needs of these market segments, competitors will follow. Chain stores have often led the way.

- *Changes in laws.* Support has decreased for the traditional religious view that a specific day should be a day of rest for one and all, regardless of religious beliefs. In a multicultural society, it is hard to decide which day should be decided as special – for observant Jews and Seventh Day Adventists, Saturday is the Sabbath; for Muslims, Friday is the holy day; and agnostics or atheists are presumed to be indifferent. There has been a gradual erosion of such laws in Western nations in recent years.

- *Economic incentives to improve the use of assets.* A great amount of money is often tied up in service facilities. The increase in costs of extending hours is often relatively small. If extending hours reduces crowding and increases revenues, then it is an attractive option. There are costs involved in

shutting down and reopening a facility like a supermarket for example. Climate control and some lighting must be left running all night, and security personnel must be paid 24/7. Therefore, even if not that many extra customers are served, there are still both operational and marketing advantages in remaining open 24 hours.

- *Availability of employees to work during "unsocial" hours.* Changing lifestyles and a desire for part-time employment have created a growing pool of people who are willing to work evenings and nights. They include students looking for part-time work outside classroom hours, people working a second job, parents with child-care responsibilities, and others who simply prefer to work at night and relax or sleep in the day.

- *Automated self-service facilities.* Self-service equipment has become increasingly reliable and user friendly. Many machines now accept card-based payments in addition to coins and banknotes. Unless a machine often requires servicing, or is easily vandalized, the extra cost of going from limited hours to 24-hour operation is not a lot. In fact, it may be simpler to leave machines running continuously than to turn them on and off.

offer a one-stop solution to both corporate clients such as corporate travel planners, wholesalers, meeting planners, and major travel organizations, and guests. Starwood has a central reservations system where individual and corporate clients can check the web site and gain access to information about facilities, rates and availability of all their hotels. Bookings and payment can also be made online. In fact, corporate customers can book online with their own confidential negotiated rates.[8]

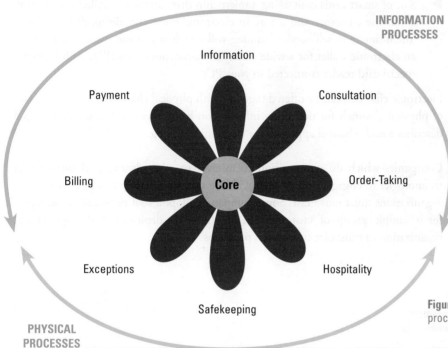

Figure 5.11 Information and physical processes of the augmented service product.

While businesses try to drive their customers to the online channel (Figure 5.12), not all customers like to use self-service equipment. Therefore, moving customers to new electronic channels may require different strategies for different segments.[9] In fact, some proportion of customers may never shift from their preferred high-contact delivery environments.

Service Delivery Innovations Facilitated by Technology

More recently, businessmen have taken advantage of the Internet to create new services. Four innovations of particular interest are:

▶ Development of "smart" cell phones and PDAs, and Wi-Fi high-speed Internet technology that can link users to the Internet wherever they may be (Figure 5.13).

Figure 5.12 Many businesses are moving their customers to the online channel.

- Usage of voice recognition technology that allows customers to give information and request service simply by speaking into a phone or microphone.

- Creation of web sites that provide information, take orders, and even serve as a delivery channel for information-based services. Web sites now are also platforms for vast social networks for individual networking, and user generated content (Figure 5.14).

- Sale of smart cards containing a microchip that can store detailed information about the customer and act as an electronic purse containing digital money. The ultimate in self-service banking will be when you can use a smart card as an electronic wallet for a wide variety of transactions, as well as refill it from a special card reader connected to your PC.

Electronic channels can be offered together with physical channels, or take the place of physical channels for delivering information-based services. Service Insights 5.3 describes a multichannel approach for electronic banking.

Companies which do not position themselves to take advantage of these newer technologies to engage the customer will lose out. In a fiercely competitive market, organizations must move fast. Some companies adopt a trial period of "prototypes" for a sample group of customers before full-scale deployment throughout the organization to minimize unforeseen problems.[10]

Figure 5.13 PDAs connect people even in remote places.

Figure 5.14 Cisco is one of the leading companies that provides integrated network solutions and services.

Multichannel Banking without Branches at First Direct

First Direct, a division of HSBC, has become famous as the originator of the concept of a bank without branches. At the beginning of 2008, it was serving more than 1.2 million customers throughout the United Kingdom (and abroad) through call centers, a web site, text messaging on cell phones, and access to HSBC's large network of ATMs.

In January 2000, First Direct described itself as "the largest virtual bank in the world." It announced that it would transform itself into an e-bank and set the standard for e-banking. At the heart of the strategy is a multi channel approach to banking. It combines First Direct's telephone banking experience with the strengths of the Internet, as well as the adaptability of cell phone technologies to deliver a superior service at extremely competitive prices. As noted by chief executive Alan Hughes:

> "We are the first bank in the world to reengineer our entire business for the e-age. The scale of the initiative creates a new category of e-banking and sets a benchmark for the industry around the globe. More than a bank, firstdirect.com will be the first Internet banking store."

By 2008, 80 percent of all customer contact with First Direct was electronic and 43 percent of sales were through e-channels. Some 885,000 customers use Internet banking and 390,000 use SMS (short message service) text messaging. The bank sent out some 2.6 million text messages a month.

A central element in this strategy is to offer Britain's most comprehensive cell phone banking service, recognizing that almost all adults in the United Kingdom either own or use a cell phone. Through SMS text messages, First Direct customers have access to mini-statements for up to three accounts and can be advised when credits or debits enter or leave the account. In addition, they are alerted automatically if their accounts go into the red. When the iPhone was launched, First Direct became the first bank to adapt its online banking so that it worked well with the iPhone.

Although person-to-person voice telephone still remains the backbone of the bank's relationship with its customers, in August 2005, the bank launched a new web chat service, allowing customers to "talk" with banking reps through a keyboard and mouse rather than by phone. It promotes this service as offering the immediacy of a phone conversation with the convenience of e-mail.

Is this non-traditional strategy working? The evidence suggests a resounding "yes." According to MORI and Research International, First Direct has been the most recommended bank in the United Kingdom for the past 16 years. First Direct had the greatest proportion of customers prepared to recommend their own bank. More than one-third of its customers was acquired through recommendations. Despite intense competition among British banks and the costs of continued investment in technology, First Direct has been profitable since 1995.

SOURCE

Cagna A.-M., & Larreche, J.-C. (2005). First Direct 2005: The most recommended bank in the world. Fontainebleau, France: INSEAD, 2005; press releases distributed on www.firstdirect.com/press/key, Accessed February 2008. Source for photo: http://www.visit4info.com/advert/First-Direct-Banking-First-Direct-Banking/7648, Accessed March 2008. This is a snapshot of a TV ad.

E-Commerce: The Move to Cyberspace

Amazon.com pioneered the concept of the virtual store. Now, there are thousands of them all over the world. Travelocity is another successful virtual store. The company markets and distributes travel-related products through its various brand web sites, including Travelocity, Site59 in the United States, lastminute.com in Europe, and Zuji in the Asia Pacific.

Among the factors luring customers into virtual stores are:

▶ Convenience,

▶ Ease of search (obtaining information and searching for desired items or services),

▶ Broader selection,

▶ Potential for better prices, and

▶ 24-hour service with prompt delivery. This is particularly appealing to customers whose busy lives leave them short of time.

Web sites are becoming increasingly sophisticated, but also more user-friendly. They often become like a well-informed sales assistant in steering customers toward items that are likely to be of interest. Some even provide the opportunity for "live" e-mail dialog with helpful customer service personnel. There are exciting recent developments that link web sites, Customer Relationship Management (CRM) systems, and mobile telephony. The integration of mobile devices is a means to following services:

1. *Access* services.

2. *Alert* customers to opportunities or problems by delivering the right information or interaction at the right time.

3. *Update* information in real time to ensure that it is continuously accurate and relevant.[11] For example, customers can set stock alerts on their broker's web site and get an e-mail or SMS alert when a certain price level is reached, or a particular transaction has been conducted. They can also obtain real-time information on stock prices. Customers can respond by accessing the brokerage and trading directly by voice or through SMS.

Figure 5.15 Yellow Pages has remained relevant by updating its content and services for today's IT-savvy, connected customer.

One of the greatest challenges that organizations face is to get customers to log on to their web sites. For instance, with more consumers being IT savvy and going online for information, the Yellow Pages directory is not as widely used as before. One of the problems with the directory is that there is long lead time before the directory is published, and information may be obsolete by the time the directory goes to print. To overcome this problem, Yellow Pages came up with a service that allows customers to log on to the Yellow Pages web site of the country. From there, customers are able to link directly to the listed merchants, and obtain further information or buy goods and services. Yellow Pages has also come up with a Global Positioning Service (GPS), where customers can click and download the information needed to pin-point a company's location (Figure 5.15).

THE ROLE OF INTERMEDIARIES

LO 4
Understand the part played by intermediaries in distributing services.

Many service organizations find it cost-effective to outsource certain tasks. These are usually supplementary service elements. For instance, despite their greater use of telephone call centers and the Internet, cruise lines and resort hotels still rely on travel agents to handle a large portion of their customer interactions. These involve giving out information, taking reservations, accepting payment, and ticketing. How should a service provider work in partnership with one or more intermediaries to deliver a complete service package to customers?

In Figure 5.16 we use the Flower of Service framework to show an example in which the core product is delivered by the original supplier, together with certain supplementary elements in the informational, consultation, and exceptions categories. Delivery of the remaining supplementary services packaged with this offering is through an intermediary. The challenge for the original supplier is to oversee the overall process. They have to make sure that each element offered by intermediaries fits the overall service concept, and creates a consistent and service experience for the customer.

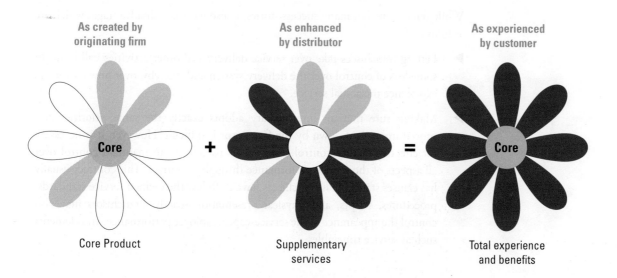

Figure 5.16 Splitting responsibilities for service delivery.

Applying the 4Ps to Services **125**

Figure 5.17 Saks has built a thriving salon network, 140 strong to date, and the Saks franchise is associated with style and award-sweeping excellence.

Franchising

Even delivery of the core product can be outsourced to an intermediary. Franchising has become a popular way to expand delivery of an effective service concept that includes all the 7*Ps*. Franchising reaches multiple sites without the level of monetary investment that would be needed for rapid expansion of company-owned and -managed sites.[12] A franchisor recruits entrepreneurs who are willing to invest their own time and finances in managing a previously developed service concept. In return, the franchisor provides training on how to operate and market the business, sells necessary supplies, and provides promotional support at a national or regional level to add to the local marketing activities. These activities are paid for by the franchisee, but must follow the copy and media guidelines of the franchisor.

Growth-oriented service firms like franchising because franchisees are highly motivated to ensure good customer service and high-quality service operations.[13] Franchising has been applied to a very wide array of both consumer and business-to-business services and now spans some 75 different product categories. New concepts are being created and commercialized all the time in countries around the world.[14] From 2003 to 2005, 900 new franchise concepts were launched in the United States. However, in 2006 alone, 300 new franchise concepts were launched. The fastest growing categories of concepts are related to health and fitness, publications, security, and consumer services.[15] One example of a successful franchise is UK's leading hair and beauty franchise group, Saks (Figure 5.17). They have an award winning international network of salons and training academies.[16]

However, there is a high drop-out rate among franchisors in the early years of a new franchise system. One-third fail within the first four years and no less than three quarters of all franchisors stop existing after 12 years.[17] Since growth is very important to achieve an efficient scale, some franchisors use a strategy known as master franchising. Master franchisees are often individuals who have already succeeded as operators of an individual franchise outlet. They are therefore given the responsibility of recruiting, training, and supporting franchisees within a given geographic area.

While franchising has many success stories, it also has some disadvantages which are as follows:

▶ Letting franchisees take over service delivery and other activities will result in some loss of control over the delivery system and, thereby, over how customers experience the actual service.

▶ Making sure that an intermediary adopts exactly the same priorities and procedures as laid down by the franchisor is difficult. However, it is necessary for effective quality control. Franchisors usually try to maintain control over all aspects of the service performance through a contract. This contract usually has clauses stating that franchisees have to follow the defined service standards, procedures, scripts, and physical presentation strictly. Franchisors may also control the appearance of the servicescape, employee performance, and elements such as service timetables.

Figure 5.18 Trucking companies license jobs to local firms in remote areas.

▶ An ongoing problem is that as franchisees gain experience, they may start to feel that they should not be paying the various fees to the franchisor. They may also believe that they can operate the business better without the restrictions imposed by the agreement, which then often leads to legal fights between the two parties.

An alternative to franchising is licensing another supplier to act on the original supplier's behalf to deliver the core product. Trucking companies regularly make use of independent agents (Figure 5.18). They do this instead of locating company-owned branches in each of the different cities they serve. They may also choose to contract with independent "owner-operators," who drive their own trucks, rather than buy their own trucks and employ full-time drivers.[18]

DISTRIBUTING SERVICES INTERNATIONALLY

LO 5

Understand the special challenges of distributing people-processing, possession-processing, and information-based services internationally.

Many service companies have an international presence. What are the alternative ways for a service company to tap the potential of international markets? It depends in part on the nature of the underlying processes and delivery system. People-processing, possession-processing, and information-based services have very different requirements on an international distribution strategy.

How Service Processes Affect International Market Entry

People processing services

The service provider needs to have a local geographic presence, stationing the necessary personnel, buildings, equipment, vehicles, and supplies within reasonably easy reach of target customers. There are three options for people processing services:

▶ *Export the service concept.* Acting alone or in partnership with local suppliers, the firm establishes a service factory in another country. The objective may be to reach out to new customers, or to follow existing corporate or individual customers to new locations (or both). This approach is commonly used by chain restaurants, hotels, car rental firms, and weight-reduction clinics, where a local presence is essential in order to be able to compete. For corporate customers, the industries are likely to be in fields like banking, professional services, and business logistics etc.

▶ *Import customers.* Customers from other countries are invited to come to a service factory in the firm's home country. Some of these customers may be mobile and may patronize a company's offerings in many different locations, and make comparisons between them. People will travel from abroad to ski at outstanding resorts, such as Whistler-Blackholm in British Columbia or Vail in Colorado. They may also travel for specialist medical treatment at famous hospitals and clinics, such as Massachusetts General Hospital or the Mayo Clinic, (Figure 5.19) to cost-effective hospitals in exotic locations like the Bumrungrad Hospital in Bangkok which we discussed in Chapter 1.

Possession-processing services

This category involves services to the customer's physical possessions. It includes repair and maintenance, cargo transport, cleaning, and warehousing. These may be restricted by geography. A local presence is required when the supplier must come to repair or maintain objects in a fixed location. This is regardless of whether customers drop off items at a service facility or personnel visit the customer's site. Sometimes, however, expert personnel may be flown in from a base in another country (e.g. repair of aircraft engines or high end machine tools). In a few instances, a transportable item of equipment may be shipped to a Foreign Service center for repair, maintenance, or upgrade. This is where global logistics firms play a part. However, there are transportation costs, customs duties, and government laws to deal with. Modern technology now allows certain types of service processes to be controlled from a distance through electronic diagnostics and transmission of so-called "remote fixes".

Figure 5.19 The Mayo Clinic's name in specialty medicine ensures a steady stream of visitors.

Information-based services

This group includes two categories, *mental processing services* (services to the customer's mind, such as news and entertainment), and *information processing services* (services to customers' intangible assets, such as banking and insurance). They are, perhaps, the most interesting category of services from the point of view of global strategy development. This is because data is transmitted or changed to create value. Information-based services can be distributed internationally in one of three ways:

▶ *Export the service to a local service factory.* The service can be made available in a local facility that customers visit. For instance, a film made in Hollywood can be shown in movie theaters around the world, or a college course can be designed in one country and then be offered by approved teachers elsewhere (Figure 5.20).

▶ *Import customers.* Customers may travel abroad to visit a specialist facility, in which case the service takes on the features of a people-processing service. For example, a large number of people travel all over the world as tourists.

▶ *Export the information via telecommunications and transform it locally.* Modern global telecommunications link intelligent machines to powerful databases, and makes it increasingly easy to deliver information-based services around the world. Rather than ship object-based services from their country of origin, the data can be downloaded from that country for physical production in local markets (even by customers themselves).

In theory, none of these information-based services require face-to-face contact with customers. All can possibly be delivered at arm's length through telecommunications or mail. Banking and insurance are good examples of services that can be delivered from other countries, with cash delivery available through global ATM networks. In practice, however, a local presence may be necessary to build personal relationships, conduct on-site research (as in consulting or auditing), or even to fulfill legal requirements.

Figure 5.20 Technology has enabled foreign language courses to be exported to a mobile, localized service factory.

LO 1 ▶ Services can be distributed through various modes. They are:

- o Customers visit the service site,

- o Service providers go to their customers, and

- o Service transactions conducted remotely (at arm's length).

The goals behind the choice of each channel differ. Convenience is a key driver of channel choice, often favoring at arm's length channels. However, consumers rely more on personnel channels when the perceived risk is high, when there are social motives behind the transaction. On the other hand, when consumers have high confidence or knowledge about the product, and are technology savvy, they are more likely to use self-service channels.

LO 2 ▶ Where should service be delivered? The place and time decisions must reflect customer needs and expectations, competitive activity, and the nature of the service operation. Deciding where to locate a service facility for customers is very different from deciding where to locate backstage elements. For the location of backstage elements, cost, productivity, and access to labor are main considerations. For location of service facility, convenience and operational requirements are main factors to consider. New distribution innovations by service firms include mini stores, sharing retail space with complementary providers, and design of multi-purpose facilities (e.g. malls in airports).

LO 3 ▶ When should service be available? Previously, services were available for about 40–50 hours a week. Now, there is a move to encourage extended operating hours. One way of catering to customer demands for greater convenience is for firms to extend their hours and days of service, with the ultimate being 24/7 service every day of the year. The use of self-service technology allows services to be offered 24/7.

▶ Another way services can be offered 24/7 is through the Internet. The Internet allows for services to be distributed through cyberspace. Virtual stores (e.g. Amazon.com) and online banks offer an alternative to traditional physical channels for delivering information-based services. Recent developments are infrastructures that link CRM systems, mobile telephones, and web sites to provide a consistent and convenient customer experience.

LO 4 ▶ Apart from firms distributing their services, intermediaries also have a role to play. Service organizations may find it cost effective to outsource certain tasks.

- o Franchising can be used to outsource the core service offering. There are advantages and disadvantages of franchising. Franchisees are highly motivated to ensure customer orientation and high quality service operations. Disadvantages of franchising include the loss of control over the delivery system and how the customers experience the actual service. Hence, franchisors often have strict contracts exercising control over all aspects of the service performance.

- o Licensing is an alternative way to distribute services. Licensing is where another supplier acts on behalf of the original supplier. Trucking companies often use this method of distribution instead of owning different operations in different cities.

LO 5 ▶ When distributing services internationally, firms need to bear in mind that people-processing, possession-processing, and information-based services have very different requirements.

- o People-processing services firms that require direct contact with the customer have several options like (1) export the service concept, (2) import the customers, and (3) transport customer to new locations.

- o Possession-processing services may need crew or equipment to be flown in to enable service completion.

- o Information-based services can be distributed in several ways: (1) export the service to a local service factory, (2) import customers, and (3) export the service via telecommunications and transform it locally.

UNLOCK YOUR LEARNING

These keywords are found within the sections of each Learning Objective (LO). They are integral in understanding the services marketing concepts taught in each section. Having a firm grasp of these keywords and how they are used is essential in helping you do well for your course, and in the real and very competitive marketing scene out there.

LO 1
1. Arbitrage
2. Arm's length transactions
3. Channel choice
4. Channel preferences
5. Convenience
6. Customers visit the service site
7. Options for service delivery
8. Self-service channels
9. Service provider visits the customer
10. Personal channels
11. Distribution

LO 2
12. "24/7" service
13. Backstage elements
14. Bricks-and-Mortar
15. Locational constraints
16. Ministores

17. Multi-site service businesses
18. Multi-purpose facilities

LO 3
19. Cyberspace
20. Multichannel approach
21. Virtual stores
22. Flower of Service

LO 4
23. Franchising
24. Franchisor
25. Franchisee
26. Intermediary
27. Licensing

LO 5
28. Export the service concept
29. International markets
30. Import customers
31. Information-based services
32. Possession-processing services
33. People-processing services

How well do you know the language of services marketing? Quiz yourself!

 Not for the academically faint-of-heart

For each keyword you are able to recall without referring to earlier pages, give yourself a point (and a pat on the back). Tally your score at the end and see if you earned the right to be called—a *services marketeer.*

SCORE

0 – 5	Services Marketing is done a great disservice.
6 – 12	The midnight oil needs to be lit, pronto.
13 – 18	I know what you *didn't* do all semester.
19 – 24	A close shave with success.
25 – 30	Now, go forth and market.
31 – 33	There should be a marketing concept named after you.

Review Questions

1. What are the different options for service delivery? For each of the options, what factors do service firms need to take into account when using that option?

2. How should service firms make decisions on the place and time of service delivery? Give examples to support your points.

3. What are the factors that a new service provider needs to take into account when setting up a virtual store? How can they lure consumers to the virtual store? Give examples.

4. Why is franchising a popular way to expand distribution of an effective service concept? What are some disadvantages of franchising?

5. How does the nature of the service affect the opportunities for internationalization?

Application Exercises

1. How can an experience or something intangible be distributed?

2. Identify three situations where you use self-service delivery. For each situation, what is your motivation for using this form of delivery? Why don't you have service personnel deliver the service for you?

3. An entrepreneur is thinking of setting up a new business. (You can choose any business). What advice would you give regarding the issues of time and place?

4. Think of three services that you buy or use mainly through the Internet. What benefits do you get from using this channel compared to alternative channels like phone, mail or branch network?

5. Select two business franchisees (other than food service), one targeted mainly at consumers and the other targeted mainly at businesses. Develop a profile of each, examining their strategy across the 7 Ps and evaluating their competitive positioning.

6. What advice would you give to (1) a weight reduction clinic, (2) a pest control company and (3) a university offering undergraduate courses about going international?

ENDNOTES

1 Ivatury, G., & Pickens, M. (2006). Mobile phone banking and low-income customers: Evidence from South Africa. white paper, *Consultative Group to Assist the Poor/The World Bank and United Nations Foundation*; Katz, R. (2006). Cell phone banking and the BOP: *Wizzit. NextBillion. net – Development Through Enterprise*, 19 June 2006. Available: http://www.nextbillion. net//blogs/2006/06/19/cell-phone-banking-and-the-bop-wizzit, Accessed February 2008; Video on YouTube, WIZZIT: Banking the unbanked in South Africa. Available: http://www.youtube. com/watch?v=2SKhCYoF0Lg. Accessed March 2008; http://www.wizzit.co.za/

2 Whiting, A., & Donthu, N. (2006). Managing voice-to-voice encounters: Reducing the agony of being put on hold. *Journal of Service Research*, 8(3), pp. 234–244.

3 This section was based on the following research: Black, N. J., Lockett, A., Ennew, C., Winklhofer H., & McKechnie, S. (2002). Modelling consumer choice of distribution channels: An illustration from financial services. *International Journal of Bank Marketing*, 20(4), pp. 161–173; Lee, J. (2002). A key to marketing financial services: The right mix of products, services, channels and customers. *Journal of Services Marketing*, 16(3), pp.238–258; Berry, L. L., Seiders, K., & Grewal, D. (2002) Understanding service convenience. *Journal of Marketing*, 66(3), pp. 1–17.

4 Lin, J. –S. C., & Hsieh, P. –L. (2006). The Role of technology readiness in customers' perception and adoption of self-service technologies. *International Journal of Service Industry Management*, 17(5), pp. 497–517.

5 Nunes, P. F., & Cespedes, F. V. (2003). The customer has escaped. *Harvard Business Review*, 81(11), pp. 96–105.

6 Jones, M. A., Mothersbaugh, F. L., & Beatty, S. E. (2004). The effects of locational convenience on customer repurchase intentions across service types. *Journal of Services Marketing*, 17(7), pp. 701–712.

7 Heskett, J. L. Sasser, W. E., Jr., & Schlesinger, L. A. (1997). *The Service Profit Chain* (pp. 218–220.). New York: The Free Press..

8 Wirtz, J., & Ho, J. P. T. (2008). Westin in Asia: Distributing Hotel Rooms Globally, In J. Wirtz & C. H. Lovelock (Eds.), *Services Marketing in Asia – A Case Book* (pp. 253–259). Singapore: Prentice Hall. Available: www.starwoodhotels.com, Accessed February 2008.

9 Recent research on the adoption of self-service technologies includes: Meuter, M. L., Bitner, M. J., Ostrom, A. L., & Brown, S. W. (2005). Choosing among alternative service delivery modes: An investigation of customer trial of self-service technologies. *Journal of Marketing*, 69(April), pp. 61–83; Curran, J. M., & Meuter, M. L. (2005). Self-service technology adoption: Comparing three technologies. *Journal of Services Marketing*, 19(2), pp. 103–113.

10 Brown, & Stanley A. (2000). *Customer Relationship Management: A Strategic Imperative in the World of e-Business* (p. 222), PriceWaterhouse Coopers: John Wiley & Sons..

11 Lemon, K. N., Newell, F. B., & Lemon, L. J. (2002). The Wireless Rules for e-Service. In R. T. Rust & P. K. Kannan (Eds.), *New Directions in Theory and Practice* (pp. 220–232). New York: Armonk, M.E. Sharpe.

12 Hoffman R. C., & Preble, J. F. (2004). Global franchising: Current status and future challenges. *Journal of Services Marketing*, 18(2), pp. 101–113.

13 Cross J., & Walker, B. J. (2000). Addressing Service Marketing Challenges Through Franchising. In T. A. Swartz & D. Iacobucci (Eds.), *Handbook of Services Marketing & Management* (pp. 473–484). Thousand Oaks, CA: Sage Publications; Altinay, L. (2004). Implementing international franchising: The role of intrapreuneurship. International *Journal of Service Industry Management*, 15(5), pp. 426–443.

14 Hoffman R. C., & Preble, J. F. (2004). Global franchising: Current status and future challenges. *Journal of Services Marketing*, 18(2), pp.101–113.

15 International Franchise Association Educational Foundation Inc., (2007). Franchise Industry Gains 300 Concepts in One Year," 19 November 2007. Available: http://www.franchise.org/Franchise-News-Detail.aspx?id=36416, Accessed March 2008.

16 www.saks.co.uk , accessed March 2008.

17 Shane S., & Spell, C. (1998). Factors for new franchise success. *Sloan Management Review, Spring*, pp. 43–50.

18 For a discussion on what to watch out for where parts & the service are outsourced, see: Johnson, L. K. (2005). Outsourcing postsale service: is your brand protected? Before you spin off repairs, or parts distribution, or customer call centers, consider the cons as well as the pros. *Harvard Business Review Supply Chain Strategy*, (July), pp. 3–5.

setting prices and

IMPLEMENTING REVENUE MANAGEMENT

LEARNING OBJECTIVES

By the end of this chapter, students should be able to:

> **LO 1** Recognize that effective pricing is central to the financial success of service firms.

> **LO 2** Outline the foundations of a pricing strategy and the various approaches to pricing a service as represented by the pricing tripod.

> **LO 3** Define different types of financial costs and explain the limitations of cost-based pricing.

> **LO 4** Understand the concept of net value and how gross value can be enhanced through value-based pricing.

> **LO 5** Describe competition-based pricing and situations where service markets are less price competitive.

> **LO 6** Describe what revenue management is and how it works.

> **LO 7** Understand the role rate fences play in effective revenue management.

> **LO 8** Be familiar with the issue of ethics related to service pricing.

> **LO 9** Put service pricing into practice.

Figure 6.1 London is home to many famous monuments, as well as the first easyInternetcafe.

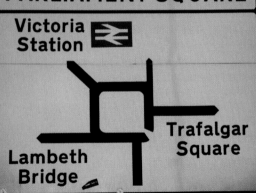

OPENING VIGNETTE[1]

DYNAMIC PRICING AT EASY INTERNET CAFE

easyInternetcafe is part of the easyGroup of companies headed by Stelios Haji-Ioannou, the Greek entrepreneur who received knighthood from Queen Elizabeth II for his contribution to entrepreneurship. The first easyInternetcafe was opened in 1999 opposite London's Victoria Station. An interesting feature of this Internet café is that it is unmanned by personnel. Vending machines are used to dispense credit to customers. There are currently 74 owned or operated easyInternetcafes in countries such as United Kingdom, Cyprus, Italy, Germany, Spain, Greece, the Netherlands, and New York in the USA, and it has about 5,200 PCs.

easyInternetcafe has many features that allow revenue management to be used successfully. Firstly, the perishable inventory. Once nobody uses the Internet access time, that hour is gone and cannot be resold. Secondly, there is relatively fixed capacity and high fixed costs. The equipment, software, and bandwidth are fixed costs that are incurred whether or not there is a customer in the store. Thirdly, demand for Internet access varies by time of the day, day of the week, months and seasons. Hence, demand is very unpredictable and uncertain. Finally, different customers may be willing to pay different amounts for one hour of Internet access time.

To cater to the different price sensitivities of their customers, there are different types of passes. Customers can either buy passes which allow unlimited access during a set period of time, or passes at the going rate. Passes sold at the going rate are priced using dynamic pricing. Users who choose the dynamic pricing options pay according to how busy the store is. The user can log on as many times as desired, until the credit expires. Hence, the more customers there are in a store, the more the user has to pay for the Internet access. The ticket price is always the same. However, if the café is very busy, then there will be fewer minutes of surfing time on the ticket. If the café is less busy, then there will be more minutes of surfing time on the ticket. In this way, when it is very busy, the queue will clear faster as each user has a shorter time and when it is less busy, each user has a longer time and demand is allowed to buildup. As a result, waiting time is also moderated. Price sensitive customers can use the café when they see that many terminals are available and those customers willing to pay more know that even during busy periods, the wait is not that long. The concept has been highly successful as a high percentage of customers think that easyInternetcafe is good value for money.

Figure 6.2 The New York easyInternetcafe.

...easyInternetcafe
is a success story
for shrewd
revenue
management...

PART II

LO 1

Recognize that effective pricing
is central to the financial
success of service firms.

EFFECTIVE PRICING IS CENTRAL TO FINANCIAL SUCCESS

Pricing is typically more complex in services than it is in manufacturing. For physical goods, the costs of creating and distributing it can be calculated. However, it is usually harder for managers to calculate the financial costs of services, as costs vary widely depending on capacity utilization. In addition, the importance of the time factor in service delivery means that speed of delivery and avoidance of waiting time often increase value. With the increase in value, customers are prepared to pay a higher price for the service.

Consumers often find service pricing difficult to understand (e.g. insurance products or hospital bills), risky (when you make a hotel reservation on three different days, it can happen that you are offered three different prices!), and sometimes even unethical (e.g. many bank customers complain about a variety of fees and charges they consivder to be unfair). In this chapter, we will learn how to have an effective pricing and revenue management strategy so that the consumer decides to buy your service.

Objectives for Establishing Prices

Before the firm can come up with an effective pricing strategy, there must be a clear understanding of a company's pricing objectives. The most common pricing objectives are related to revenue and profits; building demand, and developing a user base (Table 6.1).

Table 6.1 Objectives for pricing of services.

Revenue and Profit Objectives

Seek Profit
- Make the largest possible contribution or profit.
- Achieve a specific target level, but do not seek to maximize profits.
- Maximize revenue from a fixed capacity by varying prices and target segments over time. This is done typically using revenue management systems.

Cover costs
- Cover fully allocated costs, including corporate overhead.
- Cover costs of providing one particular service, excluding overhead.
- Cover incremental costs of selling one extra unit or to one extra customer.

Patronage and User Base-Related Objectives

Build Demand
- Maximize demand (when capacity is not a restriction), provided a certain minimum level of revenue is achieved.
- Achieve full capacity utilization, especially when high capacity utilization adds to the value created for all customers (e.g. a 'full-house' adds excitement to a theater play or basket ball game).

Build a User Base
- Encourage trial and adoption of a service. This is especially important for new services with high infrastructure costs, and for membership-type services that provide a large amount of revenues from their continued usage after adoption (e.g. cell phone service subscriptions, or life-insurance plans).
- Build market share and/or a large user base, especially if there are a lot of economies of scale that can lead to a competitive cost advantage (e.g. if development or fixed costs are high).

PRICING STRATEGY STANDS ON THREE FOUNDATIONS

 LO 2

Outline the foundations of a pricing strategy and the various approaches to pricing a service as represented by the pricing tripod.

Once the pricing objectives are understood, we can focus on the pricing strategy. The foundations of the pricing strategy can be described as a tripod. There are three legs, namely costs to the provider, competition, and value to the customer (Figure 6.3). In many service industries, pricing used to be viewed from a financial and accounting standpoint, and therefore cost-plus pricing was often used. Today, however, most services have a good understanding of value-based and competitive pricing. In the pricing tripod, the costs that a firm needs to cover usually sets a minimum price, or floor, for a specific service offering. The customer's perceived value of the offering sets a maximum, or ceiling. The price charged by competitors for similar or substitute services usually controls where the price can be set within the floor-to-ceiling range. The pricing objectives of the organization then decide where actual prices should be set, given the possible range provided by the pricing tripod analysis. Let us look at each leg of the pricing tripod in more detail in the next three sections.

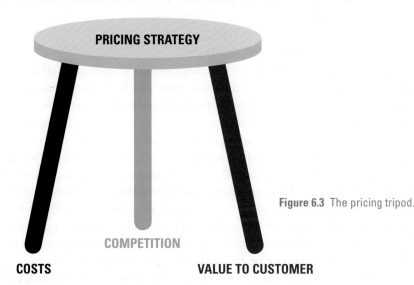

PRICING STRATEGY

COMPETITION

COSTS　　　**VALUE TO CUSTOMER**

Figure 6.3 The pricing tripod.

 LO 3

Define different types of financial costs and explain the limitations of cost-based pricing.

Cost-Based Pricing

It is usually harder to find out the costs involved in producing an intangible performance, than it is to trace the costs of producing a physical good. In addition, because of the labor and infrastructure needed to create performances, many service organizations have a much higher ratio of fixed costs to variable costs than is found in manufacturing firms (Figure 6.4).

Figure 6.4 Train services have very high infrastructure costs; variable costs of transporting an additional customer are insignificant.

Establishing the Costs of Providing Service

Even if you have already taken a marketing course, you may find it helpful to review how service costs can be estimated, using fixed, semi-variable, and variable costs. In addition, you can review how the ideas of contribution and break-even analysis can help in pricing decisions (see Marketing Review on page 139). These traditional cost-accounting approaches work well for service firms with a large proportion of variable costs and/or semi-variable costs (e.g. many professional services). For service firms with high fixed-costs and complex product lines with shared infrastructure (e.g. retail banking products), it may be worthwhile considering the more complex Activity-Based Costing (ABC) approach (Figure 6.5). ABC is a more accurate way to allocate indirect costs (overheads) for service firms. When determining the indirect cost of a service, it looks at the resources needed to perform each activity and then allocates the indirect cost to a service based on the quantities and types of activities required to perform the service. Thus, resource expenses (or indirect costs) are linked to the variety and complexity of goods and services produced and not just on physical volume. If implemented well, firms will be in a better position to estimate the costs of creating specific types of services, performing activities in different locations or serving specific customers.

Pricing Implications of Cost Analysis

To make a profit, a firm must set its price high enough to cover the full costs of producing and marketing the service. There must also be enough contribution so that there can be a desired profit margin at the predicted sales volume. Service businesses with high fixed costs include those with expensive physical facilities (such as a hospital, or a college), or a fleet of vehicles (such as an airline, or a trucking company), or a network (such as a telecommunications company, a railroad, or a gas pipeline). For such services, the variable costs of serving an extra customer may be minimal. Under these conditions, managers may feel that they have a lot of flexibility in pricing and be tempted to set a very low price to increase sales (Figure 6.6). However, there will be no profit at the end of the year unless all relevant costs have been covered. Many service businesses have gone bankrupt because they ignored this fact. Hence, firms that compete on the basis of low prices need to have a very good understanding of their cost structure and of the sales volume needed to break even at particular prices.

Figure 6.5 Housekeeping services contribute to the cost of hotel rooms.

Figure 6.6 Budget airlines like easyJet, set low prices to encourage higher sales. As a consequence, they need high load factors to break even.

Understanding **Costs**, **Contribution**, and **Break-Even Analysis**

Fixed costs are those economic costs that a supplier would continue to have (at least in the short run) even if no services were sold. These costs are likely to include rent, depreciation, utilities, taxes, insurance, salaries, and wages for managers and long-term employees, and interest payments.

Variable costs refer to the costs of serving an additional customer. Examples are making an additional bank transaction, or selling an additional seat in a theater. In many services, such costs are very low. For instance, in a theater, the cost of seating an extra patron is close to zero. More significant variable costs are associated with activities such as serving food and beverages, or installing new parts when undertaking repairs. This is because expensive physical products are often provided, in addition to labor. Just because a firm has sold a service at a price that exceeds its variable cost does not mean that the firm is now profitable. There are still fixed and semi-variable costs to be recouped.

Semi-variable costs fall in between fixed and variable costs. They are expenses that rise or fall in a stepwise fashion as the volume of business increases/decreases. Examples include adding an extra bus to meet increased demand on a specific bus route, or hiring a part-time employee to work in an accounting firm during financial year closing.

Contribution is the difference between the variable cost of selling an extra unit of service and the money received from the buyer of that service. It goes to cover fixed and semi-variable costs before creating profits.

Determining and allocating economic costs can be challenging in some service operations because of the difficulty of deciding how to assign fixed costs in a multi-service facility, such as a hospital. For instance, there are certain fixed costs for running the emergency department in a hospital. Apart from that, there are fixed costs for running the hospital, where the emergency department is a part of. How much of the hospital's fixed costs should be allocated to the emergency department? A hospital manager might use one of several ways to calculate the emergency department's share of overheads. These could include (1) the percentage of total floor space that it occupies, (2) the percentage of employee hours or payroll that it accounts for, or (3) the percentage of total patient contact hours involved. Each method is likely to yield a totally different fixed-cost allocation. One method might show the emergency department to be very profitable, another might make it seem like a loss-making operation.

Break-even analysis Managers need to know at what sales volume a service will become profitable. This is called the break-even point. The necessary analysis involves dividing the total fixed and semivariable costs by the contribution obtained on each unit of service. For instance, if a 100-room hotel needs to cover fixed and semi-variable costs of $2 million a year, and the average contribution per room-night is $100, then the hotel will need to sell 20,000 room-nights per year out of a total annual capacity of 36,500. If prices are cut by an average of $20 per room night (or variable costs rise by $20), then the contribution will drop to $80 and the hotel's break-even volume will rise to 25,000 room nights. The required sales volume needs to be related to *price sensitivity* (Will customers be willing to pay this much?), *market size* (Is the market large enough to support this level of patronage after taking competition into account?), *maximum capacity* (the hotel in our example has a capacity of 36,500 room-nights per year, assuming no rooms are taken out of service for maintenance or renovation).

LO 4

Understand the concept of net value and how gross value can be enhanced through value-based pricing.

Value-Based Pricing

Another leg of the pricing tripod is value to the customer. No customer will pay more for a service than he or she thinks it is worth. Thus, marketers need to understand how customers perceive service value in order to set an appropriate price.

Understanding Net Value

Customer definitions of value may be highly personal and vary from individual to individual. In this book, we use the definition of "value is what I get for what I give,"[2] and use the term *net value* to describe it. Net value is the sum of all the perceived benefits (gross value) minus the sum of all the perceived costs of service. The greater the positive difference between the two, the greater the net value. If the perceived costs of a service are greater than the perceived benefits, then the service will have negative net value, and the consumer will not buy. You can think of calculations that customers make in their minds as being similar to weighing materials on a pair of old-fashioned scales, with the service benefits in one tray and the costs of obtaining those benefits in the other tray (Figure 6.7). When customers look at competing services, they are basically comparing the relative net values. As we discussed in Chapter 4, a marketer can increase the value of a service by adding benefits to the core product and by improving supplementary services (Figure 6.8).

"As an alternative to the traditional 30-year mortgage, we also offer an interest-only mortgage, balloon mortgage, reverse mortgage, upside down mortgage, inside out mortgage, loop-de-loop mortgage, and the spinning double axel mortgage with a triple lutz."

Figure 6.7 Net value equals benefits minus costs.

Figure 6.8 Does adding alternatives always create value? Or can it confuse the customer?

Managing the Perception of Value

Since value is subjective, not all customers have the skills or knowledge to judge the quality and value they receive. This is true especially for credence services (discussed in Chapter 2), where customers cannot reliably assess the quality of a service even after consumption.[3] Therefore, we have to manage the perception of value.

Consider a home owner who calls an electrician to repair a defective circuit. The electrician arrives, carrying a small bag of tools. He disappears into the closet where the circuit board is located, soon locates the problem, replaces a faulty circuit breaker, and hey everything works! Only 20 minutes have passed. A few days later, the home owner is shocked to receive a bill for $90, most of it for labor charges. Not surprisingly, customers are often left feeling that they have been taken advantage of—take a look at Blondie's reaction to the plumber in Figure 6.9.

To manage the perception of value, effective communications and even personal explanations are needed to help customers understand the value they receive. What they often cannot see are the fixed costs that business owners need to cover: the office, telephone, insurance, vehicles, tools, fuel, and office support staff. The variable costs of a home visit are also higher than they appear. We can add 15 minutes of driving each way to the 20 minutes spent at the house. We then add in 5 minutes each to unload and reload needed tools and supplies from the van. In total, the labor time of 60 minutes was used for this call. Finally, the firm still has to add a margin in order to make a profit.

Figure 6.9 Blondie seeks her money's worth from the plumber.

Recently, auctions and dynamic pricing have become increasingly popular as a way to price according to value perceptions of customers. Our story on easyInternetcafe is one such example. See Service Insights 6.1 for other examples of dynamic pricing, but in the Internet environment.

Reducing Related Monetary and Non-monetary Costs

When we consider customer value, we look at customers' perceived costs. From a customer's point of view, the price charged by a supplier is only part of the costs involved in buying and using a service. There are other *costs of service*, which are made up of both the *related-monetary costs* and *non-monetary costs* incurred by customers.

Related-Monetary Costs

Customers often spend more in searching for, purchasing, and using the service, than the price paid to the supplier. For instance, the cost of an evening at the theater for a couple with young children is usually a lot more than the price of the two tickets. It can include expenses such as as hiring a babysitter, travel, parking, food, and beverages.

Dynamic Pricing on the Internet

Dynamic pricing—also known as customized or personalized pricing—is a new version of the age-old practice of price discrimination. It is popular with service suppliers because of its potential to increase profits and at the same time, provide customers with what they value. E-tailing, or retailing over the Internet, is suitable for this strategy because changing prices electronically is a simple process. Dynamic pricing enables e-tailers to charge different customers different prices for the same products. This is based on information collected about their purchase history, preferences, price sensitivity, and so on. Tickets.com gained up to 45 percent more revenue per event when pricing of concerts and events was adjusted to meet demand and supply. However, customers may not be happy.

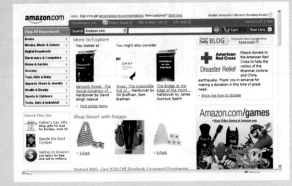

Customers of Amazon.com were upset when they learned that the online mega-store was not charging everyone the same price for the same movie DVDs. A study of online consumers by the University of Pennsylvania's Annenberg Public Policy Center found that 87 percent of respondents did not think dynamic pricing was acceptable.

Reverse Auctions

Travel e-tailers such as Priceline.com, Hotwire.com, and Lowestfare.com follow a customer-driven pricing strategy known as a reverse auction. Each firm acts as an intermediary between potential buyers who request quotations for a product or service, and multiple suppliers who quote the best price they are willing to offer. Buyers can then review the offers and select the supplier that best meets their needs. These services use different business models. While some are provided free to end users, most e-tailers either receive a commission from the supplier or do not pass on the whole savings. Others charge customers either a fixed fee or one based on a percentage of the savings.

Traditional Auctions

Other e-tailers such as eBay and Yahoo! Auctions follow the traditional online auction model. This is where bidders place bids for an item and compete with each other to determine who buys it. Marketers of both consumer and industrial products use such auctions to sell obsolete or overstock items, collectibles, rare items and second hand merchandise. This form of retailing has become very successful since eBay first launched it in 1995.

Shopbots help Consumers to Benefit from Dynamic Pricing

Consumers now have tools of their own to prevent them from being taken advantage of by the practices of dynamic pricing. One approach involves using

site, such as Dealtime.com, and run a search for the desired item. The shopbot instantly queries all the retailers selling the item, to check availability, features, and price, then presents the results in a comparison table.

There is little doubt that dynamic pricing is here to stay. With further advances in technology and wider applications, it is extending its reach to more and more service categories.

shopbots. *Shopbots* or shopping robots are basically intelligent agents that automatically collect price and product information from multiple online vendors. A customer only has to visit a shopbot

SOURCES

Biller, S., Chan, L. M. A., Simchi-Levi, D., & Swann, J. (2005). Dynamic pricing and direct-to-customer model in the automotive industry. *Electronic Commerce Research*, 5(2), pp. 309–334; Campanelli, M. (2005). Getting personal: Will engaging in dynamic pricing help or hurt your business?" *Entrepreneur*, 33(10), pp. 44–46; Melnik, M. I., & Alm, J. (2005). Seller reputation, information signals, and prices for heterogeneous coins on eBay. *Southern Economic Journal*, 72(2) pp. 305–328; Dynamic pricing schemes – Value led. *Managing Change: Strategic Interactive Marketing*, Available: www.managingchange.com/dynamic/valueled.htm, Accessed April 2008.

Non-monetary Costs

These costs reflect the time, effort, and discomfort connected to search, purchase, and use of a service. Customers sometimes refer to them collectively as "effort" or "hassle." Non-monetary costs tend to be higher when customers are involved in production (which is particularly important in people-processing services and in self-service) and must travel to the service site. Services that are high in experience and credence attributes may also create psychological costs, such as anxiety. There are four distinct categories of non-monetary costs. They are time, physical, psychological, and sensory costs.

▶ *Time costs* are part of service delivery. Today's customers often complain that they do not have enough time. Time spent on one activity means that they have to give up spending time on some other activity. Internet users are often frustrated by the amount of time spent to find information on a website.

▶ *Physical costs* (such as fatigue, discomfort) may be part of the costs of obtaining services, especially if customers must go to the service factory, if queuing is involved, and if delivery entails self-service.

PART II

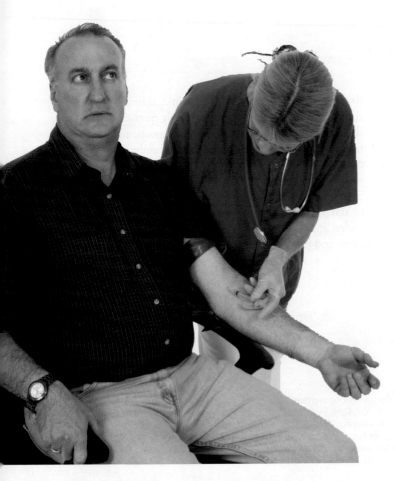

Figure 6.10 Anxiety as an important psychological factor in medical treatment.

▶ *Psychological costs* such as mental effort, perceived risk, cognitive dissonance, feelings of inadequacy, or fear are sometimes attached to buying and using a particular service (Figure 6.10).

▶ *Sensory costs* relate to unpleasant feelings affecting any of the five senses. In a service environment, these costs may include putting up with noise, unpleasant smells, too much heat or cold, uncomfortable seating, visually uninteresting environments, and even nasty tastes.

As shown in Figure 6.11, there may be costs to service users during any of the three stages of the service consumption model introduced in Chapter 2. Thus, firms have to consider (1) *search costs*, (2) *purchase and service encounter costs*, and (3) *post-purchase costs*. When you were looking at universities, how much money, time, and effort did you spend before deciding where to apply? How much time and effort would you put into selecting a new cell phone service provider or a bank?

A firm can create competitive advantage by minimizing non-monetary and related- monetary costs to increase consumer value. Possible approaches include:

▶ Working with operations experts to reduce the time required to complete service purchase, delivery, and consumption.

▶ Minimizing unwanted psychological costs of service at each stage. This can be done by getting rid of, or redesigning unpleasant or inconvenient processes, educating customers on what to expect, and retraining staff to be friendlier and more helpful.

▶ Getting rid of, or minimizing unwanted physical effort, especially during search and delivery processes.

▶ Decreasing unpleasant sensory costs of service by creating more attractive visual environments, reducing noise, installing more comfortable furniture and equipment, getting rid of offensive smells, and so on.

▶ Suggesting ways in which customers can reduce other monetary costs, including discounts with partner suppliers (for instance, parking) or offering mail or online delivery of activities that previously required a personal visit.

Perceptions of net value may vary widely between customers, or even from one situation to another for the same customer. Service markets can often be segmented by sensitivity to time savings and convenience, compared to sensitivity to price savings.[4] Consider Figure 6.12, which identifies a choice of three clinics available

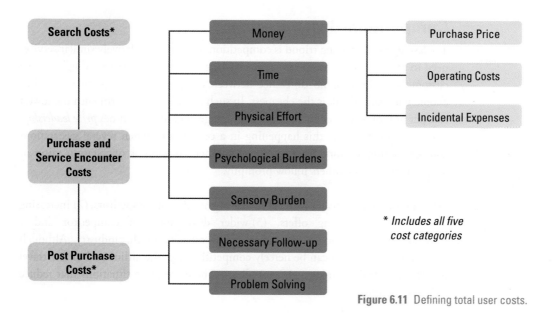

Figure 6.11 Defining total user costs.

* Includes all five cost categories

to an individual who needs to obtain a routine chest X-ray. In addition to varying dollar prices for the service, there are very different time and effort costs associated with using each service. Depending on the customer's priorities, non-monetary costs may be as important, or even more important, than the price charged by the service provider.

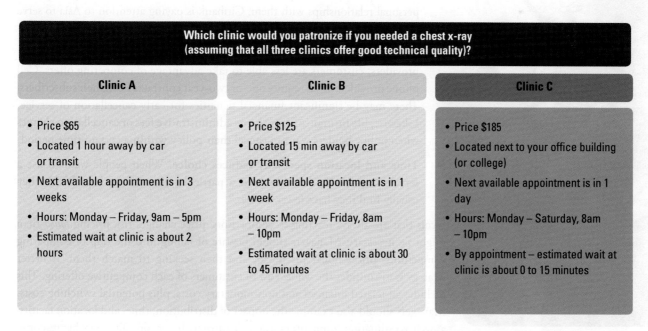

Figure 6.12 Trading off monetary and non-monetary costs.

LO 5

Describe competition-based pricing and situations where service markets are less price competitive.

Competition-Based Pricing

The last leg of the pricing tripod is competition. Firms with relatively similar services need to monitor what competitors are charging and try to price accordingly. When customers see little or no difference between competing offerings, they may just choose what they think is the cheapest. In such a situation, the firm with the lowest cost per unit of service enjoys a market advantage, and often assumes *price leadership*. You can sometimes see this happening in a certain area when several gas stations compete within a short distance of one another. As soon as one station raises or lowers its prices, the others follow promptly.

Price competition is greater with (1) increasing number of competitors, (2) increasing number of substituting offers, (3) wider distribution of competitor and/or substitution offers, and (4) increasing excess capacity in the industry. Although some service industries can be fiercely competitive (e.g. the airline and online travel industries or online brokerage),[5] not all are. There are some situations that reduce price competition:

▶ **Non-price-related costs of using competing alternatives are high**. When saving time and effort are of equal or greater importance to customers than price, the intensity of price competition is reduced.

▶ **Personal relationships matter**. In services that are highly personalized and customized, such as hair styling or family medical care, relationships with individual providers can be very important to customers (Figure 6.13). This discourages them from responding to competitive offers. Many global banks for example, are focusing on very wealthy customers and forming long-term personal relationships with them. Citibank is paying attention to Asia to serve the growing number of wealthy Indian and Chinese nationals in the region.

▶ **Switching costs are high**. When it takes time, money, and effort to switch providers, customers are less able to take advantage of competing offers. Cell phone providers often require one-or two-year contracts from their subscribers. There may be significant financial penalties for early cancellation of service. Likewise, life insurance firms charge administrative fees or cancellation charges when policy holders want to cancel their policy within a certain time period.

▶ **Time and location specificity reduces choice**. When people want to use a service at a specific location or at a particular time (or perhaps both), they usually find they have fewer choices.[6]

Firms that are always reacting to competitors' price changes risk pricing *lower* than might be necessary. Managers should beware of falling into the trap of comparing competitors' prices dollar for dollar, and then seeking to match them. A better strategy is to consider the whole cost to customers of each competitive offering. This includes all related financial and non-monetary costs, plus potential switching costs. Managers should also examine the impact of distribution, time, and location factors, as well as estimating competitors' available capacity before deciding on what response is appropriate.

Figure 6.13 Personalized hairstyling may prevent customers from switching to other services.

REVENUE MANAGEMENT: WHAT IT IS AND HOW IT WORKS?

LO 6
Describe what revenue management is and how it works.

Many service businesses now focus on strategies to maximize the revenue (or contribution) that can be obtained from a unit of available capacity at any given point in time. Revenue management is important in value creation. It ensures that capacity is better used and reserves available capacity for higher-paying segments. It is a sophisticated approach to managing supply and demand under different degrees of constraint. Airlines, hotels, and car rental firms, in particular, have become very skillful in varying their prices in response to the price sensitivity and needs of different market segments. The prices can even vary by different times of the day, week, or season.

Revenue management has been most effective when applied to operations characterized by:

▶ Relatively fixed capacity.

▶ High fixed cost structure.

▶ Perishable inventory.

▶ Variable and uncertain demand.

▶ Varying customer price sensitivity.

Industries that have successfully used revenue management include airlines, car rentals, hotels, and more recently hospitals, restaurants, golf courses, on-demand IT services, data processing centers, and even non-profit organizations (Figure 6.14).[7]

Figure 6.14 Successful coffee houses practice effective revenue management.

Reserving Capacity for High-Yield Customers

In practice, revenue management (also known as yield management) involves setting prices according to predicted demand levels among different market segments. The least price sensitive segment is the first to be provided capacity. This segment pays the highest price. Other segments follow at increasingly lower prices. As higher-paying segments often book closer to the time of actual usage, firms need to save capacity for them, instead of simply selling on a first-come-first-serve basis. For example, business travelers often reserve airline seats, hotel rooms, and rental cars at short notice. However, holiday goers may book months in advance, and convention organizers often block hotel space years in advance of a big event.

A well-designed revenue management system can predict with reasonable accuracy the number of customers who will use a given service, at a specific time, at each of several different price levels. The relevant amount of capacity at each level (known as a *price bucket*) can then be blocked. Sophisticated firms use complex mathematical models for this purpose and employ revenue managers to make decisions about inventory allocation. The objective is to maximize the revenues for the firm. Service Insights 6.2 shows how revenue management has been implemented at American Airlines, long an industry leader in the field.

Pricing Seats on Flight AA 2015

Revenue management departments use sophisticated yield management software and powerful computers to forecast, track and manage each flight on a given date separately. Let us look at American Airlines (AA) 2015, a popular flight from Chicago to Phoenix, Arizona, which departs daily at 5:30pm on the 1,370 miles (2,200 km) journey.

The 125 seats in coach (economy class) are divided into seven fare categories, referred to by yield management specialists as "buckets." There is an enormous variation in ticket prices among these seats: round-trip fares range from $238 for a bargain excursion ticket (with various restrictions and a cancellation penalty attached) all the way up to an unrestricted fare of $1,404. Seats are also available at an even higher price in the small first-class section. Scott McCartney tells how ongoing analysis by the computer program changes the allocation of seats between each of the seven buckets in economy class.

In the weeks before each Chicago-Phoenix flight, American's yield management computers constantly adjust the number of seats in each bucket, taking into account tickets sold, historical ridership patterns, and connecting passengers likely to use the route as one leg of a longer trip.

If advance bookings are slim, American adds seats to low-fare buckets. If business customers buy unrestricted fares earlier than expected, the yield management computer takes seats out of the discount buckets and preserves them for last-minute bookings that the database predicts will still show up.

With 69 of 125 coach seats already sold four weeks before one recent departure of Flight 2015, American's computer began to limit the number of seats in lower-priced buckets. A week later, it totally shut off sales for the bottom three buckets, priced $300 or less. To a Chicago customer looking for a cheap seat, the flight was 'sold out'....

One day before departure, with 130 passengers booked for the 125-seat flight, American still offered five seats at full fare because its computer database indicated 10 passengers were likely not to show up or take other flights. Flight 2015 departed full and no one was bumped.

Although AA 2015 for that date is now history, it has not been forgotten. The booking experience for this flight was saved in the memory of the yield management program to help the airline do an even better job of forecasting in the future.

SOURCE

McCartney, S. (1997). Ticket shock: Business fares increase even as leisure travel keeps getting cheaper. *Wall Street Journal*, (November). pp. A1–A10.

How does Competitors' Pricing Affect Revenue Management?

Because revenue management systems monitor booking pace, they indirectly pick up the impact of competitors' pricing. If a firm prices too low, it will experience a higher booking pace, and its cheaper seats fill up quickly. That is generally not good, as it means that a higher share of late-booking but high fare-paying customers will not be able to get their seats confirmed. They will therefore fly on competing airlines. If the initial pricing is too high, the firm will get too low a share of early booking segments (which still tend to offer a reasonable yield), and may later have to offer deeply discounted "last-minute" prices to sell excess capacity in order to obtain some contribution toward fixed costs (Figure 6.15). Some of these sales may take place through reverse auctions, using intermediaries such as Priceline.com.

Price Elasticity

For revenue management to work effectively there needs to be two or more segments that attach different values to the service and have different price elasticities. To allocate and price capacity effectively, the revenue manager needs to find out how sensitive demand is to price, and what net revenues will be generated at different prices for each target segment. The concept of elasticity is computed as follows:

$$\text{Price elasticity} = \frac{\text{Percentage change in demand}}{\text{Percentage change in price}}$$

When price elasticity is at "unity," sales of a service rise (or fall) by the same percentage that price falls (or rises). If a small change in price has a big impact on sales, demand for that product is said to be *price elastic*. If a change in price has little effect on sales, demand is described as *price inelastic*. The concept is illustrated in the simple chart presented in Figure 6.16, which shows the price elasticity for two segments. One has a highly elastic demand (a small change in price results in a big change in the amount demanded), and the other has a highly inelastic demand (even big changes in price have little impact on the amount demanded).

Figure 6.15 Price sensitive customers are encouraged to use range services during off peak timings.

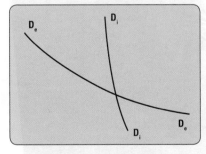

$$\text{Price Elasticity} = \frac{\text{Percentage change in demand}}{\text{Percentage change in price}}$$

PRICE PER UNIT OF SERVICE

QUANTITY OF UNITS DEMANDED

D_e : Demand is *price elastic*. Small changes in price lead to big changes in demand

D_i : Demand for service is *price inelastic*. Big changes have little impact on demand

Figure 6.16 Illustration of price elasticity.

LO 7

Understand the role rate fences play in effective revenue management.

Designing Rate Fences

Price customization is part and parcel of revenue management. This means that different customers are charged differently for what is actually the same product. As noted by Hermann Simon and Robert Dolan,

> The basic idea of price customization is simple: Have people pay prices based on the value they put on the product. Obviously you can't just hang out a sign saying "Pay me what its worth to you" or "It's $80 if you value it that much but only $40 if you don't." You have to find a way to segment customers by their valuations. In a sense, you have to "build a fence" between high-value customers and low-value customers so the "high" buyers can't take advantage of the low price.[8]

How can a firm make sure that customers willing to pay higher prices are unable to take advantage of lower price buckets? Properly designed rate fences allow customers to choose which segment they want to belong to, based on the characteristics of the service and willingness to pay. It helps companies to restrict lower prices to customers who are willing to accept certain restrictions on their purchases.

Fences can be either physical or non-physical. *Physical fences* refer to product differences that may be due to different prices, such as the seat location in a theater, or the size and furnishing of a hotel room (Figure 6.17). *Non-physical fences* refer to consumption, transaction or buyer characteristics. For example, they include staying a certain length of time in a hotel, playing golf on a weekday afternoon, cancellation or change penalties, or booking a certain length of time ahead. Examples of common rate fences are shown in Table 6.2.

Figure 6.17 Expect higher prices for seats that have a better view of your favorite performer like India Arie.

Table 6.2 Key categories of rate fences.

RATE FENCES	EXAMPLES
Physical (product-related) Fences	
• Basic product	• Class of travel (business/economy class)
	• Size of rental car
	• Size and furnishing of a hotel room
	• Seat location in a theater or stadium
• Amenities	• Free breakfast at a hotel, airport pick up, etc.
	• Free golf cart at a golf course
	• Valet parking
• Service level	• Priority wait-listing, separate check-in counters with no or only short queues
	• Improved food and beverage selection
	• Dedicated service hotlines
	• Personal butler
Non-Physical Fences	
Transaction Characteristics	
• Time of booking or reservation	• Discounts for advance purchase
• Location of booking or reservation	• Passengers booking air-tickets for an identical route in different countries are charged different prices.
	• Customers making reservations online are charged a lower price than those making reservations by phone
• Flexibility of ticket usage	• Fees/penalties for cancelling or changing a reservation (up to loss of entire ticket price)
	• Non-refundable reservations fees
Consumption Characteristics	
• Time or duration of use	• Early bird special in a restaurant before 6:00pm
	• Must stay over a Saturday night for an hotel booking.
	• Must stay at least for five nights
• Location of consumption	• Price depends on departure location, especially in international travel.
	• Prices vary by location (between cities, city center versus edges of the city)
Buyer Characteristics	
• Frequency or volume of consumption	• Member of certain loyalty-tier with the firm (e.g. Platinum member) get priority pricing, discounts or loyalty benefits
• Group membership	• Child, student, senior citizen discounts
	• Affiliation with certain groups (e.g. Alumni)
	• Corporate rates
• Size of customer group	• Group discounts based on size of group
• Geographic location	• Local customers are charged lower rates than tourists
	• Customers from certain countries are charged higher prices

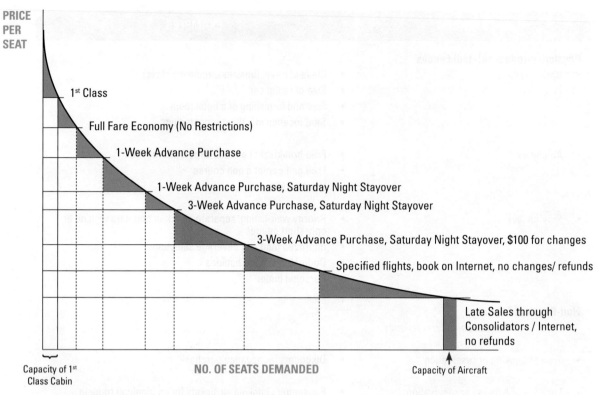

PRICE PER SEAT

1st Class

Full Fare Economy (No Restrictions)

1-Week Advance Purchase

1-Week Advance Purchase, Saturday Night Stayover

3-Week Advance Purchase, Saturday Night Stayover

3-Week Advance Purchase, Saturday Night Stayover, $100 for changes

Specified flights, book on Internet, no changes/ refunds

Late Sales through Consolidators / Internet, no refunds

Capacity of 1st Class Cabin

NO. OF SEATS DEMANDED

Capacity of Aircraft

Dark areas denote amount of consumer surplus (goal of segmented pricing is to reduce this)

Figure 6.18 Relating price buckets to the demand curve.

In summary, using a detailed understanding of customer needs, preferences, and willingness to pay, product and revenue managers can design effective products that consist of the core service, physical product features (physical fences), and non-physical product features (non-physical fences). A good understanding of the demand curve is needed so that "buckets" of inventory can be distributed to the various products and price categories. An example from the airline industry is shown in Figure 6.18.

 LO 8

Be familiar with the issue of ethics related to service pricing.

ETHICAL CONCERNS IN SERVICE PRICING

Do you sometimes have difficulty in understanding how much it is going to cost you to use a service? Do you believe that many prices are unfair? If so, you are not alone.[9] The fact is, service users cannot always be sure beforehand what they will receive in return for their payments. Many customers assume that a higher-priced service should offer more benefits and greater quality than a lower-priced one. For example, a professional, say a lawyer, who charges very high fees is assumed to be more skilled than one who is relatively inexpensive. Although price can serve as an indication of quality, it is sometimes hard to be sure if the extra value is really there.

Service Pricing is Complex

Pricing for services tend to be complex and hard to understand. Comparison across providers may even require complex spreadsheets or even mathematical formulas. In fact, complexity makes it easy (and perhaps more tempting) for firms to engage in unethical behavior. The quoted prices typically used by consumers for price comparisons may be only the first of several charges they can be billed.

For example, cell phone companies have a confusing variety of plans to meet the different needs and calling patterns of different market segments. Plans can be national, regional, or purely local in scope. The monthly fees depend on the number of minutes selected in advance. There are usually separate allowances for peak and off-peak minutes. Overtime minutes and "roaming minutes" on other carriers are charged at higher rates. Some plans allow unlimited off-peak calling, while others allow free incoming calls. Some providers charge calls per second, per six-second blocks or even per minute blocks, resulting in vastly different costs per call. Family plans let parents and children add together their monthly minutes for use on several phones, as long as the total for everyone's calling does not exceed the monthly limit allowed.

In addition, puzzling new fees have started to appear on bills (Figure 6.19), ranging from "paper bill fee" to pay for the bill itself, to strange sounding fees such as "property tax allotment," "single bill fee," and "carrier cost recovery fee." Phone bills of course include real taxes (e.g. sales tax). However, on many bills, the majority of surcharges, which users often misread as taxes, go directly to the phone company. For instance, the "property tax allotment" is nothing more than the property taxes the carrier pays, and the "carrier cost recovery fee" is a catch-all for all sorts of operating expenses.

Many people find it difficult to predict their own usage, which makes it hard to compare prices when evaluating competing suppliers, whose fees are based on a variety of usage-related factors. It is coincidence that the humorist Scott Adams (creator of Dilbert), used exclusively service examples when he "branded" the future of pricing as "confusiology". Noting that firms, such as telecommunication companies, banks, insurance firms, and other financial service providers offer nearly identical services, Adams remarks:

> You would think this would create a price war and drive prices down to the cost of providing it (that's what I learned between naps in my economic classes), but it isn't happening. The companies are forming efficient confusopolies, so customers can't tell who has the lowest prices. Companies have learned to use the complexities of life as an economic tool.[10]

One of the roles of effective government regulation, says Adams, should be to discourage this tendency for certain service industries to evolve into "confusopolies."

Figure 6.19 Complex billing structures make it difficult for customers to evaluate service value.

Piling on the Fees

Not all business models are based on getting income from sales. There is a growing trend today to have fees that sometimes have little to do with usage. The car rental industry advertises bargain rental prices and then tells customers on arrival that other fees such as collision insurance and personal insurance are compulsory. Also, staff sometimes fail to explain certain "small print" contract terms like a high-mileage charge that is added once the car exceeds a very low limit of free miles. A common practice when the car is returned is to charge fees for refueling a partially empty tank that is far more than what the driver would pay at the pump.[11]

More and more consumers find themselves facing fines and penalties. Chris Keeley, a New York University student, used his debit card to spend $230 on Christmas gifts. However, his holiday mood soured when he received a notice from his bank that he had overdrawn his checking account. Although his bank authorized each of his seven transactions, it charged him $31 per payment, totaling $217 for only $230 in purchases. Keeley insisted that he had never requested the so-called overdraft protection on his account. He wished his bank had rejected the transactions, because he would then simply have paid by credit card. He fumed, "I can't help but think they wanted me to keep spending money so that they could collect these fees."[12]

The importance of fees as a proportion of profits has increased dramatically. None of the fees cause more debate than bounce protection (i.e. the practice of allowing you to overdraw your account beyond an agreed credit line), generating some $8 billion in income for banks, and making up almost 30 percent to all their service fees. Critics feel that some banks oversell bounce protection. Regulators are particularly worried about bounce protection being offered through ATMs. For example, a customer with a balance of $300 in his account, and a $500 bounce protection could be told at the ATM that he has $800 available. If he withdrew $400, the ATM would still show available funds of $370 (after charging a fee of, for example, $30 for using the bounce protection balance) (Figure 6.20).

Some banks however, do not charge for overdraft protection. Said Dennis DiFlorio, president for retail banking at Commerce Bancorp Inc. in Cherry Hill, N.J.: "It's outrageous. It's not about customer convenience. It's just a way for banks to make money off customers." Commerce and other banks offer services that cover overdrafts automatically from savings accounts, other accounts, or even the customer's credit card, and don't charge fees for doing so.[13]

It is possible to design penalties that do not seem unfair to customers. Service Insight 6.3 describes what drives customers' fairness perceptions with service fees and penalties.

Figure 6.20 Consumers may be unaware of the high penalty fees imposed on overdrafts.

Crime and Punishment: How **Customers** respond to **Fines** and **Penalties**

Various types of "penalties" are part and parcel of many pricing schedules, and range from late fees for DVD rentals, cancellation charges for hotel bookings, to charges for late payments. Customer responses to penalties can be highly negative, and can lead to switching of provider and negative word of mouth. Young Kim and Amy Smith conducted an online survey using the Critical Incident Technique (CIT) in which the 201 respondents were asked to recall a recent penalty incident, describe the situation, and then complete a set of structured questions based on how the respondents felt and responded to that incident. Their findings showed that negative consumer responses can be reduced significantly by following these three guidelines:

1 Make Penalties Relative to the Crime Committed

The results found that customers' negative emotions to a penalty increased greatly when they found that the penalty was much larger compared to the "crime" committed. Customers' negative feelings were further increased if they were "surprised" by the penalty being suddenly charged to them. This is usually when they had not been aware of the fee or the size of the fee. These findings suggest that firms can reduce negative customer responses tremendously if amounts are seen as reasonable or fair for a given "customer lapse." The fines/fees should be communicated effectively even before an incident happens. For example, front line staff can explain at the point when a customer opens an account, the potential fines or fees that come with various "violations," such as overdrawing beyond the authorized limits, bounced checks, or late payments.

2 Consider Causal Factors and Customize Penalties

The study showed that customers' perceptions of fairness were lower, and negative responses were higher, when they perceived the causes that led to the penalty to be out of their control (e.g. "I mailed the check on time—there must have been a delay in the postal system"). To increase fairness perceptions, firms may want to identify common penalty cases which are

typically out of the control of the customer, and allow the front line to waive or reduce such fees.

In addition, it was found that customers who generally observe all the rules and therefore have not paid fines in the past, react particularly negatively should they be fined. One respondent said, "I have always made timely payments and have never been late with a payment—they should have considered this fact and waived the fee." Service firms should take customers should take into account customers' penalties history in dealing with penalties. They could offer them different treatments based on their past behavior. Perhaps, they could waive the first fine for an incident, while at the same time communicating that the next time the fee will be charged. This would improve fairness perceptions.

3 Focus on Fairness and Manage Emotions During Penalty Situations

Consumers' responses are heavily driven by fairness perceptions. Customers are likely to think that penalties are too high if they find that a penalty out of proportion compared to the damage or extra work caused by the penalized incident. One consumer complained, "I thought this particular penalty (credit card late payment) was excessive. You are paying already high interest; the penalty should have been more in line with the payment. The penalty was more than the payment!" Considering fairness perceptions would mean, for example, that the late fee for a keeping a DVD should not exceed the potentially lost rental fees during that late period.

Service companies can also make penalties seem fairer by providing enough explanations and reasons for the penalty. Ideally, penalties should be imposed for the good of other customers (e.g. we kept the room for you which we could have given to another guest on our wait list) or community. Finally, the front line should to be trained in how to handle customers, who have become angry, upset and complain about penalties (see Chapter 13 on how we recommend you to deal with such situations).

SOURCE

Young "Sally" Kim, K., & Smith, A. K., (2005). Crime and punishment: Examining customers' responses to service organizations' penalties. *Journal of Service Research*, 8(2), pp. 162–180.

Designing Fairness into Revenue Management

A well carried out revenue management strategy does not mean just blindly chasing short-term yield maximization. The following specific ways can help firms to have revenue management practices, together with customer satisfaction, trust, and good will.[14]

Figure 6.21 Limousine service providers typically charge for no-shows.

▶ **Design Price Schedules and Fences that are Clear, Logical, and Fair.** Firms should actively spell out all fees and expenses (e.g. no-show or cancellation charges) clearly in advance so that there are no surprises (Figure 6.21). For a rate fence to be perceived as fair, customers must be able to easily understand them (i.e. fences have to be transparent and upfront), see the logic in them.

▶ **Use High Published Prices and Frame Fences as Discounts.** Rate fences framed as customer gains (i.e. discounts) are generally perceived as fairer than those framed as customer losses (i.e. surcharges), even if the situations are the same in economic terms.[15] For example, a customer who goes to her hair salon on Saturdays may perceive the salon as profiteering, if she finds herself facing a weekend surcharge. However, she is likely to find the higher weekend price more acceptable, if the hair salon advertises its peak weekend price as the published price, and offers a $5 discount for weekday haircuts. Furthermore, having a high published price also helps to increase the reference price and potentially quality perceptions, in addition to the feeling of being rewarded for the weekday patronage.

▶ **Communicate Consumer Benefits of Revenue Management.** Marketing communications should position revenue management as a win-win practice. In fact, providing information about revenue management policies has increased the fairness perceptions of hotels.[16] Providing different price and value balances allows customers to self-segment and enjoy the service. It allows each customer to find the price and benefits (value) balance that best satisfies his or her needs. For example, charging a higher price for the best seats in the theater recognizes that some people are willing and able to pay more for a better location. It also makes it possible to sell other seats at a lower price. Perceived fairness is affected by what customers perceive as normal. Hence, when revenue management practices become more familiar to customers, the unfairness perceptions may decrease over time.[17]

▶ **Use Bundling to 'Hide' Discounts.** Bundling a service into a package effectively hides the discounted price. When a cruise line includes the price of air travel or ground transportation in the cruise package, the customer only knows the total price, not the cost of the individual parts. Bundling usually makes price comparisons between the bundles and its individual parts impossible. This reduces potential unfairness perceptions (Figure 6.22). The kind of bundles preferred by customers is those that reduce their search costs.[18]

▶ **Take Care of Loyal Customers.** Firms should try to retain valued customers, even to the extent of not charging the maximum possible amount on a given transaction. After all, customer perceptions of price gouging do not build trust. Yield management systems can be programmed to include "loyalty multipliers" for regular customers, so that reservations systems can give them "special treatment" status at peak times, even when they are not paying premium rates (Figure 6.23). For instance, Fedex has developed an online support system that its loyal customers can use, where efficiency and productivity for its customers can be increased.

Figure 6.22 Cruise packages bundle land tours into their total package price.

▶ **Use Service Recovery to Make Up for Overbooking.** Many service firms overbook to make allowances for anticipated cancellations and no-shows. Profits increase but so, too, does the occurrence of being unable to honor reservations. Being "bumped" by an airline, or "walked" by a hotel can lead to a loss of customer loyalty, and affect a firm's reputation negatively. Thus, it is important to back up overbooking programs with well-designed service recovery procedures, such as:

1. Give customers a choice between retaining their reservation and receiving compensation.

2. Provide sufficient advance notice so that customers will be able to make alternative arrangements.

3. If possible, offer a substitute service that delights customers.

A Westin beach resort has found that it can free up capacity by offering guests who are departing the next day, the option of spending their last night in a luxury hotel near the airport or in the city at no cost. Guest feedback on the free room, upgraded service, and a night in the city after a beach holiday has been very positive. From the hotel's point of view, this practice trades the cost of securing a one-night stay in another hotel, against that of turning away a multiple-night guest arriving that same day.

Figure 6.23 Loyal diners enjoying the premium service of being exclusively served.

PUTTING SERVICE PRICING INTO PRACTICE

Although the main decision in pricing is usually seen as how much to charge, there are other decisions to be made. There are seven questions that service marketers need to ask themselves as they prepare to create and implement a well-thought-out price strategy.

How Much to Charge?

▶ What costs are the company trying to recover? What is the specific profit margin desired?

▶ How price sensitive are the customers?

▶ What prices are charged by competitors?

▶ What discount(s) should be offered?

▶ Are psychological pricing points (e.g. $4.95 versus $5.00) usually used?

What Should Be the Specified Basis for Pricing?

A wide array of strategies are available, but must be tailored to industry characteristics. Options may include:

▶ Performance of a specific task like repairing a piece of equipment, or cleaning a jacket.

▶ Admission to a service facility like a concert, or sports event.

▶ A rate for a defined period of time—for instance, using an hour of a lawyer's time, or occupying a hotel room for a night.

▶ A pro-rated fee that is related to the monetary value of service delivery, such as a realtor's commission, which is calculated as a percentage of the selling price of a house.

▶ Consumption of physical resources, such as food, drinks, water, or natural gas.

▶ A distance-based rate, as in transportation. Freight companies often use a combination of distance (kilometers or zones) and weight or size (such as cubic volume) (Figure 6.24).

Prices for some services include separate charges for access and usage. Recent research suggests that access or subscription fees are an important driver of adoption and customer retention, whereas usage fees are much more important drivers of actual usage.[19]

An important question for service marketers is whether to charge an inclusive price for all elements (referred to as a "bundle"), or to price component elements separately. If customers prefer to avoid making many small payments, then bundled pricing may be preferable. However, if they dislike being charged for product elements they do

Figure 6.24 Shipment of goods are typically charged by a combination of distance (kilometers or zones) and weight or size (such as cubic volume).

not use, then itemized pricing may be preferable. Bundled prices offer firms a certain level of guaranteed revenue from each customer, while also providing customers a clear idea in advance of how much they can expect to pay. Unbundled pricing provides customers with the freedom to choose what to buy and pay for. For instance, many US airlines now charge economy class passengers for meals and drinks on their domestic flights.

Who Should Collect Payment?

▶ The company that provides the service.

▶ A specialist intermediary such as a travel agent, bank or retailer and so on (Figure 6.25).

▶ How should the intermediary be paid for this work? Should it be a flat fee or percentage commission?

Where Should Payment Be Made?

▶ Service delivery sites are not always conveniently located. When consumers have to purchase a service before using it, there are obvious benefits in using intermediaries that are more conveniently located.

▶ Payment can also be by mail or bank transfer.

▶ A growing number of organizations now accept Internet, telephone, and fax bookings with payment by credit card.

Figure 6.25 Travel agencies are intermediaries that help to distribute airline tickets.

When Should Payment Be Made?

▶ Customers can pay in advance (as with an admission charge, airline ticket, or postage stamps).

▶ They can also be billed once service delivery has been completed, as with restaurant bills and repair charges.

▶ Occasionally, a service provider may ask for an initial payment in advance of service delivery, with the balance being due later. This approach is quite common with expensive repair and maintenance jobs (Figure 6.26).

"Unless we receive the outstanding balance within ten days, we will have no choice but to destroy your credit rating, ruin your reputation, and make you wish you were never born. If you have already sent the seven cents, please disregard this notice."

Figure 6.26 Some firms do not leave their customers with much flexibility in dealing with late payment.

Figure 6.27 Gyms usually charge membership fees for customers to use facilities and services.

The timing of payment can affect usage pattern. From an analysis of the payment and attendance records of a Colorado-based health club, it was found that members' usage patterns were closely related to their payment schedules. When members made payments, their use of the club was highest during the months immediately following payment and then decreased steadily until the next payment. Members with monthly payment plans attended the health club much more consistently and were more likely to renew, perhaps because each month's payment encouraged them to use what they were paying for (Figure 6.27).[20]

How Should Payment Be Made?

▶ Cash may appear to be the simplest method, but it raises security problems and is inconvenient when exact change is required to operate machines.

▶ Accepting payment by check for all but the smallest purchases is now fairly widespread and offers customer benefits, although it may require controls to discourage bad checks.

Figure 6.28 Credit cards allow customers to pay more conveniently.

For example, there can be a charge for returned checks ($15–20 on top of any bank charges is not uncommon at retail stores).

▶ Credit and debit cards can be used around the world (Figure 6.28). As their acceptance has become more global, businesses that refuse to accept them increasingly find themselves at a competitive disadvantage.

▶ Other payment procedures include tokens or vouchers. Tokens with a predefined value can simplify the process of paying road and bridge tolls or bus and metro fares. Vouchers are sometimes provided by social service agencies to elderly or low-income people.

▶ Now coming into broader usage are prepayment systems based on cards that store value on a magnetic strip or in a microchip embedded within the card. Service firms that want to accept payment in this form, however, must first install card readers. To save its customers time and effort, Chase Bank has introduced credit cards with what it calls "blink," an embedded technology that can be read by a point-of-sale terminal without physically touching it (Figure 6.29).

Figure 6.29 Chase's "blink" scanning service provides card members with increased speed and convenience at the point-of-sale.

Interestingly, a recent study found that the payment method has an impact on the total spending of customers. This is especially so for spending on items that are not necessities such as spending in cafes.[21] The less tangible or immediate the payment method (e.g. payment via credit cards), the more consumers tend to spend.

How Should Prices Be Communicated to the Target Markets?

▶ Managers must decide whether or not to include information on pricing in advertising for the service. It may be suitable to relate the price to the costs of competing products.

▶ Salespeople and customer service representatives should be able to give immediate, accurate responses to customer queries about pricing, payment, and credit.

▶ Good signage at retail points of sale will save staff members from having to answer basic questions on prices.

When the price is presented in the form of an itemized bill, marketers should make sure that it is both accurate and easy to understand. Hospital bills, which may run to several pages and contain dozens of items, have been much criticized for inaccuracy (Figure 6.30). A significant number of hotel bills, despite containing fewer entries, are also inaccurate. One study estimated that business travelers in the United States may be overpaying for their hotel rooms by half-a-billion dollars a year, with 11.6 percent of all bills incorrect, resulting in an average overpayment of $11.36.[22]

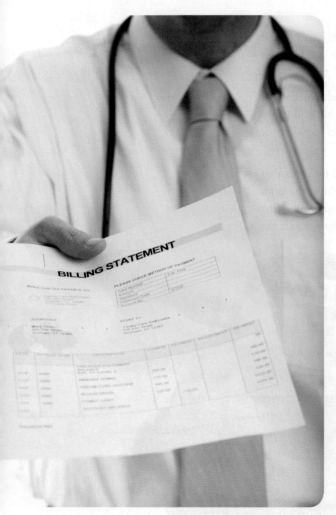

Figure 6.30 Customers may be paying more than they should for their hospital stay.

LO 1 ▶ Effective pricing is central to financial success of service firms. The objectives for establishing prices can be to generate revenue and profits, and cover costs. Pricing can also be used to build demand and develop a user base. Once the firm understands what its pricing objectives are, it needs to decide on its pricing strategy.

LO 2 ▶ The foundations of a pricing strategy are the three legs of the pricing tripod: Cost, customer value, and competition.

o The costs that a company has to cover set the floor price.

o The customer's perceived value of the offering sets a ceiling price.

o The price that the competitors charge decides where the price can be set, within the floor-to-ceiling range.

LO 3 ▶ The first leg of the pricing tripod is cost. If services have a large amount of variable costs, cost-accounting approaches work well. However, many services are complex with shared infrastructure. For these types of services, ABC is more appropriate.

LO 4 ▶ The second leg of the pricing tripod is value to the customer.

o When customers purchase a service, they are weighing its perceived benefits against its perceived cost.

o Firms need to take into account not only the direct monetary costs (i.e. the price they pay to the service firm), but they also have to consider related monetary and non-monetary costs when looking at what is the customers' perceived value.

o Since value is perceived, it can be managed and enhanced through communication and education.

LO 5 ▶ The third leg of the pricing tripod is competition. Firms with relatively similar services need to see what competitors are charging and price accordingly. In some situations, price competition is strong. However, a firm should not always focus on competitors' pricing, without considering the entire cost of the competitive offering, like the non-monetary costs.

LO 6 ▶ Revenue management is a powerful tool that maximizes revenue for the firm and can create value for its customers.

o Revenue management is a powerful tool that manages demand and prices different segments closer to their reservation prices. Prices are set according to predicted demand levels among different segments of customers. In order for revenue management to work, there must be different segments of customers with different price elasticities.

LO 7 ▶ Well designed physical and non-physical rate fences are needed to define "products" for each target segment. However, great care has to be taken in the way revenue management is implemented so that customer satisfaction and perceived fairness are maintained.

LO 8 ▶ Service firms need to be careful that their pricing schedules do not become so complex and with hidden charges that it leads to perceptions of unethical behavior. Revenue management practices in particular can be perceived as unfair. The following ways help firms to improve customers' fairness perceptions:

o Design price schedules and fences that are clear, logical and fair.

o Use published prices and frame fences as discounts.

o Communicate consumer benefits of revenue management.

o Use bundling to "hide" discounts.

o Take care of loyal customers.

o Use service recovery or make up for overbooking.

LO 9 ▶ To put the service pricing into practice, service marketers need to consider seven questions to have a well-thought-out price strategy. The questions are:

1. How much to charge?
2. What should be the specified basis for pricing?
3. Who should collect payment?
4. Where should payment be made?
5. When should payment be made?
6. How should payment be made?
7. How should prices be communicated to the target markets?

UNLOCK YOUR LEARNING

These keywords are found within the sections of each Learning Objective (LO). They are integral in understanding the services marketing concepts taught in each section. Having a firm grasp of these keywords and how they are used is essential in helping you do well for your course, and in the real and very competitive marketing scene out there.

LO 1
1. Pricing
2. Pricing objectives

LO 2
3. Ceiling
4. Floor
5. Minimum price
6. Pricing tripod

LO 3
7. Activity-based costing
8. Allocating economic costs
9. Break-even analysis
10. Contribution
11. Cost-based pricing
12. Cost-accounting
13. Fixed costs
14. Price sensitivity
15. Semi-variable costs
16. Variable costs

LO 4
17. Dynamic pricing
18. E-tailers
19. Gross value

20. Net value
21. Non-monetary costs
22. Perceived benefits
23. Perceived costs
24. Physical costs
25. Post-purchase costs
26. Psychological costs
27. Price discrimination
28. Reverse auctions
29. Shopbots
30. Sensory costs
31. Search costs
32. Service encounter costs
33. Time costs
34. Value-based pricing

LO 5
35. Competition-based pricing
36. Price competition
37. Switching costs

LO 6
38. Price elasticity
39. Price elastic
40. Price inelastic
41. Price customization

42. Revenue management
43. Yield management
44. Intermediaries

LO 7
45. Non-physical fences
46. Overbooking
47. Physical fences
48. Rate fences

LO 8
49. Bundling
50. Confusiology
51. Confusopolies
52. Discounts
53. Fees
54. Published prices
55. Surcharges
56. Fairness perceptions

LO 9
57. Bundled pricing

> How well do you know the language of services marketing? Quiz yourself!

 Not for the academically faint-of-heart

For each keyword you are able to recall without referring to earlier pages, give yourself a point (and a pat on the back). Tally your score at the end and see if you earned the right to be called—a *services marketeer.*

SCORE

0 – 9 Services Marketing is done a great disservice.

10 – 20 The midnight oil needs to be lit, pronto.

21 – 30 I know what you *didn't* do all semester.

31 – 40 A close shave with success.

41 – 51 Now, go forth and market.

52 – 57 There should be a marketing concept named after you.

Review Questions

1. Why the pricing of services are more difficult compared to pricing of goods?

2. How can the three main approaches to service pricing be used to come to a good pricing point for a particular service?

3. Why cannot we compare competitor prices dollar for dollar in a service context?

4. What is the part played by non-monetary costs in pricing of services, and how do they relate to the consumer's value perceptions?

5. What is revenue management? How does it work? What type of service operations benefit most from good revenue management systems and why?

6. How can we charge different prices to different segments of customers without them feeling cheated? How can we even charge the same customer different prices at different times, context, and/or occasions, and at the same time be seen to be fair?

7. What are the seven key decisions managers need to make when designing an effective pricing schedule?

■ WORK **YOUR** ESM ▶

Application Exercises

1. Select a service organization of your choice and find out what their pricing policies and methods are. In what way are they similar to, or different from what has been discussed in this chapter?

2. From the customer perspective, what serves to define value in the following services: (a) a hairdressing salon, (b) an audit firm, (c) a theater performance?

3. Go through recent bills that you have received from service businesses, such as those for telephone, car repair, cable TV, credit card, and so on. Evaluate each one against the following criteria:

   (a) general appearance and clarity of presentation,

   (b) easily understood terms of payment,

   (c) avoidance of confusing terms and definitions,

   (d) appropriate level of detail,

   (e) unanticipated ("hidden") charges,

   (f) accuracy,

   (g) ease of access to customer service in case of problems or disagreements.

4. How might revenue management be applied to

   (a) a professional firm (e.g. consulting),

   (b) a restaurant, and

   (c) a golf course?

5. Collect the pricing schedules of three leading cell phone service providers. Identify all the pricing dimensions (e.g. air time, subscription fees, free minutes, per second/six seconds/minute billing, air time roll-over, push e-mail, data services, and so on.) and pricing levels for each dimension (i.e. the range that is offered by the players in the market). Find out the usage profile for a particular target segment (e.g. a young executive who uses the phone mostly for personal calls, or a full-time student). Based on the usage profile, find out the lowest cost provider. Next, measure the pricing schedule preferences of your target segment (e.g. via conjoint analysis). Finally, advise the smallest of the three providers how to redesign its pricing schedule to make it more attractive to your target segment.

6. Consider a service of your choice and develop a pricing schedule. Apply the seven questions marketers need to answer to design an effective pricing schedule.

•ENDNOTES

1   Dynamic pricing – easyInternetCafe case study. *Managing Change: Strategic Interactive Marketing*, available:http://www.managingchange.com/dynamic/easyic.htm; http://www.easyeverything.com;/ http://www.stelios.com/; Accessed February 2008.

2   Zeithaml, V. (1988). Consumer perceptions of price, quality, and value: A means-end model and synthesis of evidence. *Journal of Marketing,* 52(July). pp. 2–21; Lin, C. H., wSher, P. J., & Shih, H. Y. (2005). Past progress and future directions in conceptualizing customer perceived value. *International Journal of Service Industry Management,* 16(4), pp. 318–336.

3   Mattila, A. S., & Wirtz, J. (2002). The impact of knowledge types on the consumer search process – An investigation in the context of credence services. *International Journal of Service Industry Management,* 13(3), pp. 214–230.

4   Berry, L. L., Seiders, K., & Grewal, D. (2002). Understanding service convenience. *Journal of Marketing,* 66(July), pp. 1–17.

5   Green, C. E. (2006). Demystifying dstribution: Building a distribution strategy one channel at a time. *TIG Global Special Report.* Hospitality Sale and Marketing Institute.

6   Heinonen, K. (2004). Reconceptualizing customer perceived value: The value of time and place. *Managing Service Quality,* 14(3), pp. 205–215.

7   Kimes, S. E., & Wirtz, J. (2003). Perceived fairness of revenue management in the US golf industry. *Journal of Revenue and Pricing Management,* 1(4), pp. 332–344; Metters, R., & Vargas, V. Yield. (1999). Management for the nonprofit sector. *Journal of Service Research,* 1(February), pp. 215–226; Susskind, A. M., Reynolds, D., & Tsuchiya, E. (2004). An evaluation of guests' preferred incentives to shift time-variable demand in restaurants. *Cornell Hotel and Restaurant Administration Quarterly,* 44(1), pp. 68–84; Dube, P., Hayel, Y., & Wynter, L. (2005). Yield management for IT resources on demand: Analysis and validation of a new paradigm for managing computing centres. *Journal of Revenue and Pricing Management,* 4(1), pp. 24–38.

8   Simon, H., & Dolan, R. J. (1998). Price customization. *Marketing Management* (Fall), pp. 11–17.

9   Bolton, L. E., Warlop, L., & Alba, J. W. (2003). Consumer perceptions of price (Un)fairness. *Journal of Consumer Research,* 29(4), pp. 474–491; Xia, L., Monroe, K. B., & Cox, J. L. (2004). The price is unfair! A conceptual framework of price fairness perceptions. *Journal of Marketing,* 68 (October), pp. 1–15; Homburg, C., Hoyer, W. D., & Koschate, N. (2005). Customer's reactions to price increases: Do customer satisfaction and perceived motive fairness matter? *Journal of the Academy of Marketing Science,* 33(1), pp. 36–49.

10   Adams, S. (1997). *The Dilbert™ future—Thriving on business stupidities in the 21st century* (p. 160). New York: HarperBusiness.

11   Ayres, I., & Nalebuff, B. (2003). In praise of honest pricing. *Sloan Management Review* (Fall), pp. 24–28.

12   Foust, D. (2005). Protection racket? As overdraft and other fees become huge profit sources for banks, critics see abuses. *Business Week,* (February), pp. 68–89.

13   Parts of this section are based on Foust, D. (2005). Protection racket? As overdraft and other fees become huge profit sources for banks, critics see abuses. *Business Week,* (February). pp. 68–89.

14   Wirtz, J., Kimes, S. E. Ho, J. P. T., & Patterson, P. (2003). Revenue management: Resolving potential customer conflicts. *Journal of Revenue and Pricing Management,* 2(3), pp. 216–228.

15   Shoemaker, S. (2005). Pricing and the consumer. *Journal of Revenue and Pricing Management,* 4(3), pp. 228–236.

16   Choi, S. M., & Mattila, A. S. (2005). Impact of information on customer fairness perceptions of hotel revenue management. *Cornell Hotel and Restaurant Administration Quarterly,* 46(4), pp. 444–451; Choi, S. M., & Mattila, A. S. (2006). The role of disclosure in variable hotel pricing: A cross-cultural comparison of customers' fairness perceptions. *Cornell Hotel and Restaurant Administration Quarterly,* 47(1), pp. 27–34.

17 Wirtz, J., & Kimes, S. E. (2007). The moderating role of familiarity in fairness perceptions of revenue management pricing. *Journal of Service Research,* 9(3), pp. 229–240.

18 Harris, J., & Blair, E. A. (2006). Consumer preference for product bundles: The role of reduced search costs. *Journal of the Academy of Marketing Science,* 34(4), pp. 506–513.

19 Danaher, P. J. (2002). Optimal pricing of new subscription services: An analysis of a market experiment. *Marketing Science*, 21(Spring), pp. 119–129; Fruchter, G. E., & Rao, R. C. (2001). Optimal membership fee and usage price over time for a network service. *Journal of Services Research,* 4, pp. 3–15.

20 Gourville, J., & Soman, D. (2002). Pricing and the psychology of consumption. *Harvard Business Review,* (September), pp. 90–96.

21 Soman, D. (2003). The effect of payment transparency on consumption: Quasi-experiments from the field. *Marketing Letters,* 14(3), pp. 173–183.

22 See, for example, Sharpe, A. (1997). The operation was a success: The bill was quite a mess. *Wall Street Journal,* (September) 1. Stoller, G. (2005). Hotel bill mistakes mean many pay too much. *USA Today,* (July). Accessed: www.news.yahoo.com/s.

promoting services and
EDUCATING CUSTOMERS

LEARNING OBJECTIVES

By the end of this chapter, students should be able to:

LO 1 Discuss the role of marketing communications in services.

LO 2 Understand the challenges of service communications.

LO 3 Know the 5 Ws of marketing communications planning.

LO 4 Describe the variety of marketing communication tools that can be used.

LO 5 Identify the different sources of communications messages received by the target audience and the different communication tools related to the source of communications.

LO 6 Understand the role of corporate design in communications.

OPENING VIGNETTE[1]

THE WESTIN HOTELS AND RESORTS' NEW MULTI-MILLION GLOBAL AD CAMPAIGN HELPS YOU TO EXPERIENCE THE BRAND

It was an experiential campaign to make it seem as if people were actually undergoing the experience. Imagine this. After a long tiring day at work, you take that slow walk to the subway station. When you ride on the escalator, you suddenly feel as if you are in the middle of a rushing waterfall. This is because you are looking at the escalator wrap. Somehow, you feel less tired and a little more refreshed. When you step into the train, you are a little lost for a moment and wonder

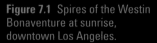

Figure 7.1 Spires of the Westin Bonaventure at sunrise, downtown Los Angeles.

where you are. The car seems transformed into a sauna. Your mind tries hard to understand what has happened. Since all the seats are taken, you walk further along and instead of the wooden panels of the sauna, you step into a striking blue environment the next car. Now, you feel as if you are in the Underwater World theme park! Curious, you decide to explore the other cars to see what you would be able to find. You discover that you can be in the green rainforest, or the white snow covered mountains. It is almost like taking a holiday around the world! After your "round the world trip," you decide to take a seat at Iceland. That is when something else catches your attention. When the train moves, you see the effects of a flower slowly bloom as the train passes by some portion of walls along the tunnel. As you journey further, you see waves crashing. By the time you leave the subway, you feel as if you have lived a lifetime of experiences that leave you feeling refreshed even though it is the end of a work day! You have just been through the Westin experience.

Westin Hotel spent $30 million on this campaign, called "This is How it Should Feel.' The campaign uses a range of traditional and non-traditional media like print, radio, online and multiplatform. There are more than 270 different visuals and 2,754 media placements. The different experiences in the train itself are part of the shuttle wrap. Apart from that, they also used escalator and column wraps. The blooming flower is part of the o-media, which uses the motion of the train to have the images on the wall of the tunnel move like a giant flipbook. They also used image shifting lenticulars (ads that change as you move) that may change from an emergency exit door to a forest. Outdoors, there were larger-than-life three dimensional billboards spread over five major cities in the United States. In Boston, for example, there are a few three-dimensional skydivers placed in front of a beautifully printed sky.

This very interesting campaign tells the guests what they will feel at a Westin. It will be a relaxing, renewing and personal experience. Starwood, the parent company, wanted to reposition and redefine the brands of hotels in its group and embarked on this campaign to reinforce Westin's new position as one of personal renewal.

> ...The sleepy routine of commuters across major cities in America is given a bit of pep by the Westin Experience...

Figure 7.3 Manhattanites explore the depths of the sea while transiting.

THE ROLE OF MARKETING COMMUNICATIONS

There is a lot of confusion over the scope of marketing communications. Some people still define this element of the services marketing mix too narrowly. Communications is more than just advertising, public relations and professional salespeople. It is for good reason that we define the marketing communication element of the 7 Ps as *Promotion and Education*. Through communication, marketers explain and promote the value proposition that their firm is offering. In the Westin campaign, they use experiential advertising to communicate an experience of renewal. It is a promise of what customers can expect if they stay at the Westin hotels.

Figure 7.4 A sales agent for an insurance company explains the available offerings to a prospective client.

Marketing communication is very important for a company's success. Without effective communication, potential customers may never learn of a service firm's existence. They may not know the offerings available and the value proposition of each of its products (Figure 7.4). Let us look at some specific roles performed by marketing communication.

Position and Differentiate the Service

Companies use marketing communications to persuade target customers that their service product offers the best solution to meet their needs, compared to the competing offerings (Figure 7.5). Communication efforts serve not only to attract new users but also to maintain contact with existing customers and build relationships with them. Marketing communications is used to convince target customers about the firm's superior performance on determinant attributes (see Chapter 3).

Help Customers to Evaluate Service Offerings and Highlight Differences that Matter

Even if customers understand what a service is supposed to do, they may find it hard to tell the difference between offerings from different suppliers. Companies may use concrete clues to communicate service performance. Examples include the quality of equipment and facilities, or employee qualifications and professionalism. Some performance attributes are easier or more appropriate to communicate than others. Airlines do not advertise safety because even the suggestion that things might go wrong makes many passengers nervous. Instead, they approach this ongoing customer concern indirectly by advertising the expertise of their pilots, the newness of their aircraft, and the skills and training of their mechanics.

search.ebay.com/hula skirts
/portable video games   /ranch land   /laptops
/mystery novels   /hedge trimmers   /swimming trunks
/baseball tickets   /golf shoes   /digital cameras
/all-terrain tires   /video cellphones   /sprinklers
/dome tents   /flip-flops   /sun hats
/stain removers   /digital sports watches /lawnmowers
                             /horseshoe sets   /artificial turf

you can get it on ebaY.

Figure 7.5 eBay brightly promotes the sheer value and range of their services.

Promote the Contribution of Service Personnel and Backstage Operations

High quality front line staff and backstage operations can be important differentiators for services. In high-contact services, front line personnel are the main source of service delivery. They often help to make the service more concrete and personal. Advertising, brochures, and websites can show customers the work that goes on "backstage" to ensure good service delivery. For example, Starbucks has publicity materials and web pages showing customers what service personnel are doing behind the scenes. Starbucks shows how coffee beans are cultivated, harvested, and produced, highlighting its use of the finest and freshest. Emphasizing the expertise and commitment of employees whom customers normally never meet may increase trust in the organization's competence and commitment to service quality.

Advertising messages set customer expectations, so advertisers must show service personnel in realistic ways. They should also inform employees about the content of new advertising campaigns or brochures that promise specific attitudes and behavior. If a firm's communications show friendly, smiling workers but most of them turn out to be glum or rude in practice, customers will be disappointed.

Add Value through Communication Content

Information and consultation are important ways to add value to a product. Potential customers may need information and advice about the kind of services available to them, the place and time of availability and the cost of these services, and the specific features, functions and service benefits that come with these services.

Facilitate Customer Involvement in Production

When customers are actively involved in service production, they need training to help them perform well. This benefits the company because it helps to improve productivity. One approach to training customers, recommended by advertising experts, is to show service delivery in action. Video is a good medium where viewers can see the sequence of events. Some dentists show their patients videos of surgical procedures before the surgery takes place so that customers know what to expect.

Marketers often use sales promotions as incentives to encourage customers to make the necessary changes in their behavior. For example, giving price discounts is one way to encourage self-service. Other incentives to change customer behavior include promotions that offer a chance to win a reward.

Stimulate or Dampen Demand to Match Capacity

Many live service performances, like a seat at the theater for a performance, or a haircut at Jean-Louis David, Europe's largest hairdresser chain, are time-specific and cannot be stored for resale at a later date. Advertising and sales promotions can help to change the timing of customer use. Low demand outside peak periods is a serious problem for service industries with high fixed costs, like hotels. One strategy is to run promotions that offer extra value, such as a room upgrade and a free breakfast, to stimulate demand without decreasing price. When demand increases and during peak periods, the number of promotions can be reduced or even eliminated.

CHALLENGES OF SERVICE COMMUNICATIONS

After having discussed the role of market communications, let us explore some of the challenges service firms face. Since services are performances rather than objects, it can be difficult to communicate their benefits to customers. This is especially true when the service does not involve any tangible actions to customers, or their possessions.[2]

Problems of Intangibility

Intangibility creates four problems for marketers: generality, non-searchability, abstractness, and mental impalpability. Table 7.1 presents the implications of each problem and proposes specific communications strategies for dealing with them.

▶ *Generality* refers to items that make up a class of objects, persons, or events. For the airline industry, we would refer to airline seats, flight attendants, and cabin service. Most consumers of the service know what they are. However, a key task for marketers is to communicate what makes a specific offering distinctly different from (and better than) competing offerings.

Table 7.1 Advertising strategies for overcoming intangibility.

Intangibility Problem Incorporeal Existence	Advertising Strategy Physical Representation	Description Show Physical Components of Service
Generality:		
• For objective claims	System documentation Performance documentation	Objectively document physical system capacity Document and cite past performance statistics
• For subjective claims	Service performance episode	Present an actual service delivery incident
Non-searchability	Consumption documentation Reputation documentation	Obtain and present customer testimonials Cite independently audited performance
Abstractness	Service consumption episode	Capture and display typical customers benefiting from the service
Impalpability	Service process episode Case history episode Service consumption episode	Present a vivid documentary on the step-by-step service process Present an actual case history of what the firm did for a specific client An articulate narration or depiction of a customer's subjective experience

SOURCE

Banwari Mittal and Julie Baker, Advertising strategies for hospitality services. *Cornell Hotel and Restaurant Administration Quarterly*, 43 (April 2002): 53. Copyright Cornell University. All rights reserved. Used by permission.

- *Non-searchability* refers to the fact that intangibles cannot be searched for or inspected before they are purchased. Physical service attributes, such as the appearance of a health club and the type of equipment installed, can be checked in advance. However, the experience of working with the trainers can only be known through experience. And as noted in Chapter 2, credence attributes are those that one must trust, such as a surgeon's skill.

- *Abstractness* refers to the lack of one-to-one connection with physical objects. Financial security or investment related matters (Figure 7.6), expert advice such as legal or medical advice are examples of such abstract concepts.

- *Mental impalpability.* Many services are sufficiently complex, multi-dimensional, or new such that it is difficult for consumers to understand what the experience of using them will be like and what benefits will result. An example of such a service would be plastic surgery.

Figure 7.6 Julius Bär, a Swiss private bank shows how the intangibility of providing excellent private banking services can be communicated.

Overcoming the Problems of Intangibility

Tangible cues and metaphors can be effective in overcoming the challenge of intangibility.

Tangible Cues

Using tangible cues is one strategy commonly used in advertising. It is helpful to include information that catches the audience's attention and will produce a strong, clear impression on the senses, especially for services that are complex and highly intangible.[3] For example, many business schools feature successful alumni to make the benefits of its education tangible and communicate what its education could do for prospective students.

Use Metaphors

A metaphor is a symbol representing something else. Some companies have created metaphors to help communicate the benefits of their service offerings. Insurance companies often use this approach to market their highly intangible products. Thus, Allstate advertises that "You're in Good Hands" and Prudential uses the Rock of Gibraltar as a symbol of corporate strength. Professional service firms sometimes use metaphors to communicate their value propositions more dramatically. To bring to life the abstract idea of helping clients achieve high performance, Accenture, an international consulting firm, features the champion golfer, Tiger Woods, in eye-catching situations (Figure 7.7).

Figure 7.7 Tiger Woods spearheads Accenture's image of high-performance businesses.

Figure 7.8 The Merrill Lynch bull is a imposing figure on the Brooklyn-Battery Tunnel toll road.

Figure 7.9 MasterCard puts no price on scaling the heights.

The Merrill Lynch bull has been a steadfast symbol for the investment bank's business philosophy, which suggests both the market bull run and a strong commitment towards investment (Figure 7.8).

Reaching the top is the metaphor employed by MasterCard to appeal to the hearts and minds of customers. The indication is that with MasterCard on your side the sky's the limit (Figure 7.9).

LO 3
Know the 5 Ws of marketing communications planning.

MARKETING COMMUNICATIONS PLANNING

After having discussed the role of market communications and how to overcome the challenge of intangibility of service offerings, we now turn our discussion to how to plan and design an effective communications strategy. Planning a marketing communications campaign requires a good understanding of the service product. It is also necessary to understand target market segments and to research such factors as:

▶ the different media through which they can be reached

▶ their awareness of the product

▶ their attitudes toward it.

Decisions include deciding on the content, structure, and style of the message to be communicated, its manner of presentation, and the media most suited to reaching the intended audience. Additional considerations include: the budget available, time frames for the campaign, and methods of measuring and evaluating performance.

The 5Ws model provides useful checklist for marketing communications planning:

Who is our target audience?

What do we need to communicate and achieve?

How should we communicate this?

Where should we communicate this?

When do the communications need to take place?

We will first consider the issues of defining the target audience and specifying communication objectives. Then we will review the wide variety of communication tools available to service marketers. Issues relating to the location and scheduling of communication activities tend to be situation-specific, so we will not address them here.

Target Audience

Prospects, users, and employees represent three broad target audiences for any services communications strategy.

▶ Prospects—Marketers do not know them. Hence, they need to use traditional communications mix, like media advertising, public relations, and use of purchased address lists.

▶ Users—They can be reached by cost effective channels, including selling efforts by customer contact personnel, point-of-sale promotions, and other information distributed during service encounters. If the firm has a membership relationship with its customers and a database containing contact information, it can distribute highly targeted information through e-mail, direct mail, or telephone.

▶ Employees—Employees serve as a secondary audience for communication campaigns through public media. Advertising can help to shape employees' behavior, as employee behavior shown in the ads can serve as a role model and benchmark. Communications can also be directed specifically at staff. These are part of an internal marketing campaign, using company-specific channels, and so are not accessible to customers. We will discuss internal marketing in Chapter 11.

Communication Objectives

After we are clear about our target audience, we need to now specify what exactly we want to achieve with this target audience. Marketers need to be clear about their goals, otherwise it will be difficult to formulate specific communications objectives and select the most appropriate messages and communication tools to achieve them. Communication objectives answer the question of what we need to communicate and achieve. Common educational and promotional objectives for service organizations include:

▶ Create memorable images of companies and their brands.

▶ Build awareness of and interest in an unfamiliar service or brand.

▶ Compare a service favorably with competitors' offerings.

- Build preference by communicating the strengths and benefits of a specific brand.

- Reposition a service relative to competing offerings (see Service Insights 7.1).

- Reduce uncertainty and perceived risk by providing useful information and advice.

- Provide reassurance, such as by promoting service guarantees.

- Encourage trial by offering promotional incentives.

- Familiarize customers with service processes in advance of use.

⠿ SERVICE INSIGHTS 7.1

UPS Repositions itself To Deliver

Founded as a messenger company in the United States in 1907, UPS has become one of the world's top service brands developing new services and expanding into new markets around the globe. In recent years, the company has had to develop communication strategies to change the perceptions of both current and potential customers. Although recognized as a leader in the ground shipping business, the company wanted wider awareness of its other services like supply chain management, multi-modal transportation, and financial services. So it started a rebranding and repositioning exercise to make sure that all UPS services were closely identified with the UPS name.

Research showed that UPS was strongly associated with the color brown, used for the paintwork on its trucks and the design of its employee uniforms. This color also gave UPS an image of being trustworthy and reliable. Seeking to clarify that UPS could do more for customers than just deliver packages, UPS adopted the tag line 'What Can Brown Do For You?' and combined it with a new slogan, "Synchronizing the world of commerce".

The company understood that changing the perception of a brand had to start with the employees first. Although it can be difficult to change people's mindsets about a company's vision, UPS succeeded. Employees accepted the new brand positioning strategy and learned to work with each other across business units. Working together, they were able to serve customers better.

Today, the company operates in more than 200 countries and territories worldwide. In 2007, it served 7.9 million customers daily and had operating revenues of close to $50 billion. UPS has a very strong retail presence, with over 4,500 retail stores, 1,300 mail boxes, 1,000 customer centers, 17,000 authorized outlets and 40,000 drop boxes. Their website has an average of 15 million tracking requests daily. The UPS jet aircraft fleet is the eighth largest in the world.

SOURCE

Vivian Manning-Schaffel. *UPS Competes to Deliver*, http://www.brandchannel.com/features_effect.asp?pf_id=210, 17 May 2004, accessed on 18 May 2007; http://www.ups.com/content/sg/en/about/facts/worldwide.html, accessed February 2008. Source for picture: http://www.ups.com/content/us/en/about/history/2007.html, accessed February 2008.

- Teach customers how to use a service to their own best advantage.

- Stimulate demand in low-demand periods and shift demand during peak periods to low-demand periods.

- Recognize and reward valued customers and employees.

THE MARKETING COMMUNICATIONS MIX

After understanding our target audience and our specific communications objectives, we now need to select a mix of cost effective communications channels. There are a number of forms of communication referred to collectively as the *marketing communications mix*. These show us the various ways we can communicate. As shown in Figure 7.10a, the mix includes personal contact, advertising, publicity and public relations, sales promotion, instructional materials, and corporate design.

Communications Sources

As shown in Figure 7.10b, the traditional communications mix shown in Figure 7.10a can also be categorized into two main channels—those that are controlled by the organization, and those that are not. Not all communications messages originate from the service provider. Rather, some messages originate from outside the organization. Furthermore, Figure 7.10b shows that messages from an internal source can be further divided into those transmitted through marketing channels (traditional media and the Internet), and those transmitted through the service firm's own service delivery channels. Let us look at the communications mix within each of these originating sources.

 LO 4

Describe the variety of marketing communications tools that can be used.

PART II

Figure 7.10a The marketing communications mix for services.

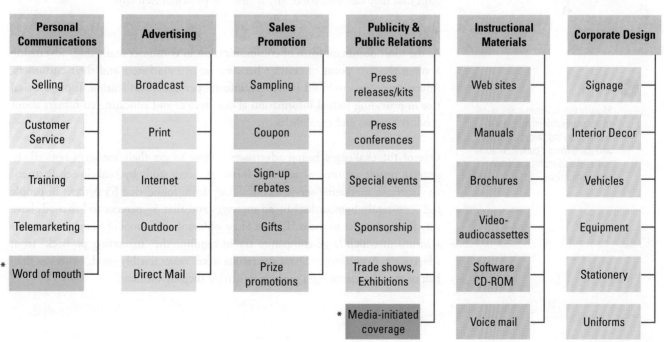

Personal Communications	Advertising	Sales Promotion	Publicity & Public Relations	Instructional Materials	Corporate Design
Selling	Broadcast	Sampling	Press releases/kits	Web sites	Signage
Customer Service	Print	Coupon	Press conferences	Manuals	Interior Decor
Training	Internet	Sign-up rebates	Special events	Brochures	Vehicles
Telemarketing	Outdoor	Gifts	Sponsorship	Video-audiocassettes	Equipment
* Word of mouth	Direct Mail	Prize promotions	Trade shows, Exhibitions	Software CD-ROM	Stationery
			* Media-initiated coverage	Voice mail	Uniforms

Key: * Denotes communications originating from outside the organization

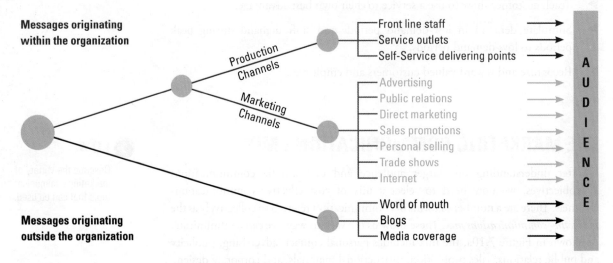

Messages originating within the organization

Production Channels
- Front line staff
- Service outlets
- Self-Service delivering points

Marketing Channels
- Advertising
- Public relations
- Direct marketing
- Sales promotions
- Personal selling
- Trade shows
- Internet

Messages originating outside the organization
- Word of mouth
- Blogs
- Media coverage

AUDIENCE

Figure 7.10b Sources of messages received by a target audience.

SOURCE

Adapted from a diagram by Adrian Palmer, *Principles of Services Marketing*, London: McGraw-Hill, 4th ed., 2005, p. 397.

Messages Transmitted through Traditional Marketing Channels

As shown in Figure 7.10b, service marketers have a wide variety of communication tools that they can use. We briefly review the principal elements.

Advertising

As the most dominant form of communication in consumer marketing, advertising is often the first point of contact between service marketers and their customers. Advertising serves to build awareness, inform, persuade, and remind. It plays a vital role in providing factual information about services and educating customers about product features and capabilities.

One of the challenges facing advertisers is how to get their messages noticed. In general, people are tired of ads in all forms. A recent study by Yankelovich Partners, an American marketing-services consultancy firm, found that 65 percent of people feel "constantly bombarded" by ad messages and that 59 percent feel that ads have very little relevance to them.[4] Robert Shaw of Cranfield School of Management runs a forum in which large companies try to monitor the "marketing payback" from advertising. According to Shaw, the results were "never terribly good," with less than half of the ads generating a positive return on their investment.[5]

LO 5

Identify the different sources of communications messages received by the target audience and the different communication tools related to the source of communications.

Marketers are trying to be more creative with their advertising to allow their messages to be more effective. They are now putting advertisements in the video games. These can even be dynamic advertisements if the games consoles are connected to the Internet.[6] (Figure 7.11)

Public Relations

PR involves efforts to generate positive interest in an organization and its products. A basic element in public relations strategy is the preparation and distribution of press releases (including photos and/or videos) that feature stories about the company, its products, and its employees. Corporate PR specialists at many service organizations also teach senior managers how to present themselves well at news conferences, or in radio and television interviews. Other widely used PR techniques include recognition and reward programs, getting testimonials from public figures, community involvement and support, fundraising, and obtaining favorable publicity for the organization through special events. Firms can also win wide exposure through sponsorship of sporting events and other high-profile activities, like the World Cup for soccer.

Figure 7.11 Avatars crowd in front of Sony BMG's media island. Virtual video game worlds like Second Life lead the new wave of dynamic in-game advertising.

Unusual activities can present an opportunity to promote a company. FedEx gained a lot of positive publicity when it safely transported two giant pandas from Chengdu, China, to the National Zoo in Washington, DC. The pandas flew in specially designed containers aboard a FedEx aircraft renamed "FedEx PandaOne." In addition to press releases, the company also featured information about the unusual shipment on a special page in its web site (Figure 7.12).

Direct Marketing

This category includes tools like e-mails, direct mailers, and telemarketing. These channels allow personalized messages to be sent to highly targeted micro-segments. Tesco is an example of a company that has used direct marketing to great success (see Service Insights 7.2).

Figure 7.12 FedEx donated the use of its extensive global network, granting the logistical resources to move the animals, which were previously housed at the Beijing Zoo and the Shanghai Zoo.

Advances in on-demand technologies like e-mail spam filters, TiVo, and podcasting allow consumers to decide how and when they prefer to be reached and by whom. This led *permission marketing* to become more widely used. In the permission marketing model, the goal is to persuade consumers to volunteer their attention. By reaching out only to individuals who have previously expressed interest in receiving a certain type of message, permission marketing enables service firms to build stronger relationships with their customers. E-mail, in combination with websites, can be integrated into a one-to-one permission-based medium.[7]

Sales Promotion

A useful way of looking at sales promotions is as a communication that comes with an incentive. Sales promotions are usually specific to a time period, price, or customer group—sometimes all three. Typically, the objective is to get customers to make a purchase decision faster or encourage customers to use a specific service sooner, in greater volume with each purchase, or more frequently. Sales promotions for service firms may take such forms as samples, coupons and other discounts, gifts, and competitions with prizes. Sales promotions need to be used with care because research shows that customers acquired through sales promotions may have lower repurchase rates and lower life time values. [8]

Some years ago, SAS International Hotels devised an interesting sales promotion targeted at older customers. If a hotel had vacant rooms, guests over 65 years of age could get a discount equivalent to their age (e.g. a 75-year old could save 75 percent of the normal room price). All went well until a Swedish guest checked into one of the SAS chain's hotels in Vienna, announced his age as 102, and asked to be paid 2 percent of the room rate in return for staying the night. This request was granted, and the energetic centenarian challenged the general manager to a game of tennis—and got that, too. (The results of the game, however, were not disclosed!) In this case, a clever promotion led to a humorous, widely reported story that placed the hotel chain in a positive light.

"I read someplace that eye contact is a very important business skill."

Figure 7.13 To persuade customers of the superiority of one's brand, body language is also important.

Personal Selling

Personal selling is the interpersonal encounter where efforts are made to educate customers and promote preference for a particular brand or product (Figure 7.13). Many firms, especially those marketing business-to-business services, have dedicated sales forces, or use agents and distributors to do the personal selling efforts on their behalf. For services that are bought less often like property, insurance and funeral services, the firm's representative may act as a consultant to help buyers make their selections. For industrial and professional firms that sell relatively complex services, customers may have an account manager they can turn to for advice, education and consultation.

However, face-to-face selling to new prospects is expensive. A lower-cost alternative is *telemarketing*. Telemarketing involves the use of the telephone to reach prospective customers. At the consumer level, there is growing frustration with telemarketing because it is often timed to reach people when they are home in the evening or at weekends (Figure 7.14).

"Before you hang up, Mrs. Johnson, are you aware that you can lose up to 50 pounds a year by listening to telemarketers instead of eating your dinner?"

Figure 7.14 Telemarketers call in the evenings.

Trade Shows

Trade shows are a popular form of publicity, especially for business-to-business services and include important personal selling opportunities (Figure 7.15). In many industries, shows receive extensive media coverage. They offer business customers an opportunity to learn about the latest offerings from a wide variety of suppliers and are one of the few occasions when large numbers of potential buyers come to the marketer rather than the other way around. A sales representative who usually reaches four to five potential customers per day may be able to get five qualified leads per hour at a show.

Messages transmitted through the Internet

Messages transmitted through the Internet can come from the company's own web site, or from advertisements it places on a variety of other sites. Internet advertising has become an important part of the communications mix for most service firms but should be part of an integrated, well-designed communications strategy.[9]

Figure 7.15 Trade shows are a good way to showcase a company's offerings.

Company's Web Site

Marketers use the Internet for a variety of communications tasks:

▶ Creating consumer awareness and interest

▶ Providing information and consultation

▶ Allowing two-way communications with customers through e-mail and chat rooms

▶ Encouraging product trial

▶ Allowing customers to place orders

▶ Measuring the effectiveness of specific advertising or promotional campaigns.

Innovative companies are continually looking for ways to improve the appeal and usefulness of their sites. The appropriate communication content varies widely from one type of service to another. A B2B site may offer visitors access to a library of technical information (e.g. Siebel or SAP both provide quite a lot of information on their customer relationship management solutions at their respective websites at www.siebel.com and www.sap.com.) By contrast, the website for a university's executive MBA program may include attractive photographs featuring the location, the facilities and past students, and short videos showing the university, its professors and facilities, student testimonials and even the graduation ceremony. (See, for example, the dual degree Executive MBA program offered by UCLA and the National University of Singapore at www.ucla.nus.edu.)

Online Advertising

There are two main types of online advertising, namely banner advertising and search engine advertising. In each instance, advertisers can include moving images and create links to more extended video presentations. The use of online advertising as part of an integrated communications strategy can bring success to a firm.

Banner Advertising

Many firms pay to place advertising banners and buttons on portals like Google, Yahoo or Netscape, as well as on other firms' web sites (Figure 7.16). The usual goal is to draw online traffic to the advertiser's own site. Advertisements are often placed from other websites that offer services that are related but do not compete directly with the firm's own services. For example, Yahoo's stock quotes page features a sequence of advertisements for various financial service providers.

Simply obtaining a large number of exposures ("eyeballs") to a banner (a thin horizontal ad running across all or part of a web page), a skyscraper (a long skinny ad running vertically down one side of a website), or a button does not necessarily lead to increases in awareness, preference, or sales for the advertiser. As a result, there is now more emphasis on advertising contracts that tie fees to marketing-relevant behavior by these visitors. These include providing the advertiser with some information about themselves or making a purchase. Internet advertisers increasingly pay only if a visitor to the host site clicks through on the link to the advertisers' site. This is similar to paying for the delivery of junk mail only to households that read it.

Search Engine Advertising

Search engines are a form of a reverse broadcast network. Instead of advertisers broadcasting their messages to consumers, search engines let advertisers know exactly what consumers want through their key word search. Advertisers can then target relevant marketing communications directly at these consumers. Advertisers have several options. They can:

▶ pay for the placement of ads to keyword searches that are related to their firm

▶ sponsor a short text message with a click-through link, located parallel to the search results

▶ buy top rankings in the display of search results through a "pay-for-placement" option. Pricing for these ads and placements can be based on either number of impressions (i.e., eyeballs) or click-throughs, both of which are achieved by placing sponsored links at the top of search results. One company that built a successful business model around highly targeted Internet advertising is Pinstorm (see Service Insights 7.3).

Figure 7.16 Web banners function similarly to traditional banners: Turning consumers' attention to the product or service and selling a pitch, though service-provider and consumer interaction is more realized with the "click through" of online advertisement.

Pinstorm—The Company that Takes the **Advertising World by Storm**

In 2005, when it was only 15 months old, Pinstorm was picked as among Asia's 100 hottest companies, by *Red Herring*, a weekly magazine that covers high-tech businesses. Pinstorm is a search engine marketing company based in India. How does a company like Pinstorm allow you to set up a marketing campaign in Google or Yahoo and achieve better results for the same amount of dollars spent?

The main income for search engines like Google or Yahoo is through the "Sponsored Links." In order for companies to appear on the first page of a Google search, they have to pay for the keywords that they think their potential customers will search for. However, the price for these keywords is not fixed. A company has to outbid other advertisers on phrases that they want to be on. As a result, common search terms are typically expensive.

Pinstorm applies the Long Tail phenomenon to keyword searches. This phenomenon is one where search terms that are low in demand or infrequently used can together make up a significant share of search terms. Pinstorm has the technology (**BroadWords**® technology) to look for the long tail of low-priced keywords that are relevant to their clients' offering.

Pinstorm has a business model that guarantees results. Clients do not have to pay if there are no results. Results by their definition could be measured by visits, unique visitors, online actions, leads or even sales. Hence, the company does everything to make sure that it gets results. Apart from picking effective words that are low-priced, they also develop effective online ads for their clients. These are tested again and again during a campaign until they find one that performs best. Pinstorm tracks millions of searches and understands demand for a particular product category and even geographical region. As a result, they are able to micro-target and micro-market. The leads they deliver to their clients are therefore self-selected and of high quality. Clients will be able to know where the leads came from, the time they visited, and the search terms used. All these kinds of information provide the clients with a lot more understanding about their customers.

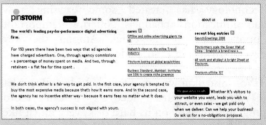

Among Pinstorm's clients are famous companies like eBay, HP, National Geographic, Dell, Qantas, and Swissotel Hotels and Resorts. They also have many clients who are not as well known yet, but Pinstorm hopes that with their help, their clients will become famous.

SOURCE

http://www.pinstorm.com, accessed June 2008; The Long Tail. *Wikipedia*, http://en.wikipedia.org/wiki/The_Long_Tail, accessed 13 August 2007.

Moving from Impersonal to Personal Communications

Communication experts divide *personal* communications, like personal selling, telemarketing, and word of mouth, and *impersonal communications,* where messages move in only one direction and are generally targeted at a large group of customers and prospects rather than at a single individual. However, technology has created a gray area between personal and impersonal communications. Think about the direct mail and e-mail messages that you have received, containing perhaps some reference to your specific situation or past use of a particular product.

Another way of personalized communications are electronic recommendation agents that are increasingly used by online retailers. Interactive software, voice recognition technology, and computer-generated voice prompts and responses can be like a two-way conversation. Recommendation agents are "virtual salespeople" who help customers make their selections from among a large number of offerings. This can be done by generating alternative lists ranked based on customers' preferences.[10] As customers become more technology savvy, more companies are beginning to experiment with web-based agents that move, speak, and even change expression.

With the advances of on-demand technologies, consumers are increasingly empowered to decide how and when they like to be reached. This development is transforming marketing communications on radio, television, the Internet and even mobile phones (see Service Insights 7.4).

⠿ SERVICE INSIGHTS 7.4

New Media and Its Implications for Marketing Communications

Technology has created some exciting new communication channels offering important opportunities for targeting. Among the key developments are TiVo, podcasting and YouTube.

TiVo (also known as Digital Video Recorder (DVR) or Personal Video) TiVo can record programs digitally on its hard disk, very much like a VCR. However, unlike a VCR, TiVo is "always on" and continuously stores up to some 30 minutes of TV programming. This means that TiVo users can pause or rewind live TV. In fact, many users begin watching a TV program after the broadcast has started so that they can fast-forward and skip the commercials. This is worrying for advertisers. Interestingly, while customers liked TiVo because it can be commercial free, TiVo is attracting marketers and advertisers as well.

Charles Schwab & Co. became the first financial-services company in June 2004 to use TiVo's new interactive technology, employing a 30-second spot featuring golfer Phil Mickelson. The spot allowed viewers to move from the commercial into a four-minute video to watch three segments hosted by the golf pro. Viewers could also order information on Schwab's golf-rewards program at the same time. The effectiveness of ads can be immediately measured based on viewer responses. Schwab began

testing large billboards and small logos that pop up as an alternative way to generate revenue. When users fast-forward, they will also see a static image ad, which is more suitable than a broken video stream.

Podcasting. This term comes from the words "iPod" and "broadcasting." It refers to a group of technologies for distributing audio or video programs over the Internet using a publisher/subscriber model. Podcasting gives broadcast radio or television programs a new method of distribution. Once someone has subscribed to a certain feed, they will automatically receive new "episodes" that become available. Podcasting is so popular that it has several variations now, including video podcasting for delivery of video clips, mobilecast for downloads onto a cell phone, and blogcast for attachment of an audio or video file to a blog. It is beneficial to include podcasting as part of a firm's marketing communications program because once a listener has subscribed to a specific show, this means the listener is interested in the topic. Hence, podcasts can reach a wide audience of listeners that have a narrow focus, more like "narrowcasting" than broadcasting. When the advertising message is more targeted, this leads to a higher return on investment for the advertising dollars spent.

YouTube. YouTube was founded in mid February 2005, and the company was bought over by Google in late 2006. YouTube is a trendy video sharing website where registered users can upload videos, and unregistered users can watch most videos and also post responses to those videos. Already in 2006, some 100 million YouTube video clips were viewed daily, and 65,000 new videos were uploaded every 24 hours. Advertisers were quick to see the advantages of using YouTube as a marketing communications channel.

The CEO of Red Hat, Matthew Szulik, used a video called "Truth Happens" to open a keynote address four years ago. That video has been viewed more than 50,000 times on YouTube. Today, the company uses YouTube, blogs and its own magazine as marketing communications tools.

Mobile advertising. Mobile advertising is a form of advertising through cell phones and other mobile wireless devices, but currently mainly targeted at cell phones. Mobile advertising is quite complex as it can involve the Internet, video, text, gaming music and much more. For example, advertisements can come in the form of an SMS, MMS, advertisements in mobile games, or videos or even some music

before a voicemail recording. Through mobile advertising and the use of a global positioning system, customers can walk into shopping malls and receive advertisements from those malls where they can activate coupons, or get discounts if they visited a particular store within the mall. What will this mean for the consumer? It might be greater convenience, more targeted advertising, or does it mean the invasion of privacy?

Web 2.0. Web 2.0 technology facilities the rise of user-generated content. This uses the power of peer to peer communication. Wikipedia and Flickr are examples of web sites that ride on the technologies offered by Web 2.0, where content is generated by multiple users and shared. Marketers cannot control what is being said. Therefore, they need to understand Web 2.0, carefully integrate it into its marketing mix, and sometimes even participate in conversations.

Social networks and communities. Internet-based virtual worlds like Second Life and social networks like Facebook offer communication and learning opportunities for marketers. In Second Life are virtual advertising firms and virtual advertising campaigns in the different communities, with business functions just like in the real world. As social networks gain popularity, marketers have begun to use applications to analyze the networks within the communities to enable them to identify those people who may be more influential in spreading the word about specific services for example. Marketers who want to take advantage of these rich networks need to remember though, that they are in a community where people would not welcome the intrusion of marketers. Hence, marketers have to come up with creative ways to engage the participants in these networks.

SOURCE

Silverthorne, S.(2004) .TiVo ready to fast forward? *HBS Working Knowledge*, (November)15; TiVo. http://www.en.wikipedia. org/wiki/TiVo, accessed June 2008; Podcast http://en.wikipedia.org/wiki/Podcast, accessed June 2008; Rumford, R.. (2005) What you don't know about podcasting could hurt your business: How to leverage & benefit from this New Media technology. Podcasting White Paper, *The Info Guru LLC*, (June); YouTube serves up 1000 million videos a day online. *USA Today*, Gannett Co. Inc, 16 July 2006; Daniels, C. (2007). Animated Conversation. *PRweek*, New Your: 25 June, 10 (25): 15; Fichter, D. (2007). Seven strategies for marketing in a Web 2.0 World. *Marketing Library Services*, 21 no. 2, (Mar/Apr) in http://www.infotoday.com/mls/mar07/Fichter. shtml, accessed June 2008; Jesdanun, A. (2007). Mobile advertising still at tryout stage. *USA Today*, 29 December, http://new. yahoo.com/s/ap/20071229/ap_on_hi_te/advertising_on_the_go, accessed December 2007; Smith, B. (2008). Mobile advertising reaches for the sky. *Wireless Week*, 15 August, http://www.wirelessweek.com/Mobile-Advertising.aspx, accessed June 2008; Mobile Advertising http://en.wikipedia.org/wiki/Mobile_advertising, accessed June 2008.

Messages Transmitted through Service Delivery Channels

This category comprises communications developed within the organization and transmitted through the channels that deliver the service itself, mainly front line staff, service outlets, and self-service delivery points.

Figure 7.17 The Salentein Winery in Argentina exudes a distinctive servicescape.

Customer Service Employees

Employees in front line positions may serve customers face-to-face or by telephone. Communication from front line staff takes the form of the core service and a variety of supplementary services, including providing information, taking reservations, receiving payments, and solving problems. New customers, in particular, often rely on customer service personnel for help in learning to use a service effectively and to solve problems. When several different products are available from the same supplier, firms encourage their customer service staff to cross-sell additional services, or to upsell to higher value services.

Service Outlets

Messages can be communicated in the form of banners, posters, signage, brochures, video screens, and audio. We will discuss in Chapter 10 the physical design of the service outlet—what we call the *servicescape*[11] (Figure 7.17).

Self-service Delivery Points

ATMs, vending machines and web sites are all examples of self-service delivery points. Promoting self-service delivery requires clear signage, step-by-step instructions (perhaps through diagrams) on how to operate the equipment, and user-friendly design.

Messages Originating from Outside the Organization

Some of the most powerful messages about a company and its products come from outside the organization and are not controlled by the marketer. They include word of mouth, blogs and media coverage.

Word of Mouth (WOM)

Word of mouth has a powerful influence on people's decisions to use (or avoid using) a service. This is because it is viewed as more believable than promotional activities of firms. In fact, the greater the risk that customers perceive in purchasing a service, the more actively they will seek and rely on WOM to guide their decision making.[12] In addition, whether or not customers are willing to give positive WOM for a firm is the single most important predictor of top-line growth.[13]

Since WOM is so powerful, some marketers use a variety of strategies to encourage existing customer to provide positive and persuasive comments.[14] These include:

- Having satisfied customers providing comments that will encourage WOM.

- Using other purchasers and knowledgeable individuals as a reference. For instance: "We have done a great job for ABC Corp., and if you wish, feel free to talk to Mr. Cabral, their MIS manager, who oversaw the implementation of our project.").

- Creating exciting promotions that get people talking about the great service that the firm provides.

- Offering promotions that encourage customers to persuade others to join them in using the service, such as "bring two friends, and the third eats for free" or "subscribe to two mobile service plans, and we'll waive the monthly subscription fee for all subsequent family members."

- Developing referral incentive schemes, such as offering an existing customer some units of free or discounted service in return for introducing new customers to the firm (Figure 7.18).

In addition to WOM, we also have word of mouse. Viral marketing has spread so fast, that firms cannot ignore it.[15] One of the early success stories of viral marketing was the Hotmail free e-mail service. The service grew from zero to 12 million users in 18 months on a very small advertising budget, thanks mostly to the inclusion of a promotional message with Hotmail's URL in every e-mail sent by its users. eBay and other electronic auction firms rely on users to rate sellers and buyers in order to build trust in the items offered on their websites.

Blogs—A New Type of Online WOM[16]

Web logs, commonly referred to a blogs, are becoming increasingly popular. They can be best described as online journals, diaries or news listings, where people can post anything, about whatever they like. Their authors, known as bloggers, usually focus on narrow topics. Blogs can be about anything, ranging from baseball and sex, to karate and financial engineering. There are a growing number of travel-oriented sites, ranging from Hotel.chatter.com (focused on boutique hotels), to CruiseDiva.com (reporting on the cruise industry), and pestiside.hu ("the daily dish of cosmopolitan Budapest"). Some sites, such as the travel-focused Tripadvisor.com, allow users to post their own reviews or ask questions that more experienced travelers may be able to answer.[17]

Marketers are interested in the way blogs have evolved into a new form of social interaction on the web. Communications include consumers' experiences with service firms and their recommendations on avoiding or buying from certain firms. In the exchange of dialog, owners of weblogs add hyperlinks into their weblogs, which allow readers to click on these hyperlinks and access information that they want to share. The additional information also influences opinions of a brand or product. Some service firms have started to monitor blogs, viewing them as a

Figure 7.18 Word of mouth can be an effective promotional tool.

Figure 7.19 Google has come on board the social and marketing phenomenon of blogging.

form of immediate market research and feedback. Some service companies have even started their own blogs, see for example Google's blog at http://googleblog.blogspot.com (Figure 7.19).

Media Coverage

A significant amount of media coverage of firms and their services is done by firms' public relations activities which inform the media about the latest news services and exciting company news. Media coverage can also take several other forms. For example, journalists responsible for consumer affairs often contrast and compare service offerings from competing organizations, identifying their strong and weak points, and offering advice on "best buys." In a more specialized context, *Consumer Reports,* the monthly publication of US-based Consumers' Union, periodically evaluates services that are offered on a national basis, including financial services and telecommunications. Furthermore, investigative reporters may conduct an in-depth study of a company, especially if they believe it is putting customers at risk, cheating them, using deceptive advertising, damaging the environment, or exploiting poor workers in developing countries.

Ethical and Consumer Privacy Issues in Communications

We have been focusing on the various communications tools and channels of communication where customers receive information about the firm. Firms, however, also need to consider the ethical and privacy issues associated with communications. It is very easy to misuse or even abuse advertising, selling, and sales promotion. Since customers often find it hard to evaluate services, they rely on marketing communication for information and advice. Communication messages often include promises about the benefits that customers will receive and the quality of service delivery. When promises are made and then broken, customers are disappointed because their expectations have not been met. Their disappointment and even anger will be even greater if they have wasted money, time, and effort and have no benefits to show in return or have actually suffered a negative impact.

Some unrealistic service promises result from poor internal communications between operations and marketing personnel concerning the level of service performance that customers can reasonably expect. In other instances, unethical advertisers and salespeople overpromise in order to get sales. Finally, there are promotions that lead people to think that they have a much higher chance of winning prizes or awards than there really is. Fortunately, there are many consumer watchdogs on the lookout for these unethical marketing practices.

Consumer Concerns about Online Privacy

Technology advances have made the Internet a very powerful threat to user privacy. Information is being collected on not just people who register and shop, or use e-mail, but also on those who are just surfing the Internet! Individuals are increasingly fearful of databases and concerned about their online privacy. Hence, they use several ways to protect themselves including.

- Providing false information about themselves.

- Using technology like anti-spam filters, e-mail shredders, and cookie-busters to hide the identity of their computers from websites.

- Refusing to provide information and avoid websites that require personal information to be disclosed.

Such consumer responses will make information collected in CRM systems inaccurate and incomplete, and even drive potential customers away from a firm's website. The result will be reduced effectiveness of a firm's customer relationship marketing and its efforts to provide customized service. There are several steps that firms can take to reduce privacy concerns.

- Firms should have a good privacy policy in place. This privacy policy should be easily noticed on the websites. It should be in a language that is easy to understand, and comprehensive enough to be effective.

- If the information being requested is highly sensitive, the information asked for should be perceived to be related to the transaction. Therefore, firms should clearly communicate why the information is needed, and how such information will benefit the consumer through more convenience, more customization, and improved offers.

- Firms should have high ethical standards of data protection. They can use third party endorsements like TRUSTe or Better Business Bureau, and have the recognizable privacy seals displayed clearly on their website.

SOURCE

Lwin, M., Wirtz, J. & Williams, J.D. (2007). Consumer online privacy concerns and responses: A power-reponsibility equilibrium perspective. *Journal of the Academy of Marketing Science*, 35.pp. 572-585; Wirtz, J., Lwin, M., & Williams, J.D. (2007). Causes and consequences of consumer online privacy concern, *International Journal of Service Industry Management*, 18(4), pp. 326-348.

A different type of ethical issue concerns privacy. The increase in telemarketing, direct mail and e-mail is frustrating for those who receive unwanted sales communications. How do you feel if your evening meal at home is interrupted by a telephone call from a stranger trying to interest you in buying services in which you have no interest? Even if you are interested, you may feel, as many do, that your privacy has been violated (see Service Insights 7.5). Trade associations like the Direct Marketing Association offer ways for consumers to remove their names from telemarketing and direct mail lists to try to decrease the growing anger towards these types of direct marketing techniques. Governments are coming up anti-spam laws to stop this intrusion into consumers' private lives. In the US, Federal Communications Commission regulations do not allow telemarketers to use equipment that automatically dials cell phone numbers to make cold calls.

Figure 7.20 The Golden Arches prominently displayed on the exterior of the Times Square McDonald's restaurant.

Figure 7.21 The Shell brand is one of the most instantly-recognizable global commercial symbols.

THE ROLE OF CORPORATE DESIGN

So far, we have focused on communications media and content, but not much on design. Corporate design is key to ensure a consistent style and message is communicated through all a firm's communications mix channels. Have you noticed how some firms stick in your mind because of the colors that they use, their logos, the uniforms worn by their personnel, and the design of their physical facilities? If you were to be asked, you would probably be able to identify the corporate colors of DHL as red and yellow. These colors are on their packages, their uniforms, and their vehicles. If you ask children worldwide to identify the McDonald's "Golden Arches," it is unlikely that any of them will get it wrong (Figure 7.20).

Many service firms use one distinctive visual appearance for all their tangible elements. The objective is to help recognition and strengthen a desired brand image. Corporate design strategies are usually created by external consulting firms and cover stationery and promotional literature, retail signage, uniforms, and color schemes for vehicles, equipment, and building interiors. Corporate design is particularly important for companies operating in competitive markets where it is necessary to stand out from the crowd and to be instantly recognizable in different locations. Companies can do that in several ways:

▶ Use of colors in corporate designs. If we look at gasoline retailing, we see BP's bright green and yellow service stations, Texaco's red, black and white, and Sunoco's blue, maroon, and yellow.

▶ Companies in the highly competitive express delivery industry tend to use their names as a central element in their corporate designs. When Federal Express changed its trading name to the more modern "FedEx," it also changed its logo to feature the new name in a distinctive logo.

▶ Many companies use a trademarked symbol, rather than a name, as their primary logo, Shell displays a yellow scallop shell on a red background. This has the advantage of making its vehicles and service stations instantly recognizable (Figure 7.21).

▶ Some companies have succeeded in creating tangible, recognizable symbols to connect with their corporate brand names. Animal motifs are common physical symbols for services. Examples include the eagles of the US Postal Service (AeroMexico and Eagle Star Insurance also feature an eagle), the lions of ING Bank and the Royal Bank of Canada, the ram of the investment firm T. Rowe Price, the Chinese dragon of Hong Kong's Dragonair and the kangaroo on Qantas Airlines. Merrill Lynch, the global financial services company, used its famous slogan, "We're Bullish on America" as the basis for its corporate symbol—a bull. Easily recognizable corporate symbols are especially important when services are offered in markets where the local language is not written in Roman script or where a significant proportion of the population is are unable to read (Figure 7.22).

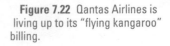

Figure 7.22 Qantas Airlines is living up to its "flying kangaroo" billing.

CHAPTER SUMMARY

LO 1 ▶ The role of service marketing communication is to position and differentiate the service, help customers to evaluate service offerings, promote the contribution of service personnel, add value through communication content, facilitate customer involvement in production, and stimulate or dampen demand to match capacity.

LO 2 ▶ The intangibility of services presents challenges for communications. To overcome the problem of intangibility, service marketers can emphasize tangible clues like its facilities, certificates and awards, or its customers. Another way of doing so is through using metaphors to communicate the value proposition, like Accenture and Julius Bär.

LO 3 ▶ After understanding the challenges of service communications, service marketers need to plan and design an effective communications strategy. They can use the 5 Ws model to guide service communications planning. The 5 Ws are:

o *Who* is our target audience?

o *What* do we need to communicate and achieve?

o *How* should we communicate this?

o *Where* should we communicate this?

o *When* do the communications need to take place?

LO 4 ▶ After understanding the target audience and knowing the communication objectives, we can use a variety of communication tools and channels for communication. Messages come from a variety of sources and the services communications is discussed within each of these originating sources:

LO 5 ▶ o Messages from traditional marketing channels. These are advertising, public relations, direct marketing, sales promotions, personal selling and tradeshows. There are also messages transmitted through the Internet using company websites, and online advertising like banner advertising and search engine advertising.

o Messages can also come from within the organization through its service delivery channels like customer servivce employees, service outlets, and self-service delivery points.

o Communicating messages originating from outside the organization include word of mouth, blogs, and media coverage.

o When designing their communication strategy, firms need to bear in mind the ethical and privacy issues in communication.

LO 6 ▶ Besides the communication tools, corporate design can also help firms to achieve a unified image in the minds of customers. Good corporate design uses a unified and distinctive visual appearance for all tangible elements, including stationery, promotional literature, retail signage, uniforms, vehicles, equipment, and building interiors.

UNLOCK YOUR LEARNING

These keywords are found within the sections of each Learning Objective (LO). They are integral in understanding the services marketing concepts taught in each section. Having a firm grasp of these keywords and how they are used is essential in helping you do well for your course, and in the real and very competitive marketing scene out there.

LO 1
1. Marketing communications
2. Promotion and education

LO 2
3. Abstractness
4. Challenges of service communications
5. Generality
6. Intangibility
7. Non-searchability
8. Mental impalpability
9. Metaphor
10. Symbol
11. Tangible cues

LO 3
12. 5Ws model
13. Communication objectives
14. Employees
15. Marketing communications planning

16. Prospects
17. Target audience
18. Users

LO 4
19. Marketing communications mix

LO 5
20. Advertising
21. Banner advertising
22. Blogs
23. Communication sources
24. Customer service "employees"
25. Direct marketing
26. Ethical issue
27. Eyeballs
28. Facebook
29. Google
30. Impersonal communications
31. Media coverage

32. Mobile advertising
33. Online advertising
34. Permission marketing
35. Personal communications
36. Personal selling
37. Podcasting
38. Privacy
39. Public relations
40. Sales promotion
41. Search engine advertising
42. Second Life
43. Employees
44. Service outlets
45. Servicescape
46. Self-service delivery points

47. Skyscraper

48. Social networks

49. Telemarketing

50. TiVo

51. Trade shows

52. Website

53. Yahoo

54. YouTube

55. Word of mouth

56. Word of mouse

 LO 6

57. Viral marketing

58. Corporate design

59. Logo

> How well do you know the language of services marketing? Quiz yourself!

⚠ **Not for the academically faint-of-heart**

For each keyword you are able to recall without referring to earlier pages, give yourself a point (and a pat on the back). Tally your score at the end and see if you earned the right to be called—a *services marketeer.*

SCORE

0 – 9	Services Marketing is done a great disservice.
10 – 20	The midnight oil needs to be lit, pronto.
21 – 30	I know what you *didn't* do all semester.
31 – 41	A close shave with success.
42 – 51	Now, go forth and market.
52 – 59	There should be a marketing concept named after you.

Review Questions

1. What role does marketing communications play in services?

2. What are some challenges in service communications and how can they be overcome?

3. Which elements of the marketing communications mix would you use for each of the following scenarios? Explain your answers.

   - A newly established hair salon in a suburban shopping center

   - An established restaurant facing declining patronage because of new competitors

   - A large, single-office accounting firm in a major city that serves primarily business clients.

4. What roles do personal selling, advertising, and public relations play in (a) attracting new customers to visit a service outlet, (b) retaining existing customers?

5. Discuss the relative effectiveness of brochures and web sites for promoting (a) a ski resort, (b) a business school, (c) a fitness centre, and (d) an online broker.

6. Why is word of mouth considered so important for the marketing of services? How can a service firm that is the quality leader in its industry encourage and manage word of mouth?

7. How can companies use corporate design to differentiate themselves?

WORK YOUR ESM

Application Exercises

1. What tangible cues could a scuba diving school or a dentist office use to position itself as something attractive to wealthy customers?

2. Describe and evaluate recent public relations efforts made by service organizations in connection with three or more of the following: (a) launching a new offering; (b) opening a new facility; (c) promoting an expansion of an existing service; (d) announcing an upcoming event; or (e) responding to a negative situation that has happened. (Pick a different organization for each category).

3. If you were exploring the institution that you are now studying in, or research the program you are now in, what could you learn from blogs and any other online word of mouth? How would that information influence the decision of a potential new applicant to your institution? Since you are a student in the institution, how accurate do you think is the information that you found online?

4. Register at Amazon.com and Hallmark.com, and analyze their permission-based communications strategy. What are their marketing objectives? Evaluate their permission-based marketing for a specific customer segment of your choice—what is excellent, what is good, and what could be further improved?

•ENDNOTES

1   Westin Turns Traditional Hotel Advertising on its Head, http://www.hotelmarketing.com/index.php/content/print/070802_westin_turns_traditional_hotel_advertising_on_its_head, 6 August 2007 (article downloaded on 13 August 2007). Source for photos: http://www.westinadvertising.com/, accessed March 2008.

2. Devlin J.F., & Azhar, S. (2004). Life would be a lot easier if we were a Kit Kat: Practitioners' views on the challenges of branding financial services successfully. *Brand Management*, 12(1), pp. 12–30.

3. Hill, D.J., Blodgett, J., Baer, R. & Wakefield, K. (2004). An investigation of visualization and documentation strategies in service advertising. *Journal of Service Research*, 7 (November), pp. 155–166; Grace, D. & O'Cass, A. (2005). Service branding: Consumer verdicts on service brands. *Journal of Retailing and Consumer Services*, 12, pp. 125–139.

4. The future of advertising—The harder hard sell. (2004, June 24). *The Economist*.

5. *The Economist*, op. cit.

6. Got game: Inserting advertisements into video games holds much promise. (2007, June 9). *The Economist*, p. 69.

7. Godin, S. & Peppers, D. (1999). *Permission marketing: Turning strangers into friends and friends into customers.* New York, Simon & Schuster.

8. Lewis, M. (2006). Customer acquisition promotions and customer asset value. *Journal of Marketing Research*, XLIII (May), pp. 195–203.

9. Lagrosen, S. (2005). Effects of the Internet on the marketing communication of service companies. *Journal of Services Marketing*, 19(2), pp. 63–69.

10. Aksoy, L., Bloom, P.N., Nicholas, H.L., & Cooil, B. (2006). Should recommendation agents think like people? *Journal of Service Research*, 8(May), pp. 297–315.

11. Bitner, M.J. (1992). Servicescapes: The impact of physical surroundings on customers and employees. *Journal of Marketing*, 56(April), pp. 57–71.

12. Bansal, H.S., & Voyer, P.A. (2000). Word-of-mouth processes within a service purchase decision context. *Journal of Service Research*, 3(2), (November 2000), pp. 166–177.

13. Reichheld, F.F. (2003). The one number you need to grow. *Harvard Business Review*, 81(12), pp. 46–55. Malcom Gladwell explains how different types of epidemics, including word-of-mouth epidemics, develop. Gladwell, M. (2000). *The Tipping Point*, N.Y.: Little Brown and Company, p.32.

14. Wirtz, J. & Chew, P. (2002). The effects of incentives, deal proneness, satisfaction and tie strength on word-of-mouth behaviour. *International Journal of Service Industry Management,* 13(2), pp. 141–162. Hogan, J.E., Lemon, K.N., Libai, B. (2004). Quantifying the ripple: Word-of-mouth and advertising effectiveness. *Journal of Advertising Research*, (September), pp 271–280.

15. Phelps, J.E., Lewis, R., Mobilio, L., Perry, D. & Raman, N. (2004). Viral marketing or electronic word-of-mouth advertising: Examining consumer responses and motivations to pass along emails. *Journal of Advertising Research*, (December), pp. 333–348; Datta, P.R., Chowdhury, D.N. & Chakraborty, B.R. (2005). Viral marketing: New form of word-of-mouth through Internet," *The Business Review*, 3(2), (Summer), pp. 69–75.

16. Thielst, C.B. (2007). Weblogs: A communication tool. *Journal of Healthcare Management*, 52, (September/October), pp. 297–289; Yates, J., Orlikowski, W.J. & Jackson, A. (2008). The six key dimensions of understanding media. *MIT Sloan Management Review*, 49(2), (Winter), pp. 62–69.

17. Kurutz, K. (2005).For travelers, blogs level the playing field. *New York Times*, (2005, August 7) pp. TR-3.

Managing the Customer Interface

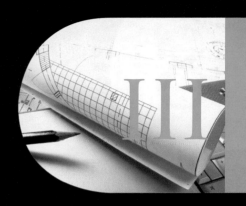

PART III focuses on how to manage the link between the customer and the service firm. It covers the additional 3Ps that are unique to service marketing and not found in goods marketing. It consists of the following four chapters:

Chapter 8 Designing and Managing Service Processes

Starts off with the design of effective delivery processes, specifying how the operating and delivery systems link together to create the value proposition. Very often, customers are involved in these processes as co-producers and badly designed processes will lead to a disappointing experience. It will also make it difficult for service personnel to do their jobs well.

Chapter 9 Balancing Demand Against Productive Capacity

Relates still to process management and focuses on managing the widely fluctuating demand and to balance that against available productive capacity. Well-managed demand and capacity leads to smooth processes with less waiting time for customers. Marketing strategies for managing demand involve smoothing demand fluctuations and inventorying demand through reservation systems and formalized queuing. Understanding customer motivations in different segments is one of the keys to successful demand management.

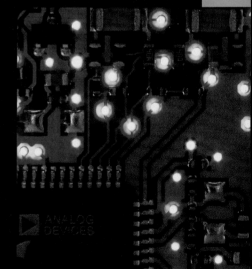

Chapter 10 Crafting the Service Environment

Focuses on the physical environment, which often creates the first impression on customers. This is also known as the servicescape, which needs to be engineered to create the right impression and facilitate effective service process delivery. The servicescape provides tangible evidence of a firm's image and service quality. Service firms need to manage it carefully, because it can have a profound impact on customers' impressions.

Chapter 11 Managing People for Service Advantage

Introduces people. People play a very important role in services marketing. Many services require direct interaction between customers and contact personnel. The nature of these interactions strongly influences how customers perceive service quality. Hence, service firms devote a significant amount of effort to recruiting, training and motivating employees. Happy employees who perform well are often a source of competitive advantage for a firm.

designing and managing
SERVICE PROCESSES

Figure 8.1 The Merlion is an enduring symbol of Singapore's transition from her humble beginnings to today's thriving services hub.

LEARNING OBJECTIVES

By the end of this chapter, students should be able to:

LO 1 Know how flowcharts are drawn and be familiar with what we can learn from flowcharting a service.

LO 2 Tell the difference between flowcharting and blueprinting.

LO 3 Develop a blueprint for a service process with all the necessary elements in place.

LO 4 Understand how to use fail-proofing to design fail points out of service processes.

LO 5 Recognize how service redesign can help improve both service quality and productivity.

LO 6 Know when customers should be viewed as "co-producers" of service and what the implications are.

LO 7 Understand and manage the factors that lead customers to accept or reject new Self-Service Technologies (SST).

OPENING VIGNETTE[1]

PROCESS REDESIGN IN SINGAPORE'S LIBRARIES

In the digital age, libraries have suffered from reduced usage. Many people now go online to obtain information. The National Library Board of Singapore (NLB) had to work hard to change people's view that the library was a place with bookshelves full of old books and unfriendly staff. They started on a plan to completely change the library system in Singapore. Part of that included redesigning its service processes. Processes are the building blocks of services. They describe the method and sequence in which service operating systems work, show how they link together to create the value proposition that has been promised to customers.

One interesting process that the NLB redesigned was the time-to-shelf process. The time-to-shelf process is the time taken from the point the book is returned, to the time it is back on the shelf. Previously, readers had to return the books to the library that they borrowed it from. With the redesign, books could be returned to any of its many libraries. In addition, books could be returned even if the library was closed. To achieve this, NLB was the first public library in the world to use the Radio Frequency Identification (RFID) technology. RFID tags were installed in its over 10 million books. As readers returned the books through book drops that looked like ATM machines, the books were scanned. Customers received an immediate message that confirmed that the book had registered as "returned." At the same time, library staffs were immediately informed which shelf the book had to be returned to, cutting time-to-shelf to below 15 minutes. Before the process redesign, a book could take up to over seven hours to be returned to the shelf!

To go one step further, one branch even pioneered "smart bookshelves." When a book was either removed or placed on a bookshelf, the RFID technology took note of it. Therefore, if a book was put in the wrong place, the bookshelf "knew" and alerted staff. With a hand-held device, the librarian could then locate the book in moments. This allowed books to be traced easily and both staff and users saved time in not having to search for specific books.

> ...NLB's process redesign has kept pace with the digital age...

It is not easy to create a service, especially one that must be delivered in real time with customers present in the service factory. Marketers and operations specialists need to work together to design services that are both satisfying for customers and efficient from the operations point of view. In the opening story, NLB redesigned the time-to-shelf process and made the job of the shelving staff more efficient. They also reduced the instances of users not being able to locate a book on the shelf even though it has the status of "available" in the catalog system. To help in designing and managing customer service processes, information about the sequence in which customers use the service, and the estimated length of time needed is important. Flowcharting helps to capture this sequence.

LO 1

Know how flowcharts are drawn and be familiar with what we can learn from flowcharting a service.

FLOWCHARTING SERVICE DELIVERY

Flowcharting is a technique for displaying the nature and sequence of the different steps in delivering service to customers. It is a way to understand the total customer service experience. Flowcharting allows us to see the way customer involvement is different for each of the four categories of services introduced in Chapter 1—people processing, possession processing, mental stimulus processing, and information processing. Let us take one example of each category—staying in a motel, getting a DVD player repaired, getting a weather forecast, and buying health insurance. Figure 8.2 displays a simple flowchart that shows what is involved in each of the four scenarios. Imagine that you are the customer. Think about your involvement in the service delivery process and the types of encounters with the organization.

▶ *Stay at a motel (people processing).* It is late evening. You are driving on a long trip and getting tired. You see a motel with a vacancy sign, and the price displayed seems very reasonable. You park your car, noting that the grounds are clean and the buildings look freshly painted. When you enter the reception area, you are greeted by a friendly clerk who checks you in and gives you the key to a room. You move your car to the space in front of the room and let yourself in. After undressing and using the bathroom, you go to bed. After a good night's sleep, you rise the next morning, shower, dress, and pack. Then you walk to the reception. There you have free coffee, juice, and donuts. After breakfast, you return your key to a different clerk, pay, and drive away.

▶ *Repair a DVD player (possession processing).* When you use your DVD player, the picture quality on the TV screen is poor. Fed up with the situation, you search the Online Yellow Pages to find a repair store in your area. At the store, the neatly-dressed technician checks your machine carefully but quickly. He tells you that it needs to be adjusted and cleaned. You are impressed by his professional manner. The estimated price seems reasonable. You are also pleased that repairs are guaranteed for three months, so you agree to the work and are told that the player will be ready in three days' time. The technician disappears into the back office with your machine and you leave the store. When you return to pick up the product, the technician explains the work that he did and demonstrates that the machine is now working well. You pay the agreed price and leave the store with your machine. Back home, you plug in the player, insert a DVD, and find that the picture is now much improved.

PEOPLE PROCESSING - STAY AT MOTEL

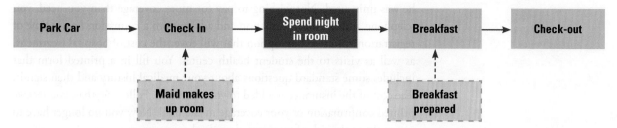

POSSESSION PROCESSING - REPAIR A DVD PLAYER

MENTAL STIMULUS PROCESSING - WEATHER FORECAST

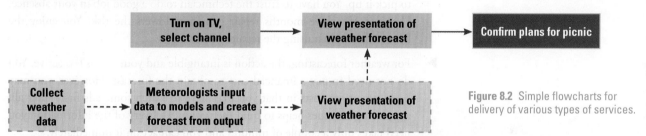

Figure 8.2 Simple flowcharts for delivery of various types of services.

INFORMATION PROCESSING - HEALTH INSURANCE

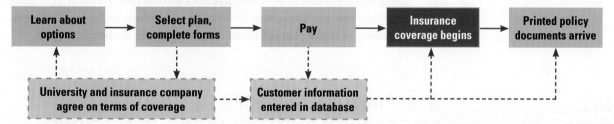

▶ *Weather forecast (mental stimulus processing).* You are planning a picnic trip to the park. However, one of your friends says she heard that it is going to be really cold this weekend. Back home that evening, you check the weather forecast on TV. The meteorologist reports that there is a cold front over the next 72 hours. However, it is north of your area. With this information, you call your friends to tell them that the picnic is on (Figure 8.3).

▶ *Health insurance (information processing).* Your university mails you a package of information before the beginning of the new semester. This package includes a student health service brochure describing a few different health insurance options available to students. Although you consider yourself very healthy, you remember the experience of a friend. Your friend recently had to pay expensive hospital bills for the

Figure 8.3 The weather forecast is an invaluable guide for an outing.

treatment of a badly fractured ankle from his own savings. This was because he was uninsured. Not wishing to pay for more coverage than you need, you telephone and ask for information and advice from a counselor. At the time of registration, you select an option that will cover the cost of hospital treatment, as well as visits to the student health center. You fill in a printed form that includes some standard questions about your medical history and then sign it. The cost of the insurance is added to your term bill. Following that, you receive printed confirmation of your coverage in the mail. Now you no longer have to worry about the risk of unexpected medical expenses.

Insights from Flowcharting

As you can see from these flowcharts, your role as a customer for each of these service products varies sharply from one category to another. The first two examples involve physical processes.

▶ At the motel you make use of a bedroom, bathroom, and other physical facilities such as parking. You have to be physically present to enjoy the benefits.

▶ Your role at the repair store, however, is limited to briefly explaining what is wrong with the machine, leaving the machine, and returning several days later to pick it up. You have to trust the technician to do a good job in your absence. However, the three months repair guarantee lowers the risk. You enjoy the benefits later when using the repaired machine.

▶ For weather forecasting, the action is intangible and your role is less active. You do not need to pay a financial cost to obtain the forecast. However, you may have some time costs in that you may have to watch some ads first. After all, advertising revenues helps to fund the station. Delivery of the information you need takes only a couple of minutes and you can act on it immediately.

▶ Getting health insurance is also an intangible action, but it takes more time and mental effort. You have to assess several options and complete a detailed application form. Then you may have to wait for the policy to be issued, and coverage to begin. Your choice of health plan will reflect the cost relative to the benefits offered.

LO 2

Tell the difference between flowcharting and blueprinting.

BLUEPRINTING SERVICES TO CREATE VALUED EXPERIENCES AND PRODUCTIVE OPERATIONS

A key tool that we use to design new services (or redesign existing ones) is known as *blueprinting*. Blueprinting is a more complex form of *flowcharting*. A flowchart describes an existing process, usually in a fairly simple form. A blueprint, however, specifies in more detail how a service process should be constructed.

Maybe you are wondering where the term blueprinting comes from and why we are using it here. The design for a new building or a ship is usually done on architectural drawings called blueprints. The term "blueprints" is used, because of the drawings used to be printed on special paper, and the drawings and notes appeared in blue. These blueprints show what the product should look like and what specifications it should follow. Unlike the architecture of a building or ship, service processes have a largely intangible structure. That makes them all the more difficult to visualize.

Hence, it is useful to use blueprint-like techniques to describe processes involving flows, sequences, relationships, and dependencies.[2]

Developing a Blueprint

How should you get started on developing a service blueprint?

 LO 3

Develop a blueprint for a service process with all the necessary elements in place.

▶ Identify all the key activities involved in creating and delivering the service.

▶ Specify the linkages between these activities.[3] Initially, it is best to keep activities at the "big picture" level. You can later "drill down" to obtain a higher level of detail. In an airline context, for instance, the passenger activity of "boards aircraft" actually represents a series of actions and can be divided into steps like wait for seat rows to be announced, give agent boarding pass for verification, walk down jetway, enter aircraft, let flight attendant verify boarding pass, find seat, stow carry-on bag, sit down (Figure 8.4).

Advantages of Blueprinting

▶ Blueprinting differentiates between what customers experience "front stage," and the activities of employees and support processes "backstage," where customers cannot see them. Between the two lies what is called the line of visibility. If a firm is too focused on operations, they may manage backstage activities well, but neglect the front stage. But it is front-stage operation that customers experience. Accounting firms, for instance, often have detailed, written procedures and standards for how to conduct an audit. However, they may lack clear standards for hosting a meeting with clients or how staff members should answer the telephone.

Figure 8.4 Baggage collection is one of the last steps in an air travel service process.

▶ Blueprints show how customers and employees interact, and how these are supported by backstage activities and systems. This can help to bring together marketing, operations and human resource management within a firm.

▶ Blueprinting highlight possible *fail points* in the process. When managers are aware of these fail points, they are better able to take steps to prevent failures, or to have back-up plans, or both. This decreases the chance of things going wrong and service failure occurring.

▶ Blueprints can also pinpoint stages in the process where customers commonly have to wait. Marketing and operational specialists can then develop standards for carrying out each activity, including times for completion of a task, and maximum wait times in between tasks (Figure 8.5).

Figure 8.5 Long waiting lines indicate operational problems that need to be addressed.

PART III

In summary, blueprints allow different groups of people in the company to participate in the service improvement process. People from different departments cooperate and work together in a relationship of interdependence. The service blueprint allows them to see the big picture, and they are able to see the part that they play in the overall service experience for the customer.[4]

Blueprinting the Restaurant Experience: A Three-Act Performance

Let us now discuss how a blueprint is done. The example is a blueprint of a high-contact, people-processing service. We look at the experience of dinner for two at Chez Jean. It is an expensive restaurant that enhances its core food service with a variety of other supplementary services (see Figure 8.8, pp. 206-209). In full-service restaurants, the cost of the food ingredients is usually about 20–30 percent of the price of the meal. The balance can be seen as the "fee" that the customer is willing to pay for renting a table and chairs in a pleasant setting, hiring the services of food preparation experts and their kitchen equipment, and providing serving staff to wait on them both inside and outside the dining room.

The key components of the blueprint, reading from top to bottom, are:[5]

1. Service standards for each front-stage activity (only a few examples are actually stated in detail in the figure).

2. Physical and other evidence for front-stage activities (stated for all steps).

3. Main customer actions (Shown by pictures).

4. Line of interaction.

5. Front-stage actions by customer contact personnel.

6. Line of visibility.

7. Backstage actions by customer contact personnel.

8. Support processes involving other service personnel.

9. Support processes involving information technology.

Reading from left to right, the blueprint shows the sequence of actions over time. In Chapter 2, we compared service performances to theater. To highlight the involvement of human actors in service delivery, we use pictures to show each of the 14 main steps involving our two customers (there are other steps not shown). We start with making a reservation and end with them leaving the restaurant after the meal. The "restaurant drama" can be divided into three "acts." These represent activities that take place before the core product is encountered, delivery of the core product (in this case, the meal), and the activities that follow, that still involve the service provider.

The "stage" or servicescape includes both the inside and outside of the restaurant. Restaurants usually decorate their front stage. They use physical evidence such as furnishings, décor, uniforms, lighting, and table settings. They may also use background music to create an environment and atmosphere that matches their market positioning (Figure 8.6).

Act I—Introductory Scenes

In this drama, Act I begins with a customer making a reservation by telephone. This action could take place hours or even days before the visit to the restaurant. In theatrical terms, the telephone conversation is similar to a radio drama. Impressions are created by the nature of the service personnel's voice, speed of response, and style of the conversation. When our customers arrive at the restaurant, a valet parks their car. They leave their coats in the coatroom and enjoy a drink in the bar area while waiting for their table. The act ends with them being brought to a table and seated.

These five steps make up the couple's first experience of the restaurant performance. Each involves an interaction with an employee—by phone or face-to-face. By the time the two of them reach their table in the dining room, they have been exposed to several supplementary services. They have also come into contact with quite a number of cast characters. This includes five or more contact personnel, as well as many other customers.

Standards can be set for each service activity, but should be based on a good understanding of guest expectations (remember our discussion in Chapter 2 of how expectations are formed). Below the line of visibility, the blueprint identifies main actions that are needed to make sure that each front-stage step is performed in a manner that meets or exceeds those expectations. These actions include recording reservations, handling customers' coats, delivery and preparation of food, maintenance of facilities and equipment, training and assignment of staff for each task, and use of information technology to access, input, store, and transfer relevant data.

Figure 8.6 The elegant table setting and interior of an upscale Chinese restaurant clearly communicates its positioning.

Act II—Delivery of the Core Product

As the curtain rises on Act II, our customers are finally about to experience the core service they came for. To keep it simple, we divide the meal into just four scenes. If all goes well, the two guests will have an excellent meal, nicely served in a pleasant atmosphere, and perhaps with a fine wine to enhance it. But if the restaurant fails to satisfy their expectations (and those of its many other guests) during Act II, it is going to be in serious trouble.

After our diners decide on their meals, they place their orders with the server (Figure 8.7). The server must then pass on the details to personnel in the kitchen, bar, and billing desk. Mistakes in the transfer of information are a frequent cause of quality failures in many organizations. Bad handwriting or unclear verbal requests can lead to delivery of the wrong items, or of the right items incorrectly prepared.

Figure 8.7 A waiter in a French restaurant taking orders from a diner.

Managing the Customer Interface **205**

Figure 8.8 Blueprinting a full-service restaurant experience.

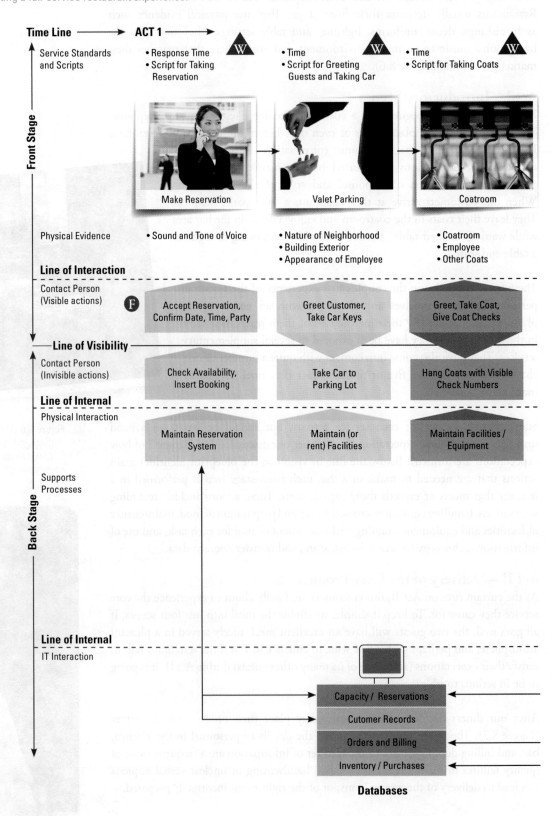

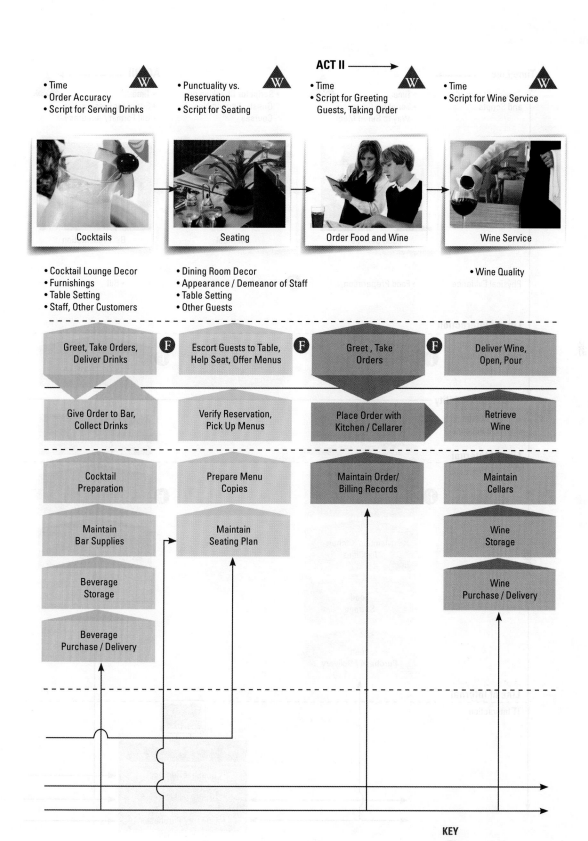

ACT II →

- Time
- Order Accuracy
- Script for Serving Drinks

- Punctuality vs. Reservation
- Script for Seating

- Time
- Script for Greeting Guests, Taking Order

- Time
- Script for Wine Service

Cocktails

Seating

Order Food and Wine

Wine Service

- Cocktail Lounge Decor
- Furnishings
- Table Setting
- Staff, Other Customers

- Dining Room Decor
- Appearance / Demeanor of Staff
- Table Setting
- Other Guests

- Wine Quality

Greet, Take Orders, Deliver Drinks

Escort Guests to Table, Help Seat, Offer Menus

Greet, Take Orders

Deliver Wine, Open, Pour

Give Order to Bar, Collect Drinks

Verify Reservation, Pick Up Menus

Place Order with Kitchen / Cellarer

Retrieve Wine

Cocktail Preparation

Prepare Menu Copies

Maintain Order/ Billing Records

Maintain Cellars

Maintain Bar Supplies

Maintain Seating Plan

Wine Storage

Beverage Storage

Wine Purchase / Delivery

Beverage Purchase / Delivery

KEY

  Points Fail

Risk of Excessive Wait (Standard times should specify limits.)

Figure 8.8 (Continued)

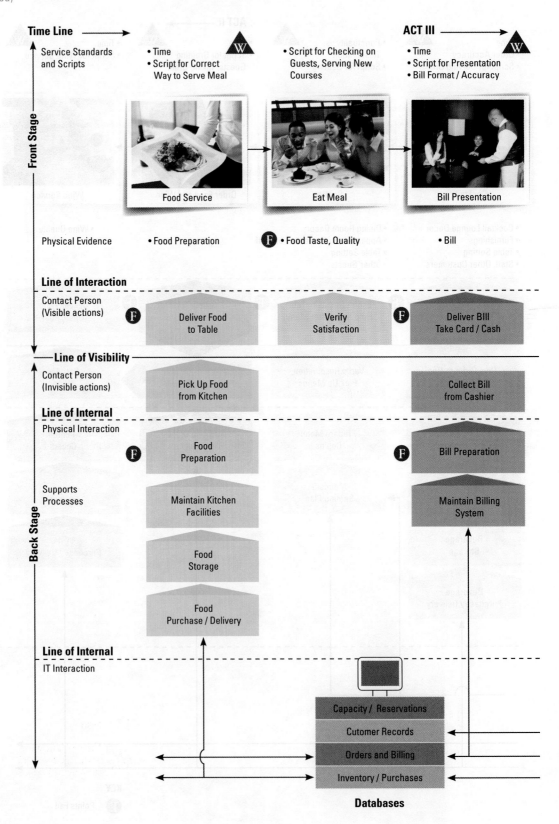

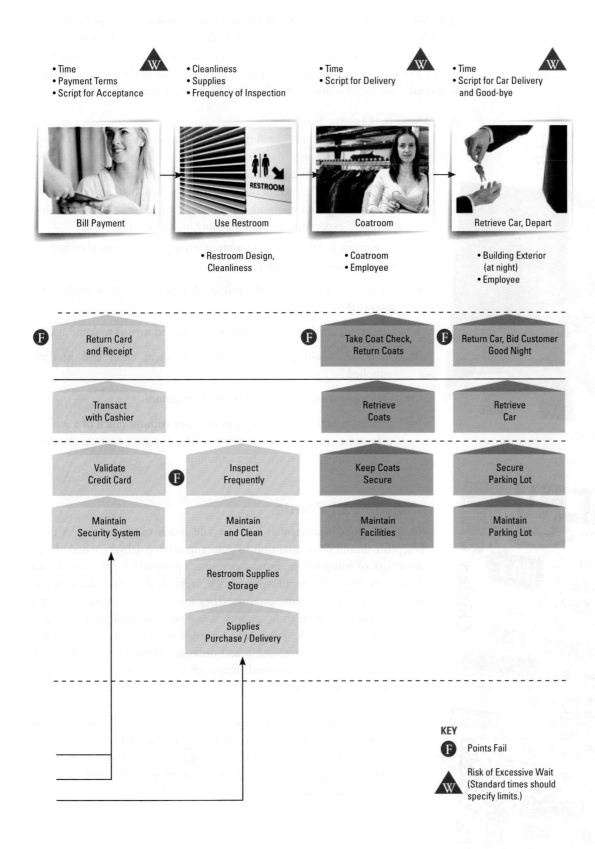

- Time
- Payment Terms
- Script for Acceptance

- Cleanliness
- Supplies
- Frequency of Inspection

- Time
- Script for Delivery

- Time
- Script for Car Delivery and Good-bye

Bill Payment

Use Restroom

Coatroom

Retrieve Car, Depart

- Restroom Design, Cleanliness

- Coatroom
- Employee

- Building Exterior (at night)
- Employee

F Return Card and Receipt

F Take Coat Check, Return Coats

F Return Car, Bid Customer Good Night

Transact with Cashier

Retrieve Coats

Retrieve Car

Validate Credit Card

F Inspect Frequently

Keep Coats Secure

Secure Parking Lot

Maintain Security System

Maintain and Clean

Maintain Facilities

Maintain Parking Lot

Restroom Supplies Storage

Supplies Purchase / Delivery

KEY

F Points Fail

W Risk of Excessive Wait (Standard times should specify limits.)

PART III

In the other scenes of Act II, our customers may assess not only the quality of food and drink—the most important dimension of all—but also the style of service and how quickly it is served (not too quickly, for guests don't want to feel rushed!). Even though a server can perform the job correctly, the experience of the customer can still be spoiled if the server is disinterested, unfriendly, or even overly friendly.

Act III—The Drama Ends

The meal may be over, but much is still taking place both front stage and backstage as the drama moves to its close. The core service has now been delivered, and we will assume that our customers are happily digesting it. Act III should be short. The action in each of the remaining scenes should move smoothly, quickly, and pleasantly, with no shocking surprises at the end. Most customers' expectations would probably include the following:

▶ An accurate bill that is easy to understand is presented quickly when the customer asks for it (Figure 8.9).

▶ Payment is handled politely and quickly (with all major credit cards accepted).

▶ The guests are thanked for their patronage and invited to come again.

▶ Customers visiting the restrooms find them clean and properly supplied.

▶ The right coats are retrieved from the coatroom.

▶ The customer's car is brought to the door without much of a wait, in the same condition as when it was left. The attendant thanks them again and wishes them a good evening.

Identify Fail Points

Running a good restaurant is not easy and much can go wrong. A good blueprint should draw attention to points in service delivery where things are at risk of going wrong. From a customer's perspective, the most serious fail points, marked in our blueprint by 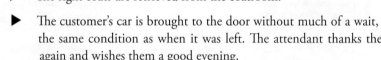, are those that will result in failure to access or enjoy the core product. They involve the reservation (Could the customer get through by phone? Was a table available at the desired time and date?, Was the reservation recorded accurately?), seating (Was a table available when promised?), and ordering (Is the menu information complete? Can it be understood? Is everything on the menu available this evening?). (Figure 8.10)

Since service delivery takes place over time, there is also the possibility of delays between specific actions, requiring the customers to wait. Common locations for such waits are identified by W. Excessive waits will annoy customers. In practice, every step in the process—both front stage and backstage—has some potential for failures and delays.

Figure 8.9 The billing process should be quick and painless to ensure customer convenience.

Figure 8.10 A disorganized menu can frustrate a customer to no end.

David Maister coined the term OTSU ("opportunity to screw up") to stress the importance of thinking about all the things that might go wrong in delivering a particular type of service.[6] It is only by identifying all the possible OTSUs associated with a particular process that service managers can put together a delivery system that is designed to avoid such problems.

Use Failure Proofing to Design Fail Points Out of Service Processes[7]

 LO 4

Understand how to use fail-proofing to design fail points out of service processes.

Once fail points have been identified, careful analysis of the reasons for failure in service processes is necessary. This analysis often reveals opportunities for "failure proofing" certain activities in order to reduce or even eliminate the risk of errors. Fail-safe methods need to be designed not only for employees but also for customers.

One of the most useful Total Quality Management (TQM) methods in manufacturing is the application of poka-yoke, or fail-safe methods to prevent errors in manufacturing processes. Richard Chase and Douglas Stewart introduced this concept to fail-safe service processes.[8]

Server poka-yokes ensure that service staffs do things correctly, as requested, in the right order and at the right speed. Examples include surgeons whose surgical instrument trays have indentations for each instrument. For a given operation, all the instruments are nested in the tray so it is clear if the surgeon has not removed all instruments from the patient before closing the incision (Figure 8.11).

Some service firms use poka-yokes to ensure that certain steps or standards in the customer-staff interaction are adhered to. A bank ensures eye contact by requiring tellers to record the customer's eye color on a checklist at the start of a transaction. Some firms place mirrors at the exits of staff areas to foster a neat appearance. Front line staff can then automatically check their appearance before greeting a customer. At one restaurant, servers place round coasters in front of those diners who have ordered a decaffeinated coffee and square coasters in front of the others.

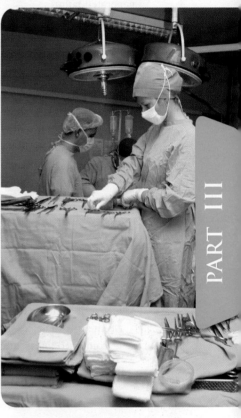

Figure 8.11 The practice of poka-yoke is observed in the operating room.

Customer poka-yokes usually focus on preparing the customer for the encounter (including getting them to bring the right materials for the transaction and to arrive on time, if applicable), understanding and anticipating their role in the service transaction, and selecting the correct service or transaction. Examples that prepare the customer for the encounter include printing dress code requests on invitations, sending reminders of dental appointments, and printing guidelines on customer cards (e.g. "please have your account and pin number ready before calling our service reps"). Poka-yokes that address customer errors during the encounter include beepers at automated teller machines (ATMs) so that customers do not forget to take their card, locks on aircraft lavatory doors that must be closed to switch on the lights. Most of the procedures seem trivial, but this is actually a key advantage of this method.

Designing poka-yokes and fail-proofing service processes is part art and part science. Service Insights 8.1 provides a three-step framework to prevent customer failures. The same three steps can also be used for addressing employee errors.

::: SERVICE INSIGHTS 8.1

Framework to Prevent Customer Failures

Companies can use service redesign to improve reliability and quality. If the service fails, they can have good service recovery procedures in place. However, it can be hard to fix failures caused by customers themselves. A good way is to employ the following three-step approach to prevent customer-generated failures.

1 Systematically collect information on the most common failure points.

2 Identify their root causes. It is important to note that an employee's explanation may not be the true cause. Instead, the cause must be investigated from the customer's point of view. Human causes of customer failure include lack of needed skills, failure to understand role, and insufficient preparation. Shortcomings in processes may often involve slowness, excessive complexity, and lack of clarity. Other causes may include weaknesses in design of the servicescape and poorly designed technology, such as self-service machines that are not user friendly.

3 Create strategies to prevent the failures identified. The five strategies listed below may need to be combined for maximum effectiveness.

(a) redesign processes (e.g. redesign customers' role as well as processes). For example, customers may now have the option of borrowing library books through vending machines, which is very different from borrowing a book from the library itself.

(b) Use technology (e.g. use information systems to help customers make choices from a large set). For example, financial service firms may use technology to help customers self-diagnose their financial needs and select a suitable portfolio of investments for retirement.

(c) Manage customer behavior (e.g. remind customers when payment is due, reward them for avoiding failure).

(d) Encourage "customer citizenship" (e.g. customers help one another to prevent failure like in weight loss programs).

(e) Improve the servicescape (e.g. impacts customer experiences and contributes to failures). Many firms forget that customers need user-friendly directional signs to help them find their way around, failing which, they might be very frustrated.

Helping customers to avoid failure can become a source of competitive advantage, especially when companies increasingly deploy self-service technologies.

SOURCE

Tax, S. S., Colgate, M., & Bowen, D. E. (2006). How to prevent your customers from failing. *Sloan Management Review,* (Spring), 30–38.

SERVICE PROCESS REDESIGN

While we can fail proof processes to decrease the chances of anything going wrong, there would come a time when processes become outdated. When this happens, service processes should be redesigned. However, that does not mean that the processes were poorly designed in the first place. Rather, changes in technology, customer needs, added service features and new offerings have made existing processes crack and creak.[9] Mitchell T. Rabkin MD, formerly President of Boston's Beth Israel Hospital (now Beth Israel Deaconess Medical Center), characterized the problem as "institutional rust" and declared: "Institutions are like steel beams—they tend to rust. What was once smooth and shiny and nice tends to become rusty."[10] He suggested that there were two main reasons for this situation. The first involves changes in the external environment. Some practices may no longer be needed. Therefore, there may be a need to redesign the underlying processes, or even create brand-new processes so that the organization can remain relevant and responsive. In healthcare, such changes may reflect new forms of competition, legislation, technology, health insurance policies, and changing customer needs (Figure 8.12).

Figure 8.12 Healthcare needs to be redesigned to meet customers' needs.

The second reason for institutional rusting occurs internally. Often, it reflects a natural weakening of internal processes, rules and regulations, or the development of unofficial standards (see Service Insights 8.2). There are many symptoms that indicate the processes are not working well and need to be redesigned. They include:

▶ A lot of information exchange.

▶ Data that is not useful.

▶ A high ratio of checking or control activities to value-adding activities.

▶ Increased processing of exceptions.

▶ Growing numbers of customer complaints about inconvenient and unnecessary procedures.

In fact, examining blueprints of existing services may suggest opportunities for product improvement. These opportunities will then result in efficiencies for the service firm and increased perception of service quality by customers.

Rooting Out **Unofficial Standards** in a Hospital

One of the special characteristics of Mitchell T. Rabkin as president of Boston's Beth Israel Hospital was his policy of regularly visiting all areas of the hospital. He usually did so unannounced. No one working at the hospital was surprised to see Dr. Rabkin drop by at almost any time of the day or night. His natural curiosity gave him a lot of insights into how effectively service procedures were working and the hardly noticeable ways in which things could go wrong. As the following story reveals, he discovered that messages often change over time.

> One day, I was in the EU [emergency unit], chatting with a house officer [physician] who was treating a patient with asthma. He was giving her medication through an intravenous drip. I looked at the formula for the medication and asked him, "Why are you using this particular cocktail?" "Oh," he replied, "that's hospital policy." Since I was certain that there was no such policy, I decided to investigate.

What had happened went something like this. A few months earlier, Resident [physician] A says to Intern B, who is observing her treat a patient: "This is what I use for asthma." On the next month's rotation, Intern B says to new Resident C: "This is what Dr. A uses for asthma." The following month, Resident C says to Intern D, "This is what we use for asthma." And finally, within another month, Intern D is telling Resident E, "It's hospital policy to use this medication."

As a result of conversations like these, well-intentioned but unofficial standards keep appearing. It is a particular problem in a place like the hospital as there isn't an inhuman policy manual where one must look up the policy for everything one does. One always has to be aware of the growth of institutional rust and to be clear about what is being done and why it is being done.

SOURCE

Lovelock, C. (1994). *Product Plus.* New York: McGraw-Hill. p. 355.

Service Process Redesign Should Improve Both Service Quality and Productivity

Managers in charge of service process redesign projects should look for opportunities to achieve a great leap in both service quality and productivity at the same time. Redesigning the ways in which tasks are performed has great potential to increase output, especially in many backstage jobs.[11] Redesign efforts typically focus on achieving the following key performance measures:

1. Increased customer satisfaction.

2. Improved productivity

3. Reduced number of service failures,

4. Reduced cycle time (i.e. the time from start of a service process to its completion) Ideally, redesign efforts achieve all the four measures simultaneously!

Service process redesign includes reconstruction, rearrangement, or substitution of service processes. Berry and Lampo identified the following five service redesign concepts: self-service, direct service, pre-service, bundled service, and physical service. We expanded some of these concepts in this section to embrace more of the productivity enhancing aspects of process redesign such as eliminating non-value adding work steps in all stages of service delivery.[12] These efforts can be grouped into a few types, including:

▶ Getting rid of non-value adding steps—Often, activities at the front-end and back-end processes of services can be simplified so that the benefit-producing part of the service encounter can be focused on. For example, a customer wanting to rent a car is not interested in filling out forms, or processing payment and check of the returned car. Service redesign simplifies these tasks by trying to get rid of non-value adding steps. Now, some car rental companies allow customers to rent a car online. The car is returned to the car park where it was collected from, the key is returned to a safe deposit box, and the customer does not have to come into contact with service personnel. The outcomes are typically increased productivity and customer satisfaction.

▶ Shifting to self-service—There can be great gains in productivity and sometimes even service quality when there is increasing self-service (Figure 8.13). For example, FedEx succeeded in shifting more than 50 percent of its transactions from its call centers to its website, thus reducing the number of employees in its call centers by some 20,000 persons.[13]

▶ Delivering direct service—This type of redesign involves bringing the service to the customer instead of bringing the customer to the service firm. This is often done to improve convenience for the customer, but can also result in productivity gains if companies can do away with expensive downtown rentals for their physical locations.

LO 5
Recognize how service redesign can help improve both service quality and productivity.

Figure 8.13 When firms shift to self-service, they may require the services of shipping firms like Cosco to help in delivering the core product to the customer.

▶ Bundling services—Bundling services involves bundling, or grouping, multiple services into one offer, for a particular customer group. Bundling can help increase productivity and customer satisfaction. The bundle is already tightly tailored for a particular segment so it fits their needs well. This makes transactions faster and reduces the marketing costs for each service.

▶ Redesigning the physical aspects of service processes—Physical service redesign focuses on the tangible elements of a service process, and includes changes to the service facilities and equipment to improve the service experience. This leads to convenience and productivity, and often also enhances the satisfaction and productivity of frontline staff.

Table 8.1 summarizes the five types of service process redesign. There is an overview of their potential benefits for the firm and its customers, and also potential challenges or limitations. You should note that these redesigns are often used in combination.

Table 8.1 Five types of service redesign.

Approach and Concept	Potential Company Benefits	Potential Customer Benefits	Challenges / Limitations
Elimination of non-value-added steps (streamlines process)	• Improved efficiency • Increases productivity • Increases ability to customize service • Differentiates company	• Improved efficiency, speed • Shift tasks from customer to service firm • Separate service activation from delivery • Customizes service	• Requires customer education and employee training to implement smoothly and effectively
Self-service (customer assumes role of producer)	• Lowers cost • Improves productivity • Enhances technology reputation • Differentiates company	• Increases speed of service • Improves access • Saves money • Increases perception of control	• Must prepare customers for the role • Limits face-to-face inter-action and opportunities tp build relationships • Harder to get customer feedback
Direct service (service delivered to the customer's location)	• Eliminates store location limitations • Expands customer base • Differentiates company	• Increases convenience • Improves access	• Imposes logistical burdens • May be costly • Needs credibility and trust
Bundled service (combines multiple services into a package)	• Differentiates company • Aids customer retention • Increases per-capita service use	• Increases convenience • Customizes service	• Requires extensive knowledge of targeted customers • May be perceived as wasteful
Physical service (manipulation of tangibles associated with the service)	• Improves employee satisfaction • Increases productivity • Differentiates company	• Increases convenience • Enhances function • Generates interest	• Easily imitated • Requires expense to effect and maintain • Raises customer expectations for the industry

THE CUSTOMER AS CO-PRODUCER

 LO 6

Know when customers should be viewed as "co-producers" of service and what the implications are.

Customers are often involved in the production of the service. Blueprinting helps to specify the role of customers in the service delivery process and allows us to see if the customer has to be actively involved in producing the service or not.

Levels of Customer Participation

Customer participation refers to the actions and resources supplied by customers during service production and/or delivery, including mental, physical, and even emotional inputs.[14] In people-processing services, there will be some form of customer participation. Customer participation in services varies widely, and can be divided into three broad levels.[15]

Low Participation Level

Employees and systems do all the work. Service products tend to be standardized. Payment may be the only thing that the customer needs to be involved in. In situations where customers come to the service factory, all that is needed is the customers' physical presence. Visiting a movie theater or taking a bus are examples. In possession-processing services such as routine cleaning or maintenance, customers can remain entirely uninvolved with the process other than allowing service providers to enter their premises, and making payment (Figure 8.14).

Moderate Participation Level

Customers need to help the firm in creating and delivering service. For example, they may need to provide information, put in personal effort, or provide physical possessions. When getting their hair washed and cut, customers must let the hairstylist know what they want and cooperate during the different steps in the process. If a client wants an accountant to prepare a tax return, she must first get the information and physical documentation that the accountant can use to prepare the return correctly. Then the customer must be prepared to answer any questions that the accountant may have.

High Participation Level

In these instances, customers work actively with the provider to co-produce the service. Service cannot be created without the customer's active participation (Figure 8.15).

Figure 8.14 Possession-processing services like gardening have little customer involvement.

Figure 8.15 Yoga classes are services that require high participation from the customer.

In fact, if customers do not play their part well, it will affect the quality of the service outcome. Marriage counseling and educational services fall into this category. In weight loss or rehabilitation, the goal is to improve the patient's physical condition. However, the patient has to play an active part to help, by perhaps closely following a dietary and exercise plan provided by the doctor. Successful delivery of many business-to-business services requires customers and providers to work closely together as members of a team, such as for management consulting and supply chain management services.

Customers as Partial Employees

Some researchers argue that firms should view customers as "partial employees," who can influence the productivity and quality of service processes and outputs.[16] This view needs a change in the way management think, as Schneider and Bowen make clear:

> If you think of customers as partial employees, you begin to think very differently about what you hope customers will bring to the service encounter. Now they must bring not only expectations and needs but also relevant service production competencies that will enable them to fill the role of partial employees. The service management challenge deepens accordingly.[17]

Effective human resource management starts with recruitment and selection. The same process should be true for "partial employees." So if co-production requires certain types of skills, firms should target their marketing efforts to get new customers who have the needed skills to do the tasks.[18] After all, many colleges do just this in their student selection process! When the relationship is not working out, there may be no choice but to end the relationship. Doctors have a legal and ethical duty to help their patients. However, the relationship will only succeed if the doctor and patient cooperate with each other (Figure 8.16). Sooner or later most doctors encounter a patient so uncooperative in terms of following a prescribed treatment, dishonest, or troublesome that the doctor simply has to ask that individual to seek care elsewhere.[19]

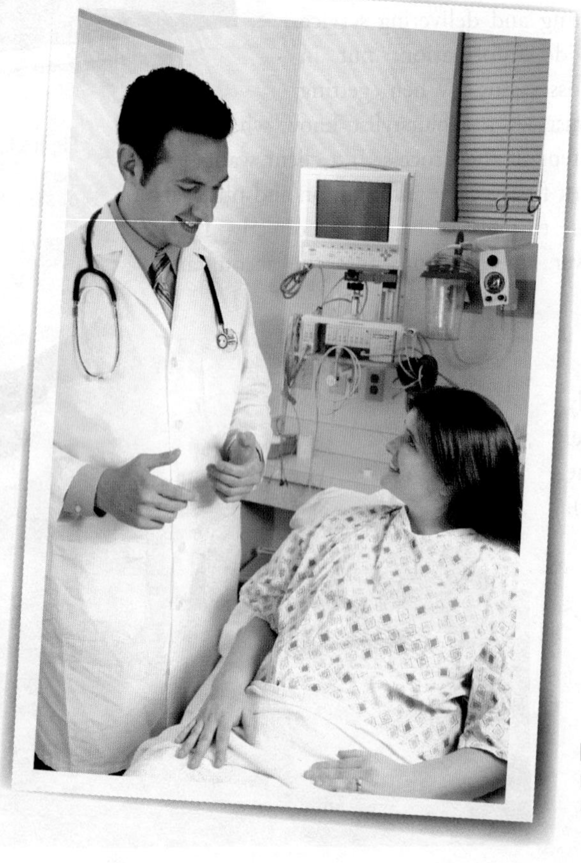

Figure 8.16 Doctor-patient relationships must be mutually cooperative for effective treatment.

SELF SERVICE TECHNOLOGIES

LO 7

Understand and manage the factors that lead customers to accept or reject new Self-Service Technologies (SSTs).

The greatest form of involvement in service production is for customers to take on the whole activity themselves. This often means they use facilities or systems provided by the service firm. The customer's time and effort replaces that of a service employee. In the case of telephone and Internet-based services, customers even provide their own terminals (Figure 8.17).

Consumers are faced with a variety of SSTs that allow them to produce a service without direct service employee involvement.[20] SSTs include automated banking terminals, self-service scanning at supermarket checkouts, self-service gasoline pumps, and automated telephone systems such as phone banking, automated hotel check-out, and numerous Internet-based services.

Information-based services can easily be offered using SSTs. These services include not only such supplementary services as getting information, placing orders and reservations and making payment, but also delivery of core products in fields such as banking, research, entertainment, and self-paced education. One innovation that has had a great impact in the Internet age has been the development of online auctions, led by eBay. No human auctioneer is needed to go between buyers and sellers. Many companies have developed strategies designed to encourage customers to serve themselves through the World Wide Web. They hope that this will result in customers reducing the use of more expensive alternatives like direct contact with employees, use of intermediaries like brokers and travel agents, or voice-to-voice telephone. However, not all customers use SSTs. Matthew Meuter and his colleagues observe: "For many firms, often the challenge is not managing the technology but rather getting consumers to try the technology."[21]

Figure 8.17 Many Internet-based services require customers to serve themselves.

Psychological Factors Related to Use of SSTs

Given the large amount of time and money needed for firms to design, implement, and manage SSTs, it is very important for service marketers to understand how consumers decide between using an SST option and relying on a human provider. We need to recognize that there are both advantages and disadvantages to using SSTs. The advantages of using SSTs are

▶ time savings,

▶ cost savings,

▶ flexibility,

▶ convenience of location,

▶ greater control over service delivery, and

▶ higher perceived level of customization.

Customers may also derive fun, enjoyment and even spontaneous delight from SST usage.[22] However, some consumers see the introduction of SSTs into the service encounters as something of a threat. If they are uncomfortable with using SSTs, they may feel anxious and stressed.[23] Some consumers see service encounters as social experiences and prefer to deal with people, whereas others avoid such contact on purpose to save time. Research has shown that a number of attitudes drive customer intentions to use a specific SST. These include global attitudes toward related service technologies, global attitudes toward the specific service firm, and attitudes toward its employees.[24]

What Aspects of SSTs Please or Annoy Customers?

Research suggests that customers both love and hate SSTs.[25] They love SSTs when:

▶ They help them to get out of difficult situations. This is often because SST machines are conveniently located and accessible 24/7. As Figure 8.18 shows, a web site is as close as the nearest computer. Therefore, this is easier to get to than the company's physical sites.

▶ Customers also love SSTs when they perform better than the service employee. For example, SSTs allow users to get detailed information and complete transactions faster than they could get through face-to-face or telephone contact. Experienced travelers rely on SSTs to save time and effort at airports, rental car facilities, and hotels. As a *Wall Street Journal* article summarized the trend, "Have A Pleasant Trip: Eliminate Human Contact."[26] Sometimes, a well-designed SST can deliver better service than a human being. Said one customer about the experience of buying convenience store items from a new model of automated vending machine, "A guy in the store can make a mistake or give you a hard time, but not the machine. I definitely prefer the machine."[27] In short, many customers like SSTs when they work well.

Figure 8.18 An Internet kiosk with a touchscreen in Vienna, Austria. The growing number of Internet kiosks available in public areas like libraries, airport halls and hotel lobbies means visiting companies online is more convenient than going to the actual site.

However, customers hate SSTs when they fail.

▶ Users get angry when they find that machines are out of service, their pin numbers are rejected, web sites are down, or tracking numbers do not work.

▶ Even when SSTs do work, customers dislike poorly designed technologies that make service processes difficult to understand and use. A common complaint is difficulty in finding one's way around a web site.

▶ Users also get frustrated when they themselves mess up, due to mistakes such as forgetting their passwords, failing to provide information as requested, or simply hitting the wrong button (Figure 8.19). Self-service logically implies that customers can cause their own dissatisfaction. But even when it is the customers' own fault, they may still blame the service provider for not providing a simpler and more user-friendly system.[28]

A problem with SSTs is that so few of them include effective service recovery systems. Very often, when the process fails, there is no simple way to solve the problem on the spot. Usually, customers are forced to telephone or make a personal visit to solve the problem. This may be exactly what they were trying to avoid in the first place! Mary Jo Bitner suggests that managers should put their firms' SSTs to the test by asking the following basic questions:[29]

▶ *Does the SST work reliably?* Firms must make sure that SSTs work as promised and that the design is user friendly for customers. Southwest Airlines' online ticketing has set a high standard for simplicity and reliability. It boasts of

Figure 8.19 Customers feel frustrated when they get stuck in poorly designed online self-service processes.

the highest percentage of online ticket sales of any airline—clear evidence of customer acceptance.

▶ *Is the SST better than the interpersonal alternative?* If it does not save time or provide ease of access, cost savings, or some other benefit, then customers will continue to use the familiar interpersonal choice. Amazon.com's success reflects its efforts to create a highly personalized, efficient alternative to visiting a retail store.

▶ *If it fails, what systems are in place to recover?* It is very important for firms to provide systems, structures, and recovery technologies that will allow timely service recovery when things go wrong (Figure 8.20). Some banks have a phone beside each ATM. This links customers to a 24-hour customer service center, if they have questions or run into difficulties. Supermarkets that have installed self-service checkout lanes usually get one employee to keep watch on the lanes. This practice combines security with customer assistance. In telephone-based service systems, well-designed voicemail menus include an option for customers to reach a customer service representative.

Figure 8.20 As a fail-safe measure, departmental stores normally have employees on standby near self-checkout lanes to react to problems.

CHAPTER SUMMARY

LO 1 ▶ Flowcharting is a technique for displaying the nature and sequence of the different steps in delivering a service to the customer. It is a simple way to understand the total customer service experience and allows us to understand the nature of customer involvement.

LO 2 ▶ Blueprinting is a more detailed form of flowcharting. It clearly shows the front-stage and backstage activities, and supplies information flows.

LO 3 ▶ o The front-stage activities in the blueprint show the overall customer experience, the desired output, and the sequence in which delivery of that output should take place. Specific times can be set for the completion of each task and the acceptable wait between each customer activity.

o The blueprint also specifies the tasks that must be performed backstage to support a particular front-stage activity.

o It identifies the need for purchase and delivery of supplies and the role of information systems.

o Finally, service standards should be established for each activity, reflecting customer expectations.

LO 4 ▶ A good blueprint draws attention to fail points in service delivery where things can go wrong. Fail-safe methods, also called poka-yokes, can then be designed to prevent such failures for both employees and customers.

The following three-step approach can be used to prevent employee and customer generated failures:

1. Collecting information on the most common fail points.
2. Identifying the root causes of those failures, and
3. Creating strategies to prevent the failures that have been identified.

LO 5 ▶ Changes in technology, customer needs and service offerings require customer service processes to be redesigned. Such service process redesign efforts aim to:

1. Increase customer satisfaction,
2. Improve productivity,
3. Reduce number of service failures, and
4. Reduce cycle time.

▶ There are five types of service process redesign. They are:

1. Elimination of non-value-adding steps (streamlining processes).
2. Shifting to self-service.
3. Delivering direct service (services delivered to the customer's location).
4. Bundling services (combining multiple services into a package).
5. Redesigning the physical aspects of service processes (e.g. service environment, and equipment).

LO 6 ▶ Customers are also often involved in service processes as co-producers and therefore can be thought of as "partial employees." Their performance affects the quality and productivity of output. Therefore, service firms need to educate and train customers so that they have the skills and motivation needed to perform their tasks well.

LO 7 ▶ The greatest form of customer involvement is self-service. Here, customers take on the entire service activity themselves. Most people welcome SSTs that offer more convenience in terms of locations served, 24/7 availability, and faster service. However, poorly designed technology and inadequate education in how to use SST can cause customers to reject SSTs.

UNLOCK YOUR LEARNING

These keywords are found within the sections of each Learning Objective (LO). They are integral in understanding the services marketing concepts taught in each section. Having a firm grasp of these keywords and how they are used is essential in helping you do well for your course, and in the real and very competitive marketing scene out there.

LO 1
1. Flowcharting
2. People processing
3. Possession processing
4. Information processing
5. Mental-stimulus processing

LO 2
6. Blueprinting

LO 3
7. Backstage
8. Components of the blueprint
9. Developing a service blueprint
10. Fail points
11. Front-stage
12. Line of visibility
13. Line of interaction
14. OTSU "Opportunity To Screw Up"
15. Support processes
16. Service performances

LO 4
17. Failure proofing
18. Fail-safe methods

19. Institutional rust
20. Poka-yoke
21. Service process redesign

LO 5
22. Bundling
23. Delivering direct service
24. Non-value adding
25. Physical service redesign

LO 6
26. Customer as co-producer
27. Customer participation
28. High participation
29. Low participation
30. Moderate participation
31. Partial employees

LO 7
32. Information-based services
33. Self-service
34. Self-service technologies

How well do you know the language of services marketing? Quiz yourself!

 Not for the academically faint-of-heart

For each keyword you are able to recall without referring to earlier pages, give yourself a point (and a pat on the back). Tally your score at the end and see if you earned the right to be called—a *services marketeer*.

SCORE

0 – 5	Services Marketing is done a great disservice.
6 – 11	The midnight oil needs to be lit, pronto.
12 – 18	I know what you *didn't* do all semester.
19 – 24	A close shave with success.
25 – 30	Now, go forth and market.
31 – 34	There should be a marketing concept named after you.

Review Questions

1. How does flowcharting help us to understand the difference between people processing services, possession processing services, mental stimulus processing services and information processing services?

2. How does blueprinting help in designing, managing and redesigning service processes?

3. How can fail-safe methods help to reduce service failures?

4. Why is process redesign necessary after some time?

5. How can customer service processes be redesigned?

6. Why do we need to think of customers as partial employees?

7. What makes customers like and use SSTs? What makes customers dislike and reject SSTs?

◀ **WORK YOUR ESM** ▶

Application Exercises

1. Prepare a blueprint for a service with which you are familiar. On completion, consider (a) what are the tangible indicators of quality from the customers' point of view considering the line of visibility, (b) whether all steps in the process are necessary, (c) the location of potential fail points and how they could be designed out of the process, or if they cannot be prevented, what service recovery procedures could be introduced, and (d) what are possible measures of process performance.

2. Think about what happens in a doctor's office when a patient comes for a physical examination. How much participation is needed from the patient in order for the process to work smoothly? If a patient refuses to cooperate, how can that affect the process? What can the doctor do in advance, to ensure that the patient cooperates in the delivery of the process?

3. Observe supermarket shoppers who use self-service checkout lanes and compare them to those who use the services of a checker. What differences do you observe? How many of those conducting self-service scanning appear to run into difficulties and how do they get their problems solved?

• ENDNOTES

1   Johnston, R., Hin, C. K., Wirtz, J., & Lovelock, C. (2007). *Singapore's libraries: Re-inventing library services: Continuity with change.* National Library Board Singapore.

2   Shostack, G. L. (1992). Understanding services through blueprinting. In T. Schwartz et al. (Eds.), *Advances in Services Marketing and Management* (pp. 75–90). Greenwich, CT: JAI Press.

3   Shostack, G. L. (1984). Designing services that deliver. *Harvard Business Review*, (January–February), pp. 133–139.

4   Bitner, M. J., Ostrom, A. L., & Morgan, F. N. (2007). Service blueprinting: A practical tool for service innovation. Working paper, Center for Services Leadership, Arizona State University.

5   We modified and simplified an approach & blueprinting originally proposed by Jane Kingman-Brundage; see Kingman-Brundage J. (1989). The ABCs of service system blueprinting. In M.J. Bitner & L. A. Crosby (Eds.), *Designing a Winning Service Strategy.* Chicago: American Marketing Association.

6   Maister, D. (1980) Now president of Maister Associates, coined the term OTSU while teaching at Harvard Business School.

7   Based in part on Chase, R. B., & Stewart, D. M. (1994). Make your service fail-safe. *Sloan Management Review* (Spring), pp. 35–44.

8   Chase, R. B., & Stewart, D. M. (1994). Make your service fail-safe. *Sloan Management Review* (Spring). pp. 35-44.

9   Wirtz, J., & Tomlin, M. (2000). Institutionalizing customer-driven learning through fully integrated customer feedback systems. *Managing Service Quality,* 10(4). pp. 205–215.

10 Rabkin, M.T.,MD, cited in Lovelock, C. H. (1994). *Product Plus* (pp. 354-55). New York: McGraw-Hill.

11 See, for example, Hammer, M., & Champy, J. (1993). *Reeingineering the corporation.* New York: Harper Business.

12 This section is partially based on Berry and Sandra K. Lampo, Teaching an old service new tricks – the promise of service redesign. *Journal of Service Research,* 2(3),(February),pp. 265–275. Berry and Lampo identified the following five service redesign concepts: self-service, direct service, pre-service, bundled service, and physical service. We expanded some of these concepts in this section to embrace more of the productivity enhancing aspects of process redesign such as eliminating non-value adding work steps in all stages of service delivery.

13 Berry, L. L., & Lampo, S. K. (2000). Teaching an old service new tricks: The promise of service redesign. *Journal of Service Research,* 2(3), pp. 265–275.

14 Rodie, A. R., & Klein, S. S. (2000). Customer participation in services production and delivery In T. A. Schwartz, & D. Iacobucci (Eds.), *Handbook of Service Marketing and Management* (pp. 111–125). Thousand Oaks, CA: Sage Publications, pp. 111–125.

15 Bitner, M. J., Faranda, W. T., Hubbert, A. R., & Zeithaml, V. A. (1997). Customer contributions and roles in service delivery. *International Journal of Service Industry Management,* 8(3), pp.193–205.

16 Bowen, D. E. (1986). Managing customers as human resources in service organizations. *Human Resources Management,* 3, pp. 371–383.

17 Schneider, B., & Bowen, D. E. *op cit,* p. 85.

18 Canziani, B. F. (1997). Leveraging customer competency in service firms. *International Journal of Service Industry Management,* 8(1). pp. 5–25.

19 Painter, K. (2003). Cutting ties to vexing patients. *USA Today,* (January). 8D.

20 Meuter, M. L., Ostrom, A. L., Roundtree, R. I., & Bitner, M. J. (2000). Self-service technologies: Understanding customer satisfaction with technology-based service encounters. *Journal of Marketing,* 64(July), pp. 50–64.

21 Meuter, M. L., Bitner, M. J., Ostrom, A. L., & Brown, S. W. (2005). Choosing among alternative service delivery modes: An investigation of customer trial of self-service technologies. *Journal of Marketing,* 69(April), pp. 61–83.

22 Dabholkar, P. A. (1996). Consumer evaluations of new technology-based self-service options: An investigation of alternative models of service quality. *International Journal of Research in Marketing,* 13, pp. 29–51; Bitner, M. J., Brown, S. W., & Meuter, M. L. (2000). Technology infusion in service encounters. *Journal of the Academy of Marketing Science,* 28(1), pp. 138–149; Dabholkar et al., 2003 *op. cit.*

23 Mick, D. G., & Fournier, S.(1998). Paradoxes of technology: Consumer cognizance, emotions, and coping strategies. *Journal of Consumer Research,* 25(September), pp. 123–143.

24 Curran, J. M., Meuter, M. L., & Surprenant, C. G. (2003). Intentions to use self-service technologies: A confluence of multiple attitudes. *Journal of Service Research,* 5(February), pp. 209–224.

25 Meuter et al, 2000; Bitner, M. J. (2001). Self-service technologies: What do customers expect? *Marketing Management,* (Spring), pp. 10–11.

26 Stringer, K. (2002, October 31). Have a pleasant trip: Eliminate all human contact. *Wall Street Journal.*

27 Rayport, L. F., & Jaworski, B. J. (2004). Best face forward. *Harvard Business Review,* 82(December).

28 Bendapudi, N., & Leone, R. P. (2003). Psychological implications of customer participation in co-production. *Journal of Marketing,* 67(January), pp. 14–28.

29 Bitner, 2001, *op.cit.*

balancing demand against
PRODUCTIVE CAPACITY

LEARNING OBJECTIVES

By the end of this chapter, students should be able to:

▶ **LO 1** Define productive capacity.

▶ **LO 2** Know the different demand-supply situations that fixed capacity firms may face.

▶ **LO 3** Use capacity management techniques to match demand variations.

▶ **LO 4** Recognize that demand varies by segment and identify the patterns of demand.

▶ **LO 5** Know the five basic ways to manage demand.

▶ **LO 6** Use marketing to reshape demand patterns.

▶ **LO 7** Inventory demand through queuing systems.

▶ **LO 8** Understand how customers feel about waiting and make waiting less burdensome for them.

▶ **LO 9** Know the benefits of having an effective reservations system and understand what is involved in designing one.

Figure 9.1 The beauty and splendor of Tungudalur, a ski resort in Westfjords, Iceland, is now enjoyed all year-long.

OPENING VIGNETTE

SUMMER ON THE SKI SLOPES

It used to be that ski resorts shut down once the snow melted and no skiing could be done on the slopes. The lifts stopped operating, the restaurants closed, and the lodges were locked until the next winter.

In due course, however, some ski operators recognized that a mountain offers summer pleasures too. They kept lodging and restaurants open for hikers and picnickers. Some even built Alpine Slides—curving tracks in which wheeled toboggans could run from the top of the mountain to the base. This created demand for tickets on the ski lifts.

The arrival of the mountain biking craze created opportunities for equipment rentals as well as chairlift rides. Killington Resort in Vermont has long encouraged summer visitors to ride to the top, see the view, and eat at the mountaintop restaurant. Now however, it also enjoys a booking business in renting mountain bikes and related equipment (such as helmets). Beside the base lodge, where racks of skis are available for rental in winter, the summer visitor can now choose from rows of mountain bikes. Once in a while, a biker will actually choose to ride up the mountain. But usually, bikers use the specially equipped lift-chairs to carry their bikes up to the top of the mountain, and then ride them down marked trails. Serious hikers do it the other way round. They climb to the top through trails—get refreshments at the restaurant, and then take the chairlift back down to the base.

Most ski resorts look for a variety of additional ways to attract guests to their hotels and rental homes during the summer. Mont Tremblant, Quebec, for instance, is located beside an attractive lake. In addition to swimming and other water sports on the lake, the resort offers visitors' activities such as a championship golf course, tennis and roller-blading. In the pedestrian village, free animation like face painting and balloon sculptures greet children and the young at heart. Hikers and vacationers ride the gondola up the mountain to catch the beautiful view or the birds of prey show.

...Ski resorts today are broadening their choice of recreation to become **four-season resorts...**

PART III

Figure 9.2. Vacationers can look forward to an activity-jammed good time in Mont Tremblant's summer calendar.

FLUCTUATIONS IN DEMAND THREATEN SERVICE PRODUCTIVITY

Many services with limited capacity face wide swings in demand. In the opening vignette, this wide swing of demand is caused by the change of seasons. This is a problem because service capacity usually cannot be kept aside for sale at a later date. The effective use of expensive productive capacity is one of the secrets of success in such businesses. The goal should be to utilize staff, labor, equipment, and facilities as *productively* as possible. For ski resort operators, they have found that the effective use of capacity post-winter requires changing the nature of the activities so that the slopes and facilities will still be utilized.

LO 1

Define productive capacity.

Defining Productive Capacity

What do we mean by productive capacity? The term refers to the resources or assets that a firm can use to create goods and services. In a service context, productive capacity can take several forms:

1. *Physical facilities designed to contain customers* and used for people-processing services or mental stimulus processing services. Examples include medical clinics, hotels, passenger aircrafts and college classrooms. The main form of capacity limitation is likely to be in terms of furnishings such as beds, rooms, or seats. In some cases, local laws may limit the number of people allowed in for health or safety reasons (Figure 9.3).

Figure 9.3 Cinemas have to follow strict safety regulations on seating capacity in case of fire emergencies.

2. *Physical facilities designed for storing or processing goods* that either belong to customers or are being offered to them for sale. Examples include pipelines, warehouses, parking lots (Figure 9.4), or railroad freight wagons.

3. *Physical equipment used to process people, possessions, or information.* Examples would include diagnostic equipment (Figure 9.5), airport security detectors, toll gates, and bank ATMs.

4. *Labor* is a key element of productive capacity in all high-contact services and many low-contact ones (Figure 9.6). If staffing levels are not high enough, customers might be kept waiting or service becomes rushed. Professional services are especially dependent on highly skilled staff to create high value-added, information-based output. Abraham Lincoln captured it well when he remarked that "A lawyer's time and expertise are his stock in trade."

5. *Infrastructure.* Many organizations depend on access to sufficient capacity in the public or private infrastructure to be able to deliver quality service to their own customers. Capacity problems of this nature may include crowded airways that lead to air traffic restrictions on flights, traffic jams on major highways, and power failures (or "brown outs" caused by reduced voltage).

Financial success in businesses that are limited in capacity depends largely on how capacity is used. If capacity is always used efficiently and profitably, that would be ideal. In practice, however, it is difficult to achieve this ideal. It is not only demand levels that change over time. Time and effort required to process each person or thing may also vary widely at any point in the process.

Figure 9.4 Car parks "store" customers' cars temporarily when they are out shopping.

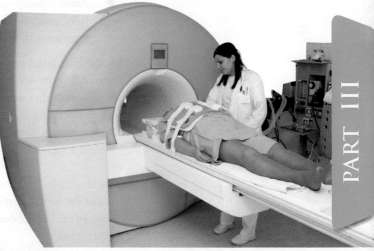

Figure 9.5 "Productive capacity" is expressed in available hours for MRI scanning equipment.

PART III

Figure 9.6 Restaurants need to ensure sufficient manpower to meet customer demands.

LO 2
Know the different demand-supply situations that fixed capacity firms may face.

From Excess Demand to Excess Capacity

For fixed capacity firms, the problem is a familiar one. "It's either feast or famine for us!" sighs the manager. "In peak periods, we're disappointing prospective customers by turning them away. And in low periods, our facilities are idle, our employees are bored, and we're losing money." In other words, demand and supply are not in balance.

At any given moment, a fixed-capacity service may face one of four conditions (see Figure 9.7):

▶ *Excess demand*—the level of demand exceeds maximum available capacity with the result that some customers are denied service and business is lost.

▶ *Demand exceeds desired capacity*—no one is actually turned away, but conditions are crowded, service quality seems lower and customers feel dissatisfied.

▶ *Demand and supply are well balanced* at the level of desired capacity. Staff and facilities are busy without being overworked and customers receive good service without delays.

▶ *Excess capacity*—demand is below desired capacity and resources are not used fully, resulting in low productivity. There is a risk that customers may find the experience disappointing or have doubts about whether the firm can survive.

Sometimes, ideal and maximum capacities are one and the same. At a live theater or sports performance, a full house is grand, since it excites the players and the audience. With most other services, you probably feel that you get better service if the facility is not operating at full capacity (Figure 9.8). The quality of restaurant service, for instance, often worsens when every table is occupied, because the staff is rushed and there is a greater likelihood of errors or delays.

There are two basic ways to overcoming the problem of varying demand. One is to adjust the level of capacity to meet changes in demand. The second approach is to manage the level of demand using marketing strategies. Many firms use a mix of both approaches.[1]

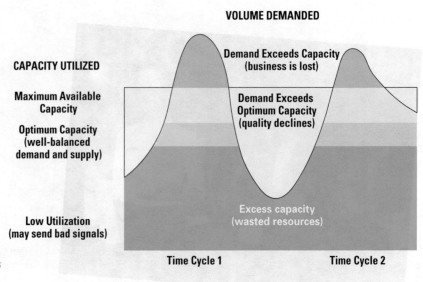

Figure 9.7 Implications of variations in demand relative to capacity.

MANAGING CAPACITY

LO 3
Use capacity management techniques to match demand variations.

Although service firms may encounter capacity limitations because of varying demand, there are ways in which capacity can be adjusted to reduce the problem. Capacity can be stretched or shrunk, the overall capacity can be adjusted to match demand, and capacity can be flexible for different segment mixes.

Capacity Levels can sometimes be Stretched or Shrunk

In this instance, nothing is done to the actual level of capacity. However, it is a case of serving more people with the same level of capacity. For example, the normal capacity for a subway car may be 40 seats and standing room for another 60 passengers with enough handrail and floor space for all. However, during rush hours, maybe up to 200 passengers can stand under sardine-like conditions (Figure 9.9).

Another way to stretch capacity within a given time frame is to use the facilities for longer periods. For example, some banks have extended their opening hours during weekdays, and even operate on weekends as well. Universities may offer evening classes and summer semester programs. Some restaurants now serve meals round the clock. Besides lunch and dinner, there is "brunch" (period likely between breakfast and lunch, 9–11.30 am), "tunch" (period likely between lunch and tea, 2–5 pm), supper (period likely between 10–1 pm) and even "after clubbing" (period likely between 2–5 am), to cater to party-goers who want to grab a bite after a night of partying and dancing.

Lastly, the average amount of time that customers (or their possessions) spend in process may be reduced. Sometimes, this is achieved by minimizing slack time. For example, a restaurant can buzz tables and seat arriving diners and present menus fast, and the bill can be presented promptly to a group of diners relaxing at the table after a meal as research has shown that the increased pace of those particular pre-process and post-process elements can be tolerated by customers.[2]

Figure 9.8 For this sushi bar in Tokyo, Japan, ideal capacity is less than maximum capacity for dining comfort.

PART III

Adjust Capacity to Match Demand

Unlike the previous option, this option involves changing the overall level of capacity to match variations in demand. This strategy is also known as *chasing demand*. There are several actions that managers can take to adjust capacity as needed.[3] These actions start from the easiest to implement, to the more difficult.

▶ *Schedule downtime during periods of low demand.* To make sure that 100 percent of capacity is available during peak periods, repair, and renovations should be done when demand is expected to be low.

Figure 9.9 Rush hour crowd stretches the capacity of train services.

Figure 9.10 Supermarket employees are crossed-trained as cashiers and stockers.

Employee holidays should also be taken during such periods. One interesting example is what happened at the height of the SARS (Severe Acute Respiratory Syndrome) crisis in Asia in 2003. Travel and tourism were badly affected. Some hotels and retailers sent staff for training or encouraged staff to take leave or time off. Others renovated their premises.

▶ *Cross-train employees.* Even when the service delivery system seems to be operating at full capacity, certain parts may not be used. If employees can be cross-trained to perform a variety of tasks, they can be shifted around when needed. This would increase the capacity of the total system. In supermarkets for instance, the manager may call on stockers to operate cash registers when checkout queues get too long. Likewise, during slow periods, the cashiers may be asked to help stock shelves (Figure 9.10).

▶ *Use part-time employees.* Many organizations hire extra workers during their busiest periods. Examples include postal workers and retail shop assistants at Christmas-time, extra staff for tax preparation service firms at the end of the financial year, and additional hotel employees during holiday periods and major conferences.

▶ *Invite customers to perform self service.* If the number of employees is limited, capacity can be increased by involving customers in the co-production of certain tasks. One way to do this is by adding self-service technologies, such as electronic kiosks at the airport for airline ticketing and check-in, or automated check-out stations at supermarkets.

▶ *Ask customers to share.* Capacity can be stretched by asking customers to share a unit of capacity that is normally for one individual. For example, at busy airports and train stations, the supply of taxis may be limited, so travelers going the same direction may be given the choice of sharing a ride at a lower rate.

▶ *Create flexible capacity.* Capacity is designed in such a way that we can move the elements to create different configurations when necessary. For example, the tables in a restaurant can be all two-seaters. When necessary, two tables can be combined to seat four, or three tables combined to seat six.

▶ *Rent or share extra facilities and equipment.* To reduce spending on fixed assets, a service business may be able to rent extra space or machines at peak times. Two firms with demand patterns where when one is high, the other is low, may enter into formal sharing agreements.

LO 4

Recognize that demand varies by segment and identify the patterns of demand.

ANALYZE PATTERNS OF DEMAND

Now let us look at the other side of the equation. In order to manage demand for a particular service, managers need to understand that demand differs by market segments, and these segments may have different demand patterns.

Demand Varies by Market Segment

Demand patterns may seem random. However, analysis will sometimes reveal that there may be a predictable demand cycle for one segment hidden within a broader pattern that seems to be irregular. Hence, it is important to break down demand on a segment-by-segment basis. For instance, a repair and maintenance shop that services industrial electrical equipment may already know that a certain amount of its work consists of regularly scheduled jobs (Figure 9.11).

The rest may come from "walk-in" business and emergency repairs. While it might seem hard to predict or control the timing and volume of such work, further analysis could show that there is more walk-in business on some days of the week than others. Emergency repairs are usually requested following damage sustained during thunderstorms (which are usually seasonal in nature and can often be predicted a day or two in advance).

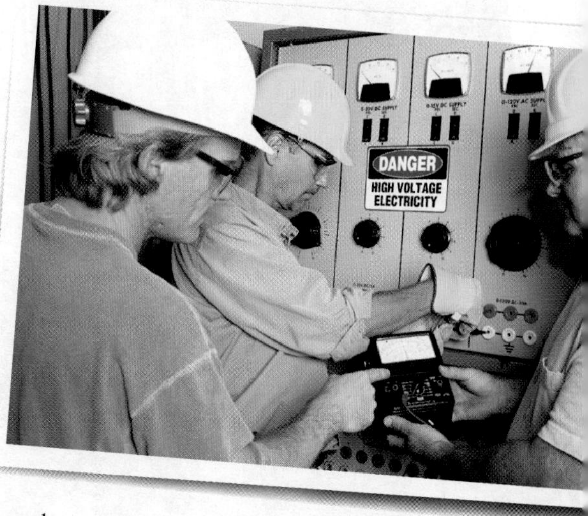

Understanding Patterns of Demand

For each market segment, managers need to know the patterns of demand. Research should begin by getting some answers to a series of important questions about the patterns of demand and their underlying causes (Table 9.1).

Figure 9.11 Scheduled maintenance checks at a power plant.

The impact of seasonal cycles is well known and affects demand for a broad range of services. Low demand in the off-season is a problem for tourism promoters. In many instances, multiple cycles may operate simultaneously. For example, demand levels for public transport may vary by time of day (highest during commute hours), day

Table 9.1 Questions about demand patterns and their underlying causes.

1. **Do demand levels follow a predictable cycle?**

   If so, is the duration of the *demand cycle*
   - One *day* (varies by hour)
   - One *week* (varies by day)
   - One *month* (varies by day or by week)
   - One *year* (varies by month or by season or reflects annual public holidays)
   - Another period

2. **What are the underlying causes of these cyclical variations?**
   - Employment schedules
   - Billing and tax payment / refund cycles
   - Wage and salary payment dates
   - School hours and vacations
   - Seasonal changes in climate
   - Occurrence of public or religious holidays
   - Natural cycles, such as coastal tides

3. **Do demand levels seem to change randomly?**

   If so, could the underlying causes be
   - Day-to-day changes in the weather
   - Health events whose occurrence cannot be pinpointed exactly
   - Accidents, fires, and certain criminal activities
   - Natural disaster (e.g., earthquakes, storms, mudslides, and volcanic eruptions)

4. **Can demand for a particular service over time be disaggregated by market segment to reflect such components as**
   - Use patterns by a particular type of customer or for a particular purpose
   - Variations in the net profitability of each completed transaction

Figure 9.12 In summer, many tourists flock to Cologne, Germany, to take in its rich heritage.

of week (less travel to work on weekends but more leisure travel), and season of year (more travel by tourists in summer) (Figure 9.12).

To understand demand patterns, firms should keep good records of each transaction. This will help them to see the demand patterns based on past experience. Sophisticated software can track customer demand patterns by date and time of day automatically. Where relevant, it is also useful to record weather conditions and other special factors (a strike, an accident, a big convention in town, a price change, launch of a competing service, and so on) that might have influenced demand.

LO 5

Know the five basic ways to manage demand.

MANAGING DEMAND

Once we have understood the demand patterns of the different market segments, we can manage demand. There are five basic ways to manage demand.

▶ *Take no action and leave demand to find its own levels.*

▶ *Reduce demand in peak periods*

▶ *Increase demand in low periods.*

▶ *Inventory demand using a queuing system.*

▶ *Inventory demand using a reservations system.*

Table 9.2 Alternate demand management strategies for different capacity situations.

Approach Used To Manage Demand	CAPACITY SITUATION RELATIVE TO DEMAND	
	Insufficient Capacity (Excess demand)	**Excess Capacity (Insufficient Demand)**
Take no Action	Unorganized queuing results (may irritate customers and discourage future use)	Capacity is wasted (customers may have a disappointing experience for services such as theater)
Reduce demand	Higher prices will increase profits; communication can encourage use in other time slots (can this effort be focused on less profitable and desirable segments?)	Take no action (but see preceding)
Increase demand	Take no action unless opportunities exist to stimulate (and give priority to) more profitable segments	Lower prices selectively (try to avoid cannibalizing existing business; ensure that all relevant costs are covered); use communications and variation in products and distribution (but recognize extra costs, if any, and make sure that appropriate trade-offs are made between profitability and use levels)
Inventory demand by reservation system	Consider priority system for most desirable segments; make other customer shift to off-peak period or to future peak	Clarify that space is available and that no reservations are needed
Inventory demand by formalized queuing	Consider override for most desirable segments; try to keep waiting customers occupied and comfortable; try to predict wait period accurately	Not applicable

Table 9.2 links these five methods to the two situations of excess demand and excess capacity. Many service businesses face both situations at different points in the cycle of demand, and should consider the use of the strategies described.

Marketing Strategies Can Reshape Some Demand Patterns

 LO 6
Use marketing to reshape demand patterns.

Some marketing mix variables can be used to encourage demand during periods of excess capacity, and decrease or shift demand during periods when there is a lack of capacity. Price is often the first variable to be proposed for bringing demand and supply into balance. However, product distribution, and communication can also be used to reshape demand patterns. Although each element is discussed separately, effective demand management efforts often need changes in two or more elements at the same time.

Use price and other costs to manage demand

One of the most direct ways of reducing excess demand at peak periods is to charge customers more money to use the service during those periods. Nonmonetary costs, too, may have a similar effect. For instance, if customers learn that they are likely

PART III

Figure 9.13 Bed and Breakfast inns are dependent on the seasonal tide of tourists.

to face increased time and effort costs during peak periods, those who dislike spending time waiting in crowded and unpleasant conditions may go at a different time. Similarly, the cheaper prices may encourage at least some people to change the timing of their behavior, whether it is shopping, travel, or sending equipment in for repair. Governments have in fact been managing demand for public health services by encouraging private health insurance, which is an indirect way of reducing the monetary costs for consumers[4].

When capacity is limited, however, the goal in a profit-seeking business should be to make as much use of the capacity as possible by making available to the most profitable segments at any given time. Airlines, for instance, hold a certain number of seats for business passengers paying full fare, and place restrictive conditions on fares for tourists (like requiring a four people to travel together to qualify for the lower fare). This is to prevent business travelers from taking advantage of cheap fares designed to attract tourists who can help fill the aircraft. Pricing strategies of this kind are known as *revenue management* and are discussed in Chapter 6.

Change product elements

Sometimes, pricing cannot be used to balance supply and demand. The opening vignette is a good example of how the service product offering was changed to encourage demand. No amount of price discounting is likely to develop business out of season and new value propositions targeted at different segments is needed (Figure 9.13).

Modify the place and time of delivery

Some firms respond to market needs by modifying the time and place of delivery. Three basic options are available.

▶ Strategy of *no change*. Regardless of the level of demand; this service continues to be offered in the same location at the same time.

▶ Strategy of *varying the times when the service is available*. For example, people usually have more time to watch movies on weekends. Therefore, there are more time slots for shows on weekends compared to weekdays. Similarly, retailers also tend to stay open till later on Fridays and Saturdays as there are more shoppers on those days.

▶ Strategy of *offering the service to customers at a new location*. One way is to operate mobile units that take the service to customers, rather than to require them to visit fixed-site service locations. This will help to decrease the number of people visiting the existing site. For example, instead of queues at car wash, the company can offer mobile car wash services.

Promotion and education

Even if the other variables of the marketing mix remain unchanged, communication efforts alone may be able to help smoothen demand. Signage, advertising, publicity, and sales messages can be used to educate customers about the timing of peak periods and encourage them to purchase the service at off-peak times. Post offices request people to "Mail Early for the Holidays." Also, any changes in pricing, product characteristics, and distribution must be communicated clearly.

::: SERVICE INSIGHTS 9.1

Discouraging demand For Non-Emergency Calls

Have you ever wondered what it is like to be the person who sends out the emergency vehicles for an emergency telephone service such as 911? People differ widely in what they consider to be an emergency.

Imagine yourself in the huge communications room at Police Headquarters in New York. A gray-haired sergeant is talking patiently by phone to a woman who has dialed 911 because her cat has run up a tree and she is afraid it is stuck there. "Ma'am, have you ever seen a cat skeleton in a tree?" the sergeant asks her. "All those cats get down somehow, don't they?" After the woman has hung up, the sergeant turns to a visitor and shrugs. "These kinds of calls keep pouring in," he says. "What can you do?" The trouble is, when people call the emergency number with complaints about noisy parties next door, pleas to rescue cats, or requests to turn off leaking fire hydrants, they may be slowing down the response times to fires, heart attacks, or violent crimes.

At one point, the situation in New York City got so bad that officials were forced to develop a marketing campaign to discourage people from making inappropriate requests for emergency assistance through the 911 number. The problem was that what might seem like an emergency to the caller—a beloved cat stuck up a tree, a noisy party that was preventing a tired person from getting needed sleep—was not a life (or property) threatening situation of the type that the city's emergency services should be called on to solve. For help in solving other problems, they were asked to call their local police station or other city agencies. The had shown below appeared on New York buses and subways.

SAVE 911 for the real thing
CALL YOUR PRECINCT OR CITY AGENCY
WHEN IT'S NOT A **DANGEROUS** EMERGENCY
(noisy party, open hydrant, abandoned car, etc.)
911 NEW YORK CITY'S DANGEROUS EMERGENCY NUMBER

Service Insights 9.1 shows how a marketing campaign was used to reduce undesirable demand and free up capacity. Many calls to 911 numbers are not really problems that fire, police, or ambulance services should be solving. Such undesirable demand can be discouraged through education and communication.

INVENTORY DEMAND THROUGH WAITING LINES AND RESERVATIONS

● LO 7
Inventory demand through queuing systems.

One of the challenges of services is that, being performances, they cannot normally be stored for later use. A hair stylist cannot pre-package a haircut for the following day. It must be done in real time. In businesses where demand regularly exceeds supply, managers can often take steps to inventory demand (keep for use later). This task can be done in two ways: (1) by asking customers to wait in line (queuing), usually on a first-come, first-served basis, or (2) by offering them the opportunity of reserving or booking capacity in advance.

Figure 9.14 Hailing a cab can be frustrating during busy stretches.

Waiting in Line

Nobody likes to be kept waiting (Figure 9.14). Yet, waiting for a service process is something that occurs everywhere. The average person may spend as much as half-an-hour per day waiting in line, which would translate to 20 months of waiting in an 80 year lifetime![5] Physical and inanimate objects wait for processing too. Customers' e-mails sit in customer service staff's inboxes, appliances wait to be repaired and checks wait to be cleared at a bank. In each instance, a customer may be waiting for the outcome of that work.

Not all queues take the form of a physical waiting line in a single location. When customers deal with a service supplier at arm's length, as in information processing services, they may use the telephone to get service. Typically, calls are answered in the order received. This often requires customers to wait their turn in a virtual line. Some physical queues are geographically dispersed. Travelers wait at many different locations for taxis.

Different Queue Configurations

There are a variety of queues and the challenge for managers is to select the most suitable one. Figure 9.15 shows diagrams of several types that you have probably experienced yourself.

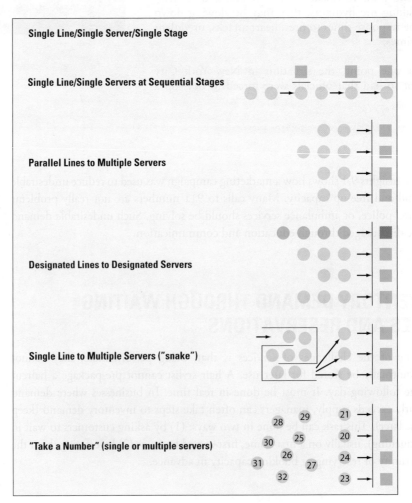

Figure 9.15 Alternative queue configuration.

- In *single line, sequential stages,* customers go through several serving operations, as in a cafeteria. Some stages however, may take longer to process than previous stages. Many cafeterias have lines at the cash register because the cashier takes longer to calculate how much you owe and to provide change than the servers take to slap food on your plate.

- *Parallel lines to multiple servers* offer more than one serving station. This allows customers to select one of several lines in which to wait. Banks and ticket windows are common examples. The disadvantage of this design is that lines may not move at equal speed. How many times have you chosen what looked like the shortest line only to watch in frustration as the lines on either side of you move at twice the speed because someone in your line has a complicated transaction?

- A *single line to multiple servers* is commonly known as a "Snake." This solves the problem of the parallel lines to multiple servers. This method is often used at post offices, banks and airport check-ins (Figure 9.16).

- *Designated lines* involve allocating different lines to specific categories of customers. Examples include express lines (for instance, 12 items or less) and regular lines at supermarket checkouts, and different check-in stations for first class, business class, and economy class airline passengers.

- *Take a number* saves customers the need to stand in a queue. This procedure allows them to sit down and relax (if seating is available) or to guess how long the wait will be and go somewhere else in the meantime (e.g. to the Starbucks around the corner). Of course, this would mean the risk losing their place if earlier customers are served faster than expected. Users of this method include large travel agents, government offices and outpatient clinics in hospitals.

- *Wait list.* Restaurants often have waitlists where people put their names down and queue. There are four common ways of wait listing. (1) Party size seating where the number of people is matched to the size of the table. (2) VIP seating involves giving special rights to favored customers. (3) Call-ahead seating allows people to telephone before arrival to hold a place in the wait list. (4) Large party reservations. If customers are familiar with wait listing techniques, they are likely to view them to be fairer. If not, large party reservations are viewed as slightly unfair, and VIP seating is viewed as especially unfair.[6]

Figure 9.16 Post offices employ the single line to multiple servers approach to ease human traffic.

A combination of the different ways to queue also exists. For instance, a cafeteria with a single serving line might offer two cash register stations at the final stage (Figure 9.17). Similarly, patients at a small medical clinic might visit a single receptionist for registration, go through multiple channels in a sequence for testing, diagnosis, and treatment, and finish by returning to a single line for payment at the receptionist's desk.

Figure 9.17 Single queuing system in cafés usually have more than one cash register stations.

Virtual Waits

One of the problems of waiting in line is the waste of customers' time. When two or more people are waiting together, it is sometimes possible for one to remain and the others to go off and do something else for a while. The "virtual queue" strategy is an innovative way to take the physical waiting out of the wait altogether. Instead, customers register their place in line on a computer, and estimates the time they will reach the front of the virtual line. Customers can then return to claim their place.[7] Service Insights 9.2 describes the virtual queuing systems used in two very different industries, namely a theme park and a call center. The concept of virtual queues has many potential applications. Cruise ships, all-inclusive resorts and restaurants can all use this strategy if customers are willing to remain within buzzing range of a pager system.

::: SERVICE INSIGHTS 9.2

Waiting in a **Virtual Queue**

Disney is well known for its efforts to provide visitors with its theme parks information on how long they may have to wait to ride a particular attraction, and for entertaining guests while they are waiting in line. However, the company found that the long waits at its most popular attractions was still a great source of dissatisfaction, and so created an innovative solution.

The concept of the virtual queue was first tested at Disney World. At the most popular attractions there, guests were able to register their place in line with a computer and were then free to use the wait time visiting other places in the park. Surveys showed that guests who used the new system spent more money, saw more attractions, and had much higher satisfaction. After further refinement, the system, now named FASTPASS, was introduced at the five most popular attractions at Disney World and subsequently extended to all Disney parks worldwide. It is now used by more then 50 million guests a year.

FASTPASS is easy to use. When guests approach a FASTPASS attraction, they are given two clear choices: Obtain a FASTPASS ticket there and return at an appointed time, or wait in a standby line. Signs indicate how long the wait is in each instance. To use the FASTPASS option, guests insert their park admission ticket into a special turnstile and receive a FASTPASS ticket specifying a return time. Guests have some flexibility because the system allows them a 60-minute window beyond the printed return time.

Just like the FASTPASS system, call centers also use virtual queues. There are many vendors selling different types of virtual queuing systems designed for call centers. The first-in, first-out queuing system is very common. When callers call in, they will hear a message that informs them of the estimated wait time for the call to be taken by an agent. The caller can (1) wait in the queue and get connected to an agent when his turn arrives, or (2) choose to receive a call back. When the caller chooses this option, he has to enter his telephone number and tell his name. He then hangs up the phone. However, his virtual place in the queue is maintained. When he is nearly at the head of the queue, the system calls the customer back and puts him at the head of the queue where an agent will attend to him next. In both situations, the customer is unlikely to complain. In the first situation, it is their choice to wait in the queue and the person can still do something else as he already knows the estimated wait time. In the second situation, the person does not have to wait for very long before reaching an agent. The call center also benefits in that there are fewer frustrated customers that may take up the valuable time of the agents by complaining about how long they have to wait. In addition, they also do not have to miss calls by customers.

SOURCE

Dickson, D., Ford, R. C., & Laval, B. (2005). Managing real and virtual waits in hospitality and service organizations. *Cornell Hotel and Restaurant Administration Quarterly*, 46(February). pp. 52–68; "Virtual Queue," Wikipedia. Available: www.en.wikipedia.org/wiki/Virtual_queuing, Accessed March 2008.

PERCEPTIONS OF WAITING TIME

LO 8
Understand how customers feel about waiting and make waiting less burdensome for them.

Research shows that people often think they have waited longer for a service than they actually did. Studies of public transportation use, for instance, have shown that travelers feel time spent waiting for a bus or train as passing one and a half to seven times more slowly than the time actually spent traveling in the vehicle.[8] People don't like wasting their time on unproductive activities. Customer dissatisfaction with delays in receiving service can often stir up strong emotions, even anger.[9]

The Psychology of Waiting

When increasing capacity or shifting demand is simply not possible or enough, service providers should try to look for ways to make waiting more bearable for customers (Figure 9.18).

David Maister and other researchers have the following suggestions on how to use the psychology of waiting to make waits less stressful and unpleasant:[10]

Figure 9.18 While waiting, time can seem to pass very slowly.

▶ *Unoccupied time feels longer than occupied time.* When you are sitting around with nothing to do, time seems to crawl. BMW car owners can wait in comfort in BMW service centers. The waiting areas are furnished with designer furniture, plasma TV mounted on walls, Wi-Fi hotspots, magazines and freshly brewed cappuccino. Similarly, most clinics provide stacks of magazines to make waiting less boring (Figure 9.19).

▶ *Solo waits feel longer than group waits.* It is nice to wait with people whom you know. Talking to friends is one way of helping to pass the time while waiting.

▶ *Physically uncomfortable waits feel longer than comfortable waits.* If people have to stand, then they are likely to complain about waiting. If the temperature is too cold or too hot, waiting will also be unpleasant.

▶ *Pre- and post-process waits feel longer than in-process waits.* Waiting to buy a ticket to enter a theme park is different from waiting to ride on a roller coaster once you are in the park.

▶ *Unexplained waits are longer than explained waits.* Have you ever been in a subway or an elevator that has stopped for no apparent reason? In addition to the worry caused by the wait, there is also added worry about what is going to happen.

▶ *Unfamiliar waits seem longer than familiar ones.* People who use a service often know what to expect, so they are less likely to worry while waiting. New users or those who use the service once in a while will wonder how long the wait is, and also wonder what will happen next.

Figure 9.19 Keeping occupied by reading magazines will make the wait for the spa treatment feel shorter.

▶ *Uncertain waits are longer than known, finite waits.* Although any wait can be frustrating, people can adjust to a wait if they know how long they need to wait. If people do not know how long the wait is then that makes them angry. Therefore, telling people how long they are likely to wait is useful information for customers. They can then make decisions on whether to wait or to come back later.

▶ *Unfair waits are longer than fair waits.* What is considered fair or unfair varies from culture to culture. In some countries, people expect everyone to wait their turn in a line and will be irritated if someone jumps ahead in the line.

▶ *Anxiety makes waits seem longer.* Can you remember waiting for someone to show at a meeting point, and worrying about whether you had gotten the time or location correct? While waiting in unfamiliar locations, especially outdoors and at night, people often worry about their personal safety.

▶ *The more valuable or important the service, the longer people will wait.* People will queue up overnight in very uncomfortable situations just to get good seats to a popular sports event.

▶ LO 9
Know the benefits of having an effective reservations system and understand what is involved in designing one.

INVENTORY DEMAND THROUGH A RESERVATIONS SYSTEM

As an alternative, or in addition to, waiting lines, reservations systems can be used to inventory demand. Ask someone what services come to mind when you talk about reservations and most likely they will talk about airlines, hotels, restaurants, car rentals, and theater seats. Suggest terms with similar meanings like "bookings" or "appointments" and they may add haircuts, visits to professionals such as doctors and consultants, and service calls to fix anything from a broken refrigerator to a computer that is not behaving properly. There are many benefits in having a reservations system.

▶ The aim of reservations is to make sure that the service is available when the customer wants it. Reservations allow demand to be controlled and smoothed out in a more manageable way.

▶ Data from reservation systems also help organizations to prepare operational and financial projections for future periods. Systems vary from a simple appointments book for a doctor's office, using handwritten entries, to a central, computerized data bank for an airline's worldwide operations.

▶ Reservations systems also benefit businesses. For example, requiring reservations for normal repair and maintenance allows management to make sure that some time will be kept free for handling emergency jobs. Since these are unpredictable, higher prices can be charged and these bring with them higher margins.

▶ Taking reservations also helps to pre-sell a service, to inform customers and to educate them about what to expect.

▶ Customers who hold reservations should be able to count on avoiding a queue, since they have been guaranteed service at a specific time.

The challenge in designing reservation systems is to make them fast and user-friendly for both staff and customers. Many firms now allow customers to make their own reservations on a website—a trend that seems certain to grow. Whether customers talk with a reservations agent or make their own bookings, they want quick answers to questions about whether a service is available at a preferred time. They also appreciate it if the system can provide further information about the type of service they are reserving. For instance, can a hotel assign a specific room on request? Or at least, can it assign a room with a view of the lake rather than one with a view of the parking lot and the nearby power station? Some businesses now in fact charge a fee for making a reservation (see Service Insights 9.3). Northwest airlines charge customers $15 if they want to reserve certain of the most desirable economy class seats, and Air Canada charges $12 for advanced seat reservations on certain flights.[11]

Reservations Strategies should focus on Yield

More and more, service firms are looking at their "yield"—that is, the average revenue received per unit of capacity. The aim is to increase the yield to the greatest amount possible, in order to improve profitability. As noted in Chapter 6, revenue management strategies that achieve this goal are widely used in industries with relatively fixed capacity such as airlines, hotels, and car rental firms.

Yield analysis forces managers to recognize the opportunity cost of allocating capacity to one customer or market segment when another segment might yield a higher rate later. Think about the following problems facing sales managers for different types of service organizations with capacity limitations:

▶ Should a railroad with 30 empty freight cars accept an immediate request for a shipment worth $1,500 per car, or hold the cars for a few more days in the hope of getting a priority shipment that would be twice as valuable?

▶ Should a print-shop process all jobs on a first-come, first-served basis, with a guaranteed delivery time for each job, or should it charge a premium rate for "rush" work, and tell customers with "standard" jobs to expect some variability in completion dates?

Decisions on such problems need to be based on good information. Good information should be based on detailed record keeping of past usage. It should also be supported by current market intelligence and good marketing sense. The decision to accept or reject business should be based on a realistic estimate of the chances of obtaining higher rated business, and awareness of the need to keep current customer relationships. Very often, firms overbook in an attempt to increase yield. Customers who are affected negatively may significantly reduce their relationships with the firm, yet those who were upgraded are only weakly positive about the firm.[12]

Figure 9.20 shows capacity allocation in a hotel setting. Demand from different types of customers varies not only by day of the week, but also by season. These allocation decisions by segment, captured in reservation databases that are available worldwide, tell reservations personnel when to stop accepting reservations at certain prices, even though many rooms may still remain unbooked. Loyalty program members, who are mainly business travelers, are obviously a very desirable segment.

Similar charts can be drawn for most businesses that face capacity limitations. In some instances, capacity is measured in terms of seats for a given performance, seat-miles, or room-nights. In others, it may be in terms of machine time, labor time, billable professional hours, vehicle miles, or storage volume—whichever is the limited resource.

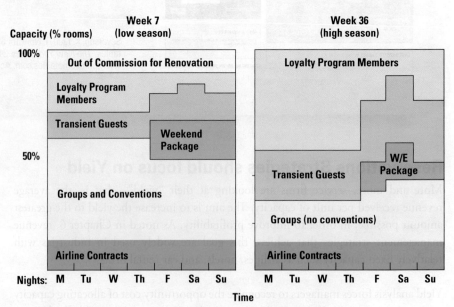

Figure 9.20 Setting capacity allocation targets by segment for a hotel.

CHAPTER SUMMARY

LO 1 ▶ There are many different forms of productive capacity in services. They are physical facilities for processing customers; physical facilities for processing goods; physical equipment for processing people, possession or information; labor and infrastructure

LO 2 ▶ At any one time, a firm that has limited capacity can face different demand-supply situations. There could be excess demand, demand that's more than ideal capacity, well balanced demand and supply, or excess capacity. When demand and supply are not balanced, firms will have idle capacity during low periods, but have to turn away customers during peak periods. This situation is not ideal. Therefore, firms should try to balance demand and supply.

To balance demand and supply, either capacity or demand can be adjusted.

LO 3 ▶ Some capacity can be stretched by having more customers during peak period as for our subway example.

Capacity can be changed to match demand in the following ways:

o   Schedule downtime during low periods.

o   Cross-train employees, use part-time employees.

o   Invite customers to perform self-service.

o   Ask customers to share capacity.

o   Design capacity to be flexible.

o   Rent or share extra facilities and equipment.

LO 4 ▶ To manage demand effectively firms need to understand demand patterns and drivers by market segment. Different segments often exhibit different demand patterns. Once firms have an understanding of the demand patterns of their market segment, they can use marketing strategies to reshape those patterns.

LO 5/6 ▶ To manage demand, a firm can:

o   Use price and other costs to manage demand.

o   Change product elements.

o   Change the time and place of delivery.

o   Inventory demand by using waiting or queuing systems.

o   Inventory demand by using reservations systems.

LO 7 ▶ When designing waiting systems, firms need to bear in mind that there are different types of queues with their respective advantages and applications. Queuing systems include single line in a sequence, parallel lines to multiple servers, single line to multiple servers, allocated lines, taking a number on a wait list.

LO 8 ▶ As long as customers have to wait in line, they are likely to get bored or frustrated. Firms need to understand the psychology of waiting and take active steps to make waiting less frustrating. We discussed 10 possible steps, including informing the customers how long the wait is, keep them occupied or entertained while they are waiting, provide them with explanation of why they have to wait, and provide customers with a comfortable seat so that they do not have to stand while waiting.

LO 9 ▶ Effective reservations systems help to reduce or even avoid customers waiting in queues. There are several benefits of having a reservations system, such as: the service is available when the customer wants it, reservations help to pre-sell capacity, and customers do not have to queue as much.

An effective reservations system should also focus on increasing yield, rather than just selling off capacity.

UNLOCK YOUR LEARNING

These keywords are found within the sections of each Learning Objective (LO). They are integral in understanding the services marketing concepts taught in each section. Having a firm grasp of these keywords and how they are used is essential in helping you do well for your course, and in the real and very competitive marketing scene out there.

LO 1
1. Productive capacity

LO 2
2. Fixed capacity
3. Ideal capacity
4. Maximum capacity

LO 3
5. Adjust capacity
6. Capacity limitations
7. Chasing demand
8. Cross-train employees
9. Flexible capacity
10. Self-service
11. Stretch capacity

LO 4
12. Patterns of demand
13. Seasonal cycles

LO 5
14. Inventorying demand
15. Manage demand

LO 7
16. Designated lines
17. Physical queues
18. Queue configurations
19. Wait list
20. Waiting line
21. Virtual waits
22. Virtue queue

LO 8
23. Psychology of waiting
24. Pre- and post-process waits

LO 9
25. Capacity allocation reservations
26. Revenue management
27. Yield analysis
28. Reservations system

How well do you know the language of services marketing? Quiz yourself!

 Not for the academically faint-of-heart

For each keyword you are able to recall without referring to earlier pages, give yourself a point (and a pat on the back). Tally your score at the end and see if you earned the right to be called—a *services marketeer.*

SCORE

0 – 5	Services Marketing is done a great disservice.
6 – 10	The midnight oil needs to be lit, pronto.
11 – 15	I know what you *didn't* do all semester.
16 – 20	A close shave with success.
21 – 25	Now, go forth and market.
26 – 28	There should be a marketing concept named after you.

Review Questions

1. What is productive capacity?

2. What is the difference between ideal capacity and maximum capacity? Provide examples of a situation where (a) the two might be the same and (b) the two are different.

3. What actions can firms take to match demand to capacity?

4. How can firms identify the factors that affect demand for their firms?

5. How can marketing strategies be used to reshape demand patterns?

6. What are the advantages and disadvantages of the different types of queuing? For which type of service might each of the queuing types be more suitable?

7. How can firms overcome some of the negative feelings that customers have about waiting?

8. What are the benefits of having an effective reservation system?

◖WORK **YOUR ESM**◗

Application Exercises

1. Explain how flexible capacity can be created in each of the following situations: (a) a local library, (b) an office-cleaning service, (c) a technical support helpdesk, (d) an interflora franchise.

2. Provide some examples of firms in your community (or region) that greatly changed their product or marketing mix in order to increase demand during low demand periods.

3. Review the ten suggestions on the psychology of waiting. Which is the most relevant in (a) a supermarket, (b) a city bus stop on a rainy, dark evening, (c) a doctor's office and (d) a ticket line for a football game that is expected to be a sell-out?

4. Give examples, based on your own experience, of a reservation system that worked really well, and of one that worked really badly. Identify and examine the reasons for the success and failure of these two systems. What recommendations would you make to both firms to improve (or further improve in case of the good example) their reservation system.

PART III

•ENDNOTES

1   Klassen, K. J., & Rohleder, T. R. (2001). Combining operations and marketing to manage capacity and demand in services. *The Service Industries Journal* 21(April). pp. 1–30.

2   Noone, B. M., Kimes, S. E., Mattila, A. S., & Wirtz, J. (2007). The effect of meal pace on customer satisfaction. *Cornell Quarterly*, 48(3). pp. 231–245.

3   Based on material in Fitzsimmons, J. A., & Fitzsimmons, M. J. (2000). Service Management: Operations, Strategy, and Information Technology, 3/E. New York: Irwin McGraw-Hill;. Earl Sasser, W. Jr. (1976). Match supply and demand in service industries. Harvard Business Review (November-December).

4   Willcox, S., Seddon, M., Dunn, S., Edwards, R. T., Pearse, J., & Tu, J. V. (2007). Measuring and reducing waiting times: A cross-national comparison of strategies. *Health Affairs*, 26(4), pp. 1078–1087.

5   Wielenga, D. (1997 November 28). Not so fine lines. *Los Angeles Times*. p. E1.

6   McGuire K. A., & Kimes, S. E. (2006). The perceived fairness of waitlist-management techniques for restaurants. *Cornell Hotel and Restaurant Administration Quarterly*, 47(May). pp. 121–134.

7   Dickson, D., Ford, R. C., & Laval, B. (2005). Managing real and virtual waits in hospitality and service organizations. *Cornell Hotel and Restaurant Administration Quarterly*, 46(February), pp. 52–68.

8   Chernow, J. R. (1981). Measuring the values of travel time savings. *Journal of Consumer Research*, 7(March), pp. 360–371. [Note: This entire issue was devoted to the consumption of time.]

9   Diaz, A. B. C., & Ruiz, F. J. M. (2002). The consumer's reaction to delays in service. *International Journal of Service Industry Management*, 13(2), pp. 118–140.

10 This section is based on: Maister, D. H. (1986). The psychology of waiting lines. In J. A. Czepiel, M. R. Solomon, & C. F. Surprenant, (Eds.), *The Service Encounter* (pp.113–123). Lexington, MA: Lexington Books/D.C. Heath; Davis, M. M., & Heineke, J. (1994). Understanding the roles of the customer and the operation for better queue management. *International Journal of Service Industry Management* 7(5). pp. 21–34; Jones, P., & Peppiat, E. (1996). Managing perceptions of waiting times in service queues. *International Journal of Service Industry Management* 7(5). pp. 47–61.

11 Carey, S. (2006). Northwest airlines to charge extra for aisle seats. *The Wall Street Journal*, 14(March).

12 Wangenheim, F. V., & Bayon, T. (2007). Behavioral consequences of overbooking service capacity. *Journal of Marketing*, 71(4), pp. 36–47.

BLANK

10

crafting the
SERVICE
ENVIRONMENT

LEARNING OBJECTIVES

By the end of this chapter, students should be able to:

LO 1 Explain the purpose of the service environment.

LO 2 Explain how the Mehrabian-Russell Stimulus-Response Model and Russell's Model of Affect help us to understand consumers' responses to service environments.

LO 3 List the dimensions of the service environment and describe their impact on behavior.

LO 4 Understand what goes into designing an effective servicescape.

OPENING VIGNETTE[1]

GUGGENHEIM MUSEUM IN BILBAO

When the Guggenheim Museum in Bilbao in northern Spain opened its doors to the public in 1997, there was praise for it from all over the world. It had a fascinating architecture that resulted in it being hailed as "the greatest building of our time" by Philip Johnson, the influential and famous American architect. It also put Bilbao on the world map as a tourist destination. Before that, most people had never heard of Bilbao. In fact, it was an industrial area with a shipyard and large warehouse districts. Its river was filled with a century of waste that had spilt into it from the factories that lined its shores. The entire city however, was transformed

Figure 10.1 The contemporary curves of the Guggenheim has drawn in large amounts of praise and crowds.

with the museum as the beginning of the city's redevelopment plan. Such a transformation is now even called the "Bilbao effect" and is being studied to understand how the wow-effect kind of architecture can transform a city.

The design of the building communicated several different kinds of messages to its audience. It is shaped like a ship and blends in with the environment of the river. The museum is a mixture of regular forms built in stone, curved forms made of titanium, and huge glass walls for natural light to penetrate the museum. Because of the glass walls, visitors inside the museum can see the surrounding hills. The titanium panels outside have been arranged to look like fish scales, keeping in tune with the image of being by the Nervion River. Outside the museum, a 43-foot-tall shaped structure of a "topiary terrier" (a breed of dog), made up of pots of fresh pansies (flowers) greets visitors. There is also a huge spider sculpture called "Maman" done by Louise Bourgeoris, the twentieth-century leading sculptor, who was born in Paris but made her home in New York.

Inside the museum is a centrally located atrium, a huge empty space that is crowned by a metal dome. From this atrium, one can visit 19 other galleries that are connected by curved walkways, glass lifts and stairways. Even the design of the galleries is meant to hint at what visitors can expect inside. The shapes of the galleries and the content of the galleries complement each other. The rectangular shaped galleries have limestone covered walls. The rectangle is a more conventional shape, and these galleries hold the classic art collections. The irregularly shaped galleries hold collections of selected living artists. There are also special galleries with no columns within the museum so that large artworks can be displayed. The structures of these galleries are also a work of art that comes from a specially designed and planned servicescape.

While not all servicescapes are great works of architecture, the Guggenheim Museum in Bilbao is. It is an attention-drawing medium that creates a message that shapes the expectations of visitors. They can look forward to an awesome experience at the museum.

...The Guggenheim in Bilbao has redefined the servicescape...

Figure 10.2 The organic nature of its architecture draws inspiration from the surrounding Nervion River.

WHAT IS THE PURPOSE OF SERVICE ENVIRONMENTS?

Designing the service environment is an art that takes a lot of time and effort, and can be expensive to implement. Service environments are also called *servicescapes*. This term is modeled after the term "landscape," but refers to a service environment. The term servicescape refers to the style and appearance of the physical surroundings and also includes other elements of the service environment that shape customers' experience.[2] Once designed and built, service environments are not easily changed.

Why do many service firms take so much trouble to shape the environment where their customers and service personnel interact? For the Guggenheim Museum in Bilbao, it was to address several of the city's problems and to create a tourist attraction. For the museum and many service firms, there are four core purposes of servicescapes:

▶ Shape customers' experience and their behavior.

▶ Support image, positioning and differentiation.

▶ Be part of the value proposition.

▶ Facilitate the service encounter and enhance productivity.

These key purposes are elaborated in the next four sections.

Shape Customers' Experiences and Behaviors

For high-contact services, the design of the physical environment and the way in which tasks are performed by customer-contact personnel jointly play a central role in shaping the nature of customers' experiences. The environment can affect a customer's perception and service experience in three important ways:

1. *As a message-creating medium,* using the elements in the environment to communicate the special nature and quality of the service experience.

2. *As an attention-creating medium,* to make the servicescape stand out from those of its competitors, and to attract customers from target segments.

3. *As an effect-creating medium,* using colors, textures, sounds, scents and spatial design to create the desired service experience, and/or to increase the desire for certain goods, services or experiences.

Figure 10.3 (a) Lobby of the Generator youth hostel, London.

For Image, Positioning and Differentiation

Often customers find it difficult to assess the quality of service performances, therefore, they use the service environment as a proxy. Well-managed firms put in a lot of effort into making sure that the environment signals quality and communicate the desired image and positioning.[3] Figure 10.3 shows the lobbies, of the Generator youth hostel in London and The Fairmont Empress in Victoria, British Columbia, Canada. These two hotels have very different target segments. One is for

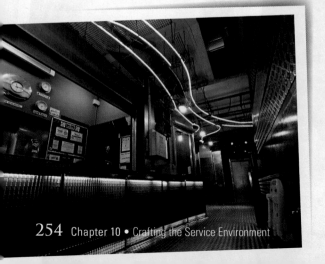

younger guests who love fun and have low budgets. The other targets the more mature and wealthy customers that include business travelers. Each servicescape clearly shows its hotel's positioning.

Part of the Value Proposition

The third purpose of the servicescape is to help to shape the desired feelings and reactions in customers and employees.[4] Perhaps the most extreme examples of servicescape come from Las Vegas. Faced with competition from numerous casinos in other locations, Las Vegas has been trying to reposition itself away from being purely an adult destination to including elements that will be enjoyed by families and convention attendees. The gambling is still there, of course. However, many of the huge hotels recently built (or rebuilt) have been transformed such that they look very impressive. The entertainment centers have erupting "volcanoes," mock sea battles, and striking reproductions of Paris, ancient Rome, the Pyramids, and Venice and its canals. The Bellagio even includes an art museum.

Figure 10.3 (b) Lobby of the Fairmont Empress, Victoria, British Columbia, Canada.

Movie theaters are discovering the power of servicescapes in an effort to attract more patrons. In the US, chains like Florida-based Muvico are trying something different. They want people to go to the movies as part of an overall entertainment experience. They have buildings with different themes, the most modern movie theaters, well-decorated bars and restaurants and supervised playrooms for children. Although their ticket prices are higher, they are still attracting the crowds. Says Muvico's CEO, Hamid Hashemi, of his competitors, "At the end of the day, you all get the same 35-mm tape…. What sets you apart is how you package it."[5] At one French opera house themed Muvico cinema (Figure 10.4), moviegoers are transported to a Beaux Arts-styled Paris Opera house, surrounded by marble friezes, columns, and ornate sculptures. Inside the auditorium, they find wide aisles and red velvet seats.

Facilitate the Service Encounter and Enhance Productivity

Finally, the servicescape is often designed to make the service encounter easier for customers and to increase productivity. Richard Chase and Douglas Stewart highlighted ways in which fail-safe methods that are part of the service environment can help to reduce service failures and support a fast and smooth service delivery process.[6] For example, some childcare centers feature outlines of specific toys on the floors and walls to show where these items should be placed after use.

Figure 10.4 The French opera house themed Muvico cinema.

UNDERSTANDING CONSUMER RESPONSES TO SERVICE ENVIRONMENTS

We now understand why service firms take so much effort to design the service environment. Why does the service environment have such important effects on people and their behaviors? The field of environmental psychology studies how people respond to particular environments and can help us to answer that question.

Feelings are a Key Driver of Customer Responses to Service Environments

Two important models help us better understand and therefore also manage consumer responses to service environments. The first, the Mehrabian-Russell Stimulus-Response Model, demonstrates that feelings or affect are central to how we respond to the different elements in the environment. The second, Russell's Model of Affect, shows how we can better understand those feelings and their effect on response behaviors.

The Mehrabian-Russell Stimulus-Response Model

Figure 10.5 displays a simple and basic model of how people respond to environments. The environment and how people view and interpret it, whether consciously or unconsciously, influences how people feel in that setting[7]. People's feelings are the central and most important element in the model, driving their responses to that environment. Similar environments can lead to very different feelings and subsequent responses. For example, we may dislike being in a crowded department store with lots of other customers, find ourselves unable to get what we want as fast as we wish, and thus seek to avoid that environment. However, if we were not in a rush and felt excited about being part of the crowd during seasonal festivities in the very same

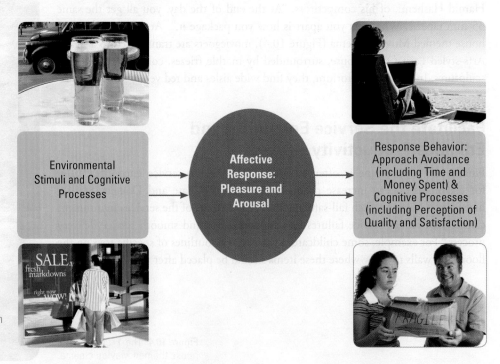

Figure 10.5 Environmental stimuli and their perception and interpretation.

environment, then we might derive feelings of pleasure and excitement that would make us want to stay and enjoy the experience.

In environmental psychology, the typical outcome variable is 'approach' or 'avoidance' of an environment. Of course, in services marketing, we can add a long list of additional outcomes that a firm might want to manage, including the amount of time and money people spend, and how satisfied they are with the service experience after they have left.

Russell's Model of Affect

Since affect or feelings are central to how people respond to an environment, we need to understand those feelings better. For this, Russell's model of affect (Figure 10.6) is widely used. It suggests that emotional responses to environments can be described along the two main dimensions of pleasure and arousal.[8] Pleasure is a direct response to the environment, depending on how much an individual likes or dislikes the environment. Arousal refers to how stimulated the individual feels, ranging from deep sleep (lowest level of internal activity) to the highest level of stimulation such as during bungee-jumping. Arousal depends largely on the information rate or load of an environment. For example, environments are stimulating (i.e. have a high information rate) when they are complex, have movement or change in it, and have novel and surprising elements.

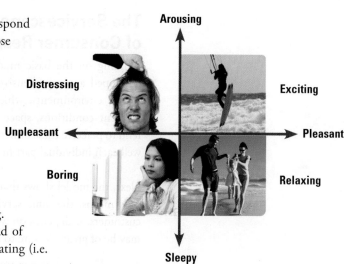

Figure 10.6 Russell's Model of Affect.

The strength of Russell's model is its simplicity. It allows a direct judgment of how customers feel while they are in a service environment. Therefore, firms can set targets for the affective states they want their customers to be in. For example, a roller-coaster operator wants its customers to feel excited (which is a relatively high arousal environment combined with pleasure). A spa may want customers to feel relaxed, a bank pleasant, and so on.

Affect and Cognitive Processes

Affect is influenced by how people sense and interpret an environment, which is their cognitive processing. The more complex a cognitive process becomes, the more powerful is its possible impact on affect. Yet this does not mean that simple cognitive processes, such as the unconscious perception of scents or music, are unimportant. In practice, most service encounters are routine. We tend to be on "autopilot" when doing the usual transactions such as using the subway, entering a fast food restaurant or a bank. On such occasions, it is the simple cognitive processes that determine how people feel. However, should higher levels of cognitive processes be set off, for instance through something surprising in the service environment, then what determines people's feelings are how they interpret this surprise.[9]

At the most basic level, pleasant environments result in approach behaviors and unpleasant ones in avoidance. Arousal increases the basic effect of pleasure on behavior. If the environment is pleasant, increasing arousal can create excitement, leading to a stronger positive response. On the other hand, if a service environment is unpleasant, increasing arousal levels would move customers into the "distressed" region. For example, loud fast-beat music would increase the stress levels of shoppers trying to make their way through crowded aisles on a pre-Christmas Friday evening. In such situations, retailers should try to lower the information load of the environment.

The Servicescape Model—An Integrative Framework of Consumer Responses to Service Environments

Building on the basic models in environmental psychology, Mary Jo Bitner has developed a comprehensive model.[10] Figure 10.7 shows the main dimensions of service environments, which she named servicescapes. These dimensions include ambient conditions, space/functionality, and signs, symbols and artifacts. People tend to perceive these dimensions as a whole. Therefore, key to effective design is how well each individual part fits together with everything else in that environment.

Next, the model shows that there are customer and employee-response moderators. This means, the same service environment can have different effects on different customers. It depends on who that customer is and what he or she likes. Rap music may be of great pleasure to some customer segments, and a torture to others.

One important contribution of Bitner's model is the addition of employee responses to the service environment. After all, employees spend much more time in the servicescape than customers do. It is therefore extremely important that designers are aware of how a particular environment enhances (or at least does not reduce) the productivity of frontline personnel and the quality of service that they deliver.

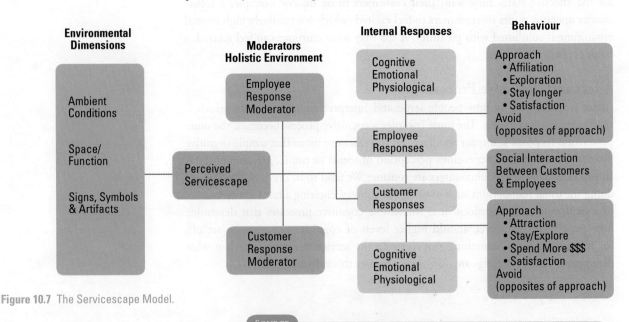

Figure 10.7 The Servicescape Model.

SOURCE

Bitner, M.J. (1992) Servicescapes: The impact of physical surroundings on customers and employees. *Journal of Marketing*, 56 (April), pp. 57–71.

Internal customer and employee responses can be grouped into cognitive responses (e.g. quality perceptions and beliefs), subsequent emotional responses (e.g. feelings and moods) and physiological responses (e.g. pain and comfort). These internal responses lead to observable behavioral responses such as avoiding a crowded departmental store, or responding positively to a relaxing environment by remaining there longer and spending extra money on impulse purchases.

DIMENSIONS OF THE SERVICE ENVIRONMENT

Service environments are complex and have many design elements that can shape customer and employee responses. Table 10.1 provides an overview of all the design elements that might be encountered in a retail outlet. In this section, we will focus on the main dimensions of the service environment in the servicescape model, which are the ambient conditions, space and functionality, and signs, symbols and artifacts.

 LO 3

List the dimensions of the service environment and describe their impact on behavior.

Table 10.1 Design elements of a retail store environment

Dimensions	Design Elements	
Exterior facilities	• Architectural style • Height of building • Size of building • Color of building • Exterior walls and exterior signs • Storefront • Marquee • Lawns and gardens	• Window displays • Entrances • Visibility • Uniqueness • Surrounding stores • Surrounding areas • Congestion • Parking and accessibility
General interior	• Flooring and carpeting • Color schemes • Lighting • Scents • Odors (e.g. tobacco smoke) • Sounds and music • Fixtures • Wall composition • Wall textures (paint, wallpaper) • Ceiling composition	• Temperature • Cleanliness • Width of aisles • Dressing facilities • Vertical transportation • Dead areas • Merchandise layout and displays • Price levels and displays • Cash register placement • Technology, modernization
Store layout	• Allocation of floor space for selling, merchandise, personnel, and customers • Placement of merchandise • Grouping of merchandise • Workstation placement • Placement of equipment • Placement of cash register	• Waiting areas • Traffic flow • Waiting queues • Furniture • Dead areas • Department locations • Arrangements within departments
Interior displays	• Point-of-purchase displays • Posters, signs, and cards • Pictures and artwork • Wall decorations • Themesetting • Ensemble	• Racks and cases • Product display • Price display • Cut cases and dump bins • Mobiles
Social dimensions	• Personnel characteristics • Employee uniforms • Crowding	• Customer characteristics • Privacy • Self-service

SOURCE

Barry Berman and Joel R. Evans, Retail management—A strategic approach, 8th ed. Upper Saddle River, NJ: Prentice Hall, 2001, p. 604; L. W. Turley and Ronald E. Milliman, "Atmospheric effects on shopping behavior: A review of the experimental literature." *Journal of Business Research*, 49 (2000): pp. 193–211.

PART III

The Impact of Ambient Conditions

Ambient conditions refer to those characteristics of the environment that relate to our five senses. Even when these conditions are not consciously noticed, they may still affect people's emotional well-being, perceptions, and even attitudes and behaviors. The ambient environment or atmosphere is made up of hundreds of design elements and details in the service environment that have to work together to create the desired service environment. An ambient condition includes lighting and color schemes, scents or smells, sounds such as noise and music, size and shapes, and air quality and temperature. These are mechanical clues that contribute to the overall customer experience.[11] They are perceived both separately and holistically. See how ambient conditions can contribute to patient recovery as described in Service Insights 10.1.

::: SERVICE INSIGHTS 10.1 •

Hospital Servicescape and Its Effects on Patients and Employees

Thankfully, most of us do not have to stay in hospitals. If it should happen to us, we hope our stay will allow us to recover in a suitable environment. But what is considered suitable in a hospital?

Patients may contract infections while in hospital, feel stressed by contact with many strangers yet bored without much to do, dislike the food, and unable to rest well. All these factors may delay a patients' recovery. Medical workers usually work under demanding conditions and may contract infectious diseases, be stressed by the emotional labor of dealing with difficult patients, or be at risk of injury when exposed to various types of medical equipment. Research has shown that more care in designing the hospital servicescape reduces these risks and contributes to patient well-being and recovery, as well as staff welfare and productivity. The recommendations include:

- Provide single-bed rooms. These can lower infections caught in the hospital, improve rest and sleep quality by lessening disturbance caused by other patients sharing the room, increase patient privacy, facilitate social support by families, and even improve communication between staff and patients.

- Reduce noise levels. This leads to decreased stress levels for staff, and improved sleep for patients.

- Provide distractions for patients, including areas of greenery and nature that they can see. This can aid patient recovery.

- Improve lighting, especially access to natural light. A lighted environment increases cheerfulness in the building. Natural lighting can lead to reduced length of stay for patients. Staff work better under proper lighting and make fewer errors.

- Improve ventilation and air filtration to reduce the transmission of airborne viruses and improve air quality in the building.

- Develop user-friendly "wayfinding" systems. Hospitals are complex buildings and it is very frustrating for the many first-time and infrequent visitors to get lost, especially when rushing to see a loved one who has been hospitalized.

- Design the layout of patient care units and the location of nurse stations to reduce unnecessary walking within the building and the tiredness and waste of time that can result. In this way, the quality of care to patients can be improved. Well-designed layouts also enhance staff communication and activities.

SOURCE

Ulrich, R., Quan, X., Zimring, C., Joseph, A., & Choudhary, R. (2004). The role of the physical environment in the hospital of the 21st century: A once-in-a-lifetime opportunity. Report to the center for health design for the *Designing the 21st Century Hospital* Project, funded by the Robert Wood Johnson Foundation. (September).

Music

Let us next discuss a number of important ambient dimensions, starting with music. Music can have powerful effects on perceptions and behaviors in service settings, even if played at barely audible volumes. The components of music include tempo, volume, and harmony, and these are perceived as a whole. The effect of music on behavior depends on the individual. Younger people tend to like different music and therefore respond differently from older people to the same piece of music.[12] Studies have found that fast tempo music and high volume music increases arousal levels.

People tend to adjust their pace, either intentionally or unintentionally, to match the tempo of music. This means that restaurants can speed up table turnover by increasing the tempo and volume of the music and serve more diners. On the other hand, they can slow diners down with slow beat music and softer volume. In fact, with slow beat music, revenues from the sale of beverages can be increased.[13] Relaxing music can lower stress levels in a hospital's surgery waiting room. Pleasant music can even improve customers' perceptions of and attitudes towards service personnel.

Would it surprise you to learn that music can also be used to discourage the wrong type of customers? Many service environments, including subway systems, supermarkets and other public locations, attract individuals who are not customers. The London Underground (subway) system makes use of classical music by Mozart and Haydn to discourage behavior like standing around doing nothing, or destroying public property. A London Underground spokesperson reports that the most effective are anything written by Mozart or sung by Pavarotti. According to Adrian North, a psychologist researching music-behavior links at Leicester University, unfamiliarity is a key factor in driving people away. When the target individuals are not used to strings and woodwind, Mozart will do (Figure 10.8).

Figure 10.8 Classical music can be used to deter vandals and loiterers.

Scent

After music, let us focus on scent as the next important ambient dimension. Specifically, we focus on ambient scent or smell, which is the one that is spread throughout an environment. It may or may not be consciously perceived by customers, and is not related to any particular product. We experience the power of smell when we are hungry and get to smell freshly baked croissants long before we pass a Delifrance Café. This smell makes us aware of our hunger and points us to the solution (i.e. walk into Delifrance and get some food). The presence of scent can have a strong impact on mood, affective and evaluative responses, and even purchase intentions and in-store behaviors.[14]

Service marketers will be interested in how to make you hungry and thirsty in the restaurant, or relax you in a dentist's waiting room. In aromatherapy, it is generally accepted that scents have special characteristics and can be used to obtain certain emotional, physiological, and behavioral responses (Figure 10.9).

Figure 10.9 Aromatherapy can induce a state of relaxation that helps one to sleep.

Table 10.2 Aromatherapy – The effects of selected fragrances on people.

Fragrance	Aroma Type	Aromatherapy Class	Traditional Use	Potential Psychological Effect on People
Eucalyptus	Camphoraceous	Toning, stimulating	Deodorant, antiseptic, soothing agent	Stimulating and energizing
Lavender	Herbaceous	Calming, balancing, soothing	Muscle relaxant, soothing agent, astringent	Relaxing and calming
Lemon	Citrus	Energizing, uplifting	Antiseptic, soothing agent	Soothing energy levels
Black pepper	Spicy	Balancing, soothing	Muscle relaxant, aphrodisiac	Balancing people's emotions

Table 10.2 shows the effects of specific scents on people as set down by aromatherapy. In service settings, research has shown that scents can have significant impact on customer perceptions, attitudes, and behaviors. For example:

▶ Gamblers put in 45 percent more quarters into slot machines when a Las Vegas casino was scented with a pleasant artificial smell. When the intensity of the scent was increased, spending jumped by 53 percent.[15]

▶ People were more willing to buy Nike sneakers and pay more for them—an average of US$10.33 more per pair—when they tried on the shoes in a floral-scented room. The same effect was found even when the scent was so light that people could not detect it, that is, the scent was unconsciously perceived.[16]

Color

In addition to music and scent, researchers have found that colors have a strong impact on people's feelings. The color system commonly used in psychological research is the Munsell System, which defines colors in terms of hue, value, and chroma.[17] Hue is the pigment of the color (i.e. the name of the color: red, orange, yellow, green, blue or violet). Value is the degree of lightness or darkness of the color. Chroma refers to hue-intensity, saturation or brilliance. High-chroma colors have a high intensity of pigmentation in them and are seen as rich and bright. Low-chroma colors are seen as dull.

Hues are classified into warm colors (red, orange and yellow hues) and cold colors (blue and green). Orange (a mix of red and yellow) is the warmest and blue is the coldest of the colors. These colors can be used to manage the warmth of an environment. For example, if a violet is too warm, you can cool it off by reducing the red. If a red is too cold, warm it up by giving it some orange.[18] Warm colors are associated not only with happy mood states, and arousal, but also increased anxiety. Cool colors reduce arousal levels and can bring out emotions such as peacefulness, calmness, love, and happiness. Table 10.3 summarizes common associations and responses to colors. Research in a service environment context has shown that despite differing color preferences, people are generally drawn to warm color environments (Figure 10.10).[19] Warm colors encourage fast decision making. In service situations, they are best suited for low-involvement decisions or impulse purchases. Cool colors are preferred when consumers need time to make high-involvement purchases.

Table 10.3 Common associations and human responses to colors.

Color	Degree of Warmth	Nature Symbol	Common Association and Human Responses to Color
Red	Warm	Earth	High energy and passion; can excite and stimulate emotions, expressions, and warmth
Orange	Warmest	Sunset	Emotions, expressions, and warmth
Yellow	Warm	Sun	Optimism, clarity, intellect, and mood-enchancing
Green	Cool	Growth, grass and trees	Nurturing, healing and unconditional love
Blue	Coolest	Sky and Ocean	Relaxation, serenity and loyality
Indigo	Cool	Sunset	Mediation and spirituality
Violet	Cool	Violet flower	Spirituality, reduces stress, can create an inner feeling of calm

Although we have an understanding of the general impact of colors, their use in any specific context needs to be approached with caution. For example, a transportation company in Israel decided to paint its buses green. This was part of an environmentalism public relations campaign. Reactions to this seemingly simple act from different groups of people were unexpectedly negative. Some customers found that green buses blended in with the environment and were therefore more difficult to see. Others felt that it represented undesirable ideas such as terrorism or opposing sports teams.

Spatial Layout and Functionality

After ambient conditions, spatial layout and functionality is another key dimension of the service environment.
They affect the user friendliness and the ability of the facility to service customers well. Spatial layout refers to the floor plan, size and shape of furnishings, counters, and possible machinery and equipment, and the ways in which they are arranged. Functionality refers to the ability of those items to make the performance of service easier. Poor layout and functionality not only affect the efficiency of the service operation, they also have direct impact on the customer experience. Tables which are too close together in a café, counters in a bank that lack privacy, uncomfortable chairs in a lecture theater, and lack of car parking space can all leave negative impressions on customers. This will affect their buying behavior and satisfaction.

Spatial layout and functionality have to deliver their part of the value proposition. For example, in a community center which aims at bringing people together to learn subjects such as a language or astrology, class rooms can be designed to make it easier to learn by having U-shaped classrooms, or arranging groups around tables.

Figure 10.10 Bright and warm colors are usually used in environments with children to provide attractive and cheery effect.

Signs, Symbols, and Artifacts

Many things in the service environment act as signals to communicate the firm's image. They also help customers find their way (e.g. to certain service counters, departments, or the exit), and to let them know the service script (e.g. for a queuing system). First time customers will automatically try to draw meaning from the signs, symbols, and artifacts to guide them through the service environment and service processes.

Signs are signals which can be used as labels (e.g. to indicate the name of the department or counter), for giving directions (e.g. entrance, exit, way to lifts and toilets), for communicating the service script (e.g. take a queue number and watch for your number to be called, or clear the tray after your meal) and behavioral rules (e.g. switch off or turn your mobile devices to silent mode during the performance, or smoking/no-smoking areas). Signs are often used to teach behavioral rules in service settings. Some signs are quite interesting and may be quite obvious, but other signs need the person to think a little before understanding the meaning (Figure 10.11).

One challenge for designers is to use signs, symbols, and artifacts to guide customers clearly through the process of service delivery. This task is especially important when there are many new customers, or many who seldom visit a service facility. It is also important in self-service situations, especially when there are few service employees available to help customers through the process.

Customers become confused when they cannot make out clear signals from a servicescape. They may become angry and frustrated as a result. Think about the last time you were in a hurry and tried to find your way through an unfamiliar hospital, shopping center or airport where the signs were not clear. At many service facilities, customers' first point of contact is likely to be the car park. As emphasized in Service Insights 10.2, the principles of effective environment design apply even in this environment.

Interestingly, symbols and artifacts related to *feng shui* are increasingly being used in some countries and organizations. *Feng Shui*, meaning "wind" and "water" in Chinese, is an ancient Chinese practice of placing and arranging spaces to create harmony (Figure 10.12). *Feng shui* elements are included in the exterior and interior design of buildings and interior decorations. The Hong Kong Tourism Board and the Peninsula Hotel's Peninsula Academy, Hong Kong, have been known to consult *feng shui* masters to create harmony amongst the elements and ensure that people feel good in the environment and prosperity to the organization.[20]

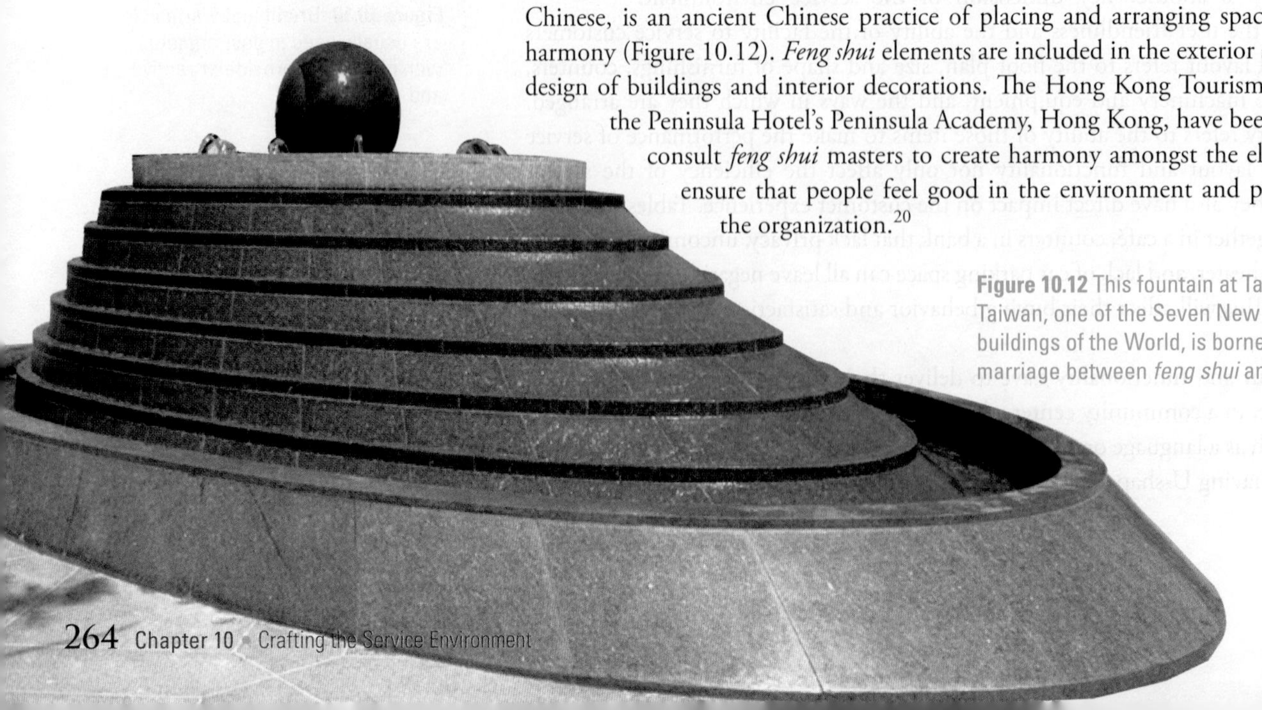

Figure 10.11 Confusing signs can lead people nowhere.

Figure 10.12 This fountain at Taipei 101, Taiwan, one of the Seven New Wonders and tallest buildings of the World, is borne out of the modern marriage between *feng shui* and architectural design.

Guidelines For **Parking Design**

Car parks play an important role at many service facilities. Effective use of signs, symbols and artifacts in a parking lot helps customers find their way. It also displays a positive image for the service firm.

- *Friendly warnings*—all warning signs should communicate a customer benefit. For instance, "Fire lane—for everyone's safety we ask you not to park in the fire lane."

- *Safety lighting*—good lighting in all areas makes life easier for customers and improves safety. Firms may want to draw attention to this with notices stating that "parking lots have been specially lit for your safety."

- *Help customers remember where they left their vehicle*—forgetting where one left the family car in a large parking structure can be a nightmare.

Many car parks have used color-coded floors to help customers remember which level they parked on. In addition, many car parks also mark sections with special symbols like different kinds of animals. This helps customers to remember not only the level, but the section where the car is parked. At Boston's Logan Airport, each level has been assigned a theme connected with Massachusetts. Examples include Paul Revere's Ride, Cape Cod, or the Boston Marathon. An image is attached to each theme—a male figure on horseback, a lighthouse, or a woman runner. While waiting for the elevator, travelers hear a few bars of music that are tied to the theme for that level. For the Boston Marathon floor, it is the theme music from *Chariots of Fire*, an Oscar-winning movie about an Olympic runner.

- *Maternity parking*—handicapped spaces are often required by law but require special stickers on the vehicle. A few thoughtful organizations have special expectant mother parking spaces, painted with a blue/pink stork. This strategy shows a sense of caring and understanding of customer needs.

- *Fresh paint*—curbs, cross walks and lot lines should be repainted regularly before any cracking, peeling, or disrepair become obvious. Repainting often give positive cleanliness signals and sends out a positive image.[21]

People are Part of the Service Environment Too

The appearance and behavior of both service personnel and customers can strengthen the impression created by a service environment, or weaken it. Dennis Nickson and his colleagues use the term "aesthetic labor" to capture the importance of the physical image of service personnel who serve customers directly.[22] Employees at Disney theme parks are called cast members. Whether the staff is acting as Cinderella, one of the seven dwarfs, or as park cleaner or the person managing Buzz Lightyear's Tomorrowland booth, these cast members must dress up and look the part. Once dressed up, they must "perform" for the guests.

Figure 10.13 Distinctive restaurant servicescapes—from table settings to furniture and room design—create different customer expectations of these two restaurants.

For customers, marketing communications may seek to attract those who will not only appreciate the ambience created by the service provider but actively enhance it by their appearance and behavior. In hospitality and retail settings, newcomers often look at the existing customers before deciding whether to patronize the service firm. Figure 10.13 shows the interior of two restaurants. Imagine that you have just entered each of these two dining rooms. How is each restaurant positioning itself within the restaurant industry? What sort of meal experience can you expect? And what are the clues that you use to make your judgments? In particular, what assumptions do you make from looking at the customers who are already seated in each restaurant?

LO 4

Understand what goes into designing an effective servicescape.

PUTTING IT ALL TOGETHER

Although individuals often look at certain aspects or individual design features of an environment, it is the total combination of features that influences consumer responses. Consumers perceive service environments as a whole (i.e. holistically).[23]

Design with a Holistic View

Whether a dark, glossy wooden floor is the perfect flooring depends on everything else in that service environment. These include the type, color scheme and materials of the furniture, the lighting, the promotional materials, the overall brand perception and positioning of the firm (Figure 10.14). Servicescapes have to be seen as a whole, which means no dimension of the design should be planned without considering other aspects, because everything depends on everything else.

As the design of the environment needs to be planned as a whole, it is more like a work of art. Therefore, professional designers tend to focus on specific types of servicescapes. For example, a handful of famous interior designers do nothing but create hotel lobbies around the world. Similarly, there are design experts, who focus only on restaurants, bars, clubs, cafés and bistros, or retail outlets, or healthcare facilities, and so forth. Spain's Guggenheim Museum, Bilbao, in the opening vignette is one such example where Frank Gehry designed the building not only for visitors to admire the works of art on display, but to also admire the architecture of the building, which is a masterpiece of art in itself.

Design from a Customer's Perspective

Many service environments are built with a focus on physical appearance. Designers sometimes forget that the most important design factor should be the customers who will be using the environment.

Figure 10.14 Arne Jacobson's enduring egg chair instantly brightens up any servicescape.

Ron Kaufman, a consultant and trainer on service excellence, experienced the following design weaknesses in two new service environments:

▶ "A new hotel just had opened in Jordan without clear signage that would guide guests from the ballrooms to the restrooms. The signs that did exist were etched in muted gold on dark marble pillars. More 'obvious' signs were apparently inappropriate amidst such elegant décor. Very swish, very chic, but who were they designing it for?"

▶ "At a new airport lounge in a major Asian city, a partition of colorful glass hung from the ceiling. My luggage lightly brushed against it as I walked inside. The entire partition shook and several panels came undone. A staff member hurried over and began carefully reassembling the panels. (Thank goodness nothing broke.) I apologized profusely. 'Don't worry,' she replied, 'This happens all the time.'" An airport lounge is a heavy traffic area. People are always moving in and out. Ron Kaufman keeps asking "What were the interior designers thinking? Who were they designing it for?"

"I am regularly amazed," declares Kaufman, "by brand new facilities that are obviously user 'unfriendly'! What were the architects thinking about? Size? Grandeur? Physical exercise? Who were they designing it for?" He draws the following key learning point: "It's easy to get caught up in designing new things that are 'cool' or 'elegant' or 'hot'. But unless you keep your customer in mind throughout, you could end up with an investment that's not."

Alain d'Astous explored environmental aspects that irritate shoppers. His findings highlighted the following common problems:

▶ *Ambient Conditions* (ordered by how negative and frequent the irritation is):

  o Store is not clean

  o Too hot inside the store or the shopping center

  o Music inside the store is too loud

  o Bad smell in the store.

- *Environmental Design Variables*:
  - o No mirror in the dressing room.
  - o Unable to find what one needs.
  - o Not enough directions within the store.
  - o Arrangement of store items has been changed.
  - o Store is too small.
  - o Finding the way in a large shopping center[24] (Figure 10.15).

Figure 10.15 Badly designed shopping centers mar the shopping experience.

Use Tools That Can Guide Servicescape Design

As a manager, how might you determine which aspects of the servicescape irritate customers and which they like? Among the tools that you can use are:

- ▶ **Careful observation** of customers' behavior and responses to the service environment by management, supervisors and frontline staff.

- ▶ **Feedback and ideas from frontline staff and customers** using a variety of research tools ranging from complaint and compliment analysis to focus groups and surveys. (This type of survey is called environmental surveys if they focus on the design of the service environment.)

- ▶ **Photo audit** is a method of asking customers to take photographs of their service experience. These photographs can be used later as a basis for further interviews of their experience, or included as part of a survey about the service experience.[25]

- ▶ **Field experiments** can be used to control specific dimensions in an environment and observe the effects. For instance, researchers can experiment with various types of music and scents, and then measure the time and money customers spend in the environment. Laboratory experiments, using slides or videos or other ways to create real-world service environments (such as computer virtual tours), can be used to examine the impact of changes in design elements. These methods are used when the real environment cannot really be controlled. Examples include testing of different color schemes, spatial layouts, or styles of furnishing.

▶ **Blueprinting** the service (described in Chapter 8) can be extended to include the physical evidence in the environment. Design elements can be noted down as the customer moves through each step of the service delivery process. Photos and videos can be attached to the blueprint to make it clearer.

Table 10.4 shows an examination of a customer's visit to a movie theater. It identifies how different environmental elements at each step were better than expected or failed to meet expectations. The service process was broken up into steps, decisions, duties, and activities, all designed to take the customer through the entire service encounter. The more a service company can see, understand, and experience the same things as its customers, the more it will be able to realize mistakes in the design of its environment and further improve on what is already working well.

Table 10.4 A visit to the movies: the service environment as perceived by the customer.

Steps in the Service Encounter	Design of the Service Environment	
	Exceeds Expectations	Fails Expectations
Locate a parking lot	Ample room in a bright place near the entrance, with a security officer protecting your valuables	Insufficient parking spaces, so patrons have to park in another lot
Queuing up to obtain tickets	Strategic placement of mirrors, posters of upcoming movies, and entertainment news to ease perception of long wait, if any; movies and time slots easily seen; ticket availability clearly communicated	A long queue and having to wait for a long while; difficult to see quickly what movies are being shown at what time slots and whether tickets are still available
Checking of tickets to enter the theater	A very well maintained lobby with clear directions to the theater and posters of the movie to enhance patrons' experience	A dirty lobby with rubbish strewn and unclear or misleading directions to the movie theater
Go to the restroom before the movie starts	Sparkling clean, spacious, brightly lit, dry floors, well stocked, nice décor, clear mirrors wiped regularly	Dirty, with an unbearable odor; broken toilets; no hand towels, soap, or toilet paper; overcrowded; dusty and dirty mirrors
Enter the theater and locate your seat	Spotless theater; well designed with no bad seats; sufficient lighting to locate your seat; spacious, comfortable chairs, with drink and popcorn holders on each seat; and a suitable temperature	Rubbish on the floor, broken seats, sticky floors, gloomy and insufficient lighting, burned-out exit signs
Watch the movie	Excellent sound system and film quality, nice audience, an enjoyable and memorable entertainment experience overall	Substandard sound and movie equipment, uncooperative audience that talks and smokes because of lack of "No Smoking" and other signs; a disturbing and unenjoyable entertainment experience overall
Leave the theater and return to the car	Friendly service staff greet patrons as they leave; an easy exit through a brightly lit and safe parking area, back to the car with the help of clear lot signs	A difficult trip, as patrons squeeze through a narrow exit, unable to find the car because of no or insufficient lighting

SOURCE

Adapted from Albrecht, S. (1996). See things from the customer's point of view —how to use The 'Cycles of Service' to understand what the customer goes through to do business with you. *World's Executive Digest.* (December) pp. 53–58

PART III

CHAPTER SUMMARY

LO 1 ▶ Service firms that understand the importance of the service environment pay careful attention in its design. Why is that so? There are four main purposes of the servicescape. They are

- o The service environment plays a major part in shaping customer perception of a firm and its image and positioning.

- o Customers often use the service environment as an important quality signal.

- o A well-designed service environment facilitates the service encounter for the customers and increases their satisfaction.

- o It also improves the productivity of the service operation.

LO 2 ▶ Why does the service environment have such an impact on behavior? Two theories from environmental psychology literature can help us to understand the effects of service environments on customers:

- o The Mehrabian-Russell Stimulus-Response model shows that environments influence peoples' affective state (or feelings). This in turn drives their behavior in that environment.

- o Russell's Model of Affect incorporates two key dimensions: pleasure and arousal, which jointly determine whether people spend more time and money in an environment, or whether they avoid it.

LO 3 ▶ The servicescape model builds on these theories and explains in a comprehensive framework how customers and service staff perceive and respond to service environments. In addition, it also shows the key dimensions of the service environments, which each can have important effects on customer responses. The key dimensions are:

- o Ambient conditions (including music, scents and colors)

- o Spatial layout and functionality

- o Signs, symbols and artifacts.

LO 4 ▶ Putting it all together is difficult as environments are perceived holistically. That means that no individual aspect of the environment should be designed without considering everything else in that environment. In fact, designing service environments is an art.

The best service environments are designed with the customer's perspective in mind. Good environments facilitate smooth movement through the service process. Tools that can be used to design good servicescapes include careful observation, feedback from frontline staff and customers, photo audits, field experiments and blueprinting.

UNLOCK YOUR LEARNING

These keywords are found within the sections of each Learning Objective (LO). They are integral in understanding the services marketing concepts taught in each section. Having a firm grasp of these keywords and how they are used is essential in helping you do well for your course, and in the real and very competitive marketing scene out there.

LO 1
1. Attention-creating medium
2. Effect-creating medium
3. Enhance productivity
4. Message-creating medium
5. Service environment
6. Servicescapes
7. Shape customers' experiences
8. Value proposition

LO 2
9. Affect
10. Approach
11. Ambient conditions
12. Arousal
13. Artifacts
14. Avoidance
15. Cognitive process
16. Customer response moderators

17. Environmental psychology
18. Employee-response moderators
19. Pleasure
20. Mehrabian-Russell Stimulus-Response Model
21. Space and functionality
22. Signs
23. Symbols
24. The Servicescape model

LO 3
25. Aromatherapy
26. Chroma
27. Color
28. Dimensions of the service environment
29. *Feng shui*
30. Floorplan
31. Harmony
32. Hue
33. Holistically
34. Lighting

35. Music
36. Munsell System
37. People
38. Scents
39. Size and shape
40. Temperature
41. Tempo
42. Value
43. Volume

LO 4
44. Blueprinting
45. Customer's perspective
46. Environmental design
47. Field experiments
48. Photo audit

How well do you know the language of services marketing? Quiz yourself!

 Not for the academically faint-of-heart

For each keyword you are able to recall without referring to earlier pages, give yourself a point (and a pat on the back). Tally your score at the end and see if you earned the right to be called—a *services marketeer.*

SCORE

0 – 8	Services Marketing is done a great disservice.
9 – 17	The midnight oil needs to be lit, pronto.
18 – 24	I know what you *didn't* do all semester.
25 – 33	A close shave with success.
34 – 42	Now, go forth and market.
43 – 48	There should be a marketing concept named after you.

Review Questions

1. What is the purpose of the service environment?

2. Describe how Mehrabian-Russell Stimulus-Response Model and Russell's Model of Affect explain consumer responses to a service environment.

3. What is the relationship or link between Russell's Model of Affect and the Servicescape Model?

4. Why is it that the responses of different customers can be vastly different to the same service environment?

5. Explain the dimensions of ambient conditions and how each can influence customer behavior in a service environment.

6. What are the roles of signs, symbols and artifacts?

7. What tools are available for aiding our understanding of customer responses, and for guiding the design and improvement of service environments?

WORK YOUR ESM

Application Exercises

1. Identify firms from three different service sectors where the service environment is a crucial part of the overall value proposition. Analyze and explain in detail the value that is being delivered by the service environment.

2. Visit a service environment, and have a detailed look around. Experience the environment and try and feel how the various design parameters shape what you feel and how you behave in that setting.

3. Visit a self-service environment and analyze how the design dimensions guide you thorough the service process. What do you find most effective for yourself, and what seems least effective? How could that environment be improved to further ease the "way-finding" for self-service customers?

4. Take a digital camera and conduct an environmental audit of a specific servicescape. Photograph examples of excellent and very poor design features. Develop concrete suggestions how this environment can be improved.

ENDNOTES

1. http://en.wikipedia.org/wiki/Guggenheim_Museum_Bilbao, Accessed March 2008; Beatriz Plaza. (2007). The Bilbao effect: *Museum News*, (September/October), 13–15, 68. Lee, D. (2007). Bilbao, 10 years later. *New York Times*, 23(September). Available: http://travel.nytimes.com/2007/09/23/travel/23bilbao.html, Accessed April 2008.

2. Bitner, M. J. (1992). Servicescapes: The impact of physical surroundings on customers and employees. *Journal of Marketing*, 56, pp. 57–71.

3. Reimer, A., & Kuehn, R. (2005). The impact of servicescape on quality perception. *European Journal of Marketing*, 39(7/8), pp. 785–808.

4. Pullman, M. E., & Gross, M. A. (2004). Ability of experience design elements to elicit emotions and loyalty behaviors. *Decision Sciences*, 35(1), pp. 551–578.

5. Cullen, L. T. (2005, August 22). Is luxury the ticket? *Time*, pp. 38–39.

6. Chase, R. B., & Stewart, D. M. (1994). Making your service fail-safe. *Sloan Management Review*, 35, pp. 35–44.

7. Donovan, R. J., & Rossiter, J. R. (1982). Store atmosphere: An environmental psychology approach. *Journal of Retailing*, 58(1), pp. 34–57.

8. Russell, J. A. (1980). A circumplex model of affect. *Journal of Personality and Social Psychology*, 39(6), pp. 1161–1178.

9. Wirtz, J., & Bateson, J. E. G. (1999). Consumer satisfaction with services: Integrating the environmental perspective in services marketing into the traditional disconfirmation paradigm. *Journal of Business Research*, 44(1), pp. 55–66.

10. Bitner, M. J. (1992). Service environments: The impact of physical surroundings on customers and employees. *Journal of Marketing*, 56(April), pp. 57–71.

11. Berry, L. L., & Carbone, L. P. (2007). Build loyalty through experience management. *Quality Progress*, 40(9), (September), pp. 26–32.

12. Oakes, S. (2000). The influence of the musicscape within service environments. *Journal of Services Marketing*, 14(7), pp. 539–556.

13. Caldwell, C., & Hibbert, S. A. (2002). The influence of music tempo and musical preference on restaurant patrons' behavior. *Psychology and Marketing*, 19(11), pp. 895–917.

14. Spangenberg, E. R., Crowley, A. E., Henderson, P. W. (1996). Improving the store environment: Do olfactory cues affect evaluations and behaviors? *Journal of Marketing*, 60(April), pp. 67–80; Bone, P. F., & Ellen, P. S. (1999). Scents in the marketplace: Explaining a fraction of olfaction. *Journal of Retailing*, 75(2), pp. 243–262; Caplan, J. (2006). Sense and sensibility. *Time*, 168(16), pp. 66–67.

15. Hirsch, A. R. (1995). Effects of ambient odors on slot machine usage in a Las Vegas casino. *Psychology and Marketing*, 12(7), pp. 585–594.

16. Hirsch, A. R., & Gay, S. E. (1991). Effect on ambient olfactory stimuli on the evaluation of a common consumer product. *Chemical Senses*, 16, p. 535.

17. Munsell, A. H. (1996). *A Munsell Color Product*. New York: Kollmorgen Corporation.

18. Holtzschuhe, L. (2006). *Understanding Color – An Introduction for Designers* (p. 51), New Jersey: John Wiley.

19. Bellizzi, J. A., Crowley, A. E., & Hasty, R. W. (1983). The effects of color in store design. *Journal of Retailing*, 59(1), pp. 21–45.

20. Available: http://www.raymond-lo.com; http://en.wikipedia.org/wiki/Feng_Shui, Accessed on April 2008.

21. Carbone, L. P., & Haeckel, S. H. (1994) Engineering customer experiences. *Marketing Management*, 3(3) (Winter), pp. 9–18; Carbone, L. P., Haeckel, S. H., & Berry, L. L. (2003). How to lead the customer experience. *Marketing Management*, 12(1).(Jan/Feb),18; Berry, L. L., & Carbone, L. P. (2007). Build loyalty through experience management. *Quality Progress*, 40(9) (September), pp. 26–32.

22. Nickson, D., Warhurst, C., & Dutton, E. (2005). The importance of attitude and appearance in the service encounter in retail and hospitality. *Managing Service Quality*, 2, pp. 195–208.

23 Mattila, A. S., & Wirtz, J. (2001). Congruency of scent and music as a driver of in-store evaluations and behavior. *Journal of Retailing*, 77, pp. 273–289.

24 d' Astous, A. (2000). Irritating aspects of the shopping environment. *Journal of Business Research*, 49, pp. 149–156; Hoffman, K. D., Kelly, S. W., & Chung, B. C. (2003). A CIT investigation of servicescape failures and associated recovery strategies, *Journal of Services Marketing*, 17(4), pp. 322–340.

25 Pullman, M. E., & Robson, S. K. A. (2007). Visual methods: Using photographs to capture customers' experience with design. *Cornell Hotel and Restaurant Administration Quarterly*, 48(2), pp. 121–144.

BLANK

11

managing people for
SERVICE
ADVANTAGE

LEARNING OBJECTIVES

By the end of this chapter, students should be able to:

LO 1 Explain why service staff is so important to the success of a service firm.

LO 2 Understand the factors that make the work of frontline staff so difficult and stressful.

LO 3 Describe the cycles of failures, mediocrity, and success in Human Resource (HR) management for service firms.

LO 4 Understand the key elements of the Service Talent Cycle and know how to get HR right in service firms.

LO 5 Know how to attract, select and hire the right people for service jobs.

LO 6 Explain the key areas in which service employees need training.

LO 7 Understand why empowerment is so important in many frontline jobs, and know the three levels of employee involvement.

LO 8 Explain how to build high-performance service delivery teams.

LO 9 Know how to motivate and energize service employees so that they will deliver service excellence and productivity.

LO 10 Understand the role of service leadership and culture in developing people for service advantage.

OPENING VIGNETTE[1]

CORA GRIFFITH — THE OUTSTANDING WAITRESS

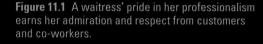

Figure 11.1 A waitress' pride in her professionalism earns her admiration and respect from customers and co-workers.

Cora Griffith is a waitress for the Orchard Café at the Paper Valley Hotel in Appleton, Wisconsin. She is excellent in her role, appreciated by first-time customers, famous with her regular customers, and admired and respected by her co-workers. Cora loves her work and it shows. She implements the following nine rules of success:

1. **Treat Customers like Family.** First-time customers are not allowed to feel like strangers. Cora smiles, chats, and includes everyone at the table in the conversation. She is as respectful to children as she is to adults and makes it a point to learn and use everyone's name. "I want people to feel like they're sitting down to dinner right at my house. I want them to feel they're welcome, that they can get comfortable, that they can relax. I don't just serve people, I pamper them."

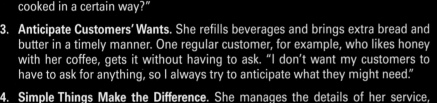

2. **Listen First.** Cora has developed her listening skills to the point that she rarely writes down customers' orders. She listens carefully and provides a customized service: "Are they in a hurry? Or do they have a special diet or like their selection cooked in a certain way?"

3. **Anticipate Customers' Wants.** She refills beverages and brings extra bread and butter in a timely manner. One regular customer, for example, who likes honey with her coffee, gets it without having to ask. "I don't want my customers to have to ask for anything, so I always try to anticipate what they might need."

4. **Simple Things Make the Difference.** She manages the details of her service, keeps track of the cleanliness of the utensils and their correct placement. The fold for napkins must be just right. She inspects each plate in the kitchen before taking it to the table. She provides crayons for small children to draw pictures while waiting for the meal. "It's the little things that please the customer."

5. **Work Smart.** Cora scans all her tables at once, looking for opportunities to combine tasks. "Never do just one thing at a time. And never go from the kitchen to the dining room empty-handed. Take coffee or iced tea or water with you." When she refills one water glass, she refills others. When clearing one plate, she clears others. "You have to be organized, and you have to keep in touch with the big picture."

6. **Keep Learning.** Cora makes it an ongoing effort to improve existing skills and learn new ones.

7. **Success is Where You Find It.** Cora is satisfied with her work. She finds satisfaction in pleasing her customers, and she enjoys helping other people enjoy. Her positive attitude is a positive force in the restaurant. "If customers come to the restaurant in a bad mood, I'll try to cheer them up before they leave." Her definition of success: "To be happy in life."

8. **All for One, One for All.** She has been working with many of the same co-workers for more than eight years. The team supports one another on the crazy days when 300 conventioneers come to the restaurant for breakfast at the same time. Everyone helps out. The wait staff cover for one another, the managers bus the tables, the chefs garnish the plates. "We are like a little family. We know each other very well and we help each other out. If we have a crazy day, I'll go in the kitchen towards the end of the shift and say, 'Man, I'm just proud of us. We really worked hard today."

9. **Take Pride in Your Work.** Cora believes in the importance of her work and in the need to do it well. "I don't think of myself as 'just a waitress'…. I've chosen to be a waitress. I'm doing this to my full potential, and I give it my best. I tell anyone who's starting out: take pride in what you do. You're never just an anything, no matter what you do. You give it your all … and you do it with pride."

Cora Griffith is a success story. She is loyal to her employer and dedicated to her customers and co-workers. Says Cora, "I have always wanted to do my best. However, the owners really are the ones who taught me how important it is to take care of the customer and who gave me the freedom to do it. The company always has listened to my concerns and followed up. Had I not worked for the Orchard Café, I would have been a good waitress, but I would not have been the same waitress."

...She is proud of being a waitress; proud of "touching lives"...

LO 1

Explain why service staff is so important to the success of a service firm.

SERVICE EMPLOYEES ARE EXTREMELY IMPORTANT

Highly capable and motivated people are at the center of service excellence and productivity. Cora Griffith in our opening vignette is a powerful demonstration of a frontline employee delivering service excellence and productivity, and at the same time having high job satisfaction. Many of the topics in Cora Griffith's nine rules of success are the result of good HR strategies for service firms. After having read this chapter, you will know how to get HR right in service firms, and how to get satisfied, loyal, motivated and productive service employees.

Why do you think service personnel are so crucially important for the success of service firms? There are the following three main reasons:

▶ Service personnel help to maintain the firm's positioning. They are:

o **A core part of the product.** Often, service employees are the most visible part of the service. They deliver the service and affect service quality greatly.

o **The service firm.** Frontline employees represent the service firm, and from a customer's perspective, is the firm.

o **The brand.** Frontline employees and service are often a core part of the brand. It is the employees who are the ones who either deliver or do not deliver the brand promise. Almost everybody can tell some horror story of a terrible experience they have had with a service business. Many of these same people can also remember a really good service experience. Service personnel typically play a prominent role in such dramas!

▶ Service personnel are a source of customer loyalty. Frontline employees see what customers need, deliver the service and build personal relationships with customers (Figure 11.2). These lead to customer loyalty.

▶ Service personnel are a key driver of the productivity of the frontline operation.

▶ Service personnel are also often crucially important for generating sales, cross-sales and up-sales.

Figure 11.2 Service personnel represent the firm and often build personal relationships with their customers.

The Frontline in Low-Contact Services

Most research in service management relates to high-contact services. However, many services are moving towards using low-contact delivery channels such as call centers, where contact is voice to voice rather than face to face. A growing number of transactions no longer even involve frontline staff. As a result, a large and increasing number of customer contact employees work by telephone or e-mail, never meeting customers face to face. Are frontline staff really that important for such services?

Few customers call the service hotline of their mobile operator, or their credit card company very often. However, these occasional service encounters with a telephone-based Customer Service Representative (CSR) often are "moments of truth" that affect how the customer views the firm (see Figure 11.3). Typically, such encounters involve an attempt by the customer to resolve a problem or make a special request. At the end of the conversation, a customer's personal feelings may range from,

"Your firm's customer service is excellent! When I need help, I can call you, and this is one important reason why I bank with you," all the way to "Your service stinks. I don't like interacting with you, and I am going to spread the word about how bad your service is!"

To ensure that the CSRs are aware of the important role they are playing—that they are not just telephone operators—contact centers could send their staff for Customer Operations Performance Center (COPC) certification (see Service Insights 11.1).

Figure 11.3 The pleasant disposition of call center staff can result in a positive "moment of truth", where a firm's service quality will be favorably perceived.

::: SERVICE INSIGHTS 11.1 •

Customer Operations Performance Center Inc. — **The Standards Body For Call Centers**

If a company is customer-centric and serious about running a best practice customer contact center, its managers could have heard of Customer Operations Performance Center Inc. (COPC Inc.). COPC Inc. is a leading call center consulting, training, certification and benchmarking company. The company sets the standards in call centers. For more than a decade, it has been helping companies around the world to ensure that they have systems in place that follow best practices. It helps companies to manage their call center operations, and improve performance, leading to increased customer satisfaction and profitability. Companies could achieve results of two to five times return on investment.

How are such results achieved? COPC Inc. has developed a set of standards called the COPC-2000® Family of Standards. It is a performance management and certification system that is the first in the industry. COPC Inc. audits companies to ensure that they continue to meet the standards, which measure all call center customer-touch activities. Among other aspects, included in the system are certification programs of various call center operations like call waiting, call pick-up and call drop; training in customer satisfaction; and Six Sigma in Call Centers.

COPC Inc. has worked with over 200 companies in 50 different countries. Global clients include Accenture, Apple, BT Group, Cable & Wireless, Citigroup, HP, Lenovo, Microsoft, NTT, Sony, Telefónica, Telstra, and Wipro.

SOURCE

Available: http://www.copc.com, accessed January 2008.

FRONTLINE WORK IS DIFFICULT AND STRESSFUL

The service-profit chain has high performing, satisfied employees as the main requirement for achieving service excellence and customer loyalty. However, these employees work in some of the most demanding jobs in service firms. We will next discuss the main reasons why these jobs are so stressful.

Boundary Spanning

The organizational behavior literature refers to service employees as boundary spanners. Boundary spanners link the inside of an organization to the outside world. Their roles often pull them in opposite directions causing frontline employees to experience role conflict and as a consequence, role stress. Let us look at the sources of role conflict in more detail.

Sources of Conflict

There are three main causes of role stress in frontline positions: Organization/Client, Person/Role, and Interclient conflicts.

Organization/Client Conflict

Customer contact personnel must attend to both operational and marketing goals. They are expected to delight customers, which takes time, yet have to be fast and efficient at operational tasks. In addition, they may be expected to sell, cross-sell and up-sell too. Sometimes, they are also responsible for enforcing pricing schedules that may upset or frustrate customers. Conflict also arises when customers request services, extras, or exceptions that are against the organizational rules. Service employees often are torn between following the company's rules and objectives, and satisfying customer demands. Organization/client conflict is more severe in service organizations that are not customer oriented.

Person/Role Conflict

Service staff have conflicts between their job requirements and their own personalities, self-perception and beliefs. For example, the job may require being pleasant even to rude customers. In non-work situations, they may even look down on such people. When their jobs force them to behave differently from what they prefer, they feel stressed.

Interclient Conflict

Conflicts between customers may result from such behaviors as smoking in non-smoking sections, jumping queues, speaking on a mobile phone in a cinema, and behaving obnoxiously in restaurants. When employees are asked to tell the other customer to behave, they may find this a stressful and unpleasant task, as it is often impossible to satisfy both sides.

In short, frontline staff may perform several roles, including producing service quality, productivity and sales. In combination, playing such roles often leads to role conflict and role stress for employees.[2] Although employees may experience conflict and stress, they are still expected to have a pleasant disposition towards the customer. We call this emotional labor, which in itself is an important cause of stress. Let us look at it in more detail in the next section.

Emotional Labor

The term *emotional labor* was first used by Arlie Hochschild in her book '*The Managed Heart.*'[3] Emotional labor occurs when there is a gap between the way frontline staff feel inside and the emotions that management requires them to display to their customers. Frontline staff are expected to be cheerful, friendly, compassionate, sincere or even humble. Although some service firms make an effort to recruit employees with such characteristics, there will definitely be situations when employees do not feel such positive emotions, yet are required to hide their true feelings in order to meet customer expectations (Figure 11.4).

The stress of emotional labor is illustrated in the following story: A flight attendant was approached by a passenger with "Let's have a smile." She replied with "Okay. I'll tell you what, first you smile and then I'll smile, okay?" He smiled. "Good," she said. "Now hold that for eight hours," and walked away.

Forward-looking companies take steps to address the problem of emotional labor. For example, Singapore Airlines (SIA) has a reputation for service excellence. Therefore, its customers tend to have very high expectations and can be very demanding. This puts a lot of pressure on its frontline. The Commercial Training Manager of Singapore Airlines explained:

> "We have a motto: 'If SIA can't do it for you, no other airline can.' So we encourage staff to try to sort things out, and to do as much as they can for the customer. Although they are very proud, and indeed protective of the company, we need to help them deal with the emotional turmoil of having to handle their customers well, and at the same time, feel they're not being taken advantage of. The challenge is to help our staff deal with difficult situations and take the brickbats."[4]

Firms need to be aware of ongoing emotional stress among their employees and to make sure that their employees are trained to handle emotional stress and to cope with pressure from customers. Figure 11.5 captures emotional labor with humor.

Figure 11.4 Put on a smile when you do not feel like it, and you may end up looking like him.

"We'd like to hire you for our Customer Service Department. It's practically impossible to look at a penguin and feel angry."

Figure 11.5 Recruiting the right employee will reduce emotional labor.

CYCLES OF FAILURE, MEDIOCRITY, AND SUCCESS

 LO 3

Describe the cycles of failures, mediocrity, and success in Human Resource (HR) management for service firms.

Having discussed the importance of frontline employees and how difficult their work is, let us look at the big picture—how poor, mediocre and excellent firms set up their frontline employees for failure, mediocrity or success. All too often, bad working environments are connected to terrible service, with employees treating customers the way their managers treat them. Businesses with high employee turnover are often stuck in what has been termed the "*Cycle of Failure.*" Others, which offer job security but are rule and procedure based, may suffer from an equally undesirable "*Cycle of Mediocrity.*" However, if managed well, there is potential for a virtuous cycle in service employment, called the "*Cycle of Success.*"[5] As we will see, employee satisfaction and customer satisfaction are highly correlated and affect each other.[6]

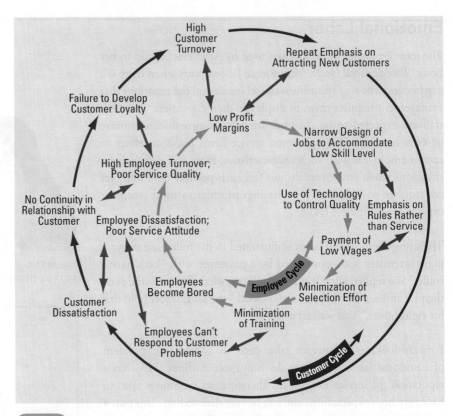

Figure 11.6 The Cycle of Failure.

The Cycle of Failure

In many service industries, the search for productivity leads to simplifying work processes and paying the lowest possible wages. Such employees perform repetitive tasks that need little or no training. Among consumer services, department stores, fast food restaurants and call center operations are often examples of this mindset (although there are notable exceptions). The cycle of failure captures the effect of such a strategy. There are two separate cycles, but they affect each other. One involves failures with employees, the second, with customers (Figure 11.6).

The *employee cycle of failure* begins with a narrow design of jobs for low skill levels. There is an emphasis on rules rather than service, and the use of technology to control quality. Low wages are paid, accompanied by little investment in selection and training. As a result, there are bored employees who lack the ability to respond to customer problems. They then become dissatisfied and develop a poor service attitude. The results for the firm are low service quality and high employee turnover. Because of low profit margins, the cycle repeats itself with the hiring of more low-paid employees to work in the same unrewarding manner (Figure 11.7). Some service firms can reach such low levels of employee morale that frontline staff engage in 'service sabotage' rather than deliver service excellence.[7]

Figure 11.7 Employees in the cycle of failure are bored and dissatisfied.

The *customer cycle of failure* begins with repeated emphasis on attracting new customers. Since the employees are dissatisfied, the customers become dissatisfied with employee performance. High staff turnover means that customers are always served by new faces, so there is no continuity. Because these customers fail to become loyal to the supplier, they turn over as quickly as the staff, requiring an ongoing search for new customers to maintain sales volume.

Many managers ignore the long-term financial effects of low-pay/high turnover human resource strategies. They often fail to measure three key cost variables: (1) the cost of constantly recruiting, hiring, and training; (2) the lower productivity of inexperienced new workers; and (3) the costs of always attracting new customers (requiring extensive advertising and promotional discounts). Also often ignored are two revenue variables: future revenue if the customer stayed loyal, and income from potential customers who are turned off by negative word of mouth.

The Cycle of Mediocrity

Another cycle is the "Cycle of Mediocrity" (Figure 11.8). It is most likely to be found in large organizations that operate on lots of rules and procedures.

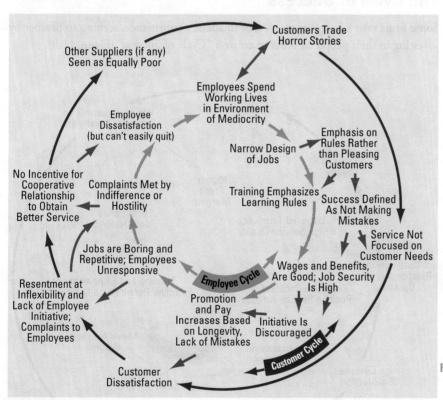

Figure 11.8 The Cycle of Mediocrity.

SOURCE

Christopher Lovelock (1995). Managing services: The human factor. In W.J. Glynn and J.G. Barnes. *Understanding Service Management* (p. 228). Chichester, O K John Wiley.

In such environments, service delivery standards tend to be rule-based. Service is standardized and the stress is on operational efficiencies. Job responsibilities are narrowly defined, and categorized by grade and scope of responsibilities. The unions also have work rules. Salary increases and promotions are largely based on how long

PART III

the person has been working in the company. Successful performance in a job is often measured by lack of mistakes, rather than by high productivity or outstanding customer service. Training focuses on learning the rules and the technical aspects of the job, not on improving relationships with customers and co-workers. Since employees are given very little freedom to do their work in the way they think is necessary or suitable, jobs tend to be boring and repetitive. However, unlike the cycle of failure, most positions provide adequate pay and often good benefits, combined with high security. Thus, employees are reluctant to leave.

Customers find such organizations frustrating to deal with. There are many rules, lack of service flexibility, and unwillingness of employees to make an effort to serve them well. There is little incentive for customers to cooperate with the organization to achieve better service. When they complain to employees who are already unhappy, the poor service attitude becomes worse. However, customers often remain with the organization as there is nowhere else for them to go. This could either be because the service provider holds a monopoly, or because all other available players are seen as being equally bad or worse.

The Cycle of Success

Some firms take a longer term view of financial performance, seeking to prosper by investing in their people in order to create a "Cycle of Success" (Figure 11.9).

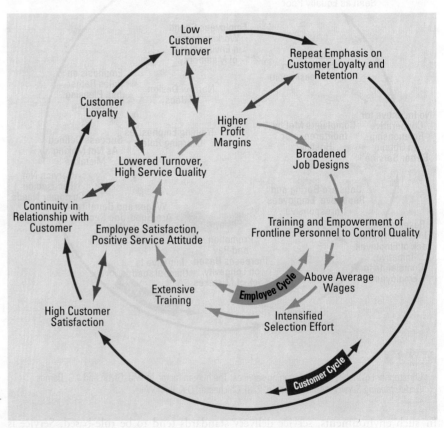

Figure 11.9 The Cycle of Success.

As with failure or mediocrity, success applies to both employees and customers. Better pay and benefits attract good quality staff. Broadened job designs are accompanied by training and empowerment practices that allow frontline staff to control quality. With more focused recruitment, intensive training and better wages, employees are likely to be happier in their work and provide higher quality service. Lower turnover means that regular customers appreciate the continuity in service relationships and are more likely to remain loyal (Figure 11.10). With greater customer loyalty, profit margins tend to be higher. The organization is free to focus its marketing efforts on strengthening customer loyalty through customer retention strategies.

Figure 11.10 DLA Piper has a dedicated team of employees who put the client's interests first, forming service relationships with customers that are likely to result in increased customer loyalty.

HUMAN RESOURCE MANAGEMENT — HOW TO GET IT RIGHT?

Any manager who thinks logically would like to operate in the Cycle of Success. What strategies will help service firms to move in that direction? Figure 11.11 shows the Service Talent Cycle which is our guiding framework for successful HR practices in service firms. We will discuss the recommended practices one by one in this section.

> **LO 4**
> Understand the key elements of the Service Talent Cycle and know how to get HR right in service firms.

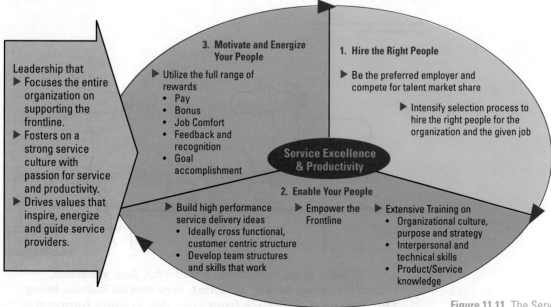

Figure 11.11 The Service Talent Cycle.

Know how to attract, select and hire the right people for service jobs.

Hiring the Right People

Employee effort is a strong driver of customer satisfaction, so it is important to have employees who are willing to put in the effort. As Jim Collins said, "The old adage, 'People are the most important asset' is wrong. The right people are your most important asset.' We would like to add to this: '… and the wrong people are a liability that is often difficult to get rid of.' Getting it right starts with hiring the right people."

Hiring the right people includes competing for applications from the best employees in the labor market, then selecting from this pool the right candidates for the specific jobs to be filled.

Be the Preferred Employer

To be able to select and hire the best people, they first have to apply for a job with you and then accept your job offer in preference to offers. That means a firm has to first compete for talent market share, or as McKinsey & Company calls it, "the war for talent."[8] To effectively compete in the labor market means having an attractive value proposition for potential employees, including a good image in the community as a place to work, and delivering high-quality products and services which make employees feel proud to be part of the team. Top people expect above average packages. In our experience, it takes a salary in the range of the 65th to 80th percentile of the market to attract top performers to top companies. See Service Insights 11.2 on how Google has become the Best Company to Work for in 2008!

Select the Right People

There is no such thing as the perfect employee (Figure 11.12). Different positions are often best filled by people with different skill sets, styles and personalities. For example, the Walt Disney Company looks at potential employees and judges how they fit into on-stage or backstage work. The job of on-stage workers, known as cast members, are given to those people with the appearance, personalities, and skills to match the job.

Copyright 2001 by Randy Glasbergen.
www.glasbergen.com

"Allen is an incredible, wonderful, fun, generous, exciting, kind, loving, brilliant, very special human being. **This personal reference from your dog is quite impressive."**

Figure 11.12 There is no such thing as a perfect employee.

Google, **the Preferred Employer**

Google was voted number one in "FORTUNE'S 100 Best Companies to Work for 2008." So, the immediate question on people's minds will be: Why so? What makes it the best? What kind of culture does the company have? What kind of benefits do the employees enjoy? What are its employees like? Employees of Google are called Googlers. They are widely perceived as fun-loving and interesting. At the same time, when it comes to work, they are achievement oriented and driven. Google's culture is one of innovation, of being non-conventional, of being different, of being fun-loving. Googlers are given the freedom to work independently. Google's experience suggests that pampering employees actually results in increased productivity and profitability. Certainly, Googlers seem willing to work long hours.

What kind of benefits do Googlers enjoy? The list is long, but top on the list is gourmet food for free, and food is just the appetizer! At the company's headquarters in Mountain View, California, the "campus" offers many free amenities, including Wi-Fi enabled shuttle buses, motorized scooters to get around, car washes, and oil changes. If Googlers are

Figure 11.13 The Google Campus, Mountain View, California.

interested in buying hybrid cars, they get a $5000 subsidy for that. Googlers have five free onsite doctors, unlimited sick days, free flu shots, gym to work out at, a pool to do laps with lifeguards on duty. For more domestic activities, there is free onsite laundry or one can drop off laundry at the dry

cleaners. There are also child care services. Pets are welcome at the work place on a temporary basis. For leisure and sports, one can play a game of pool, do some rock climbing on the wall, play a game of volleyball at the beach volleyball pit. The list goes on. As a result, Googlers can spend long and productive hours at work. But it must be noted that the benefits offered to employees working at other Google offices tend to be less significant.

Google has a new engineering headquarters in Zurich, Switzerland. Life there is just as fun. There are meeting places that are designed to look like Swiss chalets and igloos. People can get from one floor to another using fireman poles, and there is a slide that allows them to reach the cafeteria very quickly. There are other areas like a games room, a library with architecture in the style of an English country house, and an aquarium where staff can lie in a bath of red foam and look at fish if they feel much stressed out. This building was partly designed by the engineers who work there.

Figure 11.14 The slide gets people to the cafeteria quickly.

Because the firm is seen as such a desirable place to work, it can be extremely selective in its recruiting, hiring only the best and the brightest. This may work particularly well for its engineers, who tend to get the most kudos. However, despite the company's stellar reputation as an employer, some observers question whether this very positive environment can be maintained as the company grows and its workforce matures.

SOURCE

Lashinsky, A. (2007). Google is no. 1: Search and enjoy. 100 Best companies to work for: Life inside google. The perks of being a googler. *Fortune*, 10(January); Inside the Googleplex. *The Economist*, (September) 2007; Levering, R., & Moskowitz, M. (2008). 100 Best companies to work for 2008: Top 50 employers. (22 January). Available: http://money.cnn.com/galleries/2008/fortune/0801/gallery.bestcos_top50.fortune/index.html, Accessed April 2008; Wakefield, J. (2008). Google your way to a wacky office. *BBC News Website*, (13 March)., Available: http://news.bbc.co.uk/1/hi/technology/7290322.stm, Accessed April 2008.

What makes outstanding service performers so special? Often it is things that cannot be taught. It is the qualities that are part of people's personality. While good manners and the need to smile and make eye contact can be taught, warmth itself cannot.

Tools to Identify the Best Candidates

Excellent service firms use a number of methods to identify the best candidates in their applicant pool. They include observing behavior, conducting personality tests, interviewing applicants, and providing applicants with a realistic job preview.

Observe Behavior

The hiring decision should be based on the behavior that recruiters observe, not the words they hear. As John Wooden said: "Show me what you can do, don't tell me what you can do. Too often, the big talkers are the little doers."[9] Behavior can be directly or indirectly observed by using behavioral simulations or assessment centre tests. Southwest Airlines observes applicants closely during the day of interview. Also, past behavior is the best predictor of future behavior: hire the person who has won service excellence awards, received many complimentary letters and has great references from past employers that highlight relevant performance measures.

Conduct Personality Tests

Use personality tests that are related to specific jobs. For example, willingness to treat customers and colleagues with courtesy, consideration and tact, sensitivity to customer needs, and ability to communicate accurately and pleasantly are traits that can be measured.

For example, the Ritz-Carlton Hotels Group uses personality profiles to help select staff who have a natural predisposition for working well in a defined service context. Based on her experience, a successful applicant for an assistant concierge job gave the following advice: Tell the truth. These are experts; they will know if you are lying, and then she added:

> On the big day, they asked if I liked helping people, if I was an organized person and if I liked to smile a lot." "Yes, yes and yes," I said. But I had to support it with real life examples. To answer the first question for instance, I had to say a bit about the person I had helped—why she needed help, for example. The test forced me to recall even insignificant things I had done, like learning how to say hello in different languages which helped to get a fix on my character.[10]

Use Multiple, Structured Interviews

Successful recruiters use structured interviews built around job requirements. They use two or more interviewers because people tend to be more careful in their judgments when they know that another person will be judging the same applicant. Using two or more interviewers also reduces the risk of 'similar to me' biases—we all like people who are similar to ourselves (Figure 11.15).

Figure 11.15 Does the interviewee a higher chance of shaking hands on that dream position if the "similar to me" bias comes into play?

Give Applicants a Realistic Preview of the Job

During the recruitment process, service companies should let candidates know the reality of the job, thereby giving them a chance to "try on the job" and see whether

it is good fit or not. At the same time, recruiters can observe how candidates respond to the job's realities. Some candidates may withdraw if they realize the job is not a good match for them. Au Bon Pain, a chain of French bakery cafes, lets applicants work for two paid days in a café prior to the final selection interview. Managers can observe candidates in action, and candidates can assess whether they like the job and the work environment (Figure 11.16). In the ultimate recruitment and interview process, Donald Trump worked with the NBC network to produce "The Apprentice" TV show where the winner got to join the Trump organization and manage a project selected by Trump himself.

Train Service Employees Actively

 LO 6

Explain the key areas in which service employees need training.

Service champions show a strong commitment in words, dollars and action to training. They recognize that employees need to be trained in three key areas:

▶ **The Organizational Culture, Purpose and Strategy.** Training and mentoring must focus on getting emotional commitment to the firm's core strategy and promote core values. Teaching must emphasize 'what', 'why' and 'how'.[11] For example, new recruits at Disneyland attend the "Disney University Orientation." It starts with a detailed discussion of the company history and philosophy, the service standards expected of cast members and a tour of Disneyland's operations.

▶ **Interpersonal and Technical Skills.** Interpersonal skills cut across service jobs. They include visual communications skills such as making eye contact, attentive listening, body language and even facial expressions. Technical skills include all the required knowledge related to processes (e.g. how to handle a merchandized return), machines (e.g. how to operate the terminal or cash machine), and rules and regulations related to customer service processes. Both interpersonal and

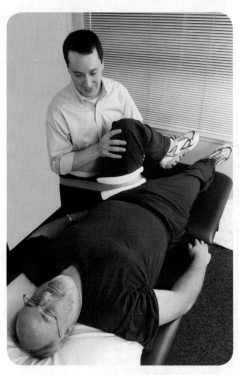

technical skills are necessary but neither alone is enough for performing a job well (Figure 11.17).

▶ **Product/Service Knowledge.** Employees must have detailed knowledge of the firm's products and services. Otherwise, they will be unable to explain product features effectively to customers, to contrast them with competing offerings, and to help customers to make the right choice. In many ways, knowledgeable staff are a key aspect of service quality. For instance, in Service Insights 11.3, Jennifer Grassano of Dial-A-Mattress coaches individual staff members on how to paint pictures in the customer's mind.

Figure 11.17 A physiotherapist displaying technical competence, as well as a warm and friendly smile.

⋮⋮⋮ SERVICE INSIGHTS 11.3

Coaching at Dial-A-Mattress

Coaching is a common method employed by services leaders to train and develop staff. Dial-A-Mattress' Jennifer Grassano is a Bedding Consultant (BC) for three days a week, and a coach to other BCs for one day a week. She focuses on staff whose productivity and sales performance are slumping.

Her first step is to listen to the BC's telephone calls with customers. She will listen for about an hour and take detailed notes on each call. The BCs understand that their calls may be monitored, but they receive no advance notice as that would defeat the purpose.

Next, she conducts a coaching session with that staff member, where strengths and areas for improvements are reviewed. Grassano knows how difficult it is to maintain a high energy level and convey enthusiasm when handling some 60 calls per shift. She likes to suggest new tactics and phrasings "to spark up their presentation." One BC was not responding effectively when customers asked why one mattress was more expensive than another. Here, she stressed the need to paint a picture in the customer's mind,

"Customers are at our mercy when buying bedding. They don't know the difference between one coil system and another. It is just like buying a carburetor for my car. I don't even know what a carburetor looks like. We have to use very descriptive words to help bedding customers make the decision that is right for them. Tell the customer that the more costly mattress has richer, finer padding with a blend of silk and wool. Don't just say the mattress has more layers of padding."

About two months after the initial coaching session, Grassano conducts a follow-up monitoring session with that BC. She then compares the BC's performance before and after the coaching session to assess the effectiveness of the training.

Grassano's experience and productivity as a BC give her the credibility as a coach. "If I am not doing well as a BC, then who am I to be a coach? I have to lead by example. I would be much less effective if I was a full-time trainer." She clearly relishes the opportunity to share her knowledge and pass on her craft.

SOURCE

Berry, L. L. (1999). *Discovering the soul of service – The nine drivers of sustainable business success.* (pp.171–172). New York: The Free Press.

The end-goal of training is to achieve and maintain desired behaviors on the job. To achieve this, practice and reminders are needed. Supervisors can meet with staff to repeat key lessons from recent complaints and compliments (Figure 11.18). Training and learning professionalizes the frontline. A waiter, who knows about food, cooking, wines, dining etiquette, and how to effectively interact with customers (even complaining ones) feels professional, has a higher self-esteem and is respected by his customers. Training thus helps to reduce person/role stress. See how Up Your Service! College enables and energizes front line employees (Service Insights 11.4).

Figure 11.18 A Formula One technician being briefed by his foreman.

::: SERVICE INSIGHTS 11.4 •

Up Your Service! College Builds Cultures that **Inspire People** to **Excel in Service**

Having a service-oriented attitude is not something that comes necessarily naturally to everyone, especially if the culture within the organization does not support a "customer first" mentality. This is where UP Your Service! College (UYSC)comes in.

"All organizations can create a sustainable competitive advantage by building a Superior Service Culture," notes Ron Kaufman, author of the bestselling book series UP Your Service! and founder of UYSC. He adds, "a powerful service reputation attracts the best customers, the most loyal employees and the highest industry margins."

UYSC combines customer service training courses with culture building activities that uplift the spirit of service throughout an organization. This creates an atmosphere where staffs are inspired to excel in service delivery to customers and to one another.

The comprehensive UYSC course curriculum includes:

Course 100: Achieving Superior Service™ teaches fundamental service principles to raise service levels and improve the customer experience at every point of contact.

Course 200: Building Service Partnerships™ demonstrates the importance of building powerful service partnerships with partners and colleagues.

Course 300: Increasing Customer Loyalty™ teaches how to increase customer loyalty, manage customer expectations and handle situations professionally when things go wrong.

These courses are closely integrated with Service Leadership Workshops, Service Momentum Events and Service Culture Building Activities. Unlike many other training programs, UYSC builds a common service language throughout all levels of the organization, resulting in everyone applying the same service principles in their work every day. The courses are facilitated by certified course leaders and feature video-based instruction by Ron Kaufman to ensure consistently high quality training.

To date, organizations using the UYSC proven curriculum include major multinationals, large domestic companies and government entities such as: Dubai Bank, Dubai Properties, Lehman Brothers International, ManuLife, Nokia, Riyadh Care Hospital, Singapore Central Provident Fund, Singapore General Hospital, Tatweer, TECOM, Wipro, and Xerox Emirates.

Figure 11.19 An Uplifting Course Leader Certification Program for managers of Lehman Brothers UK with College founder Ron Kaufman at the center.

SOURCE

Source for text: http://www.upyourservice.com/ and http://www.ronkaufman.com/, accessed April 2008. Photo Courtesy of Ron Kaufman.

LO 7

Understand why empowerment is so important in many frontline jobs, and know the three levels of employee involvement.

Empower the Frontline[12]

After being the preferred employer, selecting the right candidates and training them well, the next step is to empower the frontline. High empowerment has been linked to higher customer satisfaction.[13] In fact, nearly all excellent service firms have stories of employees who recovered failed service transactions, walked the extra mile to make a customer's day or avoided some kind of disaster for a client. To allow this to happen, employees have to be empowered. Nordstrom is a company that trains and trusts its employees to do the right thing, and empowers them to do so (see Service Insights 11.5). Employee self-direction has become increasingly important, especially in service firms. This is because frontline staff are often on their own when they face their customers.

⦂⦂⦂ SERVICE INSIGHTS 11.5

Empowerment at Nordstrom

Welcome to Nordstrom

We're glad to have you with our Company.
Our number one goal is to provide outstanding customer service.
Set both your personal and professional goals high.
We have great confidence in your ability to achieve them.

Nordstrom Rules:

Rule#1: Use your good judgment in all situations. There will be no additional rules.
Please feel free to ask your department manager, store manager, or division general manager any question at any time.

SOURCE

Robert Spector and Patrick D. McCarthy, *The Nordstrom Way*. New York: John Wiley & Sons, Inc., 2000, pp. 15–16, 95.

Research has shown that empowerment is most important when the following factors are present within the organization and its environment:

▶ The firm offers personalized, customized service and is based on competitive differentiation.

▶ The firm has extended relationships with customers rather than short-term transactions.

▶ The organization uses technologies that are complex and non-routine in nature.

- Service failures often are non-routine and cannot be designed out of the system. Front line employees have to respond fast to recover the service.

- The business environment is unpredictable and surprises are to be expected.

- Existing managers are comfortable with letting employees work on their own for the benefit of both the organization and its customers.

- Employees have a strong need to grow and deepen their skills in the work environment, are interested in working with others, and have good interpersonal and group process skills.

Levels of Employee Involvement

Empowerment can take place at several levels:

- *Suggestion Involvement* empowers employees to make recommendations through formalized programs. McDonald's for example, listens closely to its frontline. Creations ranging from Egg McMuffin, to methods of wrapping burgers without leaving a thumbprint on the bun, were invented by employees.

- *Job Involvement* represents opening up of job content. Jobs are redesigned to allow employees to use a wider range of skills. To cope with the added demands accompanying this form of empowerment, employees require training. Supervisors need to be reoriented from directing the group to supporting its performance.

- *High Involvement* gives even the lowest level employees a sense of involvement in the company's overall performance. Information is shared. Employees develop skills in teamwork, problem solving, and business operations. They participate in work-unit management decisions. There is profit sharing, often in the form of bonuses.

Southwest Airlines is an example of a high-involvement company. It trusts its employees and gives them the freedom and authority to do their jobs. Southwest mechanics and pilots feel free to help ramp agents load bags. When a flight is running late, it is not uncommon to see pilots helping passengers in wheelchairs to board the aircraft, assisting operations agents by taking boarding passes, or helping flight attendants clean the cabin between flights. In addition, Southwest employees use common sense, not rules, when it is in the best interests of the customer.

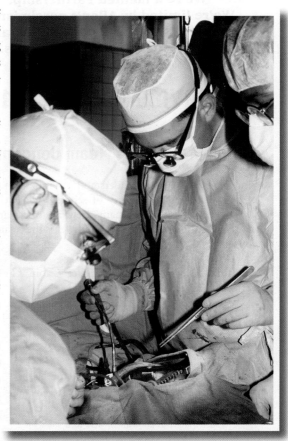

Figure 11.20 Surgical teams work under particularly demanding conditions.

Build High-Performance Service-Delivery Teams

 LO 8

Explain how to build high-performance service delivery teams.

A team has been defined as "a small number of people with complementary skills who are committed to a common purpose, set of performance goals, and approach for which they hold themselves mutually accountable."[14] Many services require people to work in teams, often across functions for well-coordinated delivery, especially when different individuals each play specialist roles. For example, healthcare services depend heavily on effective teamwork (see Figure 11.20).

**"We're a Limited Partnership.
We're limited by Allen's pessimism,
Elizabeth's abrasive personality, and
Dave's refusal to work weekends."**

Research confirms that frontline staff feel that lack of interdepartmental support prevents them from satisfying their customers (Figure 11.21).[15] In many industries, firms need to create cross-functional teams and give them the authority and responsibility to serve customers from end-to-end. Such teams are also called self-managed teams.[16]

Teams, training and empowerment go hand-in-hand. Singapore Airlines uses teams to provide emotional support, to mentor its cabin crew, and effectively assess, rewards and promote staff (see Service Insights 11.6).

Figure 11.21 Lack of cooperation within a team will present the staff from satisfying customers.

⠿ SERVICE INSIGHTS 11.6

Singapore Airlines' **Team Concept**

Singapore (SIA) Airlines understands the importance of teamwork in the delivery of service excellence. This is difficult because many crew members are scattered around the world. SIA's answer is the "team concept."

Choo Poh Leong, Senior Manager Cabin Crew Performance, explained:

> "In order to effectively manage our 6,600 crew, we divide them into teams, small units, with a team leader in charge of about 13 people. We will roster them to fly together as much as we can. Flying together, as a unit, allows them to build up camaraderie, and crew members feel like they are part of a team, not just a member. The team leader will get to know them well, their strengths and weaknesses, and will become their mentor and their counsel, and someone to whom they can turn if they need help or advice. The "check trainers" oversee 12 or 13 teams and fly with them whenever possible, not only to inspect their performance, but also to help their team develop."

> "The interaction within each of the teams is very strong. As a result, when a team leader

Figure 11.22 Cabin Crew serving in the A380 First Class Cabin.

> does a staff appraisal they really know the staff. You would be amazed how meticulous and detailed each staff record is. So, in this way, we have good control, and through the control, we can ensure that the crew delivers the promise. They know that they're being constantly monitored and so they deliver. If there are problems, we will know about them and we can send them for re-training. Those who are good will be selected for promotion."

According to Toh Giam Ming, Senior Manager Crew Performance, "What is good about the team concept is that despite the huge number of crew, people can relate to a team and have a sense of belonging—'this is my team.' And they are put together for 1–2 years and they are rostered together for about 60–70 percent of the time, so they do fly together quite a fair bit."

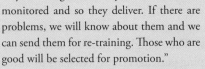

SOURCE

Wirtz, J., & Johnston, R. (2003). Singapore airlines: What it takes to sustain service excellence — A senior management perspective. *Managing Service Quality*, 13(1), pp. 10–19; Heracleous, L., Wirtz, J., & Pangarkar, N. (2006). *Flying High in Competitive Industry: Cost-Effective Service Excellence at Singapore Airlines* (pp. 145–173). Singapore: McGraw-Hill.

It is not easy to make teams work well. Skills like cooperation, listening to others, coaching and encouraging one another are needed. Team members must learn how to voice differences, tell one another hard truths, and ask tough questions. All these require training. Management also needs to set up a structure that will move the teams towards success. To succeed in the global economy, managers need to do each of the following:

▶ Identify what the team will achieve. Goals need to be defined and shared with the team members.

▶ Select team members with care. All the skills needed to achieve the goal must be found within the team.

▶ Monitor the team and its team members and provide feedback. This aligns individual goals with that of the organization.

▶ Keep team members informed of goal achievement, update them, and reward them for their efforts.

▶ Coordinate with other managers to achieve the overall company objectives.[17]

Motivate and Energize People[18]

 LO 9

Know how to motivate and energize service employees so that they will deliver service excellence and productivity.

Once a firm has hired the right people, trained them well, empowered them, and organized them in effective service delivery teams, how can it ensure that they will deliver service excellence? Motivating and rewarding strong service performers are key to success.

Unsuccessful service businesses fail to make effective use of the full range of available rewards. Money alone does not pass the test of an effective reward. Paying higher wages beyond what is seen as a reasonably fair salary may only have short term motivating effects. Performance-based bonuses have to be earned again and again, and therefore have more lasting impact. Apart from monetary rewards in the form of bonuses, lasting rewards are the job content itself, recognition and feedback, and goal achievement.

Job content
People are motivated and satisfied simply by knowing that they are doing a good job. This is true especially if

▶ the job also has a variety of different activities,

▶ needs the completion of 'whole' pieces of work,

▶ it has an impact on the lives of others,

▶ it comes with freedom and flexibility, and

▶ there is a source of direct and clear feedback about how well employees did their work (e.g. grateful customers and sales).

Feedback and recognition
Humans are social beings, and they like to feel that they belong. This is possible if there is recognition and feedback from the people around them, that is, their customers, colleagues and bosses. If employees are being recognized and thanked for service

PART III

excellence, they will want to continue achieving it. If done well, star employee of the month-type of awards recognize high performances and can be highly motivating.

Goal achievement

Goals focus people's energy. Achieving important goals is a reward in itself. Goals that are specific, difficult but achievable, and accepted by the staff are strong motivators (Figure 11.23). They result in higher performance than no goals, or unclear goals (e.g. 'do your best'), or goals that are impossible to achieve. In short, well communicated and mutually accepted goals are effective motivators.

Figure 11.23 When people are focused on goal achievement, it will motivate and energize them.

 LO 10

Understand the role of service leadership and culture in developing people for service advantage.

SERVICE LEADERSHIP AND CULTURE

To move an organization towards service excellence, we need a strong service culture that is continuously strengthened and developed by management. 'Charismatic leadership,' also called transformational leadership is needed. With this kind of leadership, staff are more likely to perform 'above and beyond the call of duty,' because it is in line with their own values, beliefs and attitudes.

Leonard Berry found some core values in excellent service firms. They included excellence, innovation, joy, teamwork, respect, moral and ethical principles, and social profit.[19] These values are part of the firms' culture. A service culture can be defined as:

▶ Shared ideas of what is important in an organization, and

▶ Shared values and beliefs of why those things are important.[20]

In order for values and beliefs to be shared by all employees, they may have to be instilled in them and employees have to be reminded of this. For example, Ritz-Carlton translated the key product and service requirements of its customers into the Ritz-Carlton Gold Standards, which include a credo, motto, three steps of service and 20 'Ritz-Carlton Basis' (see Service Insights 11.7).

Ritz-Carlton's **Gold Standards**

Ritz-Carlton's Gold Standards is the cornerstone on which Ritz-Carlton's success is founded. The devotion to the Gold Standards has seen Ritz-Carlton sweeping all the major awards in the hospitality industry. It is the first and only hotel company twice honored with the Malcolm Baldridge National Quality Award from the United States Department of Commence.

THE RITZ-CARLTON® BASICS

1. The Credo is the principal belief of our Company. It must be known, owned and energized by all.
2. Our Motto is: "We Are Ladies and Gentlemen serving Ladies and Gentlemen." As service professionals, we treat our guests and each other with respect and dignity.
3. The Three Steps of Service are the foundation of Ritz-Carlton hospitality. These steps must be used in every interaction to ensure satisfaction, retention and loyalty.
4. The Employee Promise is the basis for our Ritz-Carlton work environment. It will be honored by all employees.
5. All employees will successfully complete annual Training Certification for their position.
6. Company objectives are communicated to all employees. It is everyone's responsibility to support them.
7. To create pride and joy in the workplace, all employees have the right to be involved in the planning of the work that affects them.
8. Each employee will continuously identify defects (M.R. B.I.V.) throughout the Hotel.
9. It is the responsibility of each employee to create a work environment of teamwork and lateral service so that the needs of our guests and each other are met.
10. Each employee is empowered. For example, when a guest has a problem or needs something special, you should break away from your regular duties to address and resolve the issue.
11. Uncompromising levels of cleanliness are the responsibility of every employee.
12. To provide the finest personal service for our guests, each employee is responsible for identifying and recording individual guest preferences.
13. Never lose a guest. Instant guest pacification is the responsibility of each employee. Whoever receives a complaint will own it, resolve it to the guest's satisfaction and record it.
14. "Smile – We are on stage." Always maintain positive eye contact. Use the proper vocabulary with our guests and each other. (Use words like – "Good Morning," "Certainly," "I'll be happy to" and "My pleasure.")
15. Be an ambassador of your Hotel in and outside of the workplace. Always speak positively. Communicate any concerns to the appropriate person.
16. Escort guests rather than pointing out directions to another area of the Hotel.
17. Use Ritz-Carlton telephone etiquette. Answer within three rings with a "smile." Use the guest's name when possible. When necessary, ask the caller "May I place you on hold?"
Do not screen calls. Eliminate call transfers whenever possible. Adhere to voice mail standards.
18. Take pride in and care of your personal appearance. Everyone is responsible for conveying a professional image by adhering to Ritz-Carlton clothing and grooming standards.
19. Think safety first. Each employee is responsible for creating a safe, secure and accident free environment for all guests and each other. Be aware of all fire and safety emergency procedures and report any security risks immediately.
20. Protecting the assets of a Ritz-Carlton hotel is the responsibility of every employee. Conserve energy, properly maintain our Hotels and protect the environment.

Superior-Atlanta 898

THREE STEPS OF SERVICE

1
A warm and sincere greeting. Use the guest name, if and when possible.

2
Anticipation and compliance with guest needs.

3
Fond farewell. Give them a warm good-bye and use their names, if and when possible.

"We Are Ladies and Gentlemen Serving Ladies and Gentlemen"

THE EMPLOYEE PROMISE

At The Ritz-Carlton, our Ladies and Gentlemen are the most important resource in our service commitment to our guests.

By applying the principles of trust, honesty, respect, integrity and commitment, we nurture and maximize talent to the benefit of each individual and the company.

The Ritz-Carlton fosters a work environment where diversity is valued, quality of life is enhanced, individual aspirations are fulfilled, and The Ritz-Carlton mystique is strengthened.

THE RITZ-CARLTON®

CREDO

The Ritz-Carlton Hotel is a place where the genuine care and comfort of our guests is our highest mission.

We pledge to provide the finest personal service and facilities for our guests who will always enjoy a warm, relaxed yet refined ambience.

The Ritz-Carlton experience enlivens the senses, instills well-being, and fulfills even the unexpressed wishes and needs of our guests.

SOURCE

The Ritz-Calton Hotel Company, LLC.

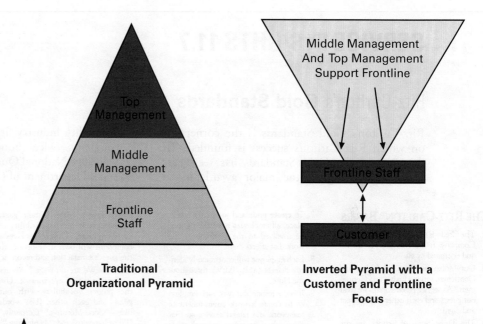

Traditional Organizational Pyramid

Inverted Pyramid with a Customer and Frontline Focus

Legend: $\updownarrow$ = Service encounters, or "Moments of Truth"

Figure 11.24 The inverted organizational pyramid.

A strong service culture is one where the entire organization focuses on the frontline, and understands that it is the lifeline of the business. Figure 11.24 shows the *inverted pyramid*, which highlights the importance of the frontline. It shows that the role of top management and middle management is to support the frontline in their task of delivering service excellence to their customers.

In firms with a passion for service, top management is informed and actively involved. They achieve this by regularly talking to and working with frontline staff and customers, even spending time serving customers themselves. For example, Disney World's management spends two weeks every year in frontline staff jobs such as sweeping streets, selling ice-cream or being the ride attendant, to gain a better understanding of what really happens on the ground. We will discuss service leadership in more detail in Chapter 15.

LO 1 ▶ Service employees are extremely important to the success of a service firm. They are

- A source of competitive positioning because they are (1) a core part of the service product, (2) they *are* the service firm in the eyes of the customer, (3) and they deliver the brand promise.

- A source of customer loyalty.

- A key driver of the productivity of the frontline operation.

- Often crucially important for generating sales, cross-sales and up-sales.

- Even in low-contact services, frontline employees are the ones who leave an impression on the customer in those 'moments of truth' encounters.

LO 2 ▶ The work of frontline employees is difficult and stressful because they are in boundary spanning positions. They are often caught in

- organization/client conflicts,

- person/role conflict, and

- interclient conflicts.

LO 3 ▶ We used three types of cycles to describe how firms can set up their front line employees for failure, mediocrity and success:

- The cycle of failure involves high employee turnover and high customer dissatisfaction and defection.

- The cycle of mediocrity offers job security, but not much scope in the job itself. There is no incentive to serve customers well.

- Successful service firms operate in the cycle of success, where employees and customers are both satisfied and happy, and firms enjoy high profitability.

LO 4 ▶ To achieve the Cycle of Success, firms should follow the prescriptions outlined in the Service Talent Cycle. It recommends that firms should

LO 5 - Work on being seen as a preferred employer, and as a result, receive a large number of applications from the best potential candidates in the labor market.

- Select the best suited candidates using screen methods such as observation, personality tests, structured interviews, and providing realistic job previews.

LO 6 - Conduct extensive training on (1) the organizational culture, purpose and strategy, (2) interpersonal and technical skills, and (3) product/service knowledge.

LO 7 - Empower the frontline so that they can respond with flexibility to customer needs and non-routine encounters and service failures.

LO 8 - Organize them into often cross-functional service delivery teams that can serve the customer from end-to-end.

LO 9 - Finally, motivate them with a full set of rewards, ranging from pay, satisfying job content, recognition and feedback, to goal accomplishment.

- Implementing the Service Talent Cycle correctly will give firms highly motivated employees who are willing and able to deliver service excellence and go the extra mile for their customers, and are highly productive at the same time.

LO 10 ▶ Top and middle management must show service leadership and:

- Focus the entire organization on supporting the front line

- Reinforce a strong service culture that emphasizes service excellence and productivity, and build employee understanding and support for the organization's goals.

- Drive values that inspire, energize and guide service providers.

UNLOCK YOUR LEARNING

These keywords are found within the sections of each Learning Objective (LO). They are integral in understanding the services marketing concepts taught in each section. Having a firm grasp of these keywords and how they are used is essential in helping you do well for your course, and in the real and very competitive marketing scene out there.

LO 1
1. Customer loyalty
2. Customer Operations Performance Center (COPC)
3. Customer service representative
4. Firm's positioning
5. Moments of truth
6. Service personnel

LO 2
7. Boundary spanners
8. Role conflict
9. Emotional labor
10. Role stress
11. Interclient conflict
12. Organization/client conflict
13. Person/role conflict

LO 3
14. Customer cycle of failure
15. Cycle of Failure
16. Cycle of Mediocrity
17. Cycle of Success
18. Employee cycle of failure

LO 4
19. Service Talent Cycle

LO 5
20. Assessment center tests
21. Behavioral simulations
22. Hiring the right people
23. Observe behavior
24. Preferred employer
25. Personality tests
26. Realistic preview
27. Structured interviews
28. Talent market share

LO 6
29. Training

LO 7
30. Empower the frontline
31. Empowerment
32. Employee involvement
33. High involvement
34. Job involvement

LO 8
35. Teams
36. Teamwork

LO 9
37. Feedback and recognition

38. Goals
39. Goal achievement
40. Job content
41. Monetary rewards
42. Motivators
43. Reward

LO 10
44. Charismatic leadership
45. Inverted pyramid
46. Inverted organizational pyramid
47. Service leadership
48. Service culture
49. Transformational leadership

How well do you know the language of services marketing? Quiz yourself!

 Not for the academically faint-of-heart

For each keyword you are able to recall without referring to earlier pages, give yourself a point (and a pat on the back). Tally your score at the end and see if you earned the right to be called—a *services marketeer.*

SCORE

0 – 8	Services Marketing is done a great disservice.
9 – 17	The midnight oil needs to be lit, pronto.
18 – 26	I know what you *didn't* do all semester.
27 – 35	By George! You're getting there.
36 – 45	Now, go forth and market.
46 – 49	There should be a marketing concept named after you.

Review Questions

1. Why are service personnel so important for service firms?

2. There is a trend of service delivery moving from high-contact to low-contact. Are service personnel still important in low-contact services? Explain your answer.

3. What is emotional labor? Explain the ways in which it may cause stress for employees in specific jobs. Illustrate with suitable examples.

4. What are the key characteristics of the Cycles of Failure, Mediocrity and Success?

5. Describe the key components of the Service Talent Cycle.

6. What can a service firm do to become a preferred employer, and as a result, receive a large number of applications from the best potential candidates in the labor market?

7. How can a firm select the best suited candidates from a large number of applicants?

8. What are the key types of training service firms should conduct?

9. What are the factors that favor a strategy of employee empowerment?

10. Identify the factors needed to make service teams successful in (a) an airline, (b) a restaurant.

11. How can frontline employees be effectively motivated to deliver service excellence and productivity?

12. How can a service firm build a strong service culture that emphasizes on service excellence and productivity?

WORK **YOUR** ESM

Application Exercises

1. An airline runs a recruiting advertisement for cabin crew that shows a picture of a small boy sitting in an airline seat and clutching a teddy bear. The headline reads: "His mom told him not to talk to strangers. So what's he having for lunch?" Describe the types of personalities that you think would be (a) attracted to apply for the job by that ad, and (b) discouraged from applying.

2. Consider the following jobs: emergency ward nurse, bill collector, computer repair technician, supermarket cashier, dentist, kindergarten teacher, prosecuting attorney, server in a family restaurant, server in an expensive French restaurant, stockbroker, and undertaker. What type of emotions would you expect each of them to display to customers in the course of doing their job? What drives your expectations?

3. Use the Service Talent Cycle as a diagnostic tool on a successful and an unsuccessful service firm you are familiar with. What recommendations would you prescribe to each of these two firms?

4. Think of two organizations you are familiar with, one that has a very good and one that has a very poor service culture. Describe the factors that contributed to shaping those organizational cultures. What factors do you think contributed most? Why?

PART III

ENDNOTES

1 L. Berry, L. L, *Discovering the Soul of Service – The Nine Drivers of Sustainable Business Success* (pp. 156–159). New York; Free Press.

2 Bowen, D. E. & Schneider, B. (1985). Boundary-spanning role employees and the service encounter: Some guidelines for management and research. In *The Service Encounter*, (pp. 127–148), J. A. Czepiel, M. R. Solomon, & C. F. Surprenant. (Eds.). Lexington Mass.: Lexington Books.

3 Hochschild, A. R. (1983). *The Managed Heart: Commercialization of Human Feeling*. Berkeley: University of California Press.

4 Wirtz, J., & Johnston, R. (2003). Singapore airlines: What it takes to sustain service excellence - A senior management perspective. *Managing Service Quality* 13(1), pp. 10–19, Heracleous, L., Wirtz, J., & Pangarkar, N. (2006). *Flying High in Competitive Industry: Cost-Effective Service Excellence at Singapore Airlines* (p. 155). Singapore: McGraw-Hill.

5 The terms "cycle of failure" and "cycle of success" were coined by Schlesinger, L. L., & Heskett, J. L. (1991). Breaking the cycle of failure in services. *Sloan Management Review* (Spring), pp. 17–28; Lovelock, C. H., (1995). Managing services: The human factor. In W. J. Glynn, & J. G. Barnes (Eds.). *Understanding Services Management* (p. 228). Chichester, UK: John Wiley & Sons.

6 Schneider, B., & Bowen, D. E. (1993). The service organization: Human resources management is crucial. *Organizational Dynamics*, 21(4) (Spring), pp. 39–52.

7 Harris, L. C., & Ogbonna, E. (2002). Exploring service sabotage: The antecedents, types, and consequences of frontline, deviant, antiservice behaviors. *Journal of Service Research*, 4(3), 163–183.

8 O'Reilly III, C. A., & Pfeffer, J. (2000). *Hidden Value – How Great Companies Achieve Extraordinary Results with Ordinary People* (p. 1). Boston, Massachusetts: Harvard Business School Press.

9 Wooden, J. (1997). A Lifetime of Observations and Reflections On and Off the Court (p. 66). Chicago: Lincolnwood.

10 Goh, S. (2001, September 5). All the right staff and Arlina Arshad, Putting your personality to the test. *The Straits Times*, 5(September), p. H1.

11 Berry, L. L. (1999). *Discovering the Soul of Service – The Nine Drivers of Sustainable Business Success* (p. 161). New York: The Free Press.

12 Parts of this section are based on Bowen, D. E., & Lawler, E. E., III, (1992). The empowerment of service workers: What, why, how and when. *Sloan Management Review*, (Spring), pp. 32–39.

13 Bradley, G. L., & Sparks, B. A. (2000). Customer reactions to staff empowerment: Mediators and moderators. *Journal of Applied Social Psychology*, 30(5), pp. 991–1012.

14 Katzenbach, J. R., & Smith, D. K. (1993). The discipline of teams. *Harvard Business Review*, (March–April), p. 112.

15 Sergeant, A., & Frenkel, S. (2000). When do customer contact employees satisfy customers? *Journal of Service Research*, 3(1) (August), pp. 18–34.

16 Jong, A. D., Ruyter, K. D., & Lemmink, J. (2004). Antecedents and consequences of the service climate in boundary-spanning self-managing service teams. *Journal of Marketing*, 68(April), pp. 18–35.

17 Osheroff, M. (2007). Teamwork in the global economy. *Strategic Finance*, 88(8) (Feb), pp. 25, 61.

18 Based on Schneider & Bowen, *Winning the Service Game*, pp. 145–173.

19 Berry, L. L. (2005). *On Great Service – A Framework for Action*, 236–237; Schwepker Jr. C. H., & Hartline, M. D. (2005). Managing the ethical climate of customer-contact service employees. *Journal of Service Research*, 7(4), pp. 377–397.

20 Schneider & Bowen, *Winning the Service Game*, p. 240.

BLANK

PART

IV

THE *ESM*
FRAMEWORK

PART I

Understanding Service Products, Consumers and Markets

Chapter 1 Introduction to Services Marketing
Chapter 2 Consumer Behavior in a Services Context
Chapter 3 Positioning Services in Competitive Markets

PART II

Applying the 4Ps to Services

Chapter 4 Developing Service Products:
Core and Supplementary Elements
Chapter 5 Distributing Service through
Physical and Electronic Channels
Chapter 6 Setting Prices and Implementing
Revenue Management
Chapter 7 Promoting Services and Educating
Customers

PART III

Managing the Customer Interface

Chapter 8 Designing and Managing Service
Processes
Chapter 9 Balancing Demand Against Productive
Capacity
Chapter 10 Crafting the Service Environment
Chapter 11 Managing People for Service Advantage

PART IV

Implementing Profitable Service Strategies

Chapter 12 Managing Relationships and Building Loyalty
Chapter 13 Complaint Handling and Service Recovery
Chapter 14 Improving Service Quality and Productivity
Chapter 15 Organizing for Change Management and Service Leadership

Implementing Profitable Service Strategies

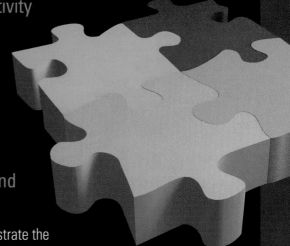

PART IV focuses on four key aspects of implementation. It consists of the following four chapters:

Chapter 12   Managing Relationships and Building Loyalty

Focuses on achieving profitability through creating relationships with customers from the right segments and then finding ways to build and reinforce their loyalty through the Wheel of Loyalty. Loyalty bonds are created to deepen the relationships with customers, but firms also have to reduce customer churn/defections. This chapter closes with a discussion of customer relationship management (CRM) systems.

Chapter 13   Complaint Handling and Service Recovery

Examines how a loyal customer base is often built from effective complaint handling and service recovery. Chapter 13 discusses consumer complaining behavior and principles of effective service recovery systems. Service guarantees are discussed as a powerful way of institutionalizing effective service recovery and as an effective marketing tool signaling high quality service.

Chapter 14   Improving Service Quality and Productivity

Deals with productivity and quality. Both productivity and quality are necessary and related to financial success in services. Chapter 14 covers service quality, diagnosing quality shortfalls using the Gap model, and strategies to close quality gaps. Customer feedback systems are introduced as an effective tool for systematically listening to and learning from customers.

Chapter 15   Organizing for Change Management and Service Leadership

Uses the service profit chain as an integrative model to demonstrate the strategic linkages involved in running a successful service organization. Implementing the service profit chain requires integration of the three key functions of marketing, operations and human resources. We discuss how to move a service organization to higher levels of performance in each functional area. The chapter closes with the role of leadership in both evolutionary and turnaround environments, and in creating and maintaining a climate for service.

12

managing
RELATIONSHIPS and BUILDING LOYALTY

LEARNING OBJECTIVES

By the end of this chapter, students should be able to:

▶ **LO 1** Recognize the important role loyalty plays in driving a service firm's profitability.

▶ **LO 2** Calculate the Life Time Value (LTV) of a loyal customer.

▶ **LO 3** Understand why customers are loyal to a particular service firm.

▶ **LO 4** Know the core strategies that are part of the Wheel of Loyalty.

▶ **LO 5** Appreciate why it is so important for service firms to target the "right" customers.

▶ **LO 6** Use service tiering to manage the customer base.

▶ **LO 7** Understand the relationship between satisfaction and loyalty.

▶ **LO 8** Know how to deepen the relationship through cross-selling and bundling.

▶ **LO 9** Understand the role of loyalty rewards in enhancing customer loyalty.

▶ **LO 10** Appreciate the power of social, customization and structural bonds in enhancing loyalty.

▶ **LO 11** Understand what factors cause customers to switch to a competitor, and how to reduce such switching.

▶ **LO 12** Understand the part played by Customer Relationship Management (CRM) systems in delivering customized services and building loyalty.

OPENING VIGNETTE[1]

HARRAH'S ENTERTAINMENT'S CUSTOMER RELATIONSHIP MANAGEMENT

Figure 12.1 From high-rollers to casual gamblers, the glittering lights of Harrah's promises customer satisfaction.

Harrah's Entertainment, the world's largest gaming company with its three main brands Harrah's, Caesar's and Horseshoe, is a leader in the use of highly sophisticated loyalty programs. Harrah's was first to launch a tiered customer loyalty program in the gaming industry. Today, it has five tiers in its program—Gold, Platinum, Diamond, Seven Stars, and Chairman's Club. The card is integrated across all its properties and services. Customers identify themselves (and earn points) at every touch point throughout the company, ranging from its gaming tables, restaurants and hotels to the gift shops and shows. The points collected can be used to obtain cash, merchandize, lodging, show tickets, vacations, and events.

What is special about Harrah's is not its loyalty program, but what it does with the information gleaned about its customers when they use their cards to earn points. At the backend, Harrah's linked all its databases from casino management, hotel reservations and events to allow it to have a holistic view of each of its customers. Harrah's now has detailed data on over 42 million of its customers. They know the personal preferences of their customers from how much they spend on each type of game, to the preferences in terms of food and drinks, as well as entertainment. Information about the customer is captured real-time.

Harrah's uses this data to drive its marketing and on-site customer service. For example, it will know when the customer wins a jackpot and can tailor a reward that celebrates that win. Harrah's knows when a particular customer is approaching his maximum gaming limit on a particular evening upon when the customer will stop playing. Just before the limit is reached, Harrah's can offer him a heavily discounted ticket via SMS time promoting a show with still available seats. This keeps the customer on the premises (and spending), and makes him feel valued as he gets a very special deal just when he wanted to stop playing. If the customer is celebrating a birthday, then the data will allow employees to know that and surprise the guest with a greeting or a special gift. When a customer makes a call to its call center, the staff have detailed real time information about a customer's preferences and spending habits and can then tailor promotions that cross-sell or up-sell its services to valued customers.

Harrah's does not do blanket promotions hitting all its customers. Rather, it uses highly targeted promotions that create the right incentives for each of its different customers. And it uses control groups to measure the success of a promotion in dollars and cents.

With its data-driven CRM, Harrah's is able to make each customer interaction a personal and differentiated one, leading to a special relationship which its customers value. As a result, Harrah's increased the share-of-wallet of its Harrah's Total Rewards card holders to over a highly impressive 50 percent.

...Harrah's hits the jackpot with its use of technological innovation to cultivate excellent customer relations...

THE SEARCH FOR CUSTOMER LOYALTY

Loyalty in a business context describes a customer's willingness to continue buying from a firm over the long-term, and recommending the firm's products to friends and associates. Customer loyalty does not just mean behavior. It includes preference, liking, and future intentions.

"Few companies think of customers as annuities," says Frederick Reichheld, author of *The Loyalty Effect*, and a major researcher in this field.[2] However, that is what a loyal customer can mean to a firm—a regular source of revenue over a period of many years. The active management of the customer base and customer loyalty is also referred to as customer asset management.[3] This is what Harrah's Entertainment is good at—managing its customer assets.

In a marketing context, the term defection is used to describe customers who stop buying from a company and transfer their brand loyalty to another supplier. Reichheld and Sasser made the term "zero defections" popular. Zero defections means keeping every customer the company can profitably serve.[4] A rising defection rate shows that something is wrong with quality, or that competitors offer better value. It also shows a fall in profits. Large customers do not just disappear overnight. They may show their increasing dissatisfaction by steadily reducing their purchases and shifting part of their business elsewhere.

LO 1
Recognize the important role loyalty plays in driving a service firm's profitability.

Why is Customer Loyalty Important to a Firm's Profitability?

How much is a loyal customer worth in terms of profits? Reichheld and Sasser analyzed the profit per customer in different service businesses. It was grouped by the number of years that a customer had been with the firm.[5] They found that the longer customers remained with a firm in each of these industries, the more profitable they became. Annual profit increases per customer are shown in Figure 12.2 for a few sample industries. The same loyalty effect was found in the internet context, where profits also increased as customers stayed longer with the firm.[6]

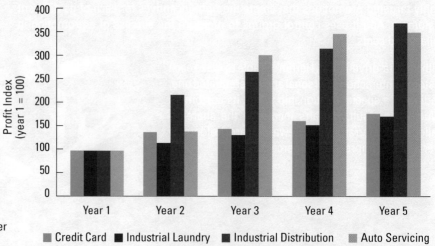

Figure 12.2 How much profit a customer generates over time.

SOURCE

Based on reanalysis of data from Reichheld, F.R., Sasser Jr., W.E., (1990). Zero defections: quality comes from services. *Harvard Business Review*, 68 (September–October), pp. 105–111.

There are four factors that cause this growth, say Reichheld and Sasser. These factors are:

1. *Profit from increased purchases* (or, in a credit card or banking environment, higher account balances). Over time, business customers often grow larger and so need to purchase in greater quantities. Individuals may also purchase more as their families grow or as they become wealthier. Both types of customers may decide to consolidate their purchases with their preferred supplier who provides high quality service.

2. *Profit from reduced operating costs*. As customers become more experienced, they make fewer demands on the supplier (for instance, less need for information and assistance, and they self-serve more via the internet). They may also make fewer mistakes when involved in operational processes. This contributes to greater productivity.

3. *Profit from referrals to other customers*. Positive word-of-mouth recommendations are such as free sales and advertising, saving the firm from having to invest as much money in these activities.

4. *Profit from price premium*. New customers often benefit from introductory promotional discounts. Long-term customers however, are more likely to pay regular prices, and when highly satisfied may even be willing to pay a price premium.[7] Moreover, when customers trust a supplier, they are more willing to pay higher prices at peak periods or for express work.

Figure 12.3 shows the relative contribution of each of these different factors over a seven-year period, based on an analysis of 19 different product categories (both goods and services). Reichheld argues that the economic benefits of customer loyalty noted above often explain why one firm is more profitable than a competitor.

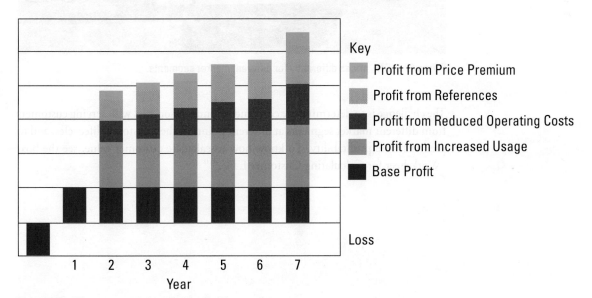

Figure 12.3 Why customers become profitable over time.

Assessing the Value of a Loyal Customer

It would be a mistake to assume that loyal customers are always more profitable than those making one-time transactions.[8] Loyal customers may not necessarily spend more than one-time buyers and in some instances loyal customers may even expect price discounts. For example, in many B2B contexts, large customers have a lot of bargaining power. Therefore, when contracts are to be renewed, they try to make sure they get lower prices. This forces suppliers to share the cost savings resulting from doing business with a large, loyal customer. DHL has found that although each of its major accounts brings a lot of business, it has below average margins. In contrast, DHL's smaller, less powerful accounts, show higher profitability[9] (Figure 12.4).

Figure 12.4 DHL prices differently for different market segments.

The challenge is to determine the costs and revenues associated with serving customers from different market segments at different points in their customer lifecycles, and to predict future profitability. To know how to calculate customer value, see the box, "Worksheet for Calculating Customer LTV."[10]

LO 2
Calculate the lifetime value
(LTV) of a loyal customer.

Worksheet for Calculating Customer Lifetime Value

Calculating customer value is an inexact science that is subject to a variety of assumptions. You may want to try varying these assumptions to see how it affects the final figures. Generally speaking, revenues per customer are easier to track on an individualized basis than are the associated costs of serving a customer, unless (1) no individual records are kept and/or (2) the accounts served are very large and all account-related costs are individually documented and assigned.

Acquisition Revenues Less Costs

If individual account records are kept, the initial application fee paid and initial purchase (if relevant) should be found in these records. Costs, by contrast, may have to be based on average data. For instance, the marketing cost of acquiring a new client can be calculated by dividing the total marketing costs (advertising, promotions, selling, etc.) devoted toward acquiring new customers by the total number of new customers acquired during the same period. If each acquisition takes place over an extended period of time, you may want to build in a lagged effect between when marketing expenditures are incurred and when new customers come on board. The cost of credit checks—where relevant—must be divided by the number of new customers, not the total number of applicants, because some applicants will probably fail this hurdle. Account set-up costs will also be an average figure in most organizations.

Annual Revenues and Costs

If annual sales, account fees, and service fees are documented on an individual-account basis, account revenue streams (except referrals) can be easily identified. The first priority is to segment your customer base by the length of its relationship with your firm. Depending on the sophistication and precision of your firm's records, annual costs in each category may be directly assigned to an individual account holder or averaged for all account holders in that age category.

Value of Referrals

Computing the value of referrals requires a variety of assumptions. To get started, you may need to conduct surveys to determine (1) what percentage of new customers claim that they were influenced by a recommendation from another customer and (2) what other marketing activities also drew the firm to that individual's attention. From these two items, estimates can be made of what percentage of the credit for all new customers should be assigned to referrals. Additional research may be needed to clarify whether "older" customers are more likely to be effective recommenders than "younger" ones.

Net Present Value

Calculating net present value (NPV) from a future profit stream will require choice of an appropriate annual discount figure. (This could reflect estimates of future inflation rates.) It also requires assessment of how long the average relationship lasts. The NPV of a customer, then, is the sum of the anticipated annual profit on each customer for the projected relationship lifetime, suitably discounted each year into the future.

Acquisition			Year 1	Year 2	Year 3	Year n
Initial Revenue		*Annual Revenues*				
Application fee[a]	————	Annual account fee[a]	————	————	————	————
Initial purchase[a]	————	Sales	————	————	————	————
		Service fees[a]	————	————	————	————
		Value of referrals[b]	————	————	————	————
Total Revenues	══════		══════	══════	══════	══════
Initial Costs	————	*Annual Costs*				
Marketing	————	Account management	————	————	————	————
Credit check[a]	————	Cost of sales	————	————	————	————
Account setup[a]	————	Write-offs (e.g., bad debts)	————	————	————	————
Less total costs	————		————	————	————	————
Net Profit (Loss)	══════		══════	══════	══════	══════

[a] If applicable.
[b] Anticipated profits from each new customer referred (could be limited to the first year or expressed as the net present value of the estimated future stream of profits through year n); this value could be negative if an unhappy customer starts to spread negative word of mouth that causes existing customers to defect.

LO 3

Understand why customers are loyal to a particular service firm.

Why are Customers Loyal?

After understanding how important loyal customers can be for the bottom line of a service firm, let us explore what it is that makes a customer loyal.

Customers are not inherently loyal to any one firm! Rather, we need to give our customers a reason to consolidate their buying with us and then stay with us. We need to create value for them to become and remain loyal. Research has shown that relationships can create value for individual consumers through such factors as inspiring greater confidence, social benefits and special treatment (see Service Insights 12.1). We will next discuss how we can systematically think about creating value for our loyal customers using the Wheel of Loyalty.

⠿ SERVICE INSIGHTS 12.1

How Customers See **Relational Benefits** in Service Industries

What benefits do customers see themselves receiving from an extended relationship with a service firm? Researchers seeking answers to this question conducted two studies. The first consisted of in-depth interviews with respondents from a broad cross-section of backgrounds. Respondents were asked to identify service providers that they used on a regular basis and invited to identify and discuss any benefits they received as a result of being a regular customer. Among some of the verbatim comments were:

▶ "I like him [hair stylist]…. He's really funny and always has lots of good jokes. He's kind of like a friend now."

▶ "I know what I'm getting—I know that if I go to a restaurant that I regularly go to, rather than taking a chance on all of the new restaurants, the food will be good."

▶ "I often get price breaks. The little bakery that I go to in the morning, every once in a while, they'll give me a free muffin and say, 'You're a good customer, it's on us today.'"

▶ "You can get better service than drop-in customers… We continue to go to the same automobile repair shop because we have gotten to know the owner on a kind of personal basis, and he… can always work us in."

▶ "Once people feel comfortable, they don't want to switch to another dentist. They don't want to train or break a new dentist in."

After evaluating and categorizing the comments, the researchers designed a second study in which they collected 299 survey questionnaires. The respondents were told to select a specific service provider with whom they had a strong, established relationship. Then the questionnaire asked them to assess the extent to which they received each of 21 benefits (derived from analysis of the first study) as a result of their relationship with the specific provider they had identified. Finally, they were asked to assess the importance of these benefits for them.

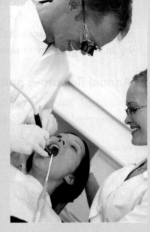

A factor analysis of the results showed that most of the benefits that customers derived from relationships could be grouped into three clusters. The first, and most important, group is concerned about what the researchers labeled confidence benefits, followed by social benefits and special treatment.

Confidence benefits included feelings by customers that in an established relationship there was less risk of something going wrong, confidence in correct performance, ability to trust the provider, lowered anxiety when purchasing, knowing what to expect, and receipt of the firm's highest level of service.

Social benefits embraced mutual recognition between customers and employees, being known by name, friendship with the service provider, and enjoyment of certain social aspects of the relationship.

Special treatment benefits included better prices, discounts on special deals that were unavailable to most customers, extra services, higher priority when there was a wait, and faster service than most customers.

SOURCE

Gwinner, K. P., Gremler, D. D., & Bitner, M. J. (1998). Relational benefits in services industries: The customer's perspective. *Journal of the Academy of Marketing Science*, 26(2), pp. 101–114.

THE WHEEL OF LOYALTY

LO 4

Know the core strategies that are part of the Wheel of Loyalty.

Building customer loyalty is difficult. Just try and think of all the service firms you yourself are loyal to. You are likely to only come up with very few examples. This shows that although firms spend huge amounts of money and effort on building loyalty, they often are not successful in building true customer loyalty.

We use the Wheel of Loyalty shown in Figure 12.5 as an organizing framework for thinking of how to build customer loyalty. It is made up of three sequential strategies.

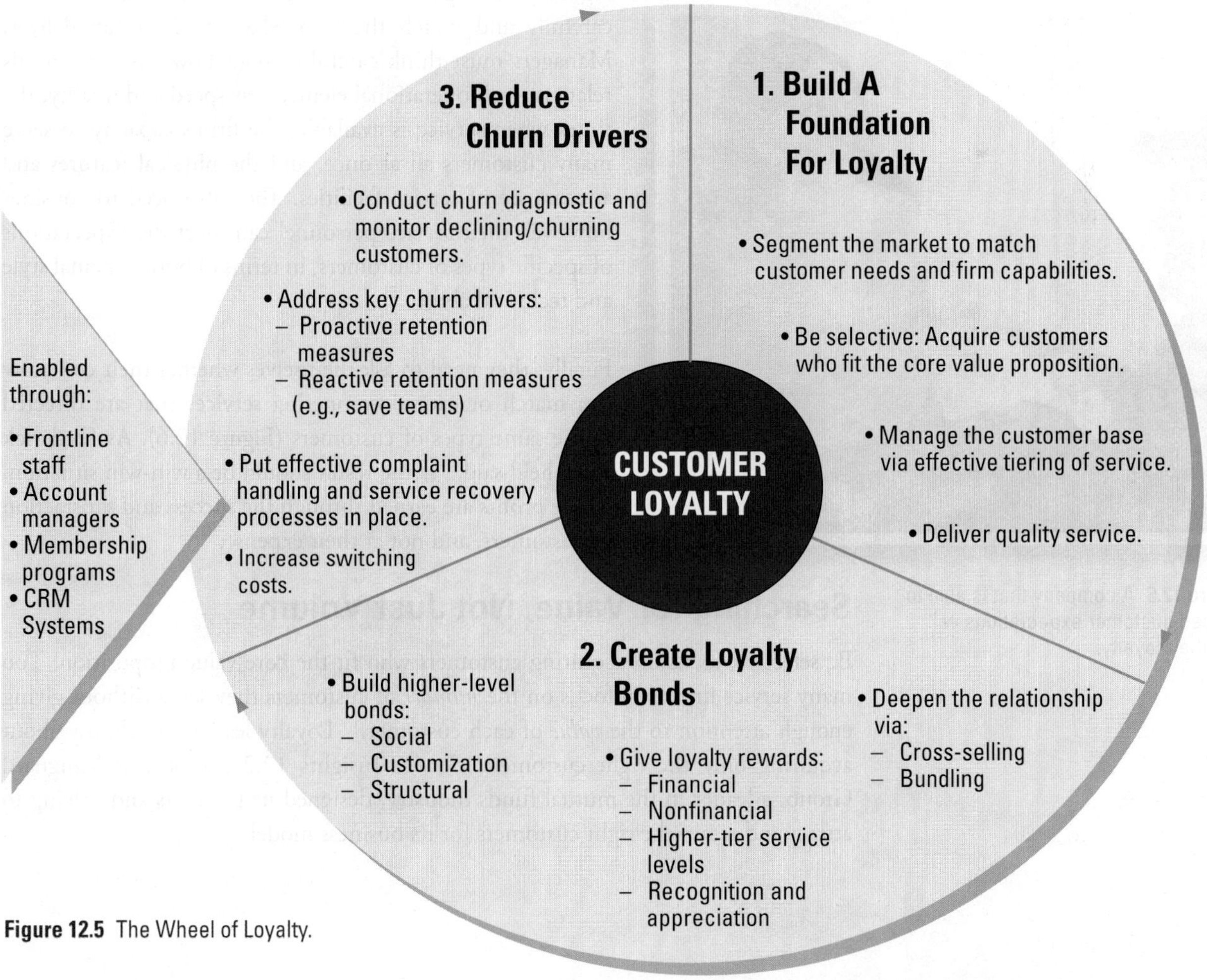
1. Build A Foundation For Loyalty
• Segment the market to match customer needs and firm capabilities.
• Be selective: Acquire customers who fit the core value proposition.
• Manage the customer base via effective tiering of service.
• Deliver quality service.
2. Create Loyalty Bonds
• Build higher-level bonds:
– Social
– Customization
– Structural
• Give loyalty rewards:
– Financial
– Nonfinancial
– Higher-tier service levels
– Recognition and appreciation
• Deepen the relationship via:
– Cross-selling
– Bundling
3. Reduce Churn Drivers
• Conduct churn diagnostic and monitor declining/churning customers.
• Address key churn drivers:
– Proactive retention measures
– Reactive retention measures (e.g., save teams)
• Put effective complaint handling and service recovery processes in place.
• Increase switching costs.
CUSTOMER LOYALTY
Enabled through:
• Frontline staff
• Account managers
• Membership programs
• CRM Systems

Figure 12.5 The Wheel of Loyalty.

PART IV

Firstly, you need a solid foundation for creating customer loyalty. This includes having the right mix of customer segments, attracting the right customers, tiering the service and delivering high levels of satisfaction. If done right, this step also generates confidence benefits as described in Service Insights 12.1.

Secondly, to truly build loyalty, a firm needs to develop close bonds with its customers. They can either deepen the relationship through cross-selling and bundling, or add value to the customer through loyalty rewards (delivering special treatment benefits) and higher level bonds (creating social benefits).

Thirdly, service marketers should identify and reduce the factors that result in "churn"—the loss of existing customers and the need to replace them with new ones. We discuss each of the components of the Wheel of Loyalty in the sections that follow.

⊙ LO 5

Appreciate why it is so important for service firms to target the "right" customers.

BUILDING A FOUNDATION FOR LOYALTY
Targeting the Right Customers

Loyalty management starts with segmenting the market to match customer needs and firm capabilities, in short, identify and target the right customers. "Who should we be serving?" is a question that every service business needs to ask regularly. Companies need to choose their target segments carefully and match them to what the firm can deliver. Managers must think carefully about how customer needs relate to such operational elements as speed and quality, the times when service is available, the firm's capacity to serve many customers all at once, and the physical features and appearance of service facilities. They also need to consider how well their service personnel can meet the expectations of specific types of customers, in terms of both personal style and technical ability.[11]

Finally, they need to ask themselves whether their company can match or exceed competing services that are directed at the same types of customers (Figure 12.6). As Frederick Reichheld said, "...the result should be a win-win situation, where profits are earned through the success and satisfaction of customers, and not at their expense."[12]

Figure 12.6 A company that is able to exceed customer expectations will win their loyalty.

Searching for Value, Not Just Volume

Be selective, focus on acquiring customers who fit the core value proposition! Too many service firms still focus on the *number* of customers they serve without giving enough attention to the *value* of each customer.[13] Loyalty leaders are choosy about acquiring only the right customers. Service Insights 12.2 shows how Vanguard Group, a leader in the mutual funds industry, designed its products and pricing to attract and retain the right customers for its business model.

Vanguard Discourages the **Acquisition of 'Wrong' Customers**

The Vanguard Group is a growth leader in the mutual fund industry. As of 25 March 2008, it has total assets of about $1.25 trillion in US mutual funds. It has built its assets by carefully targeting the right customers for its business model. Its large share of new sales and a far lower share of redemptions, which gave it a market share of net cash flows of 55 percent (new sales minus redemptions), made it the fastest growing mutual fund in its industry.

How did Vanguard achieve such low redemption rates? The secret was in its careful acquisition, and its product and pricing strategies, which encouraged the acquisition of the 'right' customers.

John Bogle, Vanguard's founder, believed in the quality of its index funds and their lower management fees would lead to higher returns over the long run. He offered Vanguard's clients low management fees through a policy of not trading (its index funds hold the market they are designed to track), not having a sales force, and spending only a small amount of what its competitors did on advertising. Another important part of keeping its costs low has been to discourage the acquisition of customers who are not long term investors.

John Bogle attributes the high customer loyalty Vanguard has achieved to placing importance on customer defections, which are redemptions in the fund context. "I watched them like a hawk," he explained, and analyzed them very carefully to make sure that Vanguard acquired the right kind of customer. Low redemption rates meant that the firm was attracting the right kind of loyal, long-term investors.

When an institutional investor redeemed $25 million from an index fund which was only bought nine months earlier, he regarded the acquisition of this customer a failure of the system. He explained, "We don't want short-term investors. They muck up the game at the expense of the long-term investor." At the end of his chairman's letter to the Vanguard Index Trust, Bogle repeated: "We urge them [short-term investors] to look elsewhere for their investment opportunities."

This care and attention to acquiring the right customers is famous. For example, Vanguard turned away an institutional investor who wanted to invest $40 million because it suspected that the customer would churn the investment within the next few weeks, creating extra costs for existing customers.

Vanguard introduced a number of changes to industry practices which discouraged active traders from buying its funds. For example, Vanguard's pricing was set up to reward loyal customers. Specifically, redemption fees were added to some funds, and for many of its funds, investors pay a one-time fee upfront. This fee goes into the funds themselves to make up for current investors' administrative costs of selling new shares. In essence, this fee subsidizes long-term investors, and penalizes short term investors. Another novel pricing approach was the creation of Admiral Shares for loyal investors, which carried an expense fee one-third less than those of ordinary shares. Combined, these pricing policies turned away heavy traders, but made the fund extremely attractive for the long term investor.

Welcome to Vanguard, the client-owned investment management company built to put your interests first®

SOURCE

Reichheld, F. F. (2001). *Loyalty Rules! How Today's Leaders Build Lasting Relationships* (pp. 24–29, 84–87, 144–145). Boston: MA, Harvard Business School Press; Available: www.vanguard.com, accessed April 2008.

PART IV

Different segments offer different value for a service firm. Like investments, some types of customers may be more profitable than others in the short term. However, others may have more room for long-term growth. Similarly, the spending patterns of some customers may be stable over time, while others may vary, spending heavily in boom times but cutting back sharply in recessions. With its customer analytics, Harrah's is able to predict spending patterns of segments based on the history of people with a similar profile. A wise marketer seeks a mix of segments in order to reduce the risks associated with variations in demand.[14]

Also, managers should not assume that the "right customers" are always high spenders. Many firms have become successful by serving customer segments that bigger players did not see as "valuable" enough. For example, Enterprise Rent-A-Car targeted customers who needed a temporary replacement car. For many years, it avoided the more traditional segment of business travelers targeted by its main competitors. Charles Schwab focused on retail stock buyers. Many professional firms target small businesses rather than large ones.

LO 6

Use service tiering to manage the customer base.

Managing the Customer Base through Effective Tiering of Service

▶ Marketers should adopt a strategic approach to retaining, upgrading, and even terminating customers. Customer retention involves developing long-term, cost-effective links with customers for the mutual benefit of both parties. However, these efforts should not target all customers with the same level of intensity. Customers can be grouped into tiers in terms of profitability. It is important for firms to understand that these tiers often have quite different service expectations and needs.[15] Zeithaml, Rust and Lemon show how this can be done through a four-level pyramid (Figure 12.7).

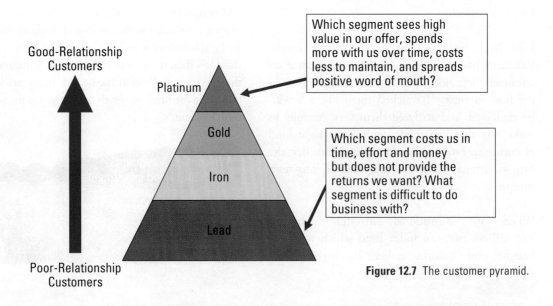

Figure 12.7 The customer pyramid.

Good-Relationship Customers

Poor-Relationship Customers

Platinum

Gold

Iron

Lead

Which segment sees high value in our offer, spends more with us over time, costs less to maintain, and spreads positive word of mouth?

Which segment costs us in time, effort and money but does not provide the returns we want? What segment is difficult to do business with?

SOURCE

Zeithaml, V. A., Rust, R. T., & Lemon, K. N. (2001). The customer pyramid: Creating and serving profitable customers. *California Management Review*, 43(4), (Summer), pp. 118–142.

- *Platinum.* These customers form a very small percentage of a firm's customer base. They are heavy users and contribute a large share of the profits. This segment is usually less price-sensitive, but expects highest service levels in return. They are likely to be willing to invest in and try new services.

- *Gold.* The gold-tier includes a larger percentage of customers than the platinum. However, individual customers contribute less profit than platinum customers. They tend to be slightly more price sensitive and less committed to the firm.

- *Iron.* These customers provide the bulk of customer base. Their numbers give the firm economies of scale. Hence, they are often important so that a firm can build and maintain a certain capacity level and infrastructure, which is often needed for serving gold and platinum customers. However, iron customers are often only marginally profitable. Their level of business is not enough for special treatment.

- *Lead.* Customers in this tier tend to generate low revenues for a firm. However, they often still require the same level of service as iron customers. Therefore, from the firm's perspective, they are a loss-making segment.

Tiering the service means that the firm delivers different services and service levels to these different customer groups. The benefit features for platinum and gold customers should be designed to encourage them to remain loyal because these customers are the very ones competitors would like most to steal. Among loyal segments, the focus should be on developing and growing the relationship, perhaps via loyalty programs.[16]

By contrast, among lead tier customers at the bottom of the pyramid, the options are either to move them to the iron segment (e.g. through increasing sales, increasing prices and/or cutting servicing costs) or to end the relationship with them. Imposing a minimum balance or fee that is waived when a certain level of revenue is generated may encourage customers who use several suppliers to consolidate their buying with a single firm. Another way to migrate customers from lead to iron is to encourage them to use low-cost service delivery channels. For instance, lead customers may be charged a fee for face-to-face interactions but the fee is waived when such customers use electronic channels. In the cellular telephone industry, for example, low-use mobile users can be encouraged to use pre-paid packages that do not require the firm to send out bills and collect payments. This also reduces the risk of bad debts on such accounts.

Occasionally customers are fired outright. ING Direct is a no frills bank. It only has a handful of basic products, and attracts customers with high interest rates (its Orange savings account pays 3 percent in May 2008,[17] which is higher than the industry average!) (Figure 12.8). To balance that generosity, its business model pushes its customers to online transactions. The bank often fires customers who do not fit its business model. When a customer calls too often (the average customer phone call costs the bank $5.25 to handle),

Figure 12.8 ING Direct offers high interest rates that keep customers happy.

PART IV

or wants too many exceptions to the rule, the banks sales associates basically say: "Look, this doesn't fit you. You need to go back to your community bank and get the kind of contact you're comfortable with." As a result, ING Direct's cost per account is only one-third of the industry average.[18]

Each service firm needs to regularly examine its customer portfolio and consider ending unsuccessful relationships. Legal and ethical considerations, of course, will determine how to take such actions. For example, a bank may introduce a minimum monthly fee for accounts with a low balance (e.g. below $1000), but for social responsibility considerations waive this fee for customers on social security.

LO 7

Understand the relationship between satisfaction and loyalty.

Customer Satisfaction and Service Quality are Prerequisites for Loyalty

The foundation for true loyalty lies in customer satisfaction. Highly satisfied or even delighted customers are more likely to become loyal apostles of a firm.[19] They consolidate their purchases with one supplier, and spread positive word-of-mouth. On the other hand, dissatisfaction drives customers away and is a key factor in switching behavior. Recent research even showed that increases in customer satisfaction lead to increases in stock prices—see Service Insights 12.3.

The satisfaction-loyalty relationship can be divided into three main zones: Defection, indifference, and affection (Figure 12.9). The *zone of defection* occurs at low satisfaction levels. Customers will switch unless switching costs are high or there are no other choices. Extremely dissatisfied customers can turn into 'terrorists' providing a lot of negative word-of-mouth for the service provider.[20] The *zone of indifference* is found at moderate satisfaction levels. Here, customers are willing to switch if they find a better choice. Finally, the *zone of affection* is located at very high satisfaction levels, where customers may have such high attitudinal loyalty that they do not look for alternative service providers. Customers who praise the firm in public and refer others to the firm are described as 'apostles.' High satisfaction levels lead to improved future business performance.[21]

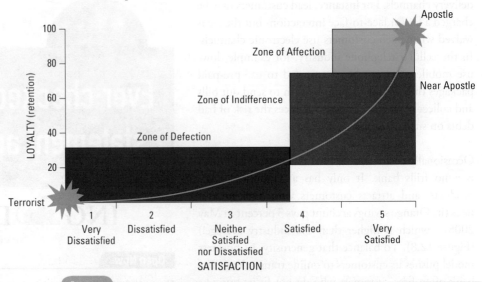

Figure 12.9 The customer satisfaction-loyalty relationship.

Customer Satisfaction and Wall Street — High Returns and Low Risk!

Do a firm's customer satisfaction levels have anything to do with its stock price? This was the interesting research question Claes Fornell and his colleagues worked on to answer. More specifically, they examined whether investments in customer satisfaction led to excess stock returns (see Figure 12.10). If yes, were these returns associated with higher risks as would be predicted by finance theory? The researchers built two stock portfolios, and measured the return and risks of the firms in those portfolios compared to the firm's American Customer Satisfaction Index (ACSI) scores.

Their findings are striking for managers and investors alike! Fornell and his colleagues discovered that the ACSI was significantly related to stock prices of the individual firms and outperformed the market. However, simply publishing the latest data on the ACSI index did not immediately move share prices. Rather share prices seemed to adjust slowly over time as firms published other results (perhaps earnings data or other 'hard' facts which may lag customer satisfaction). Therefore, acting faster than the market to changes in the ACSI index generated excess stock returns. The results are in line with research in marketing which holds that satisfied customers improve the level and the stability of cash flow.

For marketing managers, this study's findings confirm that investments (or "expenses" if you talk to accountants) in managing customer relationships and the cash flows they produce increase a firm's value. Although the results are convincing, be careful if you want to invest in firms that show high increases in customer satisfaction in future ACSI releases. Your finance friends will tell you that efficient markets learn fast! You know this has happened when you see stock prices move as a response to future ACSI releases. You can learn more about the ACSI at: www.theacsi.org.

Figure 12.10 Can customer satisfaction data help to outperform Wall Street?

SOURCE

Fornell, C., Mithas, S., Morgeson III, F. V., & Krishnan, M. S. (2006). *Journal of Marketing*, 70, (January), pp. 3–14.

STRATEGIES FOR DEVELOPING LOYALTY BONDS WITH CUSTOMERS

Having the right mix of customer segments, attracting the right customers, tiering the service and delivering high levels of satisfaction are a solid foundation for creating customer loyalty as shown in The Wheel of Loyalty in Figure 12.5. However, there is more that firms can do to 'bond' closer with their customers. Strategies for developing loyalty bonds include (1) deepening the relationship through cross-selling and bundling, (2) creating reward-based bonds through loyalty programs, and (3) higher level bonds such as social, customization and structural bonds.[22] We will discuss each of these three strategies next.

Deepening the Relationship through Cross-selling and Bundling

To tie customers closer, firms can deepen the relationship through bundling and/or cross-selling services. For example, banks like to sell as many financial products into an account or household as possible. Once a family has its current account, credit card, savings account, safe deposit box, car loan, mortgage, and so on with the same

 LO 8

Know how to deepen the relationship through cross-selling and bundling.

bank, the relationship is so deep that switching becomes a major exercise. Therefore, customers are not likely to switch unless they are very dissatisfied with the bank.

In addition to higher switching costs, there is often value for the customer when buying all particular services from a single provider. One-stop-shopping typically is more convenient and less hassle than buying individual services from different providers. When having many services with the same firm, the customer may achieve a higher service tier and receive better services, and sometimes service bundles do come with price discounts.

LO 9
Understand the role of loyalty rewards in enhancing customer loyalty.

Encouraging Loyalty Through Reward-based Bonds

Few customers buy only from only one supplier. This is especially true in situations where service delivery involves separate transactions (such as a car rental) rather than being continuous in nature (as with insurance coverage). In many instances, consumers are loyal to several brands (sometimes described as "polygamous loyalty") but avoid others. Here, the marketing goal becomes one of strengthening the customer's preference for one brand over the others and gaining a greater share of the customer's spending on that service category. This is sometimes referred to as "increasing share of wallet."

Reward-based bonds, either financial or non-financial in nature, can be used to strengthen customer's preferences. Financial bonds are built when loyal customers are rewarded with incentives with financial value. Service firms ranging from retailers (such as department stores, supermarkets, book shops, and petrol stations), to telecommunications providers, café chains to courier services and cinema chains have reward programs. Some provide their own rewards, such as free merchandise, vehicle upgrades, or free hotel rooms in vacation resorts. Others offer air miles linked to a selected frequent-flyer program. In fact, air miles have become a form of promotional currency in the service sector.

Service Insights 12.4 describes how British Airways has designed its loyalty program, the Executive Club, to encourage the loyalty of its most valuable customers.

⠿ SERVICE INSIGHTS 12.4 •

Rewarding Value of Use, not just Frequency, at British Airways

Unlike some frequent flyer programs, where customer usage is measured simply in miles, British Airways' (BA's) Executive Club members receive both *air miles* for redemption of air travel awards and *points* for silver or gold tier status for travel on BA. With the creation of the "OneWorld" airline alliance with American Airlines, Qantas, Cathay Pacific, and other carriers, Executive Club members have been able to earn miles (and sometimes points) by flying these partner airlines too.

As shown in Table 12.1, silver and gold cardholders get special benefits, such as priority reservations

and high standards of on-the-ground service. For instance, even if a gold cardholder is only traveling in economy class, he or she will be entitled to first-class standards of treatment at check-in and in the airport lounges. However, while miles can be accumulated for up to three years (after which they expire), tier status is only valid for twelve months from the time it is earned. This means that the right to special privileges must be re-earned each year. The objective of awarding tier status is to encourage passengers to concentrate their travel on British Airways, rather than to join several frequent flyer programs and collect mileage awards from all of them.

Table 12.1: Benefits Offered by British Airways to Its Most Valued Passengers.

Benefit	Silver Tier Members	Gold Tier Members
Reservations	Dedicated silver phone line	Dedicated gold phone line
Reservation assurance	If flight is full, guaranteed seat in economy when booking full fare ticket at least 24 hours in advance and checking in at least one hour in advance	If flight is full, guaranteed seat in economy when booking full fare ticket at least 24 hours in advance, and checking in at least one hour in advance
Priority waitlist and standby	Higher priority	Highest priority
Advance notification of delays over 4 hours from US or Canada	Yes	Yes
Check-in desk	Club (regardless of travel class)	First (regardless of travel class)
Lounge access	Club departure lounges for passenger and one guest regardless of class of travel	First class departure lounge for passenger and one guest, regardless of travel class; use of arrivals lounges; lounge access anytime, and allowing use of lounges even when not flying BA intercontinental flights
Preferred boarding	Board aircraft at leisure	Board aircraft at leisure
Special services assistance		Problem solving beyond that accorded to other BA travelers
Bonus air miles	+25%	+50%
Upgrade for two		Free upgrade to next cabin for member and companion after earning 2,500 tier points in one year; another upgrade for two after 3,500 points in same year. Award someone else with a Silver Partner card on reaching 4,500 points within membership year

SOURCE

British Airways Executive Club, Available: www.britishairways.com/travel/ecbenftgold/public/en_us; accessed May 2008.

Points given also vary according to the class of service. Longer trips earn more points than shorter ones (a domestic or short haul European trip in economy class generates 15 points, a transatlantic trip 60 points, and a trip from the UK to Australia, 100 points.) However, tickets at deeply discounted prices may earn fewer miles and no points at all.

To reward purchase of higher-priced tickets, passengers earn points at double the economy rate if they travel in Club (business class), and at triple the rate in First. To encourage gold and silver card holders to remain loyal, BA offers incentives for Executive Club members to retain their current tier status (or to move up from silver to gold). Silver cardholders receive a 25 percent bonus on all air miles, regardless of class of service, while gold cardholders receive a 50 percent bonus. In other words, it does not pay to spread the miles among several frequent-flyer programs!

Although the airline makes no promises on complimentary upgrades, members of BA's Executive Club are more likely to receive such invitations than other passengers. Tier status is an important consideration. Unlike many airlines, BA tends to limit upgrades to situations in which a lower class of cabin is overbooked. They do not want frequent travelers to believe that they can plan on buying a less expensive ticket and then automatically receive an upgraded seat.

PART IV

Rewards programs alone are not enough to retain the most desirable customers. If customers are dissatisfied with the quality of service they receive, or believe that they can obtain better value from another provider, they may quickly become disloyal. No service business should use a rewards program to replace high quality and good value.[23]

Non-financial rewards provide customers with benefits that cannot be translated directly into monetary terms. Examples include giving priority to loyalty program members for waitlists and queues in call centers, and access to special services. Informal loyalty rewards, sometimes found in small businesses, may take the form of giving regular customers a small treat as a way of thanking them for their business. Important intangible rewards include special recognition and appreciation. Customers tend to value the extra attention given to their needs.

LO 10

Appreciate the power of social, customization and structural bonds in enhancing loyalty.

Building Higher-Level Bonds

One objective of reward-based bonds is to encourage customers to consolidate their purchases with a single provider or at least give it the bulk of their purchases. However, reward-based loyalty programs are relatively easy for other suppliers to copy, so they seldom provide sustained competitive advantage. In contrast, higher level bonds offer a longer term competitive advantage. We will next discuss the three main types of higher level bonds which are (1) social bonds, (2) customization bonds, and (3) structural bonds.

Social Bonds

Have you ever noticed how your favorite hairdresser calls you by your name when you go for a haircut or how she asks why she hasn't seen you for a long time? Social bonds are usually based on personal relationships between providers and customers. There is an element of trust there, which is important for loyalty.[24] Social bonds are more difficult to build than financial bonds and may take longer to achieve, but they are also harder for other suppliers to imitate. A firm that has created social bonds with its customers has a better chance of keeping them for the long term. When social bonds include shared relationships (Figure 12.11) or experiences between customers, such as in country clubs or educational settings, they can be a major loyalty driver for the organization.[25]

Figure 12.11 A knowledgeable, charismatic lecturer is a huge pull for students to stay at a university beyond their undergraduate days.

Figure 12.12 Beyond a smile: Starbucks' employees are encouraged to learn their customers' preferences.

Customization Bonds

These bonds are built when the service provider succeeds in providing customized service to its loyal customers. For example, Starbucks' employees are encouraged to learn their regular customers' preferences and customize their service accordingly (Figure 12.12). Many large hotel chains capture the preferences of their customers through their loyal program databases. Firms offering customized service are likely to have more loyal customers.[26] For example, when customers arrive at their hotel, they find that their individual needs have already been met. These ranges from preferred drinks and snacks in the mini bar, to the kind of pillow they like and the newspaper they want to receive in the morning. A customer who is used to this special service may find it difficult to adjust to another provider who cannot immediately offer a similar level of service.[27]

Structural Bonds

Structural bonds are commonly seen in B2B settings. They are created by getting customers to align their way of doing things with the supplier's own processes, thus linking the customer to the firm. This situation makes it more difficult for competitors to draw them away. Examples include joint investments in projects and sharing of information, processes and equipment. Structural bonds can be created in a B2C environment, too. For instance, some car rental companies offer travelers the opportunity to create customized pages on the firm's website where they can get details of past trips including the types of cars, insurance coverage, and so forth. This simplifies and speeds up the task of making new bookings.

Have you noticed that while all these bonds tie a customer closer to the firm, they also deliver the confidence, social and special treatment benefits customers desire (refer back to Service Insights 12.1)? In general, bonds will not work well unless they also generate value for the customer!

LO 11

Understand what factors cause customers to switch to a competitor, and how to reduce such switching.

STRATEGIES FOR REDUCING CUSTOMER DEFECTIONS

So far, we have discussed drivers of loyalty and how to tie customers closer to the firm. A complementary approach is to understand the drivers for customer defections, also called customer churn, and work on reducing those drivers.

Analyze Customer Defections and Monitor Declining Accounts

The first step is to understand the reasons for customer switching. Susan Keveaney conducted a large-scale study across a range of services and found several key reasons behind customers' switch to another provider (Figure 12.13).[28] Core service failures were mentioned by 44 percent of respondents as a reason for switching; dissatisfactory service encounters by 34 percent; high, deceptive or unfair pricing by 30 percent; inconvenience in terms of time, location, or delays by 21 percent, and poor response to service failure by 17 percent. Many respondents decided to switch after a series of related incidents, such as a service failure followed by an unsatisfactory service recovery.

Mobile phone service providers regularly conduct what is called churn diagnostics. It includes the analysis of data warehouse information on customers who switched, or those whose business was decreasing. Exit interviews are conducted when customers call to cancel their subscription. Here, call center staff often have a short set of questions, which they ask when a customer cancels an account, to gain a better understanding of why customers defect. In-depth interviews of former customers by a third party research agency also help to gain a more detailed understanding of churn drivers.[29]

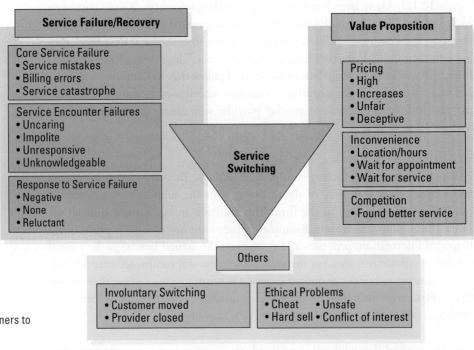

Figure 12.13 What drives customers to switch away from a service film.

Adapted from Keaveney, S. M. (1995). Customer switching behavior in service industries: An exploratory study, *Journal of Marketing*, 59(April), pp. 71–82.

Address Key Churn Drivers

Keaveney's findings show the importance of addressing some general churn drivers by delivering quality service (see Chapter 14), reducing inconvenience and other non-monetary costs, and having fair and transparent pricing (Chapter 6). There are often industry-specific churn drivers as well. For example, handset replacement is a common reason for cellular phone service subscribers to discontinue an existing relationship, as new subscription plans usually come with heavily subsidized new handsets. To prevent handset-related churn, many providers now offer handset replacement programs, offering current subscribers heavily discounted new handsets at regular intervals. Some providers even provide handsets free to high value customers or against redemption of loyalty points.

In addition to measures to prevent churn, many firms take active steps to retain customers. They train call center staff, called 'save teams,' who deal with customers who intend to cancel their accounts. The main job of save team employees is to listen to customer needs and issues, and try to address these with the key focus of retaining the customer. But be careful on how to reward save teams—see Service Insights 12.5.

⠿ SERVICE INSIGHTS 12.5 ·

Churn **Management** Gone **Wrong**

American Online (AOL) agreed to pay $1.25 million in penalties and costs, and to change some of its customer service practices to settle an investigation by the State of New York. About 300 subscribers filed complaints with the state attorney general's office, saying that AOL ignored their demands to cancel the service and stop billing them.

What went wrong? AOL had rewarded its call centre employees for 'saving' customers who called in to cancel their service. Employees could earn high bonuses if they were able to persuade half or more of such customers to stay with the firm. As claimed by the attorney general's office, this may have led AOL's employees to make it difficult for customers to cancel their service. As a response, AOL agreed to a settlement to have service cancellations requests recorded and verified through a third-party monitor. It also agreed to provide up to four

months of refunds to all New York subscribers who claim that their cancellations had been ignored. Former Attorney General Eliot Spitzer said in a statement, "This agreement helps to ensure that AOL will strive to keep its customers through quality service, not stealth retention programs."

SOURCE

The Associated Press (2005)."AOL to pay $1.25M to settle spitzer probe." *USA Today*, (August), p. 5B.

Implement Effective Complaint Handling and Service Recovery Procedures

Effective complaint handling and excellent service recovery are central to keeping unhappy customers from switching providers. Well-managed firms make it easy for customers to voice their problems and respond with suitable service recovery strategies. In that way, customers will remain satisfied, and this will reduce the intention to switch.[30] We will discuss how to do that effectively in Chapter 13.

Increase Switching Costs

Another way to reduce churn is to increase switching barriers.[31] Many services have natural switching costs. For instance, it takes customers time and effort to change a primary banking account, especially when many direct debits, credits, and other related banking services are tied to that account. Also, many customers are not willing to learn about the products and processes of a new provider.[32] Loyalty programs add to switching costs for many customers as they do not want to loose their higher tier status or forfeit loyalty points already collected.

Switching costs can also be created by having contractual penalties for switching, such as the transfer fees payable to some brokerage firms for moving shares and bonds to another financial institution. However, firms need to be careful not to be seen as holding their customers hostage. A firm with high switching barriers and poor service quality is likely to generate negative attitudes and bad word-of-mouth.

⊙ **LO 12**

Understand the part played by Customer Relationship Management (CRM) systems in delivering customized services and building loyalty.

CRM: CUSTOMER RELATIONSHIP MANAGEMENT SYSTEMS

Service marketers have understood for some time the power of relationship management, and certain industries have applied it for years. Examples include the corner grocery store, the neighborhood car repair shop, and providers of banking services to high net-worth clients. However, mention CRM, and immediately costly and complex IT systems and infrastructure come to mind. But CRM is actually the whole process by which relations with the customers are built and maintained.[33] It is an integrated framework (Figure 12.14). It should be seen as enabling the successful implementation of the Wheel of Loyalty.

Common Objectives of CRM Systems

CRM systems allow capturing customer information, and delivering it to the various touch points. From a customer perspective, well-implemented CRM systems deliver customization and personalization. This means that at each transaction, the relevant account details, knowledge of customer preferences and past transactions, or history of a service problem are at the finger tips of the person serving the customer. This can result in a vast service improvement and increased customer value. Personalization and improved communication will result in more loyalty.[34]

From a company perspective, CRM systems allow the company to better understand, segment, and tier its customer base, better target promotions and cross-selling, and even implement churn-alert systems that signal if a customer is in danger of

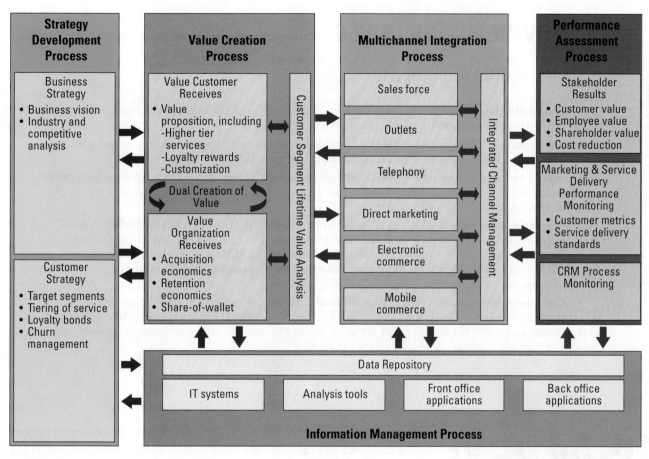

Figure 12.14 An integrated framework for CRM strategy.

SOURCE

Adapted from Payne, A. & Frow, P. (2005) A strategic framework for customer relationship management, *Journal of Marketing*, 69 (October), pp. 167–176.

defecting.[35] It is important to note that CRM should offer a 360° holistic view of the customer where everyone in the company – be it the front line, middle management, or senior management – and even stakeholders in the company (vendors, suppliers or business partners) have the same view of the customer. Service Insights 12.6 highlights some common CRM applications.

What does a Comprehensive CRM Strategy Include?[36]

Rather than viewing CRM as a technology, we should view it as a system that focuses on the profitable development and management of customer relationships. Figure 12.14 provides five key processes involved in a CRM strategy:

1. *Strategy development* involves the analysing of business strategy, including the company's vision, industry trends, and competition. It is usually the responsibility of top management. The business strategy should be guiding the development of the customer strategy, including the choice of target segments, customer base tiering, the design of loyalty bonds and churn management (as discussed in the Wheel of Loyalty, Figure 12.5).

PART IV

Figure 12.15 Airport self-check-in represents another service touch point that needs to be integrated into an airline's CRM system.

2. *Value creation* translates business and customer strategies into value propositions for customers and the firm. The value created for customers includes all the benefits that are delivered through priority tiered services, loyalty rewards, and customization and personalization. The value created for the firm includes reduced customer acquisition and retention costs, increased share-of-wallet, and reduced customer serving costs. Customers need to participate in CRM (e.g. through volunteering information) so that they benefit from the firm's CRM strategy. CRM seems most successful when there is a win-win situation for the firm and its customers.[37]

3. *Multichannel integration.* Most service firms interact with their customers through a variety of channels, including multiple face-to-face outlets, call centers, self-service machines, and the Internet. It is difficult to serve customers well across these channels. CRM's channel integration offers a 'unified customer interface' that delivers customization and personalization.

4. *Information management.* Service delivery across many channels depends on the firm's ability to collect customer information from all channels at the various touch points (Figure 12.15). The information management process includes:

- the data repository which contains all the customer data
- IT systems including IT hardware and software
- analytical tools such as data mining packages

- specific application packages such as campaign management analysis, credit assessment, customer profiling, and churn alert systems

- front office applications, which support activities that involve direct customer contact, including sales force automation and call center management applications

- back office applications, which support internal customer related processes, including, logistics, procurement and financial processing.

5. *Performance assessment* must address three important questions.

- Is the CRM strategy creating value for its key stakeholders (i.e. customers, employees and shareholders)?

- Are the marketing objectives (ranging from customer acquisition, share-of-wallet, retention to customer satisfaction) and service delivery performance objectives (e.g. call center service standards such as call waiting) being achieved?

- Is the CRM process itself performing up to expectations?

Common Failures in CRM Implementation

Unfortunately, most of the CRM implementations in the past have failed. According to the Gartner Group, the implementation failure rate is 55 percent and Accenture claims it to be around 60 percent. Common reasons for CRM failures include:[38]

▶ Viewing CRM as driven by technology. It is easy to let the focus shift towards technology, with the result that the IT department rather than senior management or the marketing department takes the lead in coming up with the CRM strategy. This often results in a lack of direction, understanding of customers and markets during implementation.

▶ Lack of customer focus. Many firms implement CRM without the goal of allowing improving service delivery for valued customers across all delivery channels.

▶ Not enough understanding of customer LTV. Marketing does not take into account the different profitability of different customers. Furthermore, servicing costs of different customers are often not well captured (e.g. by using activity based costing as discussed in Chapter 6).

▶ Inadequate support from top management. Without ownership and active involvement of top management, the CRM implementation will not be successful.

▶ Lack of coordination. There is a need for coordination within the organization, between the different entities that are involved in the implementation.[39]

▶ Failing to reengineer business processes. It is nearly impossible to implement CRM successfully without redesigning customer service and back-office processes. Many implementations fail because CRM is being fitted into existing processes, rather than redesigning the processes to fit a customer-centric CRM implementation. Redesigning also requires changes in management and employee involvement and support, which are often lacking.

Figure 12.16 The phone operator on the line practises CRM in real time.

▶ Underestimating the challenges in data integration. Firms frequently fail to integrate customer data that usually are scattered all over the organization. However, a key to taking advantage of the full potential of CRM is to make customer knowledge available in real time to all employees who need it (Figure 12.16).

In the long run, firms can put their CRM strategies at risk if customers believe that CRM is being used in a way that is harmful to them.[40] Examples include feeling that they are not being treated fairly (including not being offered attractive pricing or promotions that are offered, for example, to new accounts, but not to existing customers), and potential privacy concerns (see Service Insights 12.7). Being aware and actively avoiding these weaknesses is a first step towards successful CRM implementation.

⠿ SERVICE INSIGHTS 12.7 •

CRM *Extreme – A Glimpse into Ordering Pizza in 2015*

Operator: "Thank you for calling Pizza Delight. Linda speaking, how may I help you?"

Customer: "Good evening, can I order …"

Operator: "Sir, before taking your order, could I please have the number of your multi-purpose smart card?"

Customer: "Hold on …. it's ehm … 4555 1000 9831 3213"

Operator: "Thank you! Can I please confirm you're Mr. Thompson calling from 10940 Wilford Boulevard. You are calling from your home number 432-3876, your cellphone number is 992-4566, and your office number is 432-9377."

Customer: "How in the world did you get my address and all my numbers?"

Operator: "Sir, we are connected to the Integrated Customer Intimacy System."

Customer: "I would like to order a large seafood pizza …"

Operator: "Sir, that's not a good idea."

Customer: "Why not?"

Operator: "According to your medical records, you have very high blood pressure and a far too high cholesterol level, Sir"

Customer: "What?.... Then what do you recommend?"

Operator: "Try our Low Fat Soybean Yoghurt Pizza. You'll like it."

Customer: "How do you know?"

Operator: "You borrowed the book "Popular Soybean Dishes" from the City Library last week, Sir."

Customer: "OK, I give up....Get me three large ones then. How much will that be?"

Operator: "That should be enough for your family of 8, Sir. The total is $47.97."

Customer: "Can I pay by credit card?"

Operator: "I'm afraid you'll have to pay us cash, Sir. Your credit card is over the limit and your checking account has an overdue balance of $2,435.54. That's excluding the late payment charges on your home equity loan, Sir."

Customer: "I guess I'll have to run to the ATM and withdraw some cash before your guy arrives."

Operator: "You can't do that, Sir. Based on the records, you've reached your daily machine withdrawals limit for today"

Customer: "Never mind, just send the pizzas. I'll have the cash ready. How long is it gonna take?"

Operator: "About 45 min, Sir; but if you don't want to wait you can always come and collect it on your Harley, registration number L.A.6468 …"

Customer: "#@$#@%^%%@"

Operator: "Sir, please watch your language. Remember, on 28th April 2011 you were convicted of using abusive language at a traffic warden …"

Customer: (Speechless)

Operator: "Is there anything else, Sir?"

SOURCE

This story was adapted from various sources, including www.lawdebt.com/gazette/nov2004/nov2004.pdf accessed on June 2008; and a video created by the American Civil Liberties Union (ACLU) available at http://www.aclu.org/pizza. This video aims to show the threats to consumers' privacy caused by CRM. ACLU is a non-profit organization that challenges government's and corporations' aggressive collection of information on people's personal life and habits. .

How to get CRM Implementation Right

In spite of the many horror stories of millions of dollars sunk into unsuccessful CRM projects, more and more firms are getting it right. "No longer a black hole, CRM is becoming a basic building block of corporate success."[41] Experienced McKinsey consultants believe that even CRM systems that have not yet shown results can still be turned around. They recommend taking a step back and focusing on how to build customer loyalty, rather than focusing on the technology itself.[42] Many successful CRM implementations are highly focused and narrow in scope. Often, they focus on clearly defined problems within the customer relationship cycle. These narrow CRM strategies often reveal additional opportunities for further improvements, which taken together, can over time develop into broad CRM implementation extending across the entire company.[43]

Among the key questions managers should ask when defining their customer relationship strategy are:

1. How should our value proposition change to increase customer loyalty?

2. How much customization or one-to-one marketing and service delivery is suitable and profitable?

3. What is the increase in profit from increasing the share-of-wallet with our current customers? How much does this change by customer tier and/or segment?

4. How much time and resources can we provide to CRM right now?

5. If we believe in CRM, why have we not taken more steps in that direction in the past? What can we do today to develop customer relationships without spending on technology?[44]

Answering these questions may lead to the conclusion that a CRM system may at the moment not be the best investment or highest priority. In any case, we emphasize that the system is merely a tool to drive the strategy, and must thus be customized to deliver that strategy (Figure 12.17).

Figure 12.17 CRM can help companies create two-way channels with customers so that firms have a bigger picture of their needs, wants, and buying patterns.

CHAPTER SUMMARY

LO 1 ▶ Customer loyalty is an important driver of a service firm's profitability. The profits derived from loyal customers come from:

- o increased purchases
- o reduced operation costs
- o referral to other customers
- o price premiums

LO 2 ▶ However, it is not true that loyal customers are always more profitable. They may expect price discounts for staying loyal. To truly understand the profit impact of the customers, firms need to learn how to calculate the LTV of their customers.

LO 3 ▶ Customers are only loyal if there is a benefit for the customer. Common benefits customers see in being loyal include:

- o Confidence benefits, including feeling that there is less risk of something going wrong, ability to trust the provider, and receipt of the firm's highest level of service.
- o Social benefits, including being known by name, friendship with the service provider, and enjoyment of certain social aspects of the relationship.
- o Special treatment benefits, including better prices, extra services, and higher priority.

LO 4 ▶ It is not easy to build customer loyalty. The Wheel of Loyalty offers a systematic framework that guides firms on how to do so. The framework has three components that follow a sequence.

- o First, firms need to build a foundation for loyalty without which loyalty cannot be achieved. The foundation delivers confidence benefits to its loyal customers.
- o Once the foundation is laid, firms can then create loyalty bonds to strengthen the relationship. Loyalty benefits deliver social and special treatment benefits.
- o Finally, besides focusing on loyalty, firms also have to work on reducing customer churn.

▶ To build the foundation for loyalty, firms need to:

LO 5
- o Segment the market and target the "right" customers. Firms need to choose their target segments carefully and match them to what the firm can do best.
- o Firms need to examine customer value, instead of just going for customer volume.

LO 6
- o Manage the customer base via service tiering. The Customer Pyramid divides the customer base into four tiers, namely platinum, gold, iron and lead. It helps to tailor strategies to the different service tiers. The higher tiers offer higher value for the firm, but also expect higher service levels. For the lower tiers, the focus should be on increasing profitability through building volume, increasing prices, cutting servicing costs, and as a last resort even terminating unprofitable relationships.

LO 7
- o Finally, firms have to understand that the foundation for true loyalty lies in customer satisfaction and service quality. The satisfaction-loyalty relationship can be divided into three main zones: defection, indifference and affection. Only highly satisfied or delighted customers will be truly loyal.

▶ Loyalty bonds are used to build relationships with customers. There are three different types of customer bonds:

LO 8
- o Cross-selling and bundling deepen relationships that make switching more difficult and often increase convenience through one-stop shopping.

LO 9
- o Reward-based bonds aim at building share-of-wallet through financial and non-financial rewards, higher-tier service levels and recognition and appreciation

LO 10
- o Higher level bonds include social, customization and structural bonds.

LO 11 ▶ The final step in the Wheel of Loyalty is to understand what causes customers to leave and then systematically reduce these churn drivers.

- o Customers may leave because of core service failures, dissatisfaction with some service encounters, perceptions that pricing is deceptive and unfair, inconvenience, and poor response to service failures.
- o To prevent customers from switching, firms should have good complaint handling and service recovery processes in place.
- o Firms can also increase customers' switching costs.

LO 12 ▶ Finally, CRM systems should be seen as enabling the successful implementation of the Wheel of Loyalty. CRM systems are particularly useful when firms have to serve large numbers of customers across many delivery channels.

▶ An effective CRM strategy includes five key processes: (1) strategy development, (2) value creation, (3) multi-channel integration, (4) information management, and (5) performance assessment.

UNLOCK YOUR LEARNING

These keywords are found within the sections of each Learning Objective (LO). They are integral in understanding the services marketing concepts taught in each section. Having a firm grasp of these keywords and how they are used is essential in helping you do well for your course, and in the real and very competitive marketing scene out there.

1. Loyalty
2. Customer asset management
3. Defection
4. Zero defections

LO 1 5. Customer Lifetime Value

LO 4 6. Foundation for Loyalty
7. Wheel of Loyalty
8. Loyalty rewards

LO 5 9. Loyalty leaders
10. Target the right customers

LO 6 11. Four-level pyramid
12. Gold
13. Iron
14. Lead
15. Platinum
16. Tiering of service

LO 7 17. Apostles
18. Bundling
19. Cross-selling
20. Loyalty bonds
21. Satisfaction-loyalty relationship
22. Zone of defection
23. Zone of indifference
24. Zone of affection
25. Loyalty programs

LO 8 26. Polygamous loyalty
27. Reward-based bonds

LO 10 28. Customization Bonds
29. Structural bonds
30. Social bonds

LO 11 31. Complaint handling
32. Customer churn
33. Customer defections
34. Customer switching
35. Churn diagnostic
36. Churn drivers
37. Industry-specific churn drivers
38. Reduce churn
39. Save teams
40. Service recovery
41. Swtiching barriers

LO 12 42. Churn-alert systems
43. Common CRM applications
44. CRM
45. CRM systems
46. CRM strategy
47. Customization

48. Customer acquisition
49. Data mining packages
50. Data repository
51. Information management
52. IT systems
53. Multichannel integration
54. Performance assessment
55. Personalization
56. Reasons for CRM failures
57. Relationship management
58. Strategy development
59. Share-of-wallet
60. Value creation

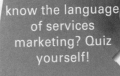

How well do you know the language of services marketing? Quiz yourself!

⚠ **Not for the academically faint-of-heart**

For each keyword you are able to recall without referring to earlier pages, give yourself a point (and a pat on the back). Tally your score at the end and see if you earned the right to be called—a *services marketeer*.

SCORE

0 – 10	Services Marketing is done a great disservice.
11 – 19	The midnight oil needs to be lit, pronto.
20 – 29	I know what you *didn't* do all semester.
30 – 39	By George! You're getting there.
40 – 50	Now, go forth and market.
51 – 60	There should be a marketing concept named after you.

PART **IV**

Review Questions

1. Why is customer loyalty an important driver of profitability for service firms?

2. Why is targeting the 'right customers' so important for successful CRM?

3. How can a firm calculate the LTV of its customers?

4. How do the various strategies described in the Wheel of Loyalty relate to one another?

5. How can a firm build a foundation for loyalty?

6. What is tiering of services? Explain why it is used and what its implications are for firms and their customers.

7. Identify some key measures that can be used to create customer bonds and encourage long-term relationships with customers.

8. What are the arguments for spending money to retain existing customers who are at risk of switching to a competitor?

9. What is the role of CRM in delivering a customer relationship strategy?

WORK YOUR ESM

APPLICATION QUESTIONS

1. Identify three service businesses that you buy from regularly. Now, for each business, complete the following sentence: "I am loyal to this business because _____ _____."

2. What conclusions do you draw about (a) yourself as a consumer, and (b) the performance of each of the businesses in Exercise 1? Judge whether any of these businesses managed to develop a sustainable competitive advantage through the way it won your loyalty.

3. Identify two service businesses that you have used several times but have now stopped buying from (or will stop buying from). Complete the sentence: "I stopped using (or will soon stop using) this organization as a customer because _____ _____."

4. Again, what conclusions do you draw about yourself and the firms in Exercise 3? How could each of these firms avoid your defection?

5. Evaluate the strengths and weaknesses of two loyalty or frequent user programs, each one from a different service industry. Assess how each program could be improved further.

6. Approach service employees in two firms with implemented CRM systems. Ask the employees about their experience of using these systems, and whether the CRM systems help them in understanding their customers better. Does this lead to improved service experiences for their customers? Do interview them about potential concerns and improvement suggestions they may have about their organizations' CRM systems.

•ENDNOTES

1   Sarner, A. (2001) Harrah's success is no crapshoot – it's solid CRM. Gartner Research, 19 (June),ID Number: CS-13-5933; Stanley, T. (2006) High-stakes analytics. Optimize: Business Strategy & Execution for CIOs, (February). www.cognos.com/company/success/harrahs.html, accessed April 2008; Voight, J. (2007)Total rewards pays off for Harrah's. Brandweek.com, 17, (September). www.brandweek.com/bw/news/recent_display.jsp?vnu_content_id=1003641351, accessed April 2008; Hoover, J.N. (2007) 2007 Chief Of The Year: Tim Stanley. InformationWeek, 8. (December) www.informationweek.com/story/showArticle.jhtml?articleID=204702770, accessed May 2008, www.harrahs.com, accessed May 2008.

2   Reichheld, F. F., & Teal, T. (1996). *The Loyalty Effect*. Boston: Harvard Business School Press.

3   Bolton, R., Lemon, K. N., & Verhoef, P. C. (2004). The theoretical underpinnings of customer asset management: A framework and propositions for future research. *Journal of the Academy of Marketing Science*, 32(3), pp. 271–292.

4   Reichheld, F. F., & Sasser, Jr., W. E. (1990). Zero defections: Quality comes to services. *Harvard Business Review*, (October), pp. 105–111.

5   *Ibid*

6   Reichheld, F. F., & Schefter, P. (2002). E-loyalty – your secret weapon on the web. *Harvard Business Review*, (July–August), pp. 105–113.

7   Homburg, C., Koschate, N., & Hoyer, W. D. (2005). Do satisfied customers really pay more? A study of the relationship between customer satisfaction and willingness to pay. *Journal of Marketing*, 69(April), pp. 84–96.

8   Dowling, G. R., & Uncles, M. (1997). Do customer loyalty programs really work? *Sloan Management Review*, (Summer), pp. 71–81; Reinartz, W., & Kumar, V. (2002). The mismanagement of customer loyalty. *Harvard Business Review*, (July), pp. 86–94. Reinartz, W. J., & Kumar, V. (2000). On the profitability of long-life customers in a noncontractual setting: An empirical investigation and implications for marketing. *Journal of Marketing*, 64 (October), pp. 17–35.

9   Wirtz, J., Sen, I., & Singh, S. (2005). Customer asset management at DHL in Asia. In J. Wirtz., & C. Lovelock, (Eds.). (pp. 379–396). *Services Marketing in Asia – A Case Book,* Singapore: Prentice Hall.

10   For a discussion on how to evaluate the customer base of a firm, see Gupta, S., Lehmann, D. R., & Stuart, J. A. (2004). Valuing customers. *Journal of Marketing Research*, 41(1), pp. 7–18.

11   It has even been suggested to let "chronically dissatisfied customer go to allow front-line staff focus on satisfying the 'right' customers," see Woo. K. S., & Fock, H. K.Y. (2004). Retaining and divesting customers: An exploratory study of right customers, "At-Risk" right customers, and wrong customers. *Journal of Services Marketing*, 18(3), pp. 187–197.

12   Reichheld, F. F. (201). *Loyalty Rules – How Today's Leaders Build Lasting Relationships* (45). Boston: MA, Harvard Business School Press,

13   Liu, Y. (2007). The long-term impact of loyalty programs on consumer purchase behavior and loyalty. *Journal of Marketing*, 71(4), (October), pp. 19–35.

14   Dhar, R., & Glazer, R. (2003). Hedging customers. *Harvard Business Review,* 81 (May), pp. 86–92.

15   Zeithaml, V. A., Rust, R. T., & Lemon, K. N. (2001). The customer pyramid: Creating and serving profitable customers. *California Management Review*, 43(4), (Summer), pp. 118–142.

16   Reinartz, W. J., & Kumar, V. (2003). The impact of customer relationship characteristics on profitable lifetime duration. *Journal of Marketing*, 67(1), pp. 77–99.

17   Available: http://home.ingdirect.com/about/about.asp?s=InternetRichMedia, accessed May 2008.

18   Esfahani, E. (2004). How to get tough with bad customers. *ING Direct,* (October); Available: http://home.ingdirect.com, accessed on 19 October 2007.

19   Not only is there a positive relationship between satisfaction and share of wallet, but the greatest positive impact is seen at the upper extreme levels of satisfaction. For details, refer to Keiningham, T. L.,Munn, T. P., & Evans, H. (2003). The impact of customer satisfaction on share of wallet in a business-to-business environment. *Journal of Service Research*, 6(1), 37–50.

20   Wangenheim, F. V. (2005). Postswitching negative word of mouth. *Journal of Service Research,* 8(1), pp. 67–78.

21   Morgan, N. A., & Rego, L. L. (2006).The value of different customer satisfaction and loyalty metrics in predicting business performance. *Marketing Science*, 25(5), (September–October), pp. 426–439.

22   Berry, L. L., & Parasuraman, A. (1991). Three levels of relationship marketing. *Marketing Services – Competing through Quality* (pp. 136–142). New York, NY: The Free Press; Zeithaml, V. A., Bitner, M. J., & Gremler, D. D. (2006). *Services Marketing* (pp. 196–201). (4th ed.), New York, NY: McGraw-Hill.

23 See for example: Skogland, I., & Siguaw, J. (2004). Are your satisfied customers loyal? *Cornell Hotel and Restaurant Administration Quarterly*, 45(3), pp. 221–234.

24 Ndubisi, N. O. (2007). Relationship marketing and customer loyalty. *Marketing Intelligence & Planning*, 25(1), pp. 98–106.

25 Rosenbaum, M. S., Ostrom, A. L., & Kuntze, R. (205). Loyalty programs and a sense of community. *Journal of Services Marketing*,19(4), pp. 222–233; Szmigin, I., Canning, L., & Reppel, A. E. (2005). Online community: Enhancing the relationship marketing concept through customer bonding. *International Journal of Service Industry Management*, 16(5), pp. 480–496; & Roos, I., Gustafsson, A., & Edvardsson, B. (2005). The role of customer clubs in recent telecom relationships. *International Journal of Service Industry Management*, 16(5), pp. 436–454; Pitta, D., Franzak, F., Fowler, D. (2006). A strategic approach to building online customer loyalty: Integrating customer profitability tiers. *Journal of Consumer Marketing*, 23(7), pp. 421–429.

26 Ferguson, R., & Hlavinka, K. (2006). The long tail of loyalty: How personalized dialogue and customized rewards will change marketing forever. *Journal of Consumer Marketing*, 23(6), pp. 357–361.

27 Peppers, D., & Rogers, M. (1999). *The One-to-One Manager*. New York: Currency/Doubleday.

28 Keaveney, S. M. (1995). Customer switching behavior in service industries: An exploratory study. *Journal of Marketing*, 59,(April), pp. 71–82.

29 For a more detailed discussion of situation-specific switching behavior, refer to Roos, I., Edvardsson, B., & Gustafsson, A. (2004). Customer switching patterns in competitive and noncompetitive service industries. *Journal of Service Research*, 6(3), pp. 256–271.

30 Walsh, G., Dinnie, K., & Wiedmann, K. P. (2006). How do corporate reputation and customer satisfaction impact customer defection? A study of private energy customers in Germany. *Journal of Services Marketing*, 20(6), pp. 412–420.

31 Lee, J., Lee, J., & Feick, L. (2001). The impact of switching costs on the consumer satisfaction-loyalty link: Mobile phone service in France. *Journal of Services Marketing*, 15(1), pp. 35–48, & Lam, S. Y., Shankar, V., Erramilli, M. K., & Murthy, B. (2004). Customer value, satisfaction, loyalty, and switching costs: An illustration from a business-to-business service context. *Journal of the Academy of Marketing Science*, 32(3), pp. 293–311.

32 Lee, M., & Cunningham, L. F. (2001). A cost/benefit approach to understanding loyalty. *Journal of Services Marketing*, 15(2), pp. 113–130. Bell, S. J., Auh, S., & Smalley, K. (2005). Customer relationship dynamics: Service quality and customer loyalty in the context of varying levels of customer expertise and switching costs. *Journal of the Academy of Marketing Science*, 33(2), pp. 169–183.

33 For an excellent book on CRM see: Kumar, V., & Reinartz, W. J. (2006). *Customer Relationship Management: A Database Approach*. Hoboken, NJ: John Wiley & Sons.

34 Ball, D., Coelho, P. S., & Vilares, M. J. (2006). Service personalization and loyalty. *Journal of Services Marketing*, 20(6), pp. 391–403.

35 Quiring, K. N., & Mullen, N. K. (2002). More than data warehousing: An integrated view of the customer. John G. Freeland, (Ed.). In: *The Ultimate CRM Handbook – Strategies & Concepts for Building Enduring Customer Loyalty & Profitability* (pp. 102–108). New York: McGraw-Hill.

36 Payne, A., & Frow, P. (2005). A strategic framework for customer relationship management. *Journal of Marketing*, 69(October), pp. 167–176.

37 Boulding, W., Staelin, R., Ehret, M., & Johnston, W. J. (2005). A customer relationship management roadmap: What is known, potential pitfalls, and where to go. *Journal of Marketing*, 69(4), pp. 155–166.

38 Kale, S. H. (2004). CRM failure and the seven deadly sins. *Marketing Management*, (September/October), pp. 42–46.

39 Bohling T. et. al. (2006). CRM implementation: Effectiveness issues and insights. *Journal of Service Research*, 9(2), (November), pp. 184–194.

40 Boulding, W., Staelin, R., Ehret, M., & Johnston, W. J. (2005). A customer relationship management roadmap: What is known, potential pitfalls, and where to go. *Journal of Marketing*, 69(4), pp. 155–166.

41 Rigby, D. K., & Ledingham, D. (2004). CRM done right. *Harvard Business Review*, (November), pp. 118–129.

42 Ebner, M., Hu, A.,Levitt, D., & McCrory, J. (2002). How to rescue CRM?. *The McKinsey Quarterly* 4, (Technology).

43 Rigby, D. K., & Ledingham, D. (2004). CRM done right. *Harvard Business Review*, (November), pp. 118–129.

44 Rigby, D. K., Reichheld, F. F., & Schefter, P. (2002). Avoid the four perils of CRM. *Harvard Business Review*, (February), p. 108.

BLANK

13

complaint handling and
SERVICE RECOVERY

LEARNING OBJECTIVES

By the end of this chapter, students should be able to:

> **LO 1** List the actions that customers may take in response to service failures.

> **LO 2** Describe the key aspects of complaining behavior.

> **LO 3** List the guidelines companies can use to handle complaining customers and recover from a service failure.

> **LO 4** Know how customers respond to effective service recovery.

> **LO 5** Know how to design an effective service recovery system.

> **LO 6** Recognize the power of service guarantees, when firms should offer them and whether it is wise to make them unconditional.

> **LO 7** Be familiar with the different groups of jaycustomers and understand how to manage them effectively.

Figure 13.1 JetBlue's reputation for customer service excellence was temporarily grounded.

OPENING VIGNETTE[1]

TOO LITTLE, TOO LATE – JETBLUE'S SERVICE RECOVERY

It was a terrible ice storm in the East Coast of the United States. Hundreds of passengers were trapped for 11 hours inside JetBlue planes at the John F. Kennedy International Airport in New York. These passengers were furious! No one in JetBlue did anything to get the passengers off the planes. On top of that, JetBlue cancelled more than 1,000 flights over six days, leaving many more passengers stranded. This

incident in February 2007 cancelled out many positive things JetBlue had done to become one of the strongest customer service brands. JetBlue was originally going to be ranked number four by *Business* Week in a list of top 25 customer service leaders, but it was pulled from the rankings after the incident. What happened?

These was no service recovery plan. No one, not the pilot, flight attendants nor station manager had the power to get the people off the plane. Even though JetBlue later offered refunds and travel vouchers, it did not serve to reduce the anger of the passengers who had been stuck for so many hours. David Neeleman, JetBlue's CEO, sent a personal e-mail to all customers in its database to explain what caused the problem, apologized profusely, and detailed its service recovery efforts. He even appeared on late-night television to apologize and admitted that the airline should have had better contingency planning to get the passengers off the plane. The airline still had a long way to go to repair the damage done to its reputation.

Slowly, the airline rebuilt its reputation, starting with its new Customer Bill of Rights. This bill required the airline to provide vouchers or refunds in certain situations when flights were delayed. Neeleman also changed information systems to keep track of the locations of its crew, upgraded the website to allow online rebooking, and trained staff at the headquarters to help out at the airport when needed. What remains to be seen is whether this former customer service champion will be able to climb its way back up to the heights it fell from.

CUSTOMER COMPLAINING BEHAVIOR

When the incident with JetBlue occurred, they received many customer complaints. No service firm can deliver service that satisfies all customers 100 percent of the time. Chances are that you yourself will not be satisfied with at least some of the services you receive. How do you respond to your dissatisfaction with a service?

LO 1
List the actions that customers may take in response to service failures.

Customer Response Options to Service Failures

Figure 13.3 shows the actions that a customer may take in response to a service failure.

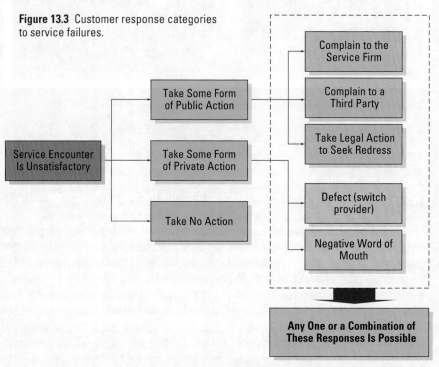

Figure 13.3 Customer response categories to service failures.

▶ Take some form of public action (including complaining to the firm or to a third party, such as a customer affairs or body that controls the industry, or even civil or criminal courts).

▶ Take some form of private action (including leaving the supplier).

▶ Take no action (Figure 13.4).

It is important to remember that any one or a combination of actions can be taken by the customer. Managers need to be aware that the impact of a defection can go far beyond the loss of that customer's future revenue stream. Angry customers often tell many other people about their problems. The Internet allows unhappy customers to reach thousands of people by posting complaints on bulletin boards or setting up web sites to talk about their bad experiences with specific organizations.

Figure 13.4 Some customers may just be frustrated but will not take any action to complain, as seen here in an interaction with an online service.

Understanding Customer Responses to Service Failures

 LO 2
Describe the key aspects of complaining behavior.

To be able to deal effectively with dissatisfied and complaining customers, managers need to understand key aspects of complaining behavior, starting with the questions below.

Why Do Customers Complain? In general, studies of consumer complaining behavior have identified four main purposes for complaining.

▶ *Obtain compensation.* Often, consumers complain to recover some economic loss by seeking a refund, compensation, and/or to have the service performed again.

▶ *Release their anger.* Some customers complain to rebuild self-esteem and/or to release their anger and frustration. When service processes are too rule focused and unreasonable, or when employees are rude, the customers' self-esteem, self-worth, or sense of fairness can be negatively affected. They may become angry and emotional.

▶ *Help to improve the service.* When customers are highly involved with a service (e.g. at a college, an alumni association, or their main banking connection), they give feedback to try and contribute toward service improvements.

▶ *Because of concern for others.* Finally, some customers are motivated by concern for others. They want to spare other customers from experiencing the same problems and may feel good raising a problem to improve a service.

What Proportion of Unhappy Customers Complain? Research shows that on average, only 5–10 percent of customers who have been unhappy with a service actually complain.[2] One of the authors of this book analyzed the complaints a public bus company received. There were about three complaints for every million passenger trips. Assuming two trips a day, a person would need 1,370 years (roughly 27 lifetimes) to make a million trips. In other words, the rate of complaints was incredibly low, given that public bus companies are usually not known for service excellence.

Why Don't Unhappy Customers Complain? They do not wish to take the time to write a letter, send an e-mail, fill out a form, or make a phone call, especially if they do not see the service as important enough to make that effort. Many customers are unsure of whether there will be some result from the complaint. They believe that no one would be concerned about their problem or be willing to deal with it. In some situations, people simply do not know where to go or what to do. In addition, many people feel that complaining is unpleasant and would like to avoid the stress of a confrontation (Figure 13.5).[3]

Who is Most Likely to Complain? Research shows that people in higher social and economic classes are more likely to complain than those in lower classes. Their better education, higher income and greater social involvement give them the confidence, knowledge and motivation to speak up when they encounter problems.[4]

"Thank you for calling our Customer Service Department. This call may be recorded for our new CD, America's Funniest Tantrums."

Figure 13.5 Customers often view complaining as difficult and unpleasant.

Figure 13.6 Customer complaining over the phone.

Where Do Customers Complain? Studies show that the majority of complaints are made at the place where the service is received. One of the authors of this book recently completed a consulting project developing and implementing a customer feedback system. He found that over 99 percent of customer feedback was given face-to-face or over the phone to customer service representatives (Figure 13.6). Only less than 1 percent of all complaints were submitted via e-mail, letters or feedback cards. Also, customers tend to use non-interactive channels to complain (e.g. e-mail or letters) when they mainly want to vent their anger and frustration. However, they use interactive channels such as face to face or the telephone when they want a problem to be fixed.[5] In practice, even when customers do complain, managers often do not hear about the complaints made to frontline staff, especially if there is no customer feedback system in place to manage these complaints.

What Do Customers Expect Once They have made a Complaint? When a service failure occurs, customers expect to be treated fairly. Stephen Tax and Stephen Brown found that as much as 85 percent of the satisfaction with a service recovery was due to three dimensions of fairness, as shown in Figure 13.7:

▶ *Procedural justice* concerns the policies and rules that any customer will have to go through in order to seek service recovery. Here, customers expect the firm to take responsibility. This is the key to the start of a fair procedure, followed by a convenient and responsive recovery process. That includes flexibility of the system, and consideration of customer inputs into the recovery process.

▶ *Interactional justice* involves the employees of the firm who provide the service recovery and their behavior toward the customer. Giving an honest explanation for the failure and making an effort to solve the problem are very important. And the recovery effort itself must be perceived as genuine, fair, and polite.

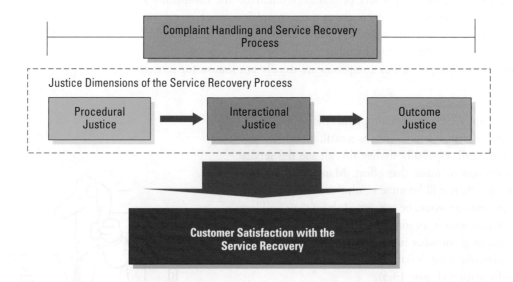

Figure 13.7 Three dimensions of perceived fairness over service recovery processes.

SOURCE

From MIT *Sloan Management Review.* Copyright 1998 by Massachusettes Institute of Technology. All rights reserved. Distributed by Tribune Media Services.

▶ *Outcome justice* concerns the compensation that a customer receives as a result of the losses and inconveniences caused by the service failure. This includes compensation for not only the failure, but also time, effort and energy spent during the service failure and the process of service recovery.

Dealing with Complaining Customers and Recovering from a Service Failure

How should service employees deal with complaining customers? It starts with *not* taking complaints personally but professionally. Both managers and frontline employees must be prepared to deal with angry customers who may sometimes behave in insulting ways toward service personnel who are not at fault in any way (Figure 13.8). The best perspective to take is that customers who complain give a firm the chance to correct problems, restore relationships with the complainer, and improve future satisfaction for all. As one successful manager remarked, "Thank goodness I've got a dissatisfied customer on the phone! The ones I worry about are the ones I never hear from." Service Insights 13.1 provides specific guidelines to help solve problems effectively and recover from a service failure.

Current customers are a valuable asset base. Therefore, managers need to develop effective procedures for service recovery when they have unsatisfactory experiences. Effective service recovery can stop dissatisfied customers from switching to another service provider.[6] Service recovery is the systematic effort by a firm to correct a problem following a service failure. In every organization, things that have a negative impact on its relationships with customers may happen. The true test of a firm's commitment to service *quality* is not in the advertising promises. It is in the way it responds when things go wrong for the customer.

▶ **LO 3**
List the guidelines companies can use to handle complaining customers and recover from a service failure.

Copyright 2006 by Randy Glasbergen.
www.glasbergen.com

"Who picked 'I Can't Get No Satisfaction' to be our on-hold music?"

Figure 13.8 Employees must be prepared to deal with angry customers in a satisfactory manner.

CUSTOMER RESPONSES TO EFFECTIVE SERVICE RECOVERY

After having looked at complaining customers and how best to recover from service failure, let us explore how customers respond to a good service recovery.

▶ **LO 4**
Know how customers respond to effective service recovery.

Impact of Effective Service Recovery on Customer Loyalty

When complaints are satisfactorily resolved, there is a much higher chance that the customers involved will remain loyal. TARP research found that intentions to repurchase for different types of products was only 9 percent when customers experienced a major problem and dissatisfaction but they did not complain. If customers complained and the company offered a sympathetic ear but was not able to deal with the complaint to the satisfaction of the customer, the repurchase rate increased to 19 percent. If the complaint could be dealt with to the satisfaction of the customer, retention jumped to 54 percent. The highest retention rate of 82 percent was achieved when problems were fixed quickly, usually on the spot![7]

PART IV

Guidelines for the Front Line: How to Handle Complaining Customers and Recover from a Service Failure.

1 *Act fast.*[8] If the complaint is made during service delivery, then time is very important to achieve a full recovery. When complaints are made after the fact, many companies try to respond within 24 hours, or sooner.

2 *Acknowledge the customer's feelings.* This helps to build an emotional connection, the first step in rebuilding a relationship that has some problems.

3 *Do not argue with customers.* The goal should be to gather facts to reach a solution that is accepted by the firm and the customer. It is not advisable to argue and prove that the customer is wrong. Arguing gets in the way of listening and seldom reduces anger.

4 *Show that you understand the problem from the customer's point of view.* Seeing situations through the customers' eyes is the only way to understand what they think has gone wrong and why they are upset. Service personnel should avoid jumping to conclusions with their own interpretations.

5 *Clarify the truth and sort out the cause.* A failure may result from inefficiency of service, misunderstanding by customers, or the misbehavior of a third party. If you have done something wrong, apologize immediately in order to win the understanding and trust of the customer. The more the customer can forgive you, the less he expects to be compensated. Do not act as if you are trying to defend yourself. Acting that way may suggest that the organization has something to hide or is not willing to fully look into the situation.

6 *Give customers the benefit of the doubt.* Not all customers are truthful and not all complaints are genuine. However, customers should be treated as though they have a valid complaint until clear evidence proves that it is not true. If a lot of money is involved (as in insurance claims or potential lawsuits), careful investigation needs to be carried out. If the amount involved is small, it may not be worth arguing about a refund or other compensation. However, it is still a good idea to check records to see if there is a past history of doubtful complaints by the same customer.

7 *Propose the steps needed to solve the problem.* When solutions are not immediately available, tell the customers how the firm intends to take action to deal with the problem. This also sets expectations about the time involved (so firms should be careful not to overpromise!).

8 *Keep customers informed about the progress.* Nobody likes being left in the dark. Uncertainty causes people to be anxious and stressed. Therefore, people should be kept informed about what is going on regularly.

9 *Consider compensation.* When customers do not receive the service outcomes that they have paid for, or have suffered serious inconvenience and/or loss of time and money because the service failed, there should either be a monetary payment or some other compensation (e.g. upgrade on a flight or a free dessert in a restaurant). This type of recovery may also reduce the risk of legal action by angry customers.

10 *Continue trying to regain customer goodwill.* When customers have been disappointed, one of the hardest things to do is to restore their confidence and keep the relationship going. Firms must try to calm the customers and to convince them that actions are being taken to avoid the same problem in the future.

11 Truly exceptional recovery efforts can be extremely effective in building loyalty and referrals.

Self-check the system and improve it. After the customer has left, you should check to see whether the service failure was caused by an accidental mistake or system problems. Use every complaint to perfect the whole service system. Even if the complaint is found to be a misunderstanding by customers, it also means that a part of your communications may not be effective.

When a dissatisfied customer defects, the firm loses more than just the value of the next transaction. It may also lose a long-term stream of profits from that customer. In addition, it may lose profits from anyone else who switches suppliers or is stopped from doing business with that firm because of negative comments from an unhappy friend. The conclusion is that complaint handling should be seen as a profit center and not a cost center. However, as can be seen in Service Insights 13.2, many organizations have not accepted the idea that it pays to invest in service recovery to protect those long-term profits.

⋮⋮⋮ SERVICE INSIGHTS 13.2

Common Service **Recovery Mistakes**

Here are some typical service recovery mistakes made by many organizations:

▶ **Managers do not consider evidence that shows that service recovery provides a significant financial return.** Rather, many organizations have focused on cost cutting. They do not take active steps to keep their profitable customers.

▶ **Companies do not focus enough on preventing service problems from occurring in the first place.** Having fewer problems greatly reduces the burden on front-line staff. However, preventive measures cannot eliminate all problems, so the need for good service recovery systems remains.

▶ **Service employees fail to display good attitudes.** The three most important things in service recovery are attitude, attitude and attitude. No matter how well designed and well-planned a service recovery system may be, it will not work well without a friendly and "smile-in-the-voice" attitude from front-line employees.

▶ **Organizations fail to make it easy for customers to complain or give feedback.** Although some improvement can be seen, such as hotels and restaurants offering comment cards, research shows that a large proportion of customers still complain of being unaware of what feedback channels could help them get their problems resolved.

SOURCE

Stiefbold, R. (2003). Dissatisfied customers require service recovery plans. *Marketing News*, 37(22), (October), pp. 44–45.

The Service Recovery Paradox

The service recovery paradox refers to the effect that sometimes, customers who experience a service failure and then have it resolved to their full satisfaction are more likely to make future purchases than customers who have no problem in the first place. Therefore, service recovery has been referred to as an opportunity to impress a customer one wishes one hadn't had in the first place.

A study of repeated service failures in a retail banking context showed that the service recovery paradox was true for the first service failure that was recovered to customers' full satisfaction.[9] However, when a second service failure occurred, the paradox disappeared. Furthermore, customers' expectations were raised after they experienced a very good recovery. Thus, excellent recovery becomes the standard they expect for dealing with future failures.

Whether a customer comes out delighted from a service recovery probably also depends on how serious the failure was, and whether the failure can be recovered. No one can replace spoilt wedding photos, a ruined holiday, or an injury caused by some service equipment. In such situations, it is hard to imagine anyone being truly delighted even when a most professional service recovery is conducted.[10] In conclusion, the best strategy is to do it right the first time!

LO 5

Know how to design an effective service recovery system.

PRINCIPLES OF EFFECTIVE SERVICE RECOVERY SYSTEMS

Given that service recovery is so important, how should we do it effectively? We next discuss the three guiding principles for providing effective service recovery: Make it easy for customers to give feedback, put in place a system that allows effective service recovery, and decide on suitable compensation levels.

Make It Easy for Customers to Give Feedback

How can managers encourage unhappy customers to complain about service failures? The best way is to deal with why they are not willing to complain. Table 13.1 shows general steps that can be taken to overcome those reasons we had identified earlier in this chapter. Many companies have improved their complaint-collection procedures by:

▶ Adding special toll-free phone lines (see Figure 13.9 for a tongue-in-cheek example of what not to do!).

▶ Having feedback links on their web sites.

▶ Having customer comment cards displayed very obviously in their branches.

Table 13.1 Strategies to reduce the barriers to customer complaint

Complaint Barriers for Dissatisfied Customers	Strategies to Reduce These Barriers
Inconvenience • Hard to find the right complaint procedure • Effort involved in complaining	**Make Feedback Easy and Convenient** • Put customer service hotline numbers, e-mail and postal addresses on all customer communications materials
Doubtful Pay Off • Uncertain if action will be taken by the firm to address the problem	**Assure that Feedback is Taken Seriously** • Have service recovery procedures in place, communicate this to customers • Feature service improvements based on customer feedback
Unpleasantness • Fear of being treated rudely • Hassle, embarrassment	**Make Feedback Experience Positive** • Thank customers for their feedback • Train frontline employees not to hassle • Allow anonymous feedback

© Randy Glasbergen.
www.glasbergen.com

"Thank you for calling. Please leave a message. In case I forget to check my messages, please send your message as an audio file to my e-mail, then send me a fax to remind me to check my e-mail, then call me back and remind me to check my fax."

Figure 13.9 Unhappy customers who call to complain should not be made more frustrated.

Put in Place a System that Allows Effective Service Recovery

Recovering from service failures requires commitment, planning, and clear guidelines. Specifically, effective service recovery procedures should be: (1) proactive, (2) planned, (3) trained, and (4) empowered.

Service Recovery Should Be Proactive

Service recovery needs to be on the spot and proactive (i.e. before customers have a chance to complain). Service Insights 13.3 is an example of how service recovery can be proactive.

Service personnel should be able to sense signs of dissatisfaction and ask whether customers might be experiencing a problem. For example, a waiter may ask a guest who has eaten only half of his dinner, "Is everything all right, Sir?" The diner may

Effective Service Recovery in **Action**

The lobby is deserted. It is not hard to overhear the conversation between the night manager at the Marriott Long Wharf Hotel in Boston and the late arriving guest.

"Yes, Dr. Jones, we've been expecting you. I know you are scheduled to be here three nights. I'm sorry to tell you, Sir, but we are booked solid tonight. A large number of guests we assumed were checking out did not. Where is your meeting tomorrow, Sir?"

The doctor told the clerk where it was.

"That's near the Omni Parker House! That's not very far from here. Let me call them and get you a room for the evening. I'll be right back."

A few minutes later the desk clerk returned with the good news.

"They're holding a room for you at the Omni Parker House, sir. And, of course, we'll pick up the tab. I'll forward any phone calls that come here for you. Here's a letter that will explain the situation and expedite your check-in, along with my business card so you can call me directly here at the front desk if you have any problems."

The doctor's mood was moving from exasperation toward calm. But the desk clerk was not finished with the encounter. He reached into the cash drawer. "Here are two $10 bills. That should more than cover your cab fare from here to the Parker House and back again in the morning. We don't have a problem tomorrow night, just tonight. And here's a coupon that will get you complimentary continental breakfast on our concierge level on the fifth floor tomorrow morning … and again, I am so sorry this happened."

As the doctor walks away, the night manager turns to the desk clerk, "Give him about 15 minutes and then call to make sure everything went okay."

A week later when it was still a peak period for hotels in that city, the same guest is in a taxi en route to the same hotel. Along the way, he tells his colleague about the great service recovery episode he had witnessed the week before. The pair arrive at the hotel and make their way to the front desk—ready to check in.

They are greeted with unexpected news: "I am so sorry, gentlemen. I know you were scheduled here for two nights. But we are booked solid tonight. Where is your meeting scheduled tomorrow?"

The would-be guests exchange a rueful glance as they give the desk clerk their future plans. "That's near the Meridian. Let me call over there and see if I can get you a room. It won't but take a minute." As the clerk walks away, the tale teller says, "I'll bet he comes back with a letter and a business card."

Sure enough, the desk clerk returns to deliver the solution; not a robotic script but all the elements from the previous week's show were on display. What the tale teller thought he witnessed the previous week was pure desk-clerk initiative, he now realized was planned, a spontaneous-feeling yet predetermined response to a specific category of customer problem.

SOURCE

Zemke, R., & Bell, C. R. (2000). *Knock Your Socks Off Service Recovery.* New York: AMACOM, pp. 59–60.

say, "Yes, thank you, I'm not that hungry," or "The steak is well done but I asked for medium-rare; I don't really like it." The latter response gives the waiter a chance to recover the service, rather than have an unhappy diner leave the restaurant and potentially not return. Service Insights 13.4 describes how service recovery procedures can not only be proactive, but customers can decide if they have been inconvenienced and decide on the compensation they want to receive!

Recovery Procedures Need to Be Planned

Back up plans have to be developed for service failures, especially for those that occur regularly and cannot be designed out of the system. Revenue management practices in the travel and hospitality industries often result in overbooking. Therefore, travelers are denied boarding the plane, or hotel guests do not have rooms although they had a confirmed seat or reservation. Firms should identify the most common service problems such as overbooking and develop solution sets for employees to follow. In contact centers, the customer service representatives have prepared scripts to guide them in a service recovery situation.

Recovery Skills Must Be Taught

Customers and employees easily feel insecure at the point of service failure because things are not turning out as expected. Effective training of how to handle recovery solution sets (e.g. for routine service failure as in our hotel example in Service Insights 13.3) and non-routine service failures allows frontline staff to turn distress into delight with confidence and skill.

Recovery Requires Empowered Employees

Employees should be given the freedom to use their judgment and communication skills to develop solutions that will satisfy complaining customers. This is especially true for out-of-the-ordinary failures where a firm may not have developed and trained possible solution sets. At the Ritz-Carlton and Sheraton hotels, staff are given the freedom to be proactive, rather than reactive. They take ownership of the situation and help resolve the customers' problems to the best of their ability.

How Generous Should Compensation Be?

How much compensation should a firm offer when there has been a service failure? The following general rules can help to answer these questions:

▶ **What is the positioning of your firm?** If a firm is known for service excellence and charges a high premium for quality, then customers will expect service failures to be rare. In this case, the firm should make a great effort to recover the few failures that do occur and be prepared to offer something of greater value. However, in a mass market business, customers are likely to accept compensations like a free coffee or dessert as fair.

▶ **How severe was the service failure?** The general guideline is "let the punishment fit the crime." Customers expect less for minor inconveniences (here, often a sincere apology will do), but much more if there was major damage in terms of time, effort, annoyance or anxiety.

▶ **Who is the affected customer?** Long-term customers and those who spend heavily at a service provider expect more, and it is worth making an effort to save their business. One-time customers tend to demand less, and also contribute less to the profits of a firm. Hence, compensation can be less, but should still be fair. There is always the possibility that a first-time user will become a repeat customer if treated fairly.

Overly generous compensation is not only expensive but may even be negatively interpreted by customers.[11] It may lead customers to become suspicious about the motives of the firm (e.g. avoid law suits). Also, over-generosity does not seem to result in higher repeat purchase rates than just offering a fair compensation. There is also the risk that a reputation for over-generosity might encourage dishonest customers to "seek" service failures.

LO 6

Recognize the power of service guarantees, when firms should offer them and whether it is wise to make them unconditional.

SERVICE GUARANTEES

One way for particularly customer-focused firms to institutionalize professional complaint handling and effective service recovery is service guarantees. In fact, a growing number of companies offer customers a service guarantee. The guarantee promises that if service delivery fails to meet certain standards, the customer is entitled to one or more forms of compensation, such as an easy-to-claim replacement, refund, or credit. A well-designed service guarantee not only facilitates effective service recovery, but also institutionalizes learning from service failures and subsequent system improvements.

The Power of Service Guarantees

Service guarantees are powerful tools for both promoting and achieving service quality for the following reasons:[12]

1. Guarantees force firms to focus on what their customers want and expect in each element of the service.

2. Guarantees set clear standards. These tell customers and employees what the company stands for. Compensations made to customers cause managers to take guarantees seriously, because they highlight the financial costs of quality failures.

3. Guarantees require the development of systems for getting meaningful customer feedback and acting on it.

4. Guarantees force service organizations to understand why they fail and encourage them to identify and overcome potential fail points.

5. Guarantees build "marketing muscle" by reducing the risk of the purchase decision and building long-term loyalty.

Sara Björlin Lidén and Per Skålén found that even when dissatisfied customers were unaware that a service guarantee existed before making their complaints, they were impressed to learn that the company had a pre-planned procedure for handling failures and to find that their complaints were taken seriously.[13]

The benefits of service guarantees can be seen clearly in the case of Hampton Inn's 100 percent Satisfaction Guarantee ("If you're not 100 percent satisfied, you don't pay"—see Figure 13.10). Many guests choose to stay at a Hampton Inn because they know they will be satisfied.

How to Design Service Guarantees

Some guarantees are simple and unconditional. Others appear to have been written by lawyers and contain many restrictions. Compare the examples in Service Insights 13.5 and ask yourself which guarantee gives you more trust and confidence, and would make you like to do business with that firm.

Figure 13.10 The 100% Hampton Guarantee is Hampton Inn's dedication to quality service. Guests are provided perks such as free high-speed Internet access and daily hot breakfast buffets.

::: SERVICE INSIGHTS 13.5

Examples of Service Guarantees

MFA GROUP INC. (PROFESSIONAL EMPLOYEE RECRUITMENT AGENCY)

An Unconditional Guarantee

We 'put our money where our mouth is', in two ways, not just one:

1. Money back

We offer an unconditional money back guarantee—if at any point during the search process you are unhappy with progress, simply address the fact with us and if you are still not 100 percent satisfied after that discussion, we will cheerfully and unconditionally, refund every cent you have paid as a retainer. No quibble, no hassle, guaranteed period.

2. Twelve-month candidate guarantee

All candidates placed by us are guaranted for a full 12 months. If, during this period they leave your firm, for any reason whatsoever, we will conduct an additional search, completely free of charge, until a suitable replacement has been found.

L.L BEAN'S GUARANTEE

Our Guarantee. Our products are guaranteed to give 100 percent satisfaction in every way. Return anything purchased from us at any time if it proves otherwise. We do not want you to have anything from L.L. Bean that is not completely satisfactory.

EXCERPT FROM THE "QUALITY STANDARD GUARANTEES" FROM AN OFFICE SERVICES COMPANY

1. We guarantee 6-hour turnaround on documents of two pages or less (does not include subsequent client changes or equipment failures).

2. We guarantee that there will be a receptionist to greet you and your visitors during normal business hours … (short breaks of less than five minutes are not subject to this guarantee).

3. You will not be obligated to pay rent for any day on which there is no a manager on site to assist you (lunch and reasonable breaks are expected and not subject to this guarantee).

MERCHANTS HOME LOAN (PROVIDER OF HOME MORTGAGE LOANS)

1st Rate Service Guarantee

This document represents Merchants Home Loan, Inc.'s and "Your Loan Officer's" commitment to providing "The Customer" with unparalleled customer service not only through this closing but long after, as your mortgage loan consultant.

If within 30 days from the date of closing "The Customer" does not feel that Merchants Home Loan, Inc. and "Your Mortgage Loan Officer" merited their full commission on the mortgage loan, "Your Loan Officer" will refund "The Customer" $500.

If "The Customer" feels that Merchants Home Loan, Inc. and "Your Mortgage Loan Officer" have met or exceeded your expectations, then "The Customer" agrees to refer three prospective customers for home equity loans or any type of home loan to Merchants Home Loan, Inc. and "Your Loan Officer".

Please review the following criteria to determine the level of service received:

▶ All phone calls and e-mails were returned during the same business day (if received prior to 3:30p.m CST)

▶ You were educated and you understood the mortgage loan process

▶ Closing documents were reviewed prior to closing

▶ You were treated courteously and respectfully during the entire process by the loan officer and the loan processor

▶ Proper notification of any home loan program changes

The following information represents Merchants Home Loan, Inc's responsibility to this mortage loan transcation:

▶ Merchants will request the proper documentation needed to process the home loan

▶ Merchants will have an appraisal performed on the property by an independent state certified appraiser

▶ Merchants will request that a title insurance policy be ordered on the property by an independent title company

▶ Merchants will have a highly skilled loan processor prepare all paperwork for an underwriter to review and gather any remaining documents required by the said underwriter

▶ A merchants closing coordinator will schedule your closing and confirm that the final documents have been received at the title company

The following information represents "The Customer's" responsibility to this loan transaction:

▶ "The Customer" will promptly return all required loan disclosure documents along with all income, asset, and credit documents required to approve the mortgage loan

▶ "The Customer" will comply with all requests for additional documentation by the loan processor

▶ "The Customer" agrees to be forthright about all aspects of his home loanfile

▶ On refinancing loan, "The Customer" agrees to schedule the appraisal within two business days

SOURCE

Printed in all L. L. Bean catalogs and on the company's website,
www.llbean.com/customerService/aboutLLBean/guarantee.html, accessed April 2008.
http://www.merchantshomeloan.com/first_rate.asp, accessed April 2008.
Reproduced in Shapiro, E. C., Fad Surfing in the Boardroom. Reading, MA: Addison-Wesley, 1995: 18.
http://www.merchantshomeloan.com/first_rate.asp, accessed April 2008.

Both the L.L. Bean and MFA Group guarantees are powerful, with no conditions attached and earn trust. In fact, L.L. Bean was ranked number two in customer service in 2008.[14] The other guarantees are weakened by the many conditions. Service guarantees should be designed to meet the following criteria:[15]

1. **Unconditional**—Whatever is promised in the guarantee should be without conditions and there should not be any bit of surprise for the customer.

2. **Easy to understand and communicate**—to the customer so that he is clearly aware of the benefits that can be gained from the guarantee.

3. **Meaningful to the customer**—in that the guarantee is on something important to the customer and the compensation should be more than enough to compensate for a service failure.

4. **Easy to invoke**—It should be easy for the customer to invoke the guarantee. They should not need to put in a lot of effort to do so. It should be the service provider who puts in the effort to make sure that the customer can make a claim on the guarantee if something really did go wrong.

5. **Easy to collect**—If a service failure occurs, the customer should be able to easily collect on the guarantee without problems.

6. **Credible**—The guarantee should be believable (Figure 13.11).

Figure 13.11 To leave a clear stamp of service guarantee on customers, the guarantee must be unconditional, meaningful, credible, easily understood, invoked, and collected on.

Is Full Satisfaction the Best You can Guarantee?

Full satisfaction guarantees have generally been considered the best possible design. However, customers may raise questions such as "What does full satisfaction mean?" or "Can I invoke a guarantee when I am dissatisfied, although the fault does not lie with the service firm?" A new type of guarantee, called the "combined guarantee," addresses this issue. It combines the wide scope of a full satisfaction guarantee with the low uncertainty of specific performance standards, and appears to be more effective than either a full satisfaction or an attribute-specific guarantee design. Table 13.2 shows examples of the various types of guarantees.

Table 13.2 Types of service guarantees

Term	Guarantee Scope	Example
Single attribute-specific guarantee	One key attribute of the service is covered by the guarantee.	"Any of three specified popular pizzas is guaranteed to be served within 10 minutes of ordering on working days between 12 A.M. and 2 P.M. If the pizza is late, the customer's next order is free."
Multiattribute-specific guarantee	A few important attributes of the service are covered by the guarantee.	Minneapolis Marriott's guarantee: "Our quality commitment to you is to provide: • A friendly, efficient check-in • A clean, comfortable room, where everything works • A friendly efficient check-out If we, in your opinion, do not deliver on this commitment, we will give you $20 in cash. No questions asked. It is your interpretation."
Full-satisfaction guarantee	All aspects of the service are covered by the guarantee. There are no exceptions.	Lands' End's guarantee: "If you are not completely satisfied with any item you buy from us, at any time during your use of it, return it and we will refund your full purchase price. We mean every word of it. Whatever. Whenever. Always. But to make sure this is perfectly clear, we've decided to simplify it further. GUARANTEED. Period."
Combined guarantee	All aspects of the service are covered by the full-satisfaction promise of the guarantee. Explicit minimum performance standards on important attributes are included in the guarantee to reduce uncertainty.	Datapro Information Services guarantees "to deliver the report on time, to high quality standards, and to the contents outlined in this proposal. Should we fail to deliver according to this guarantee, or should you be dissatisfied with any aspect of our work, you can deduct any amount from the final payment which is deemed as fair."

SOURCE

Wirtz, J. & Kum, D. (2002). Designing service guarantees—Is full satisfaction the best you can guarantee? *Journal of Services Marketing*, 15(4), pp. 282–299.

Is it Always Suitable to Introduce a Service Guarantee?

A guarantee is not always appropriate. Amy Ostrom and Christopher Hart list a number of situations in which a guarantee is not suitable.[16]

▶ Companies that already have a strong reputation for service excellence may not need a guarantee. In fact, it might not fit their image to offer one. Rather, best practice service firms will be expected to do what is right without offering a service guarantee.

▶ A firm whose service is currently poor must first work to improve quality to a level above what is guaranteed. Otherwise, too many customers will invoke the guarantee with serious cost implications.

▶ Service firms whose quality is truly uncontrollable because of external forces like the weather, should not offer a guarantee.

▶ When consumers see little financial, personal, or physiological risk associated with purchasing and using a service, a guarantee adds little value but still costs money to design, implement, and manage.

PART IV

LO 7

Be familiar with the different groups of jaycustomers and understand how to manage them effectively.

JAYCUSTOMERS[17]

While we discussed the importance of professional complaint handling and service recovery, we have to acknowledge that not all complaints are honest. When firms have generous service recovery policies or offer guarantees there is always the fear that some customers may take advantage. Also, not all complaining customers are right or reasonable in their behavior, and some may actually be the cause of other customer complaints. We refer to such people as jaycustomers.

A jaycustomer is someone who acts in a thoughtless or abusive way, causing problems for the firm, its employees, and other customers. Every service has its share of jaycustomers. Jaycustomers are undesirable. At best, a firm should avoid attracting them in the first place, and at worst, a firm needs to control or prevent their abusive behavior. Let us first describe the main types of jaycustomers before we discuss how to deal with them.

Seven Types of Jaycustomers

We discuss here seven broad categories of jaycustomers front line employees have to deal with.

The Cheat

There are many ways in which customers cheat service firms. Cheating ranges from writing compensation letters with the sole purpose of exploiting service recovery policies and cheating on service guarantees, to inflating or faking insurance claims and "wardrobing" (that is, using the purchase generously and return of used clothing),[18] The following quotes describe the thinking of these customers nicely:

> *"On checking in to a hotel I noticed that they had a 100 percent satisfaction or your money back guarantee, I just couldn't resist the opportunity to take advantage of it, so on checking out I told the receptionist that I wanted a refund as the sound of the traffic kept me awake all night. They gave me a refund, no questions asked. These companies can be so stupid they need to be more alert."[19]*

> *"I've complained that service was too slow, too quick, too hot, too cold, too bright, too dark, too friendly, too impersonal, too public, too private... it doesn't matter really, as long as you enclose a receipt with your letter, you just get back a standard letter and gift coupon."[20]*

Firms cannot easily check whether a customer is faking dissatisfaction or truly is unhappy. At the end of this section we will discuss how to deal with this type of consumer fraud.

The Thief

This jaycustomer has no intention of paying and steals goods and services. Shoplifting is a major problem in retail stores. For those with technical skills, it is sometimes possible to bypass electricity meters, make telephone calls free of charge, or bypass normal cable TV feeds. Riding free on public transportation, sneaking into movie theaters, or not paying for restaurant meals are also popular. Finding out how people steal a service is the first step in preventing theft or catching thieves and charging them in court if necessary. However, firms must take into account that there are some honest but absent-minded customers who forget to pay.

The Rule Breaker

Many service businesses need rules of behavior for employees and customers to guide them safely through the various steps of the service encounter. Some of these rules are set down by government agencies for health and safety reasons. Air travel provides one of the best examples of rules designed to ensure safety.

Rules set by service providers are meant to help smooth operations, avoid unreasonable demands on employees, prevent misuse of products and facilities, protect themselves legally, and discourage individual customers from misbehaving. Ski resorts, for instance, are getting tough on careless skiers. Skiers can be seriously injured or even killed if they crash into each other. Therefore, ski patrol members must sometimes take on a policing role. Just as dangerous drivers can lose their licenses, dangerous skiers can lose their lift tickets (Figure 13.12).

Figure 13.12 Dangerous skiers are rule breakers who pose a danger to others and need to be policed.

There are risks attached to making lots of rules. The firm may be too inflexible. Instead of being customer-oriented, employees become like police officers, making sure that customers follow all the rules. The fewer the rules, the clearer the important ones can be.

The Belligerent

You have probably seen him (or her) in a store, at the airport, in a hotel or restaurant. The person is shouting angrily, or maybe mouthing insults, threats, and curses. Service personnel are often abused, even when they are not to be blamed. If an employee lacks the power to resolve the problem, the belligerent may become madder still, even to the point of physical attack. Unfortunately, when angry customers yell at service personnel, the latter sometimes responds in the same way. This can lead to arguments and reduce the likelihood of solving the problem (Figure 13.13).

Figure 13.13 Confrontations between customers and service employees can easily escalate.

What should an employee do when an aggressive customer does not listen? In a public place, the main aim should be to move the person away from other customers. Sometimes supervisors may have to settle disagreements between customers and staff members. At other times, they need to support the employee's actions. If a customer has physically attacked an employee, then it may be necessary to get security officers or the police.

Telephone rudeness poses a different problem. One way to handle customers who continue to shout at a telephone-based employee is for the latter to say firmly, "This conversation isn't getting us anywhere. Why don't I call you back in a few minutes when you've had time to digest the information?" In many cases, a break to think is exactly what is needed.

The Family Feuders

People who get into arguments (or worse) with other customers—often members of their own family—make up a subcategory of belligerents we call family feuders. If employees try to help, it may calm the situation or actually make it worse. Some situations require detailed analysis and a carefully thought out response. Others, like customers starting a food fight in a nice restaurant (yes, such things do happen!), require almost immediate response. Service managers in these situations need to be prepared to think on their feet and act fast.

The Vandal

The level of physical abuse to service facilities and equipment is truly surprising. Soft drinks are poured into bank cash machines; there are burn holes from cigarettes on carpets, tablecloths, and bedcovers; hotel furniture are broken; telephone handsets are torn off; glass is smashed and fabrics are torn. The list is endless. Customers do not cause all of the damage, of course. Bored or drunk young people are the source of much exterior vandalism. However, much of the problem does come from paying customers who choose to misbehave.

Figure 13.14 Installing a sophisticated surveillance system can discourage vandalism.

The best cure for vandalism is prevention. Improved security discourages some vandals (Figure 13.14). Good lighting helps, as well as open design of public areas. Companies can choose vandal-resistant surfaces and protective coverings for equipment. Educating customers on how to use equipment properly can reduce the likelihood of abuse or careless handling. Finally, customers can be made to provide security deposits or signed agreements in which they agree to pay for any damage that they cause.

The Deadbeat

They are the ones who delay payment. Once again, preventive action is better than a cure. A growing number of firms insist on pre-payment. Any form of ticket sale is a good example of this. Direct marketing organizations ask for your credit card number as they take your order. The next best thing is to present the customer with a bill immediately on completion of service. If the bill is to be sent by mail, the firm should send it fast, while the service is still fresh in the customer's mind.

Customers may have good reason for the delay and acceptable payment arrangements can be worked out. There may be other aspects to think about too. If the client's problems are only temporary ones, what is the long-term value of maintaining the relationship? Will it create positive goodwill and word-of-mouth to help the customer work things out? If creating and maintaining long-term relationships is the firm's goal, they need to explore working with the customer toward a solution.

Dealing with Consumer Fraud

Dishonest customers may steal from the firm, refuse to pay for the service, pretend to be dissatisfied, or cause service failures to occur on purpose. They are the ones where it is not worth the firm's effort to recover service failure. In fact, it would benefit the firm if they switched to another provider. What steps can a firm take to protect itself against such behavior (see Service Insights 13.6)?

Tracking down **Guests Who Cheat**

As part of its guarantee tracking system, Hampton Inn has developed ways to identify guests who appeared to be cheating—using aliases or various dissatisfaction problems to invoke the guarantee repeatedly in order to get the cost of their room refunded. Guests showing high invocation trends receive personalized attention and follow-up from the company's Guest Assistance Team. Wherever possible, senior managers telephone these guests to ask about their recent stays. The conversation might go as follows: "Hello, Mr. Jones. I'm the director of guest assistance at Hampton Inn, and I see that you've had some difficulty with the last four properties you've visited. Since we take our guarantee very seriously, I thought I'd give you a call and find out what the problems were."

The typical response is dead silence! Sometimes the silence is followed by questions of how headquarters could possibly know about their problems. These calls have their humorous moments as well. One individual, who had invoked the guarantee seventeen times in what appeared to be a trip that took him across the United States and back, was asked, innocuously, "Where do you like to stay when you travel?" "Hampton Inn," came the enthusiastic response. "But," said the executive making the call, "Our records show that the last seventeen times you have stayed at a Hampton Inn, you have invoked the 100 percent Satisfaction Guarantee." "That's why I like them!" proclaimed the guest (who turned out to be a long-distance truckdriver).

SOURCE

Hart C. W., & Long, E., (1997). *Extraordinary Guarantees,* New York: AMACOM.

The working assumptions should be "if in doubt, believe the customer." However, the company has to have a database to keep track of how often customers invoke service guarantees, or payments to make up for service failure. For example, one Asian airline found that the same customer lost his suitcase on three flights in a row. The chances of this truly happening are probably lower than winning in the national lottery, so frontline staff were made aware of this individual. The next time he checked in his suitcase, the check-in staff video-taped the suitcase almost from check-in to pickup in the baggage claim at the destination. It turned out that a companion collected the suitcase and took it through while the traveler again made his way to the lost-baggage counter to report his missing suitcase. This time, the police were waiting for him and his friend.

Recent research shows that the amount of a guarantee payout (e.g. whether it is a 10 percent or 100 percent money-back guarantee) had no effect on consumer cheating. However, if the consumer intended to buy again from the firm, their intention to cheat is greatly reduced. These findings show that: (1) managers can implement and gain the bigger marketing benefits of 100 percent money-back guarantees or generous service recovery policies without worrying that the large payouts would increase cheating; and (2) generous recovery or guarantees can be offered to regular customers or as part of a membership program, since repeat customers are unlikely to cheat on service guarantees. A further finding was that customers were also not willing to cheat if the service quality provided was truly high than when it was just satisfactory. This implied that truly excellent services firms have less to worry than the average provider.[21]

CHAPTER SUMMARY

LO 1 ▶ When customers are dissatisfied, they have several alternatives. They can complain, spread negative word of mouth, and/or switch to another supplier.

LO 2 ▶ To effectively manage complaining behavior, firms need to understand why customers complain and what they expect in response. There are many aspects to customer complaining behavior:

- Some customers want compensation, others seek to release their anger; still others hope to see future improvements in the service.
- In practice, most dissatisfied customers do not complain. Some may not know where to complain while others may find it inconvenient or unpleasant.
- The people who are most likely to complain tend to be better educated, have higher income and are more socially involved.

▶ Once customers make a complaint, they expect service suppliers to deal with them in a fair manner along three dimensions of fairness:

- Procedural fairness—customers expect the firm to have a convenient, responsive and flexible service recovery process.
- Interactional justice—here, customers expect an honest explanation, a genuine effort to solve the problem, and fair and polite treatment.
- Outcome justice—customers expect a compensation that reflects the loss and inconvenience suffered as a result of failure.

LO 3 ▶ The guidelines to handle customer complaints and service recovery are:

- Act fast
- Acknowledge the customer's feelings
- Do not argue with the customer
- Show that you understand the problem from each customer's point of view
- Clarify the truth and sort out the cause

- Give customers the benefit of the doubt
- Propose the steps needed to solve the problem
- Keep customer informed of progress
- Consider compensation
- Continue trying to regain customer goodwill
- Self-check the system and improve it.

LO 4 ▶ The correct way to look at service recovery is to see it as an opportunity to retain a valued customer. When customers complain, they give the firm a chance to correct problems, restore the relationship with the complainer and improve future satisfaction.

LO 5 ▶ Effective service recovery systems:

- Make it easy for customers to give feedback,
- Are proactive and well planned,
- Involve carefully trained and empowered employees, and
- Provide compensation for service failure.

▶ How generous should compensation be? Compensation for service failure should be higher if a firm is known for service excellence, if the service failure is serious, and if the customer is more valuable.

LO 6 ▶ Service guarantees are a powerful way to institutionalize professional complaint handling and service recovery. Service guarantees set clear standards for the firm, and they also reduce customers' risk perceptions and can build long-term loyalty.

LO 7 ▶ Not all complaining customers are honest, some may just want to take advantage of the firm. These customers are called jaycustomers. There are seven groups of jaycustomer: the cheat, the thief, the rule breaker, the belligerent, the family feuders, the vandals and the deadbeat.

▶ The different types of jaycustomers cause different problems to firms and may spoil the experience of other customers. Hence, firms need to manage their behavior, even if that means blacklisting them from using the firm's facilities.

UNLOCK YOUR LEARNING

These keywords are found within the sections of each Learning Objective (LO). They are integral in understanding the services marketing concepts taught in each section. Having a firm grasp of these keywords and how they are used is essential in helping you do well for your course, and in the real and very competitive marketing scene out there.

LO 1
1. Public action
2. Private action
3. Service failure

LO 2
4. Complaining behavior
5. Purposes for complaining
6. Compensation
7. Concern for others
8. Dimensions of fairness
9. Improve the service
10. Interactive channels
11. Interactional justice
12. Non-interactive channels
13. Outcome justice
14. Procedural justice

LO 3
15. Handle complaining customers
16. Service recovery

LO 4
17. Complaint handling

18. Customer loyalty
19. Retention rate
20. Service recovery mistakes
21. Service recovery paradox

LO 5
22. Complaint-collection procedures
23. Effective service recovery systems
24. Effective service recovery procedures
25. Fair compensation
26. Generous compensation

LO 6
27. 100 percent satisfaction guarantee
28. Combined guarantee
29. Full satisfaction guarantees
30. Power of service guarantees
31. Service guarantee

32. Unconditional

LO 7
33. Jaycustomers
34. The belligerent
35. The cheat
36. The deadbeat
37. The family feuders
38. The rulebreaker
39. The thief
40. The vandal

How well do you know the language of services marketing? Quiz yourself!

 Not for the academically faint-of-heart

For each keyword you are able to recall without referring to earlier pages, give yourself a point (and a pat on the back). Tally your score at the end and see if you earned the right to be called—a *services marketeer.*

SCORE

0 – 6	Services Marketing is done a great disservice.
7 – 13	The midnight oil needs to be lit, pronto.
14 – 20	I know what you *didn't* do all semester.
21 – 27	By George! You're getting there.
28 – 33	Now, go forth and market.
34 – 40	There should be a marketing concept named after you.

Review Questions

1. How do customers typically respond to service failures?

2. Why don't many more unhappy customers complain? What do customers expect the firm to do once they have made a complaint?

3. What is the service recovery paradox? Under what conditions is this paradox most likely to hold? When is it not likely to be true?

4. What could a firm do to make it easy for dissatisfied customers to complain?

5. Why should a service recovery strategy be proactive, planned, trained and empowered?

6. How generous should compensation be for a service failure?

7. How should service guarantees be designed?

8. Under what conditions is it not suitable to introduce a service guarantee?

9. What are the different types of jaycustomers and how can a service firm deal with the behavior of such customers?

Application Exercises

1. Think about the last time you experienced a dissatisfactory service experience. Did you complain? Why? If you did not complain, explain why not.

2. When was the last time you were truly satisfied with an organization's response to your complaint? Describe in detail what happened and what made you feel satisfied.

3. What would be an appropriate service recovery policy for a wrongly bounced check for (a) your local savings bank, (b) a major national bank, (c) a high-end private bank? Please explain your reasoning.

4. Design an effective service guarantee for a service with high perceived risk. Explain why and how your guarantee would (a) reduce perceived risk of potential customers, and (b) why current customers would like being offered this guarantee although they already use the service and therefore are likely to already perceive lower levels of risk.

5. Identify the possible behavior of jaycustomers for a service of your choice. How can the service process be designed to minimize or control the behavior of jaycustomers?

• ENDNOTES

1. "An Extraordinary Stumble at JetBlue," Business Week, 5 March 2007, http://www.businessweek.com/magazine/content/07_10/b4024004.htm, accessed April 2008; Tschohl, J. (2007). "Too little, too late: Service recovery must occur immediately – as JetBlue discovered." *Service Quality Institute*, (May), Available: http://www.customer-service.com/articles/JetBlueBlues.aspx, Accessed on April 2008.

2. Tax, S. S., & Brown, S. W. (1998). Recovering and learning from service failure. *Sloan Management Review, 49(1)*, (Fall), pp. 75–88.

3. A penny for your thoughts: When customers don't complain. In Knowledge@W.P. Carey, 27 September 2006, http://knowledge.wpcarey.asu.edu/article.cfm?articleid=1303#, accessed April 2008; Stephens, N., & Gwinner, K. P. (1998). Why don't some people complain? A cognitive-emotive process model of consumer complaining behavior. *Journal of the Academy of Marketing Science, 26(3)*, pp. 172–189.

4. Stephens, N. (2000). Complaining. In T. A. Swartz & D. Iacobucci (Eds.). *Handbook of Services Marketing and Management* (p. 291). California: Thousand Oaks, Sage Publications; Bodey, K., & Grace, D. (2006). Segmenting service "complainers" and "non-complainers" on the basis of consumer characteristics. *Journal of Services Marketing, 20(3)*, pp. 178–187.

5. Mattila, A., & Wirtz, J. (2004). Consumer complaining to firms: The determinants of channel choice. *Journal of Services Marketing, 18(2)*, pp. 147–155; Snellman, K., & Vihtkari, T. (2003). Customer complaining behavior in technology-based service encounters. *International Journal of Service Industry Management, 14(2)*, pp. 217–231.

6. White, L., & Yanamandram, V. (2007). A model of customer retention of dissatisfied business services customers. *Managing Service Quality, 17(3)*, pp. 298–316.

7. Goodman, J. (1999). Basic facts on customer complaint behavior and the impact of service on the bottom line. *Competitive Advantage*, (June), pp. 1–5.

8. Hocutt, M. A., Bowers, M. R., & Donavan, D. T. (2006). The art of service recovery: Fact or fiction?. *Journal of Service Research, 20(3)*, pp. 199–207.

9. Maxham III, J. G., & Netemeyer, R. G. (2002). A longitudinal study of complaining customers' evaluations of multiple service failures and recovery efforts. *Journal of Marketing, 66(4)*, pp. 57–72.

10. Andreassen, T. W. (2001). From disgust to delight: Do customers hold a grudge? *Journal of Service Research, 4(1)*, pp. 39–49. (Other studies also confirmed that the service recovery paradox does not hold universally).

11. Estelami, H., & Maeyer, P. D. (2002). Customer reactions to service provider overgenerosity. *Journal of Service Research, 4(3)*, pp. 205–217.

12. Hart, C. W. (1990). The power of unconditional service guarantees. *Harvard Business Review*, (July–August), pp. 54–62.

13. Lidén, S. B., & Skålén, P. (2003). The effect of service guarantees on service recovery. *International Journal of Service Industry Management, 14(1)*, pp. 36–58.

14. Gregor, J. M. (2008). Customer service champs. special report. (February), *Business Week*.

15. Hart, C. W. The power of unconditional service guarantees. *Op Cit*

16. Ostrom, A. L., & Hart, C. (2000). Service guarantee: Research and practice. In T. Schwartz, & D. Iacobucci, (Eds.). *Handbook of Services Marketing and Management* (pp. 299–316), California: Thousand Oaks, Sage Publications.

17. This section is adopted from Lovelock, C. (1994). *Product Plus*. New York: McGraw-Hill.

18. Harris, Lloyd C. & Reynolds, K. L. (2003). The consequences of dysfunctional customer behavior. *Journal of Service Research, 6(2)*, pp. 144–161; Wirtz, Jochen & Kum, D. (2004). Consumer cheating on service guarantees. *Journal of the Academy of Marketing Science, 32(2)*, pp. 159–175; Accenture Inc. (2003, February 12), "One-Fourth of Americans Say It's Acceptable to Defraud Insurance Companies, Accenture Survey Finds," press release, (Accessed April 10, 2008), [available at http://newsroom.accenture.com/article_display.cfm?article_id=3970]; Wujin, C., Gerstner, E., & Hess, J. D. (1998). Managing dissatisfaction: How to decrease customer opportunism by partial refunds. *Journal of Service Research, 1(2)*, pp. 140–155.

19. Reynolds, K. L., & Harris, L. C. (2005). When service failure is not service failure: An exploration of the forms and motives of "illegitimate" customer complaining. *Journal of Services Marketing, 19(5)*, p. 326.

20. Harris, Lloyd C. & Reynolds, K. L. (2004). Jay customer behavior: An exploration of types and motives in the hospitality industry. *Journal of Services Marketing, 18(5)*, p. 339.

21. Wirtz, J., & Kum, D. (2004). Consumer cheating on service guarantees. *Journal of the Academy of Marketing Science, 32(2)*, pp. 159–175.

CHAPTER

14

improving

SERVICE
QUALITY and
PRODUCTIVITY

LEARNING OBJECTIVES

By the end of this chapter, students should be able to:

LO 1 Understand what is meant by both productivity and quality in a service context.

LO 2 Know the different perspectives and measures of service quality.

LO 3 Be familiar with the Gap Model for identifying and correcting service quality problems.

LO 4 Understand the difference between hard and soft measures of service quality.

LO 5 Explain the key objectives of effective customer feedback systems.

LO 6 Be familiar with soft measures and the mix of customer feedback collection tools.

LO 7 Be familiar with hard measures of service quality and control charts.

LO 8 Understand three important tools to analyze service problems (i.e. the fishbone diagram, pareto analysis, and blue printing).

LO 9 Understand the financial implications of quality improvements.

LO 10 Know how to define and measure productivity.

LO 11 Be familiar with the key methods of improving service productivity.

LO 12 Know how productivity improvements impact quality and value.

LO 13 Understand how TQM, ISO 9000, Malcolm-Baldrige Approach and Six Sigma relate to managing and improving service quality and productivity.

PART IV

BUILDING MARKETING COMPETENCE IN A FERRY COMPANY

Sealink British Ferries, whose routes linked Britain to Ireland and several European countries, was a poor service quality provider. Sealink used a top-down, military-style structure that focused on the operational aspects of ship movements. The quality of customers' experiences was not its focus. Sealink was then acquired by the Swedish company Stena Line, which is today one of the world's largest car-ferry operators. In contrast to Sealink, Stena had a whole department constantly focusing on how to improve service quality.

Before the takeover, Sealink did not focus on punctual or reliable operations, and ferries were often late. Customer complaints were ignored, and there was little pressure from customer service managers to improve the situation. After the takeover, things started to change. They solved the problem of late departures and arrivals by concentrating on individual problem areas. On one route, for instance, the port manager involved all operational staff and gave each person "ownership" of a particular aspect of the improvement process. They kept detailed records of each sailing, together with reasons for late departures. They also kept track of competitors' performance. In this way, staff members in different job positions had close links with each other. Customer service staff also learnt from experience. Within two years, the Stena ferries on this route were operating at close to 100 percent punctuality.

On-board service was another area chosen for improvement. Historically, customer service managers did what was convenient for staff rather than customers. This meant that staff could be having meal breaks at times when customer demand for service was greatest. As one observer noted, "customers were ignored during the first and last half hour on board, when facilities were closed.... Customers were left to find their own way around [the ship].... Staff only responded to customers when [they] initiated a direct request and made some effort to attract their attention."

Figure 14.1 The London Bridge is just one of many scenic spots on Stena Line's extensive ferry route that runs across Europe.

Figure 14.2 Stena Line's leading status is attributed to its on-board service excellence.

After Stena Line Took over, personnel from each on-board functional area had to choose a particular area for service quality and productivity improvements, and work in small groups to achieve this. Initially, some teams were more successful than others, resulting in differing levels of service from one ship to another. After that, managers shared ideas and experiences, learning from each others' successes and failures, and made further changes on their individual ships.

By 2008, Stena Line had 35 ships sailing on 18 routes, carrying about 16 million passengers and 3 million vehicles each year. They included three of the world's largest fast ferries. Stena was a leader in all its markets. The company's focus was on constant service and product improvement. Says the company's website:

> "The phrase Making Good Time summarises the core of the Stena Line business in three words: fast, enjoyable and efficient sea travel.... Today's customers are looking for more. Basic factors such as punctuality, safety, clean and well-equipped ferries with good service are now taken for granted, so at Stena Line we're trying even harder to give guests that little extra so they'll want to travel with us again. A way of meeting these new demands is to develop new products and services, and to further customize our offers to suit different requirements. Our ambition is that everyone should find a travel offer in our selection that they like."

...The phrase *Making Good Time* summarises the core of the Stena Line business in three words: fast, enjoyable and efficient sea travel...

INTEGRATING SERVICE QUALITY AND PRODUCTIVITY STRATEGIES

The Stena Line is an excellent example that shows how improving service quality and productivity can turn around a failing business! We will learn in this chapter that quality and productivity are twin paths to creating value for both customers and companies. In broad terms, quality focuses on the benefits created for the customer's side of the equation. Productivity looks at the financial costs of the firm. If we make service processes more efficient and increase productivity, this may not result in a better quality experience for customers. Likewise, getting service employees to work faster to increase productivity may sometimes be welcomed by customers. However, at other times it may make them feel rushed and unwanted. Thus, marketing, operations, and human resource managers should work together to look at quality and productivity improvement strategies together rather than in isolation. They need to ensure that they can deliver quality experiences more efficiently to improve the long-term profitability of the firm.

Figure 14.3 Service quality can be difficult to manage for the fussy diner.

WHAT IS SERVICE QUALITY?

What do we mean when we speak of service quality? Company personnel need a common understanding in order to address issues such as the measurement of service quality, finding out the causes of service quality problems, and the design and implementation of corrective actions. As suggested humorously by the restaurant illustration in Figure 14.3, service quality can be difficult to manage, even when failures are tangible in nature.

 LO 2
Know the different perspectives and measures of service quality.

Different Perspectives of Service Quality

The word *quality* means different things to different people depending on the context. Common perspectives on quality include.[2]

1. *The transcendent view* of quality is that people will learn to recognize quality only through the experience gained from being exposed to it again and again. This viewpoint is often applied to the performing and visual arts. However, it is not very useful nor helpful to suggest that managers or customers will know quality when they see it.

2. The *manufacturing-based approach* is supply based. It looks mainly at engineering and manufacturing practices. In services, we would say that this approach looks at quality from the operations perspective. It focuses on meeting internally developed standards. These standards are usually set with the goals of increasing productivity and decreasing costs.

3. *User-based definitions* see that quality lies in the eyes of the beholder. This subjective, demand-oriented view recognizes that different customers have different needs and wants.

4. *Value-based definitions* define quality in terms of value and price. By considering the trade-off between the benefits the customer obtains and the price he pays, quality comes to be defined as "affordable excellence."

These different views of quality sometimes lead to disagreements between managers in different functional departments. In this chapter, we define service quality from the user's perspective as consistently meeting or exceeding customer expectations (Figure 14.4).

Dimensions of service quality

Valarie Zeithaml, Leonard Berry, and A. Parasuraman have done a lot of research on service quality. They identified ten dimensions used by consumers to evaluate service quality (Table 14.1). In subsequent research, they found a high degree of correlation between several of these variables and so combined them into five broad dimensions:

► Tangibles (appearance of physical elements)

► Reliability (dependable and accurate performance)

► Responsiveness (promptness and helpfulness)

► Assurance (credibility, competence, courtesy and security)

► Empathy (good communications, customer understanding and easy access).[3]

Figure 14.4 IBM's partnership with healthcare providers gives them a platform to exceed patient expectations.

Table 14.1 Generic dimensions used by customers to evaluate service quality.

Dimensions	Characteristics	Queries
Tangibles	Appearance of physical facilities, equipment, personnel, and communication materials	Are the hotel's facilities attractive? Is my accountant dressed appropriately? Is my bank statement easy to understand?
Reliability	Ability to perform the promised service dependably and accurately	Does my lawyer call me back when promised? Is my telephone bill free of errors? Is my TV repaired right the first time?
Responsiveness	Willingness to help customers and provide prompt service	When there is a problem, does the firm resolve it quickly? Is my stockbroker willing to answer my questions? Is the cable TV company willing to give me a specific time when the installer will show up?
Assurance • Credibility	Trustworthiness, believability, honesty of the service provider	Does the hospital have a good reputation? Does my stockbroker pressure me to buy? Does the repair firm guarantee its work?
• Security	Freedom from danger, risk, or doubt	Is it safe for me to use the bank's ATMs at night? Is my credit card protected against unauthorized use? Can I be sure that my insurance policy provides complete coverage?

PART IV

Dimensions	Characteristics	Queries
• Competence	Possession of the skills and knowledge required to perform the service	Can the bank teller process my transaction without fumbling around? Is my travel agent able to obtain the information I need when I call? Does the dentist appear to be competent?
• Courtesy	Politeness, respect, consideration and friendliness of contact personnel	Does the flight attendant have a pleasant demeanor? Are the telephone operators consistently polite when answering my calls? Does the plumber take off muddy shoes before stepping on my carpet?
Empathy		
• Access	Approachability and ease of contact	How easy is it for me to talk to a supervisor when I have a problem? Does the airline have a 24-hour toll-free phone number? Is the hotel conveniently located?
• Communication	Listening to customers and keeping them informed in a language they can understand	When I have a complaint, is the manager willing to listen to me? Does my doctor avoid using technical jargon? Does the electrician call when he or she is unable to keep a scheduled appointment?
• Understanding the customer	Making the effort to know customers and their needs	Does someone in the hotel recognize me as a regular customer? Does my stockbroker try to determine my specific financial objectives? Is the moving company willing to accommodate my schedule?

 LO 3

Be familiar with the Gap Model for identifying and correcting service quality problems.

THE GAP MODEL – A CONCEPTUAL TOOL TO IDENTIFY AND CORRECT SERVICE QUALITY PROBLEMS

After understanding what service quality is, let us explore a model that allows us to identify and correct service quality problems. This model, called the Gap Model, was first developed by Zeithaml, Berry and Parasuraman with five gaps. Figure 14.5 extends and refines their framework to identify five possible gaps within the service organization that together lead to the sixth and most serious final gap, the service quality gap. The final gap is defined as the difference between what customers expected and what they think was delivered.[4]

Let us explore the six gaps in more detail:

Gap 1—the knowledge gap is the difference between what senior management believes customers expect and what customers actually need and expect.

Gap 2—the policy gap is the difference between management's understanding of customers' expectations and the service standards they set for service delivery. We call it the policy gap because the management made a policy decision not to deliver what they think customers expect. Reasons for setting standards below customer expectations are typically cost and feasibility considerations.

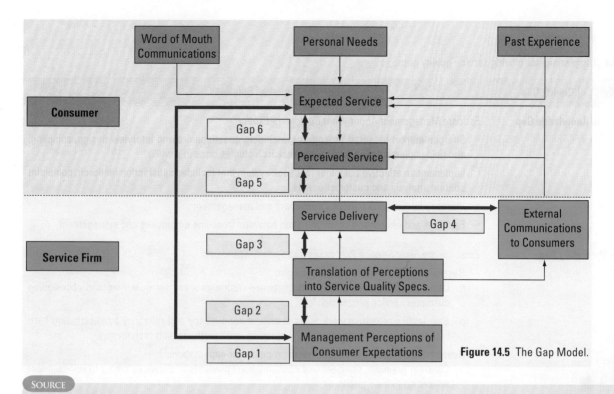

SOURCE

Adapted from the original 5-gaps model developed by Parasuraman, A., Zeithaml, V. A., & Berry, L. L. (1985). A conceptual model of service quality and its implications for future research. *Journal of Marketing* 49, (Fall), pp. 41–50; Zeithaml, V. A., Bitner, M. J., & Gremler, D. (2006). *Services Marketing: Integrating Customer Focus Across the Firm* (p. 46.). NY: McGraw Hill/Irwin. A further gap (Gap 5) was added by Christoper Lovelock (1994), *Product Plus* (p. 112). NY: McGraw Hill.

Figure 14.5 The Gap Model.

Gap 3—the delivery gap is the difference between service standards and the service delivery teams' actual performance on these standards.

Gap 4—the communications gap is the difference between what the company communicates and what it actually delivers to the customer. This gap is caused by two sub-gaps.[5] Firstly, the internal communications gap is the difference between what the company's advertising and sales personnel think are the product's features, performance, and service quality level and what the company is actually able to deliver. Secondly, the overpromise gap which can be caused by advertising and sales personnel being assessed by the sales they generate. This can lead them to overpromise. Finally, the interpretation gap is the difference between what a service provider's communication efforts (in advance of service delivery) actually promise and what a customer thinks was promised by these communications.

Gap 5—the perceptions gap is the difference between what is actually delivered and what customers feel they have received because they are unable to accurately judge service quality accurately.[6]

Gap 6—the service quality gap is the difference between what customers expect to receive and their perception of the service that is actually delivered.

Core Ways to Close Six Quality Gaps

Gaps at any point can damage relationships with customers. The Service Quality Gap 6 is the most important. The main goal in improving service quality is to close or narrow this gap as much as possible. However, to achieve this, service organizations usually need to work on closing the other five gaps. Improving service quality requires identifying the causes of each of the gaps and then developing ways to close them. We summarize suggestions on how to close the six quality gaps in Table 14.2.

PART IV

Table 14.2 Suggestions for closing service quality gaps.

Types of Quality Gap	Proposed Solutions
Gap 1—The Knowledge Gap	*Educate Management About What Customers Expect* • Sharpen market research procedures, including questionnaire and interview design, sampling, and field implementation, and repeat research studies once in a while • Implement an effective customer feedback system that includes satisfaction research, complaint content analysis and customer panels • Increase interactions between customers and management • Facilitate and encourage communication between front-line employees and management

Gap 2—The Policy Gap	*Establish the Right Service Processes and Specify Standards*
	• Get the customer service processes right:
	  o Use a rigorous, systematic, and customer-centric process for designing and redesigning customer service processes.
	  o Standardize repetitive work tasks to ensure consistency and reliability by substituting hard technology for human contact and improving work methods (soft technology).
	• Develop tiered service products that meet customer expectations:
	  o Consider premium, standard and economy-level products to allow customers to self-segment according to their needs, or
	  o Offer customers different levels of service at different prices
	• Set, communicate and reinforce measurable customer-oriented service standards for all work units:
	  o Establish for each step in service delivery a set of clear service quality goals that are challenging, realistic and explicitly designed to meet customer expectations.
	  o Ensure that employees understand and accept goals, standards, and priorities

Gap 3—The Delivery Gap	*Ensure that Performance Meets Standards and that Customers Understand the Quality Level Delivered*
	• Ensure that customer service teams are motivated and able to meet service standards:
	  o Improve recruitment with a focus on employee-job fit; select employees for the abilities and skills needed to perform their job well.
	  o Train employees on the technical and soft skills needed to perform their assigned tasks effectively, including interpersonal skills, especially for dealing with customers under stressful conditions.
	  o Clarify employee roles and ensure that employees understand how their jobs contribute to customer satisfaction; teach them about customer expectations, perceptions and problems.
	  o Build cross-functional service teams that can offer customer-centric service delivery and problem resolution.
	  o Empower managers and employees in the field by pushing decision-making power down the organization.
	  o Measure performance; provide regular feedback and reward customer service team performance as well as individual employees and managers on attaining quality goals.
	• Install the right technology, equipment, support processes and capacity:
	  o Select the most appropriate technologies and equipment for enhanced performance.
	  o Ensure that employees working on internal support jobs provide good service to their own internal customer, the front-line personnel.
	  o Balance demand against productive capacity.
	• Manage customers for service quality:
	  o Educate customers so that they can perform their roles and responsibilities in service delivery effectively.

Types of Quality Gap	Suggest Solutions

Gap 4—The Communications Gap	*Close the Internal Communications Gap by ensuring that Communications Promises are Realistic and Correctly understood by Customers*
	
	 • Educate managers responsible for sales and marketing communications about operational capabilities:
	    o Seek inputs from front-line employees and operations personnel when new communications programs are being developed.
	    o Let service providers preview advertisements and other communications before customers are exposed to them.
	    o Get sales staff to involve operations staff in face-to-face meetings with customers.
	    o Develop internal educational and motivational advertising campaigns to strengthen understanding and integration among the marketing, operations, and human resource functions, and to standardize service delivery across different locations.
	
	 • Ensure that communications content sets realistic customer expectations.
	
	 • Be specific with promises and manage customers' understanding of communication content:
	    o Pretest all advertising, brochures, telephone scripts and web site content prior to external release to see if target audience interpret them as the firm intends (if not, revise and retest). Make sure that the advertising content reflects those service characteristics that are most important to customers. Let them know what is not possible and why.
	    o Identify and explain in real time the reasons for shortcomings in service performance, highlighting those that cannot be controlled by the firm.
	    o Document beforehand the tasks and performance guarantees that are included in an agreement or contract. After the completion of the work, explain what work was performed in relation to a specific billing statement.

Gap 5—The Perception Gap	*Tangibilize and Communicate the Service Quality Delivered*
	 • Make service quality tangible and communicate the service quality delivered:
	    o Develop service environments and physical evidence cues that are consistent with the level of service provided.
	    o For complex and credence services, keep customers informed during service delivery on what is being done, and give briefings after the delivery so that customers can appreciate the quality of service they received.
	    o Provide physical evidence (e.g. for repairs, show customers the damaged components that were removed).

Gap 6—The Service Gap	Close Gaps 1 to 5 to consistently meet Customer Expectations Gap 6 is the accumulated outcome of all the preceding gaps. It will be closed when Gaps 1 to 5 have been addressed.

SOURCE

Adapted and extended from Zeithaml, V. A., Parasuraman, A., & Berry, L. L. (1990). *Delivering service quality: Balancing customer perceptions and expectations.* New York: The Free Press; Zeithaml, V. A., Bitner, M. J., & Gremler, D. (2006). *Services marketing: Integrating customer focus across the firm*, (4th ed.). New York: McGraw-Hill, 2006, Chapter 2. The remaining prescriptions were developed by the authors.

MEASURING AND IMPROVING SERVICE QUALITY

We have now understood the Gap Model and the general prescriptions on how to close the six quality gaps. Let us next discuss how to use measurement to guide our service quality improvement efforts. It is commonly said that 'what is not measured is not managed.' Without measurement, managers cannot be sure whether service quality gaps exist, where they exist, and what possible corrective actions should be taken. Measurement is also needed to see whether goals for improvement are being met after changes have been carried out.

Soft and Hard Service Quality Measures

LO 4

Understand the difference between hard and soft measures of service quality.

Customer-defined standards and measures of service quality can be grouped into two broad categories: 'soft' and 'hard.' Soft standards and their measures are those that cannot easily be observed and must be collected by talking to customers, employees, or others. As noted by Valarie Zeithaml and Mary Jo Bitner, "Soft standards provide direction, guidance and feedback to employees on ways to achieve customer satisfaction and can be quantified by measuring customer perceptions and beliefs."[7] SERVQUAL (see Appendix 14.1) is an example of a complex soft measurement system, and we will discuss a cocktail of customer feedback tools later in this chapter.

Hard standards and measures are characteristics and activities that can be counted, timed, or measured through audits. Such measures may include the number of telephone calls that were dropped while the customer was on hold, the temperature of a particular food item, the number of trains that arrived late, the number of bags lost, or the number of patients who made a complete recovery following a specific type of surgery. The challenge for service marketers is to make sure that operational measures of service quality consider the effect of customer input. Organizations that are known for excellent service make use of both soft and hard measures. These organizations are good at listening to both their customers and their customer-contact employees.

We will next give you a comprehensive overview of soft measures in the section on customer feedback, followed later by a section on hard measures.

LEARNING FROM CUSTOMER FEEDBACK[8]

How can companies measure their performance against soft standards of service quality? According to Leonard Berry and A. Parasuraman:

> [C]ompanies need to establish ongoing listening systems using multiple methods among different customer groups. A single service quality study is a snapshot taken at a point in time and from a particular angle. Deeper insight and more informed decision making come from a continuing series of snapshots taken from various angles and through different lenses, which form the essence of systematic listening.[9]

In this section we will discuss how customer feedback can be systematically collected, analyzed and passed on to the relevant departments through a Customer Feedback System (CFS) to achieve customer-driven learning and service improvements.[10]

Key Objectives of Effective CFSs

"It is not the strongest species that survive, nor the most intelligent, but the ones most responsive to change," wrote Charles Darwin. Similarly, many planners have concluded that in increasingly competitive markets, the best competitive advantage for a firm is to learn and change faster than the competition.[11] Effective CFSs facilitate fast learning. Their objectives usually fall into the following three main categories.

 LO 5

Explain the key objectives of effective customer feedback systems.

Assessment and benchmarking of service quality and performance

The objective is to answer the question, "How satisfied are our customers?" This objective includes learning about how well a firm performed in comparison to its main competitor(s), how it performed in comparison to the previous year (or quarter, or month), and where the firm wants to be the following year. Benchmarking does not only have to be with companies from the same industry. Southwest Airlines benchmarks Formula One pit-stops for speedy turnaround of aircraft; Pizza Hut benchmarks Federal Express for on-time package delivery; and Ikea examines the military for excellence in coordination and logistics management.[12]

Customer-driven learning and improvements

Here, the objective is to answer the questions, "What makes our customers happy or unhappy?" and "What are the strengths we need to maintain, and where and how do we need to improve?" For this, more detailed information on processes and products is required to guide a firm's service improvement efforts, and to see which areas have possible high returns on quality investment.

Creating a customer-oriented service culture

This objective is concerned with focusing the organization on customer needs and customer satisfaction, and moving the entire organization towards a service quality culture.

Of the three objectives just discussed, firms seem to be doing well on the first, but to be missing great opportunities in the other two. Neil Morgan, Eugene Anderson and Vikas Mittal concluded in their research on Customer Satisfaction Information Usage (CSIU) the following:

> *Many of the firms in our sample do not appear to gain significant customer-focused learning benefits from their CS [customer satisfaction] systems, because they are designed to act primarily as a control mechanism [i.e. our assessment or benchmarking]. ... [Firms] may be well served to reevaluate how they deploy their existing CSIU resources. The majority of CSIU resources ... are consumed in CS data collection. This often leads to too few resources being allocated to the analysis, dissemination, and utilization of this information to realize fully the potential payback from the investment in data collection.*[13]

Use a Mix of Customer Feedback Collection Tools

 LO 6

Be familiar with soft measures and the mix of customer feedback collection tools.

What tools can firms use to listen and learn? Reene Fleming, soprano, America's beautiful voice once said, "We singers are unfortunately not able to hear ourselves sing. You sound entirely different to yourself. We need the ears of others – from outside ..." Likewise, firms need to listen to the voice of the customer.

Table 14.3 Strengths and weaknesses of key customer feedback collection tools.

Collection Tools	Level of Measurement			Actionable	Representative, Reliable	Potential for Service Recovery	First-Hand Learning	Cost-Effectiveness
	Firm	Process	Transaction specific					
Total market survey (including competitors)	●	○	○	○	●	○	○	○
Annual survey on overall satisfaction	●	◐	○	○	●	○	○	○
Transactional survey	●	●	◐	◐	●	○	○	○
Service feedback cards	◐	●	●	◐	◐	●	◐	●
Mystery shopping	○	◐	●	●	○	○	◐	○
Unsolicited feedback (e.g., complaints)	○	◐	●	●	○	●	◐	●
Focus group discussions	○	◐	●	●	○	◐	●	◐
Service reviews	○	◐	●	●	○	●	●	◐

Legend: ● meets requirements fully; ◐ moderately; ○ hardly at all.

SOURCE

Adapted from Wirtz, J., & Tomlin, M. (2000). Institutionalizing customer-driven learning through fully integrated customer feedback systems. *Managing Service Quality*, 10(4), 210.

Table 14.3 gives an overview of typically used feedback tools and their ability to meet various requirements. Recognizing that different tools have different strengths and weaknesses, service marketers should select a mix of customer feedback collection tools that jointly deliver the needed information. As Leonard Berry and Parasuraman observe, "Combining approaches enables a firm to tap the strengths of each and compensate for weaknesses."[14]

Total Market Surveys, Annual Surveys, and Transactional Surveys

Total market surveys and annual surveys typically measure satisfaction with all major customer service processes and products.[15] The level of measurement is usually at a high level, with the objective of obtaining a global index or indicator of overall service satisfaction for the entire firm.

Overall indices such as these tell how satisfied customers are, but not why they are happy or unhappy. There are limits to the number of questions that can be asked about each individual process or product. For example, a typical retail bank may have 30–50 key customer service processes (e.g. from car loan applications, to cash deposits at the teller). Many surveys have room for only one or two questions per process (e.g. how satisfied are you with our ATM services?) and cannot address issues in greater detail.

In contrast, transactional surveys, also called intercept surveys, are typically conducted after customers have completed a particular transaction (Figure 14.6). At this point, if time allows, they may be asked about the process in some depth. Such feedback can tell the firm why customers are happy or unhappy with the process, and usually shows how customer satisfaction can be improved.

All three survey types are representative and reliable when designed properly. Representativeness and reliability are required for: (1) accurate assessment of where the company, a process, branch or individual stands relative to quality goals (having a representative and reliable sample means that observed changes in quality scores are not the result of sample biases and/or random errors); and (2) evaluation of individual service employees, service delivery teams, branches and/or processes, especially when incentive schemes are linked to such measures. The methodology has to be water-tight if staff are to trust and buy into the results, especially when a survey delivers bad news.

Service Feedback Cards

This powerful and inexpensive tool involves giving customers a feedback card (or an online pop-up form, e-mail or SMS) following completion of a major service process and inviting them to return it by mail or other means to a central customer feedback unit (Figure 14.7). For example, a feedback card can be attached to each housing loan approval letter or to each hospital invoice. These cards are a good indicator of process quality and provide feedback on what works well and what does not. However, respondents who are very satisfied or very dissatisfied are likely to be over-represented among the respondents, which affect the reliability and representativeness of this tool.

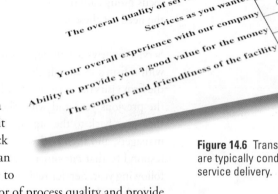

Figure 14.6 Transactional surveys are typically conducted following service delivery.

Mystery Shopping

Service businesses often use this method to determine whether frontline staff are displaying desired behaviors. Because the number of mystery calls or visits is usually small, no individual survey is reliable or representative. However, if a particular staff member performs well (or poorly) month after month, managers can judge with reasonable confidence that this person's performance is good (or poor).

Unsolicited Customer Feedback

Customer complaints, compliments and suggestions can be transformed into a stream of information that can be used to help monitor quality, and highlight improvements needed to the service design and delivery. Complaints and compliments are rich sources of detailed feedback on what makes customers unhappy and what delights them. Similar to feedback cards, unsolicited feedback is not a reliable measure of overall customer satisfaction, but it is a good source of improvement ideas.

Figure 14.7 The widespread use of SMS text messaging allows for convenient M-feedback.

Detailed customer complaint and compliment letters, recorded telephone conversations, and direct feedback from employees can serve as an excellent tool for communicating internally what customers want, and allow employees and managers at all levels to "listen" to customers first hand. For example, Singapore Airlines prints complaint and compliment letters in its monthly employee magazine Outlook. Southwest Airlines shows staff videotapes of customers providing feedback. Seeing actual customers giving comments about their service leaves a much deeper and lasting impression on staff and encourages them to improve further.

For complaints, suggestions, and inquiries to be useful as research input, they have to be channeled into a central collection point, logged, grouped, and analyzed.[16] That requires a system for capturing customer feedback where it is made, and then reporting it to a central unit.

Focus Group Discussions and Service Reviews

Both tools give great insights on potential service improvements and ideas. Typically, focus groups are organized by key customer segments or user groups to understand the needs of these users.

Service reviews are in-depth one-on-one interviews, usually conducted once a year with a firm's most valuable customers (Figure 14.8). Usually, a senior executive of the firm visits the customers and discusses issues such as how well the firm performed the previous year and what should be maintained or changed. That senior person then goes back to the organization and discusses the feedback with his/her account managers, and then both write a letter back to the client detailing how the firm will respond to that customer's service needs and how the account will be managed the following year. Service reviews focus on retention of the most valuable customers and get high marks for service recovery potential.

Figure 14.8 Service review being conducted with an important B2B customer.

As we noted earlier, there are advantages in using a mix of feedback tools. Service Insights 14.1 features FedEx's excellent CFS which combines various customer feedback collection tools with a detailed process performance measurement system.

Analysis, Reporting and Dissemination of Customer Feedback

Choosing the relevant feedback tools and collecting customer feedback is meaningless if the company is unable to pass the information to the relevant parties to take action. Hence, to drive continuous improvement and learning, a reporting system needs to deliver feedback and its analysis to frontline staff, process owners, branch or department managers and top management.

::: SERVICE INSIGHTS 14.1 ·

FedEx's Approach to Listening to the **Voice of the Customer**

"We believe that service quality must be mathematically measured" declares Frederick W. Smith, Chairman, President and CEO of FedEx Corp. The company has a commitment to clear quality goals, followed up with continuous measurement of progress against those goals. This practice forms the foundation for its approach to quality.

Since FedEx had systematically catalogued customer complaints, it was able to develop what CEO Smith calls the "Hierarchy of Horrors," which referred to the eight most common complaints by customers: (1) wrong day delivery, (2) right day, late delivery, (3) pick-up not made (4) lost package, (5) customer misinformed by FedEx, (6) billing and paper work mistakes, (7) employee performance failures, and (8) damaged packages. This list was what FedEx built its CFS on.

FedEx refined the list of "horrors" and developed the Service Quality Indicator (SQI), a 12-item measure of satisfaction and service quality from the customers' viewpoint. In addition to the SQI, which has been modified over time to reflect changes in both procedures, services, and customer priorities, FedEx uses a variety of other ways to capture feedback.

Customer Satisfaction Survey – This telephone survey is conducted on a quarterly basis with several thousand selected customers from its key segments. The results are passed on to senior management on a quarterly basis.

Targeted Customer Satisfaction Survey – This survey covers specific customer service processes and is conducted on a semi-annual basis with clients who have experienced one of the FedEx processes within the last three months.

FedEx Center Comment Cards – Comment cards are collected from each FedEx store. The results are analyzed twice a year and passed on to managers in charge of the centers.

Online Customer Feedback Surveys – FedEx has regular studies to get feedback for its online services (e.g. such as package tracking), as well as studies on new products.

The information from these various customer feedback measures has helped FedEx to maintain a leadership role in its industry and played an important role in enabling it to receive the prestigious Malcolm Baldridge National Quality Award.

SOURCE

Blueprints for service quality: The federal express approach. AMA Management Briefing, New York: *American Management Association*, 1991, pp. 51–64; Rosencrance, L. (2000). Betasphere delivers fedex some customer feedback. *Computerworld*, 14(14), p. 36.

The feedback loop to the frontline should be immediate for complaints and compliments. In addition, we recommend three types of service performance reports to provide the information necessary for service management and team learning.

1. A monthly Service Performance Update provides process owners with timely feedback on customer comments and operational process performance. Here, the feedback is provided to the process manager, who can in turn discuss them with his or her service delivery team.

2. A quarterly Service Performance Review provides process owners and branch or department managers with trends in process performance and service quality.

3. An annual Service Performance Report shows top management the status and long-term trends relating to customer satisfaction with the firm's services.

The reports should be short and reader-friendly, focusing on key indicators and providing easily understood comments.

 LO 7
Be familiar with hard measures of service quality and control charts.

HARD MEASURES OF SERVICE QUALITY

Having learnt about the various tools for collecting soft service quality measures, let us explore hard measures in more detail. Hard measures usually refer to operational processes or outcomes. They include data such as uptime, service response times, failure rates, and delivery costs. In a complex service operation, a few measures of service quality will be recorded at many different points. In low-contact services, in which customers are not deeply involved in the service delivery process, many operational measures apply to backstage activities.

FedEx was one of the first service companies to understand the need for a firm-wide index of service quality that included all the key activities that had an impact on customers (see Service Insights 14.1). By publishing a single, composite index regularly, senior managers hoped that all FedEx employees would work towards improving quality. The firm recognized the danger of using percentages as targets, because they might lead to self-satisfaction. In an organization as large as FedEx, which ships millions of packages a day, even delivering 99 percent of packages on time or having 99.9 percent of flights arrive safely would lead to terrible problems. Instead, the company decided to approach quality measurement from the baseline of zero failures. The design of this "hard" index reflected the findings of extensive "soft" customer research on what is important to customers, and it is being adjusted regularly based on new research insights.

How can we show performance on hard measures? For this, *control charts* are a simple method of displaying performance on hard measures over time against specific quality standards. The charts can be used to monitor and communicate individual variables or an overall index. Since they are visual, trends are easily identified. Figure 14.9 shows an airline's performance on the important hard standard of on-time departures. The trends displayed suggest that this issue needs to be addressed by management, as performance is not consistent and not very satisfactory. Of course, control charts are only as good as the data on which they are based.

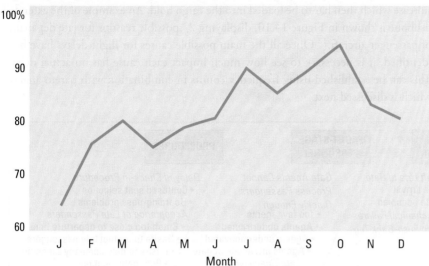

Flights Departing Within 15 Minutes of Schedule

Figure 14.9 Control chart for departure delays showing percentage of flights departing within 15 minutes of schedule.

TOOLS TO ANALYZE AND ADDRESS SERVICE QUALITY PROBLEMS

LO 8

Understand three important tools to analyze service problems (i.e. the fishbone diagram, pareto analysis, and blue printing).

After having assessed service quality using soft and hard measures, how can we now drill deeper to identify common causes of quality shortfalls and take corrective actions? After all, maintaining customers' goodwill after a service failure depends on keeping promises like "we're taking steps to ensure that it doesn't happen again!" With prevention in mind, let us look briefly at some tools for finding out the root causes of specific service quality problems.

The Fishbone Diagram

Cause-and-effect analysis uses a technique first developed by the Japanese quality expert, Kaoru Ishikawa. Groups of managers and staff brainstorm all the possible reasons that might cause a specific problem. The reasons are then classified into one of the five groupings—Equipment, Manpower (or People), Material, Procedures, and Other—on a cause and effect chart, popularly known as a fishbone diagram because of its shape. This technique has been used for many years in manufacturing and, more recently, also in services.

To apply this tool better to the service organizations, we show an extended framework that has eight rather than five groupings.[17] "People" has been broken into Front-Stage Personnel and Backstage Personnel. This highlights the fact that front-stage service problems are often experienced directly by customers, whereas backstage failures tend to show up more indirectly through a ripple effect. "Information" has been taken from "Procedures." This recognizes the fact that many service problems result from information failures. For example, these failures happen because front-stage personnel do not tell customers what to do and when.

In manufacturing, customers do not really affect the day-to-day operational processes. However, in a high-contact service, they are involved in front-stage operations. If they do not play their own parts correctly, they may reduce service productivity and cause quality problems for themselves and other customers. For instance, an aircraft can be delayed if a passenger tries to board at the last minute with an oversized suitcase which then has to be loaded into the cargo hold. An example of the extended fishbone is shown in Figure 14.10, displaying 27 possible reasons for late departures of passenger aircraft.[18] Once all the main possible causes for flight delays have been identified, it is necessary to see how much impact each cause has on actual delays. This can be established using frequency counts in combination with pareto analysis which is discussed next.

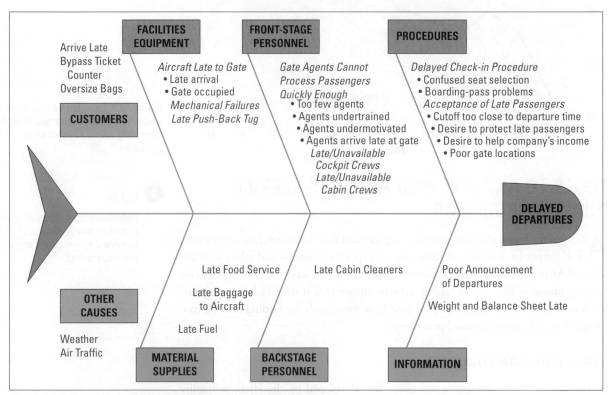

Figure 14.10 Cause-and-effect chart for flight departure delays.

Pareto Analysis

Pareto Analysis (named after the Italian economist who first developed it) identifies the main causes of observed outcomes. This type of analysis often reveals that around 80 percent of the value of one variable (in this instance, number of service failures) is caused by only 20 percent of the causal variable (i.e. number of possible causes as identified by the fishbone diagram).

In the airline example, findings showed that 88 percent of the company's late departing flights from the airports it served were caused by only four (15 percent) of all the possible factors. In fact, more than half the delays were caused by a single factor: acceptance of late passengers (situations when the staff held a flight for one more passenger who was checking in after the official cutoff time).

On such occasions, the airline made a friend of that late passenger, but risked frustrating all the other passengers who were already onboard, waiting for the aircraft to depart. Other major delays included waiting for pushback (a vehicle must arrive to pull the aircraft away from the gate), waiting for fueling, and delays in signing the weight and balance sheet (a safety requirement relating to the distribution of the aircraft's load that the captain must follow on each flight). Further analysis, however, showed that the reasons are slightly different from one airport to another (see Figure 14.11).

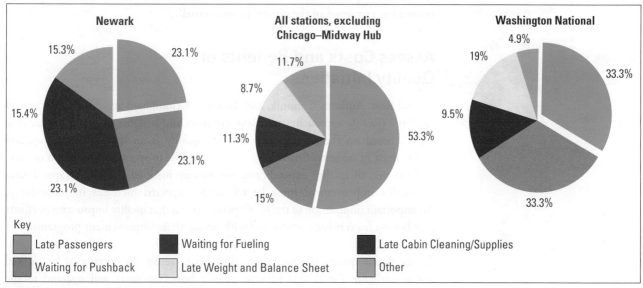

Figure 14.11 Analysis of causes of flight departure delays.

Combining the Fishbone diagram and Pareto analysis serves to identify the main causes of service failure.

Blueprinting—A Powerful Tool for Identifying Fail Points

Fishbone diagrams and pareto analyses tell us the causes and importance of quality problems. Blueprints drill down further to precisely show where exactly in a service process the problem was caused. Blueprints identify the potential *fail points* where failures are most likely to occur, and service process redesign teams can then work on designing those failpoints out of the system (see the Poka Yoke method described in Chapter 8).

Blueprints also help us to understand how failures at one point (such as incorrect entry of an appointment date) may have an effect later in the process (the customer arrives at the doctor's office and is told the doctor is unavailable). Using frequency counts, managers can identify the types of failures that happen most often and thus need urgent attention. Knowing what can go wrong and where is an important first step in preventing service quality problems. See also Chapter 8 where we describe in more detail of what a blueprint is and how it can be used to design and redesign customer service processes.

RETURN ON QUALITY

We now understand how to drill down to specific quality problems, and we can use the learning from Chapter 8 on how to design and redesign improved service processes. However, the picture is not complete yet without

 LO 9

Understand the financial implications of quality improvements.

understanding the financial implications related to quality improvements. Many firms pay a lot of attention on improving service quality. However, quite a few of them have been disappointed by the results. Even firms recognized for service quality efforts have sometimes run into financial difficulties. This is partly because they spent too much on quality improvements. In other instances, such results show poor or incomplete execution of the quality program itself.

Assess Costs and Benefits of Quality Initiatives

Roland Rust, Anthony Zahonik, and Timothy Keiningham argue for a "Return on Quality" (ROQ) approaches to assess the costs and benefits of quality initiatives. This is based on the assumptions that (1) quality is an investment, (2) quality efforts must make sense financially, (3) it is possible to spend too much on quality, and (4) not all quality expenditures are equally justified.[19] Hence, expenditures on quality improvement must be related to expected increases in profitability. An important implication of the ROQ perspective is that quality improvement efforts may benefit from being coordinated with productivity improvement programs.

To see if new quality improvement efforts make sense, the costs must be worked out beforehand. Firms also have to predict how customers will respond to the improvement efforts. Will the program allow the firm to attract more customers (e.g. through word-of-mouth of current customers), increase share-of-wallet, and/or to reduce defections? If so, how much additional net income will be generated?

With good documentation, it is sometimes possible for a firm that operates in a number of locations to examine past experience and judge the strength of a relationship between specific service quality improvements and revenues (see Service Insights 14.2).

::::: SERVICE INSIGHTS 14.2 •

Quality of Facilities and Room Revenues at Holiday Inn

To find out the relationship between product quality and financial performance in a hotel context, Sheryl Kimes analyzed three years of quality and operational performance data from 1135 franchised Holiday Inn hotels in the United States and Canada.

Indicators of product quality came from the franchisor's quality assurance reports. These reports were based on unannounced, semi-annual inspections by trained quality auditors who were rotated among different regions and who inspected and rated different quality dimensions of each hotel. Sheryl Kimes used twelve of these quality dimensions in her study: two relating to the guest rooms (bedroom and bathroom) and ten relating to commercial areas (e.g. exterior, lobby, public restrooms, dining facilities, lounge facilities, corridors, meeting area, recreation area, kitchen, back of house). Each quality dimension usually included 10–12 individual items that could be passed or failed. The inspector noted the number of defects for each dimension and the total number for the entire hotel.

Holiday Inn Worldwide also provided data on revenue per available room (RevPAR) at each hotel. To compensate for differences in local conditions, Kimes analyzed sales and revenue statistics obtained from thousands of US and Canadian hotels and reported in the monthly Smith Travel

Accommodation Reports (a widely used service in the travel industry). This data enabled Kimes to calculate the RevPAR for the immediate midscale competitors of each Holiday Inn hotel. The results were then used to make the RevPARs comparable across all Holiday Inns in the sample. The average daily room rate at the time was about $50.

For the purposes of the research, if a hotel had failed at least one item in an area, it was considered "defective" in that area. The findings showed that as the number of defects in a hotel increased, the RevPAR decreased. Quality dimensions that showed quite a strong impact on RevPAR were the exterior, the guest room, and the guest bathroom. Even a single defect resulted in a statistically significant reduction in RevPAR. However, the combination of defects in all three areas showed an even larger effect on RevPAR over time. Kimes calculated that the average annual revenue impact on a defective hotel was a revenue loss of $204,400 compared to a non-defective hotel.

Using a ROQ perspective, the results showed that the main focus of increased expenditures on housekeeping and preventive maintenance should be the hotel exterior, the guest rooms, and bath rooms.

SOURCE

Kimes, S. E. (1999). The relationship between product quality and revenue per available room at holiday inn. *Journal of Service Research*, 2, (November), 138–144.

Determine the Optimal Level of Reliability

How far should we go in improving service reliability? A company with poor service quality can often achieve big jumps in reliability with relatively modest investments in improvements. As illustrated in Figure 14.12, initial investments in reducing service failure often bring dramatic results, but at some point diminishing returns set in as further improvements require increasing levels of investment, even becoming prohibitively expensive. What level of reliability should we target?

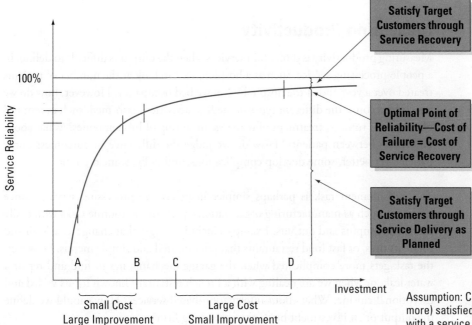

Figure 14.12 When does improving service reliability become uneconomical?

Typically, the cost of service recovery is lower than the cost of an unhappy customer. This suggests a strategy of increasing reliability up to the point that the incremental improvement equals the cost of service recovery or the cost of failure. Although this strategy results in a service that is less than 100 percent failure free, the firm can still aim to satisfy 100 percent of its target customers by ensuring that either they receive the service as planned or, if a failure occurs, they obtain a satisfying service recovery (see Chapter 13).

LO 10

Know how to define and measure productivity.

DEFINING AND MEASURING PRODUCTIVITY

We highlighted in the introduction of this chapter that we need to look at quality and productivity improvement strategies together rather than in isolation. A firm needs to ensure that it can deliver quality experiences more efficiently to improve its long-term profitability. Let us first discuss what productivity is and how it can be measured.

Defining Productivity in a Service Context

Simply defined, productivity measures the amount of output produced relative to the amount of inputs used. Hence, improvements in productivity require an increase in the ratio of outputs to inputs. This ratio can be improved by cutting the resources required to create a given volume of output, or by increasing the output obtained from a given level of inputs.

What do we mean by "input" in a service context? Input varies according to the nature of the business. It may include labor (both physical and intellectual), materials, energy, and capital (consisting of land, buildings, equipment, information systems, and financial assets).

Measuring Productivity

Measuring productivity is difficult in services when the output is difficult to define. In a people-processing service, such as a hospital, we can look at the number of patients treated over a year and at the hospital's average bed occupancy. However, how do we take into account the different types of medical activities performed, such as removal of cancerous tumors, treatment of diabetes, or setting of broken bones? What about differences between patients? How do we judge the difference in outcomes? Some patients get better, some develop complications, and sadly, some even die.

The measurement task is perhaps simpler in possession-processing services, since many are, such as manufacturing organizations, performing routine tasks with easily measurable inputs and outputs. Examples include garages that change a car's oil and rotate its tires, or fast food restaurants that offer limited and simple menus. However, the task gets more complicated when the garage mechanic has to find and repair a water leak, or when we are dealing with a French restaurant known for its varied and exceptional cuisine. What about information-based services? How should we define the output of an investment bank or a consulting firm?

Service Efficiency, Productivity and Effectiveness

When we look at the issue of productivity, we need to differentiate productivity, efficiency, and effectiveness.[20] Productivity is the financial value of outputs to inputs. Efficiency involves comparison to a standard which is usually time-based. For example, how long does it take for an employee to perform a particular task compared to a set standard? Effectiveness can be defined as the degree to which an organization is meeting its goals (Figure 14.13).

Classical techniques of productivity measurement focus on outputs rather than outcomes. This means that efficiency is stressed, but effectiveness is neglected. Services tend to be variable. However, traditional measures of service output tend to ignore variations in the quality or value of service, thus ignoring effectiveness. In freight transport, for instance, a ton-mile of output for freight that is delivered late is treated the same for productivity purposes as a similar shipment delivered on time.[21]

Another method—counting the number of customers served per unit of time—suffers from the same weakness. What happens when an increase in customers served is at the expense of perceived service quality? For example, suppose a hairdresser usually serves three customers per hour. However, she can increase her output to one every 15 minutes by using a faster but noisier hairdryer, reducing conversation with the customer, and by rushing her customers. Even if the haircut itself is just as good, the delivery process may be perceived as functionally inferior, leading customers to rate the overall service experience less positively (Figure 14.14). In this example, productivity and efficiency have been achieved, but not effectiveness.

In the long run, organizations that are more effective in consistently delivering outcomes desired by customers should be able to command higher prices for their output. Therefore, there is a need to stress effectiveness and outcomes. When looking at productivity, we also need to focus on quality and value.

"If you're losing patience with our endless automated system and need to run outside and scream, press 44. If you're feeling better now and wish to continue, press 45..."

Figure 14.13 Productivity for the firm may result in customer frustration when they cannot talk to service personnel.

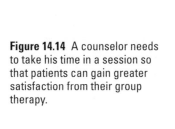

Figure 14.14 A counselor needs to take his time in a session so that patients can gain greater satisfaction from their group therapy.

PART IV

LO 11

Be familiar with the key methods of improving service productivity.

IMPROVING SERVICE PRODUCTIVITY

Intensive competition in many service sectors pushes firms to continually seek ways to improve their productivity.[22] This section discusses various possible ways to improve productivity.

General Productivity Improvement Strategies

Traditionally, operations managers have been in charge of improving service productivity. They usually take the following actions like:

▶ Careful control of costs at every step in the process.

▶ Reduce waste of materials and labor.

▶ Matching productive capacity to average levels of demand rather than peak levels, so that workers and equipment are not underemployed for long periods.

▶ Replacement of workers by automated machines and customer-operated Self-Service Technologies (SSTs).

▶ Providing employees with equipment and data that help them to work faster and/or to a higher level of quality.

▶ Teaching employees how to work more productively (faster is not necessarily better if it leads to mistakes or unsatisfactory work that has to be redone).

▶ Broadening the variety of tasks that a service worker can perform to get rid of bottlenecks and wasteful downtime. With this, managers can assign workers wherever they are most needed.

▶ Installing expert systems that allow para-professionals to take on work previously performed by more experienced individuals earning higher salaries.

Although improving productivity can be approached in small steps, major gains often require redesigning entire customer service processes (e.g. Figure 14.15). Service process redesign is discussed in depth in Chapter 8.

Figure 14.15 Long queues and bottlenecks point to problems within the service process design.

Customer-driven Ways to Improve Productivity

In situations where customers are deeply involved in the service production process (typically, people-processing services), operations managers should be looking at how customer inputs can be made more productive. Marketing managers should be thinking about what marketing strategies should be used to influence customers to behave in more productive ways. Some of these ways include:

▶ **Changing the Timing of Customer Demand.** The issues that relate to managing demand in capacity-constrained service businesses is discussed in detail in Chapter 9.

▶ **Involve Customers More in Production.** Customers who assume a more active role in the service production and delivery process can take over some labor tasks from the service organization. Benefits for both parties may result when customers perform self-service. Many technological innovations are designed to get customers to perform tasks previously undertaken by service employees (e.g. see Figure 14.16). The issues related to customers playing a more active role as co-producers of the service are discussed in detail in Chapter 8. Quality and productivity improvements often depend on customers' willingness to learn new procedures, follow instructions, and interact cooperatively with employees and other people.

▶ **Ask Customers to Use Third Parties.** In some instances, managers may be able to improve service productivity using third parties. Specialist intermediaries may enjoy economies of scale, allowing them to perform the task more cheaply than the core service provider. This allows the service provider to focus on quality and productivity in its own area of expertise. An example of an intermediary is a travel agency (Figure 14.17).

Figure 14.16 Self-service pumps with credit card readers have increased gas station productivity.

Figure 14.17 This travel agency in South Norwood, Massachusetts, is an intermediary that helps South Americans plan their holidays. It employs Portugese-speaking agents and displays the flag of Brazil prominently.

LO 12

Know how productivity improvements impact quality and value.

How Productivity Improvements Impact Quality and Value

Resource inputs should be used to produce outcomes that are desired by customers. As firms make productivity improvements, they need to examine the impact on the customer experience.

How Backstage Changes May Impact Customers

Some backstage changes may affect customers directly and are noticed by them, but others may not. If airline mechanics develop a method for servicing jet engines more quickly, without needing increased wage rates or material costs, the productivity improvement has no impact on the customer's service experience.

Other backstage changes, however, may have a ripple effect that extends to the front stage and affects customers. Marketers should keep track of these suggested backstage changes, and prepare customers for them. At a bank, for instance, the goal of installing new computers and printers may improve internal quality controls and reduce the cost of preparing monthly statements. However, this new equipment may change the way bank statements look. If customers are likely to notice such changes, an explanation may be needed. If the new statements are easier to read and understand, it may be worth positioning the change as a service improvement.

Front Stage Efforts to Improve Productivity

In high-contact services, many productivity improvements are quite visible. Some changes simply require acceptance by customers. Others need customers to change their behavior. If a lot of changes are suggested, then it makes sense to conduct market research first to see how customers may react. Failure to think about impacts on customers may result in a loss of business and cancel out expected productivity gains. Service Insights 14.3 identifies ways of addressing customer resistance to change, particularly when the innovation requires a major change in customer behavior. Once the nature of the changes has been decided, marketing communication can help prepare customers for the change, explaining the reasons, the benefits, and what customers will need to do differently in the future.

A Caution on Cost Reduction Techniques

Service productivity improvements usually focus on getting rid of waste and reducing labor costs if it does not involve new technology. Reducing front stage staffing either means that the remaining employees have to work harder and faster, or that there are not enough personnel to serve customers fast at busy times. Although employees may be able to work faster for a short period of time, few can do that for long periods. They become tired, make mistakes, and treat customers in a cold manner. Workers who are trying to do two or three things at the same time may do a poor job of each task. Too much stress leads to dissatisfaction and frustration. A better way is to search for service process redesign opportunities that lead to great improvements in productivity and at the same time increase service quality. Biometrics is set to become a new technology that may allow both (see Service Insights 14.4).

Managing Customers' Reluctance to Change

Customers may not like changes in familiar environments and may have set patterns of behavior. This often blocks efforts to improve productivity and even quality. The following six steps can help smooth the path of change.

1. **Develop customer trust.** It is more difficult to introduce productivity-related changes when people do not trust the institution that introduced it. Customers' willingness to accept change may be closely related to the degree of goodwill they have towards the organization.

2. **Understand customers' habits and expectations.** People often get into a set way of using a particular service, with certain steps being taken in a specific sequence. Innovations that interfere with these familiar ways are likely to face resistance unless consumers are carefully advised about what changes to expect.

3. **Pretest new procedures and equipment.** To find out possible customer reactions to new procedures and equipment, marketing researchers can use concept and laboratory testing and/or field testing. If service personnel are going to be replaced by automatic equipment, it is necessary to create designs that customers of almost all types and backgrounds will find easy to use. Even the phrasing of instructions needs careful thought.

4. **Publicize the benefits.** Introduction of self-service equipment or procedures requires consumers to perform part of the task themselves. Although this additional "work" may have benefits such as extended service hours, time savings, and (in some instances) monetary savings, these benefits may not be obvious. They have to be promoted. Useful strategies may include use of mass media advertising, on-site posters and signage, and personal communications to inform people of the innovation, stir their interest in it, and explain the specific benefits to customers of changing their behavior and using new delivery systems.

5. **Teach customers to use innovations and promote trial.** To help customers to accept new procedures and technology, service personnel should demonstrate the new equipment and answer questions. This helps customers to feel more confident in using the equipment. For web-based innovations, it is important to provide access to e-mail, chat or even telephone-based assistance. Promotional incentives and price discounts may also serve to encourage trial. Once customers have tried a self-service option, especially an electronically based one, and found that it works well, they will be more likely to use it regularly in the future.

6. **Monitor performance and continue to seek improvements.** Introducing quality and productivity improvements is an ongoing process. The competitive edge gained by productivity improvements may quickly disappear as other firms use similar or better procedures. Therefore, service managers have to work hard to keep improving continuously. If customers do not like the new procedures, they may change back to their previous behavior. It is important to continue keeping watch on utilization over time.

PART IV

Biometrics – The **Next Frontier** in Driving Productivity and **Service Quality?**

Intense competitive pressures and extremely low margins in service industries do not allow firms to increase costs to improve quality. Rather, the trick is to always look for ways to achieve great improvements in service quality and efficiency at the same time. This is something Wirtz and Heracleous termed cost-effective service excellence. The Internet has in the past allowed many firms to do just that. It has changed industries including financial services, book and music retailing, and travel agencies. Biometrics may be the next major technology driving further service and productivity improvements in the service sector.

Biometrics is the identification of individuals based on a physical characteristic or trait. Physical characteristics include finger prints, facial recognition, hand geometry or the structure of the iris. Traits include signature formation, keystroke patterns or voice recognition. Biometrics, as something you are, is both more convenient and safer than something you know (passwords or pieces of personal information) or something you have (card keys, smart cards or tokens). There is no risk of forgetting, losing, copying, loaning, or getting your biometrics stolen (Figure 14.18).

Applications of biometrics range from controlling access to service facilities (used by Disneyworld to provide access to season pass holders), voice recognition at call-centers (used by the Home Shopping Network and Charles Schwab to allow fast and hassle-free client identification), self-service access to safe deposit vaults at banks (used by the

Bank of Hawaii and First Tennessee Bank), and cashing checks in supermarkets (used by Kroger, Food 4 Less and BI-LO).

So far, many biometrics-based trials focus on improving security. However, biometrics can offer service excellence through faster and more convenient service—just imagine looking into a camera at an ATM and scanning your finger print instead of carrying an ATM card and having to remember a password! Can you think of other services where firms might be able to use biometrics to achieve service excellence while also improving productivity and security?

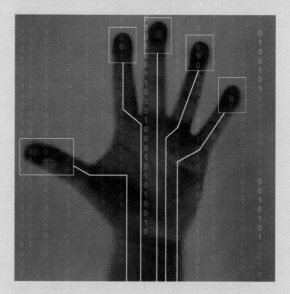

Figure 14.18 Customers cannot forget or lose their biometrics!

SOURCE

Heracleous, L., Wirtz J., & Pangarkar, N. (2006). *Flying High in a Competitive Industry – Cost-effective Service Excellence at Singapore Airlines* (pp. 104–112), Singapore: McGraw Hill; Wirtz, J., & Heracleous, L.(2005). Biometrics meets services. *Harvard Business Review*, (February) pp. 48–49; Heracleous, L., & Wirtz, J. (2006). Biometrics – The next frontier in service excellence, productivity and security in the service sector. *Managing Service Quality*, 16(1).

CHAPTER SUMMARY

LO 1 ▶ Quality and productivity are twin paths for creating value for the customer.

- o Quality focuses on the benefits created for customers, and productivity affects the financial costs to the firm.

- o Both quality and productivity have to be looked at in combination or there might be a case where productivity gains for the firm result in decreased value for the customer.

LO 2 ▶ There are different ways of looking at service quality. For this text, we adopt the view of the user's perspective where the firm should meet or exceed customer expectations.

▶ Service quality consists of five main dimensions: (1) tangibles, (2) reliability, (3) responsiveness, (4) assurance and (5) empathy.

LO 3 ▶ An important tool to identify and correct service quality problems is the Gap Model. There are six gaps:

- o Gap 1 – the knowledge gap

- o Gap 2 – the policy gap

- o Gap 3 – the delivery gap

- o Gap 4 – the communications gap

- o Gap 5 – the perceptions gap

- o Gap 6 – the service quality gap. It is the most important gap. In order to close Gap 6, all other five gaps have to be closed first.

LO 4 ▶ Service quality needs to be measured so that improvements can be made. There are both hard and soft measures and related standards of service quality. Soft measures are usually based on perceptions of and feedback from customers and employees. In contrast, hard measures can be counted, timed or observed.

LO 5 ▶ Feedback from customers should be systematically collected via CFS. The objectives of a CFS fall into three main categories:

- o Assessment and benchmarking of service quality and performance.

- o Customer-driven learning and improvement.

- o Creating a customer-oriented service culture.

LO 6 ▶ There are a variety of tools that firms can use to collect customer feedback. They include:

- o Total Market Surveys (including competitors),

- o Annual Surveys on Overall Satisfaction,

- o Transactional Surveys,

- o Service Feedback Cards,

- o Mystery Shopping,

- o Unsolicited Customer Feedback (e.g. complaints),

- o Focus Group Discussions, and

- o Service Reviews.

▶ A reporting system is needed to channel the feedback collected to the relevant parties to take action. Often, various types of service performance reports are used, including (1) the monthly Service Performance Update, (2) quarterly Service Performance Review, and (3) annual Service Performance Report.

LO 7 ▶ How can we show performance on hard measures? Control charts are a simple method of displaying performance on hard measure over time against specific quality standard.

LO 8 ▶ Key tools to analyze and address important service quality problems include:

- o fishbone diagram,

- o pareto analysis, and

- o blueprinting.

LO 9 ▶ There are financial implications related to service quality improvements. ROQ is an approach to assess the costs and benefits of quality initiatives.

LO 10 ▶ Productivity is the other path to increase firm and customer value. Productivity measures the amount of output relative to the amount of inputs used.

PART IV

▶ Productivity is often hard to define in a service context. Service firms have to be aware of the three main related concepts of:

- o service productivity (e.g. input/output ratio),

- o efficiency (e.g. speed of delivery), and

- o effectiveness (e.g. customer satisfaction with the outcome).

▶ Firms which strive to be more efficient and effective in consistently delivering outcomes desired by customers will be more successful. Therefore, when looking at productivity and efficiency, we also need to focus on quality and value.

LO 11 ▶ General methods to improve productivity include:

- o Controlling costs,

- o Reducing waste,

- o Matching capacity to demand,

- o Replacing labor with machines,

- o Teaching employees to work more productively, and

- o Using expert systems so that paraprofessionals can do the work.

▶ The customer-driven methods to improve productivity include:

- o Changing the timing of customer demand,

- o Involving customers more in co-production of the service, and

- o Getting customers to use third parties.

LO 12 ▶ When improvements are being made to productivity, firms need to bear in mind that both backstage and front stage improvements could have an impact on service quality and the customer experience. If an improvement requires customers to change their behavior, then customers need to be educated on how they should behave and how the change will benefit them.

Review Questions

1. What is the relationship between service quality, productivity and marketing?

2. What are the gaps that can occur in service quality and the steps that service marketers can take to close them?

3. Why are both "soft" and "hard" measures of service quality needed?

4. What are the main objectives of customer feedback systems?

5. What customer feedback collection tools do you know? What are the strengths and weaknesses of each of these tools?

6. What are the main tools service firms can use to analyze and address service quality problems?

7. Why is productivity a difficult issue to address for service firms?

8. What are the key tools for improving service productivity?

9. How do concepts such as TQM, ISO 9000, Malcolm-Baldrige Approach, and Six Sigma relate to managing and improving productivity and service quality? (Refer to the appendix.)

◖ WORK **YOUR ESM** ◗

Application Exercises

1. What are the five dimensions of service quality? What do they mean in the context of (a) an industrial repair shop, (b) a retail bank, (c) a Big 4 accounting firm?

2. Collect a few customer feedback forms and tools (e.g. customer feedback cards, questionnaires, and online forms) and explain how the information gathered with those tools can be used to achieve the three main objectives of effective CFSs.

3. Think about your own recent experiences as a service consumer. For which dimensions of service quality have you most often experienced a large gap between your expectations and your perceptions of the service performance? What do you think might be the underlying causes? What steps should management take to improve quality?

4. In what ways can you, as a consumer, help to improve productivity for two service organizations that you go to? What special characteristics of each service make some of these actions possible?

5. Do a literature search and identify the important factors for a successful implementation of ISO 9000, the Malcolm-Baldrige Model and Six Sigma in service firms. (Refer to the appendix.)

PART IV

MEASURING SERVICE QUALITY USING SERVQUAL

To measure customer satisfaction with various aspects of service quality, Valarie Zeithaml and her colleagues developed a survey research instrument called SERVQUAL (Table 14.4).[23] In its basic form, the scale contains 21 perception items and a series of expectation items that examine the five dimensions of service quality described earlier (Table 14.1).

Table 14.4 The SERVQUAL Scale

The SERVQUAL scale includes five dimensions: tangibles, reliability, responsiveness, assurance, and empathy. Within each dimension, several items are measured on a 7-point scale, from strongly agree to strongly disagree, for a total of 21 items.

SERVQUAL Questions
Note: For actual survey respondents, instructions are also included, and each statement is accompanied by a seven-point scale ranging from "strongly agree = 7" to "strongly disagree = 1." Only the end points of the scale are labeled; there are no words above the numbers 2 through 6.

Tangibles
- Excellent banks (refer to cable TV companies, hospitals, or the appropriate service business throughout the questionnaire) will have modern-looking equipment.
- The physical facilities at excellent banks will be visually appealing.
- Employees at excellent banks will be neat in appearance.
- Materials (e.g. brochures or statements) associated with the service will be visually appealing in an excellent bank.

Reliability
- When excellent banks promise to do something by a certain time, they will do so.
- When customers have a problem, excellent banks will show a sincere interest in solving it.
- Excellent banks will perform the service right the first time.
- Excellent banks will provide their services at the time they promise to do so.
- Excellent banks will insist on error-free records.

Responsiveness
- Employees of excellent banks will tell customers exactly when service will be performed.
- Employees of excellent banks will give prompt service to customers.
- Employees of excellent banks will always be willing to help customers.
- Employees of excellent banks will never be too busy to respond to customer requests.

Assurance
- The behavior of employees of excellent banks will instill confidence in customers.
- Customers of excellent banks will feel safe in their transactions.
- Employees of excellent banks will be consistently courteous with customers.
- Employees of excellent banks will have the knowledge to answer customer questions.

Empathy
- Excellent banks will give customers individual attention.
- Excellent banks will have operating hours convenient to all their customers.
- Excellent banks will have employees who give customers personal attention.
- The employees of excellent banks will understand the specific needs of their customers.

SOURCE

Adapted from Parasuraman, A., Zeithaml, V.A., & Berry, L. (1988). SERVQUAL: A multiple item scale for measuring consumer perceptions of service quality. *Journal of Retailing*, 64, pp. 12–40.

SERVQUAL has been widely used, but there are a number of limitations to this measure. Therefore, today, the majority of researchers using SERVQUAL omits from, add to, or change the list of statements to measure service quality in their specific context.[24] These different findings show that it is difficult to measure customer perceptions of quality. Zeithaml, Berry, and Parasuraman's achievement has been in identifying some of the key underlying constructs in service quality. However, there is a need to customize dimensions and measures to the research context.[25]

SYSTEMATIC APPROACHES TO PRODUCTIVITY AND QUALITY IMPROVEMENT AND PROCESS STANDARDIZATION

Many tools and concepts introduced in this chapter originate from Total Quality Management (TQM), ISO 9000, Six Sigma and the Malcolm-Baldrige Model. We discuss each of these approaches and relate them back to the service quality context in the following sections.

Total Quality Management

Total Quality Management (TQM) concepts were originally developed in Japan. They are widely used in manufacturing, and more recently also in service firms, including educational institutions (see Service Insights 14.5). Some concepts and tools of TQM can be directly applied to services. TQM tools such as control charts, flow charts, fish bone diagrams, and so on are being used by service firms with great results for monitoring service quality and finding out the root causes of specific problems. Twelve important dimensions have been identified for the successful implementation of TQM in a service context: (1) top management commitment and visionary leadership, (2) human resource management, (3) technical system, including service process design and process management, (4) information and analysis system, (5) benchmarking, (6) continuous improvement, (7) customer focus, (8) employee satisfaction, (9) union intervention and employee relations, (10) social responsibility, (11) servicescapes, and (12) service culture.[26] In fact, TQM and marketing together help to make the process of value creation and delivery more efficient.[27] TQM can help organizations to attain service excellence and be a continued source of value creation for its stakeholders through the feeding of innovative processes for the firm.[28]

ISO 9000 Certification

More than 90 countries are members of ISO (the International Organization for Standardization based in Geneva, Switzerland). The organization promotes standardization and quality to make it easier for international trade. ISO 9000 is made up of requirements, definitions, guidelines, and related standards to provide an independent assessment and certification of a firm's quality management system. The official ISO 9000 definition of quality is: "The totality of features and characteristics of a product or service that bear on its ability to satisfy a stated or implied need. Simply stated, quality is about meeting or exceeding your customer's needs and requirements." To ensure quality, ISO 9000 uses many TQM tools and participating firms use them often.

Service firms were late in adopting the ISO9000 standards and the majority (around two thirds) of the total 510,616 organizations that had been certified by ISO9000 by the end of year 2001 were in manufacturing industries.[29] Major service sectors that have adopted ISO9000 certification include wholesale and retail firms, IT service providers, health care providers, consultancy firms, and educational institutions. By adopting ISO 9000 standards, service firms, especially small ones, can make sure that their services meet customer expectations and also achieve improvements in productivity.

> **LO 13**
>
> Understand how TQM, ISO 9000, Malcolm-Baldrige Approach and Six Sigma relate to managing and improving service quality and productivity.

PART IV

TQM in Educational Institutions

The world is becoming increasingly competitive. Educational institutions are also moving in that direction as they compete for student numbers. Higher educational institutions understand and have started to accept that they have to be more customer-centric in their approach to increase customer satisfaction. What however, is the meaning of service quality in a higher educational institution? Sakthivel, Rajendran and Raju proposed a TQM model with five variables that measure different dimensions of service quality in an institution of higher learning, and suggest that these variables will increase student satisfaction. The five variables are:

- Commitment of top management. Top management has to walk the talk and make sure that what is preached is really practiced.

- Course delivery. While institutions of higher learning hire people with expert knowledge, there is a need that such expert knowledge can be transmitted expertly, with passion.

- Campus facilities. Attention needs to be focused on having excellent infrastructure and facilities for student learning as well as their extra-curricular activities. These facilities also have to be properly maintained.

- Courtesy. This is a positive attitude towards students that will create a friendly learning environment.

- Customer feedback and improvement. Continuous feedback from students can lead to improvement in the process of achieving service excellence.

They studied engineering students from a mix of ISO and non-ISO institution. Their findings showed that while all five variables together did predict student satisfaction, two variables were more important in affecting student satisfaction. The variables were commitment of top management and campus facilities. Top management needs to be committed to quality assurance in making sure the other variables are in place to improve the student experience. In general, they also found that ISO 9001:2000 certified institutions were moving towards TQM and offering a better quality of education than non-ISO institutions.

Figure 14.19 Institutions of higher learning should have excellent facilities to increase student satisfaction.

SOURCE

Sakthivel, P. B., Rajendran, G., & Raju, R. (2005). TQM implementation and students' satisfaction of academic performance. *The TQM Magazine*, 17(6). pp. 673–589.

Malcolm-Baldrige Model Applied to Services

The Malcolm-Baldrige National Quality Award (MBNQA) was developed by the National Institute of Standards and Technology (NIST) with the goal of promoting best practices in quality management, and recognizing and publicizing quality achievements among US firms.

While the framework is general and does not differentiate between manufacturing and service organizations, the award has a specific service category. The model can be used to create a culture of ongoing service improvements. Major services firms that have won the award include Ritz-Carlton, FedEx and AT&T (Figure 14.20). Research has confirmed that using this framework can improve organizational performance.[30]

Figure 14.20 Promotions such as the Home Technology Makeover where recipients can receive 12-months free U-verse TV, Internet services, and a host of prizes, have garnered AT&T the MBNQA as well as new supporters.

The Baldrige Model judges firms on seven areas: (1) leadership commitment to a service quality culture; (2) planning for improvement, including service standards, performance targets and measurement of customer satisfaction, defects, cycle-time and productivity; (3) information and analysis that will help the organization to collect, measure, analyze and report strategic and operational indicators; (4) human resources management that allows the firm to deliver service excellence, ranging from hiring the right people, to involvement, empowerment, and motivation; (5) process management, including monitoring, continuous improvement and process re-design; (6) customer and market focus that allows the firm to determine customer requirements and expectations; and finally (7) business results.[31] Countries other than the US have similar quality awards that follow the MBNQA model.

Six Sigma Applied to Service Organizations

The Six Sigma approach was originally developed by Motorola to improve product quality and reduce warranty claims. Other manufacturing firms soon used the approach to reduce defects in a variety of areas.

Subsequently, service firms also used Six Sigma strategies to reduce defects and cycle times, and improve productivity.[32] As early as 1990, GE Capital applied Six Sigma methodologies to reduce the costs of selling consumer loans, credit card insurance, and payment protection. Its President and COO Denis Nayden said,

"Although Six Sigma was originally designed for manufacturing, it can be applied to transactional services. One obvious example is in making sure the millions of credit card and other bills GE sends to customers are correct, which drives down our costs of making adjustments. One of our biggest costs in the financial business is winning new customers. If we treat them well, they will stay with us, reducing our customer-origination costs."[33]

PART IV

A Six Sigma standard means achieving a quality level of only 3.4 defects per million opportunities (DPMO). To understand how strict this target is, think about mail deliveries. If a mail service delivers with 99 percent accuracy, it misses 3000 items out of 300,000 deliveries. However, if it achieves a Six Sigma performance level, only one item out of this total will go missing!

Over time, Six Sigma has developed from a defect reduction approach to an overall business improvement approach. As defined by Pande et al.,

> "Six Sigma is a comprehensive and flexible system for achieving, sustaining and maximizing business success. Six Sigma is uniquely driven by close understanding of customer needs, disciplined use of facts, data and statistical analysis, and diligent attention to managing, improving, and reinventing business processes."[34]

Process improvement and process design/redesign form the foundation of the Six Sigma approach. Process improvement identifies and gets rid of the root causes of the service delivery problems, and thereby improving service quality. Process design/redesign works together with process improvement. If a root cause cannot be identified or effectively gotten rid of within the existing processes, either new processes are *designed* or existing process are *redesigned* to fully or partially address the problem.

The most popular Six Sigma improvement model used for analyzing and improving business processes is the DMAIC model, shown in Table 14.5. DMAIC stands for **D**efine the opportunities, **M**easure key steps/inputs, **A**nalyze to identify root causes, **I**mprove performance, and **C**ontrol to maintain performance.

Table 14.5 Applying the DMAIC Model to process improvement and redesign.

	Process Improvement	Process Design/Redesign
Define	• Identify the problem • Define requirements • Set goals	• Identify specific or broad problems • Define goal/change vision • Clarify scope and customer requirements
Measure	• Validate problem/process • Refine problem/ goal • Measure key steps/inputs	• Measure performance to requirements • Gather process efficiency data
Analyze	• Develop causal hypothesis • Identify root causes • Validate hypothesis	• Identify best practices • Assess process design • Refine requirements
Improve	• Develop ideas to measure root causes • Test solutions • Measure results	• Design new process • Implements new process, structures and systems
Control	• Establish measures to maintain performance • Correct problems as needed	• Establish measures and reviews to maintain performance • Correct problems as needed

SOURCE

Reproduced from Pande, P., Neuman, R.P., & Cavanagh, R.R. (2000). *The Six Sigma Way.* New York: McGraw-Hill.

Which Approach Should We Use?

As there are various approaches to systematically improving a service firm's service quality and productivity, the question of which approach should be adopted arises – TQM, ISO9000, the Malcolm-Baldrige model, or Six Sigma? TQM can be applied at differing levels of complexity and basic tools such as flow charting, frequency charts and fishbone diagrams probably should be adopted by any type of service firm. ISO9000 seems the next level of commitment and complexity, followed by the Malcolm-Baldrige Model and finally Six Sigma.

Any one of the approaches can be a useful framework for understanding customer needs, analyzing processes and improving service quality and productivity. Firms can choose a particular program, depending on their own needs and desired level of sophistication. Each program has its own strengths, and firms can use more than one program to add on to the other. For example, the ISO9000 program can be used for standardizing the procedures and process documentation. Six Sigma and Malcolm-Baldrige programs can be used to improve processes and to focus on performance improvement across the organization.

The key success factor of any of these programs depends on how well the particular quality improvement program is part of the overall business strategy. Firms who implement one of these programs due to peer pressure or just as a marketing tool will be less likely to succeed than firms who view these programs as important development tools.[35] Service champions make best practices in service quality management a core part of their organizational culture.[36]

The National Institute of Standards and Technology (NIST), which organizes the Malcolm-Baldrige Award program, has an index called the "Baldrige-Index" of Malcolm-Baldrige Award winners. It was observed that winners always outperformed the S&P 500 index.[37] Sadly, the two-time winner of the award, Motorola has been suffering financially and losing market share. It is partly due to the failure to keep up with new technology. Success cannot be taken for granted. Commitment and constant improvement that follow changing markets, technologies and environments are keys for sustained success (Figure 14.21).

Figure 14.21 When commitment and constant improvement meet head-on the challenge of changing markets, technologies and environments, success becomes a clearer picture.

PART IV

These key words are found within the sections of each Learning Objective (LO). They are integral in understanding the services marketing concepts taught in each section. Having a firm grasp of these keywords and how they are used is essential in helping you do well for your course, and in the real and very competitive marketing scene out there.

LO 1
1. Quality
2. Productivity
3. Service quality

LO 2
4. Assurance
5. Dimensions of service quality
6. Empathy
7. Manufacturing-based approach
8. Perspectives on quality
9. Reliability
10. Responsiveness
11. Tangibles
12. Transcendent view
13. User-based definitions
14. Value-based definitions

LO 3
15. Close service quality gaps
16. Gap 1—the knowledge gap
17. Gap 2—the policy gap
18. Gap 3—the delivery gap
19. Gap 4—the communications gap
20. Gap 5—the perception gap
21. Gap 6—the service gap
22. Overpromise gap
23. The interpretation gap
24. The internal communications gap
25. The Gap Model
26. Customer-driven learning
27. Customer feedback
28. Customer feedback system
29. Soft standards

LO 5
30. Benchmarking
31. Customer-oriented service culture

LO 6
32. Annual surveys
33. Customer feedback collection tools
34. Focus group discussions
35. Mix of feedback tools
36. Mystery shopping
37. Representativeness
38. Service feedback cards
39. Service reviews
40. Service performance update
41. Service performance review
42. Service performance report
43. Total market surveys
44. Transactional surveys
45. Unsolicited customer feedback

LO 7
46. Control charts
47. Hard measures of service quality

LO 8
48. Blueprinting
49. Cause-and effect analysis
50. Fail points
51. Pareto analysis
52. The Fishbone Diagram

LO 9
53. Return on Quality

LO 10
54. Efficiency
55. Effectiveness
56. Measuring productivity

LO 11
57. Improve productivity

LO 12
58. Cost-effective service
59. Cost reduction techniques
60. Service process redesign
61. Biometrics
62. SERVQUAL
63. The SERVQUAL Scale

LO 13
64. DMAIC Model
65. ISO9000 Certification
66. Malcolm-Baldrige National Quality Award
67. Six Sigma
68. Total Quality Management

How well do you know the language of services marketing? Quiz yourself!

⚠ **Not for the academically faint-of-heart**

For each keyword you are able to recall without referring to earlier pages, give yourself a point (and a pat on the back). Tally your score at the end and see if you earned the right to be called—a *services marketeer*.

SCORE

0 – 11	Services Marketing is done a great disservice.
12 – 23	The midnight oil needs to be lit, pronto.
24 – 35	I know what you *didn't* do all semester.
36 – 47	By George! You're getting there.
48 – 59	Now, go forth and market.
60 – 68	There should be a marketing concept named after you.

ENDNOTES

1   Adapted from Gilmore, A. (1998). Service marketing management competencies: A Ferry Company example. *International Journal of Service Industry Management*, 9(1), pp. 74–92; Available: www.stenaline.com, accessed June 2008.

2   Garvin, D. A. (1988). *Managing Quality*. New York: The Free Press; Keleman, M. L. (2003). *Managing Quality* (pp. 9–15). Sage Publications.

3   Zeithaml, V. A., Parasuraman, A., & Berry, L. L. (1990). *Delivering Quality Service*. New York: The Free Press.

4   Parasuraman, A., Zeithaml, V. A., & Berry, L. L. (1985). A conceptual model of service quality and its implications for future research. *Journal of Marketing 49*, (Fall), pp. 41–50; Zeithaml, V. A., Berry, L. L., & Parasuraman, A. (1988). Communication and control processes in the delivery of services. *Journal of Marketing 52*, (April), pp. 36–58.

5   The sub-gaps in this model are based on the 7-gaps model. Lovelock, C. (1994). *Product Plus* (p. 112). New York: McGraw-Hill.

6   The perception gap in this model are based on the 7-gaps model. Lovelock, C. (1994). *Product Plus* (p. 112). New York: McGraw-Hill.

7   Zeithaml, V. A., Bitner, M. J., & Gremler, D. D. (2006). *Services Marketing* 4/E (p. 192). New York: McGraw-Hill.

8   This section is partially based on Wirtz, J., & Tomlin, M. (2000). Institutionalizing customer-driven learning through fully integrated customer feedback systems. *Managing Service Quality*, 10(4), pp. 205–215.

9   Berry, L. L., & Parasuraman, A. (1997). Listening to the customer—the concept of a service quality information system. *Sloan Management Review*, (Spring), pp. 65–76.

10   Customer listening practices have been shown to affect service performance, growth and profitability, see: Glynn, W. J., Búrca, S. D., Brannick, T., Fynes, B., & Ennis, S. (2003). Listening practices and performance in service organizations. *International Journal of Service Industry Management*, 14(3), pp. 310–330.

11   Baker W. E., & Sinkula J. M., (1999). The synergistic effect of market orientation and learning orientation on organizational performance. *Journal of the Academy of Marketing Science*, 27(4), pp. 411–427.

12   Kaufman, R. (2005). *Up Your Service*, Ron Kaufman Pte Ltd.

13   Morgan, N. A., Anderson, E. W., & Mittal, V. (2005). Understanding firms' customer satisfaction information usage. *Journal of Marketing*, 69(July), pp. 131–151.

14   Berry, L. L., & Parasuraman, A. (1997) provides an excellent overview of all key research approaches discussed in this section plus a number of other tools in their paper, Listening to the customer – The concept of a service quality information system. *Sloan Management Review*, (Spring), pp. 65–76.

15   For a discussion on suitable satisfaction measures, see Wirtz, J., & Chung, L. M. (2003). An examination of the quality and context-specific applicability of commonly used customer satisfaction measures. *Journal of Service Research*, 5(May), pp. 345–355.

16   Johnston, R., & Mehra, S. (2002). Best-practice complaint management. *Academy of Management Executive*, 16(4), pp. 145–154.

17   Lovelock, C. (1994). *Product Plus: How Product + Service = Competitive Advantage* (p. 218). New York: McGraw-Hill.

18   These categories and the research data that follow have been adapted from information in Wyckoff, D. D. (2001). New tools for achieving service quality. *Cornell Hotel and Restaurant Administration Quarterly* (August–September), pp. 25–38.

19   Rust, R. T., Zahonik, A. J., & Keiningham, T. L. (1995). Return on quality (ROQ): Making service quality financially accountable. *Journal of Marketing* 59 (April), pp. 58–70; Rust, R. T. Moorman, C., & Dickson, P. R. (2002). Getting return on quality: Revenue expansion, cost reduction, or both?. *Journal of Marketing*, 66 (October), pp. 7–24.

20   Klassen, K. J., Russell, R. M., & Chrisman, J. J. (1998). Efficiency and productivity measures for high contact services. *The Service Industries Journal*, 18(October), pp. 1–18.

21   Heskett, J. L. (1986). *Managing in the Service Economy*. New York: The Free Press.

22   For a more in depth discussion on service productivity, refer to Swank, C. K. (2003). The lean service machine. *Harvard Business Review*, 81(10), pp. 123–129.

23   Parasuraman, A., Zeithaml, V. A., & Berry, L. L. (1988). SERVQUAL: A multiple item scale for measuring consumer perceptions of service quality. *Journal of Retailing*, 64, pp. 12–40; Parasuraman, A., Zeithaml, V. A. & Malhotra, A. (2005). E-S-QUAL: A multiple-item scale for assessing electronic service quality. *Journal of Service Research*, 7(3), pp. 213–233; Wolfinbarger, M. F., & Gilly, M. C. (2003). eTailQ: Dimensionalizing, measuring, and

predicting etail quality. *Journal of Retailing*, 79(3), pp. 183–198; Collier, J. E., & Bienstock, C. C. (2006). Measuring service quality in e-retailing. *Journal of Service Research*, 8(3), (February), pp. 260–275.

24 See for example, Smith, A. M. (1995). Measuring service quality: Is SERVQUAL now redundant? *Journal of Marketing Management*, 11(Jan/Feb/April), pp. 257–276; Mels, G., Boshoff, C., & Nel, D. (1997). The dimensions of service quality: The original European perspective revisited. *The Service Industries Journal*, 17(January), pp. 173–189.

25 See for example, Mels, G., Boshoff, C., & Nel, D. (1997). The dimensions of service quality: The original European perspective revisited. *The Service Industries Journal*, 17(January), pp. 173–189.

26 Sureshchandar, G. S., Rajendran, C., & Anantharaman, R. N. (2001). A holistic model for total service quality. *International Journal of Service Industry Management*, 12(4), pp. 378–412.

27 Mele, C. (2007). The synergic relationship between TQM and marketing in creating customer value. *Managing Service Quality*, 17(3), pp. 240–258.

28 Mele, C., & Colurcio, M. (2006). The evolving path of TQM: Towards business excellence and stakeholder value. *International Journal of Quality and Reliability Management*, 23(5), pp. 464–489.

29 ISO (2001), The ISO survey of ISO 9000 and ISO14000 certificates (Eleventh cycle), International Organization for Standards, Geneva, 2001.

30 Goldstein, S. M., & Schweikhart, S. B. (2002). Empirical support for the Baldrige award framework in U.S. hospitals. *Health Care Management Review*, 27(1), pp. 62–75.

31 Shirks, A., Weeks, W. B., & Stein, A. (2002). Baldrige-based quality awards: Veterans health administration's 3-year experience. *Quality Management in Health Care*, 10(3), pp. 47–54; National Institute of Standards and Technology, "Baldrige FAQs," Available: http:www.nist.gov./public_affairs/factsheet/baldfaqs.htm. Accessed January 11, 2006.

32 Biolos, J. (2002). Six sigma meets the service economy. *Harvard Business Review*, (November), pp. 3–5.

33 Harry, M., & Schroeder, R. (2000). Six Sigma – *The Breakthrough Management Strategy Revolutionizing the World's Top Corporations* (p. 232). New York: Currency.

34 Pande, P. S., Neuman, R. P., & Cavanagh, R. R. (2000). *The Six Sigma Way: How GE, Motorola, and Other Top Companies Are Honing their Performance*. New York: McGraw-Hill .

35 Dick, G., Gallimore, K., & Brown, J. C. (2001). ISO9000 and quality emphasis: An empirical study of front-room and back room dominated service industries. *International Journal of Service Industry Management*, 12(2), pp. 114–136; & Hughes, A., & Halsall, D. N. (2002). Comparison of the 14 deadly diseases and the business excellence model. Total Quality Management, 13(2), pp. 255–263.

36 Enz, C. A., & Siguaw, J. A. (2000). Best practices in service quality. *Cornell Hotel and Restaurant Administration Quarterly*, (October), pp. 20–29.

37 Eight NIST stock investment study. USA: Gaithersburg, National Institute of Standards and Technology, March 2002.

BLANK

organizing for change management
and SERVICE
LEADERSHIP

LEARNING OBJECTIVES

By the end of this chapter, students should be able to:

▶ **LO 1** Understand the prescriptions of the service-profit chain for service management.

▶ **LO 2** Appreciate that the marketing, operations and human resource management functions in service organizations need to work closely together.

▶ **LO 3** Be familiar with the four levels of service performance and know how to move a firm to a level of higher performance.

▶ **LO 4** Explain what leadership involves.

▶ **LO 5** List the leadership qualities.

▶ **LO 6** Understand the role service leaders play in building success within their organizations.

▶ **LO 7** Understand the relationship between leadership, culture and climate.

OPENING VIGNETTE[1]

LEADERSHIP AND COMPANY CULTURE AT IKEA NORTH AMERICA

IKEA North America was listed in *Fortune* magazine's list of 100 Best Companies to work for in 2007. Who is leading the company? Pernille Spiers-Lopez, a native of Denmark, joined IKEA North America in 1990 as the marketplace manager for its West Coast stores. She worked her way up and became its President in 2001. Pernille Spiers-Lopez has certain personal values that have influenced the culture at IKEA North America.

Figure 15.1 IKEA has stamped its imprint on the world furnishings market.

IKEA has a strong culture of caring for its employees. This results from Ms. Spiers-Lopez's own personal values. She believes strongly that family should be the number one priority, and so tries to keep regular hours at work and avoid business travel on weekends. She also expects those employees who have families to make them a priority. Recognizing her caring for the family lives of her employees, Ms. Spiers-Lopez was given the Family Champion Award by *Working Mother*. Under her leadership, IKEA North America also provides benefits offered by few retail stores in the United States. For example, even part-timers who work 20 hours a week have full medical and dental insurance, which covers their partners and children.

What according to Ms. Spiers-Lopez are characteristics of effective leadership?

- Being authentic and not afraid to face mistakes and change one's mind.

- Trusting the people around, and being trusted.

- Self-examination and personal values.

...Among *Fortune's* 100 best **companies to work for, IKEA** preaches, and practises, a strong culture of care and concern for its employees...

Figure 15.2 IKEA offers vast benefits and opportunities for both customers and employees alike.

PART IV

EFFECTIVE MARKETING LIES AT THE HEART OF VALUE CREATION

Ms. Spiers-Lopez in our opening vignette showed a strong focus on the welfare of her employees. Yet other service leaders focus on customers. For example, consultants and authors Don Peppers and Martha Rogers stated that "Businesses succeed by getting, keeping, and growing customers,"[2] They elaborated:

> Investors today want executives to demonstrate that their companies can make money and grow, the old-fashioned way—by earning it from the value proposition they offer customers. They want a firm's customers to buy more, to buy more often, and to stay loyal longer. They want a firm to show that it can go out and get more customers.

What is the link between Spiers-Lopez's focus on employees and Peppers and Rogers' focus on customers? In fact, both are crucially important and success in one area rubs off on the other. This is clearly shown in the Service-Profit Chain model we will discuss next.

LO 1

Understand the prescriptions of the service profit chain for service management.

The Service-Profit Chain

James Heskett and his colleagues at Harvard argue that when service companies put employees and customers first, there is a big change in the way they manage and measure success. In their Service-Profit Chain model, they relate profitability, customer loyalty, and customer satisfaction to the value created by satisfied, loyal and productive employees (see Figure 15.3).[3]

Figure 15.3 The Service-Profit Chain.

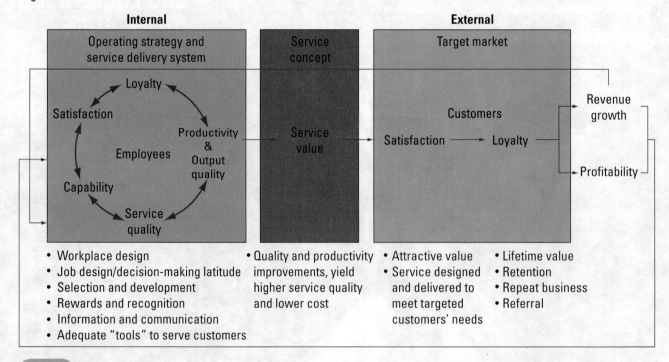

Table 15.1 Links in the Service-Profit Chain.

1. Customer loyalty drives profitability and growth
2. Customer satisfaction drives customer loyalty
3. Value drives customer satisfaction
4. Quality and productivity drive value
5. Employee loyalty drives service quality and productivity
6. Employee satisfaction drives employee loyalty
7. Internal quality drives employee satisfaction
8. Top management leadership underlies the chain's success

SOURCE

Heskett et al., J. L. (1994). Putting the service profit chain to work. *Harvard Business Review*, (March April); Heskett, J. L., Sasser, W. E., & Schlesinger, L. L. (1997). *The Service Profit Chain*, Boston: Harvard Business School Press.

Table 15.1 provides a useful summary of the links in the Service-Profit Chain. Working backwards from the goal of revenue growth and profitability, links 1 and 2 focus on customers. Firms need to identify and understand customer needs, and invest to make sure that customers stay with the firm (see Chapters 12 and 13). In addition, they should have new performance measures that keep track of satisfaction and loyalty among both customers and employees.[4] Link 3 focuses on the value for customers created by the service concept and the extended services marketing mix (Chapters 4 to 11). It also focuses on the need for investments to continually improve both service quality as well as productivity (Chapter 14).

Another set of service leadership behaviors (links 4–7) relate to employees and include organizational focus on the front line. The design of jobs should offer greater freedom for employees. Managers with potential should also be developed. This category also stressed the idea that paying higher wages actually decreases labor costs because of reduced turnover, higher productivity, and higher quality (Chapter 11). Underlying the chain's success (link 8) is top management leadership (as we will discuss later in the present chapter).

Getting the Service-Profit Chain Creates Shareholder Value

Firms that do it right will be rewarded by an increase in the value attached to the organization itself, which is shown in public companies by their stock price. As demonstrated by American Customer Satisfaction Index (ACSI) research, most service industries show a strong relationship between customer satisfaction and shareholder value (Figure 15.4).

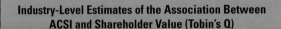

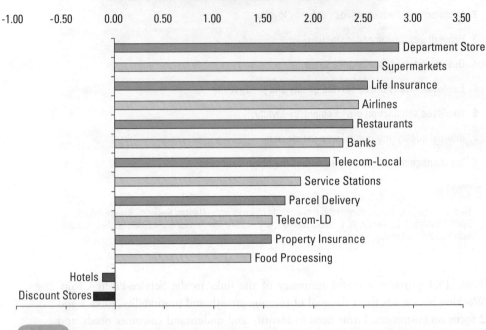

Figure 15.4 Customer satisfaction is closely linked to shareholder value in most service industries.

SOURCE

Claes Fornell et al., *The American Customer Satisfaction* Index at Ten Years. ACSI, 2005: 42 (service industry data extracted from larger table).

LO 2

Appreciate that the marketing, operations and human resource management functions in service organizations need to work closely together.

INTEGRATING MARKETING, OPERATIONS, AND HUMAN RESOURCES

The relationships in the Service Profit Chain show that in service firms, three management functions play very important and interrelated roles in meeting the needs of service customers: marketing, operations, and human resources (HR). Figure 15.5 shows how the departments depend on each other.

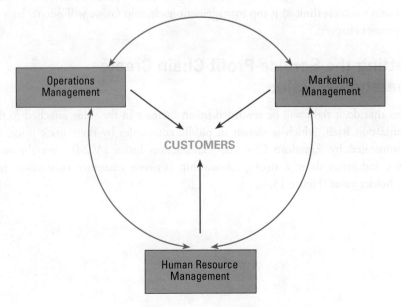

Figure 15.5 Marketing, operations and human resources functions must collaborate to serve the customer.

Service Leaders Have the Marketing, Operations and Human Resources Functions Tightly Integrated

An organization that is recognized as a service leader offers its customers superior value and quality. It has marketing strategies that beat the competition. It is seen as a leader in operations too. It is respected for very good operational processes and innovative use of technology. Finally, it is recognized as an outstanding place to work. It leads its industry in human resource management practices and has loyal, productive, and customer-oriented employees. Clearly, implementation of the Service Profit Chain requires a complete understanding of how marketing, operations, and human resources each relate to a company's strategy, and together contribute to creation of value. Finally, and perhaps most importantly, an effective leadership team with a clear vision of what it takes to succeed is needed to attain success.

How are Marketing, Operations and Human Resources Linked?

In what ways do the departments depend on each other? As we have seen, many service firms, especially those involving people-processing services, are actually "factories in the field." Customers enter whenever they need the service. When customers are actively involved in production and the service output is consumed as it is produced, the services marketing function depends on the procedures, personnel, and facilities managed by operations. In a high-contact service, the quality and commitment of the labor force have become a major source of competitive advantage. Service organizations cannot afford to have HR specialists who do not understand customers. When employees understand and support the goals of their organization, have the skills and training needed to succeed in their jobs, and recognize the importance of creating and maintaining customer satisfaction, both marketing and operations activities should be easier to manage.

Each of the three functions should have requirements and goals that relate to customers and also contribute to the mission of the firm. They can be expressed generally as follows:

▶ **The Marketing Function.** To target the types of customers whom the firm is able to serve and create ongoing relationships with them. This can be achieved by delivering a carefully defined service product package in return for a price that offers value to customers and profits to the firm. Customers will recognize this package as being one of quality that delivers solutions to their needs and is better than that offered by other competing firms (Figure 15.6).

Figure 15.6 UPS always aims to deliver value to suit the needs of their B2B customers.

▶ **The Operations Function.** To create and deliver the service package to targeted customers. This is done by selecting those operational techniques that allow the firm to continuously meet customer-driven cost, schedule, and quality goals. The techniques should also allow the business to reduce its costs through continuing improvements in productivity. The chosen operational methods will match skills that employees and intermediaries currently have, or can be trained to develop. The firm will have the resources to support these operations with the necessary facilities, equipment, and technology (Figure 15.7). At the same time, the firm will avoid negative impacts on employees and the broader community.

▶ **The Human Resources Function.** To recruit, train, and motivate front line employees, service delivery team leaders, and managers who can work well together for a satisfactory pay package. These employees have to balance the twin goals of customer satisfaction and operational effectiveness. Employees will want to stay with the firm and to improve their own skills because they value the working environment, appreciate the challenges they face, and take pride in the services they help to create and deliver.

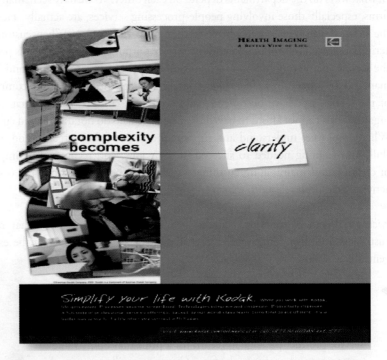

Figure 15.7 Kodak offers hospitals services that streamline processes, integrate technologies, and improve overall productivity.

Do We Need Additional Skill Sets Besides Marketing, Operations and Human Resources?

Services systems are becoming increasingly complex! Many services are crucially dependent on information technology and communications infrastructures (e.g. in global financial service firms), large and complex facilities (e.g. in integrated airport infrastructures), and complex process engineering (e.g. complex supply chains in B2B contexts), and so on. At a higher level, services is evolving into a science where is it necessary to have experts in their own fields who have knowledge that cuts across the different disciplines, such as information technology, engineering, and service management (see Service Insights 15.1).

CREATING A LEADING SERVICE ORGANIZATION

So far, we have discussed the service-profit chain which prescribes best practice management thinking about how to run a service firm, and the need for integration across functions and discipline to be able to create an effective service-profit chain for a service business. Let us next explore what it takes to move a firm from being a service loser to becoming a service leader.

⠿ SERVICE INSIGHTS 15.1

IBM's Service Science Initiative

Services contribute to more than 70 percent of the GDP in the economies of the developed world, and even in developing economies, the service sector is growing in importance. However, organizations have many functional departments, such as marketing, logistics and research that work independently, rather than jointly together. Even business schools train their graduates in specific disciplines such as accounting, finance, marketing, and operations management, but often lack the knowledge about how to integrate across functions. Furthermore, they tend to know even less about other important disciplines, such as on information technology or process engineering, that are also necessary for designing and managing complex service systems well.

IBM recognized this problem and has been leading the world in its new initiative on service science, which IBM termed Service Science, Management and Engineering (SSME). SSME combines knowledge in computer science, operations research, engineering, business strategy, management science, social and cognitive science and legal science, so that the necessary skills are being developed for the service economy. IBM has been mobilizing universities all over the world to collaborate with them.

Today, Service Science has become a part of the curriculum in many universities around the world. These universities focus on interdisciplinary research and teaching so that they are able to produce the 'T' graduates—those who not only have in-depth knowledge in one specialized area, but also have sufficient knowledge that cuts across several disciplines so that experts from these various disciplines can work together well.

Service science is an approach to enable us to study, design and manage effective service systems that create value for our customers. Companies that recognize this will hire graduates with the necessary knowledge and skills in service science so that they can have an edge in the competitive service economy. By studying services marketing, you have made a first step toward becoming familiar with service science, but you need to be aware that all these other disciplines are also important and you should work on picking up the key concepts in those other fields too!

SOURCE

"Are We Ready for 'SERVICE'?" *ThinkTank*, 10 October 2005, Available: www.research.ibm.com/ssme/20051010_services. shtml, Accessed April 2008; Davis, M. M., & Berdrow, I. (2008). Service science: Catalyst for change in business school curricula. *IBM Systems Journal*, 47(1), pp. 29–39;. Larson, R. C. (2008). Service science: At the intersection of management, social, and engineering sciences. *IBM Systems Journal*, 47(1), pp. 41–51.

LO 3

Be familiar with the four levels of service performance and know how to move a firm to a level of higher performance.

From Losers to Leaders: Four Levels of Service Performance

Service leadership is not based on excellent performance in one single area, but across a few areas. To capture this performance spectrum, we need to judge the firm within each of the three functional areas described earlier—marketing, operations, and human resources. Table 15.2 changes and extends an operations-oriented framework proposed by Richard Chase and Robert Hayes.[5] Service performers are grouped into four levels: loser, nonentity, professional, and leader. At each level, there is a short description of a typical firm across twelve aspects.

Table 15.2 Four levels of service performance level.

Level	1. Loser	2. Nonentity
Marketing Function		
Role of marketing	Tactical role only; advertising and promotions lack focus; no involvement in product or pricing decision	Uses mix of selling and mass communication, using simple segmentation strategy; makes selective use of price discounts and promotions; conducts and tabulates basic satisfaction surveys
Competitive appeal	Customers patronize firm for reasons other than performance	Customers neither seek nor avoid the firm
Customer profile	Unspecified; a mass market to be served at a minimum cost	One or more segments whose basic needs are understood
Service quality	Highly variable, usually unsatisfactory. Subservient to operations priorities	Meets some customer expectations; consistent on one or two key dimensions, but not all
Operations Function		
Role of operations	Reactive; cost oriented	The principal line management function: creates and delivers product, focuses on standardization as key to productivity, defines quality from internal perspective
Service delivery (front-stage)	A necessary evil. Locations and schedules are unrelated to preferences of customers, who are routinely ignored	Sticklers for tradition; "If it ain't broke, don't fix it"; tight rules for customers; each step in delivery run independently
Backstage operations	Divorced from front-stage; cogs in a machine	Contributes to individual front-stage delivery steps but organized separately; unfamiliar with customers
Productivity	Undefined; managers are punished for failing to stick within budget	Based on standardization; rewarded for keeping costs below budget
Introduction of new technology	Late adopter, under duress, when necessary for survival	Follows the crowd when justified by cost savings
Human Resources Function		
Role of human resources	Supplies low-cost employees who meet minimum skill requirements for the job	Recruits and trains employees who can perform competently
Workforce	Negative constraint: poor performers, do not care, disloyal	Adequate resource, follows procedures but uninspired; turnover often high
Frontline management	Controls workers	Controls the process

3. Professional	4. Leader
Marketing Function	
Has clear positioning strategy against competition; uses focused communications with distinctive appeals to clarify promises and educate customers; pricing is based on value; monitors customer usage and operates loyalty programs; uses a variety of research techniques to measure customer satisfaction and obtain ideas for service enhancements; works with operations to introduce new delivery systems	Innovative leader in chosen segments, known for marketing skills; brands at product/process level; conducts sophisticated analysis of relational databases as inputs to one-to-one marketing and proactive account management; uses state-of-the art research techniques; uses concept testing, observation, and use of lead customers as inputs to new-product development; close to operations/HR
Customers seek out the firm, based on its sustained reputation for meeting customer expectations	Company's name is synonymous with service excellence; its ability to delight customers raises expectations to levels that competitors can't meet
Groups of individuals whose variation in needs and value to the firm are clearly understood	Individuals are selected and retained based on their future value to the firm, including their potential for new service opportunities and their ability to stimulate innovation.
Consistently meets or exceeds customer expectations across multiple dimensions	Raises customer expectations to new levels; improves continuously
Operations Function	
Plays a strategic role in competitive strategy; recognizes trade off between productivity and customer-defined quality; willing to outsource; monitors competing operations for ideas, threats	Recognized for innovation, focus, and excellence; an equal partner with marketing and HR management; has in-house research capability and academic contacts; continually experimenting
Driven by customer satisfaction, not tradition; willing to customize, embrace new approaches; emphasis on speed, convenience, and comfort	Delivery is a seamless process organized around the customer; employees know whom they are serving; focuses on continuous improvement
Process is explicitly linked to front-stage activities; sees role as serving "internal customers," who in turn serve external customers	Closely integrated with front-stage delivery, even when geographically far apart; understands how own role relates to overall process of serving external customers; continuing dialog
Focuses on reengineering backstage processes; avoids productivity improvements that will degrade customers' service experience; continually refining processes for efficiency	Understands concept of return on quality; actively seeks customer involvement in productivity improvement; ongoing testing of new processes and technologies
An early adopter when IT promises to enhance service for customers and provide a competitive edge	Works with technology leaders to develop new applications that create first-mover advantage; seeks to perform at levels competitors cannot match
Human Resources Function	
Invests in selective recruiting, ongoing training; keeps close to employees, promotes upward mobility; strives to enhance quality of working life	Sees quality of employees as strategic advantage; firm is recognized as outstanding place to work; HR helps top management to nurture culture
Motivated, hard working, allowed some discretion in choice of procedures, offers suggestions	Innovative and empowered; very loyal, committed to firm's values and goals; creates procedures
Listens to customers; coaches and facilitates workers	Source of new ideas for top management; mentors, workers to enhance career growth, value to firm

PART IV

Under the marketing function, we look at the role of marketing, competitive appeal, customer profile, and service quality. Under the operations function, we look at the part of operations, service delivery (front stage), backstage operations, productivity, and introduction of new technology. Finally, under the human resources function, we examine the role of HRM, the workforce, and frontline management. The goal is to get some idea of what needs to be changed in firms that are not performing as well as they might.

Service Losers

These firms are at the bottom. They fail in marketing, operations, and human resource management alike. Customers buy from them because there is usually no other choice. This is a reason why losers continue to survive. New technology is only introduced under pressure, and the uncaring workforce has a negative impact on performance. The cycle of failure presented earlier in (Figure 11.6 p. 282), describes how such organizations behave in relation to employees and what the consequences are for customers.

Service Nonentities

Although there is still a lot of room for improvement, nonentities get rid of the worst features of losers. As shown in Table 15.2, nonentities have a traditional operations mindset where cost savings can be obtained through standardization. Their marketing strategies are simple. The roles of human resources and operations can be summarized respectively, by the ideals "adequate is good enough" and "if it ain't broke, why fix it." Consumers neither seek nor avoid such organizations. Managers may talk about improving quality and other goals, but are unable to set clear priorities, to have a clear direction, nor gain the respect and commitment of their employees (Figure 15.8). A few firms may compete in this way and you will find it difficult to tell one from the other. They may use price discounts to try to attract new customers. The cycle of mediocrity (Figure 11.8 p. 283),— shows the human resources environment of many such firms and its consequences for customers.

© 2002 Randy Glasbergen.
www.glasbergen.com

"Pardon me! If I suck the enthusiasm out of a new employee too quickly, I get gas!"

Figure 15.8 Having good managerial-employee dynamics is no laughing matter.

Service Professionals

These organizations have a clear market positioning strategy. Customers within the target segments look for these firms based on their reputation for meeting expectations. Marketing uses targeted communications, and pricing is based on value to the customer. There is research to measure customer satisfaction and obtain ideas for service improvement. Operations and marketing work together to introduce new delivery systems. They also recognize the trade off between productivity and customer-defined quality. There are clear links between backstage and front stage activities. There is investment in human resource management. *The Cycle of Success* (Figure 11.9, p. 283) shows the HR strategies that lead to a high level of performance by most employees of firms in the service professionals category. They have a positive impact on customer satisfaction and loyalty.

Service Leaders

These organizations are the best in their respective industries. Service professionals are good, but service leaders are outstanding. When we think of service leaders, we think of Starbucks, Ritz Carlton and Southwest Airlines. Their company names are linked to service excellence and an ability to delight customers. Service leaders are innovative in each functional area of management, and also have excellent internal communications and coordination among the three functions. This is made possible through a relatively flat organizational structure and use of teams to a great extent.

Marketing efforts by service leaders make use of CRM systems that offer insights about customers on an one-to-one basis. Concept testing, observation, and contacts with lead customers are used in the development of new, breakthrough services that respond to previously unrecognized needs. Operations specialists work with technology leaders around the world to develop new applications that will create a first mover advantage. As a result the firm can perform at levels that competitors cannot hope to reach for a long period of time. Internally, there are clear standards and standardized processes that employees can follow, and this facilitates the work of employees.[6] Senior executives see quality of their employees as an important competitive advantage. HRM works with them to develop and maintain a service-oriented culture and to create an outstanding working environment that attracts and retains the best people. The employees themselves are committed to the firm's values and goals. Because they are involved, empowered and quick to take on change, they are a continuous source of new ideas. (Figure 15.9)

Figure 15.9 Good HRM produces engaged and encouraged employees that serve the company cause better.

Moving to a Higher Level of Performance

Firms can move up or down the performance ladder. Organizations that focus on satisfying their current customers may miss important changes in the marketplace and find themselves turning into has-beens. These businesses may continue to serve a loyal but decreasing group of customers, but are unable to attract new consumers with different expectations. Companies whose original success was based on a specific technological processes may find that competitors have managed to find higher-performing alternatives. Organizations whose management has worked for years to build up a loyal workforce with a strong service ethic may find that such a culture can be quickly destroyed as a result of a merger or acquisition that brings in new leaders with different focus or who emphasize short-term profits.

In most markets, we find companies that are moving up the performance ladder. They put in effort to coordinate their marketing, operations, and human resource management functions in order to gain better competitive positions and better satisfy their customers.

LO 4

Explain what leadership involves.

IN SEARCH OF HUMAN LEADERSHIP

So far, we have discussed how we can move a firm from being a service loser to becoming a service leader. However, it still requires human leaders to take them in the right direction, set the strategic goals, and make sure that suitable strategies are implemented throughout the organization. We will discuss in the following sections "what is leadership?," "what are leadership qualities?," and "the role leaders have in shaping a culture and climate for service excellence."

Leadership versus Management

Leadership relates to the development of vision and strategies, and giving people the freedom and flexibility to overcome obstacles and make the vision happen. *Management*, on the other hand, involves keeping the current situation going through planning, budgeting, organizing, staffing, controlling, and problem solving. Says Kotter:

> Leadership works through people and culture. It's soft and hot. Management works through hierarchy and systems. Its harder and cooler…The fundamental purpose of management is to keep the current system functioning. The fundamental purpose of leadership is to produce useful change, especially non-incremental change. It's possible to have too much or too little of either. Strong leadership with no management risks chaos; the organization might walk right off a cliff. Strong management with no leadership tends to entrench an organization in deadly bureaucracy.[7]

However, leadership is a necessary and growing part of managerial work because the rate of change has been increasing (Figure 15.10). Kotter declares that effective top executives may now spend up to 80 percent of their time leading; double the figure required not that long ago. Even lower level management staff may spend at least 20 percent of their time on leadership.

Figure 15.10 A company culture can be dynamic when leadership and management skills work in hand-in-glove.

Setting Direction versus Planning

People often confuse these two activities. Planning, according to Kotter, is a management process, designed to produce orderly results, not change. To set direction, leaders look for patterns and relationships that help to explain things and suggest future trends. Direction setting creates visions and strategies. These describe a business, technology, or corporate culture in terms of what it should become over the long term. Planning follows and works together with direction setting. It serves as a useful reality check and a road map for strategic execution. A good plan shows how the mission can be achieved using existing resources or identifying possible new sources.

Many of the best visions and strategies are not extraordinarily innovative. They actually combine some basic understanding and use that to come up with a realistic competitive strategy that serves the interests of customers, employees, and stockholders. Some visions, however, fall into the category that Gary Hamel and C. K. Pralahad describe as "stretch." This means that it is a challenge to achieve new levels of performance and competitive advantage that might, at first sight, seem to be out of the organization's reach.[8] Stretching to achieve such goals requires reexamining the traditional ways of doing business, and maximizing existing resources through partnerships. (see Service Insights 15.2)**.** It also requires creating the energy and the will among managers and employees alike to perform at higher levels than they believe themselves to be able to do.

Can **Cirque Du Soleil** Stretch Further?

Who would have believed in the mid-1980s that Le Club des Talons Hauts (The High Heels Club), a small group of French-speaking street performers who walked on stilts and lived in a youth hostel near Quebec City, Canada, would one day become the world-famous Cirque du Soleil? With its unique mix of music, dance, and acrobatics, but no animals, the Cirque du Soleil (Circus of the Sun) has created a new category of live entertainment attended by millions around the world. "People said we reinvented the circus-we didn't reinvent the circus," declares president Guy Laliberté:

> We repackaged a way of presenting the circus show in a much more modern way…We took an art form that was known, that had a lot of dust on it, where people had forgotten it could be something other than what they knew, and we organized for ourselves a new creative platform.

To achieve its present fame, featuring six touring shows and six permanent shows with partnering resorts—five with Las Vegas casino hotels and one at Walt DisneyWorld resort in Florida—the Cirque has had to face and resolve financial, managerial, and artistic problems. For the well-paid performers, who include many former Olympic athletes, the idea of stretch (both physically and in the psychological sense) is very important to their professional lives. "Creative people always need new challenges," says COO Daniel Lamarre.

Cirque du Soleil faces new competitors today, including two that have emerged from its home-turf. Cirque Éloize and Cirque Éos were both started by the growing supply of graduates from two recently formed circus schools in Quebec. Cirque copycats can also be found in France and Argentina. An even greater challenge comes from the US Company, Feld Enterprises that owns the famous Ringling Bros. and Barnum & Bailey Circus. Feld has created a new production called Barnum's Kaleidoscope. This production replaces the traditional circus performers with a mix of acrobatic performers and live music at much higher admission prices.

Cirque du Soleil has grown in recent years by adding new shows with new partner resorts. In 2006, it launched *Love*, a show based on the music of the Beatles, making the Mirage casino its fifth partner in Las Vegas. But an important question for Cirque is: Where will future growth come from as its core market becomes more crowded? New competition is pushing up the cost of finding and keeping top performers. It is unclear how much longer the privately-held Canadian company can continue filling 1000-seat theaters at high admission prices with just slight changes on the same product. Continued development will be needed.

Figure 15.11 Cirque du Soleil's blend of circus and theater has captivated a contemporary audience.

SOURCE

David, R. J., & Motamedi, A. (2004). Cirque du soleil: Can it burn brighter? *Journal of Strategic Management Education*, 1(2), pp. 369–382; Available: www.cirquedusoleil.com, Accessed on June 2008.

Individual Leadership Qualities

⊙ **LO 5**
List the leadership qualities.

The topic of leadership has been widely written on. It has even been described as a service in itself.[9] There are many definitions of leadership. The various definitions contain three common elements: 1) it involves a group. Leadership cannot exist without the cooperation of the employees; 2) it is goal-directed. Leaders influence their followers toward the achievement of certain goals and visions. 3) there is some hierarchy in the group. Sometimes, the hierarchy is one where the leader is clearly at the top while at other time, it is informal.[10] The late Sam Walton, founder of the Wal-Mart retail chain, saw managers as "servant leaders."[11] The following are some qualities that effective leaders in a service organization should have:

▶ Love for the business. Excitement about the business will encourage individuals to teach the business to others and to pass on to them the art and secrets of operating it.

▶ Service leaders need to see service quality as the foundation for competing.[12]

▶ Recognizing the key part played by employees in delivering service, service leaders need to believe in the people who work for them and pay special attention to communicating with employees.

▶ Many outstanding leaders are driven by a set of core values which they pass on in the organization.[13] For example, in the opening vignette, Pernille Spiers-Lopez is a lady who puts her family as top priority. This is also the culture at IKEA, North America, where there is a strong stress on work-life balance.

▶ Effective leaders have a talent for communicating with others in a way that is easy to understand. They know their audiences and are able to communicate even complicated ideas in just a few phrases.[14] Effective communication is probably a leader's most important skill to inspire an organization to create success.

▶ Effective leaders are able to ask great questions and get answers from the team, rather than just rely on themselves to dominate the decision-making process.[15]

▶ Effective leaders need to know the purpose of the existence of the company, and to be able to formulate and implement strategy, watching over it daily and living with it over time.[16] The best CEO is able to reset their goals and will not stick to a decision that was right for yesterday, but not for tomorrow (Figure 15.12).[17]

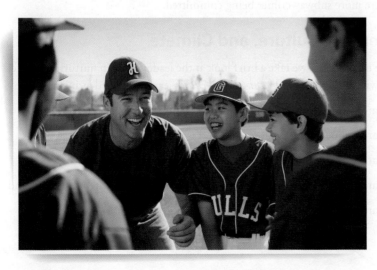

Figure 15.12 When leaders can effectively communicate a clear and exciting vision for the future, people listen, and follow attentively.

PART IV

In organizations with many levels of management, it is often assumed that leadership at the top is enough. However, as Sandra Vandermerwe points out, forward-looking service businesses need to be more flexible. Today's greater focus on using teams within service businesses means that

> [L]eaders are everywhere, disseminated throughout the teams. They are found especially in the customer facing and interfacing jobs in order that decision-making will lead to long-lasting relationships with customers…leaders are customer and project champions who energize the group by virtue of their enthusiasm, interest, and know-how.[18]

▶ **LO 6**

Understand the role service leaders play in building success within their organizations.

Role Modeling Desired Behavior

One of the qualities of successful leaders is that they are able to display the behavior that they expect of managers and other employees. In other words, they act as role models. Often, this requires "management by walking around," popularized by Thomas Peters and Robert Waterman in their book *In Search of Excellence.*[19] Walking around involves regular visits, sometimes unannounced, to various areas of the company's operation. This provides understanding of both backstage and front-stage operations, the ability to observe and meet both employees and customers, and an opportunity to see how corporate strategy is carried out at the front line. Sometimes, this may lead to the discovery that changes are needed in that strategy. It is very encouraging for service personnel to meet the CEO on such a visit. It also provides an opportunity for role modeling. Service Insights 15.3 describes how the CEO of a major hospital learned the power of role modeling early in his service there.

Chan Kim and Renée Mauborgne, both professors at INSEAD, highlight the work of William Bratton, who became famous during a 20-year police career in Boston and New York. Bratton believed in putting his key managers face-to-face with the problems that were of greatest concern to the public. When he became chief of the New York Transit Police, Bratton found that none of the senior staff officers used the subway. So he required all transit police officials, including himself, to ride the subway to work and to meetings, even at night, instead of traveling in cars provided by the city. In that way, senior officials experienced the reality of the problems faced by millions of ordinary citizens and by police officers who strove to keep order.[20] His managers were able to deploy their police officers more effectively, to areas where there were more subway crimes being committed.

▶ **LO 7**

Understand the relationship between leadership, culture and climate.

Leadership, Culture, and Climate

To close this chapter, we take a brief look at the leader's role in nurturing an effective culture within the firm.[21] *Organizational culture* can be defined as including:

▶ Shared understanding regarding what is important in the organization

▶ Shared values about what is right and wrong,

▶ Shared understanding about what works and what does not work,

▶ Shared beliefs, and assumptions about *why* these things are important, and

▶ Shared styles of working and relating to others.

A Hospital President Learns the **Power** of **Role Modeling**

During his 30-year service as president of Boston's Beth Israel Hospital (now Beth Israel-Deaconess Medical Center), Mitchell T. Rabkin, MD, was known for regularly spending time making visits to all parts of the hospital. "You learn a lot from 'management by walking around'," he said. "And you're also seen. When I visit another hospital and am given a tour by its CEO, I watch how that CEO interacts with other people, and what the body language is in each instance. It's very revealing. Even more, it's very important for role modeling." To stress that point, Dr Rabkin liked to tell the following story against him.

People learn to *do* as a result of the way they see you and others *behave*. An example from the Beth Israel that's now almost apocryphal–but *is* true–is the story of the bits of litter on the floor.

One of our trustees, the late Max Feldberg, head of the Zayre Corporation, asked me one time to take a walk around the hospital with him and inquired, "Why do you think there are so many pieces of paper scattered on the floor of this patient care unit?"

"Well, it's because people don't pick them up," I replied.

He said, "Look, you're a scientist. We'll do an experiment. We'll walk down this floor and we'll pick up every other piece of paper. And then we'll go upstairs, there's another unit, same geography, statistically the same amount of paper, but we won't pick up anything."

So this 72-year-old man and I went picking up alternate bits of the litter on one floor and nothing on the other. When we came back 10 min later, virtually all the rest of the litter on the first floor had been removed and nothing, of course, had changed on the second.

And "Mr. Max" said to me, "You see, it's not because *people* don't pick them up, it's because *you* don't pick them up. If you're so fancy that you can't bend down and pick up a piece of paper, why should anybody else?"

SOURCE

Lovelock, C. (1994). *Product Plus: How Product + Service = Competitive Advantage*. New York: McGraw-Hill,.

Changing an organization to develop a new culture along each of these five aspects is not easy even for the most gifted leader. Some organizations are run by independent-minded professionals from different fields. These professionals are more concerned about how they are viewed by fellow professionals in the same field in other institutions. This situation is found not only in professional firms but also in colleges and universities, major hospitals, and large museums.

Organizational climate is the surface layer on top of the organization's culture that can be felt and seen. Among six key factors that influence an organization's working environment are its *flexibility* (how free employees feel to innovate); their sense of *responsibility* to the organization; the level of *standards* that people set; the perceived suitability of *rewards*; the *clarity* people have about mission and values; and the level of *commitment* to a common purpose.[22] Once the values of the organization are part of the hearts and minds of its employees, they can work independently and yet be collaborative as they are all thinking with the mission and goals.[23] From an employee perspective, this climate is directly related to managerial policies and procedures, especially those linked to human resource management. In short, climate represents the shared views of employees about the practices, procedures, and types of behaviors that get rewarded and supported in a particular setting.

PART IV

Many climates often exist at the same time within a single organization. A climate must relate to something specific—for instance, service, support, innovation, or safety. A climate for service refers to employee views of those practices, procedures, and behaviors that are expected with regard to customer service and service quality, and that get rewarded when performed well. A service-oriented culture includes clear marketing goals and a strong drive to be the best in delivering superior value or service quality[24] (Figure 15.13).

Leaders are responsible for creating cultures and the service climates that go along with them. Why are some leaders more effective than others in bringing about a desired change in climate? As presented in Service Insights 15.4, research suggests that it may be a matter of style.

Creating a new climate for service, based on an understanding of what is needed for market success, may require a complete rethink of human resource management activities, operational procedures, and the firm's reward and recognition policies. Newcomers to an organization must quickly familiarize themselves with the existing culture. Otherwise, they will find themselves being led by it rather than leading through it and, if necessary, changing it.

Figure 15.13 The Singapore Girl of Singapore Airlines in their iconic Sarong Kebaya enjoys a worldwide reputation for providing superior passenger service.

::::: SERVICE INSIGHTS 15.4 •

The Impact of **Leadership Styles** on **Climate**

Daniel Goleman, an applied psychologist at Rutgers University, identified six styles of leadership. He investigated how successful each style has proved to be in affecting climate or working atmosphere. This was based on a major study of the behavior and impact on their organizations on thousands of executives.

Coercive leaders demand immediate obedience ("Do what I tell you"). They were found to have a negative impact on climate. Goleman comments that this controlling style is useful only in a crisis or in dealing with problem employees. Pace setting leaders set high standards for performance. They are very energetic. This style can be summarized as "Do as I do, now." This style too, was found to have a negative impact on climate. In practice, the pace setting leader may destroy morale by assuming too much, too soon, of subordinates—expecting them to know already what to do and how to do it. When others turn out to be less capable than expected, the leader may start focusing on details and micromanaging. This style is likely to work only

when seeking to get quick results from a highly motivated and skilful and experienced team.

The research found that the most effective style for achieving a positive change in climate came from *authoritative leaders* who have the skills and personality to move people toward a vision. These leaders build confidence using a "Come with me" approach. The research also found that three other styles had quite positive impacts on climate: *affiliative leaders* who believe that "People come first," seeking to create harmony and build emotional bonds; *democratic leaders* who looked for agreement through participation ("What do you think?"); and *coaching leaders* who work to develop people for the future and whose style might be summarized as "Try this."

SOURCE

Goleman, D. (2007). Leadership that gets results. *Harvard Business Review*, 78, (March–April), pp. 78–93.

Leadership in the Future[25]

What are some aspects of leadership that will be different from what we are used to today? There are two main interlinked areas, which are collective genius and leadership from behind.

▶ Leaders may come from emerging countries with very different styles because they come from different cultures. For example, in Africa, leadership is often based on the principle of "I am because we are." In one successful Indian company, the employee is first, and the customer is second. It works on a model of distributed leadership, where leaders of various groups share leadership with the CEO.

▶ Traditionally, leaders set a course and inspired people to follow. In the future, because of business diversity and interdependence between various parties, the leadership style needs to be more collaborative, using a team approach to problem solving. In fact, there are many knowledgeable and talented people who will not follow if leaders lead from the position of authority. Instead, we have a process of collective genius.

▶ Leadership from behind is one where the leader is not afraid of sharing power with others. They need to create a context where people are willing to lead and different people can be leading at different points of time depending on their knowledge. Leadership then becomes a collective activity (Figure 15.14). If necessary, the leader who leads from behind can also lead from the front, like in moments of crisis.

▶ In future, innovation will be the way for companies to move forward in the competitive arena. This also calls for leading from behind as innovation is a creative process that requires taking advantage of the talents of a diverse group of people. This group of people will see that their collective efforts can yield results that are far superior than their individual efforts.

Figure 15.14 In the global commercial melting pot, innovative leadership can inspire a diverse team of talent into achieving far more than individual effort.

PART IV

CHAPTER SUMMARY

LO 1 ► The Service-Profit Chain shows that service leadership in an industry requires high performance in several related areas.

- o Customer relationships must be managed effectively and there must be strategies to build loyalty.

- o Value must be created and delivered to the target customers, in ways that lead them to see the offering as better than that of competitors.

- o There must be continuous improvement to service quality and productivity.

- o Employees must be enabled and motivated.

- o Top management's leadership need to drive and support all the components of the Service-Profit Chain.

LO 2 ► To implement the Service-Profit Chain, the marketing, operations, and human resource management functions need to work closely together in well-coordinated ways.

LO 3 ► Not all firms follow the Service-Profit Chain. Rather, there are four levels of service performance, and only the last two follow the Service-Profit Chain's principles. They are: (1) Losers, (2) Nonentities, (3) Professionals, and (4) Service Leaders:

- o Losers survive because customers have no choice but to buy from them.

- o Service nonentities are functioning in the cycle of mediocrity.

- o Service professionals function in the cycle of success, and

- o Service leaders are the best in their respective industries.

► We contrasted the description and actions of a service leader against professionals, nonentities and losers along the three functions of marketing, operations and human resources management.

► What does it take for a firm to move from being a service loser to becoming a service leader? It is the senior management, the human leaders who can communicate a vision and at the same time set the strategic goals, develop the strategies to achieve those goals, and then ensure the successful implementation of that strategy.

LO 4 ► There is a difference between leading and managing. Leadership is needed for the development of vision and strategies, while management keeps the current situation going. Leadership is a necessary and growing part of managerial work so both are necessary.

LO 5 ► The qualities leaders in service organizations should have include:

- o Love for the business.

- o The perspective that service quality is a key foundation for success.

- o A strong belief in the people who work for them, and recognize the importance of the frontline.

- o A set of core values they pass on to the organization.

- o Effective communication skills, which is probably a leader's most important skill to inspire an organization to create success.

- o Ability to ask great questions and get answers from the team.

- o Understand the purpose and existence of the company and reset their goals for change when needed.

LO 7 ► Leaders need to develop a strong organizational culture so that everyone:

- o Agrees to what is important to the company and why it is important.

- o Has shared values about what is right and wrong.

- o Has a shared understanding of what works and what does not, and

- o Has shared styles of working.

► Organizational climate is the surface layer on top of the culture. Organizational climate is related to the company's policies and procedures, especially those in human resources. To create a climate for service depends a lot on having the right human resource and reward policies in place.

► Leadership styles are likely to change with the changing business environment. In future, leadership may have to embrace two further key principles, that of collective genius and leadership from behind.

UNLOCK YOUR LEARNING

These keywords are found within the sections of each Learning Objective (LO). They are integral in understanding the services marketing concepts taught in each sector. Having a firm grasp of these keywords and how they are used is essential in helping you do well for your course, and in the real and very competitive marketing scene out there.

LO 1
1. American Customer Satisfaction Index (ACSI)
2. Service leadership
3. Service-profit chain

LO 2
4. Human resources
5. Human resources function
6. Marketing
7. Marketing function
8. Operations
9. Operations function
10. Service science
11. SSME

LO 3
12. Performance ladder
13. Service leaders
14. Service leadership
15. Service losers
16. Service nonentities

17. Service professionals

LO 4
18. Direction setting leadership
19. Management
20. Planning

LO 5
21. Effective leaders
22. Leadership qualities

LO 6
23. Management by walking around
24. Role modeling

LO 7
25. Affiliative leaders
26. Authoritative leaders
27. Clarity
28. Coaching leaders
29. Coercive leaders
30. Commitment
31. Collective genius

32. Democratic leaders
33. Flexibility
34. Leadership from behind
35. Organizational culture
36. Organizational climate
37. Pacesetting leaders
38. Responsibility
39. Rewards
40. Standards
41. Service-oriented culture

How well do you know the language of services marketing? Quiz yourself!

 Not for the academically faint-of-heart

For each keyword you are able to recall without referring to earlier pages, give yourself a point (and a pat on the back). Tally your score at the end and see if you earned the right to be called—a *services marketeer.*

SCORE

0 – 6	Services Marketing is done a great disservice.
7 – 13	The midnight oil needs to be lit, pronto.
14 – 21	I know what you *didn't* do all semester.
22 – 28	By George! You're getting there.
29 – 36	Now, go forth and market.
39 – 41	There should be a marketing concept named after you.

Review Questions

1. What are the implications of the Service-Profit Chain for service management?

2. Why do the marketing, operations, and human resource management functions need to be closely coordinated in service businesses?

3. What are the causes of tension among the marketing, operations, and human resource functions? Provide specific examples of how these tensions might vary from one service industry to another.

4. How are the four levels of service performance defined? Based on your own service experiences, provide an example of a company for each category

5. What is the difference between leadership and management? Explain with examples.

6. Why is role modeling a desirable quality in leaders?

7. What is the relationship among leadership, climate and culture?

▌ WORK YOUR ESM ▐

Application Exercises

1. Analyze a service firm along the key aspects of the Service-Profit Chain. Assess how well the firm is performing at the various components of the Service-Profit Chain, and make specific suggestions for improvements.

2. Contrast the roles of marketing, operations, and human resources in (1) a gas station chain, (2) a web-based brokerage firm, and (3) an insurance company.

3. Select a company you believe would belong to the loser or nonentity category. Use the dimensions described in Table 15.2 and make recommendations how the firm could move up the performance ladder.

4. What is the role of senior management in moving a firm toward consistently delivering service excellence?

5. Profile a person whose leadership skills have played an important part in the success of a service organization. Identify personal characteristics that you consider important.

6. What are in your opinion the key drivers of success for service firms? Try and develop a causal model that explains the important drivers of success for a service firm.

ENDNOTES

1   *Fortune*, "100 Best Companies to Work for 2007," http://money.cnn.com/magazines/fortune/bestcompanies/2007/, accessed 2 June 2008; Knowledge@Wharton, "IKEA: Furnishing Good Employee Benefits Along with Dining Room Sets," http://knowledge.wharton.upenn.edu/article.cfm?articleid=959, Accessed 2 June 2008; Wang, J. (2006) "Learning from the best: Speaker profiles for August 8 women's leadership exchange conference," *Long Beach Business Journal*, (July), pp. 3–4.

2   Peppers, D., & Rogers, M. (2005). *Return on Customer* (p. 1). New York: Currency Doubleday.

3   Heskett., J. L., Jones, T. O., Loveman, G. W., Sasser, W. E., Jr., & Schlesinger, L. A. (1994). Putting the service profit chain to work. *Harvard Business Review*, (March/April); Heskett, J. L., Sasser, W. E., Jr., & Schlesinger, L. A. (1997). *The Service Profit Chain*. New York: The Free Press.

4   Note that a relationship between employee satisfaction and customer satisfaction may be more likely in high-contact situations where employee behaviour is an important aspect of the customers' experience. See Silvestro, R., & Cross, S. (2000). Applying the service-profit chain in a retail environment: Challenging the satisfaction mirror. *International Journal of Service Industry Management*, 11(3), pp. 244–268

5   Chase, R. B., & Hayes, R. H. (1991). Beefing up operations in service firms. *Sloan Management Review*, (Fall), pp. 15–26.

6   Kanter, R. M. (2008). Transforming giants. *Harvard Business Review*, (January), pp. 43–52.

7   Kotter, J. P. (1999). *What Leaders Really D* (pp. 10–11). Boston: Harvard Business School Press.

8   Hamel, G., & Prahlahad, C. K. (1994). *Competing for the Future*. Boston: Harvard Business School Press.

9   See for instance, the special issue on Leadership as a service. (Celeste Wilderom, guest editor), *International Journal of Service Industry Management, Vol. 3, No. 2, 1992*.

10 Nahavandi, A. (2006). *The Art and Science of Leadership* (p. 4). New Jersey: Pearson Education Inc.

11 Heskett, J. L., Sasser, W. E., Jr., & Schlesinger, L. A. *The Service Profit Chain* (p. 236)

12 Berry, L. L. (1995). *On Great Service* (p. 9). New York: The Free Press.

13 Berry, L. L. (1999). *Discovering the Soul of Service* (pp. 44, 47). New York: The Free Press; Abrashoff, D. M. (2001). Retention through redemption. *Harvard Business Review*, (February), pp. 136–141, which provides a fascinating example on successful leadership in the U.S. Navy.

14 Blagg, D., & Young, S. (2001). What makes a leader? *Harvard Business School Bulletin*, (February), pp. 31–36.

15 Hamm, J. (2006). The five messages leaders must manage. *Harvard Business Review*, (May), pp. 115–123.

16 Montgomery, C. A. (2008). Putting leadership back into strategy. *Harvard Business Review*, (January), pp. 54–60.

17 Nadler, D. A. (2007). The CEO's 2nd act. *Harvard Business Review*, (January), pp. 66–72.

18 Vandermerwe, S. (1993). *From Tin Soldiers to Russian Dolls*, Oxford, UK: Butterworth-Heinemann, p. 129.

19 Peters, T. J. & Waterman, R. H. (1982). *In Search of Excellence* (p. 122). New York: Harper & Row.

20 Kim, W. C., & Mauborgne, R. (2003). Tipping point leadership. *Harvard Business Review*, 81(April), pp. 61–69.

21 This section is based, in part, on Schneider, B., & Bowen, D. E. (1995). Winning the Service Game. Boston: Harvard Business School Press; & Bowen, D. E., Schneider, B., & Kim, S. S. (2000). Shaping service cultures through strategic human resource management. In T. Schwartz, & D. Iacobucci. (Eds.). *Handbook of Services Marketing and Management* (pp. 439–454). Thousand Oaks, CA: Sage Publications.

22 Goleman, D. (2000). Leadership that gets results. *Harvard Business Review*, 78(March–April), pp. 78–93.

23 Kanter, R. M. (2008). Transforming giants. *Harvard Business Review*, (January), pp. 43–52

24 Kasper, H. (2002). Culture and leadership in market-oriented service organizations. *European Journal of Marketing*, 36(9/10), pp. 1047–1057.

25 Hill, L. A. (2008). Where will we find tomorrow's leaders? *Harvard Business Review*, (January), pp. 123–129.

Sullivan Ford Auto World[1]

Christopher Lovelock

A young health care manager unexpectedly finds herself running a family-owned car dealership that is in financial trouble. She is very concerned about the poor performance of the service department and wonders whether a turnaround is possible.

Viewed from Wilson Avenue, the Sullivan Ford Auto World dealership presented a festive sight. Flags waved and strings of triangular pennants in red, white, and blue fluttered gaily in the late afternoon breeze. Rows of new model cars and trucks gleamed and winked in the sunlight. Geraniums graced the flowerbeds outside the showroom entrance. A huge rotating sign at the corner of Wilson Avenue and Route 78 sported the Ford logo and identified the business as Sullivan Ford Auto World. Banners below urged "Let's Make a Deal!"

Inside the handsome, high-ceilinged showroom, four of the new model Fords were on display—a dark-green Explorer SUV, a red Mustang convertible, a white Focus sedan, and a red Ranger pickup truck. Each vehicle was polished to a high sheen. Two groups of customers were chatting with salespeople, and a middle-aged man sat in the driver's seat of the Mustang, studying the controls.

Upstairs in the comfortably furnished general manager's office, Carol Sullivan-Diaz finished running another spreadsheet analysis on her laptop. She felt tired and depressed. Her father, Walter Sullivan, had died four weeks earlier at the age of 56 of a sudden heart attack. As executor of his estate, the bank had asked her to temporarily assume the position of general manager of the dealership. The only visible change that she had made to her father's office was installing an all-in-one laser printer, scanner, copier, and fax, but she had been very busy analyzing the current position of the business.

Sullivan-Diaz did not like the look of the numbers on the printout. Auto World's financial situation had been deteriorating for 18 months, and it had been running in the red for the first half of the current year. New car sales had declined, dampened in part by rising interest rates. Margins had been squeezed by promotions and other efforts to move new cars off the lot. Reflecting rising fuel prices, industry forecasts of future sales were discouraging, and so

were her own financial projections for Auto World's sales department. Service revenues, which were below average for a dealership of this size, had also declined, although the service department still made a small surplus.

Had she had made a mistake last week, Carol wondered, in turning down Bill Froelich's offer to buy the business? Admittedly, the amount was substantially below the offer from Froelich that her father had rejected two years earlier, but the business had been more profitable then.

THE SULLIVAN FAMILY

Walter Sullivan had purchased a small Ford dealership in 1983, renaming it Sullivan's Auto World, and had built it up to become one of the best known in the metropolitan area. In 1999, he had borrowed heavily to purchase the current site at a major suburban highway intersection, in an area of the city with many new housing developments.

There had been a dealership on the site, but the buildings were 30 years old. Sullivan had retained the service and repair bays, but torn down the showroom in front of them, and replaced it with an attractive modern facility. On moving to the new location, which was substantially larger than the old one, he renamed his business Sullivan Ford Auto World.

Everybody had seemed to know Walt Sullivan. He had been a consummate showman and entrepreneur, appearing in his own radio and television commercials and was active in community affairs. His approach to car sales had emphasized promotions, discounts, and deals in order to maintain volume. He was never happier than when making a sale.

Carol Sullivan-Diaz, aged 28, was the eldest of Walter and Carmen Sullivan's three daughters. After obtaining a bachelor's degree in economics, she had gone on to take an MBA degree and had then embarked on a career in health care management. She was married to Dr. Roberto Diaz, a surgeon at St. Luke's Hospital. Her 20-year old twin sisters, Gail and Joanne, who were students at the state university, lived with their mother.

In her own student days, Sullivan-Diaz had worked part-time in her father's business on secretarial and bookkeeping tasks, and also as a service writer in the service department, so she was quite familiar with the operations of the dealership. At business school, she had decided on a career in health care management. After graduation, she had worked as an executive assistant to the president of St. Luke's, a large teaching hospital. Two years later, she joined Heritage Hospitals, a large multi-hospital facility that also provided long-term care, as assistant director of marketing, a position she had now held for almost three years. Her responsibilities included designing new services, complaint handling, market research, and introducing an innovative day care program for hospital employees and neighbourhood residents.

Carol's employer had given her a six-week leave of absence to put her father's affairs in order. She doubted that she could extend that leave much beyond the two weeks still remaining. Neither she nor other family members were interested in making a career of running the dealership. However, she was prepared to take time out from her health care career to work on a turnaround if that seemed a viable proposition. She had been successful in her present job and believed it would not be difficult to find another health management position in the future.

THE DEALERSHIP

Like other car dealerships, Sullivan Ford Auto World operated both sales and service departments, often referred to in the trade as "front end" and "back end," respectively. Both new and used vehicles were sold, since a high proportion of new car and van purchases involved trading in the purchaser's existing vehicle. Auto World would also buy well-maintained used cars at auction for resale. Purchasers who decided that they could not afford a new car would often buy a "preowned" vehicle instead, while shoppers who came in looking for a used car could sometimes be persuaded to buy a new one. Before being put on sale, used vehicles were carefully serviced, with parts being replaced as needed. They were then thoroughly cleaned by a detailer whose services were hired as required. Dents and other blemishes were removed at a nearby body shop and occasionally the vehicle's paintwork was resprayed, too.

The front end of the dealership employed a sales manager, seven salespeople, an office manager, and a secretary. One of the salespeople had given notice and would be leaving at the end of the following week. The service department, when fully staffed, consisted of a service manager, a parts supervisor, nine mechanics, and two service writers. The Sullivan twins often worked part-time as service writers, filling in at busy periods, when one of the other writers was sick or on vacation, or when—as currently—there was an unfilled vacancy. The job entailed scheduling appointments for repairs and maintenance, writing up each work order, calling customers with repair estimates, and assisting customers when they returned to pick up the cars and pay for the work that had been done.

Sullivan-Diaz knew from her own experience as a service writer that it could be a stressful job. Few people liked to be without their car, even for a day. When a car broke down or was having problems, the owner was often nervous about how long it would take to get it fixed and, if the warranty had expired, how much the labor and parts would cost. Customers were quite unforgiving when a problem was not fixed completely on the first attempt and they had to return their vehicle for further work.

Major mechanical failures were not usually difficult to repair, although the parts replacement costs might be expensive. It was often the "little" things like water leaks and wiring problems that were the hardest to diagnose and correct, and it might be necessary for the customer to return two or three times before such a problem was resolved. In these situations, parts and materials costs were relatively low, but labor costs mounted up quickly, being charged out at US$75 an hour. Customers could sometimes be quite abusive, yelling at service writers over the phone or arguing with service writers, mechanics, and the service manager in person.

Turnover in the service writer job was high, which was one reason why Carol—and more recently her sisters—had often been pressed into service by their father to "hold the fort" as he described it. More than once, she had seen an exasperated service writer respond sharply to a complaining customer or hang up on one who was being abusive over the telephone. Gail and Joanne were currently taking turns to cover the vacant position, but there were times when both of them had classes and the dealership had only one service writer on duty.

By national standards, Sullivan Ford Auto World stood toward the lower end of medium-sized dealerships, selling around 1,100 cars a year, equally divided between new and used vehicles. In the most recent year, its revenues totaled US$26.6 million from new and used car sales and US$2.9 million from service and parts—down from US$30.5 million and US$3.6 million, respectively, in the previous year. Although the unit value of car sales was high, the margins were quite low, with margins for new cars being substantially lower than for used ones. Industry guidelines suggested that the contribution margin (known as the departmental selling gross) from car sales should be about 5.5 percent of sales revenues, and from service, around 25 percent of revenues. In a typical dealership, 60 percent of the selling gross had traditionally come from sales and 40 percent from service, but the balance was shifting from sales to service. The selling gross was then applied to fixed expenses, such as administrative salaries, rent or mortgage payments, and utilities.

For the most recent 12 months at Auto World, Sullivan-Diaz had determined that the selling gross figures were 4.6 percent and 24 percent, respectively, both of them lower than in the previous year and insufficient to cover the dealership's fixed expenses. Her father had made no mention of financial difficulties and she had been shocked to learn from the bank after his death that Auto World had been two months behind in mortgage payments on the property. Further analysis also showed that accounts payable had also risen sharply in the previous six months. Fortunately, the dealership held a large insurance policy on Sullivan's life, and the proceeds from this had been more than sufficient to bring mortgage payments up to date, pay down all overdue accounts, and leave some funds for future contingencies.

OUTLOOK

The opportunities for expanding new car sales did not appear promising, given declining consumer confidence and recent layoffs at several local plants that were expected to hurt the local economy. However, promotional incentives had reduced the inventory to manageable levels. From discussions with Larry Winters, Auto World's sales manager, Sullivan-Diaz had concluded that costs could be cut by not replacing the departing sales representative, maintaining inventory at its current reduced level, and trying to make more efficient use of advertising and promotion. Although Winters did not have Walter's exuberant personality, he had been Auto World's leading sales representative before being promoted, and had shown strong managerial capabilities in his current position.

As she reviewed the figures for the service department, Sullivan-Diaz wondered what potential might exist for improving its sales volume and selling gross. Her father had never been very interested in the parts and service business, seeing it simply as a necessary adjunct of the dealership. "Customers always seem to be miserable back there," he had once remarked to her. "But here in the front end, everybody's happy when someone buys a new car." The service facility was not easily visible from the main highway, being hidden behind the showroom. Although the building looked old and greasy, the equipment itself was modern and well maintained. There was sufficient capacity to handle more repair work, but a higher volume would require hiring one or more new mechanics.

Customers were required to bring cars in for servicing before 8:30 A.M. After parking their cars, customers entered the service building by a side door and waited their turn to see the service writers, who occupied a cramped room with peeling paint and an interior window overlooking the service bays. Customers stood while work orders for their cars were prepared. Ringing telephones frequently interrupted the process. Filing cabinets containing customer records and other documents lined the far wall of the room.

If the work were of a routine nature, such as an oil change or tune up, the customer was given an estimate immediately. For more complex jobs, they would be called with an estimate later in the morning once the car had been examined. Customers were required to pick up their cars by 6:00 P.M. on the day the work was completed. On several occasions, Carol had urged her father to computerize the service work order process, but he had never acted on her suggestions, so all orders continued to be handwritten on large yellow sheets, with carbon copies below.

The service manager, Rick Obert, who was in his late forties, had held the position since Auto World opened at its current location. The Sullivan family considered him to be technically skilled, and he managed the mechanics effectively. However, his manner with customers could be gruff and argumentative.

CUSTOMER SURVEY RESULTS

Another set of data that Sullivan-Diaz had studied carefully were the results of the customer satisfaction surveys that were mailed to the dealership monthly by a research firm retained by the Ford USA.

Purchasers of all new Ford cars were sent a questionnaire by mail within 30 days of making the purchase and asked to use a five-point scale to rate their satisfaction with the dealership sales department, vehicle preparation, and the characteristics of the vehicle itself.

The questionnaire asked how likely the purchaser would be to recommend the dealership, the salesperson, and the manufacturer to someone else. Other questions asked if the customers had been introduced to the dealer's service department and been given explanations on what to do if their cars needed service. Finally, there were some classification questions relating to customer demographics.

A second survey was sent to new car purchasers nine months after they had bought their cars. This questionnaire began by asking about satisfaction with the vehicle and then asked customers if they had taken their vehicles to the selling dealer for service of any kind. If so, respondents were then asked to rate the service department on 14 different attributes—ranging from the attitudes of service personnel to the quality of the work performed—and then to rate their overall satisfaction with service from the dealer.

Customers were also asked about where they would go in the future for maintenance service, minor mechanical and electrical repairs, major repairs in those same categories, and bodywork. The options listed for service were selling dealer, another Ford dealer, "some other place," or "do-it-yourself." Finally, there were questions about overall satisfaction with the dealer sales department and the dealership in general, as well as the likelihood of their purchasing another Ford product and buying it from the same dealership.

Dealers received monthly reports summarizing customer ratings of their dealership for the most recent month and for several previous months. To provide a comparison with how other Ford dealerships performed, the reports also included regional and national rating averages. After analysis, completed questionnaires were returned to the dealership; since these included each customer's name, a dealer could see which customers were satisfied and which were not.

In the 30-day survey of new purchasers, Auto World achieved better than average ratings on most dimensions. One finding which puzzled Carol was that almost 90 percent of respondents answered "yes" when asked if someone from Auto World had explained what to do if they needed service, but less than a third said that they had been introduced to

someone in the service department. She resolved to ask Larry Winters about this discrepancy.

The nine-month survey findings disturbed her. Although vehicle ratings were in line with national averages, the overall level of satisfaction with service at Auto World was consistently low, placing it in the bottom 25 percent of all Ford dealerships. The worst ratings for service concerned promptness of writing up orders, convenience of scheduling the work, convenience of service hours, and appearance of the service department. On length of time to complete the work, availability of needed parts, and quality of work done ("was it fixed right?"), Auto World's rating was close to the average. For interpersonal variables such as attitude of service department personnel, politeness, understanding of customer problems, and explanation of work performed, its ratings were relatively poor.

When Sullivan-Diaz reviewed the individual questionnaires, she found that there was a wide degree of variation between customers' responses on these interpersonal variables, ranging all the way across a 5-point scale from "completely satisfied" to "very dissatisfied." Curious, she had gone to the service files and examined the records for several dozen customers who had recently completed the nine-month surveys. At least part of the ratings could be explained by which service writers the customer had dealt with. Those who had been served two or more times by her sisters, for instance, gave much better ratings than those who had dealt primarily with Jim Fiskell, the service writer who had recently quit.

Perhaps the most worrying responses were those relating to customers' likely use of Auto World's service department in the future. More than half indicated that they would use another Ford dealer or "some other place" for maintenance service (such as oil change, lubrication, or tune-up) or for minor mechanical and electrical repairs. About 30 percent would use another source for major repairs. The rating for overall satisfaction with the selling dealer after nine months was below average and the customer's likelihood of purchasing from the same dealership again was a full point below that of buying another Ford product.

OPTIONS

Sullivan-Diaz pushed aside the spreadsheets she had printed out and shut down her laptop. It was time to go home for dinner. She saw the options for the dealership as basically twofold: either prepare the business for an early sale at what would amount to a distress price, or take a year or two to try to turn it around financially. In the latter instance, if the turnaround succeeded, the business could subsequently be sold at a higher price than it presently commanded, or the family could install a general manager to run the dealership for them.

Bill Froelich, owner of another nearby dealership plus three more in nearby cities, had offered to buy Auto World for a price that represented a fair valuation of the net assets, according to Auto World's accountants, plus $250,000 in goodwill. However, the rule of thumb when the auto industry was enjoying good times was that goodwill should be valued at $1,200 per vehicle sold each year. Carol knew that Froelich was eager to develop a network of dealerships in order to achieve economies of scale. His prices on new cars were very competitive and his nearest dealership clustered several franchises—Ford, Lincoln-Mercury, Volvo, and Jaguar—on a single large property.

AN UNWELCOME DISTURBANCE

As Carol left her office, she spotted the sales manager coming up the stairs leading from the showroom floor. "Larry," she said, "I've got a question for you."

"Fire away!" replied the sales manager.

"I've been looking at the customer satisfaction surveys. Why aren't our sales reps introducing new customers to the folks in the Service Department? It's supposedly part of our sales protocol, but it only seems to be happening about one-third of the time!"

Larry Winters shuffled his feet. "Well, Carol, basically I leave it to their discretion. We tell them about service, of course, but some of the guys on the floor feel a bit uncomfortable taking folks over to the service bays after they've been in here. It's quite a contrast, if you know what I mean."

Suddenly, the sound of shouting arose from the floor below. A man of about 40, wearing a windbreaker and jeans, was standing in the doorway yelling at one of the salespeople. The two managers could catch snatches of what he was saying, in between various obscenities:

". . . three visits. . . still not fixed right. . . service stinks. . . who's in charge here?" Everybody else in the showroom had stopped what they were doing and had turned to look at the newcomer.

Winters looked at his young employer and rolled his eyes. "If there was something your dad couldn't stand, it was guys like that, yelling and screaming in the showroom and asking for the boss. Walt would go hide out in his office! Don't worry, Tom'll take care of that fellow and get him out of here. What a jerk!"

"No," said Sullivan-Diaz, "I'll deal with him! One thing I learned when I worked at St. Luke's was that you don't let people yell about their problems in front of everybody else. You take them off somewhere, calm them down, and find out what's bugging them."

She stepped quickly down the stairs, wondering to herself, "What else have I learned in health care that I can apply to this business?"

Exhibit 1: Marketing cars is a different proposition to marketing services for the same vehicles.

STUDY QUESTIONS

1. How does marketing cars differ from marketing service for those same vehicles?

2. Compare and contrast the sales and service departments at Auto World.

3. From a consumer perspective, what useful parallels do you see between operating a car sales and service dealership and operating health services?

4. What advice would you give to Carol Sullivan-Diaz?

Four Customers in Search of Solutions[1]

Christopher Lovelock, Jochen Wirtz and Patricia Chew

Four telephone subscribers from suburban Munich call to complain about a variety of problems. How should the telephone company respond to each?

Among the many customers of Telekom Bavaria are four individuals living in Haar in a middle-class suburb close to Munich, Germany. Each of them has a telephone-related problem and decides to call the company about it.

Andreas Werden

Andreas Werden grumbles constantly about the amount of his home telephone bill (which is, in fact, in the top 2 percent of all household phone bills in Haar). There are many calls to countries in Southeast Asia on weekday evenings, almost daily calls to Schwabing (another district in Munich, not far from Haar) around mid-day, and calls to Frankfurt most weekends. Mr Werden also uses the phone for his Internet modem. One day, Mr Werden receives a telephone bill which is even larger than usual. On reviewing the bill, he is convinced that he has been overcharged, so he calls Telekom Bavaria's customer service department to complain and request an adjustment.

Erika Mueller

Erika Mueller has missed several important calls recently because the caller received a busy signal. She phones the telephone company to determine possible solutions to this problem. Ms. Mueller's telephone bill is at the median level for a household subscriber. Most of the calls from her house are local, but there are occasional international calls to France, where her sister has migrated to. She does not subscribe to any value-added services.

Anna Bauer

During the past several weeks, Mrs. Bauer has been distressed to receive a series of obscene telephone calls. It sounds like the same person each time. She calls the telephone company to see if they can put a stop to this harassment. Her phone bill is in the bottom 10 percent of all household subscriber bills and almost all calls are local.

Konrad Fichtner

For more than a week, the phone line at Konrad Fitchtner's house has been making strange humming and crackling noises, making it difficult to hear what the other person is saying. After two of his friends comment on these distracting noises, Mr. Fichtner calls Telekom Bavaria and reports the problem. His guess is that it is being caused by the answering machine, which is getting old and sometimes loses messages. Mr. Fichtner's phone bill is at the 75th percentile for a household subscriber. Most of the calls are made to locations within Haar and Munich, usually at evenings and weekends, although there are a few calls to Berlin too. He went to university there and he likes to keep in touch with some of his former classmates.

STUDY QUESTIONS

1. Based strictly on the information in the case, how many possibilities do you see to segment the telecommunications market?

2. As a customer service rep at the telephone company, how would you address each of the problems and complaints reported?

3. Do you see any marketing opportunities for Telekom Bavaria in any of these complaints?

---

[1] © 2009 Christopher H. Lovelock, Jochen Wirtz and Patricia Chew

Banyan Tree: Branding the Intangible[1]

Jochen Wirtz

Banyan Tree Hotels and Resorts had become a leading player in the luxury resort and spa market in Asia. As part of its growth strategy, Banyan Tree had launched new brands and brand extensions that included resorts, spas, residences, destination club memberships, retail outlets, and even museum shops. Now, the company was preparing to aggressively grow its global footprint in the Americas, Caribbean, Europe and the Middle East while preserving its distinctive Asian identity and strong brand image of Banyan Tree.

A brand synonymous with private villas, tropical garden spas, and retail galleries promoting traditional craft, Banyan Tree Hotels and Resorts received its first guest in 1994 in Phuket, Thailand. Since then, it has grown into a leading manager and developer of niche and premium resorts, hotels and spas in Asia Pacific. Despite having minimal advertising, Banyan Tree achieved global exposure and a high level of brand awareness through the company's public relations and global marketing programs. Much interest was also generated by the company's socially responsible business values and practices caring for the social and natural environments. With a firm foothold in the medium-sized luxury resorts market, the company introduced a new and contemporary brand Angsana in 2000 to gain a wider customer base. In 2003, the company launched Colours of Angsana, a boutique collection of small hotels and resorts offering an experience centred on cultural tourism and soft adventure. As the resorts market became increasingly crowded with similar competitive offerings, lured by the success of Banyan Tree, the company had to contemplate about expanding its business and preserving its distinct identity. Banyan Tree and Angsana resorts were expanding geographically outside of Asia and also into the urban hotel market in major cities throughout the world. With around 50 hotels and resorts scheduled to open over the next three years, Banyan Tree faced the challenge of translating and maintaining the success of a niche Asian hospitality brand into various market segments on a global scale.

COMPANY BACKGROUND

By end of 2007, Banyan Tree Holdings Ltd (BTHL) managed and/or had ownership interests in 23 resorts and hotels, 64 spas, 66 retail galleries, and two golf courses in more than 50 locations in 19 countries. Since its establishment in 1994,

the company's flagship brand, Banyan Tree, has won some three hundred international tourism, hospitality, design, and marketing awards, some of which include the "Best Resort Hotel in Asia-Pacific" (Phuket) for four consecutive years from Business Traveller Awards since 2002, "Seychelles' Best Resort" and "Seychelles' Best Spa" from World Travel Awards (2003), and "Best Hotels for Rooms" (Bangkok) from UK Conde Nast Traveller (2006).[2]

BTHL was founded by Ho Kwon Ping, a travel enthusiast and former journalist, and his wife Claire Chiang, a strong advocate of corporate social responsibility. Prior to entering the hotels and resorts business, Ho spent some 15 years managing the family business, which was into everything imaginable, such as commodities, food products, consumer electronics, and property development, competing mainly on cost, and was not dominant in any particular country or industry, while Claire Chiang was deeply involved in sociology and social issues. The closing of a factory in Thailand one year after its opening—because it lost out to other low-cost producers in Indonesia—was the last straw for Ho, who then realized that a low-cost strategy was not only difficult to follow but would also lead nowhere. Determined to craft out something proprietary that would allow the company to become a price maker rather than a price taker, Ho decided that building a strong brand was the only way for him to maintain a sustainable competitive advantage.

The idea of entering the luxury resorts market was inspired by the gap in the hotel industry that giant chains such as the Hilton and Shangri-La could not fill. There existed a market segment that wanted private and intimate accommodation without the expectation of glitzy chain hotels. This was fueled by the sharp price gap between the luxurious Aman Resorts and other resorts in the luxury resorts market. For example, the Amanpuri in Thailand, one of Aman's resorts, charged in 2004, a rack rate for its villas ranging from US$650 to over US$7,000 a night, whereas the prices of other luxury resorts, such as the Shangri-La Hotel and Phuket Arcadia Beach Resort by Hilton in Thailand were priced below US$350. Noticing the big difference in prices between Aman Resorts and the other resorts in the luxury resorts market, Ho saw potential for offering an innovative niche product that could also bridge the price gap in this market. Seasoned travellers themselves, Ho and Chiang backpacked throughout the world in their youth. Their extensive experiences are evident in their non-conforming beliefs that resorts should provide more than just accommodation. Ho and Chiang hit upon the idea of building a resort comprising individual villas, local-inspired architectural design and positioned as a romantic and intimate escapade for guests. Banyan Tree had moved up its positioning into the higher end of the luxury market, and by 2008 its rack rates were typically between US$1,200 and 7,000 for the resort in Phuket, and between Euros 1,500 and 4,200 for the resort in the Seychelles.

Operations at Banyan Tree began with only one resort in Phuket, situated on a former mining site once deemed too severely ravaged to sustain any form of development by a United Nations Development Program planning unit and the Tourism Authority of Thailand. It was a bold decision, but the company, together with Ho, Chiang, and Ho's brother Ho Kwon Cjan, restored it after extensive rehabilitation works costing a total of US$250 million. So successful was Banyan Tree Phuket when it was finally launched that the company worked quickly to build two other resorts, one at Bintan Island in Indonesia and the other at Vabbinfaru Island in The Maldives. The company has never looked back since. Even though Asia's travel industry experienced periodic meltdowns such as the Asian Economic Crisis in 1997/8, the September 11 attacks on the World Trade Center in 2001, the dot.com crisis in 2001/2, Severe Acute Respiratory Syndrome (SARS) in 2003, and the Tsunami on 26 December 2004, no employee was retrenched and room rates at Banyan Tree rose steadily.

BRAND ORIGINS

Known as Yung Shue Wan in the local dialect, Banyan Tree Bay was a fishing village on Lamma Island in Hong Kong, where Ho and his wife Chiang lived for three idyllic years before he joined the family business. Despite the village's modest and rustic setting, they remember it to be a sanctuary

of romance and intimacy. The large canopies of the Banyan Tree also showed semblance of the shelter afforded by Asia's tropical rainforests. Ho and Chiang thus decided to name their resort Banyan Tree, and position it as a sanctuary for the senses.

THE SERVICE OFFERING

Unlike most other resorts then, Banyan Tree resorts comprised individual villas that came with a private pool, jacuzzi, or spa treatment room, each designed to offer guests exclusivity and utmost privacy. For example, a guest could skinny-dip in the private pool within his villa without being seen by other guests, putting him in a world of his own (see Exhibit 1).

Exhibit 1: World of privacy in a double pool villa at Banyan Tree Phuket.

All Banyan Tree hotels and resorts were designed around the concept of providing "a sense of place" to reflect and enhance the culture and heritage of the destination. This is reflected in the architecture, furnishings, landscape, vegetation and the service offers. To create a sense of exotic sensuality and ensure the privacy of its guests, the resorts are designed to blend into the natural landscape of the surrounding environment and use the natural foliage and boulders as the privacy screen (see Exhibit 2 showing Banyan Tree Seychelles). The furnishings of Banyan Tree villas were deliberately native to convey the exoticism of the destination with its rich local flavor and luxurious feel. The spa pavilions in Seychelles were constructed around the large granite boulders and lush foliage to offer an outdoor spa experience in complete privacy. The resorts' local flavor were also reflected in the services offered, some of which were unique to certain resorts. Employees were allowed to vary the service delivery process according to local culture and practices, as long as these were consistent with the brand promise of romance and intimacy. Thus, in Phuket, for instance, a couple could enjoy dinner on a traditional Thai long tail boat accompanied by private Thai musicians while cruising instead of dining in a restaurant. Banyan Tree Phuket also offered wedding packages in which couples were blessed by Buddhist monks. In the Maldives, wedding ceremonies could be conducted underwater among the corals. Guests could also choose to dine in a castaway sandbank with only their private chefs and the stars for company, and watch the sunset toasting champagne on a Turkish gulet returning from a trip watching a school of spinner dolphins.

Exhibit 2: Banyan Tree Seychelles blends well into its natural environment.

Products and services were conceived with the desired customer experience in mind. One such product was the "Intimate Moments" package, specially created for couples. This was presented as a surprise when guests returned to find their villas decorated with lit candles, incense oil lamps burning, flower petals spread throughout the room, satin sheets on the decorated bed, a chilled bottle of champagne or wine and titbits placed next to the outdoor bath which itself is decorated with flowers and candles and bath oils. The couple was presented with a variety of aromatic massage oils to further inspire those intimate moments.

Another draw of the resorts was the Banyan Tree Spa, found at every Banyan Tree property. The pioneer of the tropical garden spas concept, Banyan Tree Spas offered a variety of aromatic oil massages, and face and body beauty treatments using traditional Asian therapies, with a choice of indoors or outdoors treatment. The spa products used were natural, indigenous products, made from local herbs and spices. Non-clinical in concept, Banyan Tree Spas relied mainly on the "human touch" instead of energy-consuming high-tech equipment. The spa experience was promoted as a sensorial,

intimate experience that would rejuvenate the "body, mind, and soul," and was mainly targeted at couples who would enjoy their treatments together.

Exhibit 3: Banyan Tree spa pavilion with a view.

In line with Banyan Tree's ethos of conserving local culture and heritage, and help promote cottage crafts, Chiang founded the Banyan Tree Gallery, a retail outlet showcasing indigenous crafts. Banyan Tree Gallery outlets were set up in each resort. Items sold were made by local artisans, and included traditionally woven handmade fabrics, garments, jewellery, handicrafts, tribal art, and spa accessories, such as incense candles and massage oils, which guests could use at home to recreate the Banyan Tree experience.

Exhibit 4: A contemporary Asian shopping experience with a strong sense of corporate responsibility at Banyan Tree Gallery.

Embarking on projects to support the various communities in the locations where Banyan Tree resorts are situated, Banyan Tree Gallery worked closely with village cooperatives and not for profit craft marketing agents to provide gainful employment to the artisans. While acting as a marketing channel for Asian crafts like basket weaving, hill tribe cross-stitching and lacquer ware, Banyan Tree Gallery also educated its customers about the crafts with an accompanying write-up. In the course of Banyan Tree Gallery's operations, the community outreach extended from across Thailand to Laos, Cambodia, India, Nepal, Sri Lanka, Indonesia, Malaysia and Singapore.

The result of Banyan Tree's efforts was "a very exclusive, private holiday feeling," as described by one guest. Another guest commented, "It's a treat for all the special occasions like honeymoons and wedding anniversaries. It's the architecture, the sense of place and the promise of romance."

MARKETING BANYAN TREE

In the first two years when Banyan Tree was launched, the company's marketing communications was managed by an international advertising agency. The agency also designed the Banyan Tree logo shown in Exhibit 5, and together with the management came up with the marketing tagline "Sanctuary for the Senses."

Exhibit 5: Banyan Tree Logo.

Though furnished luxuriously, Banyan Tree resorts were promoted as providing romantic and intimate "smallish" hotel experiences, rather than luxurious accommodation as touted by most competitors then. "Banyan Tree Experiences" was marketed as intimate private moments. The resorts saw themselves as setting the stage for guests to create those unforgettable memories.

When Banyan Tree was first launched, extensive advertising was carried out for a short period of time to gain recognition in the industry. Subsequently, the company scaled down on advertising and kept it minimal, mainly in high-end travel magazines in key markets. The advertisements were visual in nature with succinct copy or showcase the awards and accolades won. Exhibit 6 shows a Banyan Tree advertisement highlighting the award-winning Banyan Tree Spa.

Exhibit 6: Advertisement showcasing "Spa of the Year" award from Conde Nast Traveler.

Brand awareness for Banyan Tree was generated largely through public relations and global marketing programs. For example, relationships with travel editors and writers were cultivated to encourage visits to the resorts. This helped increase editorial coverage on Banyan Tree, which management felt was more effective in conveying the "Banyan Tree Experience" from an impartial third-party perspective. Its website www.banyantree.com increasingly drove online bookings and provided vivid information about the latest offerings of Banyan Tree's fast growing portfolio.

The management of marketing activities was centralized at the Singapore headquarters for consistency in brand building. BTHL appointed a few key wholesalers in each targeted market, and worked closely with them to promote sales. Rather than selling through wholesale and retail agents who catered to the general market, BTHL chose to work only with agents specializing in exclusive luxury holidays targeted at wealthy customers. Global exposure was also achieved through Banyan Tree's membership in the Small Luxury Hotels and Leading Hotels of the World. Targeting high-end consumers, they represent various independent exclusive hotels and have sales offices in major cities around the world.

The end of 2007 marked a new stage of Banyan Tree's global expansion, with the launch of its own GDS code "BY." GDS is a Global Distribution System that is used by travel providers to process airline, hotel, car rental reservations across 640,000 terminals of travel agents and other distribution partners around the world. Prior to BY, Banyan Tree was represented by its marketing partners, Leading Hotels of the World (LW) and Small Luxury Hotels (LX),. Now, Banyan Tree had its unique identity on the GDS code, further strengthening its brand presence and customer ownership. Banyan Tree now had enough critical mass to ensure the economic feasibility of a GDS private label. The acquisition of its own GDS code meant that Banyan Tree was transitioning from a relatively small regional player to a global brand in the eyes of the travel industry.

BRAND VALUES

Banyan Tree embraced certain values, such as actively caring for the natural and human environment, and revitalizing local communities, which in turn created pride and respect among staff. The company hoped to build the brand on values that employees and customers could identify with and support as part of their own life values. A dedicated corporate social responsibility committee, headed by Chiang featuring General Managers and valued associates from each resort, was formed to focus on these issues with both a regional overview and simultaneously local perspectives. Thus, the company worked actively to preserve, protect, and promote the natural and human environments in which Banyan Tree resorts were located.

Preserving the Environment

Resorts were built using local materials as far as possible, and at the same time minimizing the impact on the environment. At Banyan Tree Bintan, for example, the 70 villas located in a rainforest were constructed around existing trees, cutting down as few trees as possible, to minimize the impact the resort had on the natural environment. The villas were built on stilts and platforms to avoid cutting trees and possible soil erosion. At Banyan Tree Maldives Vabbinfaru and Banyan Tree Seychelles, fresh water supply was obtained by the more expensive method of desalination, instead of extracting water from the underground water-table, which risked long term disruption of the ecological system. Toiletries, such as shampoo, hair conditioner, bath foam, and body lotion, provided in the resorts were non-toxic and biodegradable, and filled in reusable containers made from celadon or ceramic. Refuse was recycled where possible and

treated through an in-house incinerator system otherwise. Waste water was also treated and recycled in the irrigation of resort landscapes.

Through the retail arm Banyan Tree Gallery, the human environment efforts were evident in the active sourcing of traditional crafts from indigenous tribes to provide gainful employment. These employment opportunities provided a source of income for the tribes and, at the same time, preserve their unique heritage.

In line with the Banyan Tree Group's Green Imperative initiative, Banyan Tree Gallery constantly used eco-friendly and recycled materials in the development of its merchandise. Examples included photo frames made using discarded telephone directories, elephant dung paper stationary, and lead-free celadon and ceramic spa amenities. Unique collections like the black resin turtles stationary range and leaf-inspired merchandise were created to promote environmental awareness, and were accompanied by a write-up to educate the consumer on the targeted conservation campaign. The galleries did not carry products made from shell or ivory in support of animal rights.

Creating Brand Ownership Among Employees

All employees were trained in the basic standards of five-star service establishments, which included greeting guests, remembering their first names, and anticipating their needs. In addition, some employees got a taste of the "Banyan Tree Experience" as part of their training. The management believed that the stay would help employees understand better what guests will experience, and, in return, enhance their delivery of special experiences for the guests.

Although the management imposed strict rules on the administration of the resorts, employees were empowered to exercise creativity and sensitivity. For example, the housekeeping teams were not restricted by a standard bed decoration. Rather, they were given room for creativity although they had general guidelines for turning the bed to keep in line with the standards of a premium resort. Banyan Tree invested liberally in staff welfare. Employees were taken to and from work in air-conditioned buses, and had access to various amenities, including good-quality canteens, medical services and child care facilities. Staff dormitories had televisions, telephones, refrigerators, and bathrooms attached. The company's generous staff welfare policies apparently paid off. Ho said, "The most gratifying response is the sense of ownership that our staff began to have. It's not a sense of financial ownership, but they actually care about the property. In our business, service and service standards do not always mean the same thing as in a developed country, where standards are measured by efficiency and productivity, by people who are already quite well-versed in a service culture. We operate in places that, sometimes, have not seen hotels. People come from villages. What we need—more than exact standards—is for them to have a sense of hospitality, a sense that the guest is an honored person who, by virtue of being there, is able to give a decent livelihood to the people who work. This creates a culture in which everybody is friendly and helpful.

Involving Guests in Environmental Conservation

Part of the company's corporate social responsibility initiatives were designed to encourage environmental conservation and help ecological restoration. To create greater environmental awareness, Banyan Tree organized activities that involved interested guests in their research and environmental preservation work. In the Maldives, for instance, guests were invited to take part in the coral transplantation program (see Exhibit 7 for a picture of guest involvement in the long running coral planting programme). Guests who participated in the program were then encouraged to return several years later to see the progress of their efforts. Guests were also offered free marine biology sessions allowing them to learn more about the fascinating marine life and its conservation. Guests also had an opportunity to take part in the Green Sea Turtle Headstarting Projects. The response from guests was tremendously positive.

In 2002, Banyan Tree established The Green Imperative Fund (GIF) to further support community-based and environmental initiatives in the regions where it has a presence. Guests were billed US$2 per room night at Banyan Tree properties and US$1 at Angsana properties (of which they could opt out if they wished) and the company matched dollar for dollar. Details of the program were communicated to guests through various methods, including sandfilled turtles and in-villa turn down gifts.

Guests were generally happy to know that their patronage contributed to meaningful causes, like the construction of new schools for the local community, the restoration of coral reefs, and helped ensure the longevity of local village crafts.

Exhibit 7: Guest participate in planting corals at Banyan Tree Maldives and Angsana Ihuru.

Involving the Local Community

In addition to engaging local craftsmen to produce indigenous art and handicrafts for sale at its galleries, Banyan Tree also involved the local community in all aspects of its business, even as the resorts were being built. Villas were constructed with as much indigenous material as possible, most of which was supplied by local traders. Traditional arts and handicrafts that complemented the villas' aesthetics were also purchased from local artisans.

The company believed in building profitable resorts that would benefit the surrounding environment and contribute to local economies through the creation of employment and community development projects. Thus, besides providing employment for the local community, the company brought business to the local farmers and traders by making it a point to purchase fresh produce from them. Wherever possible, the company supported other regional tourism ventures that would benefit the wider local community and enhance the visitor's experience. The Banyan Tree Maldives Marine Laboratory is a prime example, being the first fully equipped private research facility to be fully funded and operated by a resort. The Lab seeks to lead conservation efforts in the Maldives to protect and regenerate coral and marine life for the future of the tourism industry as well as to promote awareness and education about this field to the local community.

Recognizing that the disparity in lifestyles and living standards between guests and the local community might create a sense of alienation within the local community, a Community Relations Department was set up to develop and manage community outreach programs. After consultations with community stakeholders a number of funding scholarships for needy children were given, a school and child care center were built, lunches and parties for the elderly were hosted, and local cultural and religious activities were supported.

GROWING BANYAN TREE

In 2002, BTHL took over the management of a city hotel in the heart of Bangkok from Westin Hotel Company. The hotel was rebranded as Banyan Tree Bangkok, after extensive renovation works were completed to upgrade the hotel's facilities, build new additional spa amenities and a Banyan Tree Gallery. This was the first Banyan Tree hotel to be located in the city area, unlike the other beachfront Banyan Tree properties. Banyan Tree planned to open city hotels in Seoul, Beijing, Shanghai, and Hangzhou, and Angsana expanded into Dubai and London.

As the Banyan Tree brand became established, the company began expanding its network of spas and retail outlets. Stand-alone Banyan Tree Spas and Banyan Tree Galleries were set up as separate ventures, independent of Banyan Tree hotels and resorts, in various cities such as Singapore, Shanghai, Sydney, India and Dubai, operating either in other hotels or as stand-alone outlets. Its most recent spa was The World Spa by Banyan Tree, located on board of the ResidenSea, a residential cruise ship, offering Banyan Tree signature spa treatments to the world's only resort community travelling the globe.

To support its fast growing spa business, in 2007 Banyan Tree opened two new spa academies in Lijiang, China, and Bangkok, Thailand, in addition to the Spa Academy located in Phuket that was opened already in 2001.

Exhibit 8: Extending the Banyan Tree Maldives experience onboard the Banyan Velaa.

INTRODUCING NEW BRANDS

After establishing a foothold in the luxury resorts market, BTHL introduced the Angsana brand, in response to demand from hotel operators in Asia who were keen to introduce spa services in their hotels. As the positioning of these hotels did not fit that of Banyan Tree, the company decided to launch a new brand, Angsana, a more contemporary and affordable brand than Banyan Tree, to run as stand-alone spa businesses in other hotels.

Exhibit 9: Angsana Maldives Ihuru.

The first Angsana Spa was opened in 1999 at Dusit Laguna, one of several hotels at Laguna Phuket, an integrated resort development with shared facilities located at Bang Tao Bay in Thailand. The Angsana Spa was so well received that the company quickly set up five other such spas in various hotels in Thailand. In 2000, BTHL opened its first Angsana Resort & Spa, complete with an Angsana Gallery, located less than one kilometer away from Banyan Tree Bintan in Indonesia.

In 2003, BTHL launched Colours of Angsana to penetrate the soft adventure and cultural tourism market, catering to the more adventurous segment of the market. Colours of Angsana was launched as a boutique product line of Angsana, and comprised a collection of individual hotels and resorts, each with their own identity, situated at more offbeat and exotic locations, and priced more affordably than Banyan Tree.

Also in 2003, Banyan Tree launched the Museum Shop by Banyan Tree—a joint partnership with Singapore's National Heritage Board to showcase Asia's rich and diverse cultural heritage through unique museum-inspired merchandise. Designed to inspire and educate shoppers, Museum Shop by

Banyan Tree makes history more accessible and approachable to the layperson. By 2008, Banyan Tree had in total over 30 retail outlets, ranging from Banyan Tree Galleries, Banyan Tree Spa Galleries, Museum Shops, and Library Shops to Elements by Banyan Tree. Angsana had its own range of retail shops with a total of 35 outlets, ranging from Angsana Galleries to Angsana Spa Galleries.

Banyan Tree Galleries are the retail outlets supporting the hotels, while Banyan Tree Spa Galleries support the spa outlets, selling more spa-focused merchandise, such as signature aromatherapy amenities, essential oils, candles, and body care products. Museum Shops by Banyan Tree are located in various museums in Singapore and the merchandise sold will be inspired by the artefacts exhibited in the respective museums. The Library Shops were created in partnership with the National Library Board (NLB) and sells both NLB and Banyan Tree branded merchandise. The Elements galleries sell specialized merchandise such as jewelry and fashion items.

THE ROAD AHEAD

To diversify its geographic spread, Ho plans to venture into locations in South America, Southern Europe, and the Middle East, where he hopes to replicate Banyan Tree's success throughout Asia. However, given the higher costs of doing business in the Americas and Europe, would the same strategy that had brought fame and success to Banyan Tree in Asia be workable in the rest of the world? Ho's ultimate vision is "to string a necklace of Banyan Tree Resorts around the world; not quantity, but a number of jewels that form a chain around the world." In 2008 alone, Banyan Tree had signed management contracts that would expand its operations to at least an additional 50 Banyan Tree and Angsana properties by 2011. Of the properties under development, the majority were resorts and/or integrated resorts, and approximately 10 were city hotels.

While expanding the company's network of hotels and resorts, spas, and retail outlets, Ho has to be mindful of the brands' focus and be careful not to dilute the brands. He also has to consider the strategic fit of the company's portfolio of brands, which comprised Banyan Tree, Angsana and Colours of Angsana.

Banyan Tree certainly stood out among its competitors in the resorts industry when it was first launched. Since then, its success had attracted various competitors who offer similar products and services. Thus, it is imperative that Banyan Tree retains its competitive advantage to prevent losing its distinctive position in the market.

STUDY QUESTIONS

1. What are the main factors that contributed to Banyan Tree's success?

2. Evaluate Banyan Tree's brand positioning and communications strategies. Can Banyan Tree maintain its unique positioning in an increasingly overcrowded resorts market?

3. Discuss whether the brand portfolio of Banyan Tree, Angsana and Colours of Angsana, as well as the product portfolio of beach resorts and city hotels, spas, galleries and museum shops fit as a family. What are your recommendations to Banyan Tree for managing these brands and products in future?

4. What effect does the practice of corporate social responsibility have on brand equity?

5. What potential problems do you foresee in bringing Banyan Tree to the Americas, Europe and the Middle East. How could Banyan Tree address those issues?

[1] © 2009 by Jochen Wirtz

Jochen Wirtz is Associate Professor of Marketing and Academic Director of the UCLA – NUS Executive MBA Program at the National University of Singapore.

The support and feedback of the management of Banyan Tree Hotels & Resorts in the writing of this case is gratefully acknowledged.

[2] The complete list of awards won by Banyan Tree can be found on the company's Web site at www.banyantree.com.

Ginger: Smart Basics™

Dr Mukta Kamplikar[1]

Roots Corporation Limited develops and operates a fast-expanding chain of economy hotels across India under the "Ginger" brand. There is currently a lack of competition in the branded economy hotels segment and Ginger is the only branded economy hotel chain in India. The Ginger hotels are built around a concept that provides facilities to meet the key needs of today's traveler, at affordable rates. Ginger faces challenges in different aspects of its business as it aims to deliver consistently, quality service to the customer and manage customer expectations.

COMPANY BACKGROUND

Roots Corporation Limited (RCL) is a wholly-owned subsidiary of The Indian Hotels Company Limited (IHCL). IHCL is a part of the Tata Group of companies (see www.tata.com), India's premier business house. Taj Hotels Resorts and Palaces comprises 77 hotels, 7 palaces, 6 private islands and 12 resorts in 40 locations across India with an additional 18 international hotels in the Maldives, Mauritius, Malaysia, Australia, UK, US, Bhutan, Sri Lanka, Africa, and the Middle East.

Incorporated on 24 December 2003, Roots Corporation Limited operates the first-of-its-kind category of Smart Basics™ hotels across India. Launched in June 2004, the Smart Basics™ concept created a revolution in the world of Indian hospitality. Roots Corporation Limited develops and operates a fast-expanding chain of economy hotels across India under the "Ginger" brand. The company either owns/leases land on which it develops and operates hotels and has now started entering into joint developments where the owner brings in the land and bare shell and leases the same to the company. The company's recent growth has been organic, through developing and operating hotels in new cities or by going for additional hotels in existing markets; thus expanding the geographic reach of the hotel chain. The company intends to develop and operate additional hotels under both business models to maintain or achieve a dominant position in every market covered by their Ginger hotel chain.

Exhibit 1: The proportion of hotel segments across Indian cities.

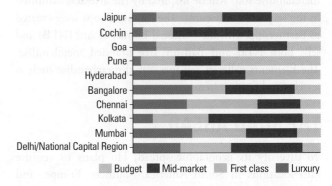

The Economy Segment

Historically, hotel development projects in India generally focused on upscale hotels that were primarily targeted at international tourists and corporate travelers. New hotels will be concentrated in 18 main cities over the next 10 years, as shown in the following chart.

Exhibit 2: Projected hotel expansion rate over 10 years.

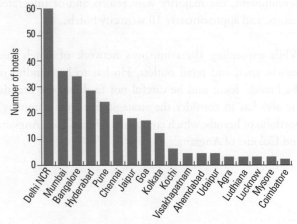

Source: *HVS International.*

Between 2007 and 2010, supply will increase in all categories of hotels, as shown in the chart below.

Exhibit 3: Projected supply increase in all categories of hotel.

	Existing Supply	Proposed Supply	Increase over Five Year	Development of Supply	Luxury	First Class	Mid-market	Budget
Agra	1,336	384	28.7%	69%	-	-	37.5%	62.5%
Ahmedabad	519	462	89.0%	48%	-	32.5%	15.6%	51.9%
Bangalore	1,906	7,794	408.9%	55%	31.1%	16.7%	37.0%	14.2%
Chennai	2,075	4,407	212.4%	36%	28.0%	38.0%	23.1%	10.9%
Delhi (NCR)	7,030	10,856	154.4%	74%	24.8%	27.0%	38.2%	10.0%
Goa	2,252	2,632	116.9%	18%	12.4%	43.6%	25.6%	18.4%
Hyperabad	1,442	7,408	513.7%	57%	25.4%	34.4%	21.3%	18.8%
Jaipur	1,298	2,770	213.4%	42	11.7%	36.3%	26.0%	26.0%
Kolkata	1,354	2,465	182.1%	61%	11.2%	29.4%	49.7%	9.7%
Mumbai	7,402	9,318	125.9%	36%	30.8%	28.9%	26.7%	13.6%
Other Cities	8,056	6,870	85.3%	47%	3.9%	18.6%	24.0%	53.5%

Source: *HVS International.*

While growth is expected in the upscale hotels, the growth in the economy segment is still minimal. While several chains, both domestic and international, have announced plans for development of hotels in this segment, visible action on the ground is limited.

Economy hotel chains in India mainly target value-conscious domestic business and leisure travelers who demand convenient lodging, a consistent product and high-quality services. According to a study conducted by Ginger, currently, 37 percent of economy hotel guests are individual business travelers, 23 percent are contract corporate customers and 20 percent are individual leisure travelers. Economy hotel chains aim to satisfy customers' basic accommodation needs with affordable pricing, a comfortable lodging experience and a standardized service-product.

Lack of competition in the branded economy hotels segment is a great opportunity for Ginger.

COMPETITION

The lodging industry in India is highly fragmented and competitive, and competition is expected to persist and intensify.

Currently, Ginger competes with three-star full-service hotels from the unorganized sector (these are hotels developed and operated as standalone hotels with no chain/hotel group

affiliations as opposed to Ginger hotels, which are part of a network of hotels). Going forward we see competition continuing from the unorganized section of the market as well as from newer international and local hotel companies who have announced their intent to set-up hotels across the country in the value segment. The market is witnessing a fair amount of activity in this segment of the hotel market.

Some of the companies who have announced plans to establish a presence in the country are shown in Exhibit 4.

Exhibit 4: Lodging brands venturing into India.

Brand	Promoters	Plans
Formule 1	Accor in a joint venture with Emaar MGF	100 hotels in the next decade
Easy Hotels	Isthitmar, Dubai	New look pod hotels
Sleep Inn	Choice Hotels with Gupta Group	10 hotels by 2010; first hotels to be in Tirupati and Vizag
Tune Hotels	Air Asia, Malaysia	First hotel to be in Goa
Red Fox	Lemon Tree partnered by Warburg Pincus	10 hotels by 2010
Peppermint	Royal Orchid Hotels	50 hotels by 2010; bids for 11 hotels on Railway land are held up; first hotel open in Hyderabad
Kamfotel	Kamat Hotels	50 hotels in the next five years; focused on West coast; tie-up with ONGC /MRPL
Days Inn / Super 8	Wyndham with Gammon	38 hotels by 2011
Premier Travel Inn	Whitbread in a joint venture with Emaar MGF	80 hotels in 10 years
City Max Hotels	Landmark Group, Dubai	20 hotels by 2009
Travelodge	DIC	No numbers mentioned
Campanile	Starwood	No numbers mentioned

While some developments have started in the mid-market segment with Lemon Tree Hotels, Ibis (Accor), Keys (Bergruen Hotels), Day Hotels (Dawnay Day), Hometel (Sarovar Group), Hilton Garden Inn Hotels (DLF) and Taj Gateway Hotels, not much activity is visible at the economy end of the spectrum. This is possibly on account of the high prices of real estate.

Ginger: Smart Basics™ **447**

Ginger—The Service Concept

The concept of Ginger was developed in association with renowned corporate strategy thinker, Dr C. K. Prahalad, and the hotels were indigenously designed and developed by the Indian Hotels Company Limited. The Ginger hotels are built around a concept that provides facilities to meet the key needs of today's traveler, at affordable rates. Smart Basics™ is a philosophy of providing intelligent, thought-out facilities and services at a 'value' pricing and reflects the new spirit in which people live and work today. It signifies the emerging lifestyle which is visible in the degree to which individuals have taken control of their various activities viz. the use of e-mail instead of letters, as also the use of mobile phones, conference calls and video conferences to get things done quickly and efficiently. Essentially, it is simplicity and convenience in ease of doing business (awareness, booking channels, payment gateways); informality, style, warmth and modernity in its approach to product design, service philosophy and affordability in pricing.

The first of the Smart Basics™ hotel was launched in Bangalore and was called indiOne. When the test marketing of the concept was completed, there were slight changes to improve the hotel facilities and services. After that, the Smart Basics™ concept was rolled out across India. This category of hotels was launched with a new name, Ginger hotels, in line with the fresh, simple yet stylish and warm world of Smart Basics™. An up-and-coming category of hotels, Ginger definitely signifies simplicity, convenience, informality, style, warmth, modernity and affordability.

The target segment for Ginger is the large growing middle class with increasing disposable incomes. They are the class of travelers who would spend on travel but not on luxury accommodations. These travelers look for value-for-money accommodation that is clean and secure and also include international travelers looking for hygienic accommodation in the smaller cities.

Ginger is the only branded economy hotel chain in India with a nationwide network of 12 hotels, with an additional 20 hotels under development as of 31 May, 2008. Their early-mover status in many markets and established regional operational synergy has enabled Ginger to develop and operate hotels efficiently and successfully in targeted markets. As the only branded economy hotel chain in India, the chain has been able to establish credibility with property owners and secure desirable properties on favorable lease terms. The economy segment (3-star) is better protected against and more resilient to the volatility in the hospitality segment as compared to the upscale segment.

THE OFFERING—SMART BASICS™

Ginger hotels designed their facilities and services to include The Square Meal™—a multi-cuisine restaurant, on-site cyber café, a meeting room (that seats 10 people), laundry facility (same day delivery), on-site ATM, a Gymnasium, secure parking and Doctor-on-call. Ginger lays special emphasis on environmental and ecological issues through the use of compact fluorescent lights (CFL), well utilized natural lighting, auto-time management for air-conditioning and energy-efficient hydro-pneumatic systems.

Ginger provides single rooms for the lone traveler; twin rooms with separate beds for those who travel together; double rooms with a queen-size bed; and special rooms for the specific needs of the physically challenged. The rooms are packed with electronic locking systems, cable TV, Internet connectivity, a mini fridge, tea/coffee makers, self controlled air-conditioners, an ergonomic work area, and a 17-inch flat screen TV. Each room has branded toiletries, 24-hour hot and cold running water, a shower area, and bath and hand towels.

Exhibit 5: Smart Basics™ amenities.

To ensure safety, Ginger is equipped with 24-hour security, closed-circuit TV to maintain records of all visitors, swipe card locks and digital safes located at a Give 'n' Take™ counter at the lobby. In addition, it has supporting infrastructural facilities including administrative offices, kitchens, housekeeping, HVAC facilities, diesel generators for emergency power supply, water treatment plant, sewage treatment plant, etc.

Ginger has outsourced food and beverage to partners operating on a revenue-share model, which includes Café Coffee Day in selected properties. Ginger also offers other facilities like "SMART Wellness", which is an Ayurvedic wellness facility for business travelers at a low cost. This has been developed with Arya Vaidya Pharmacy at all business-cum-leisure locations.

Ginger has introduced "SMART Sleep," which includes a posture-pedic mattress for absorbing and redistributing pressure from the body weight, a tropical duvet and an anti-allergy pillow. The company has also introduced self-operated vending machines that accept Indian currency for customer's convenience. The company is now developing a "SMART Shower". The organization believes that a customer's sleep and bath are his most important needs at their hotels. Going forward, Ginger plans to develop its own range of merchandise that will be offered in its hotels and on its website. The merchandise is to include their bath collection, bedding collection, furnishings and décor, apparel, accessories, travel accessories and etc.

Ginger intends to increase their revenue per available room by adopting a flexible pricing approach/policy, which will be linked to the occupancy levels in the individual hotels.

Ginger operates predominantly in a large geography of non-metros with uncontested market opportunity.

Exhibit 7: The Ginger Development Map

Signed up for 2 properties in Hyderabad

EMPLOYEES AND TRAINING

Ginger believes that their ability to attract good talent, train and retain employees is critical for their growth strategy, as people are critical to maintaining the quality and consistency of their services, and thereby their brand and reputation. The business model of Ginger uses a fair amount of outsourcing. Only about 10 managers per hotel are on the payrolls of Ginger, while all other facilities like kitchen, restaurant, backend maintenance, are outsourced. Ginger has a total of about 175 permanent employees. Since housekeeping and food and beverage are outsourced operations, these employees are on the vendors' payrolls. Ginger tries to leverage on hotel management schools to develop a management talent pool with sufficient capacity to meet the demands presented by their rapid growth. The company aims to recruit, train and retain the best talent through a multi-step recruiting and training process, and career advancement opportunities. Ginger has implemented extensive training programs and periodic tests for managerial and other hotel-based staff primarily through training partners. New unit managers of the hotels are required to undergo a two-month training, during which they receive training in managing all core aspects of the hotel operations, as well as the company culture and philosophy.

In addition to training, Ginger has implemented periodic web-based tests to assess the relevant knowledge and skills of their managerial and other employees. The company uses performance-linked compensation structure, career-oriented training and career advancement opportunities as key drivers to motivate its employees.

Ginger's challenge is also to ensure that the outsourced partner delivers up to the service standards that was agreed upon. To be able to create/modify the outsourced partner's systems and processes to its needs in order to deliver consistent good quality of service to the customer is critical. Since each person in the system is working towards the same goal of delighting the customer, there are few differences in terms of the employee profiles between employees of the outsourced partner and the employees on the payrolls of Ginger. It is important to ensure that the people working for the outsourced partner see themselves as a part of the same team. It is also important that the outsourced partner sees the advantages in following the policies, processes and systems of Ginger.

Ginger operates in a large geography of smaller cities where the profiles of employees in terms of their exposure to technology, comfort with modern amenities, etc. are different from that of a metropolitan city. The challenge therefore lies in getting these employees to perform up to expectations. To design systems to recruit the right kind of people and provide the right kind of training to employees is a challenge for Ginger because, while the developmental inputs do not need to be the same across unit locations, the output in terms of consistent service to fulfill customer needs has to be fairly identical.

Additionally, acquiring professionally qualified employees locally (in remote areas and non-metro cities) and retaining talent at those locations is an area of concern. In their endeavor to retain talent, Ginger makes efforts to ensure that employees see additional value in non-monetary rewards like developing employees competencies by making this visible to their employees through certifications, etc. But to be able to consistently ensure this across locations remains a challenge. If there is attrition, to be able to train and retrain employees (since the numbers are very small) at remote locations becomes very difficult. Ginger's people challenges are thus attracting talent and keeping them continuously motivated, given the vast opportunities for most of their young talent. Ginger training head, Bhanot, says:

"We are cost conscious and so we need to use unconventional methods of recruitment because conventional methods like placement agencies turn out to be very expensive. We recruit through Careers@Ginger, our recruitment portal, and about 48 percent of recruitment happens through this site. The rest of the recruitment is through referral programmes (with rewards for referring). These methods have been successful. We also build relationships with business schools and our employees go to colleges and partner with them by linking with their syllabi, calling students for get-togethers, using students as summer interns; instead of going once in a year like most companies do. We try to build relationships before the recruitment even starts. We also try to address the challenge of keeping our young staff motivated by giving them opportunities to learn and grow by continuously upgrading their skills. We are a budget hotel and we have chosen e-learning initiatives to cut costs. We have in-house training, induction, training operations and e-learning modules (based on customer feedback systems) and program content is created internally."

CENTRALIZED HOTEL MANAGEMENT

Personnel at corporate office perform strategic planning, finance, project development, sales and marketing, training and other functions and guide, support and monitor the on-site hotel operations and executives. The key elements of Ginger's centralized hotel management program are:

Budgeting and Monitoring

The annual budget is based on historical operating performance of the hotel, planned targeted marketing, planned renovations, operational efficiencies and local market conditions.

Quality Assurance and Training–Quality standards

These have been defined for all aspects of hotel operations, covering housekeeping and hotel maintenance, as well as ensuring compliance with these quality standards. A set of procedural manuals have been created and employees are trained to ensure the effectiveness and uniformity through the human resources department at our corporate office as well as through outsourced training vendors. The compliance with quality standards is monitored through both scheduled and unannounced visits and reviews conducted periodically at each hotel. Employees are required take periodic tests (including e-certification) in order to monitor compliance with quality standards.

In addition, the practice of mystery audits and tracking customer comments through guest comment cards, and the direct solicitation of guest opinions regarding specific items, allows Ginger to improve services and amenities at each hotel across the chain. To maintain a competitive edge and enhance their hotels' appeal the company requires each hotel to allocate a fixed percentage of their revenue for periodic renovation and replacement of furnishings and equipment to maintain the quality and standards of its facilities. Ginger has implemented a centralized procurement system (where possible, along with the parent company, IHCL) to obtain the best pricing available for the quality of goods sourced to the hotels and to minimize the operating expenses. Ginger supports local sales efforts of each of its hotels along with corporate office sales executives who develop and implement new marketing programs, and monitor and respond to specific market needs and preferences.

MARKETING GINGER

Ginger's core targeted customers consist of corporate customers, value-oriented individual SME business travelers and leisure travelers seeking comfortable and convenient lodging at an affordable price. Ginger reviews hotel pricing twice a year and typically adjust room rates annually based on the local market conditions of the city and the specific location of each hotel. The corporate office team and the city and hotel managers jointly develop tailored marketing plans to drive sales for each hotel and in each city. Ginger operates in a large geography of non-metropolitan cities like Agartala, Nashik, Bhubhaneshwar and Durgapur where profiles of customer in terms of their exposure to technology, comfort with modern amenities, etc. are different. The challenge therefore lies in customer responses to these.

Ginger is currently using the following distribution channels which includes online media.

- Website—Internet Booking Engine hosted on the Ginger website is one of the main channels used for making the bookings.

- Large travel agencies and smaller travel agents.

- Call Center—Ginger currently has a call center which can be reached through a toll-free number.

- Travel portals and other travel related websites.

- Distribution partners—Partners like BPCL, which is currently rolling out Travel Desks in various BPCL petrol pumps across the country, is also used as a channel for distribution.

Access to these channels enhances occupancy rates of the units (hotels) on a day-to-day basis.

The Ginger brand, trade names, trademarks, trade secrets and other intellectual properties are used to distinguish and protect their technology platforms, services and products from those of their competitors. This also contribute to their competitive advantage in the economy-hotel segment of the lodging industry in India. These intellectual properties are currently owned by the parent company, Indian Hotels Company Limited. To protect the Ginger brand and other intellectual properties, they rely on laws governing trademarks, trade secrets and copyrights as well as imposing confidentiality obligations on their employees, contractors and others. Ginger has registered trademarks in India, including " GINGER " and a registered domain name viz. www.gingerhotels.com.

Ginger's corporate marketing and advertising programs are designed to enhance consumer awareness and preference for the Ginger brand—which is to offer the best value, convenience and comfort in the economy hotel segment of the Indian lodging industry; and to encourage customers' use of their centralized reservation system. Marketing and advertising efforts include outdoor advertisements, distribution of flyers and other marketing collateral on their hotel properties, television, Internet, radio advertising, print advertising in consumer media, promotional events, special holiday promotions and joint promotional activities.

In reshaping customers' expectations to make the brand endearing, Ginger does not provide room service, valet and concierge, and communicates the message "Please help yourselves" through its advertisements. The advertisements convey that since none of the above facilities are provided by the hotel, the customer saves on tips. However, there is clearly an expectation-perception gap as the Indian customer is still uncomfortable with the concept of Smart Basics™. They grapple with "there was nobody to receive me," "nobody gave me water in the room," "I called 7 times and the room boy did not turn up." Ginger sees many customers each day who enter the hotel not knowing what to expect. The many complaints on the websites and complaints registered across the counters at the hotels have to do with services Ginger does not provide (by design) rather than dissatisfactions caused by Ginger's service.

Creating awareness for the Ginger brand at this point in time is a challenge, and since the business model does not allow huge expenditure on media, innovative promotion is needed. Ginger made quirky use of outdoor media by materializing the idea of using a life-size 3-dimensional hoarding of some parts of the hotel, including getting someone to live in it. This was taken across a couple of metros for promotion and received extensive coverage in the electronic media.

Ginger needs to ensure their customers come in recognizing and knowing what they should be expecting from the hotel. The challenge is not only in communication through advertisements, but also to communicate it clearly when a customer checks in. Ginger's ability to communicate clearly what the customer can expect is an area of concern. This is because there is a tendency not to explain either because the customer does not have the patience to listen or there is a fear of losing this customer. Ginger has been trying to plug this by educating the customer before he/she checks in

by having commercials playing in the hotel, training front line managers to give clear messages to the customer as to what Ginger can deliver, and communicating this through advertising.

STUDY QUESTIONS

1. What is Ginger's service concept? Use the Flower of Service to aid you in your answer.

2. How does Ginger create customer value?

3. How can Ginger manage customer expectations more effectively?

4. Evaluate Ginger's brand positioning and communications strategy. Given that the number of players in the budget hotels market is increasing, how can Ginger sustain its unique positioning?

5. Ginger faces challenges relating to people. How can they overcome these challenges?

6. What are the key challenges in the way to service excellence for Ginger? Give recommendations to Ginger to overcome these challenges?

---

[1] © 2009 Dr Mukta Kampllikar, Senior Practice Consultant, Tata Management Training Center, Pune, India.

Managing Word of Mouth: The Referral Incentive Program That Backfired[1]

Patricia Chew and Jochen Wirtz

Nguyen Trung Hung stared in dismay at the field-test reports on his desk. He was the Sales and Promotions Manager at AHL Insurance Corporation, the fifth-largest insurance company in Vietnam, and he had been the main driving force behind the company's new initiative to expand its customer base through the implementation of a "recommend-a-friend" incentive program, the first of its kind in the industry. Before the actual implementation of the program, the company had conducted a three-month field test and offered the incentive program to a small number of customers in each of the four segments it had identified in its database.

A referral incentive program was introduced, but resulted in fewer referrals than expected, especially from the desired target segments!

Based on the success of similar programs in the banking and mobile phone industries, he had thought that the initiative would be a runaway success. Results, however, were far below expectations, although the program was not a complete failure. There were referrals generated, but it was mainly from the low-yield segment of its customer base. Moreover, its higher-revenue customers, who had traditionally generated the highest number of referrals, seemed to have generated less rather than more referrals during the referral-program trial period.

BACKGROUND OF AHL INSURANCE CORPORATION

AHL Insurance Corporation had its humble beginnings as an automobile insurer in Huế, the capital city of Thua Thien-Hue province in 1985. The founder, Nguyen Anh Dung, was an insurance salesman who decided to start his own business in Huế, believing that it was a niche market with a lot of untapped potential. Since then, the company has grown tremendously. Over the years, it expanded its markets and product lines to meet the changing needs of its customers. Today, it has 13 offices at different cities in Vietnam, like Hanoi, Ho Chi Minh City, Ha Phong, Da Nang, Can Tho and Huế. There are currently more than 22,000 independent agents serving the needs of its customers.

The mission of AHL is to provide quality service and build relationships with its customers through mutual trust, and integrity. AHL aims to be the customer's first and best choice and maintain its position of leadership as a comprehensive provider of insurance products, and it has a variety of insurance products to meet both the personal and business needs of its customers.

The main strengths of AHL lie not only in the diversity of its products, but also in the excellent customer service provided by its agents. On top of that, in an industry where some firms have gained a bad reputation by making it difficult for its customers to make insurance claims, AHL actually trains dedicated agents to explain the little details of claims to its customers and these agents also help customers to expedite the claims process. As a result, it has earned the trust and loyalty of its customers over the years.

CUSTOMER SEGMENTS

When the idea of "recommend-a-friend" program was first brought up, the company used its sophisticated Customer Relationship Management (CRM) system to segment its customers into four groups. The "Apostles" were customers who had been with the company for over ten years, and they had basically consolidated most of their insurance purchases with AHL. Besides themselves, their family members had also purchased various kinds of insurance products from AHL, ranging from life insurance, investment-linked plans, retirement plans and children's education plans to property liabilities, automobile insurance, etc. Those "Apostles" running their own businesses would also buy products like group insurance packages, commercial property liabilities and disability packages from AHL. They were not price sensitive and were willing to pay a premium for a customized insurance plan to meet their individual needs. One distinguishing feature of the "Apostles" was the fact that they really helped to "sell" AHL to their family members, friends and associates. This was the group of customers that had traditionally generated the most referrals for AHL to date. As is typical of most companies, this group of customers generated about 80 percent of the company's revenue.

The "Loyals" were customers who had been with AHL for more than seven years on average. Compared to the "Apostles", they bought fewer kinds of products, and generated fewer referrals. They generally consolidated their insurance purchases with a few companies and were reluctant to pay a premium for customized plans, preferring to buy the standardized ones. The "Leads" were termed so because of their seeming inertia. They usually bought only personal insurance products, and may have one or two insurance policies that are long-term in nature, like the life, health, endowment or retirement insurance plans. When agents tried to sell them other kinds of plans, they were not open to the idea. Like the "Loyals," they also tended to use several insurance companies to meet their insurance needs based on price and coverage, but were not as price sensitive as the "Butterflies." In terms of referrals, this group would provide the occasional referral. Lastly, the "Butterflies" was the group of customers who bought the occasional short-term insurance policies like travel-related products, and might hold long-term policies from other insurance companies. This group of customers was highly price sensitive. They would flock to wherever there were any deals or promotional incentives on insurance plans.

The "Recommend-a-Friend" Incentive Program

The program was based on a points system. Points were awarded on the basis of profitability and term of the insurance products sold. The higher the sum assured, and the longer the insurance coverage, the more points the referrer could collect. The points system was transparent as the referrer could check beforehand how many points they would get if their friends bought a certain kind of product or plan from AHL. Points could be accumulated and exchanged for a variety of gifts featured in a glossy and attractive catalog.

For example, with 50,000 points, which is the highest number of points one could accumulate for a single referral, one could exchange for a branded watch costing US$800. Other products of lesser value in the catalog included Seiko watches; Samsonite travel luggage; Parker pens; Nokia mobile phones; electrical goods like shavers, blenders, juicers, vacuum cleaners, microwave ovens, toasters and television sets; DVD and CD players; restaurant vouchers, etc. In all, there were about 300 items in the catalog. The lowest number of points awarded was 50 points, for short-term travel insurance plans.

Referrals

Thus far, the "Butterflies" and "Leads" had generated the most referrals since the launch of the "recommend-a-friend" referral incentive program. However, since they themselves usually did not purchase the high-sum-assured policies, or long-term policies, their friends were also people who bought similar kinds of policies. As a result, short-term policies like travel policies that cover a few days, or up to one year, and child care policies that are typically no longer than two years, have been very popular. These policies typically did not produce high profit margins for the company, and the insured values tended to be lower.

What was alarming was the fact that the number of referrals from the "Apostles" had fallen since the start of the program. Nguyen Trung Hung had expected that this group would be motivated to refer even more friends to AHL. Their recommendations usually resulted in individuals buying policies that were long-term, and of high sums assured, thus generating higher profits for the company. Exhibit 2 details the results of the referrals in the three months of the field test. 500 customers from each of the four segments were selected to participate in the field test. For each segment, a control group consisting also of 500 customers was selected and monitored during the market testing.

INITIAL INTERVIEW RESULTS

Three months after the launch of the program, Nguyen Trung Hung had asked his marketing managers to conduct some interviews with customers from various segments, to get their views about the program (Exhibit 3). As a result, about 30 in-depth individual interviews were conducted with customers from each of the four segments, in their homes. Exhibit 3 shows some verbatim comments by the respondents.

FUTURE DIRECTION

Nguyen Trung Hung knew that before the next meeting with the Marketing Director, he had to come up with a report about the results of the field test, and also provide possible solutions to the problem. He was up for a promotion and did not want this project to affect his chances. What should he do next? Why were the results the way they were? Should he abandon the program even though approximately US$50,000 had been invested in it? Alternatively, should he change certain features of the program before relaunching it so that it is more targeted, because the different segments of customers seemed to react quite differently to the program? Was there a need for more market research to see what each group of customers would prefer in a referral incentive program?

STUDY QUESTIONS

1. Analyze the field test data and derive key managerial conclusions from them.

2. What course of action would you recommend to Nguyen Trung Hung? Determine his options, and assess the pros and cons of each option, and then recommend one course of action to him.

Exhibit 1: Marketing managers conduct interviews with customers to elicit feedback about the referral program.

Exhibit 2: Referral frequency and value index by customer segment.

	Apostles	Control Group	Loyals	Control Group	Leads	Control Group	Butterflies	Control Group
Number of referrals during the 3 months before the test	22	21	17	15	3	4	1	1
Number of referrals during the 3 test months	15	19	11	14	8	3	16	1
Conversion rate (i.e. customers who actually took up a policy)	32%	33%	27%	28%	18%	22%	12%	18%
Average policy value sold (US$'000)	173	185	143	148	59	65	33	41

Note: The index refers to the rebased number of referrals received per 1,000 customers per year. The average policy value closed by the referred customer is shown in thousand U.S. dollars ('000).

Exhibit 3: Verbatim comments about the incentive program.

Apostles	Loyals	Leads	Butterflies
"…I would only recommend if I thought it was good for the person. I would not do anything in a self-serving way…." 39, marketing manager	"…the gifts they offer. I have enough junk in my house already, I don't need anymore of it." 29, unemployed	"…the kind of thing, I leave it to the individual, I don't push…." 26, administrative assistant	"…I will definitely be motivated to get in those customers because the incentive is very relevant to me…I'll definitely do it fast–speak to anyone close to me and not so close to me…" 22, student
"….It's almost like a forced recommendation because, ultimately, you think there is something to benefit yourself. I do the recommendation out of helping somebody…." 64, businesswoman	"….I will not go out of my way to recommend just to obtain the incentive. That would be a waste of my time. I do have better things to do with my time." 32, home maker	"…the reward that I have makes me want to tell others…" 18, student	"…When they started the program, I email everyone on my mailing list. I'm aiming to get the Tag Heuer. It would indeed be a dream for me!" 20, waitress
"…I'm not the kind who looks at incentives. I look at ties. If the person is close to me… and he needs an insurance, then I will want to help him out by giving him advice on what to buy…" 35, banquet manager	"…if the company was good, they wouldn't need an incentive program. When they do that, I start to have doubts about them, and am worried about my investment…" 35, IT executive	…I'm excited by incentives. I love the incentives in the catalog. I would definitely recommend it to anyone who is interested…" 22, clerical assistant	"…I'm saving a lot. I like the feeling of exchanging points for something that I don't have to pay money for." 35, home maker
"…being a businessman who is time scarce, I never bother with it…" 56, businessman	"…I recommend my friends because the agents and customer service officers provide good service. I don't care if I get the incentive or not…" 27, professional sportsman	"…I've already gotten my friends and family to buy some insurance, and I got a Swatch watch in return. Isn't that wonderful?" 26, sales executive	"…since it's free, why don't I take advantage of it right? It would be stupid not to." 25, security guard
"…it's the service that the company has been providing that I like. It's not what they are offering…." 41, management consultant	"…the incentives that they are offering are just not worthwhile in the time that I would have to spend getting what they offer." 46, director	"…if it wasn't for the rewards, I would not have told others about the company." 40, home maker	"…whichever company is giving away freebies, I always try to take advantage of that…it saves me a lot of money. I'll queue up overnight if I have to." 19, student
"…I can buy those things with my own money. Why should I then be motivated to recommend based on the gifts?" 44, pilot	"…I think the incentive is immaterial…I will take it as an extra bonus. In the first place, we're doing word of mouth already all the time for people unknowingly…" 32, teacher		

Captial One: Launching a Mass Media Campaign[1]

Richard Ivey School of Business
The University of Western Ontario

IVEY

At the end of March 2005, Clinton Braganza, Senior Brand Manager, was preparing to present his recommendations to his Canadian senior management team at Capital One's Toronto office. Braganza had been tasked with determining Capital One's strategy for its first mass media advertising campaign in Canada. He had spent the last few months conducting and analyzing consumer research, and had started to adapt several U.S. and U.K. television ads for use in Canada.

Capital One's intent was to maintain its competition with Canadian banks, which defined the objective of this mass media advertising campaign: *To raise Capital One's awareness and communicate a position in the marketplace in order to achieve growth, and change the market's perception of it's financial products.*

With a limited budget, Braganza knew he could not invest in all the options in front of him. To design his strategy, Braganza revisited the consumer research findings he had compiled. Braganza faced three major challenges:

1. Choosing the appropriate target segments.

2. Selecting different types of advertisements for a nationwide launch.

3. Drafting an advertising plan that will best deliver the message to Capital One's target audience groups.

THE CANADIAN BANKING INDUSTRY

In 2005, the Canadian banking industry was made up of 13 domestic banks, 34 foreign bank subsidiaries and 11 foreign bank branches. The six major domestic banks—Royal Bank, Bank of Montreal, TD Canada Trust, Canadian Imperial Bank of Commerce, Scotiabank and National Bank—accounted for more than 90 percent of the assets held by the banking industry. In Canada, these six banks operated a total of 8,000 branches and nearly 17,000 automated banking machines. The other seven domestic banks were significantly smaller and, as a group, accounted for less than two percent of the total assets held by the Canadian banking industry. With a combined seven percent share, foreign banks that operated in Canada accounted for the remaining assets of the Canadian banking industry.

93 percent of Canadians had banking relationships, and it was common for customers to consolidate their mortgage, car loan, personal loan, line of credit, investments and credit card at the same retail bank.

In contrast, the US retail banking industry was less consolidated, owing to the legacy of interstate banking regulations and the preference of US consumers to use different financial institutions for their various financial needs.

Credit Cards

Credit cards provided consumers a means of payment, a source of consumer loans and were used as marketing tools by companies. By 2005, credit cards were accepted at more than 1.1 million merchant outlets in Canada. Issued through banks and financial services firms, credit cards belonged to one of the following payment solution organizations: Visa, MasterCard (the two most dominant players), American Express or Diners Club. Merchants remit between one and two percent of the total transaction charged to Visa or MasterCard. The exact fee charged varies depending on the size of the merchant, with larger firms paying close to one percent and smaller firms paying close to two percent. In Canada, the 23 principal issuers of Visa or MasterCard branded credit cards were banks, credit unions, caisses populaires and retailers. For an overview of Visa and MasterCard statistics, see Exhibit 1 on page 463. For the market shares of Visa and MasterCard, see Exhibit 2 on page 464.

The Canadian credit card industry had been traditionally controlled by the six major banks, but had, in recent years, experienced higher levels of competition because of several US-based players such as Capital One and MBNA, who had entered the market. Between 1996 and 2004, as the number of Visa and MasterCard issuers grew from 15 to 23, the circulation of cards in Canada grew from 30.2 million to 53.4 million. In 2004, about 23.2 million of these credit card accounts were considered "active," which meant they held balances, including those that were paid off every month.

A common trait shared by US and Canadian retail banks was their tendency to run their credit card business as part of an integrated operation. Managers at North American retail banks relied on a combination of these four objectives to run their line of business and optimize profits:

1. Improving marketing to new accounts

2. Retaining existing accounts

3. Minimizing credit losses

4. Minimizing costs

Retail banks in both countries primarily tended to market their credit cards to their own customers through their extensive branch networks. In addition to their trusted brand names, retail banks had lower costs of capital—up to 75 basis points lower than the US issuers, such as Capital One and MBNA. It was not surprising to see that retail banks garnered the greatest share of new acquisitions in 2004. More than half of the 2004 card applications were received through store and bank branch channels (see Exhibit 3 on page 464).

Credit Card Customers

Customers were typically divided into three categories depending on their default risk:

- Super prime

- Prime

- Sub prime

At one extreme, super prime customers were considered a low risk for default; at the other end, sub prime customers were considered a high risk for default. As a result, Canadian retail banks typically offered credit cards only to prime or super prime customers. For a look at selected statistics available on the three segments, see Table 1.

Table 1: Risk profile of customers.

Risk Segment	Risk Score	% of Cdn Adults	Average Credit Card Debt	Average Credit Available on Credit Cards	Average Number of Credit Cards
Sub prime	<660	17%	$4,500	$6,600	1.8
Prime	660–719	17%	$5,300	$12,500	2.2
Super prime	>720	66%	$2,000	$13,700	1.8

Source: Equifax eIB Tool, June 2005.

Within each segment, customers could be further divided into "transactors" and "revolvers." *Transactors* typically paid off their entire credit balance every month and tended to avoid interest charges. *Revolvers* generally carried a balance from one month to the other and would pay their minimum monthly payments (which was two or three percent of the total amount owed) but not their full amount. Because customers paid interest on the balances they carried forward, as a group, *revolvers* were a significant source of revenue for credit companies. An Ipsos Reid survey estimated that the average customer carried a balance between $2,400 and $2,900 (see Exhibit 4 on page 464).

Customers who had more credit cards were likely to have higher monthly spends (see Exhibit 5 on page 464). Regardless of how many credit cards customers possessed, however, they typically relied on one primary card. While customers had key reasons for using their primary cards, some were willing to replace their primary card with another if they were offered the right value proposition. (see Exhibit 6 on page 465).

CAPITAL ONE

In 2005, Capital One had a global customer base of 49 million and managed loans of US$105 billion. In addition to issuing credit cards, Capital One offered other financial products and services such as auto loans, home equity loans, small business loans, instalment loans, consumer financing for elective medical and dental procedures and savings products.

Established in 1995, Capital One had developed into a global diversified financial services provider with operations in the United States, Canada and the United Kingdom. The firm was founded by Richard Fairbank on his belief that the power of information, technology, testing and great people could be combined to deliver highly customized financial products directly to customers. Capital One was known for its proprietary Information-Based Strategy (IBS), which referred to its practice of relying heavily on data to make management decisions. Using scientific testing on a large scale, Capital One gathered huge amounts of information to help tailor products and services to the individual consumer, rather than simply offering one product to broad socio-economic groups. Capital One attributed its financial services success to its focus on information technology, customer acquisition and customer retention. Less than one decade after it had been established, Capital One joined the Fortune 500.

In 1996, Capital One entered Canada but, unlike its US parent, the focus was on issuing credit cards. With a foothold in Canada, Capital One leveraged its IBS to take advantage of the opportunity to offer all Canadians, in all risk segments, low-interest rates and access to credit. Capital One's initial strategy was to present a unique credit card offer to Canadians. When it began operations, Capital One relied on an initial 9.9 percent introductory offer to rapidly gain market share. As a comparison, its competitors were offering fixed-rate credit cards with interest rates of 16 percent and higher. In subsequent years, Capital One's low-price offerings became attractive to prime customers who "revolved." For the sub prime segment—a segment the major banks tended to ignore—Capital One offered products not previously available, giving sub prime customers an opportunity to build their credit history.

Canadians responded to Capital One's unique products and by 2004, they had US$2.4 billion in outstanding balances. To manage its growth, Capital One increased its staff to 100 employees in its Toronto office. Capital One's main focus in 2005 was to establish a clear positioning in the marketplace and to expand its credit card product offerings and channels to acquire new customers.

The Capital One Customer

Capital One customers used credit cards for several reasons:

- For convenience

- To avoid carrying cash

- To keep track of expenses

- For collecting loyalty reward points

If customers chose not to use credit cards, they either wanted to avoid interest and debt, or had a preference for cash or debit payment methods. It was noted that, Capital One customers were as equally likely to use credit cards for special occasion purchases as they were for business-related purchases; whereas, the general populace was more likely to use credit cards for the latter purpose[2]. For a list of Capital One credit cards available to Canadian consumers, see Exhibit 7 on page 465.

Customer Acquisition and Retention Using IBS

Capital One relied heavily on its IBS for growth. An entrepreneurial structure supported the culture of testing and learning, which was at the heart of the IBS. The responsibilities for the two core activities of customer acquisition and retention resided with the Acquisitions division and the Account Management division, respectively. Capital One built consumer tests, analyzed and applied results from large quantities of data to reduce credit risk, provided customized products for consumers and improved operational efficiency.

In the United States, Capital One combined public bureau data with its private data. In contrast, the Canadian branch only had access to bureau data in Canada after a consumer had completed an application for a credit card. Thus, from a consumer targeting perspective, Capital One felt that the management of direct mail was its largest tactical challenge across all segments. As a result, to better target consumers with appropriate direct mail, Capital One had to rely on other means to segment consumers. By actively testing a wide variety of products and service features, marketing channels (in Canada, Capital One utilized both direct mail and the Internet to solicit applications) and other aspects of offerings, Capital One enhanced the response levels and maximized returns on investment within its underwriting parameters.

Credit evaluation began during the application process. Generally credit card issuers used a combination of credit bureau information, statistical models and decision rules to approve or decline applicants. These procedures were constantly changing in response to dynamic market conditions and new insights.

Driving innovation was always a key concern at Capital One, because it was the foundation of the company's success. Communicating Capital One's innovation was equally important, as Sartaj Alag, President of the Canadian branch of Capital One, pointed out:

> "How do we come up with an advertising strategy that: 1) speaks directly to our target segment, 2) is distinctive from our competitors, and 3) is a position we can immediately deliver on?"

Youssef Lahrech, Capital One's Head of Marketing and Analysis in Canada added:

> "How can Capital One change Canadian consumers' negative attitude towards credit cards through our advertising campaign? Can Capital One build one campaign for all consumer segments or do we need to differentiate our ads?"

To determine whether their programs were on the right track, Capital One relied on quantitative measures, such as net present value per marketing dollar. After a customer was acquired, the Account Management Division ran tests to determine which marketing programs would either increase revenues or decrease default. Some of these programs included building balances, credit line increases and cross-selling products.

DAY-TO-DAY CHALLENGES

Competitive Responses by Retail Banks

In 2004, major banks continued to issue the majority of new credit cards. With their infrastructure of branches and relationships with banking customers, acquisition costs for banks were lower than similar costs for US credit card issuers. To respond to products offered by US issuers, retail banks did not have to innovate, advocate or educate. All they had to do was watch and follow. For example, while balance transfers used to be a market niche for Capital One, retail banks had since entered the market.

Although Capital One was constantly inventing new products to keep ahead of its competitors, one advantage it maintained over retail banks was its ability to target offers to select consumers. A second advantage that favored Capital One was its expertize in credit cards, among other financial services offered. Because retail banks ran their credit card operations as part of a diversified portfolio of products, they seemed not inclined to grow their credit card operations if it meant cannibalizing other products in their portfolio.

A Focused Operation That Had Not Partnered With a Rewards Program

For other card issuers, a strong rewards program, such as Air Canada's Aeroplan (to which 21 percent of all Canadian card holders belonged in 2004, up from 12 percent in 2002), provided quantifiable incentives to customers to increase their spending in the hunt for reward miles. Such programs also allowed partners to exchange mailing lists. There were several rewards programs in Canada other than Aeroplan, including Air Miles (by Loyalty Management Group), Hudson's Bay Company's HBC Rewards and Club Z program, Shoppers Drug Mart's Optimum program and Canadian Tire money. 23 percent of respondents cited the availability of a rewards program as a reason for using their primary credit card. By 2005, Capital One had built a strong business without having to rely on a rewards program or a partner in Canada.

Working Without Physical Branches

Capital One's lack of physical branches in Canada posed a unique challenge. Without face-to-face contact, several Capital One associates reasoned that, it could be difficult to build a relationship with customers who appreciated and fulfilled their needs.

Substitutes for Credit Cards

For customers who used credit cards purely as transaction vehicles, cash, checks, debit cards and direct deposits were used as substitutes. Although they did not demonstrate a cardholder's creditworthiness, debit cards allowed consumers to withdraw cash from the point of sale, giving them "cash back," while making purchases. For customers who carried balances on their credit cards, product substitutes included bank lines of credit, bank instalment loans, home equity loans (with lower interest rates), retail lay-away plans, retail store credit (such as Leon's and The Brick), cash advances against pay checks from companies such as Money Mart, and vehicle loans from automobile manufacturers or leasing organizations such as GE Capital.

THE MARKETING AND PROMOTIONS CHOICES

Capital One's global value proposition had been centered on the tagline "What's in Your Wallet?" positioning Capital One as offering "great value without the hassle." This proposition had been conveyed to customers through a series of long-running television ads in the United States and, more recently, in the United Kingdom. In both the United States and the United Kingdom, Capital One's locally made advertisements had proven extremely successful, with awareness levels of 98 percent in the United States and 95 percent in the United Kingdom. Up until now, Canadians primarily knew Capital One as a price player, with some Canadians aware of "great value without the hassle" because of US advertising spillover.

Braganza wondered about the implications of using the US positioning in Canada, and asked himself several questions:

- Does "great value" refer to price or should it refer to rewards?

- How important were rewards to Canadians and what were the implications for Capital One?

- What were the "hassles" that Canadian consumers wanted to avoid and how could Capital One show that it was providing "great value without the hassle" to Canadians?

To sum it up, was "great value" the right positioning for Capital One in Canada?

Apart from determining the right positioning, Braganza also had to decide if he would adapt US and or UK advertisements, or develop advertisements unique to Canada. He recalled that consumer packaged goods companies (Procter & Gamble, for example) developed a significant portion of their advertising in the United States, and then adapted the same advertisement for various countries. In contrast, MasterCard's "priceless" campaign, gave flexibility to individual countries' organizations to develop their own

unique advertisements based on a common global theme (tagline: "There are some things money can't buy; for everything else, there's MasterCard").

Braganza projected a minimum of four months to develop new advertising. He would need to find and hire an advertising agency, organize consumer research and obtain internal approvals at various stages. These tasks would require Capital One to shift precious marketing management resources from other programs designed to enhance customer acquisition and retention. And, according to Millward Brown's research, there was a greater than 50 percent probability that a new advertisement in the financial services industry would score below the Canadian average. But the opportunity to develop an advertisement that truly "cut through the clutter" of average advertising had a strong appeal. Adapting a US or UK advertisement would include paying licensing fees and could be accomplished in four weeks or less. However, it was not clear if the portfolio of available advertisements would enable Capital One to meet its objectives in the Canadian market.

But which segment should Capital One focus on? According to the Canadian test results, the various executions appealed to different target segments. Although competitors had largely ignored the sub prime customer (who seemed more responsive to offers), Capital One could also target prime and super prime customers (who were less responsive to offers, and were targeted by retail banks). Also should Capital One aim to book additional accounts or target existing customers? Put another way, should the television advertisements boost Capital One's direct mail response rate, or should they encourage current customers to use their cards more often?

Generally, different advertisement executions were needed to achieve either target. For example, focusing on an introductory interest rate could be enticing to new customers but not to existing ones. However, there were some advertisements—such as those focusing on fraud protection—that could be used for either segment. But would focusing on fraud protection be too general? Also, could any of the UK and US advertisements be relevant to a Canadian audience? Capital One was a relatively small player in Canada, as could be seen by Canada's contribution to the firm's overall loan portfolio (see Exhibit 8 on page 466).

With regard to executing the strategy, John McNain, head of Brand and New Ventures at Capital One, wondered:

"How do we build a sustainable brand in Canada yet recognize our current limitations such as resources, infrastructure and product offerings? Also, how do we balance the growth of general awareness versus quickly demonstrating the returns from a more direct advertising campaign? We have to consider three dimensions. First, geography: Should we target just Toronto or the entire country? Second, how do we target our customer segments—Do we offer something general or consider a rewards or price play? Third, to what extent should our advertisements target new accounts or existing customers?"

CONCLUSION

Braganza knew that a presentation to Capital One's senior management team would be more convincing if he could back up his recommendations with numbers and logic. While other firms could choose to invest in brand development over a longer time frame, Capital One's senior management team would want to see how the company's investment would pay out in the short to medium term. Braganza knew that advertising in the United States and United Kingdom would continue— clear evidence that their campaigns were paying out. But Braganza did not want to focus solely on payout because it could compromise Capital One's brand-building efforts. His challenge was to balance the needs of driving new customer signups with the longer term goals of influencing customer behavior, increasing satisfaction rates and reducing attrition.

Braganza outlined the decisions he faced:

• On which customer segments should Capital One focus?

• What value proposition should Capital One be signaling to these segments?

• What advertisements should be used to deliver these messages, and what customization efforts were needed?

Braganza took a look at the competitive media spend for Canadian credit cards, as compiled by Nielsen, a media research firm (see Exhibit 9 on page 467). Next, he looked at a list of competitive cards and their features, as can be seen in Exhibit 10 on page 468. He also reviewed results from Capital One's UK and US advertising copy tests in Canada for both the prime and sub prime segments (see Exhibit 11 on page 470).

This was the first time that Capital One would be investing in mass media advertising. Braganza wanted to recommend the best set of options to his senior management team.

STUDY QUESTION

1. Given the objectives of the mass media advertising campaign, how can each of the three challenges faced by Clinton Braganza be addressed?

Exhibit 12: Brand-building a credible credit card line involves consideration of key factors like customer segments, value proposition and advertisement scope.

CANADIAN BANKERS ASSOCIATION
Credit Card Statistics - VISA and MasterCard

Fiscal Year Ended Oct 31	Number of Cards in Circulation [1a] (Millions)	*No. of Accts with balances (Millions), including those that are paid off every month [1b]	Net Retail Volume [2] (Billions)	Average Sale	% Delinquency 90 Days & over [3][7]	Number of Cards Fraudulently used [2]	$ Amount of Fraudulent Accounts written off [6] (Millions)	Merchant Outlets [5]	VISA/MCI Principal Issuers
1977	8.2		$3.61	$30.46	1.3%	-	-	271,150	-
1978	9.0		$4.90	$32.50	1.3%	-	-	290,692	-
1979	9.9		$6.64	$35.72	1.2%	-	-	322,115	-
1980	10.8		$8.82	$39.47	1.3%	-	-	347,845	-
1981	12.0		$10.59	$42.43	1.0%	-	-	371,831	-
1982	11.6		$13.83	$50.30	1.7%	-	$15.88	382,206	-
1983	12.1		$14.84	$49.88	0.9%	19,200	$17.39	419,610	10
1984	13.1		$16.92	$52.05	0.7%	21,332	$16.79	442,928	10
1985	14.0	7.3	$19.35	$51.90	0.7%	21,026	$17.54	527,042	10
1986	15.5	7.9	$23.01	$55.15	0.8%	22,326	$18.61	571,771	10
1987	17.6	8.8	$26.37	$58.52	0.7%	23,913	$15.78	642,429	12
1988	19.4	9.5	$30.33	$61.90	0.7%	25,773	$15.63	646,844	13
1989	20.4	10.3	$36.10	$66.00	0.9%	30,919	$19.20	709,674	14
1990	23.2	11.1	$38.60	$67.22	1.8%	32,851	$28.90	786,288	14
1991	24.3	11.8	$40.45	$67.40	1.3%	53,968	$44.60	857,159	14
1992	24.4	12.2	$43.10	$69.30	1.0%	61,234	$63.50	896,365	14
1993	25.0	12.4	$47.90	$70.50	0.7%	63,442	$75.20	904,689	13
1994	27.5	13.2	$55.10	$72.40	0.9%	63,635	$70.60	955,993	13
1995	28.8	13.6	$61.26	$74.51	0.9%	66,109	$72.64	981,851	13
1996	30.2	14.1	$67.70	$77.80	1.0%	77,740	$83.60	1,076,694	15
1997	31.9	15.0	$76.00	$82.50	0.9%	89.982	$88.08	1,106,141	17
1998	35.3	16.0	$84.10	$89.96	0.9%	126,384	$104.80	1,143,110	19
1999	37.7	17.3	$94.30	$90.35	0.9%	132,836	$134.10	1,139,228	18
2000	40.1	18.5	$109.87	$95.57	0.7%	112,070	$156.38	1,187,745	19
2001	44.1	19.6	$121.82	$99.16	0.8%	116,139	$142.27	1,206,779	19
2002	49.4	20.8	$135.69	$100.51	0.7%	136,598	$128.42	1,265,157	23
2003	50.4	22.2	$150.49	$102.00	0.8%	146,310	$138.60	1,187,384	23
2004	53.4	23.2	$168.78	$104.00	0.8%	177,081	$163.18	1,128,410	23

Note: (1a) As at last day of the fiscal year-end

(1b) As at last day of the fiscal year-end, including accounts with balances paid off every month.

(2) Reported total for the fiscal year.

(3) Percentage of outstandings as at fiscal year-end.

(4) Total of Net Retail Volume ($ sales) and cash advance volume ($).

(5) Merchants accepting VISA and/or MASTERCARD. Note that merchants accepting both cards have been reported by each plan. To estimate # of merchant outlets accepting VISA or MASTERCARD, divide Merchants Outlets by 2 and multiply by 1.1.

(Exhibit 1 continues on next page)

(6)   Includes total cardholder and merchant fraud for the fiscal year.

(7)   Effective October 31, 1991, a new interpretation of "90 days & over" was adopted. This resulted in a one-time reduction in the delinquency ratio of approx. 0.2%.

PRINCIPAL VISA AND MASTERCARD ISSUERS:

VISA   Bank of America, Bank of Nova Scotia, Caisses Populaires Desjardins, CIBC, Citizens Bank of Canada, Home Trust, Laurentian Bank, Royal Bank, TD Bank, US Bank, Vancouver City Savings Credit Union.

MCI   Alberta Treasury Branches, Bank of Montreal, Canadian Tire Acceptance Ltd, Capital One, Citibank Canada, Credit Union Electronic Transaction Services Inc., G.E. Capital Corp., MBNA Canada., National Bank of Canada, President's Choice Financial, Wells Fargo/Trans Canada, Sears Canada

(Data from Affiliated Issuers reported through Principal Issuers)

Source: Canadian Bankers Association, Table includes data from all VISA & MASTERCARD issuers.

Exhibit 2: Card ownership in Canada.

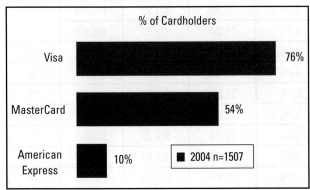

Souce: *Ipsos-Reid.*

Exhibit 4: Reported value of card balance.

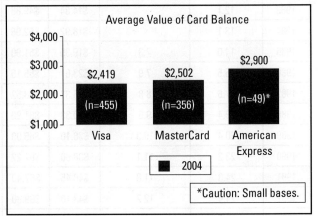

Souce: *Ipsos-Reid.*

Exhibit 3: Distribution channels for card applications.

Channel used:	2002 (n=289)	2003 (n-256)	2004 (n=322)
	%	%	%
In store	26	26	32
At bank branch	20	17	26
Kiosk/shopping centre	-	-	3
Through the mail	33	26	18
Inbound telephone	9	6	10
Outbound telephone	4	7	4
Over the Internet	3	6	7

Souce: *Ipsos-Reid.*

Exhibit 5: Reported monthly personal spend on all cards.

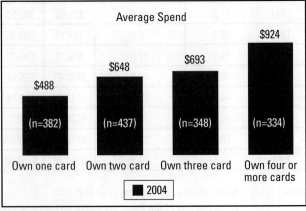

Souce: *Ipsos-Reid.*

Exhibit 6: Reasons for using/switching primary card.

% of Primary Cardholders:	Reason for Using (n=1477)	Reason for Switching (n=238)
	%	%
REWARD PROGRAMS	23	27
COST	11	19
BANK RELATIONSHIP	16	13
CONVENIENCE	14	13
USAGE	8	1
CREDIT/LIMIT	3	4
ONLY CARD I HAVE	15	-

Source: *Ipsos-Reid.*

Exhibit 7: Capital One's credit cards available to Canadians.

Credit Card	Capital One® Low-Rate Platinum MasterCard®	Capital One 1% Cash Rebate Platinum MasterCard	Capital One Gold MasterCard	Capital One Secured MasterCard
This card is right for you if	You have excellent crediit and have had Canadian cards for at least 3 years	You have excellent credit and have had Canadian cards for at least 3 years	You would like to strengthen your credit and have had Canadian cards for at least 3 years	You want to establish credit
Annual Purchase Rate	6.99%	17.90%	9.9% until May 2006; 19.8% variable thereafter (a variable annual interest rate of Canadian prime plus 15.55%, currently equal to 19.8% as of July 2005)	19.8% variable (a variable annual interest rate of Canadian Prime plus 15.55%, currently equal to 19.8% as of July 2005)
Annual Fee	None	None	$59	$59
Security Funds Required	None	None	None	Either $75 or $200

Source: *www.capitalone.ca, accessed January 27, 2006.*

Exhibit 8: Capital One financial corporation: Contribution by geographic region (in US$).

	2004 December 31		2003 December 31	
	Loans	Percentage of Total	Loans	Percentage of Total
Geographic Region:				
Domestic				
South	$25,034,582	31.34%	$23,262,643	32.65%
West	$15,873,159	19.88%	$14,662,193	20.58%
Midwest	$15,220,162	19.06%	$13,643,202	19.15%
Northeast	$13,198,619	16.53%	$12,029,894	16.89%
Total Domestic	$69,326,522	86.81%	$63,597,932	89.27%
International				
U.K.	$8,163,109	10.22%	$5,546,644	7.78%
Canada	$2,360,297	2.96%	$1,935,396	2.72%
Other	$11,371	.01%	$164,824	0.23%
Total international	$10,534,777	13.19%	$7,646,864	10.73%
	$79,861,299	100.00%	$71,244,796	100.00%
Less securitzation adjustments	($41,645,708)		($38,394,527)	
Total	$38,215,591		$32,850,269	

Source: *Capital One Annual Report*.

Exhibit 9: Nielson 2004 competitive media spend.

Company	Total Media ($) MT Shr %		Daily Paper ($)	Magazine ($)	Out of Home ($)	Radio ($)	Total TV ($)	Network TV ($)	Selective TV ($)
(JETSGO CORPORATION)	25,000	0	0	0	25,000	0	0	0	0
ALASKA AIR GROUP, INC	592,699	0.8	222,202	0	0	10,650	359,847	0	359,847
AMERICAN EXPRESS COMPANY	13,477,478	17.2	4,433,944	2,049,491	519,502	215,011	6,259,530	5,373,450	886,080
BANK OF AMERICA	56,792	0.1	0	0	0	56,792	0	0	0
BANK OF NOVA SCOTIA	330,160	0.4	29,524	15,316	0	0	285,320	193,616	91,704
BAYVIEW CREDIT UNION	3,303	0.0	3,303	0	0	0	0	0	0
BENQ AMERICA CORP	4,757	0.0	0	4,757	0	0	0	0	0
BMO FINANCIAL GROUP	3,221,715	4.1	2,355,300	191,540	0	372,866	302,009	294,529	7,480
CANADIAN AUTOMOBILE ASSOCIATION	43,069	0.1	0	26,673	0	0	16,396	0	16,396
CANADIAN COOPERATIVE AGRICULTURAL FINAN	30,179	0.0	0	0	30,179	0	0	0	0
CANADIAN IMPERIAL BANK OF COMMERCE	7,068,982	9.0	2,122,847	1,910,396	293,255	758,920	1,983,564	1,349,306	634,258
CANADIAN TIRE CORPORATION LIMITED	41,304	0.1	41,304	0	0	0	0	0	0
CHOICE REWARDS	42,783	0.1	39,079	3,704	0	0	0	0	0
CITIGROUP INC	373,472	0.5	56,234	11,520	305,718	0	0	0	0
CORP-RATE	2,998	0.0	0	2,998	0	0	0	0	0
CREDIT UNION ELECTRONIC TRANSACTION SERV	14,578	0.0	14,578	0	0	0	0	0	0
DEXIT INC	563,220	0.7	0	0	357,452	205,768	0	0	0
GM GROUP	1,945,383	2.5	873,921	1,043,734	23,960	3,768	0	0	0
GROUPE MARIE CLAIRE, LE	20,552	0.0	0	20,552	0	0	0	0	0
ISLAND SAVINGS CREDIT UNION	7,834	0.0	7,834	0	0	0	0	0	0
KOOTENAY SAVINGS CREDIT UNION	3,055	0.0	3,055	0	0	0	0	0	0
MASTERCARD INTERNATIONAL INC	10,717,720	13.7	787,066	111,522	127,325	187,701	9,504,106	5,692,158	3,811,948
MBNA CANADA BANK	576,959	0.7	246,342	0	0	0	330,617	68,981	261,636
MORGAN STANLEY & CO LTD	116	0.0	0	0	0	0	116	0	116
MOUVEMENT DES CAISSES DESJARDINS	534,326	0.7	249,425	17,264	267,637	0	0	0	0
NATIONAL BANK OF CANADA	284,991	0.4	138,877	146,114	0	0	0	0	0
PATTISON GROUP, JIM	40,223	0.1	40,223	0	0	0	0	0	0
PETRO CANADA LTD	4,065,060	5.2	1,642,395	0	0	695,976	1,727,689	667,088	1,059,601
RBC FINANCIAL GROUP	9,670,473	12.3	3,920,508	1,017,955	296,857	540,463	3,894,690	2,904,384	990,306
RONA INC	4,037	0.0	4,037	0	0	0	0	0	0
SEARS CANADA INC	77,305	0.1	77,305	0	0	0	0	0	0
SOLSTICE PUBLISHING ING	4,320	0.0	0	4,320	0	0	0	0	0
TD BANK FINANCIAL GROUP	4,020,993	5.1	1,988,483	1,018,804	287,718	276,230	449,758	449,758	0
VALERO ENERGY CORPORATION	33,396	0.0	0	0	0	33,396	0	0	0
VISA INTERNATIONAL	20,448,857	26.1	1,461,989	1,286,796	135,213	354,561	17,210,298	12,548,090	4,662,208
WESTON LIMITED, GEORGE	3,334	0.0	3,334	0	0	0	0	0	0
TOTAL	78,351,423	100.0	20,763,109	8,883,456	2,669,816	3,712,102	42,322,940	29,541,360	12,781,580

Source: *Nielsen Media Reserach Canada.*

Credit Cards*	Interest Rate	annual Fee	Insurance Programs	Reward Programs	Guaranteed Hotel Reservations	Emergency Card Replacement	Discounts
BMO Bank of Montreal							
Mosaik MasterCard (customizable) 12 different combinations possible	Variable	Yes	✓	✓			
CIBC							
Visa Cards							
Aventura Gold	19.5%	120	✓	✓	✓	✓	
Aerogold	19.5%	120	✓	✓	✓	✓	
Aero Classic	19.5%	29		✓		✓	
Classic	18.5%	Free	✓		✓	✓	✓
Select	10.5%	29	✓		✓	✓	✓
Dividend	19.5%	Free	✓		✓	✓	✓
Dividend Platinum	19.5%	79	✓		✓	✓	✓
Gold	18.5%	99	✓	✓		✓	✓
Shoppers Optimum	19.5%	Free	✓	✓		✓	✓
Classic for Students	18.5%	Free	✓			✓	✓
US Dollar	18.5%	35	✓			✓	✓
Royal Bank							
RBC Rewards Cards							
Visa Platinum Avion	19.5%	120	✓	✓	✓	✓	✓
Visa Platinum Preferred	18.5%	110	✓	✓	✓	✓	✓
Visa Gold Preferred	18.5%	110	✓	✓	✓	✓	✓
Visa Classic II	18.5%	35	✓	✓	✓	✓	✓
Visa Classic II Student	18.5%	35	✓	✓	✓	✓	✓
RBC Rewards Visa Classic	18.5%	Free	✓	✓	✓	✓	✓
US Dollar Visa Gold (US$)	18.5%	65	✓		✓	✓	
RBC Mike Weir Visa Card	19.5%	35	✓	✓	✓	✓	✓
Partner Rewards Cards							
Aadvantage Visa Gold	20.5%	70	✓	✓	✓	✓	✓
British Airways Visa Platinum	20.5%	75	✓	✓	✓	✓	✓
Cathay Pacific Visa Platinum	20.5%	75	✓	✓	✓	✓	✓
Esso Visa	18.5%	Free	✓	✓	✓	✓	✓
Starbucks Duetto Visa Card	19.5%	Free	✓	✓	✓	✓	✓
Everday Convenience Cards							
Visa Platinum	18.5%	Free	✓		✓	✓	✓
Visa Gold	18.5%	Free	✓		✓	✓	✓
Visa Classic Low Rate	11.5%	20	✓		✓	✓	✓

Visa Classic	18.5%	Free	✓		✓	✓	✓
Visa Classic Student	18.5%	Free	✓		✓	✓	✓
Scotiabank							
Visa Cards							
ScotiaGold Preferred Visa	17.9%	95	✓	✓	✓	✓	✓
No-Free ScotiaGold Visa	18.5%	Free	✓		✓	✓	✓
Scotia Moneyback Visa	17.9%	8 or Free		✓	✓	✓	✓
ScotiaLine Visa	Variable	Free	✓		✓	✓	✓
Scotia Value Visa	10.4%-12.9%	29			✓	✓	✓
TD Canada Trust							
Reward Cards							
TD Gold Travel Visa	19.5%	120	✓	✓	✓	✓	✓
TD Gold Elite Visa	19.5%	99	✓	✓	✓	✓	✓
The GM Card	19.5%	Free	✓	✓	✓	✓	✓
Low Rate Cards							
TD Emerald Visa**	7.15%-12.15%	25	✓		✓	✓	✓
Other Cards							
TD Green Visa Card	19.8%	Free	✓		✓	✓	✓
TD Gold Select Visa	19.8%	Free	✓		✓	✓	✓
TD U.S. Dollar Advantage Visa (US$)	18.5%	25	✓		✓	✓	✓
Small Business Credit Cards							
TD Business Visa Card	19.8%	50	✓		✓	✓	✓
TD Venture Line of Credit Visa	9.3%	Free			✓	✓	✓
					✓	✓	✓

**Based on TD Prime of 5.25%

Source: *This list was created from information gathered from the various bank websites on 20th Feb 2006. Some features may differ from card to card, and between banks. In addition, more features may be available than are depicted in this list.*

Exhibit 11: Canadian test scores for Capital One ads.

The Link™ Copy Test was designed to provide a complete understanding of how an ad is likely to perform in-market. It provides both evaluative and diagnostic measures and uses a standard questionnaire targeted at a custom sample. Respondents are screened against appropriate criteria; exposed to a reel of four ads with the Test Ad in the second position; re-exposed to the first ad and asked warm-up questions; re-exposed to the Test Ad and asked a full set of questions; and then re-exposed to the Test Ad again for Interest Trace. Link quantifies branded impact through the Awareness Index (AI). AI is the awareness generated per 100 Gross Rating Points (GRPs). The AI indicates how efficient the ad is at generating awareness. The components of the AI are as follows:

- Branding: Is the brand integral to the storyline? Does the brand play the 'hero'? Is the brand character a fit with the brand? Are there brand cues such as colors, icons, mnemonics, music/jingles, slogans, executional branding (e.g. Gap), package shots?

- Enjoyment: Do the aspects of the creative lead to the ad's enjoyment? Some include: music, talent, animals, kids, scenery/visuals, storyline, humor, surprise

- Active Involvement: Determine the ad's ability to engage the viewer; its 'stopping power'; its style or message of ad; the level of emotional involvement. The ad can also be negatively involving. For many brands, this is not desirable.

Millward Brown relied on its large database of ads tested: 11,000 tests had been conducted worldwide and, of those, over 600 tests had been in Canada, with two-thirds being English ads.

Source: *Millward Brown*.

Below are the Canadian test scores for Capital One's US and UK commercials.

Prime + Super Prime Segments		Bee	Catapault	Cinderella	Crab	Envelope	Poppers	Troll	Visigoths	Canada*
(Percent of respondents agreeing)										Ever Aired Norms
Branded Name	Branding (Most important)	44	42	38	40	37	30	45	42	38
	Enjoyment (2ndary importance)	42	45	50	44	35	30	45	37	39
	Involving/Unique/Interesting	56	56	58	55	50	38	55	60	55
	Irritating/Unpleasant/Disturbing	2	10	12	2	5	2	25	13	7
Communication	Unaided recall	36	38	45	35	35	30	50	40	37
	Aided recall	57	44	65	68	49	35	70	55	49

*Average for all industry ads tested by Millward Brown

Underserved Segments		Bee	Catapault	Cinderella	Crab	Envelope	Poppers	Troll	Visigoths	Canada*
(Percent of respondents agreeing)										Ever Aired Norms
Branded Name	Branding (Most important)	45	42	38	40	37	30	43	38	38
	Enjoyment (2ndary importance)	45	50	50	55	39	30	55	45	39
	Involving/Unique/Interesting	57	56	58	55	57	35	55	60	55
	Irritating/Unpleasant/Disturbing	2	10	15	2	5	2	20	13	7
Communication	Unaided recall	34	34	40	32	37	25	55	50	37
	Aided recall	55	47	70	48	49	32	75	69	49

Source: *Casewriter*
Note: Results have been disguised, including Canada Ever Aired Norms.

---

[1] To order copies or request permission to reproduce materials, contact Ivey Publishing, Ivey Management Services, c/o Richard Ivey School of Business, The University of Western Ontario, London, Ontario, Canada, N6A 3K7; phone (519) 661-3208; fax (519) 661-3882; e-mail cases@ivey.uwo.ca.

Revenue Management of Gondolas: Maintaining the Balance Between Tradition and Revenue[1]

Sheryl E. Kimes

A ride on a gondola, one of the historical black boats of Venice, is considered by many to be part of the quintessential Venice experience. However, while demand for gondola rides is extremely high, the number of boats has dropped from several thousand gondolas in the 18th century to about 400 today. In addition, there is pressure to maintain some of the tradition associated with the gondolas, so increasing revenue is tricky.

The question now is how can a balance between tradition and revenue be maintained.

Although Venice is considered to be one of the most beautiful and romantic cities in the world, modern Venice has faced many challenges, including a loss of population to other parts of Italy and physical damage from flooding, pollution, and age. The basis of the Venetian economy is tourism and the beauty of the architecture and canals and the many art and cultural attractions draw 20 million visitors per year, from around the world.

Venice is set on over 100 islands interconnected by about 150 canals. All transportation within the city is either by boat or on foot. A ride on a gondola, one of the historical black boats of Venice, is considered by many to be part of the quintessential Venice experience. Although the demand for gondola rides is extremely high, the number of boats has dropped from several thousand gondolas in the 18th century to about 400 today. Gondolas are regulated by the City of Venice and there is a strong desire to maintain their tradition; but at the same time, the economic impact on the city and its population is considerable. The question is how to best balance the maintenance of tradition with the economic impact on the gondolier and the city.

TOURISM IN VENICE

Venice receives over 20 million tourists per year of which less than half (8.7 million) spend the night there. About 80 percent of the tourists come from outside of Italy. Venice has one of the highest ratios of tourists to local residents (89 visitors for every 100 Venetians—the highest in Europe). During busy periods (the summer, over Christmas and during Carnivale), over 40,000 people per day enter the city. Since 2004, there has been a 30 percent increase in the number of overnight stays. Americans represent the largest proportion of overnight tourists. The number of Japanese tourists dropped by 7 percent in 2006; but the number of Russians increased by 31 percent, Spanish by 18 percent and French by 11 percent.

Exhibit 1: The Venetian city center skyline.

THE GONDOLA

The first mention of the gondola was in 1094, but gondolas became popular during the 15th century and helped people better maneuver around the canals of Venice. Gondolas are designed to navigate the shallow narrow canals of Venice and are strictly bound by tradition. The gondolas are 11 meters long, 1.4 meters wide and weigh about 500 kilograms. The left side is higher than the right side by 24 centimeters and the bottoms are flat so that they can function in the very shallow water (sometimes much less than a meter deep). The gondolas are constructed of 280 pieces of 8 different types of wood and only have metal in the head and stem of the boat. Gondolas are traditionally black and take about 3–6 months to build at a cost of approximately 20,000 to 30,000 Euros.

Exhibit 2: Gondolas moored at San Marco, Venice.

Gondoliers

Gondolas are owned and steered by gondoliers. Their numbers have dropped from several thousand in the 18th century to only 425 today. Gondoliers are usually male and must have been born in Venice. Traditionally, being a gondolier was passed from one generation to the next, but in recent years, this has changed because many young people have decided to take more lucrative and less physically demanding jobs. To become a gondolier, potential applicants take a test that measures their boat-handling skills, their language ability, their knowledge of the city and their ability to work with tourists.

Exhibit 3: Venetian gondolier dressed in traditional outfit.

Gondoliers are divided into 10 traghetti (or ferry stations). Each traghetto elects representatives (called barcali) who represent the traghetto to the government. Gondola rides are available at about eight stazi (ferry stations) throughout the city.

THE ROLE OF GONDOLAS IN TOURISM

Gondolas were once the primary source of transportation in Venice, but with the advent of faster and less expensive motorboats and vaporetti (a form of water-based bus), have become more of a tourist activity than a source of transportation.[2] During the 1920s, it was thought that gondolas would disappear and a lively debate ensued with even Mussolini chiming in that the gondola tradition needed to be preserved. Even by the late nineteen century, Mark Twain had commented that gondolas were little more than an anachronism.

As mass tourism increased, the design and operation of gondolas were altered in order to be able to accommodate more tourists and generate additional revenue. The boats were lengthened and narrowed and a more elaborate oar link was developed so that the gondola could be steered by one oarsman. These modifications, along with a few other design changes provided more space for passengers. In addition, as the amount of motorized boat traffic increased, it has become more difficult to safely maneuver the gondolas through the narrow canals.

Pricing and Distribution

By 1930, tour guides such as Baedeker's listed gondola prices by the hour and by the trip, and by 1945, the gondola trips were based more on the experience rather than actual transportation to a destination.

Since World War II, the tourist demand for gondola rides has been extremely high and the posted rates have increased accordingly. Whereas the posted rate was US$0.42 for 50 minutes in 1930; it reached US$1.00 by 1945, US$5.00 by 1965; and had climbed to US$70 by 1999.

The price of gondola rides is regulated by the city. Day rates are 80 Euros for 40 minutes for a maximum of six passengers, while night rates (7 P.M. – 8 A.M.) are 20 Euros higher. Although the rates are regulated, they are not always followed, and many prices are set through negotiation. Due to the popularity of gondola rides, it is quite possible to share the gondola with strangers.

Gondolas are typically booked in one of three ways: either directly with the gondolier, through a hotel or through a third party travel agency. Hotels and travel agencies often package the gondola ride with other services such as a dinner or music and take a sizable commission.

About 80 percent of gondola business comes from tour operators. Typically, tour operators either package the gondola ride with other travel options such as hotel rooms, bus tours and transfers or sell them separately. In the former case, customers do not even know the cost of the gondola ride because it is included in the package price.

Even when customers can see the price, it is generally on a per person basis, so that the price does not seem exorbitant. That being said, the rates are based on six people per gondola. Given that tour operator rates range from 35 Euros to over 70 Euros per person, the revenue associated with one 50-minute gondola ride is substantial. The tour operator passes along some of this revenue to the stazi who in turn distribute it to the gondolas, but still is able to maintain a very good profit margin even after covering costs.

The gondoliers seem to like working with the tour operators because of the guaranteed business and steady stream of business. In addition, much of the tour operator business arrives en masse which makes it easier and more efficient to fill and dispatch gondolas. Still, the tour operator profit margin is high and there may be opportunities for the stazi to increase revenue.

Carovane (caravans) of multiple gondolas (sometimes up to 30) are often used to keep groups together and to increase efficiency. Sometimes an accordionist and singer are provided for the entire carovana (at a cost of about 150 Euros). Sending out a large carovana requires a great deal of coordination because of the need to quickly load and unload customers. Gondolas are not the most stable of boats for customers to board and retired gondoliers are assigned to assist with loading and unloading.

The carovane follow a set route and can easily return to the dock within 50 minutes for the next group of passengers. Each of the stazi has different routes which are designed to ensure a smooth flow and to avoid traffic tie-ups with vaparettos and other commercial boats.

Demand and Revenue

Firm statistics on the number of gondola rides do not exist, but it is estimated that about one-quarter of all tourists take a gondola ride. In 2004, it was estimated that there were at least 3 million gondola rides. Even with a rate of US$20 per person, this is a sizable business.

Gondolas generate income for not only the gondoliers, the ganzeri (usually retired gondoliers who help with the boats) and the group leaders of the stazi but also for the boat construction trade (including the boatyard, the oar markers, the smiths and the gilders), but also provide jobs and revenue for hat makers and tailors (who supply the traditional gondolier uniform) and generate a sizable amount of souvenir sales.

THE DILEMMA

Although the demand for gondola rides is extremely high, capacity issues seem to be constraining the number of rides that can be offered. This, combined with the pressure to maintain some of the tradition associated with the gondolas, makes increasing revenue tricky. Still, the revenue provided by the gondola industry is substantial and plays an important role in the Venice economy. How should they proceed?

INTERESTING WEBSITES ON GONDOLAS

- http://www.gondolaonline.org/03.html
- http://findarticles.com/p/articles/mi_qn4159/is_20040829/ai_n12760617
- http://www.news.com.au/story/0,23599,21067634-27984,00.html
- http://www.gondolavenezia.it/history_tariffe.asp?Pag=43
- http://www.venicewelcome.com/servizi/tour-ing/venicewalktours.htm
- http://researchnews.osu.edu/archive/venice.htm

STUDY QUESTIONS

1. What can be done to increase the capacity of gondolas? What revenue impact would this have?

2. How can you balance revenue maximization with the maintenance of cultural heritage? Is it possible? If so, what would you recommend?

3. Consider the pricing structure of the gondolas. What sort of changes would you recommend? How would customers react? What revenue impact would your recommendations have?

---

[1] © 2009 by Sheryl E. Kimes. Cornell University School of Hotel Administration

[2] Much of the discussion on the next two pages is taken from Robert C. Davis & Garry R. Marvin, 2004, *Venice: The Tourist Maze*. Berkeley, California: University of California Press.

The Accra Beach Hotel: Block Booking of Capacity During a Peak Period[1]

Sheryl E. Kimes, Jochen Wirtz and Christopher Lovelock

Cherita Howard, Sales Manager for the Accra Beach Hotel, a 141-room hotel on the Caribbean island of Barbados, was debating about what to do about a request from the West Indies Cricket Board. The Board wanted to book a large block of rooms more than six months ahead, during several of the hotel's busiest times, and was asking for a discount. In return, it promised to promote the Accra Beach in all advertising materials and television broadcasts as the host hotel for the upcoming West Indies Cricket Series, an important international sporting event.

THE HOTEL

The Accra Beach Hotel and Resort had a prime beachfront location on the south coast of Barbados, just a short distance from the airport and the capital city of Bridgetown. Located on 3½ acres of tropical landscape and facing one of the best beaches on Barbados, the hotel featured rooms offering panoramic views of the ocean, pool or island.

Exhibit 1: Beach view of The Accra Beach Hotel

The centerpiece of its lush gardens was the large swimming pool, which had a shallow bank for lounging plus a swim-up bar. In addition, there was a squash court and a fully equipped gym. Golf was also available only 15 minutes away at the Barbados Golf Club, with which the hotel was affiliated.

Exhibit 2: Pool view of The Accra Beach Hotel

The Accra Beach had two restaurants and two bars, as well as extensive banquet and conference facilities. It offered state-of-the-art conference facilities to local, regional and international corporate clientele and had hosted a number of large summits in recent years. Three conference rooms, which could be configured in a number of ways, served as the setting for large corporate meetings, training seminars, product displays, dinners, and wedding receptions. A business center provided guests with Internet access, faxing capabilities, and photocopying services.

The hotel's 122 standard rooms were categorized into three groups—Island View, Pool View, and Ocean View)—and there were also 13 Island View Junior Suites, and six Penthouse Suites, each decorated in tropical pastel prints and handcrafted furniture. All rooms were equipped with cable/satellite TV, air-conditioning, ceiling fans, hair-dryer, coffee percolator, direct-dial telephone, bath-tub/shower and a balcony.

Standard rooms were configured with either a king-size bed or two twin beds in the Island and Ocean View categories, while the Pool Views had two double beds. The six Penthouse Suites, which all offered ocean views, contained all the features listed for the standard rooms plus added comforts. They were built on two levels, featuring a living room with a bar area on the third floor of the hotel and a bedroom accessed by an internal stairway on the fourth floor. These suites also had a bathroom containing a Jacuzzi, shower stall, double vanity basin and a skylight.

The thirteen Junior Suites were fitted with a double bed or two twin beds, plus a living room area with a sofa that can be converted to another bed.

HOTEL PERFORMANCE

The Accra Beach enjoyed a relatively high occupancy rate, with the highest occupancy rates achieved from January through March and the lowest generally during the summer (Exhibit 3 on page 477). The hotel's average room rates followed a similar pattern, with the highest room rates (US$150 – $170) being achieved from December through March but relatively low rates (US$120) during the summer months (Exhibit 4 on page 478). The hotel's RevPAR (revenue per available room—a product of the occupancy rate times the average room rate) showed even more variation, with RevPARs exceeding US$140 from January through March but falling to less than US$100 from June through October (Exhibit 5 on page 478). The rates on the Penthouse suites ranged from US$310 to US$395, while those on the junior suites ranged from US$195 to US$235. Guests had to pay Barbados Value-Added Tax (VAT) of 7.5 percent on room charges and 15 percent on meals.

The Accra Beach had traditionally promoted itself as a resort destination, but in the last few years, it has been promoting its convenient location and had attracted many business customers. Cherita works extensively with tour operators and corporate travel managers. The majority of hotel guests were corporate clients from companies such as Barbados Cable & Wireless, and the Caribbean International Banking Corporation (Exhibit 6 on page 478). The composition of hotel guests had changed drastically over the past few years. Traditionally, the hotel's clientele had been dominated by tourists from the UK and Canada, but during the past few years, the percentage of corporate customers had increased dramatically. The majority of corporate customers come for business meetings with local companies.

Sometimes, guests who were on vacation (particularly during the winter months) felt uncomfortable finding themselves surrounded by business people. As one vacationer put it, "There's just something weird about being on vacation and going to the beach and then seeing suit-clad business people chatting on their cell phones." However, the hotel achieved a higher average room rate from business guests than vacationers and had found the volume of corporate business to be much more stable than that from tour operators and individual guests.

THE WEST INDIES CRICKET BOARD

Cherita Howard, the hotel's Sales Manager, had been approached by the West Indies Cricket Board (WICB) about the possibility of the Accra Beach Hotel serving as the host hotel for the following spring's West Indies Cricket Home Series, an important international sporting event among cricket-loving nations. The location of this event rotated among several different Caribbean nations and Barbados would be hosting the next one, which would feature visiting teams from India and New Zealand.

Cherita and Jon Martineau, General Manager of the hotel, both thought that the marketing exposure associated with hosting the teams would be very beneficial for the hotel but were concerned about accepting the business because they knew from past experience that many of the desired dates were usually very busy days for the hotel. They were sure that the rate that the WICB was willing to pay would be lower than the average rate of US$140– $150 they normally achieved during these times. In contrast to regular guests, who could usually be counted upon to have a number of meals at the hotel, team members and officials would probably be less likely to dine at the hotel because they would be on a per diem budget. On average, both corporate customers and vacationers spend about US$8 per person for breakfast and about US$25 per person for dinner (per person including VAT). The margin on food and beverage is approximately 30 percent. About 80 percent of all guests have breakfast at the hotel and approximately 30 percent of all guests dine at the hotel (there are many other attractive restaurant options nearby). Mr. Martineau thought that only about 25 percent of the cricket group would have breakfast at the hotel and maybe only about 10 percent would dine at the hotel. Also, they worried about how the hotel's other guests might react to the presence of the cricket teams. Still, the marketing potential for the hotel was substantial. The WICB had promised to list the Accra Beach as the host hotel in all promotional materials and during the televised matches.

The West Indies Home Series was divided into three parts, and each would require bookings at the Accra Beach Hotel. The first part pitted the West Indies team against the Indian team and would run from April 24 to May 7. The second part featured the same two teams and would run from May 27 to May 30. The final part showcased the West Indies team against the New Zealand team and would run from June 17 to 26 June.

The WICB wanted 50 rooms (including two suites at no additional cost) for the duration of each part and was willing to pay US$130 per night per room. Both breakfast and VAT were to be included and each team had to be housed on a single floor of the hotel. In addition, the WICB insisted that laundry service for team uniforms (cricket teams typically wear all-white clothing) and practice gear be provided at no additional charge for all team members. Cherita estimates that it will cost the hotel about US$20 per day if they can do the laundry in-house, but about US$200 per day if they have to send it to an outside source.

Cherita called Ferne Armstrong, the Reservations Manager of the hotel, and asked her what she thought. Like Cherita, Ferne was concerned about the possible displacement of higher-paying customers, but offered to do further investigation into the expected room sales and associated room rates for the desired dates. Since the dates were over six months in the future, Ferne had not yet developed forecasts. But she was able to provide data on room sales and average room rates from the same days of the previous year (Exhibit 7 on page 479).

Soon after Cherita returned to her office to analyze the data, she was interrupted by a phone call from the head of the WICB wanting to know the status of his request. She promised to have an answer for him before the end of the day. As soon as she hung up, Jon Martineau called and chatted about the huge marketing potential of being the host hotel.

Cherita shook her head and wondered, "What should I do?"

STUDY QUESTIONS

1. What factors lead to variations in demand for rooms at a hotel such as the Accra Beach?

2. Identify the various market segments currently served by the hotel. What are the pros and cons of seeking to serve customers from several segments?

3. What are the key considerations facing the hotel as it reviews the booking requests from the West Indies Cricket Board?

4. What action should Cherita Howard take and why?

Exhibit 3: Accra Beach Hotel monthly occupancy rate.

Year	Month	Occupancy
2 Years Ago	January	87.7%
2 Years Ago	February	94.1%
2 Years Ago	March	91.9%
2 Years Ago	April	78.7%
2 Years Ago	May	76.7%
2 Years Ago	June	70.7%
2 Years Ago	July	82.0%
2 Years Ago	August	84.9%
2 Years Ago	September	64.7%
2 Years Ago	October	82.0%
2 Years Ago	November	83.8%
2 Years Ago	December	66.1%
Last Year	January	87.6%
Last Year	February	88.8%
Last Year	March	90.3%
Last Year	April	82.0%
Last Year	May	74.7%
Last Year	June	69.1%
Last Year	July	76.7%
Last Year	August	70.5%
Last Year	September	64.7%
Last Year	October	71.3%
Last Year	November	81.7%
Last Year	December	72.1%

Exhibit 4: Accra Beach Hotel average daily room rate (ADR).

Year	Month	Average Room Rate (in US$)
2 Years Ago	January	$159.05
2 Years Ago	February	$153.73
2 Years Ago	March	$157.00
2 Years Ago	April	$153.70
2 Years Ago	May	$144.00
2 Years Ago	June	$136.69
2 Years Ago	July	$122.13
2 Years Ago	August	$121.03
2 Years Ago	September	$123.45
2 Years Ago	October	$129.03
2 Years Ago	November	$141.03
2 Years Ago	December	$152.87
Last Year	January	$162.04
Last Year	February	$167.50
Last Year	March	$158.44
Last Year	April	$150.15
Last Year	May	$141.79
Last Year	June	$136.46
Last Year	July	$128.49
Last Year	August	$128.49
Last Year	September	$127.11
Last Year	October	$132.76
Last Year	November	$141.86
Last Year	December	$151.59

Note: Average Room Rate (ADR) is inclusive of VAT.

Exhibit 5: Accra Beach Hotel revenue per available room (RevPAR).

Year	Month	Revenue per Available Room (in US$)
2 Years Ago	January	$139.49
2 Years Ago	February	$144.66
2 Years Ago	March	$144.28
2 Years Ago	April	$120.96
2 Years Ago	May	$110.45
2 Years Ago	June	$96.64
2 Years Ago	July	$100.15
2 Years Ago	August	$102.75
2 Years Ago	September	$79.87
2 Years Ago	October	$105.80
2 Years Ago	November	$118.18
2 Years Ago	December	$101.05
Last Year	January	$141.90
Last Year	February	$148.67
Last Year	March	$143.02
Last Year	April	$123.12
Last Year	May	$105.87
Last Year	June	$94.23
Last Year	July	$98.55
Last Year	August	$90.59
Last Year	September	$82.24
Last Year	October	$94.62
Last Year	November	$115.89
Last Year	December	$109.24

Note: RevPAR refers to revenue per available room and is computed by multiplying the room occupancy rate (see Exhibit 1) with the average room rate (Exhibit 2). Revenue per available room is inclusive of VAT.

Exhibit 6: Clientele of Accra Beach Hotel

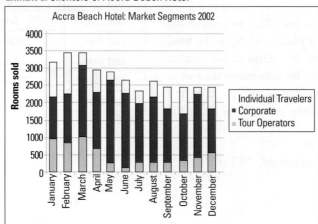

Exhibit 7: Room sales and average daily room rates for same periods in previous year.

Date of WICB Home Series	Rooms Sold in Last Year During the Same Period	Average Daily Room Rate (ADR) in US$
Part 1		
4/24	141	$138.68
4/25	138	$129.00
4/26	135	$137.60
4/27	134	$145.13
4/28	123	$142.98
4/29	128	$133.30
4/30	141	$127.93
5/1	141	$133.30
5/2	141	$103.08
5/3	139	$131.15
5/4	112	$126.85
5/5	78	$135.45
5/6	95	$139.75
5/7	113	$148.35
Part II		
5/27	99	$140.83
5/28	114	$141.90
5/29	114	$146.20
5/30	125	$146.20
Part III		
6/17	124	$134.38
6/18	119	$131.15
6/19	112	$135.45
6/20	119	$119.33
6/21	125	$118.25
6/22	116	$112.88
6/23	130	$113.95
6/24	141	$108.58
6/25	141	$118.25
6/26	125	$123.63

Note: ADR excludes VAT of 7.5 percent.

Note: Certain data have been disguised.

[1] © 2009 by Sheryl E. Kimes, Jochen Wirtz and Christopher H. Lovelock

Aussie Pooch Mobile[1]

Christopher Lovelock and Lorelle Frazer

After creating a mobile service that washes dogs outside their owners' homes, a young entrepreneur has successfully franchised the concept. Her firm now has more than 100 franchises in many parts of Australia, as well as a few in other countries. She and her management team are debating how best to plan future expansion.

Elaine and Paul Beal drew up in their 4 × 4 outside 22 Ferndale Avenue, towing a bright blue trailer with red and white lettering. As Aussie Pooch Mobile franchisees whose territory covered four suburbs of Brisbane, Australia, they were having a busy day. It was only 1:00 P.M. and they had already washed and groomed 16 dogs at 12 different houses. Now they were at their last appointment—a 'pooch party' of ten dogs at number 22, where five other residents of the street had arranged to have their dogs washed on a fortnightly basis.

Prior to their arrival outside the house, there had been ferocious growling and snarling from a fierce-looking Rottweiler. But when the animal caught sight of the brightly-colored trailer, he and two other dogs in the yard bounded forward eagerly to the chain link fence, in a flurry of barking and wagging tails.

Throughout residential areas of Brisbane and in a number of other Australian cities, dogs of all shapes and sizes were being washed and groomed by Aussie Pooch Mobile franchisees. By early 2002, the company had grown to over 100 franchisees and claimed to be "Australia's largest mobile dog wash and care company." A key issue facing its managing director, Christine Taylor, and members of the management team was how to plan and shape future expansion.

COMPANY BACKGROUND

Located in Burpengary, Queensland, just north of Brisbane, Aussie Pooch Mobile Pty. Ltd. (APM) was founded in 1991 by Christine Taylor, then aged 22. Taylor had learned customer service early, working in her parents' bait and tackle shop from the age of 8. Growing up in an environment with dogs and horses as pets, she knew she wanted to work with animals and learned dog grooming skills from working in a local salon. At 16, Chris left school and began her own grooming business on a part-time basis, using a bathtub in the family garage. Since she was still too young to drive,

her parents would take her to pick up the dogs from their owners. She washed and groomed the animals at home and then returned them.

Once Taylor had learned to drive and bought her own car, she decided to take her service to the customers. So she went mobile, creating a trailer in which the dogs could be washed outside their owners' homes and naming the fledgling venture "The Aussie Pooch Mobile". Soon, it became a full-time job. Eventually, she found she had more business than she could handle alone, so hired assistants. The next step was to add a second trailer. Newly married, she and her husband, David McNamara, ploughed their profits into the purchase of additional trailers and gradually expanded until they had six mobile units.

The idea of franchising came to Taylor when she found herself physically constrained by a difficult pregnancy:

> "David would go bike riding or head to the coast and have fun with the jet ski and I was stuck at home and felt like I was going nuts, because I'm a really active person. I was hungry for information on how to expand the business, so I started researching other companies and reading heaps of books and came up with franchising as the best way to go, since it would provide capital and also allow a dedicated group of small business people to help expand the business further."

As existing units were converted from employees to franchisee operations, Taylor noticed that they quickly became about 20 percent more profitable. Initially, APM focused on Brisbane and the surrounding region of southeast Queensland. Subsequently, it expanded into New South Wales and South Australia in 1995, into Canberra, Australian Capital Territory (ACT), in 1999, and into Victoria in 2000 (Exhibit 1). Expansion into Western Australia was expected in mid 2002. In 1996, a New Zealand

Exhibit 1: Map of Australia.

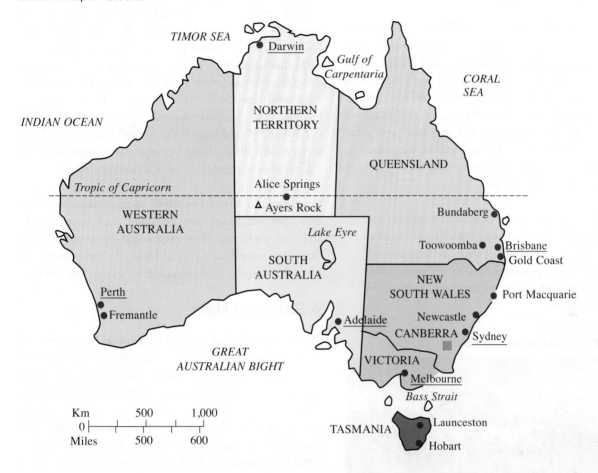

division of the firm was launched in Tauranga, a small city some 200 km southeast of Auckland, under the name Kiwi Pooch Mobile. In 2001 Aussie Pooch Mobile launched into the United Kingdom, beginning with a town in northern England. Soon, there were four operators under a master franchisee. The following year saw the official launch of The Pooch Mobile Malaysia, also under a master franchisee.

By early 2002, the company had 125 mobile units in Australia, of which 55 were located in Queensland, 42 in New South Wales, 8 in ACT, 12 in South Australia and 8 in Victoria. In addition, representatives operated another six company-owned units. The company bathed more than 20,000 dogs each month and had an annual turnover of some $3 million.[2] APM was a member of the Franchise Council of Australia and complied with the Franchising Code of Conduct. The management team consisted of Chris Taylor as managing director and David McNamara as

director responsible for overseeing trailer design and systems support. Each state had its own manager and training team. The central support office also housed staff who provided further assistance to managers and franchisees.

Expansion had benefitted from the leverage provided by several master franchisees, who had obtained the rights to work a large territory and sell franchises within it. Said Taylor:

"I look at the business as if it's my first child. I see it now starting to get into those early teens where it wants to go alone, but it still needs me to hold its hand a little bit, whereas initially it needed me there the whole time. With the support staff we have in place, the business is now gaining the support structure it needs to work without me. This is what I am aiming towards. I appreciate that a team of people can achieve much more than one person alone."

The Service Concept

Aussie Pooch Mobile specialised in bringing its dog washing services to customers' homes. Dogs were washed in a hydrobath installed in a specially-designed trailer, which was parked in the street. The trailer had partly open sides and a roof to provide protection from sun and rain (Exhibit 2). Apart from flea control products and a few grooming aids, APM did not attempt to sell dog food and other pet supplies. The company had resisted the temptation to diversify into other fields. "Our niche is in the dog bathing industry," declared Chris Taylor:

> "I don't want us to be a jack of all trades because you'll never be good at anything. We now have an exclusive range of products that customer demand has driven us to providing, but we still work closely with vets and pet shops and are by no means a pet shop on wheels."

Exhibit 2: The Aussie Pooch Mobile trailer.

In contrast to retail pet service stores, where customers brought their animals to the store or kennel, APM brought the service to customers' homes, with the trailer being parked outside on the street. The use of hydrobath equipment, in which warm, pressurized water was pumped through a shower head, enabled operators to clean dogs more thoroughly than would be possible with a garden hose. The bath was designed to rid the dog of fleas and ticks and improve its skin condition as well as to clean its coat and eliminate smells. Customers supplied water and electrical power.

The fee paid by customers varied from $15–$30 per dog, depending on breed and size, condition of coat and skin,

behaviour, and geographic location, with discounts for multiple animals at the same address. On average, regular customers paid a fee of $25 for one dog, $47 for two, and $66 for three. At "pooch parties," a concept developed at APM, the homeowner acting as host typically received one complimentary dogwash at the discretion of the operator. Additional services, for which an extra fee was charged, included the recently introduced aromatherapy bath ($2.50) and blow drying of the animal's coat for $5-10 (on average, $8). Blow drying was especially recommended in cool weather to prevent the animal from getting cold.

Operators also offered free advice to customers about their dogs' diet and health care, including such issues as ticks and skin problems. They encouraged customers to have their dogs bathed on a regular basis. The most commonly scheduled frequencies were once every two or four weeks.

A Satisfied User

The process of bathing a dog involved a sequence of carefully coordinated actions, as exemplified by Elaine Beal's treatment of Zak, the Rottweiler. "Hello my darling, who's a good boy?" crooned Elaine as she patted the enthusiastic dog, placed him on a leash and led him out through the gate to the footpath on this warm, sunny day. Paul busied himself connecting hoses and electrical cords to the house, while Elaine began back-combing Zak's coat in order to set it up for the water to get underneath. She then led the now placid dog to the hydrobath inside the trailer, where he sat patiently while she removed his leash and clipped him to a special collar in the bath for security. Meanwhile the water had been heating to the desired temperature.

Over the next few minutes Elaine bathed the dog, applied a medicated herbal shampoo to his coat and rinsed him thoroughly with the pressure driven hose (Exhibit 3). After releasing Zak from the special collar and reattaching his leash, she led him out of the hydrobath and onto the footpath, where she wrapped him in a chamois cloth and dried him. Next, she cleaned the dog's ears and eyes with disposable baby wipes, all the time continuing to talk soothingly to him. She checked his coat and skin to ensure that there were no ticks or skin problems, gave his nails a quick clip, and sprayed a herbal conditioner and deodoriser onto Zak's now gleaming coat and brushed it in. Returning Zak to the yard and removing the leash, Elaine patted him and gave him a large biscuit, specially formulated to protect the animal's teeth.

Exhibit 3: A Labrador Retriever receives a bath in a Aussie Pooch Mobile hydrobath.

THE AUSTRALIAN MARKET

Australia's population of 19.3 million in 2001 was small in relation to the country's vast land area of 7.7 million km² (almost three million square miles). By contrast, the United States had a population 15 times that of Australia on a land area, including Alaska and Hawaii, of 9.2 million km². A federal nation, Australia was divided into six states—New South Wales (NSW), Victoria, Queensland, South Australia, Western Australia, and the island of Tasmania—plus two territories: the large but thinly populated Northern Territory and the small Australian Capital Territory (ACT) which contained the federal capital, Canberra, and its suburbs and was an enclave within NSW. The average annual earnings for employed persons were $35,000.

With much of the interior of the continent uninhabitable and many other areas inhospitable to permanent settlement, most of the Australian population was concentrated in a narrow coastal band running clockwise from Brisbane on the southeast coast through Sydney and Melbourne to Adelaide,

the capital of South Australia. Some 2700 km (1600 miles) to the west lay Perth, known as the most isolated city in the world. A breakdown of the population by state and territory is shown in (Exhibit 4). The northern half of the country was in the tropics, Brisbane and Perth enjoyed a subtropical climate, and the remaining major cities had a temperate climate (Exhibit 5). Melbourne was known for its sharp fluctuations in temperature.

Exhibit 4: Population of Australia by state and territory, June 2001.

State/Tereitory	Population (000)
New South Wales	6,533
Victoria	4,829
Queensland	3,628
South Australia	1,502
Western Australia	1,910
Tasmania	470
Australian Capital Territory	314
Northern Territory	198
Australia Total	*19,387*

Source: *Australian Bureau of Statistics 2001.*

Exhibit 5: Average temperatures for principal Australian cities (in degrees Celsius)*

	July (Winter)		January (Summer)	
	High	Low	High	Low
Adelaide, SA	14.9	6.9	27.9	15.7
Brisbane, Qld	20.6	9.5	29.1	20.9
Cariberra, ACT	11.5	0.0	28.5	13.6
Darwin, NT	30.7	19.7	32.4	25.2
Hobart, Tas	12.3	4.0	22.3	11.9
Melbourne, Vic	12.9	5.2	26.0	13.5
Perth, WA	17.7	8.1	31.5	16.9
Sydney, NSW	16.9	6.9	26.3	18.6

Souce: *Australian Bureau of Meteorology, www.bom.gov.au.*
*Celsius to Fahrenheit Conversion: 0°C = 32°F, 10°C = 50°F, 20°C = 68°F, 30°C = 86°F.

There were about four million domestic dogs in the country and approximately 42 percent of the nation's 7.4 million households owned at least one. Ownership rates were slightly above average in Tasmania, the Northern Territory and Queensland, and somewhat below average in Victoria and the ACT. In 1995, it was estimated that Australians spent an estimated $1.3 billion on dog-related goods and services, of which 46 percent went to dog food, 22 percent to veterinary services, 12 percent to dog products and equipment, and 11 percent to other services, including washing and grooming (Exhibit 6).

Exhibit 6: Distribution of consumer expenditures on dog-related goods and services, 1995.

Product/Service	Allocation
Dog food	46%
Vet charges	21%
Dog products	10%
Dog equipment	2%
Dog services	11%
Pet purchases	5%
Other expenses	4%
Total dog-related expenditures	*$1.3 billion*

Source: *BIS Shrapnell Survey 1995.*

Franchising in Australia

By the beginning of the 21st Century, the Australian franchising sector had reached a stage of early maturity. McDonald's, KFC and Pizza Hut opened their first outlets in Australia in the 1970s. These imported systems were followed by many home-grown business format franchises such as Just Cuts (hairdressing), Snap Printing, Eagle Boys Pizza, and VIP Home Services, all of which grew into large domestic systems and then expanded internationally, principally to New Zealand and Southeast Asia.

In 2002, Australia boasted approximately 700 business format franchise systems holding over 50,000 outlets. Although the United States had many more systems and outlets, Australia had more franchisors per capita, reflecting the relative ease of entry into franchising in this country. Most of the growth in franchising had occurred in business format franchising as opposed to product franchising.

Business format franchises provided franchisees with a full business system and the rights to operate under the franchisor's brand name, whereas product franchises merely allowed independent operators to supply a manufacturer's product, such as car dealerships or soft-drink bottlers. Typically, franchisees were required to pay an upfront franchise fee (averaging $30,000 in service industries and $40,000 in retailing) for the right to operate under the franchise system within a defined geographic area. This initial fee was included in the total start-up cost of the business (ranging from around $60,000 in the service sector to more than $200,000 in the retail industry). In addition, franchisees paid a royalty on all sales and an ongoing contribution towards advertising and promotional activities that were designed to build brand awareness and preference. Would-be franchisees who lacked sufficient capital might be able to obtain bank financing against personal assets such as property or an acceptable guarantor.

Franchising Trends

The rapid growth of franchising had been stimulated in part by demographic trends, including the increase in dual-income families, which had led to greater demand for outsourcing of household services such as lawn mowing, house cleaning and pet grooming. Some franchise systems offered multiple concepts under a single corporate brand name. For instance, VIP Home Services had separate franchises available in lawn mowing, cleaning, car washing and rubbish removal. Additional growth came from conversion of existing individual businesses to a franchise format. For instance, Eagle Boys Pizza had often approached local pizza operators and offered them the opportunity to join this franchise.

Almost half the franchise systems in Australia were in retail trade (32 percent non-food and 14 percent food). Another large and growing industry was the property and business services sector (20 percent), as shown in (Exhibit 7). Most franchisees were ex-white collar workers or blue collar supervisors who craved independence and a lifestyle change.

Exhibit 7: Distribution of franchise systems in Australia by industry, 1999.

Industry	Percentage
Retail trade—non-food	31
Property and business services	20
Retail trade—food	14
Personal and other services	7
Construction and trade services	6
Accommodation, cafes and restaurants	4
Education	4
Cultural and recreation services	4
Unclassified	3
Manufacturing and printing	3
Finance and insurance	2
Transport and storage	1
Communication services	1
Total—all industries	*100%*

Source: *Lorelle Frazer and Colin McCosker, Franchising Australia 1999, Franchise Council of Australia/University of Southern Queensland, Toowoomba, 1999, p. 39.*

Over the years, Australia's franchising sector had experienced a myriad of regulatory regimes. Finally in 1998, in response to perceived problems in many franchising systems, the federal government introduced a mandatory Franchising

Code of Conduct, administered under the Trade Practices Act. Among other things, the Code required that potential franchisees be given full disclosure about the franchisor's background and operations prior to signing a franchise agreement. In contrast, the franchising sector in the United States faced a patchwork of regulations that varied from one state to another. Yet in the United Kingdom, there were no specific franchising regulations beyond those applying to all corporations operating in designated industries.

Master franchising arrangements had become common in Australian franchise systems. Under master franchising, a local entrepreneur was awarded the rights to sub-franchise the system within a specific geographic area, such as an entire state. Because of Australia's vast geographic size it was difficult for a franchisor to monitor franchisees who were located far from the head office. The solution was to delegate to master franchisees many of the tasks normally handled by the franchisor itself, making them responsible for recruiting, selecting, training and monitoring franchisees in their territories, as well as overseeing marketing and operations.

Not all franchisees proved successful and individual outlets periodically failed. The main reasons for failure appeared to be poor choice of location or territory and a franchisee's own shortcomings. In addition to the obvious technical skills required in a given field, success often hinged on possession of sales and communication abilities. Disputes in franchising were not uncommon, but could usually be resolved internally without recourse to legal action. The causes of conflict most frequently cited by franchisees related to franchise fees and alleged misrepresentations made by the franchisor. By contrast, franchisors cited conflicts based on lack of adherence to the system by franchisees.

Australia was home to a number of internationally-known franchise operators, including Hertz Rent-a-Car, Avis, McDonald's, KFC, Pizza Hut, Subway, Kwik Kopy and Snap-on Tools. By contrast, most Burger King outlets operated under the name Hungry Jack's, an acquired Australian chain with significant brand equity.

Jim's Group

One of Australia's best known locally-developed franchisors was Melbourne-based Jim's Group, which described itself as one of the world's largest home service franchise organizations. The company had originated with a mowing service started by Jim Penman in Melbourne in 1982 when he abandoned ideas of an academic career after his PhD thesis was rejected. In 1989, Penman began franchising the service, now known as Jim's Mowing, as a way to facilitate expansion. The business grew rapidly, using master franchisees in different regions to recruit and manage individual franchisees. The company's dark green trucks, displaying a larger-than-life logo of Penman himself, bearded and wearing a hat, soon became a familiar sight on suburban streets around Melbourne. Before long, the franchise expanded to other parts of Victoria and then to other states.

Over the following years, an array of other home-related services were launched under the Jim's brand, including Jim's Trees, Jim's Paving, Jim's Cleaning, Jim's Appliance Repair, and Jim's Floors. Each service featured the well-recognized logo of Jim Penman's face on a different coloured background. Jim's Dogwash made its debut in 1996, employing a bright red, fully enclosed trailer, emblazoned by a logo that had been amended to show Jim with a dog. By early 2002, Jim's Group comprised more than two dozen different service divisions, over ninety master franchisees, and some 1,900 individual franchisees. In many instances, master franchisees were responsible for two or more different service divisions within their regions. Jim's Group's philosophy was to price franchises according to local market conditions. If work in a prospective territory were easy to find but franchisees hard to attract, the price might be lowered somewhat, but not too much, otherwise the company felt there would be insufficient commitment.

In recent years, Jim's Group had expanded overseas. In New Zealand, it had six master franchisees and 232 franchisees and offered mowing, tree work, cleaning, and dogwashing services. It had also established a significant presence for Jim's Mowing in the Canadian province of British Columbia. But attempts to launch Jim's Mowing in the United States had failed due to difficulty in finding good operators.

Jim's Dogwash had over 60 franchises operating in Australia (primarily in Victoria) and New Zealand. This firm's experience had shown that growth was hampered by the shortage of suitable franchisees, since operators needed to be dog lovers with a background in dog care.

FRANCHISING STRATEGY AT AUSSIE POOCH MOBILE

New APM franchisees were recruited through newspaper advertisements and "advertorials" as well as by word of mouth. The concept appealed to individuals who sought to become self-employed but wanted the security of a proven business system rather than striking out entirely on their own. Interested individuals were invited to meet with a representative of the company to learn more. If they wished to proceed further, they had to complete an application form and submit a deposit of $250 to hold a particular area for a maximum of four weeks, during which the applicant could further investigate the characteristics and prospects of the designated territory. This fee was credited to the purchase cost of the franchise if the applicant decided to proceed or returned if the applicant withdrew. A new franchise cost $24,000 (up from $19,500 in 1999). An additional 10 percent had to be added to this fee to pay the recently introduced federal goods and services tax (GST). Exhibit 8 identifies how APM costed out the different elements.

Exhibit 8: Aussie Pooch Mobile: Breakdown of franchise purchase cost, 2002 vs. 1999.

Item	1999		2002	
	$	$	$	$
Initial training		2,200.00		2,200.00
Initial franchise fee		4,021.50		6,173.00
Guaranteed income		5,000.00		N/A
Exclusive territory plus trailer registration		N/A		6,600.00
Fixtures, fittings, stock, insurance etc:				
Aussie Pooch Mobile trailer and hydrobath	4,860.00		5,340.00	
Consumables (shampoo, conditioner, etc.)	160.00		230.00	
Trade equipment and uniforms	920.00		881.65	
Insurance	338.50	6,278.50	575.35	7,027.00
Initial advertising		2,000.00		2,000.00
Total franchise cost*		$19,500.00		$24,000.00

*Total franchise costs excludes 10% GST, introduced in July 2000.

Selection Requirements for Prospective Franchisees

The company had set a minimum educational requirement of passing Year 10 of high school (or equivalent). Taylor noted that successful applicants tended to be outdoor people who shared four characteristics:

> "They are self motivated and outgoing. They love dogs and they want to work for themselves. Obviously, being great with dogs is one part of the business— our franchisees understand that the dog's even an extended member of the customer's family—but it's really important that they can handle the bookwork side of the business as well, because that's basically where your bread and butter is made."

Other desirable characteristics included people skills and patience, plus a good telephone manner. Would-be franchisees also had to have a valid driver's license, access to a vehicle that was capable of towing a trailer, and the ability to do this type of driving in an urban setting. Originally, Taylor had expected that most franchisees would be relatively young, with parents being willing to buy their children a franchise and set them up with a job, but in fact only about half of all franchisees were aged 21–30; 40 percent were aged 31–40 and 10 percent were in their forties or fifties. About 60 percent were female.

Potential franchisees were offered a trial work period with an operator to see if they liked the job and were suited to the business, including not only skills with both animals and people but also sufficient physical fitness.

In return for the franchise fee, successful applicants received the rights to a geographically defined franchise, typically comprising about 12,000 homes. Franchisees also obtained an APM trailer with all necessary products and solutions to service the first one hundred dogs, plus red uniform shirts and cap, advertising material, and stationery. The trailer was built to industrial grade standards and its design included many refinements developed by APM in consultation with franchisees to simplify the process of dog washing and enhance the experience for the animal. Operators were required to travel with a mobile phone, which they had to pay for themselves.

In addition to franchised territories, APM had six company-owned outlets. These were operated by representatives, who leased the territory and equipment and in return paid APM 25 percent of the gross weekly revenues (including GST). Taylor had no plans to increase the number of representatives. The reps were generally individuals who either could not currently afford the start-up cost or who were being evaluated by the company for their suitability as franchisees. Typically, reps either became franchisees within about six months or left the company.

Assisting New Franchisees

The franchisor provided two weeks' pre-opening training for all new franchisees and representatives also spent about

10 hours with each one to help them open their new territories. Training topics included operational and business procedures, effective use of the telephone, hydrobathing techniques, dog grooming techniques, and information on dog health and behaviour. Franchisees were given a detailed operations manual containing 104 pages of instructions on running the business in accordance with company standards.

To help new franchisees get started, APM placed advertisements in local newspapers for a period of 20 weeks. It also prepared human interest stories for distribution to these newspapers. Other promotional activities at the time of launch included distributing pamphlets in the territory and writing to local vets and pet shops to inform them of the business. APM guaranteed new franchisees a weekly income of $600 for the first ten weeks and paid for a package of insurance policies for six months, after which the franchisee became responsible for the coverage.

Fees and Services

Ongoing support by the franchisor included marketing efforts, monthly newsletters, a telephone hotline service for advice, an insurance package, regular (but brief) field visits, and additional training. If a franchisee fell sick or wished to take a vacation, APM would offer advice on how to best deal with this situation, in many cases being able to organise a trained person to help out. It also organized periodic meetings for franchisees in the major metropolitan areas at which guest presenters spoke on topics relating to franchise operations. Previous guest speakers had included veterinarians, natural therapists, pharmacists, and accountants. More recently, APM had offered one-day seminars, providing more team support and generating greater motivation than the traditional meeting style.

In return for these services, franchisees paid a royalty fee of 10 percent of their gross weekly income, plus an advertising levy of an additional 2.5 percent. Income was reported on a weekly basis and fees had to be paid weekly. In addition to these fees, operating costs for a franchisee included car-related expenses, purchase of consumable products such as shampoo, insurance, telephone, and stationery. Exhibit 9 shows the average weekly costs that a typical franchisee might expect to incur.

Exhibit 9: Average annual operating expenses for an Aussie Pooch Mobile franchisee, 1999 vs. 2002.

Expense	1999 $	2002 $
Consumable products	3,552	2,880
Car registration	430	430
Car insurance	500	500
Fuel	2,400	3,360
Insurance	642	1,151
Repairs and maintenance	1,104	1,104
Phone, stationery, etc.	1,440	1,920
Communication levy	624	624
Franchise royalties	4,416	5,583
Advertising levy	1,104	1,395
Total	*$16,212*	*$18,947*

Franchisees included several couples, like the Beals, but Taylor believed that having two operators work together was not really efficient, although it could be companionable. Paul Beal, a retired advertising executive, had other interests and did not always accompany Elaine. Some couples split the work, with one operating three days a week and the other three or even four days. All franchisees were required to be substantially involved in the hands-on running of the business; some had more than one territory and employed additional operators to help them.

To further support individual franchisees, APM had formed a Franchise Advisory Council, composed of a group of experienced franchisees who had volunteered their time to help other franchisees and the system as a whole. Each franchisee was assigned to a team leader, who was a member of the FAC. The Council facilitated communications between franchisees and the support office, meeting with the managers every three months to discuss different issues within the company.

MARKETING AND COMPETITION

The company advertised Aussie Pooch Mobile service in the Yellow Pages as well as paying for listings in the White Pages of local phone directories. It promoted a single telephone number nationwide in Australia, staffed by an answering service 24 hours a day, seven days a week. Customers paid only a local call charge of 25 cents to access this number. They could leave their name and telephone number, which would then be electronically sorted and forwarded via alphanumeric pagers to the appropriate franchisee, who would then return the call to arrange a convenient appointment time. APM also offered expert advice on local advertising and promotions, and made promotional products and advertising templates available to franchisees. Other corporate communications activities included maintaining the web site www.hydrobath.com, distributing public relations releases to the media, and controlling all aspects of corporate identity such as trailer design, business cards, and uniforms.

"I try to hold the reins pretty tightly on advertising matters," said Taylor, noting that the franchise agreement required individual franchisees to submit their plans for promotional activities for corporate approval. She shook her head as she remembered an early disaster, involving an unauthorized campaign by a franchisee who had placed an offer of a free dog wash in a widely distributed coupon book. Unfortunately, this promotion had set no expiration date or geographic restriction, with the result that customers were still presenting the coupon more than a year later across several different franchise territories.

With APM's approval, some franchisees had developed additional promotional ideas. For example, Elaine and Paul Beal wrote informative articles and human interest stories about dogs for their local newspaper. When a client's dog died, Elaine sent a sympathy card and presented the owner with a small tree to plant in memory of the pet.

Developing a Territory

Obtaining new customers and retaining existing ones was an important aspect of each franchisee's work. The brightly colored trailer often attracted questions from passers-by and presented a useful opportunity to promote the service. Operators could ask satisfied customers to recommend the service to their friends and neighbors. Encouraging owners to increase the frequency of washing their dogs was another way to build business. Knowing that a dog might become lonely when its owner was absent and was liable to develop behavior problems, Elaine Beal sometimes recommended the acquisition of a "companion pet." As Paul remarked, "Having two dogs is not twice the trouble, it halves the problem!"

However, to maximize profitability, franchisees also had to operate as efficiently as possible, minimizing time spent in non-revenue producing activities such as travel, set up, and socializing. As business grew, some franchisees employed additional operators to handle the excess workload, so that the trailer might be in service extended hours, seven days a week. Eventually, a busy territory might be split, with a portion being sold off to a new franchisee.

APM encouraged this practice. The company had found that franchisees reached a comfort zone at about 80 dogs a week and then their business stopped growing because they could not physically wash any more dogs. Franchisees could set their own price when selling all or part of a territory and APM helped them to coordinate the sale. When a territory was split, a franchisee was usually motivated to rebuild the remaining half to its maximum potential.

Competition

Although many dog owners had traditionally washed their animals themselves (or had not even bothered), there was a growing trend towards paying a third party to handle this task. Dog washing services fell into two broad groups. One consisted of fixed-site operations to which dog owners brought their animals for bathing. The location of these businesses included retail sites in suburban shopping areas, kennels, and service providers' own homes or garages. The second type of competition, which had grown in popularity in recent years, consisted of mobile operations that traveled to customers' homes.

With few barriers to entry, there were numerous dog washing services in most major metropolitan areas. Many of these services included the word "hydrobath" in their names. In Brisbane, for example, the Yellow Pages listed 19 mobile suppliers in addition to APM and 26 fixed-site suppliers, a few of which also washed other types of animals (Exhibit 10). The majority of dog washing services in Australia were believed to be stand-alone operations, but there were other franchisors in addition to Aussie Pooch Mobile. Of these, the most significant appeared to be Jim's Dogwash and Hydrodog.

(A) Services including the word "mobile" in their names

A & Jane's Mobile Dog Wash
A Spotless Dog Mobile Hydrobath
Akleena K9 Mobile Hydrobath
Alan's Mobile Dog and Cat Wash
Fancy Tails Mobile Hydrobath
Fido's Mobile Dog Wash and Clipping
Go-Go's Mobile Pet Parlour
Happy Pets Mobile Hydrobath
Itch-Eeze Mobile Dog Grooming and Hydrobath Service
James' Mobile Pet Grooming and Hydrobath
My Pets Mobile Hydrobath
Paw Prints Mobile Dog Grooming
Preen A Pooch-Mobile
Rainbow Mobile Dog Wash
Redlands Mobile Pet Grooming and Hydrobath
Sallie's Mobile Dogwash
Scrappy Doo's Mobile Hydrobath
Superdog Mobile Hydrobath
Western Suburbs Mobile Dog Bath

(B) Other listings containing the words "bath," "wash," 'hydro," or similar allusions

Aussie Dog Hydrobath
Budget K9 Baths
Conmurra Hydrobaths
Dandy Dog Hydrobath
Dial A Dogwash
Doggy Dunk
Flush-Puppy
Heavenly Hydropet
Helen's Hydrobath
Herbal Dog Wash
Home Hydrobath Service
Hydro-Hound
Jo's Hydrowash
K9 Aquatics
K9 Kleeners
Keep Em Kleen
Maggie's Shampooch
Nome's Turbo Pet Wash
P.R. Turbo Pet Wash
Paws in More Hydrobath and Pet Care Services
Puppy Paws Dog Wash
Splish Splash Hydrobath
Scrubba Dub Dog
Soapy Dog
Super Clean Professional Dog Wash
Tidy Tim's Hydrobath

Source: *Yellow Pages Online, March 2002 under "Dog & Cat Clipping & Grooming" (excludes services delivered only to cats).*

Jim's Dogwash (part of Melbourne-based Jim's Group) had nine master franchisees and 52 franchises in Australia and four masters and nine franchisees in New Zealand (Exhibit 11). Jim's expansion strategy had been achieved in part by creating smaller territories than APM and pricing them relatively inexpensively, in order to stimulate recruitment of new franchisees. A territory, typically encompassing about 2,000 homes, currently sold for $10,000 (comprising an initial franchise fee of $6,000, $3000 for the trailer, and $1000 for other equipment) plus 10 percent GST. Jim's fee for washing a dog, including blow drying, ranged from $28 to $38. However, the firm did not offer aromatherapy or anything similar.

Exhibit 11: Profile of Jim's Group franchisees.

Location	All Master Franchisees	Master Dogwash Franchisees	Individual Dogwash Franchisees
Victoria	41	6	36
New South Wales + ACT	8	1	7
Queensland	6	1	4
West Australia	13	—	3
South Australia	6	1	4
Tasmania	1	—	—
Northern Territory	1	1	2
Australia	*83*	*9*	*52*
New Zealand	6	4	9
Canada	1	—	—
Grand Total	*90*	*13*	*61*

Source: *Jim's Group website, www.jims.net, accessed January 2002.*

Another franchised dogwashing operation was Hydrodog, based on the Gold Coast in Queensland with 49 units in Queensland, 9 in New South Wales, 8 in Western Australia and one each in Victoria, South Australia, and the Northern Territory. Hydrodog began franchising in 1994. By 2002, a new franchise unit cost $24,950 (including GST), of which $10,800 was accounted for by the initial franchise fee for a 10,000-home territory. In addition to their dog grooming services, which included blowdrying and ranged in price from $15 to $40, Hydrodog franchisees sold dog food products, including dry biscuits and cooked or raw meats (chicken, beef or kangaroo). They did not offer aromatherapy.

DEVELOPING A STRATEGY FOR THE FUTURE

Managing continued expansion presented an ongoing challenge to the directors of Aussie Pooch Mobile. However, as Chris Taylor pointed out, "You can be the largest but you may not be the best. Our focus is on doing a good job and making our franchisees successful."

To facilitate expansion outside its original base of southeast Queensland, APM had appointed a franchise sales manager in Sydney for the New South Wales market and another in Melbourne for both Victoria and South Australia. One question was whether to adopt a formal strategy of appointing master franchisees. Currently, there were master franchises on the Gold Coast (a fast-growing resort and residential area southeast of Brisbane), in the ACT, and in the regional cities of Toowoomba and Bundaberg in Queensland, and in Newcastle and Port Macquarie in New South Wales.

For some years, Taylor had been attracted by the idea of expanding internationally. In 1996, the company had licensed a franchisee in New Zealand to operate a subsidiary named Kiwi Pooch Mobile. However, there was only one unit operating by early 2002 and she wondered how best to increase this number. Another subsidiary had been established as a master franchise in the French province of New Caledonia, a large island northeast of Australia. Launched in late 2000 under the name of La Pooch Mobile; it had one unit. Another master franchise territory had been established in Malaysia in late 2001 and there were two units operating in 2002.

In 2001, APM had granted exclusive rights for operation in the United Kingdom to a British entrepreneur, who operated under the name The Pooch Mobile. Thus far, four units were operating in the English county of Lincolnshire, some 200 km (125 miles) north of London. This individual noted that English people traditionally washed their dogs very infrequently, often as little as once every two to three years, but once they had tried The Pooch Mobile, they quickly converted to becoming monthly clients, primarily for the hygiene benefits.

As the company grew, the directors knew it was likely to face increased competition from other providers of dogwashing services. But as one successful franchisee remarked: "Competition keeps us on our toes. It's hard being in the lead and maintaining the lead if you haven't got anybody on your tail."

STUDY QUESTIONS

1. How did Christine Taylor succeed in evolving the local dogwashing service she developed as a teenager into an international franchise business?

2. Compare and contrast the tasks involved in recruiting new customers and recruiting new franchisees

3. From a franchisee's perspective, what are the key benefits of belonging to the APM franchise in (a) the first year and (b) the third and subsequent years?

4. In planning for future expansion, what strategy should Taylor adopt for APM and why?

Biometric Meets Services[1]

Jochen Wirtz and Loizos Heracleous

Biometric devices that scan fingerprints, palm, retinas, and faces are already revolutionizing security. The killer application however, may be locking in business, not locking out bad guys. Singapore Airline has begun using biometrics to enhance customer service. Other companies could do the same, customizing and streamlining the way people buy clothing, healthcare, financial services, even a cup of coffee.

With today's focus on security, demand is booming for biometric devices that can look at your features and decide if you are who you say you are. Machines that scan fingerprints, palms, retinas and faces are cropping up in airports, banks, hotels, and even supermarkets to improve security and prevent fraud and theft. But while biometrics may make things safer, security will not be the killer app. Using a fingerprint scan to pen a locker— as visitors to the Statue of Liberty now do—is not fundamentally different from (or easier than) using a key. It is just more secure.

But using biometrics to enhance the customer experience will change the manner in which companies do business. Imagine an airline that uses scans of fingerprints and faces to allow travelers to breeze through check-in, customs, security and boarding in under 60 seconds and automatically get seat assignments based on their preferences. Who wouldn't choose that carrier over its competitors?

Singapore Airlines (SIA) and its hub, Changi Airport, are collaborating on just such a system, betting on biometrics to improve productivity, reduce costs, lure fliers with unprecedented service, and enhance security to boot. In November 2005, SIA and Changi launched a six-month pilot test of Fully Automated Seamless Travel (FAST) involving 9,000 SIA frequent fliers. Each received a smart card encoded with fingerprint and facial data. At check-in, these travelers simply walk through a separate gateway, slide their cards through a reader, and have their fingerprints and faces scanned. If the card data match the holder's features, the system clears security and immigration, recommends preferred seats, and prints boarding passes. The entire process takes less than a minute, compared with a current average of 8 to 15 minutes. SIA and Changi are exploring a similar system for baggage handling; passengers would be able to skip lines and drop off biometrically tagged luggage outside the terminal, to be reunited with it—after scanning—at the destination.

While the airline rolls out these beta tests, it is studying other ways biometrics could enhance service, including speeding ticketing and payment, customizing loyalty-program services, and improving the efficiency of call centers through voice recognition.

Biometrics' ability to improve service delivery in other industries, we believe, will be limited less by technology, regulation, or public acceptance than by imagination. Any service offering in which knowledge of customers' identities and preferences could be used to customize and streamline sales is a candidate. Imagine the principles demonstrated in the SIA-Changi experiment applied to the process by which customers buy clothing, financial services, health care—even a personalized cup of coffee.

In a recent retreat, an SIA task force identified 113 potential uses for biometrics in its business. If that is 113 more than you have thought of, you have got some thinking to do.

STUDY QUESTIONS

1. Discuss productivity gains, security improvement and customer service benefits that biometrics-based services could potentially deliver for ATM-based services, call-centers and a large coffee house chain.

2. What would be the greatest implementation challenges from (a) service process and (b) customer acceptance perspectives?

3. How would you address the service process and customer acceptance challenges identified?

Shouldice Hospital Limited (Abridged)[1]

James Heskett and Roger Hallowell

Two shadowy figures, enrobed and in slippers, walked slowly down the semi-darkened hall of the Shouldice Hospital. They did not notice Alan O'Dell, the hospital's Managing Director, and his guest. Once they were out of earshot, O'Dell remarked good naturedly, "By the way they act, you'd think our patients own this place. And while they're here, in a way they do." Following a visit to the five operating rooms, O'Dell and his visitor once again encountered the same pair of patients still engrossed in discussing their hernia operations, which had been performed the previous morning.

HISTORY

An attractive brochure that was recently printed, although neither dated nor distributed to prospective patients, described Dr. Earle Shouldice, the founder of the hospital:

Dr. Shouldice's interest in early ambulation stemmed, in part, from an operation he performed in 1932 to remove the appendix from a seven-year-old girl and the girl's subsequent refusal to stay quietly in bed. In spite of her activity, no harm was done, and the experience recalled to the doctor the postoperative actions of animals upon which he had performed surgery. They had all moved about freely with no ill effects.

By 1940, Shouldice had given extensive thought to several factors that contributed to early ambulation following surgery. Among them were the use of a local anesthetic, the nature of the surgical procedure itself, the design of a facility to encourage movement without unnecessarily causing discomfort, and the post operative regimen. With these things in mind, he began to develop a surgical technique for repairing hernias[2] that was superior to others; word of his early success generated demand.

Dr. Shouldice's medical license permitted him to operate anywhere, even on a kitchen table. However, as more and more patients requested operations, Dr. Shouldice created new facilities by buying a rambling 130-acre estate with a 17,000-square foot main house in the Toronto suburb of Thornhill. After some years of planning, a large wing was added to provide a total capacity of 89 beds.

Dr. Shouldice died in 1965. At that time, Shouldice Hospital Limited was formed to operate both the hospital and clinical facilities under the surgical direction of Dr. Nicholas Obney. In 1999, Dr. Casim Degani, an internationally-recognized authority, became surgeon-in-chief. By 2004, 7,600 operations were performed per year.

THE SHOULDICE METHOD

Only external (vs. internal) abdominal hernias were repaired at Shouldice Hospital. Thus most first-time repairs, "primaries," were straightforward operations requiring about 45 minutes. The remaining procedures involved patients suffering recurrences of hernias previously repaired elsewhere.[3] Many of the recurrences and very difficult hernia repairs required 90 minutes or more.

In the Shouldice method, the muscles of the abdominal wall were arranged in three distinct layers, and the opening was repaired, each layer in turn, by overlapping its margins as the edges of a coat might be overlapped when buttoned. The end result reinforced the muscular wall of the abdomen with six rows of sutures (stitches) under the skin cover, which was then closed with clamps that were later removed. (Other methods might not separate muscle layers, often involved fewer rows of sutures, and sometimes involved the insertion of screens or meshes under the skin.)

A typical first-time repair could be completed with the use of pre-operative sedation (sleeping pill) and analgesic (pain killer) plus a local anesthetic, an injection of Novocain in the region of the incision. This allowed immediate post-operative patient ambulation and facilitated rapid recovery.

The Patients' Experience

Most potential Shouldice patients learned about the hospital from previous Shouldice patients. Although thousands of doctors had referred patients, doctors were less likely to recommend Shouldice because of the generally regarded simplicity of the surgery, often considered a "bread and butter" operation. Typically, many patients had their problem diagnosed by a personal physician and then contacted Shouldice directly. Many more made this diagnosis themselves.

The process experienced by Shouldice patients depended on whether or not they lived close enough to the hospital to visit the facility to obtain a diagnosis. Approximately 10 percent of Shouldice patients came from outside the province of Ontario, most of these from the United States. Another 60 percent of patients lived beyond the Toronto area. These out-of-town patients often were diagnosed by mail using the Medical Information Questionnaire shown in Exhibit 1 on page 495. Based on information in the questionnaire, a Shouldice surgeon would determine the type of hernia the respondent had and whether there were signs that some risk might be associated with surgery (for example, an overweight or heart condition, or a patient who had suffered a heart attack or a stroke in the past six months to a year, or whether a general or local anesthetic was required). At this point, a patient was given an operating date and sent a brochure describing the hospital and the Shouldice method. If necessary, a sheet outlining a weight-loss program prior to surgery was also sent. A small proportion was refused treatment, either because they were overweight, represented an undue medical risk, or because it was determined that they did not have a hernia.

Arriving at the clinic between 1:00 P.M. and 3:00 P.M. the day before the operation, a patient joined other patients in the waiting room. He or she was soon examined in one of the six examination rooms staffed by surgeons who had completed their operating schedules for the day. This examination required no more than 20 minutes, unless the patient needed reassurance. (Patients typically exhibited a moderate level of anxiety until their operation was completed.) At this point it occasionally was discovered that a patient had not corrected his or her weight problem; others might be found not to have a hernia at all. In either case, the patient was sent home.

After checking administrative details, about an hour after arriving at the hospital, a patient was directed to the room number shown on his or her wrist band. Throughout the process, patients were asked to keep their luggage (usually light) with them.

All patient rooms at the hospital were semiprivate, containing two beds. Patients with similar jobs, backgrounds, or interests were assigned to the same room to the extent possible. Upon reaching their rooms, patients busied themselves unpacking, getting acquainted with roommates, shaving themselves in the area of the operation, and changing into pajamas.

At 4:30 P.M., a nurse's orientation provided the group of incoming patients with information about what to expect, including the need for exercise after the operation and the daily routine. According to Alan O'Dell, "Half are so nervous they don't remember much." Dinner was then served, followed by further recreation, and tea and cookies at 9:00 P.M. Nurses emphasized the importance of attendance at that time because it provided an opportunity for pre-operative patients to talk with those whose operations had been completed earlier that same day.

Patients to be operated on early were awakened at 5:30 A.M. to be given pre-op sedation. An attempt was made to schedule operations for roommates at approximately the same time. Patients were taken to the preoperation room where the circulating nurse administered Demerol, an analgesic, 45 minutes before surgery. A few minutes prior to the first operation at 7:30 A.M., the surgeon assigned to each patient administered Novocain, a local anesthetic, in the operating room. This was in contrast to the typical hospital procedure in which patients were sedated in their rooms prior to being taken to the operating rooms.

Upon completion of their operation, during which a few patients were "chatty" and fully aware of what was going on, patients were invited to get off the operating table and walk to the post operation room with the help of their surgeons. According to the Director of Nursing:

> "Ninety-nine percent accept the surgeon's invitation. While we use wheelchairs to return them to their rooms, the walk from the operating table is for psychological as well as physiological [blood pressure, respiratory] reasons. Patients prove to themselves that they can do it, and they start their all-important exercise immediately."

Throughout the day after their operation, patients were encouraged to exercise by nurses and housekeepers alike. By

9:00 P.M. on the day of their operations, all patients were ready and able to walk down to the dining room for tea and cookies, even if it meant climbing stairs, to help indoctrinate the new "class" admitted that day. On the fourth morning, patients were ready for discharge.

During their stay, patients were encouraged to take advantage of the opportunity to explore the premises and make new friends. Some members of the staff felt that the patients and their attitudes were the most important element of the Shouldice program. According to Dr. Byrnes Shouldice, son of the founder, a surgeon on the staff, and a 50 percent owner of the hospital:

> "Patients sometimes ask to stay an extra day. Why? Well, think about it. They are basically well to begin with. But they arrive with a problem and a certain amount of nervousness, tension, and anxiety about their surgery. Their first morning here they're operated on and experience a sense of relief from something that's been bothering them for a long time. They are immediately able to get around, and they've got a three-day holiday ahead of them with a perfectly good reason to be away from work with no sense of guilt. They share experiences with other patients, make friends easily, and have the run of the hospital. In summer, the most common after-effect of the surgery is sunburn."

The Nurses' Experience

Thirty four full-time-equivalent nurses staffed Shouldice each 24 hour period. However, during non-operating hours, only six full-time-equivalent nurses were on the premises at any given time. While the Canadian acute-care hospital average ratio of nurses to patients was 1:4, at Shouldice the ratio was 1:15. Shouldice nurses spent an unusually large proportion of their time in counseling activities. As one supervisor commented, "We don't use bedpans." According to a manager, "Shouldice has a waiting list of Nurses wanting to be hired, while other hospitals in Toronto are short-staffed and perpetually recruiting."

The Doctors' Experience

The hospital employed ten full-time surgeons and eight part-time assistant surgeons. Two anesthetists were also on site. The anesthetists floated among cases except when general anesthesia was in use. Each operating team required a surgeon, an assistant surgeon, a scrub nurse, and a circulating nurse. The operating load varied from 30 to 36 operations per day. As a result, each surgeon typically performed three or four operations each day.

A typical surgeon's day started with a scrubbing shortly before the first scheduled operation at 7:30 A.M. If the first operation was routine, it usually was completed by 8:15 A.M. At its conclusion, the surgical team helped the patient walk from the room and summoned the next patient. After scrubbing, the surgeon could be ready to operate again at 8:30 A.M. Surgeons were advised to take a coffee break after their second or third operation. Even so, a surgeon could complete three routine operations and a fourth involving a recurrence and still be finished in time for a 12:30 P.M. lunch in the staff dining room.

Upon finishing lunch, surgeons not scheduled to operate in the afternoon examined incoming patients. A surgeon's day ended by 4:00 P.M. In addition, a surgeon could expect to be on call one weekday night in ten and one weekend in ten. Alan O'Dell commented that the position appealed to doctors who "want to watch their children grow up. A doctor on call is rarely called to the hospital and has regular hours." According to Dr. Obney:

> "When I interview prospective surgeons, I look for experience and a good education. I try to gain some insight into their domestic situation and personal interests and habits. I also try to find out why a surgeon wants to switch positions. And I try to determine if he's willing to perform the repair exactly as he's told. This is no place for prima donnas."

Dr. Shouldice added:

> "Traditionally a hernia is often the first operation that a junior resident in surgery performs. Hernia repair is regarded as a relatively simple operation compared to other major operations. This is quite wrong, as is borne out by the resulting high recurrence rate. It is a tricky anatomical area and occasionally very complicated, especially to the novice or those doing very few hernia repairs each year. But at Shouldice Hospital a surgeon learns the Shouldice technique over a period of several months. He learns when he can go fast and when he must slowdown. He develops a pace and a touch. If he encounters something unusual, he is encouraged to consult immediately with other surgeons. We teach each other and try to encourage a group effort. And he learns not to take risks to achieve absolute perfection. Excellence is the enemy of good."

Exhibit 1: Medical information questionnaire.

SHOULDICE HOSPITAL

7750 Bayview Avenue
Box 379, Thornhill, Ontario L3T 4A3 Canada
Phone (418) 889-1125

(Thornhill - One Mile North Metro Toronto)

MEDICAL

INFORMATION

Patients who live at a distance often prefer their examination, admission and operation to be arranged all on a single visit — to save making two lengthy journeys. The whole purpose of this questionnaire is to make such arrangements possible, although, of course, it cannot replace the examination in any way. Its completion and return will not put you under any obligation.

Please be sure to fill in both sides.

This information will be treated as confidential.

(continued on next page)

FAMILY NAME (Last Name)	FIRST NAME	MIDDLE NAME

STREET & NUMBER (or Rural Route or P.O. Box) | Town/City | Province/State

| County | Township | Zip or Postal Code | Birthdate: Month | Day | Year |

Married or Single | Religion

Telephone
Home _____ if none, give
Work _____ neighbour's number _____

NEXT OF KIN: Name _____ Address _____ Telephone #

Date form completed

INSURANCE INFORMATION: Please give name of Insurance Company and Numbers.

HOSPITAL INSURANCE: (Please bring hospital certificates) | OTHER HOSPITAL INSURANCE

O.H.I.P. Number | BLUE CROSS Number | Company Name | Policy Number

SURGICAL INSURANCE: (Please bring insurance certificates) | OTHER SURGICAL INSURANCE

O.H.I.P. Number | BLUE SHIELD Number | Company Name | Policy Number

WORKMEN'S COMPENSATION BOARD | Approved | Social Insurance (Security) Number
Yes | No

Claim No.

Occupation | Name of Business | Are you the owner? If Retired – Former Occupation
Yes | No

How did you hear about Shouldice Hospital? (If referred by a doctor, give name & address)

Are you a former patient of Shouldice Hospital? | Yes | No | Do you smoke? | Yes | No

Have you ever written to Shouldice Hospital in the past? | Yes | No

What is your preferred admission date? (Please give as much advance notice as possible)

No admissions Friday, Saturday or Sunday.

FOR OFFICE USE ONLY

Date Received | Type of Hernia | Weight Loss

lbs.

Consent to Operate ☐ | Special Instructions | Approved

Heart Report ☐

Referring Doctor Notified | Operation Date

THIS CHART IS FOR EXPLANATION ONLY

Ordinary hernias are mostly either at the navel ("belly-button") - or just above it

or down in the groin area on either side

An "Incisional hernia" is one that bulges through the scar of any other surgical operation that has failed to hold - wherever it may be.

THIS IS YOUR CHART – PLEASE MARK IT!

(MARK THE POSITION OF EACH HERNIA YOU WANT REPAIRED WITH AN "X")

APPROXIMATE SIZE...
Walnut (or less)
Hen's Egg or Lemon
Grapefruit (or more)

ESSENTIAL EXTRA INFORMATION

Use only the sections that apply to your hernias and put a ✓ in each box that seems appropriate.

NAVEL AREA (AND JUST ABOVE NAVEL) ONLY
Is this navel (bellybutton) hernia your FIRST one?

Yes ☐   No ☐

If it's NOT your first, how many repair attempts so far? ☐

GROIN HERNIAS ONLY

	RIGHT GROIN		LEFT GROIN	
	Yes	No	Yes	No
Is this your FIRST GROIN HERNIA ON THIS SIDE?	☐	☐	☐	☐

How many hernia operations in this groin already?   Right ☐   Left ☐

DATE OF LAST OPERATION [_____]

INCISIONAL HERNIAS ONLY (the ones bulging through previous operation scars)

Was the original operation for your Appendix? ☐ , or Gallbladder? ☐
or Stomach? ☐ , or Prostate? ☐ , or Hysterectomy? ☐ , or Other? ☐

How many attempts to repair the hernias have been made so far? ☐

PLEASE BE ACCURATE!: Misleading figures, when checked on a admission day, could mean postponement of your operation till your weight is suitable.

HEIGHT......ft.......ins.   WEIGHT........lbs.Nude   Recent gain?.........lbs.
or just pyjamas   Recent loss?.........lbs.

Waist (muscles relaxed)..........ins.   Chest (not expanded)...........ins.

GENERAL HEALTH

Age.........years   is your health now GOOD ☐ , FAIR ☐ , or POOR ☐

Please mention briefly any severe past illness – such as a "heart attack" or a "stroke", for example, from which you have now recovered (and its approximate date)...........

We need to know about other present conditions, even though your admission is NOT likely to be refused because of them.

Please tick ☑ any condition for which you are having regular treatment:

Blood Pressure ☐
Excess body fluids ☐
Chest pain ("angina") ☐
Irregular Heartbeat ☐
Diabetes ☐
Asthma & Bronchitis ☐
Ulcers ☐
Anticoagulants ☐
(to delay blood-clotting or to "thin the blood")
Other...... ☐

Name of any prescribed pills, tablets or capsules you take regularly -

Did you remember to MARK AN "X" on your body chart to show us where each of your hernias is located?

Chief Surgeon Degani assigned surgeons to an operating room on a daily basis by noon of the preceding day. This allowed surgeons to examine the specific patients that they were to operate on. Surgeons and assistants were rotated every few days. Cases were assigned to give doctors a non-routine operation (often involving a recurrence) several times a week. More complex procedures were assigned to more senior and experienced members of the staff. Dr. Obney commented:

"If something goes wrong, we want to make sure that we have an experienced surgeon in charge. Experience is most important. The typical general surgeon may perform 25 to 50 hernia operations per year. Ours perform 750 or more."

The 10 full-time surgeons were paid a straight salary, typically $144,000.[4] In addition, bonuses to doctors were distributed monthly. These depended on profit, individual productivity, and performance. The total bonus pool paid to the surgeons in a recent year was approximately $400,000. Total surgeon compensation (including benefits) was approximately 15 percent more than the average income for a surgeon in Ontario.

Training in the Shouldice technique was important because the procedure could not be varied. It was accomplished through direct supervision by one or more of the senior surgeons. The rotation of teams and frequent consultations allowed for an ongoing opportunity to appraise performance and take corrective action. Whereever possible, former Shouldice patients suffering recurrences were assigned to the doctor who performed the first operation "to allow the doctor to learn from his mistake." Dr. Obney commented on being a Shouldice surgeon:

"A doctor must decide after several years whether he wants to do this for the rest of his life because, just as in other specialties—for example, radiology—he loses touch with other medical disciplines. If he stays for five years, he doesn't leave. Even among younger doctors, few elect to leave."

THE FACILITY

The Shouldice Hospital contained two facilities in one building—the hospital and the clinic. On its first-level, the hospital contained the kitchen and dining rooms. The second level contained a large, open lounge area, the admission offices, patient rooms, and a spacious glass-covered Florida room. The third level had additional patient rooms and recreational areas. Patients could be seen visiting each others' rooms, walking up and down hallways, lounging in the sunroom, and making use of light recreational facilities ranging from a pool table to an exercycle. Alan O'Dell pointed out some of the features of the hospital:

"The rooms contain no telephone or television sets. If a patient needs to make a call or wants to watch television, he or she has to take a walk. The steps are designed specially with a small rise to allow patients recently operated on to negotiate the stairs without undue discomfort. Every square foot of the hospital is carpeted to reduce the hospital feeling and the possibility of a fall. Carpeting also gives the place a smell other than that of disinfectant.

This facility was designed by an architect with input from Dr. Byrnes Shouldice and Mrs. W. H. Urquhart (the daughter of the founder). The facility was discussed for years and many changes in the plans were made before the first concrete was poured. A number of unique policies were also instituted. For example, parents accompanying children here for an operation stay free. You may wonder why we can do it, but we learned that we save more in nursing costs than we spend for the parent's room and board."

Patients and staff were served food prepared in the same kitchen, and staff members picked up food from a cafeteria line placed in the very center of the kitchen. This provided an opportunity for everyone to chat with the kitchen staff several times a day, and the hospital staff to eat together. According to O'Dell, "We use all fresh ingredients and prepare the food from scratch in the kitchen."

The Director of Housekeeping pointed out:

"I have only three on my housekeeping staff for the entire facility. One of the reasons for so few housekeepers is that we don't need to change linens during a patient's four-day stay. Also, the medical staff doesn't want the patients in bed all day. They want the nurses to encourage the patients to be up socializing, comparing notes [for confidence], encouraging each other, and walking around, getting exercise. Of course, we're in the rooms straightening up throughout the day. This gives the housekeepers a chance to josh with the patients and to encourage them to exercise."

The clinic housed five operating rooms, a laboratory, and the patient-recovery room. In total, the estimated cost to furnish an operating room was $30,000. This was considerably less than for other hospitals which require a bank of equipment with which to administer anesthetics for each room. At Shouldice, two mobile units were used by the anesthetists when needed. In addition, the complex had one "crash cart" per floor for use if a patient should suffer a heart attack or stroke.

ADMINISTRATION

Alan O'Dell described his job:

"We try to meet people's needs and make this as good a place to work as possible. There is a strong concern for employees here. Nobody is fired. [This was later reinforced by Dr. Shouldice, who described a situation involving two employees who confessed to theft in the hospital. They agreed to seek psychiatric help and were allowed to remain on the job.] As a result, turnover is low.

Our administrative and support staff are non-union, but we try to maintain a pay scale higher than the union scale for comparable jobs in the area. We have a profit-sharing plan that is separate from the doctors'. Last year the administrative and support staff divided up $60,000.

If work needs to be done, people pitch in to help each other. A unique aspect of our administration is that I insist that each secretary is trained to do another's work and in an emergency is able to switch to another function immediately. We don't have an organization chart. A chart tends to make people think they're boxed in jobs.[5] I try to stay one night a week, having dinner and listening to the patients, to find out how things are really going around here."

Operating Costs

The 2004 budgets for the hospital and clinic were close to $8.5 million[6] and $3.5 million, respectively.[7]

THE MARKET

Hernia operations were among the most commonly performed operations on males. In 2000 an estimated 1,000,000 such operations were performed in the United States alone. According to Dr. Shouldice:

"When our backlog of scheduled operations gets too large, we wonder how many people decide instead to have their local doctor perform the operation. Every time we've expanded our capacity, the backlog has declined briefly, only to climb once again. Right now, at 2,400, it is larger than it has ever been and is growing by 100 every six months."

The hospital relied entirely on word-of-mouth advertising, the importance of which was suggested by the results of a poll carried out by students of DePaul University as part of a project (Exhibit 3 on page 500 shows a portion of these results). Although little systematic data about patients had been collected, Alan O'Dell remarked that "if we had to rely on wealthy patients only, our practice would be much smaller."

Patients were attracted to the hospital, in part, by its reasonable rates. Charges for a typical operation were four days of hospital stay at $320 per day, and a $650 surgical fee for a primary inguinal (the most common hernia). An additional fee of $300 was assessed if general anesthesia was required (in about 20% of cases). These charges compared to an average charge of $5,240 for operations performed elsewhere.

Round-trip fares for travel to Toronto from various major cities on the North American continent ranged from roughly $200 to $600.

The hospital also provided annual checkups to alumni, free of charge. Many occurred at the time of the patient reunion. The most recent reunion, featuring dinner and a floor show, was held at a first-class hotel in downtown Toronto and was attended by 1,000 former patients, many from outside Canada.

Exhibit 2: Organization Chart.

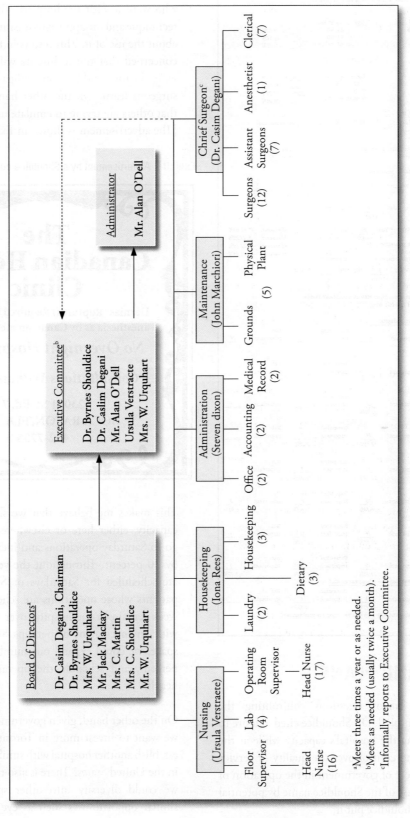

Board of Directors[a]

Dr Casim Degani, Chairman
Dr. Byrnes Shouldice
Mrs. W. Urquhart
Mr. Jack Mackay
Mrs. C. Martin
Mrs. C. Shouldice
Mr. W. Urquhart

Executive Committee[b]

Dr. Byrnes Shouldice
Dr. Caslim Degani
Mr. Alan O'Dell
Ursula Verstracte
Mrs. W. Urquhart

Administrator
Mr. Alan O'Dell

Nursing
(Ursula Verstraete)

Floor
Supervisor

Head
Nurse
(16)

Lab
(4)

Operating
Room
Supervisor

Head Nurse
(17)

Housekeeping
(Iona Rees)

Laundry
(2)

Dietary
(3)

Housekeeping
(3)

Administration
(Steven dixon)

Office
(2)

Accounting
(2)

Medical
Record
(2)

Maintenance
(John Marchiori)

Grounds

Physical
Plant
(5)

Chief Surgeon[c]
(Dr. Casim Degani)

Surgeons
(12)

Assistant
Surgeons
(7)

Anesthetist
(1)

Clerical
(7)

[a]Meets three times a year or as needed.
[b]Meets as needed (usually twice a month).
[c]Informally reports to Executive Committee.

Direction: For each question, please place a check mark as it applies to you.

1. Sex Male _41_ 95.34%
   Female _2_ 4.65%

2. Age 20 or less ____
   21–40 _4_ 9.30%
   41–60 _17_ 39.54%
   61 or more _22_ 51.16%

3. Nationality
   Directions: Please place a check mark in nation you represent and please write in your province, state or country where it applies.

   Canada _38_ Province _88.37%_
   America _5_ State _11.63%_
   Europe ___ Country ___
   Other ___

4. Education level
   Elementary _5_ 11.63%
   High School _18_ 41.86%
   College _1980_ 30.23%
   Graduate work _7_ 16.28%

5. Occupation _____

6. Have you been overnight in a hospital other than Shouldice before your operation? Yes _31_ No _12_

7. What brought Shouldice Hospital to your attention?
   Friend _23_ 53.49% Doctor _9_ 20.93% Relative _7_ 16.28% Article ___ Other _4_ (Please explain) 9.30%

8. Did you have a single _25_ 58.14% or double _18_ 41.86% hernia operation?

9. Is this your first Annual Reunion? Yes _20_ 46.51% No _23_ 53.49%
   If no, how many reunions have you attended? ____
   2–5 reunions – 11 47.63%
   6–10 reunions – 5 21.73%
   11–20 reunions – 4 12.39%
   21–36 reunions – 3 13.05%

10. Do you feel that Shouldice Hospital cared for you as a person?
    Most definitely _37_ 86.05% Definitely _6_ 13.95% Very little ___ Not at all ___

11. What impressed you the most about your stay at Shouldice? Please check one answer for each of the following.

A. Fees charged for operation and hospital stay
   Very Important _10_ Important _3_ Somewhat Important _6_ Not Important _24_

B. Operation Procedure
   Very Important _33_ 76.74% Important _9_ 20.93% Somewhat Important _1_ 2.33% Not Important ___

C. Physician's Care
   Very Important _31_ 72.10% Important _12_ 27.90% Somewhat Important ___ Not Important ___

D. Nursing Care
   Very Important _28_ 65.12% Important _14_ 32.56% Somewhat Important _1_ 2.32% Not Important ___

E. Food Service
   Very Important _23_ 53.48% Important _11_ 25.59% Somewhat Important _7_ 16.28% Not Important _2_ 4.65%

F. Shortness of Hospital Stay
   Very Important _17_ 39.53% Important _15_ 34.88% Somewhat Important _8_ 18.60% Not Important _3_ 6.98%

G. Exercise; Recreational Activities
   Very Important _17_ 39.53% Important _14_ 32.56% Somewhat Important _12_ 27.91% Not Important ___

H. Friendships with Patients
   Very Important _25_ 58.15% Important _10_ 23.25% Somewhat Important _5_ 11.63% Not Important _3_ 6.98%

I. "Shouldice Hospital hardly seemed like a hospital at all."
   Very Important _25_ 58.14% Important _13_ 30.23% Somewhat Important _5_ 11.63% Not Important ___

12. In a few words, give the MAIN REASON why you returned for this annual reunion.

PROBLEMS AND PLANS

When asked about major questions confronting the management of the hospital, Dr. Shouldice cited a desire to seek ways of increasing the hospital's capacity while at the same time maintaining control over the quality of service delivered, the future role of government in the operation of the hospital, and the use of the Shouldice name by potential competitors. As Dr. Shouldice put it:

"I'm a doctor first and an entrepreneur second. For example, we could refuse permission to other doctors who want to visit the hospital. They may copy our technique and misapply it or misinform their patients about the use of it. This results in failure, and we are concerned that the technique will be blamed. But we're doctors, and it is our obligation to help other surgeons learn. On the other hand, it's quite clear that others are trying to emulate us. Look at this ad. [The advertisement is shown in Exhibit 4.]

Exhibit 4: Advertisement by a Shouldice competitor.

This makes me believe that we should add to our capacity, either here or elsewhere. Here, we could go to Saturday operations and increase our capacity by 20 percent. Throughout the year, no operations are scheduled for Saturdays or Sundays, although patients whose operations are scheduled late in the week remain in the hospital over the weekend. Or, with an investment of perhaps $4 million in new space, we could expand our number of beds by 50 percent, and schedule the operating rooms more heavily.

On the other hand, given government regulation, do we want to invest more in Toronto? Or should we establish another hospital with similar design, perhaps in the United States? There is also the possibility that we could diversify into other specialties offering similar opportunities such as eye surgery, varicose veins, or diagnostic services (e.g. colonoscopies).

For now, we're also beginning the process of grooming someone to succeed Dr. Degani when he retires. He's in his early 60s, but at some point we'll have to address this issue. And for good reason, he's resisted changing certain successful procedures that I think we could improve on. We had quite a time changing the schedule for the administration of Demerol to patients to increase their comfort level during the operation. Dr. Degani has opposed a Saturday operating program on the premise that he won't be here and won't be able to maintain proper control."

Alan O'Dell added his own concerns:

"How should we be marketing our services? Right now, we don't advertise directly to patients. We're even afraid to send out this new brochure we've put together, unless a potential patient specifically requests it, for fear it will generate too much demand. Our records show that just under 1 percent of our patients are medical doctors, a significantly high percentage. How should we capitalize on that? I'm also concerned about this talk of Saturday operations. We are already getting good utilization of this facility. And if we expand further, it will be very difficult to maintain the same kind of working relationships and attitudes. Already there are rumors floating around among the staff about it. And the staff is not pleased."

Exhibit 5: The Shouldice Hospital grounds is a haven for rest and recuperation.

The matter of Saturday operations had been a topic of conversation among the doctors as well. Four of the older doctors were opposed to it. While most of the younger doctors were indifferent or supportive, at least two who had been at the hospital for some time were particularly concerned about the possibility that the issue would drive a wedge between the two groups. As one put it, "I'd hate to see the practice split over the issue."

STUDY QUESTIONS

1. What is the market for this service? How successful is Shouldice Hospital?

2. Define the service model for Shouldice. How does each of its elements contribute to the hospital's success?

3. As Dr. Shouldice, what actions, if any, would you like to take to expand the hospital's capacity and how would you implement such changes?

[1] Professor James Heskett prepared the original version of this case, "Shouldice Hospital Limited," HBS No. 683-068. This version was prepared jointly by Professor James Heskett and Roger Hallowell (MBA 1989, DBA 1997). HBS cases are developed solely as the basis for class discussion. Cases are not intended to serve as endorsements, sources of primary data, or illustrations of effective or ineffective management.

[2] Most hernias, knows as external abdominal hernias, are protrusions of some part of the abdominal contents through a hole or slit in the muscular layers of the abdominal wall which is supposed to contain them. Well over 90% of these hernias occur in the groin area. Of these, by far the most common are inguinal hernias, many of which are caused by a slight weakness in the muscle layers brought about by the passage of the testicles in male babies through the groin area shortly before birth. Aging also contributes to the development of inguinal hernias. Because of the cause of the affliction, 85% of all hernias occur in males.

[3] Based on tracking of patients over more than 30 years, the gross recurrence rate for all operations performed at Shouldice was 0.8%. Recurrence rates reported in the literature for these types of hernia varied greatly. However, one text stated, "In the United States the gross rate of recurrence for groin hernias approaches 10%."

[4] All monetary references in the case are to Canadian dollars. $1 US equaled $1.33 Canadian on February 23, 2004.

[5] The chart in Exhibit 2 was prepared by the case writer, based on conversations with hospital personnel.

[6] This figure included a provincially mandated return on investment.

[7] The latter figure included the bonus pool for doctors.

Red Lobster[1]

Christopher Lovelock

A peer review panel of managers and service workers from a restaurant chain must decide whether or not a waitress has been unfairly fired from her job.

"It felt like a knife going through me!" declared Mary Campbell, 53, after she was fired from her waitressing job at a restaurant in the Red Lobster chain. But instead of suing for what she considered unfair dismissal after 19 years of service, Campbell called for a peer review, seeking to recover her job and three weeks of lost wages.

Three weeks after the firing, a panel of employees from different Red Lobster restaurants was reviewing the evidence and trying to determine whether the server had, in fact, been unjustly fired for allegedly stealing a guest comment card completed by a couple of customers whom she had served.

PEER REVIEW AT DARDEN INDUSTRIES

Red Lobster was owned by Darden Industries, which also owned other restaurant chains like Olive Garden, Bahama Breeze, Smokey Bones Barbeque and Grill and Seasons 52. The company, which has more than 65,000 employees, had adopted a policy of encouraging peer review of disputed employee firings and disciplinary actions several years earlier. The company's key objectives were to limit worker lawsuits and ease workplace tensions.

This case is based on information in a story by Margaret A. Jacobs in the Wall Street Journal. Personal names have been changed. AQ Can Margaret Jacobs be considered the author of this case?

Advocates of the peer review approach, which had been adopted at several other companies, believed that it was a very effective way of channeling constructively the pain and anger that employees felt after being fired or disciplined by their managers. By reducing the incidence of lawsuits, a company could also save on legal expenses.

A Darden spokesperson stated that the peer review program had been "tremendously successful" in keeping valuable employees from unfair dismissal. Each year, about 100 disputes ended up in peer review, with only 10 subsequently resulting in lawsuits. Red Lobster managers and many employees also credited peer review with reducing racial tensions. Ms. Campbell, who said she had received dozens of calls of support, chose peer review over a lawsuit not only because it was much cheaper, but "I also liked the idea of being judged by people who know how things work in a little restaurant."

THE EVIDENCE

The review panel included a General Manager, an Assistant Manager, a server, a hostess, and a bartender, who had all volunteered to review the circumstances of Mary Campbell's firing. Each panelist had received peer review training and was receiving regular wages plus travel expenses. The instructions to panelists were simply to do what they felt was fair.

Campbell had been fired by Jean Larimer, the General Manager of the Red Lobster in Marston, where the former worked as a restaurant server. The reason given for the firing was that Campbell had asked the restaurant's hostess, Eve Taunton, for the key to the guest comment box and stolen a card from it. The card had been completed by a couple of guests whom Campbell had served and who seemed dissatisfied with their experience at the restaurant. Subsequently, the guests learned that their comment card, which complained that their prime rib of beef was too rare and their waitress was "uncooperative," had been removed from the box.

Jean Larimer's testimony

Larimer, who supervised 100 full and part-time employees, testified that she had dismissed Campbell after one of the two customers complained angrily to her and her supervisor. "She [the guest] felt violated," declared the manager, "because her card was taken from the box and her complaint about the food was ignored." Larimer drew the panel's attention to the company rule book, pointing out that Campbell had violated the policy that forbade removal of company property.

Mary Campbell's testimony

Campbell testified that the female customer had requested that her prime rib be cooked "well done" and then subsequently complained that it was fatty and undercooked. The waitress told the panel that she had politely suggested that "prime rib always has fat on it," but arranged to have the meat cooked some more. However, the woman still seemed unhappy. She poured some steak sauce over the meat, but then pushed away her plate without eating any of the food. When the customer remained displeased, Campbell offered her a free dessert. But the guests decided to leave, paid the bill, filled out the guest comment card, and dropped it in the guest comment box.

Exhibit 1: The Restaurant scene becomes the testing ground for the validity of peer review.

Admitting that she was consumed by curiosity, Campbell asked Eve Taunton, the restaurant's hostess, for the key to the box. After removing and reading the card, she pocketed it. Her intent, she declared, was to show the card to Ms. Larimer, who had been concerned earlier that the prime rib served at the restaurant was overcooked, not undercooked. However, she forgot about the card and later, accidentally, threw it out.

Taunton's testimony

At the time of the firing, Taunton, a 17-year old student, was working at Red Lobster for the summer. "I didn't think it was a big deal to give her [Campbell] the key," she said. "A lot of people would come up to me to get it."

THE PANEL DELIBERATES

Having heard the testimony, the members of the review panel had to decide whether Ms. Larimer had been justified in firing Ms. Campbell. The panelists' initial reactions to the situation were split by rank, with the hourly workers supporting Campbell and the managers supporting Larimer. But then the debate began in earnest in an effort to reach consensus.

STUDY QUESTIONS

1. What are the marketing implications of this situation?

2. Evaluate the concept of peer review. What are its strengths and weaknesses? What type of environment is required to make it work well?

3. Review the evidence. Do you believe the testimony presented?

4. What decision would you make and why?

[1] © 2009 Christopher H. Lovelock. This case is based on information in a story by Margaret A. Jacobs in *The Wall Street Journal*. Personal names have been changed.

Menton Bank[1]

Christopher Lovelock

Problems arise when a large bank, attempting to develop a stronger customer service orientation, enlarges the tellers' responsibilities to include selling activities.

" **I**'m concerned about Karen," said Margaret Costanzo to David Reeves. The two bank officers were seated in the former's office at Menton Bank. Costanzo was a Vice President of the bank and manager of the Victory Square branch, the third largest in Menton's large branch network. She and Reeves, the branch's Customer Service Director, were having an employee appraisal meeting. Reeves was responsible for the customer service department, which coordinated the activities of the Customer Service Representatives (CSRs, formerly known as tellers) and the Customer Assistance Representatives (CARs, formerly known as new accounts assistants).

Costanzo and Reeves were discussing Karen Mitchell, a 24-year-old customer service representative, who had applied for the soon-to-be-vacant position of head CSR. Mitchell had been with the bank for three and a half years. She had applied for the position of what had then been called head teller a year earlier, but the job had gone to a candidate with more seniority. Now, that individual was leaving—his wife had been transferred to a new job in another city—and the position was once again open. Two other candidates had also applied for the job.

Both Costanzo and Reeves agreed that, against all criteria used in the past, Karen Mitchell would have been the obvious choice for head teller. She was both fast and accurate in her work, presented a smart and professional appearance, and was well liked by customers and her fellow CSRs. However, the nature of the teller's job had been significantly revised nine months earlier to add a stronger marketing component. CSRs were now expected to offer polite suggestions that customers use Automated Teller Machines (ATMs) for simple transactions. They were also required to stimulate customer interest in the broadening array of financial services offered by the bank. "The problem with Karen," as Reeves put it, "is that she simply refuses to sell."

THE NEW FOCUS ON CUSTOMER SERVICE AT MENTON BANK

Although it was the largest bank in the region, Menton had historically focused on corporate business and its share of the retail consumer banking business had declined in the face of aggressive competition from other financial institutions. Three years earlier, the Board of Directors had appointed a new Chief Executive Officer (CEO) and given him the mandate of developing a stronger consumer orientation at the retail level. The goal was to seize the initiative in marketing the ever-increasing array of financial services now available to retail customers. The CEO's strategy, after putting in a new management team, was to begin by ordering an expansion and speed-up of Menton's investment in electronic delivery systems, which had fallen behind the competition. To achieve this strategy, a new banking technology team had been created.

During the past eighteen months, the bank had tripled the number of ATMs located inside its branches, replacing older ATMs with the latest models featuring color touch screens and capable of a broader array of transactions. Menton was already a member of a several ATM networks, giving its customers access to freestanding 24-hour booths in shopping centers, airports, and other high-traffic locations. The installation of new ATMs was coupled with a branch renovation program, designed to improve the physical appearance of the branches. A pilot program to test the impact of these "new look" branches was already underway. In the longer term, top management intended to redesign the interior of each branch. As more customers switched to electronic banking from remote locations, the bank planned to close a number of its smaller branches.

Another important move had been to introduce automated telephone banking, which allowed customers to check account balances and to move funds from one account to another by touching specific keys on their phone in response to the instructions of a computerized voice. This service was available 24/7 and utilization was rising steadily. Customers could also call a central customer service office to speak with a bank representative concerning service questions or problems with their accounts, as well as to request new account applications or new checkbooks, which would be sent by mail. This office currently operated on weekdays from 8:00 A.M. to 8:00 P.M. and on Saturdays from 8:00 A.M. to 2:00 P.M., but Menton was evaluating the possibility of expanding the operation to include a broad array of retail bank services, offered on a 24-hour basis.

The technology team had completely redesigned the bank's web site to make it possible to offer what were described as the region's most "user-friendly" Internet banking services. Customers had online access to their accounts and could also obtain information about bank services, branch locations and service hours, location of ATMs, as well as answers to commonly asked questions. Finally, the bank had recently started issuing new credit cards containing chips imbued with radio-frequency identification (RFID), which speeded transactions by allowing customers to wave their cards close to a special reader rather than having to swipe them in the traditional way. All these actions seemed to be bearing fruit. In the most recent six months, Menton had seen a significant increase in the number of new accounts opened, as compared to the same period of the previous year; and quarterly survey data showed that Menton Bank was steadily increasing its share of new deposits in the region.

CUSTOMER SERVICE ISSUES

New financial products had been introduced at a rapid rate. But the bank found that many existing "platform" staff—known as new accounts assistants—were ill equipped to sell these services because of lack of product knowledge and inadequate training in selling skills. As Costanzo recalled:

> "The problem was that they were so used to sitting at their desks waiting for a customer to approach them with a specific request, such as a mortgage or car loan, that it was hard to get them to take a more positive approach that involved actively probing for customer needs. Their whole job seemed to revolve around filling out forms or responding to prompts on their computer screens. We were way behind most other banks in this respect."

As the automation program proceeded, the mix of activities performed by the tellers started to change. A growing number of customers were using the ATMs, the website, and automated telephone banking for a broad array of transactions, including cash withdrawals and deposits (from the ATMs), transfers of funds between accounts, and requesting account balances. The ATMs at the Victory Square branch had the highest utilization of any of Menton's branches, reflecting the large number of students and young professionals served at that location, Costanzo noted that customers who were older or less well-educated seemed to prefer being served by "a real person, rather than a machine." They were particularly reluctant to make deposits via an ATM.

A year earlier, the head office had selected three branches, including Victory Square, as test sites for a new customer service program, which included a radical redesign of the branch interior. The Victory Square branch was in a busy urban location, about one mile from the central business district and less than 10-minutes' walk from the campus of a large university. The branch was surrounded by retail stores and close to commercial and professional offices. The other test branches were among the bank's larger suburban offices in two different metropolitan areas and were located in a shopping mall and next to a big hospital, respectively.

As part of the branch renovation program, each of these three branches had previously been remodeled to include no fewer than four ATMs (Victory Square had six), which could be closed off from the rest of the branch so that they would remain accessible to customers 24 hours a day. Further remodeling was then undertaken to locate a customer service desk near the entrance; close to each desk were two electronic information terminals, featuring color touch screens that customers could activate to obtain information on a variety of bank services. The teller stations were redesigned to provide two levels of service: an express station for simple deposits and for cashing of approved checks, as well as regular stations for the full array of services provided by tellers. The number of stations open at a given time was varied to reflect the volume of anticipated business and staffing arrangements were changed to ensure that more tellers were on hand to serve customers during the busiest periods. Finally, the platform area in each branch was reconstructed to create what the architect described as "a friendly, yet professional appearance."

HUMAN RESOURCES

With the new environment came new training programs for the staff of these three branches and new job descriptions and job titles: customer assistance representatives (for the platform staff), customer service representatives (for the tellers), and customer service director (instead of assistant branch manager). The head teller position was renamed head CSR. Details of the new job descriptions are shown in the Appendix. The training programs for each group included sessions designed to develop improved knowledge of both new and existing retail products. (CARs received more extensive training in this area than did CSRs.) The CARs also attended a 15-hour course, offered in three separate sessions, on basic selling skills. This program covered key steps in the sales process, including building a relationship, exploring customer needs, determining a solution, and overcoming objections.

The sales training program for CSRs, by contrast, consisted of just two 2-hour sessions designed to develop skills in recognizing and probing customer needs, presenting product features and benefits, overcoming objections, and referring customers to CARs. All staff members in customer service positions participated in sessions designed to improve their communication skills and professional image: clothing and personal grooming and interactions with customers were all discussed. The trainer said, "Remember, people's money is too important to entrust to someone who doesn't look and act the part!"

CARs were instructed to rise from their seats and shake hands with customers. Both CARs and CSRs were given exercises designed to improve their listening skills and their powers of observation. All employees working in places where they could be seen by customers were ordered to refrain from drinking soda and chewing gum while on the job. (Smoking by both employees and customers had been banned some years earlier under the bank's smoke-free office policy.)

Although Menton Bank's management anticipated that most of the increased emphasis on selling would fall to the CARs, they also foresaw a limited selling role for the customer service representatives, who would be expected to mention various products and facilities offered by the bank as they served customers at the teller windows. For instance, if a customer happened to say something about an upcoming vacation, the CSR was supposed to mention traveler's checks. If the customer complained about bounced checks, the CSR should suggest speaking to a CAR about opening a personal line of credit that would provide an automatic overdraft protection. If the customer mentioned investments, the CSR was expected to refer him or her to a CAR who could provide information on money market accounts, certificates of deposit, or Menton's discount brokerage service. All CSRs were supplied with their own business cards. When making a referral, they were expected to write the customer's name and the product of interest on the back of a card, give it to the customer and send that individual to the customer assistance desks.

In an effort to motivate CSRs at the three branches to sell specific financial products, the bank experimented with various incentive programs. The first involved cash bonuses for referrals to CARs that resulted in sale of specific products. During a one-month period, CSRs were offered a $50 bonus for each referral leading to a customer opening a personal line of credit account. The CARs received a $20 bonus for each account they opened, regardless of whether or not it came as a referral or simply a walk-in. Eight such bonuses were paid to CSRs at Victory Square, with three each going to just two of the full-time CSRs, Jean Warshawski and Bruce Greenfield. Karen Mitchell was not among the recipients. However, this program was not renewed, since it was felt that there were other, more cost-effective means of marketing this product. In addition, Reeves, the Customer Service Director, had reason to believe that Bruce Greenfield had colluded with one of the CARs, his girlfriend, to claim referrals which he had not, in fact, made. Another test branch reported similar suspicions of two of its CSRs

A second promotion followed and was based on allocating credits to the CSRs for successful referrals. The value of the credit varied according to the nature of the product — for instance, a debit card was worth 500 credits—and accumulated credits could be exchanged for merchandise gifts. This program was deemed ineffective and discontinued after three months. The basic problem seemed to be that the value of the gifts was seen as too low in relation to the amount of effort required. Other problems with these promotional schemes included lack of product knowledge on the part of the CSRs and time pressures when many customers were waiting in line to be served.

The bank had next turned to an approach which, in David Reeves' words, "used the stick rather than the carrot." All CSRs had traditionally been evaluated half-yearly on a variety of criteria, including accuracy, speed, quality of interactions with customers, punctuality of arrival for work, job attitudes, cooperation with other employees, and professional image. The evaluation process assigned a number of points to each criterion, with accuracy and speed being the most heavily weighted. In addition to appraisals by the Customer Service Director and the branch manager, with input from the head CSR, Menton had recently instituted a program of anonymous visits by what was popularly known as the "mystery client." Each CSR was visited at least once a quarter by a professional evaluator posing as a customer. This individual's appraisal of the CSR's appearance, performance, and attitude was included in the overall evaluation. The number of points scored by each CSR had a direct impact on merit pay raises and on selection for promotion to the head CSR position or to platform jobs.

To encourage improved product knowledge and "consultative selling" by CSRs, the evaluation process was revised to include points assigned for each individual's success in sales referrals. Under the new evaluation scheme, the maximum number of points assignable for effectiveness in making sales—directly or through referrals to CARs—amounted to 30 percent of the potential total score. Although CSR-initiated sales had risen significantly in the most recent half-year, Reeves sensed that morale had dropped among this group, in contrast to the CARs, whose enthusiasm and commitment had risen significantly. He had also noticed an increase in CSR errors. One CSR had quit, complaining about too much pressure.

KAREN MITCHELL

Under the old scoring system, Karen Mitchell had been the highest-scoring teller/CSR for four consecutive half-years. But after two half-years under the new system, her ranking had dropped to fourth out of the seven full-time tellers. The top-ranking CSR, Mary Bell, had been with Menton Bank for sixteen years, but had declined repeated invitations to apply for a head teller position, saying that she was happy where she was, earning at the top of the CSR scale, and did not want "the extra worry and responsibility." Mitchell ranked first on all but one of the operationally related criteria (interactions with customers, where she ranked second), but sixth on selling effectiveness (Exhibit 1 on page 512).

Costanzo and Reeves had spoken to Mitchell about her performance and expressed disappointment. Mitchell had informed them, respectfully but firmly, that she saw the most important aspect of her job as giving customers fast, accurate, and courteous service, telling the two bank officers:

"I did try this selling thing but it just seemed to annoy people. Some said they were in a hurry and couldn't talk now; others looked at me as if I were slightly crazy to bring up the subject of a different bank service than the one they were currently transacting. And then, when you got the odd person who seemed interested, you could hear the other customers in the line grumbling about the slow service.

Really, the last straw was when I noticed on the computer screen that this woman had several thousand in her savings account so I suggested to her, just as the trainer had told us, that she could earn more interest if she opened a money market account. Well, she told me it was none of my business what she did with her money, and stomped off. Don't get me wrong, I love being able to help customers, and if they ask for my advice, I'll gladly tell them about what the bank has to offer."

SELECTING A NEW HEAD CSR

Two weeks after this meeting, it was announced that the head CSR was leaving. The job entailed some supervision of the work of the other CSRs (including allocation of work assignments and scheduling part-time CSRs at busy periods or during employ vacations), consultation on—and, where possible, resolution of—any problems occurring at the teller stations, and handling of large cash deposits and withdrawals by local retailers (see position description in the Appendix on page 509). When not engaged on such tasks, the head CSR was expected to operate a regular teller window.

The pay scale for a head CSR ranged from US$10.00–US$15.00 per hour, depending on qualifications, seniority, and branch size, as compared to a range US$8.40–US$12.00 per hour for CSRs. The pay scale for CARs ranged from US$9.20–US$13.50. Full-time employees (who were not unionized) worked a 40-hour week, including some evenings until 6:00 P.M. and certain Saturday mornings. Costanzo indicated that the pay scales were typical for banks in the region, although the average CSR at Menton was better qualified than those at smaller banks and therefore higher on the scale. Karen Mitchell was currently earning US$10.80 per hour, reflecting her education, which included a diploma in business administration, three-and-a-half years' experience, and significant past merit increases. If promoted to head CSR, she would qualify for an initial rate of US$12.50 an hour. When applications for the positions closed, Mitchell was one of three candidates. The other two candidates were Jean Warshawski, 42, another CSR at the Victory Square branch; and Curtis Richter, 24, the head CSR at one of Menton Bank's small suburban branches, who was seeking more responsibility.

Warshawski was married with two sons in school. She had started working as a part-time teller at Victory Square some three years previously, switching to full-time work a year later in order, as she said, to put away some money for her boys' college education. Warshawski was a cheerful woman with a jolly laugh. She had a wonderful memory for people's names and Reeves had often seen her greeting customers on the street or in a restaurant during her lunch hour. Reviewing her evaluations over the previous three years, Reeves noted that she had initially performed poorly on accuracy and at one point, when she was still a part-timer, had been put on probation because of frequent inaccuracies in the balance in her cash drawer at the end of the day. Although Reeves considered her much improved on this score, he still saw room for improvement. The Customer Service Director had also on occasion, reprimanded her for tardiness during the past year. Warshawski attributed this to health problems with her elder son who, she said, was now responding to treatment.

Both Reeves and Costanzo had observed Warshawski at work and agreed that her interactions with customers were exceptionally good, although she tended to be overly chatty and was not as fast as Karen Mitchell. She seemed to have a natural ability to size up customers and to decide which ones were good prospects for a quick sales pitch on a specific financial product. Although slightly untidy in her personal appearance, she was very well organized in her work and was quick to help her fellow CSRs, especially new hires. She was currently earning US$10.20 per hour as a CSR and would qualify for a rate of US$12.10 as head CSR. In the most recent six months, Warshawski had ranked ahead of Mitchell as a result of being very successful in consultative selling (Exhibit 1 on page 512).

Richter, the third candidate, was not working in one of the three test branches, and so had not been exposed to the consultative selling program and its corresponding evaluation scheme. However, he had received excellent evaluations for his work in Menton's small Longmeadow branch, where he had been employed for three years. A move to Victory Square would increase his earnings from US$11.20 to US$12.10 per hour. Reeves and Costanzo had interviewed Richter and considered him intelligent and personable. He had joined the bank after dropping out of college midway through his third year, but had recently started taking evening courses in order to complete his degree. The Longmeadow branch was located in an older part of town, where commercial and retail activities were rather stagnant. This branch (which was rumored to be under consideration for closure) had not yet been renovated and had no ATMs, although there was an ATM accessible to Menton customers one block away. Richter supervised three CSRs and reported directly to the branch manager, who spoke very highly of him. Since there were no CARs in this branch, Richter and another experienced CSR took turns to handle new accounts and loan or mortgage applications.

Costanzo and Reeves were troubled by the decision that faced them. Prior to the bank's shift in focus, Mitchell would have been the natural choice for the head CSR job which, in turn, could be a stepping stone to further promotions, including CAR, Customer Service Director, and, eventually, Manager of a small branch or a management position in the head office. Mitchell had told her superiors that she was interested in making a career in banking and that she was eager to take on further responsibilities.

Compounding the problem was the fact that the three branches testing the improved branch design and new customer service program had just completed a full year of the test. Costanzo knew that sales and profits were up significantly at all three branches, relative to the bank's performance as a whole. She anticipated that top management would want to extend the program system-wide after making any modifications that seemed desirable.

STUDY QUESTIONS

1. Identify the steps taken by Menton Bank to develop a stronger customer orientation in its retail branches.

2. Compare and contrast the jobs of CAR and CSR. How important is each (a) to bank operations and (b) to customer satisfaction?

3. Evaluate the strengths and weaknesses of Karen Mitchell and other candidates for head CSR.

4. What action do you recommend for filling the head CSR position?

---

[1] © 2009 Christopher H. Lovelock

APPENDIX—MENTON BANK: JOB DESCRIPTIONS FOR CUSTOMER SERVICE STAFF IN BRANCHES

Previous Job Description for Teller

FUNCTION: Provides customer services by receiving, paying out, and keeping accurate records of all money involved in paying and receiving transactions. Promotes the bank's services.

Responsibilities

1. Serves customers:

   - Accepts deposits, verifies cash and endorsements, and gives customers their receipts.

   - Cashes checks within the limits assigned or refers customers to supervisor for authorization.

   - Accepts savings deposits and withdrawals, verifies signatures, and posts interest and balances as necessary.

   - Accepts loan, credit card, utility, and other payments.

   - Issues money orders, cashier's checks, traveler's checks, and foreign currency

   - Reconciles customer statements and confers with bookkeeping personnel regarding discrepancies in balances or other problems.

   - Issues credit card advances.

2. Prepares individual daily settlement of teller cash and proof transactions.

3. Prepares branch daily journal and general ledger.

4. Promotes the bank's services:

   - Cross-sells other bank services appropriate to customer's needs.

   - Answers inquiries regarding bank matters.

   - Directs customers to other departments for specialized services.

5. Assists with other branch duties:

   - Totals receipts at night and mail deposits.

   - Reconciles ATM transactions.

   - Provides safe deposit services.

   - Performs secretarial duties.

New Job Description for Customer Service Representative

FUNCTION: Provides customers with the highest quality services, with special emphasis on recognizing customer need and cross-selling appropriate bank services. Plays an active role in developing and maintaining good relations.

Responsibilities

1. Presents and communicates the best possible customer service:

   - Greets all customers with a courteous, friendly attitude.

   - Provides fast, accurate, friendly service.

   - Uses customer's name whenever possible.

2. Sells bank services and maintains customer relations:

   - Cross-sells retail services by identifying and referring valid prospects to a CAR or customer service director. When time permits (no other customers waiting in line), should actively cross-sell retail services.

   - Develops new business by acquainting non-customers with bank services and existing customers with additional services that they are not currently using.

3. Provides a prompt and efficient operation on a professional level:

   - Receives cash and/or checks for checking accounts, savings accounts, taxes withheld, loan payments, Mastercard and Visa, mortgage payments, money orders, traveler's checks, cashier's checks.

   - Verifies amount of cash and/or checks received, being alert to counterfeit or fraudulent items.

   - Cashes checks in accordance with bank policy. Watches for stop payments and holds funds per bank policy.

   - Receives payment of collection items, safe deposit rentals, and other miscellaneous items.

   - Confers with head CSR or Customer Service Director on non-routine situations.

- Sells traveler's checks, money orders, monthly transit passes, and cashier's checks and may redeem coupons and sell or redeem foreign currency.

- Prepares coin and currency orders as necessary.

- Services, maintains, and settles ATMs as required.

- Ensures only minimum cash exposure, necessary for efficient operation, is kept in cash drawer; removes excess cash immediately to secured location.

- Prepares accurate and timely daily settlement of work.

- Performs bookkeeping and operational functions as assigned by Customer Service Director.

New Job Description for Head Customer Service Representative

FUNCTION: Supervises all CSRs in the designated branch office, ensuring efficient operation and the highest-quality service to customers. Plays an active role in developing and maintaining good customer relations. Assists other branch personnel on request.

Responsibilities

1. Supervises the CSRs in the branch:

   - Allocates work, coordinates work flow, reviews and revises work procedures.

   - Ensures teller area is adequately and efficiently staffed with well-trained, qualified personnel. • Assists CSRs with more complex transactions.

   - Resolves routine personnel problems, referring more complex situations to Customer Service Director.

   - Participates in decisions concerning performance appraisal, promotions, wage changes, transfers, and termination of subordinate CSR staff.

2. Assumes responsibility for CSRs' money:

   - Buys and sells money in the vault, ensuring adequacy of branch currency and coin supply.

   - Ensures that CSRs and cash sheets are in balance.

   - Maintains necessary records, including daily branch journal and general ledger.

3. Accepts deposits and withdrawals by business customers at the commercial window.

4. Operates teller window to provide services to retail customers (see Responsibilities for CSRs).

New Job Description for Customer Assistance Representative

FUNCTION: Provides services and guidance to customers/prospects seeking banking relationships or related information. Promotes and sells needed products and responds to special requests by existing customers.

Responsibilities

1. Provides prompt, efficient, and friendly service to all customers and prospective customers:

   - Describes and sells bank services to customers/prospects who approach them directly or via referral from customer service reps or other bank personnel.

   - Answers customers' questions regarding bank services, hours, etc.

2. Identifies and responds to customers' needs:

   - Promotes and sells retail services and identifies any existing cross-sell opportunities.

   - Opens new accounts for individuals, businesses, and private organizations.

   - Prepares temporary checks and deposit slips for new checking/NOW accounts.

   - Sells checks and deposit slips.

   - Interviews and takes applications for and pays out on instalment/charge card accounts and other credit-related products.

   - Certifies checks.

   - Handles stop payment requests.

   - Responds to telephone mail inquiries from customers or bank personnel.

   - Receives notification of name or address changes and takes necessary action.

   - Takes action on notification of lost passbooks, credit cards, ATM cards, collateral, and other lost or stolen items.

   - Demonstrates ATMs to customers and assists with problems.

   - Coordinates closing of accounts and ascertains reasons.

3. Sells and services all retail products:

- Advises customers and processes applications for all products covered in CAR training programs (and updates).

- Initiates referrals to the appropriate department when a trust or corporate business need is identified.

New Job Description for Customer Service Director

FUNCTION: Supervises CSRs, CARs, and other staff as assigned to provide the most effective and profitable retail banking delivery system in the local marketplace. Supervises sales efforts and provides feedback to management concerning response to products and services by current and prospective banking customers. Communicates goals and results to those supervised and ensures operational standards are met in order to achieve outstanding customer service.

Responsibilities

1. Supervises effective delivery of retail products:

- Selects, trains, and manages CSRs and CARs.

- Assigns duties and work schedules.

- Completes performance reviews.

2. Personally, and through those supervised, renders the highest level of professional and efficient customer service available in the local marketplace:

- Provides high level of service while implementing most efficient and customer-sensitive staffing schedules.

- Supervises all on-the-job programs within office.

- Ensures that outstanding customer service standards are achieved.

- Directs remedial programs for CSRs and CARs as necessary.

3. Develops retail sales effectiveness to the degree necessary to achieve market share objectives:

- Ensures that all CSRs and CARs possess comprehensive product knowledge.

- Directs coordinated cross-sell program within office at all times.

- Reports staff training needs to branch manager and/or regional training director.

4. Ensures adherence to operational standards:

- Oversees preparation of daily and monthly operational and sales reports.

- Estimates, approves, and coordinates branch cash needs in advance.

- Oversees ATM processing function.

- Handles or consults with CSRs/CARs on more complex transactions.

- Ensures clean and business-like appearance of the branch facility.

5. Informs branch manager of customer response to products:

- Reports customer complaints and types of sales resistance encountered.

- Describes and summarizes reasons for account closings.

6. Communicates effectively the goals and results of the bank to those under supervision:

- Reduces office goals into a format which translates to goals for each CSR or CAR.

- Reports sales and cross-sell results to all CSRs and CARs.

- Conducts sales- and service-oriented staff meetings with CSRs/CARs on a regular basis.

- Attends all scheduled customer service management meetings organized by regional office.

Exhibit 1: Performance scores of the CSRs

Menton Bank: Summary of performance evaluation scores for customer service representatives at Victory Square branch during latest two half-year periods.

CSR Name[3]	Length of Full-Time Bank Service	Operational Criteria[1] (max.: 70 points)		Selling Effectiveness[2] (max.: 30 points)		Total Score	
		1st Half	2nd Half	1st Half	2nd Half	1st Half	2nd Half
Mary Bell	16 years, 10 months	65	64	16	20	81	84
Scott Dubois	2 years, 3 months	63	61	15	19	78	80
Bruce Greenfield	12 months	48	42	20	26	68	68
Karen Mitchell	3 years, 7 months	67	67	13	12	80	79
Sharon Rubin	1 year, 4 months	53	55	8	9	61	64
Swee Hoon Chen	7 months	—	50	—	22	—	72
Jean Warshawski	2 years, 1 month	57	55	21	28	79	83

Note: 1. *Totals based on sum of ratings points against various criteria, including accuracy, work production, attendance and punctuality, personal appearance, organization of work, initiative, cooperation with others, problem-solving ability, and quality of interaction with customers.*

2. *Points awarded for both direct sales by CSR (e.g. traveler's checks) and referral selling by CSR to CAR (e.g. debit card, certificates of deposit, personal line of credit).*

3. *Full-time CSRs only (part-time CSRs were evaluated separately).*

Exhibit 2: Bank tellers today are expected to shoulder wider job responsibilities to meet the demand for greater customer service orientation.

Mr Mahaleel Goes to London[1]

Christopher Lovelock

A senior account officer at an international bank is about to meet a wealthy Asian businessman who is seeking funding for a buyout of his company. The prospective client has already visited a competing bank.

It was a Friday in mid-February and Mr. Kadir Mahaleel, a wealthy businessman from the Southeast Asian nation of Tailesia, was visiting London on a trip that combined business and pleasure. Mahaleel, who held a doctorate from the London School of Economics and had earlier been a Professor of International Trade and a government trade negotiator, was the founder of Eximsa, a major export company in Tailesia. Business brought him to London every two or three months. These trips provided him the opportunity to visit his daughter, Leona, the eldest of his four children, who lived in London. Several of his ten grandchildren were attending college in Britain. Among his favorite was his grandson Anson. He was especially proud of Anson, who was a student at the Royal Academy of Music. In fact, this trip had been specially scheduled to coincide with a violin recital by Anson at 2:00 P.M. on this day.

The primary purpose of Mahaleel's visit was to resolve a delicate matter regarding his company. He had decided that the time had come to retire and wished to make arrangements for the company's future. His son, Victor, was involved in the business and ran Eximsa's trading office in Europe. Unfortunately, Victor was in poor health and could not take over the company. Mahaleel believed that a group of loyal employees were interested in buying his company if the necessary credit could be arranged.

Before leaving Tailesia, Mahaleel had discussed the possibility of a buyout with his trusted financial adviser, Li Sieuw Meng, who recommended that he talk to several banks in London because of the potential complexity of the business deal:

"The London banks are experienced in buyouts. Also, you need a bank that can handle the credit for the interested buyers in New York and London, as well as Asia. Once the buyout takes place, you'll have significant cash to invest. This would be a good time to review your estate plans as well."

Referring Mahaleel to two competitors, The Trust Company and Global Private Bank, Li added:

"I've met an account officer from Global who called on me several times. Here's his business card. His name is Miguel Kim. I've never done any business with him, but he did seem quite competent. Unfortunately, I don't know anyone at the Trust Company, but here's their address in London."

After checking into the Savoy Hotel in London the following Wednesday, Mahaleel telephoned Kim's office. Since Kim was out, Mahaleel spoke to the account officer's secretary, described himself briefly, and arranged to stop by Global's Lombard Street office around mid-morning on Friday.

On Thursday, Mahaleel visited The Trust Company. The two people he met were extremely pleasant and had spent some time in Tailesia. They seemed very knowledgeable about managing estates and gave him some good recommendations about handling his complex family affairs. However, they were clearly less experienced in handling business credit, his most urgent need.

The next morning, Mahaleel had breakfast with Leona. As they parted, she said, "I'll meet you at 1:30 P.M. in the lobby of the Savoy, and we'll go to the recital together. We mustn't be late if we want to get front-row seats."

On his way to Global Private Bank, Mahaleel stopped at Mappin & Webb's jewelry store to buy his wife a present for their anniversary. His shopping was pleasant and leisurely. He purchased a beautiful diamond necklace that he knew his wife would like. When he emerged from the jewelry store, he was caught in an unexpected snow flurry. He had difficulty finding a taxi and his arthritis started acting up, making walking to the nearest tube station out of question. At last, he caught a taxi and arrived at the Lombard Street location of Global Bancorp about noon. After going into the street-level branch of Global Retail Bank, he was redirected by a security guard to the Private Bank offices on the second floor.

He arrived at the Private Bank's reception area at 12:15 P.M. The receptionist greeted him and contacted Miguel Kim's secretary, who came out promptly to see Mahaleel, and declared:

> "Mr. Kim was disappointed that he couldn't be here to welcome you, Mr Mahaleel, but he had a lunch appointment with one of his clients that was scheduled over a month ago. He expects to return at about 1:30 P.M. In the meantime, he has asked another senior account officer, Sophia Costa, to assist you."

Exhibit 1: Receiving a client on short notice would require a bank's vice-president to rely on all her expertise and experience to clinch the deal.

Sophia Costa, 41, was the Vice President of the bank and had worked for Global Bancorp for 14 years (two years longer than Miguel Kim). She had visited Tailesia once, but had not met Mahaleel's financial adviser nor any member of the Mahaleel family. An experienced relationship manager, Costa was knowledgeable about offshore investment management and fiduciary services. Miguel Kim had looked into her office at 11:45 A.M. and asked her if she would cover for him in case a prospective client, a Mr. Mahaleel, whom he had expected to see earlier, should happen to arrive. He told Costa that Mahaleel was a successful Tailesian businessman planning for his retirement, but that he had never met the prospect personally, and then rushed off to lunch.

The phone rang in Costa's office and she reached across the desk to pick it up. It was Kim's secretary. "Mr Mahaleel is in reception, Ms. Costa."

STUDY QUESTIONS

1. Prepare a flowchart of Mr. Mahaleel's service encounters.

2. Putting yourself in Mahaleel's shoes, how do you feel (both physically and mentally) after speaking with the receptionist at Global? What are your priorities right now?

3. As Sophia Costa, what action would you take in your first five minutes with Mahaleel?

4. What would constitute a good outcome of the meeting for both the client and the bank? How should Costa try to bring about such an outcome?

---

[1] © 2009 Christopher H. Lovelock.

CASE 15

GoodLife Fitness Clubs[1]

Gordon H.G. McDougall

Originating from a single, 2000 square foot club in London in 1979, GoodLife Fitness has emerged as one of the largest groups of fitness clubs in Canada. A brand synonymmous with an unequalled level of educated fitness professionals and high-quality equipment and standards.

"These retention rates are poor. I need to do a better job of keeping members," thought Krista Swain, manager of the GoodLife Kitchener Fitness Club in Kitchener, Ontario, as she reviewed her retention rates for the 1999–2000 fiscal year.

As she was analyzing the report, Jane Riddell, chief operating officer, entered her office. Krista looked up and said, "Hi Jane. I've just been looking over the retention rates for the clubs. I'm not happy with my numbers."

"Neither is the head office," Jane replied, "and that's why I'm here today. You run one of our best clubs, and yet your retention rates are around 60 percent, the average for the 40 GoodLife Clubs. We lose 40 percent of our members each year. By improving your club's retention rates from 60 percent to 65 percent, based on last year's figures, gross revenues would increase by over $35,000[2]. You are one of our top performers, and you should be leading the way."

"I agree," said Krista. "We have to figure out how to keep the members enthused and show that the club offers them value."

"That's what I wanted to hear," replied Jane. "As a first step, let's both think about this and meet again next week with some ideas. Then I'd like you to prepare a retention plan that will be the model for all the clubs."

THE FITNESS MARKET

In a national study, the Canadian Fitness and Research Institute found that most Canadians believed that physical activity was beneficial in preventing heart disease or other chronic conditions, in reducing stress, and in maintaining the ability to perform everyday tasks with aging. However, physical inactivity remained pervasive in Canada, with 63 percent of adults age 18 and older still considered insufficiently active for optimal health benefits in 1998.[3]

The study also revealed that for a variety of reasons most Canadians tended to "talk" positively about the importance of physical activity but didn't "walk the talk." The most popular physical recreation activities were walking (86 percent of Canadians had participated at least once in this activity within the past 12 months), gardening (75 percent), swimming (57 percent), bicycling (55 percent) and home exercise (50 percent). Exercise class/aerobics was ranked thirteenth (21 percent) with significantly more women (33 percent) than men (9 percent) participating.

Although the overall physical activity of Canadians was relatively low, the fitness market was growing at approximately 6 percent a year. The growth was due to demographic changes (baby boomers were increasingly interested in maintaining a good level of physical fitness), marketing (increasing numbers of health/fitness clubs extolling the benefits of fitness through their programs), and individuals selecting fitness clubs over other physical activities as their choice for exercise.

Industry estimates were that about 10 percent of the Canadian population belonged to a health club. However, there was considerable "churning" (the percentage of members lost in a month or year); many Canadians had good intentions and joined a club, only to leave at the end of their membership for a variety of reasons. Industry research revealed the following major reasons for leaving; decline in interest, took too much time, too hard and didn't like the club. It was estimated that on an annual basis the average health/fitness club in Canada lost between 36 to 45 percent of its members.

Another reason for the high average churn rates was that many clubs, referred to as "factories," did not take a professional approach in managing their operations. Typically, a sports personality (e.g., a retired hockey player) would own these "factories" and offer low initial memberships to get people into the club. These clubs had few trained instructors, frequent equipment breakdowns, and poor facilities maintenance. These clubs often failed within a year or two, leaving customers with a valid membership and no facility.

GOODLIFE FITNESS

The Philosophy and Goals

In March 1979, David Patchell-Evans established GoodLife as a sole proprietorship. "Patch," as he was called, saw an opportunity. Canadian fitness clubs were largely cash and sales oriented with little emphasis on scientific fitness or member retention. By May 2000, Patch had built this privately owned fitness company to over 40 clubs (10 were franchises, the rest were company owned) in Ontario and Quebec. GoodLife had the largest group of fitness clubs in Canada with over 70,000 members. (The Appendix: Muscle Mania on page 522 provides more details on the philosophy and growth of the GoodLife Clubs.)

From the beginning, the company's goal was to provide the best in equipment, facilities, and service with a well-trained staff. The goal was based on high-quality service with education and training, superior cleanliness, and programs that made the individual a member for life based on their "needs and goals." The GoodLife motto, "Measurable Constant Improvement," underlaid its plan to grow to 100 clubs by 2004.

Head Office

The head office was located at the Galleria Mall Fitness Club in London, Ontario. Head office personnel numbered approximately 40, led by "Patch," Jane Riddell, chief operating officer, and Maureen Hagen, national director of fitness. Head office's main role was to provide leadership and support for the franchisees and company-owned clubs. Among the group's major activities were determining the advertising strategy, designing new fitness programs, ensuring that all clubs maintained quality standards, providing training programs for staff, and keeping all club managers abreast of the latest trends and issues in the fitness industry.

One of Jane Riddell's responsibilities was the design and management of GoodLife University, where each month 50 to 60 new associates went through a 1-week program. The training included an orientation to GoodLife (basic knowledge of GoodLife and its philosophy), personal training (skills required to assist members as a personal trainer), and computer program training. When club managers hired the associates, they typically spent their first few weeks "learning the ropes" at the club and then attended the university program. Jane led some of the training sessions and evaluated the participants, some of whom failed and left GoodLife.

Jane was generally pleased with the caliber of the participants. She rated about 70 percent of them as good to great and 30 percent as poor. In the past, the GoodLife clubs had focused on hiring physical education and kinesiology graduates. However, as the economy improved in the late 1990s, these graduates chose other job opportunities, requiring GoodLife to broaden its hiring criteria. Now GoodLife hired individuals with the "right" attitude (i.e., customer focused). However, the attitude of some new employees was that this was not a "real" job or a career. Rather it was a fun place to be for awhile, a "cool," easy job until they got a "real" job. Jane felt that this was part of the issue of employee retention at GoodLife. In the past 2 years, employee turnover had increased, and last year 600 employees (out of a total of 1,400) had left GoodLife. Jane estimated that most of the employee retention problem was GoodLife's "fault"—they either hired the wrong people, or didn't do enough to keep them.

Advertising spending, at 6 percent of revenues, used a "call to action" versus a "branding" approach. The call to action used variations on "$99 for 99 days," "one month free," "no initiation fee," or "save now".

The company allocated advertising expenditures by season (winter, 40 percent; summer, 25 percent; and October to December, 35 percent), which reflected the general interest level of people in joining a fitness club. Each month headquarters evaluated each club on sales targets—the new members obtained through internal marketing (e.g., referrals or *Yellow Pages*), external marketing (e.g., newspaper, flyers, radio, or television), and walk-ins (e.g., potential member walks into the club and asks about memberships). This information, along with conference calls with the regions, set the regional advertising allocation.

GoodLife's commitment to club members, staff, and community resulted in numerous awards and achievements. GoodLife was the first to bring many innovations to the fitness industry, including the Fit Fix training concept and the PUNCH program. GoodLife raised over $500,000 annually for various charities and supported a wide range of community activities.

The GoodLife Staff

GoodLife's size (over 1,400 associates) and rapid growth provided many opportunities for advancement. The career path at GoodLife could take an associate to any number of areas: group exercise classes, personal training, sales, administration, management, accounting, and even to owning one of the clubs.

Compensation consisted of a base salary plus club sales commissions and bonuses. The club sales commissions were based on the number of memberships sold per week against a target. Depending on the type of membership sold and/or specialty programs sold, the associate could receive a commission on sales ranging from 5 percent to 15 percent. Bonuses were based on weekly targets set for the individual club. Depending on the hours and shifts worked by the staff, if the goals were met, the staff member could earn a bonus of $15 or $25 per week. As well, there was an employee referral bonus: Any current staff member who referred an individual for employment with GoodLife could receive a bonus of $100, or $200 for individuals hired on a part-time or full-time basis. Finally, there were incentive programs for good ideas. The rewards, called "Patch Bucks," could be redeemed for fitness conferences.

GoodLife offered company awards on a monthly and yearly basis. On a monthly basis, awards were given to (1) group exercise coordinator (gift and plaque), (2) manager of the month ($200 and plaque), (3) associate ($100 and plaque), (4) sales manager ($200 and plaque), (5) sales associate ($100 and plaque), (6) personal training associate ($100 and plaque), and (7) customer service representative ($100 plus plaque). On a yearly basis, awards were given to (1) manager (free fitness conference, valued at $2,500), (2) group exercise instructor, and (3) group exercise coordinator.

GOODLIFE KITCHENER

The New Location

In September 1998, the GoodLife Kitchener Club reopened on the second floor of an indoor mall in downtown Kitchener, Ontario. Prior to that, it was located two blocks away in a relatively small (12,000 square feet) and poorly designed facility. The new facility was larger (30,000 square feet), had an open concept design, and an extensive range of equipment and programs. Over the next 18 months, membership increased dramatically under Krista Swain's

guidance. As of May 2000, the club had 3,500 members, an increase of 2,300 over the original 1,200 members who moved from the old club.

Krista, a 1995 graduate in kinesiology and physical education from Wilfrid Laurier University in Waterloo, Ontario, worked for GoodLife as a fitness instructor while she was attending the university. After graduation, she joined the GoodLife Waterloo Club as a service trainer. In addition, she handled corporate sales for the GoodLife Women Only Club in Kitchener. Within 10 months, she was appointed manager of the GoodLife Kitchener Club and was actively involved in the transition from the old to the new location. When asked how she had rapidly advanced to club manager, she said:

> "I have a passion for fitness and I'm committed to the company. I'm convinced that the GoodLife values, mission, and philosophy are right; I truly feel that we are helping people at GoodLife. I like working with people. My role is to be a coach and mentor, and I lead by example. I think the staff understand my goals and respect me because I respect them. Sometimes I can't believe what the staff are willing to do to help the club and the members. But I'll also say, if you are not a top performer, you won't fit in at GoodLife."

In early 2000, the Kitchener club was signing up over 230 new members per month (Exhibit 1 on the following page). At the same time, the club was losing about 100 members per month for a net gain of about 130 members. On an annual basis, the club was losing 40 percent of its members. Overall, the rapid growth in membership had a very positive impact on revenues, which increased by over 60 percent between June 1999 and March 2000 (Exhibit 2 on the following page).

The Associates

The Kitchener club's 40 associates (10 full-time, 30 part-time) worked in four groups: sales, customer service, personal training, and service.

- The four sales associates (all full-time) were responsible for getting new members.

- Customer service employees, who were primarily part-time, worked the front desk.

- Personal trainers worked with individual club members on fitness programs.

- Service employees introduced new members to the club and its philosophy through a series of programs on fitness and equipment use.

All employees were involved in selling. Although the sales associates were dedicated to selling new memberships, the personal trainers spent time encouraging members to sign up for personal training. The customer service employees would sell tanning programs and other services to members. Typically, each group or individual had sales targets and earned bonuses and commissions based on meeting those targets.

Exhibit 1: GoodLife Kitchener Club—Membership by Month.

Month	Members Lost During Month	Members Gained During Month	Net Members Gained During Month	Members (at end of month)	Retention Rate per Year (%)	Loss Rate per Month (%)
March '99	–	–	–	1900	–	–
April '99	58[a]	163	105	2005	63.5[b]	3.0
May '99	61	158	97	2102	64.0	3.0
June '99	73	156	83	2185	59.4	3.4
July '99	75	155	80	2263	60.9	3.3
August '99	68	150	82	2341	65.2	2.9
September '99	70	168	98	2423	64.8	2.9
October '99	108	196	88	2521	48.5	4.3
November '99	91	220	129	2609	57.9	3.5
December '99	90	223	133	2738	60.1	3.3
January '00	103	244	141	2871	56.4	3.6
February '00	99	238	139	3012	60.1	3.3
March '00	113	234	121	3151	56.4	3.6
Annual Average					59.8[c]	3.4

[a] At the beginning of April, the club had 1,900 members. The monthly loss rate for April is 3.0% (based on a yearly retention rate for April of 63.5%, which is a yearly loss rate of 36.5%). The club lost 1,900 x .03 = 58 members in April.

[b] 63.5% of the members as of April '98 were still members as of April '99; 36.5% were no longer members.

[c] The average retention rate for the year shown in 59.8%; average loss rate per month is 3.4% (1−.598 = .402/12).

Source: GoodLife Fitness Clubs.

Exhibit 2: GoodLife Kitchener Club—Selected Revenues and Expenses.

	June 30 '99 Month	June 30 '99 YTD (12 months)	March 31 '00 Month	March 31 '00 YTD (9 months)
Revenues	(%)	(%)	(%)	(%)
Membership	88.9	88.2	86.9	83.3
Services[a]	9.3	10.2	11.9	15.5
Other	1.8	1.6	1.2	1.2
Total Revenues	100.0	100.0	100.0	100.0
Expenses				
Sales Wages and Commissions[b]	10.5	12.1	8.3	8.9
Service Wages and Commissions[c]	9.0	7.1	5.3	12.3
Service and Other[d]	19.4	28.6	20.4	17.1
Total Direct Expenses	38.9	47.8	34.0	38.3
Manager Controlled[e]	9.2	15.6	4.8	10.4
Adminisrative[f]	31.8	31.1	26.3	32.6
Total Expenses[g]	79.9	94.5	65.1	81.3
Members	2,200		3,200	
Total Revenue ($)	120,000	1,004,000	195,000	1,177,000

[a] Includes personal training, specialty programs, tanning, and pro shop
[b] Related to new membership sales
[c] Includes personal training and member services
[d] Includes service staff wages and expenses
[e] Includes utilities, supplies and services
[f] Includes advertising, administrative management, rent, realty taxes, equipment leasing
[g] Not included are depreciation, amortization, interest, and taxes

Source: GoodLife Fitness Clubs.

Most of the employees earned a base salary of $8 per hour plus bonuses if they achieved the weekly targets. As an example, a sales associate might have a target of eight new members per week. If the target were achieved or exceeded, the associate could earn $1,250 or more every 2 weeks. Customer service staff could earn up to $25 per week if they met targets that included phoning members to remind them of upcoming events, encouraging them to use the club, and selling various club products and services such as tanning. Personal trainers could make up to $27 per hour for personal training in addition to their base pay of $8 per hour. The more members the trainer signed up, the more hours he/she spent in personal training.

Through these incentive programs GoodLife encouraged its staff, particularly the sales associates, to be entrepreneurial. As Krista often said, "The staff have to make things happen; they can't wait for them to happen. Both GoodLife and the staff do better when they make things happen."

As noted, GoodLife had formal training programs for new employees. In addition, Krista spent time with the new employees teaching them the technical side of the job and establishing the norms and culture of the club. By emphasizing what was important to her, Krista hoped they would understand the importance of excellent customer service. "If I can show the new employees what's important to me, and get them to trust me, they come on board and are part of the team. For example, we hold weekly staff meetings where we discuss a number of issues, including how to improve the club. People don't miss the meetings. Every once in a while, a new associate decides not to come to the meetings. The team lets him or her know that's not acceptable. Those people either become part of the team or decide to leave GoodLife."

Employee turnover at the Kitchener GoodLife Club was slightly better than the average across all the GoodLife clubs. In the past year, Krista had a turnover of about 35 percent, with the rate for full-time slightly lower than for part-time. Part-time turnover was higher, in part, because many of the part-time employees were students who left to go to university or left after completing their degree programs.

Like Jane Riddell, Krista was concerned about employee turnover, but she wasn't sure what actions could improve the situation. She had noticed that some new employees were surprised at the amount of selling involved in their positions. She also felt that some employees were not satisfied with the base salary of $8 per hour.

Typically, when an employee left, Krista needed to hire a new associate relatively quickly. She would place an ad in

the local paper, *The Record*; get some applications; conduct interviews; and hire the individual she felt was most suited for the position. With full-time employees, Krista was not always happy with the pool of applicants she interviewed, but there was always the pressure of filling the job, which had to be balanced against the quality of the applicants. With the economy improving and a low local unemployment rate, it was sometimes difficult to attract high-quality applicants.

The Members

Most new members joined the club through referrals. When an individual asked about joining the club, a sales associate would show them the club and discuss the benefits of membership and the GoodLife philosophy. Assuming the individual decided to join, the sales associate would ask if he or she had any friends who might be interested in joining the club and, if so, they would receive a free membership for 1 week. Typically, the associate tried to get five referrals. The associate would then contact these people, offer the free 1-week membership, and set up a meeting with them if they accepted. The cycle was repeated with each new member. On average, the sales associates converted between one or two of the five contacts to new members. Referrals generated between 60 percent and 80 percent of all new members.

The price for a new membership varied depending on the promotion option. The two main options were (1) a $199 initiation fee, the first 6 months free, and $40 per 4 weeks after that or (2) the initiation fee was waived and the member paid $40 per 4 weeks. Payments were on a biweekly basis through an automatic payment plan that the member signed. The new member also paid a total of $54 for the membership card ($15) and a processing fee ($39). A new member could also decide to join for a 3-month period for $180. Members could also decide to pay once a year and not use the automatic payment plan.

When an individual joined the club, an associate from the service group would take the new member through three programs as an introduction to the club and the GoodLife approach to a healthy lifestyle. The three programs were (1) Fit Fix 1—an introduction to strength training, (2) Cardio—basic information about cardiovascular training principles, and (3) Fit Fix 2—adding exercises to your program. Any new member could also have a fitness assessment (including resting heart rate and body fat measurements). After 6 weeks, the new member could also have a second fitness assessment to track his/her progress.

The club offered a wide range of cardio equipment, weights, and personal training programs. Members could participate in over 20 aerobics programs each week, from Steps 'n Abs to Circuit Training to Newbody to PUNCH. On average, 12 members were participating in each program. Typically, members had been going to these programs for years, and few new members joined any program. The club attempted to address this issue with new members by having a "new members only" aerobics class. On average, the club would get 50 new members to sign up for the program, 15 would show up for the first class, and it would be down to six people when the class ended in 12 weeks.

This issue reflected a broader problem common to most of the GoodLife Clubs, often referred to as the "20-20-60 phenomenon." Twenty percent of the club members were hard-core fitness and health people. These members came three or more times a week, were serious about their training, and would tolerate a lot (such as uneven service) as long as it didn't interfere with their training. The second 20 percent were the new members. They were enthusiastic, wanted to get fit, and over time they either became committed or not. The largest group, the remaining 60 percent, were those members who came on an irregular basis. The club staff didn't know their names; these members often were not sure how the equipment worked or what they should be doing; and they often wouldn't ask for help. Even when they stopped coming, this group kept their membership for a period until they decided to cancel. When one came to cancel, an associate tried to get her or him to stay, usually with little success.

Krista and other associates at GoodLife believed that getting members to feel that they were part of the GoodLife Club was important in retaining them. Krista believed that many of the 60 percent probably never felt they were part of the club because they didn't know many or any of the other members or the staff. Krista remembered that although many of the 1,200 members from the old club liked the new facility, they felt that the club was more impersonal. In particular, as the membership grew, the "original" members felt less at home. Krista estimated that, within a year, about 50 percent of these members had left the club.

The advertising for GoodLife consisted of an ad in the *Yellow Pages* and ads in a local free weekly newspaper, *The Pennysaver*. Local businesses were targeted with brochures offering specials. Krista felt that most of the new members came from the referral program and *Pennysaver* ads (Exhibit 2). As she said, "*The Pennysaver* ads get the phones ringing."

Although Krista believed that overall the members were satisfied with the club, she felt there was always room for improvement. For example, members sent her about 14 written complaints or concerns every week through the suggestion box. Each week, the front office staff received about a dozen verbal complaints. Most complaints or concerns dealt with equipment problems (e.g., equipment not working properly) and a few dealt with staff (e.g., a particular staff member was not friendly). Krista dealt with the complaints as they arose.

COMPETITION

In the Kitchener/Waterloo (K/W) area (Kitchener and Waterloo are twin cities), there were about 15 fitness/exercise clubs serving a population base of 450,000 people. The Kitchener GoodLife Club had four major competitors:

- The two YMCAs in K/W offered aerobic programs and had workout areas. The "Ys" had a good reputation as being friendly, family-oriented clubs. The annual membership fee ranged from $400 to $650 depending on the type of membership and the services requested.

- The International Family Fitness Centre was also located in downtown Kitchener within three blocks of the GoodLife Club. It offered equivalent facilities to the GoodLife Club, was of a similar size, and had over 40 programs a week. Its membership rates were very similar to those of GoodLife.

- Popeye's Gym previously had a reputation as a male-oriented facility where bodybuilders worked out. However, the image was slowly changing to a men's and women's fitness club that offered aerobic programs and a variety of weight and training machines. It was located approximately 3 kilometres from downtown Kitchener and was open 24 hours a day. The membership fees were approximately $350 per year.

CUSTOMER RETENTION

As Krista prepared for the meeting with Jane, she knew that improved customer retention rates were possible but was uncertain as to what actions would be most effective. She identified three major areas that she could address: employee turnover, a new bonus system, and swipe card technology.

Employee turnover, at over 40 percent, created a lack of stability at the club. Every time a new employee started, he or she did not know any members. Over time, the new employee would learn the members' names (often those who visited frequently). If the employee left, so did the knowledge. Krista had always felt that members would have a greater sense of "belonging" to the club if the front desk staff could greet them by name. Although many of the front desk staff knew some of the members by name (most of these members were the hard-core regulars who came frequently), most of the front desk staff were part-time associates or had recently joined GoodLife; therefore, they knew relatively few members by name. Further, because most of the "60 percent" group came infrequently, few staff knew their names.

Krista had two ideas for reducing employee turnover, both based on increasing wages. Increasing the hourly base rate from $8 to $9 for most employees (excluding managers and sales associates) would add about $4,000 per month to wage costs. The problem was that, although she knew that employee turnover would decline, she did not know by how much, nor did she know the effect on retention rates. A second option was to focus only on the front desk employees who greeted members. Increasing their rate to $9 would increase monthly wage costs by about $1,000. She preferred this option because the front desk associates greeted all the members as they entered and swiped their card. With the increase in their wages, Krista would ensure that the front desk staff knew that an important part of their job was to greet members by name.

Next, Krista considered introducing a bonus plan for increasing customer retention. Virtually all the targets and bonuses at GoodLife focused on increasing sales, reflecting, in part, Patch's aggressive growth targets. Although she did not have a specific plan in mind, Krista felt that an allocation of at least $1,000 to bonuses for increased retention was feasible. Her initial idea was that for every percent increase in retention rates per month (e.g., from 60 percent to 61 percent), staff would receive $200 in bonuses. Krista was uncertain how the target should be set—on an individual or group basis. The front desk staff had the most contact with members, but potentially all the employees could be involved. What was important to Krista was that the associates have a goal and a bonus attached to customer retention. She knew that this plan would get the associates to focus more of their efforts on customer retention.

Krista felt that better use of the swipe card information could improve retention. Members swiped their membership card when they visited the club. A valid card allowed a member to go through a turnstile; a nonvalid card (because it had expired) did not release the turnstile. Krista knew that other information (e.g., number of member visits) was available, but no one at the club or head office had developed a software program to track member visits. Krista contacted two software companies, one of which offered a membership management program that would provide interface with swipe scanners and provide reports on members' frequency of visits, along with a host of other member information. The cost ranged from $3,500 for a license for five sites up to $8,500 for unlimited site use.

One of the targets for the front desk associates was to make "motivation" calls to members each week. Associates would call a specified number of members to reach their target. The associates would begin anywhere on the member list (a binder at the front desk) and begin calling members to encourage them to use the facilities or inform them of special events. After the call, the associate would record the date called and his or her name next to the member's name. Ideally, all members were called once every 6 weeks, but this didn't always happen.

With the new software system, reports could identify members who had not visited the club for a particular period. Staff could then contact members who had not visited for a specific time period, such as 3 weeks or 4 weeks. Krista felt that this would substantially improve the existing approach and would improve member retention rates.

Krista knew that there were other available approaches or tactics to improve retention rates. In particular, any activities that built a greater sense of "community" would increase interaction between members and a sense of "belonging." But it was difficult to find the time to figure it out. Managing a club with 3,500 members kept her very busy making sure everything was running smoothly, and she spent most of her time "doing" not "planning."

A week later, Jane met Krista in her office. Jane started the conversation. "Let me review the situation. As I mentioned last week, if we could improve your club's retention rates from 60 percent to 65 percent, based on last year's numbers, gross revenues would increase by more than $35,000. In this business, most of the costs tend to be fixed, probably about 60 percent of revenues, so most of the revenue would be profits. If we could do that for all the clubs, it would be great for business, and I think we would have more satisfied members. Just to put this in perspective, on average, we have about 2,000 members per club."

Jane continued, "In the past year, the story has been about the same for most of our clubs. For every 100 new members signed up each month, we have about 40 people who don't renew or cancel their membership. We spend a lot on marketing to get them in the door. Then we spend time with them setting up an exercise or training program. They are enthusiastic to begin with; then they stop coming to classes or exercise. They cancel or don't renew when their membership comes up. When they cancel, we ask them why they are leaving. The most common reasons are that they don't have enough time or they can't fit it into their schedule. I think that about 30 percent of the time, they have a good reason for leaving, such as they are moving out of town. I think that 70 percent of the time, we could have done something to keep them with the club.

"From a head office point of view, we have had a number of debates about the amount of advertising we do, which is about 6 percent of revenues. That's a lot of money and sometimes we think that we should be spending more of that in staff training. Another question is—what type of training would be most effective?

"Let me mention one other issue we are concerned about," Jane continued. "We don't use the swipe card to collect data. We need to do more with that."

"That was one of my thoughts," Krista replied. She then told Jane about the software program's capabilities and costs.

"Very interesting," replied Jane. "That's certainly something to consider." Krista then presented her other ideas to Jane. As she finished, Krista said, "I think my cost estimates wouldn't be too far out of line for our average club."

Then Krista added, "Sometimes I think that maybe we should focus more on service than sales. As an example, my front desk staff have sales targets and other assignments as well as greeting members. Also, there are few opportunities for the staff to walk around and just talk to our members and see how they are doing. That's why I suggested a bonus plan based on increasing retention rates. We have very aggressive growth targets for each club and plan to add a lot more clubs. As an organization, we are really getting stretched. Most of our time is spent on growth, not service."

"Yes, but the strategy has worked well so far," Jane replied. "I'm not sure if we could justify adding more staff to focus on service; we would need to see a payback. But it's an another interesting idea."

Krista and Jane continued the discussion and then decided that Krista would prepare a customer retention plan for the Kitchener GoodLife Club with the goal of increasing retention rates by 5 percentage points or more within 6 months. "I want to at least get the average retention up to 65 percent," Jane said. "As I mentioned last week, we'll use this plan as the model for all the clubs."

As Jane left, she said, "Krista, I have every confidence in you. I'm going to send an assistant manager from the other Kitchener club down here to help you run the club while you work on the plan. I look forward to positive results."

After Jane left, Krista sat down and began thinking about the approaches she could take to increase retention rates. She had always liked a challenge, and she knew that she would do her best to meet this one.

APPENDIX: MUSCLE MANIA[4]

David Patchell-Evans may not be a natural athlete, but he's a confirmed fitness fanatic. He works and dreams physical fitness. Even his vacations are spent pursuing extreme sports such as mountain climbing or skiing. But that wasn't always the case. In his first year at university, a motorcycle accident paralyzed the right side of his body. Following extensive rehabilitation, Patchell-Evans was determined to return to full physical fitness. He took up rowing and eventually became a five-time Canadian rowing champion and a member of the 1980 Canadian Olympic team.

Those experiences taught Patchell-Evans the role health and fitness play in creating a satisfying life and fostered a life-long commitment to sell the idea to others. In 1979 he bought a workout club in London, Ontario, and began implementing his vision: to provide customers with an affordable club offering state-of-the-art equipment and, more importantly, knowledgeable staff eager to teach them how to get the most from it. "The opportunity in the marketplace," he says, "was to provide service."

In an industry notorious for dubious claims and fly-by-night operators, GoodLife Fitness Clubs has built its business on highly trained staff, innovative programming, and reinvesting in its facilities. In 20 years, it has become Canada's largest health club chain, with 42 clubs, 100,000 members, and 1998 sales of $40 million. In an industry that's adding new clubs and members at 9 percent a year, GoodLife is growing at almost three times that rate. By 2004 Patchell-Evans goal is to have 100 facilities.

To reach the goal Patchell-Evans will rely on the same philosophies on which the chain was founded: providing health, fitness, and self-esteem so that people feel better about themselves. It's part of the strategy to raise the bar of service excellence and bring a new professionalism to an industry where clubs were traditionally run by sports jocks with little business training. The GoodLife philosophy of ensuring consistently high standards in every club goes a long way to building brand loyalty among the members. "When people work out, they want to know that the shower will be clean, the equipment is going to work, and the staff know what they are talking about."

That philosophy has served GoodLife well as the chain expanded, opening new clubs and buying others that were doing poorly in strong locations. "One of the ways we grew in the early days was to take over clubs that really nobody else wanted to touch," Says Jane Riddell, GoodLife's vice president and director of franchising. "A classic example is our club at the corner of Queen and Yonge Street in downtown Toronto. When we took over the club, the membership was languishing around 100, and the facility was losing $60,000 a month. The club needed refurbishment and new equipment, but it had huge potential, with its high-profile location in a dense work population." GoodLife invested $400,000 and the facility is one of the firm's most financially successful clubs with a membership of 3,000.

One fitness expert says, "GoodLife developed a niche underneath the well-established clubs. Patchell-Evans runs a professional organization and he has a well-honed management style that includes business and financial acumen. The old-style clubs were run by squash players or golfers." One example was the innovative client billing system. While most fitness clubs demanded on up-front annual fee, Patchell-Evans debited monthly membership fees ranging from $30 to $50. Members like the system because it eliminates the needs for large up-front payments, and it stabilizes cash flow for GoodLife, which is attractive to lenders and investors.

The key to any fitness club's success is attracting and keeping members. At GoodLife it starts with the staff. Some 75 percent of its 1,200 employees hold kinesiology or physical education degrees. In addition to competitive salaries, staff benefit from ongoing training—GoodLife's annual education and training budget exceeds $2.4 million—and recognition for individual achievement, such as a weekly top performer's list. "Good staff retention leads to good membership retention," says Jane Riddell. "Members don't have a relationship with a treadmill or a whirlpool. They have a relationship with the staff." That commitment to human resources gives GoodLife an edge, says the industry expert. "GoodLife has good equipment, but they also have a very proactive staff with an attitude that says they want to help you out. The club's employee training program is probably more extensive than any other in the industry. It's difficult for an independent operator to compete with this."

In 1998 GoodLife was recognized for its mandate to provide leading edge programs. The U.S.–based International Dance Exercise Association named the club's fitness director, Maureen Hagen, program director of the year for her creative programming and leadership abilities. Hagan's innovations include Newbody, a low-impact, cardiovascular conditioning class designed for both fit and "underactive" participants.

Programming and services are also tailored to fit the demographics of each club. Some 70 percent of members are women, reflecting the club's focus on aerobics programs, to which women tend to gravitate. To ensure that women enjoy a high comfort level, GoodLife designated more than a dozen clubs for women only, where they are provided with such services as daycare, tanning facilities, and individual change rooms. GoodLife was one of the first clubs to develop the trend to women-only sections and clubs. As an example, GoodLife recently spent $500,000 upgrading the facility and equipment of a women's club in Cambridge, Ontario (Exhibit 3).

Exhibit 3: Identifying and tailoring programs and services that appeal to selected demographics is a chief concern for fitness clubs.

This formula to exceed customers' expectations is the foundation for GoodLife's aggressive growth plans for the future. Two trends will help the growth: industry consolidation, where GoodLife has achieved a critical mass, and an expanding market, where the number of people who will work out in clubs will increase substantially because the baby boomers want to stay in shape.

A challenge for Patchell-Evans is finding staff to keep pace with growth. "There was a time," he says, "when we had a bigger pool of people waiting for the next manager's job." To that end he says GoodLife will focus on giving staff the skills and knowledge they need to get to a higher level within the firm. "Staying on the cutting edge of the industry is a challenge, but it's also a passion for me," says Patchell-Evans. "Running a business is like a sport. You're driven to go fast, go hard, and find the ways you can do it better."[4]

STUDY QUESTIONS

1. Why do people join and leave a fitness club? What ar the major challenges facing fitness clubs in general?

2. What are the major challenges facing Goodlife?

3. Why has GoodLife been successful?

4. Evaluate the strengths and weaknesses of GoodLife's customer acquisition and retention strategies.

5. Calculate the revenues the net profits at GoodLife Kitchener if retention rates were 65 percent and 70 percent versus 60 percent in the past year?

6. What is the average long-term value of a member at GoodLife in terms of total revenue at 60 percent, 70 percentand 80% retention rates?

7. Evaluate the major options considered by Krista, assuming an average GoodLife Club with 2,000 members. Then, what overall plan would you recommend that GoodLife pursue in increasing customer retention rates? Be specific in your recommendations and be prepared to justify them.

---

[1] Reprinted by permission from the *Case Research Journal*. Copyright © 2008 by Gordon H.G. McDougall and the North American *Case Research Association*. All rights reserved.
[2] All monetary references in the case are to Canadian dollars. $1US equaled $1.33 Canadian on February 23, 2004.
[3] Canadian Fitness and Research Institute, *Canadian Physical Activity Monitor*, 1998.
[4] Excerpts from Louise Dearden, "Muscle Mania," *Profit*, May, 1999, pp. 46–49.

Customer Asset Management at DHL in Asia[1]

Jochen Wirtz, Indranil Sen and Sanjay Singh[2]

DHL serves a wide range of customers, from global enterprises, to the occasional customer who ships the odd one or two documents a year. To be able to effectively manage such a diverse customer base, DHL implemented sophisticated customer segmentation cum loyalty management system. The focus of this system is to assess the profitability from its customers, reduce customer churn, and increase DHL's share of shipments.

COMPANY BACKGROUND AND MARKET ENVIRONMENT

DHL, the international air express and logistics company, serves a wide range of customers, from global enterprises with sophisticated and high volume supply-chain solutions shipping anything from spare parts to documents, to the occasional customer who ships the odd one or two documents a year. Exhibit 1 shows some of DHL's logistics operations. To be able to effectively manage such a diverse customer base, DHL implemented a sophisticated customer segmentation cum loyalty management system. The focus of this system is to assess the profitability from its customers, reduce customer churn, and increase DHL's share of shipments.

Exhibit 1: An aerial view of DHL's logistics operations.

Customer Segmentation

To achieve this, the first task was to segment its customers into actionable segments with distinct needs. DHL defined three main segments. Firstly, 'Strategic Customers' are extremely high volume shippers with a full range of logistics

solutions and express-shipment needs. This segment consists approximately of DHL's top 250 customers worldwide, which are mostly large multinationals. Secondly, the 'Relationship Customers' segment consists of customers who use DHL to ship their products and documents regularly, but with a lower volume than the Strategic Customers segment and also not as much sophisticated supply chain needs. Finally, the 'Direct Customers' segment ships infrequently with DHL. The customer segmentation can be represented in the form of the familiar customer pyramid in Exhibit 2.

Exhibit 2: Customer Pyramid.

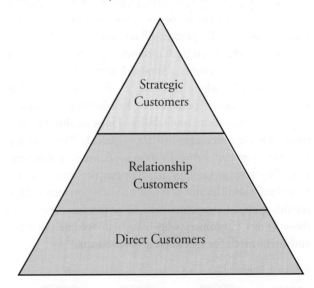

These segments are further divided into sub-segments based on the kind of service required (see Exhibit 3 on the following page). The needs of Direct Customers and many of the Relationship Customers often are fully met by DHL's basic products. For Relationship customers with special needs, DHL also offers some special programs like direct distribution to its partners, test services and parts distribution to fulfill these needs. Strategic Customers virtually always use customized solutions, like providing bulk-breaking facilities and planned production support for precision delivery schedules, and DHL aims to meet their entire express delivery needs.

Exhibit 3: Customer Subsegmentation.

	Strategic Customers	Relationship Customers	Direct Customers
Basic Products			
Special Programs			
Customized Solutions			

Customers using DHL's basic products find it easier to switch as switching costs are low and all key competitors also offer similar products. In contrast, the switching costs are significantly higher for customers with special programs, and highest for clients using customized solutions.

Exhibit 4 shows some output of DHL's segmentation analysis for one of its country markets. The majority of revenue and profits were derived from only 18 percent of its Relationship Customers. The Direct Customer segment consisted of 75 percent of the total customer base and contributed only 15 percent of revenues and 30 percent of profits. The Strategic Customer segment contributed only 6 percent to profits. Similar patterns were observed for all countries where this analysis was conducted. The verdict seems clear: Focus on the Relationship Customers segment for maximum profitability. However this does not mean that the other segments are neglected. The Strategic Customer segment, being the most loyal, needs deployment of leading edge technology and best practice infrastructure to maintain their loyalty as future business potential is high for this group. Extra effort need to be put into upgrading those Direct Customers who have high volume potential and latent needs for special program products.

Exhibit 4: Segment Analysis.

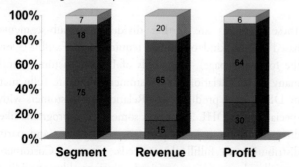

■ Direct Customers ■ Relationship Customers ▢ Strategic Customers

Loyalty Management System: Further Categorization of Segments

In order to focus service and sales staff on customer retention and development, it was necessary to get more information about these customers and hence each of these segments was further classified into six categories and the data used to take corrective and proactive measures to enhance customer loyalty.

Lost

The customer in this category has stopped shipping with DHL, for external reasons like customer having gone into liquidation, or for internal reasons like service performance failure, or increase in prices, etc. Once the reason is identified, it is easier to control internal reasons and reduce customer churn. Sales and service staff then focus on regaining potentially profitable accounts.

Decreased-performer

This category refers to customers who have shipped considerably less over a given period compared to a similar period in the past. Again, the reasons for down trading may be external or internal to DHL. The decreased performer in each segment triggers an alarm bell to warn the sales staff of impending customer churns. This means that they can proactively take action to retain the customer, especially if the reasons were internal.

Maintained

This category is for customers who continue to trade within a given bandwidth of shipment volume.

Increased-performer

The customer in this category has shipped considerably more over a given period. Again, the reasons for increased performance may be external or internal. Follow-up work is done to identify the causes for increase in volumes and particularly whether the up-trading is a result of a DHL initiative. The successful initiatives are further improved to gain better results.

New

This category is for any customer who has shipped for the first time with DHL. Special efforts are made by the sales staff to make them permanent customers.

Regained

This customer was previously 'Lost' but has re-commenced shipping with DHL recently. The reasons for this renewed activity may be external, (e.g. renewed business activity of a lapsed customer) or internal (e.g. the shipment was made as a result of reactive measures by DHL to regain the customer).

The data collected is graphically represented for each segment, as given in Exhibit 5, and reported to sales, marketing and customer service departments and senior management. This made it easy to understand the impact of the change in customer base and an increased percentage of decreased-performers should immediately cause the sales and customer service staff to take corrective action.

The classification and the data reported for each customer meant that the sales force was forewarned about potential customer defections; and could take corrective actions and identify service performance shortcomings and customer dissatisfaction leading to more proactive measures in the future. The data also made it possible to calculate the defection rate of customers for each tier of the customer pyramid, and to calculate the lifetime value of each segment. The change in lifetime value of all customers gives the management an idea of the revenue and profit implications of its marketing and service initiatives.

Exhibit 5: Direct Customers — Segment Analysis.

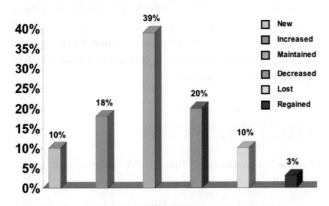

The expected increase or decrease in revenue for the month is also calculated and represented graphically, as shown in Exhibit 6, giving the impact of the change in the customer segment portfolio on DHL's revenues.

Exhibit 6: Relationship Customers — Estimated Revenues.

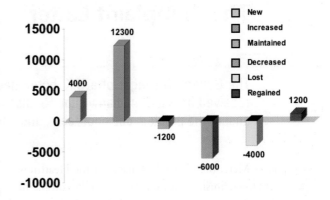

Similarly, the sales staff can study the reasons for up-trading for each customer and tap the remaining potential for further up trading. This program also helps the company send targeted communication to the customers, based on the classification of each segment instead of general communication to all customers thereby making communication cost effective.

After a short period of implementation, this initiative had already started yielding impressive results, and further modules were being developed and pilot tested for potential roll-out.

STUDY QUESTIONS

1. What do you see as the main challenges in implementing this segmentation in DHL's customer database?

2. How would you recommend DHL to address those challenges?

3. What are the various possible practical applications of this segmentation methodology by other functional departments, (e.g. sales, customer service, etc.)?

---

[2] Jochen Wirtz is Associate Professor of Marketing at the NUS Business School, National University of Singapore; Indranil Sen was the Research & Planning Manager Asia Pacific who was in charge of designing and implementing DHL's loyalty marketing across Asia, and Sanjay Singh was studying for his MBA at the NUS Business School while this case was written.

The Complaint Letter[1]

T. F. Cawsey and G. H. McDougal[1]

The General Manager of a U.K. hotel[2] needs to decide how to respond to a complaint letter received from a Canadian visitor. He also needs to decide on what actions to take internally to ensure the problem does not recur, and what implications this might have for the hotel staff.

As Andres Metz, the General Manager of the Heathrow ATMI Hotel, finished a second reading of the complaint letter (Exhibit 1), he was very concerned. The series of events described in the letter indicated that the hotel employees had failed to perform the basic services for this guest. There were as well, potential systems problems that needed examination. While Andres knew it was only one letter, it suggested significant issues that needed attention.

The Heathrow ATMI Hotel, a 578 guest-room hotel, targeted the business travellers. Extensive renovations had been completed recently and a marketing campaign announcing the new improvements had been launched. The hotel itself was billed as a "contemporary upscale hotel" offering two restaurants, three lounges or bars and a conference and training centre. The hotel staff spoke Afrikaans, Arabic, Chinese, Dutch, English, French, German, Greek, Hindi, Italian, Japanese, Maltese, Portuguese, Punjabi, Russian, Spanish and Swahili and were well trained to serve the needs of international travelers.

ATMI Hotels was a subsidiary of a global hotel company which owned or leased over 2,500 hotels worldwide. The ATMI Division, headed by Christopher Britton, was operated as an independent business unit. Recently, the operating profit for the unit was up over 50 percent, driven by market share gains in the United Kingdom. ATMI took third place in an industry rating of business hotel chains in the UK.

The strategy of ATMI's parent was to:

- Strengthen our portfolio of strongly differentiated brands through increased room night delivery to franchisees, enhanced hotel management skills and brand innovation.

- Grow our management and franchised fee income by exploiting significant potential in the *upscale* segment worldwide and building large scale, strong *mid-scale* positions in major world markets.

- Focus the organization by containing or reducing operating costs through simplification, reduction of asset ownership, infrastructure improvements and investing in the skills of our people.

- Continue to reduce capital by selling the real estate assets of the majority of our hotel portfolio while retaining management or franchise agreements in most cases. Ownership of assets will continue only if assets present strategic brand value for the group.

- Return excess funds to shareholders or reinvest in growth opportunities, while maintaining appropriate efficient debt levels

As Andres reviewed the letter, he remembered the "hospitality promise"—"If any part of your stay is not satisfactory, we promise to make it right or you won't pay for that part of your stay." He wondered how to respond and what action he should take with hotel staff.

STUDY QUESTIONS

1. What are the issues that Mr. Metz should note and be concerned with?

2. How credible is the evidence provided by the letter? That is, does it form the basis for action or is it part of the background noise of running a complex service operation such as the hotel in this case?

3. What services marketing concepts can help us to understand the situation faced by the Hotel Manager?

Mr. Christopher Britton   September 8, 2004
Chief Operating Officer
ATMI Hotels
368 Bridgeport Avenue
Rummidge, England

Dear Sir;

As a customer of yours, I want to provide you with our experiences at ATMI Hotels Heathrow on 24 August of this year. Initially, I had not planned to do anything but since then I have reflected on my experience and finally decided I needed to provide you with feedback – particularly given the "hospitality promise" on your web site.

My wife and I arrived at the hotel around 10 p.m. after a flight from Canada and the usual tiring immigration procedures, baggage check and struggle to finding your hotel. On arrival, we hoped to check in and proceed to our room quickly as we had been up since 5 a.m. our time.

As I entered the hotel, I was somewhat apprehensive because a busload of tourists had arrived just ahead of us. However, they gathered to one side of the hotel lobby and I was able to line up at one of the three open check-in lines. The initial greeting was courteous and appropriate. We were checked in and the desk person asked if we wanted a room upgrade. After I clarified that this would cost money, I declined the offer.

We then went to our room on the third floor, I believe, and discovered the room was a disaster, totally not made up. I phoned the switchboard and was put through to reception immediately. There were profuse apologies and we were told that someone would be up immediately with another key.

Within 5 minutes, someone did meet us with a key to a room on the fifth floor, a quick, fast response.

However, when we got to the new room, it was not made up! If anything it was worse. Frankly, I did not want to touch anything in that room but did go to the phone.

I phoned the switchboard. The operator said, "This shouldn't have happened. I will put you through to the night manager." I said that was not necessary. I just wanted a room.

However, the operator insisted and I was put through to the night manager. Again, there were profuse apologies and the manager said, "This shouldn't have happened. I will fix this and get right back to you." I indicated that I just wanted a room – I didn't want the organization fixed, just a room. The manager repeated, "I will get right back to you."

We waited 5, 10, 15 minutes. Inexplicably, the manager did not return the call even though he said he would.

Finally around 20 minutes later, I phoned switchboard again. I said we were waiting for a room and that the night manager had promised to call me back. The operator said, "This is probably my fault as I was doing work for the assistant manager." I did not and do not understand this part of the conversation but again, I was told that they would call right back. Again, I repeated that "I just need a room."

I waited another 5 minutes – it was now 11 p.m. at night and we were quite tired – there was no return phone call.

My wife and I went down to reception and again lined up. After a brief time, we were motioned forward by the person who initially registered us. I explained that we needed a room. He said "You were taken care of. You got a room." I replied: "No, I did not have a room, I just had two rooms that were not made up and we needed a clean one for the night."

Again there were profuse apologies. The reception person then said "Excuse me, just for a moment so I can fix this." I said "Really, I just would like a room." The person at the reception desk went around the corner and began to yell at someone working there. This went on for a several minutes. He then returned to his station, called me forward again, apologized again and located a third room for us. As well, he gave us coupons for a complimentary breakfast.

The third room was made up. We had hoped for an upgrade but this was clearly not the case. The room looked clean but was "more tired" than the previous rooms. The carpets were a bit worn and the wallpaper was faded. However, it was clean and we were delighted to find a place to sleep.

In the middle of the night, I woke up and went to the washroom. I noticed that the invoice for the room had been delivered to our room. To my absolute shock, a 72 £[3] "room change" charge was added to the price of our room.

I woke early the next morning (because we had to catch an early plane to Paris) to discuss this charge with someone at reception. One person was serving a hotel guest and I waited for a few minutes until the same reception person from the previous night came to the desk. He motioned me forward and then immediately left to open up the five or six other computer stations in the reception area. He had a tendency to not make eye contact. This may have been a cultural phenomenon or it may have been his dismay at having to deal with me again. I cannot say.

I showed him the invoice. He said, "Oh, there will be no charge for that room." I said that I was concerned as the invoice did show the charge. He said," It is taken care of". I said" Regardless, I would like something to prove that there would not be another charge to my credit card." After one further exchange and insistence on my part, he removed the charge from my invoice.

My wife and I had breakfast and appreciated it being complimentary. We were able to get to the airport in time for our flight.

We thought that you would want to know of our experience. Customer service is a critical part of the hospitality industry and I am certain that ATMI Hotels would wish feedback on experiences such as these.

I look forward to your reply.

Yours truly,

Dr. Mark Hankins
666 Newberry Dr.
Kitchener, Ontario
Canada

cc.   General Manager
        ATMI Hotel
        London Heathrow
        22 Uphill Road
        Heathrow, England

        Guest Relations Department
        ATMI Hotels
        17 Cedar Road
        Birmingham, England

CASE 18

The Accellion Service Guarantee[1]

Jochen Wirtz and Jill Klein

A high-technology company introduces what it considers to be a bold service quality guarantee to communicate its commitment to service excellence to customers, prospects, and its own employees.

Accellion was a young high-technology firm with leading-edge technology in the distributed file storage, management and delivery market space. Still new to the industry, the firm aimed to become the global backbone for the next generation of Internet-based applications.

Accellion's main value proposition to the world's largest enterprises ("the Global 2000"), as well as to Internet-based providers of premium content, was to allow them to serve their users faster, increase operational efficiencies, and lower total costs. Specifically, Accellion customers could improve the access time for downloading and uploading files by more than 200 percent How was this performance improvement achieved? It was achieved by locating an intelligent storage and file management system at the "edges of the Internet" and thereby delivering content from regions located closer to the end-user. The typical time-consuming routing through many servers and hubs could be avoided using Accellion's infrastructure.

The need for an Internet infrastructure to deliver high bandwidth content to end-users had never been greater. There was a trend towards multimedia and personalized web content, all of which could not be delivered efficiently by existing infrastructure, which routed data through the congested network of servers that form the backbone of the Internet. This prompted Accellion to develop and launch a new service: distributed file storage, management and delivery. Accellion provided an applications platform that resided on independent servers, which were directly connected to the users' Internet Service Providers (ISPs), thereby avoiding the congested "centers" of the Internet. This decreased access time allowed Accellion to distribute specialized content and applications more efficiently.

To effectively market Accellion's value proposition, Warren J. Kaplan, Accellion's CEO, and S. Mohan, its Chief Strategist and Founder, felt that in addition to its leading-edge technology, key success factors for Accellion's aggressive growth strategy were excellence in service delivery and high customer satisfaction. They envisioned that customers would prefer to leverage Accellion's technology and partnerships instead of having to manage the details of deploying, maintaining and upgrading their own storage infrastructure for distributed Internet applications. To build a customer-driven culture and to communicate service excellence credibly to the market, Accellion aimed to harness the power of service guarantees.

Cost-effective services for improving performance and reliability were becoming critical as the widespread use of multimedia and other large files increased exponentially. The value proposition was clearly attractive, but how could Accellion convince prospective clients that its technology and service actually could deliver what they promised?

Mohan felt that a Quality of Service (QoS) Guarantee would be a powerful tool to make its promises credible and, at the same time, push his team to deliver what has been promised. Mark Ranford, Accellion's Director for Product Management, and Mohan spearheaded the development of the QoS Guarantee. They launched the QoS Guarantee (shown in Exhibit 1 on page 532) stating that "it is a revolutionary statement of our commitment to the customer to do whatever it takes to ensure satisfaction." The official launch of the guarantee was announced to all staff by e-mail (Exhibit 2 on page 533).

Their QoS Guarantee, however, was just part of Accellion's push for operational excellence. Many factors worked together to keep the company focused on its clients and providing the best possible service, so that the staff could create a large and loyal customer base for their innovative product. Thus, it was very important to raise awareness about Accellion's unique value proposition and convince the early adopters of the advantages.

Accellion's customers reacted positively. One customer stated, "Hey look at this. I haven't seen anything like it. No one offers 100 percent availability. That's tremendous." Another customer exclaimed, "You must really be confident in your service. This really is risk free now, isn't it?" Accellion was committed to its guarantee and strongly believed that having the best network and technology partners would enable it to deliver on its promise.

STUDY QUESTIONS

1. What is the marketing impact of a well-designed service guarantee?

2. Evaluate the design of Accellion's guarantee shown in Exhibit 1. How effective will it be in communicating service excellence to potential and current customers? Would you recommend any changes in its design or implementation?

3. Will the guarantee be successful in creating a culture for service excellence within Accellion? What else may be needed for achieving such a culture?

4. Do you think customers might take advantage of this guarantee and "stage" service failures to invoke the guarantee? If yes, how could Accellion minimize potential cheating on its guarantee?

Exhibit 1: Accellion's service guarantee.

QUALITY OF SERVICE GUARANTEE

The Accellion Quality of Service Guarantee defines Accellion's assurance and commitment to provide the customer with value-added Service and is incorporated into Accellion's Customer Contract. The definition of terms used herein is the same as those found in the Customer Contract.

1. **Performance Guarantee**

   Accellion guarantees that the performance of the Network in uploading and downloading content, as a result of using the Accellion Service, will be no less than 200 percent of that which is achieved by a benchmark origin site being accessed from the edges of the Internet. For all purposes herein, performance measurement tests will be conducted by Accellion.

2. **Availability Guarantee**

   Accellion guarantees 100 percent Service availability, excluding *Force Majeure* and Scheduled Maintenance for Customers who have opted for our replication services.

3. **Customer Service Guarantee**

   Should Accellion fail to meet the service levels set out in aforementioned Sections 1 and 2, , Accellion will credit the customer's account with one (1) month's service fee for the month affected when the failure(s) occurred, provided the Customer gives written notice to Accellion of such failure within five (5) days from the date such failure occurred. The Customer's failure to comply with this requirement will forfeit the Customer's right to receive such credit.

   Accellion will notify the Customer no less than 48 hours (2 days) in advance of Scheduled Maintenance. If the Service becomes unavailable for any other reason, Accellion will promptly notify the Customer and take all necessary action to restore the Service.

   Accellion maintains a 24-hour support center and will provide the Customer with a response to any inquiry in relation to the Service in no more than 2 hours from the time of receipt of such query by customer service.

---

4. **Security and Privacy Policy**

   Accellion has complete respect for the Customer's privacy and that of any Customer data stored in Accellion servers. The Accellion Service does not require Customers to provide any end-user private details for the data being stored on the servers. All information provided to Accellion by the Customer is stored for the customer's sole benefit. Accellion will not share, disclose or sell any personally identifiable information to which it may have access and will ensure that the Customer's information and data [are] kept secure.

   Disclosure of Customer's information or data in Accellion's possession shall only be made where such disclosure is necessary for compliance with a court order, to protect the rights or property of Accellion and to enforce the terms of use of the Service as provided in the Contract.

   Accellion will ensure that the Customer's information and data [are] kept secure and protected from unauthorized access or improper use, which includes taking all reasonable steps to verify the Customer's identity before granting access.

Exhibit 2: E-mail to all Accellion staff announcing the launch of the QoS guarantee.

Dear Team,

I am pleased to forward to everyone our industry's leading Quality of Service guarantee (QoS). Please read it over very carefully. You will find it to be very aggressive, and it puts the ownership on everyone in this company to deliver. Customers don't want a Service Level Agreement (SLA); they just want their network up and running all the time. That is why we have created this no questions asked guarantee. This type of guarantee has proven successful in other industries where service is key to success (e.g. Industry Leaders such as Gartner Group, LL Bean, Nordstrom, etc.).

As a member of the Accellion team, you are key to our client's satisfaction.

Thanks in advance for your support in making our clients and ourselves successful.

Exhibit 3: Accellion's QoS 100 percent availability guarantee instills client confidence in their internet-based file storage and management services.

[1]© 2003 by INSEAD, Fontainebleau, and © 2009 by Jochen Wirtz and Jill Klein.
This case is an updated version of a case previously in the INSEAD case series. The authors gratefully acknowledge the invaluable support by S. Mohan, Accellion's Chief Strategist and Founder, and Vice-Chairman of the Board of Directors, for his assistance and feedback to earlier versions of this case.

Using Technology to Revolutionize the Library Experience of Singaporean Readers[1]

Chai Kah Hin, Jochen Wirtz and Robert Johnston

Changing lifestyles and changing ways of learning and entertainment posed challenges to the National Library Board (NLB) of Singapore. As a response, NLB has transformed its library services through clever use of the latest technologies by closely focusing on their customers' needs.

Over the last two decades public libraries in many parts of the world have been suffering from a decline in usage and the shrinking of public funding. Libraries are often shut when people want to use them. When they are open, they are often a disappointment. They are seen as places with high shelves full of old books, with queues to borrow or return books, staffed by unhelpful or unapproachable staff who insist that users are quiet. Furthermore, libraries are increasingly under threat from the Internet as an easy to use and efficient source of information, and by bookshops which are becoming much more welcoming places for browsing through books.

To change this image, the National Library Board of Singapore (NLB) has been making innovative use of a range of technologies to expand its services, to encourage much greater use of the libraries and to reduce costs and increase efficiency dramatically. The NLB was the first public library in the world to prototype radio-frequency identification (RFID) to create its Electronic Library Management System (ELiMS), borrowing the idea when RFID was being experimented in supermarkets. RFID is an electronic system for automatically identifying items. It uses RFID tags, or transponders, which are contained in smart labels consisting of a silicon chip and coiled antenna. They receive and respond to radio-frequency queries from an RFID transceiver, which enables remote automatic retrieval, and storage and sharing of information. Unlike barcodes, which need to be manually scanned, RFID simply broadcasts its presence and automatically sends data about the item to electronic readers. This technology is already in use in mass transit cashless ticketing systems, ski resort lift passes and security badges for controlled access to buildings.

The National Library Board has installed RFID tags in its 10 million books making it one of the largest users of

RFID tags in the world. Customers now have to spend little time queuing; book issuing is automatic, as are book returns. Indeed, books can be returned to any book drop at any library where RFID enables fast and easy sorting. Dr Varaprasad, the chief executive, explained:

"Customers can drop off books at anytime of day or night at the drop off points located on the outside of libraries. Indeed, the process is now so well designed that books dropped off one day are on the shelves at the right library by 8.00 the following morning or within minutes if it is from that branch."

From the outside, the book drop looks like an ATM machine, but with a large hole covered by a flap. The user places the book in the box below the flap, the book is scanned using RFID and a message on the screen instantly confirms that the book has been deleted from the user's account. In the Jurong Community Library, for example, staffs are located right behind the book drop. They take the book and as they pass it by their table, it is automatically scanned and they are informed about the required location of the book; the library to which it belongs or if it belongs to Jurong, the shelf to which it has to be returned. If it belongs to another library, it is placed in plastic trays which, when full, are placed in a wheeled container which the post office collects and automatically sorts and returns to the appropriate library using the existing postal system and the Library's RFID technology. If the book belongs to that library, it is placed on the appropriate shelf in front of the sorter. Other library staffs then take the books from the shelves and return them to the correct shelf in the public part of the library. A returned book can be back on the library shelf within minutes (Exhibit 1 on next page).

These RFID tags also lead to the introduction of Smart Shelves, currently on trial run at the Lee Kong Chian Reference Library at Bra Basah. By placing RFID readers in the form of bookends on book shelves, users can immediately know the exact shelf where the book is, through the computerized catalog system. The system allows the users to remember only a simple shelf number (e.g M2) instead of the long Dewey Decimal labelling (e.g. 656.159.230.123). This innovation, developed by the Institute for Inforcomm Research Singapore, also brings great benefits to the library staff. The system helps librarians re-shelf misplaced books easily and also reduces yearly stock-taking from 20 man-hours to just 4 hours, done fully by computers. In addition, with the new system, the library can now track more accurately the popularity of reference books as Smart Shelf automatically makes a note every time the book is taken from the shelf. Previously, staffs had to rely on counting the books left on tables or returning trolleys at the end of the day, which is not a very accurate measure. As a reference library, its books are strictly for use within the premises.

Exhibit 1: Smart Shelf with RFID technology[2].

Prior to the installation of the Smart Shelf system, all the libraries in NLB used a less high-tech but equally innovative way of ensuring that books were placed properly on the shelf. In most libraries, books were sorted by staff and located by users using codes typed or written on the bottom of the spine. While this universal system was also used by the NLB, it was supported by color coding, with each classification, subject, and sub-subject given a different color. Thus, it was easier for users to find the area they were looking for and library staff could easily spot a misplaced book by the break in the colour coding across the shelf. This innovative idea was actually proposed by a library staff whose work included long hours of placing books on the proper shelf (Exhibit 2).

Exhibit 2: Can you spot the wrong book?[2]

The NLB has also launched a mobile service via SMS (text messaging). This allows users to manage their library accounts anytime and anywhere through their mobile phones. They can check their loan records, renew their books, pay library payments, and get reminder alerts to return library items before the due date.

To meet the lifestyle of busy executives working in the Central Business District and to avoid the high cost of renting space in commercial buildings, the library has developed the concept of book dispensers, aimed at those people who won't or don't come into the library. Mr Chan Ping Wah, NLB's assistant chief executive, explained:

"There are, for example, thousands of people working in the CBD (Central Business District) who don't come to the Library. They say, "I go to work everyday. I am very busy. Don't expect me to come to the Library as well'. We could put a book dispenser in the CBD, just like a drinks machine, together with a book drop, and fill it with business books, self-development books, and management magazines. Imagine you are going off for lunch and you work in the CBD. You pass the dispenser, push in your library card, and press the number, out pops the book – 10 seconds – that's all. You go and eat, read the book and drop it in as you go past. It's that easy. Seventy to eighty per cent of these people do not come to the Library, so I have two choices, either build a library in the CBD, which will cost me S\$10m, or take a small selection of material to them. These people are only interested in a very small proportion of our stock, so I can select the ones they might want and we can easily and frequently change the selection. This has to be a much better and cheaper alternative. And, I can reproduce this idea at MRT stations for example. You take the MRT, pass a dispenser, get a book and drop it off at another MRT station, that day or another day. We could put lots of these dispensers around the country, targeted at specific groups."

Exhibit 3: A book-dispensing machine offering a 24/7 borrowing service for the contemporary book-thumber.

Perhaps crucially, NLB did not pursue hi-tech for technology's sake. The organisation focused on adapting technologies to drive customer value and fully recognized that different users may have different levels of comfort with using technology. Dr Varaprasad, CEO of NLB, explained:

"We had to be very careful that we do not alienate or intimidate customers with our use of technology. When you go to our libraries you now see computer screens for returning books, borrowing books, searching for books, creating and checking your accounts, and even paying fines! This is fine for people, especially younger people who are comfortable with this sort of technology but not for everyone, especially older people or those who do not read or write in English. To help these people, we enlisted a group of volunteers to get them familiar with the new technology. Indeed we used a group of senior citizen volunteers who were comfortable with the technology to help those that were not, until they became confident."

The end result? A world-class library, winner of the Singapore Innovation Award in 2001 and Singapore Quality Award in 2004, highly regarded by librarians around the world and featured in teaching case studies at top business schools such as Harvard Business School and INSEAD. Dr. Varaprasad added:

"Innovations that you see in the Library today— lifestyle libraries complete with cafes, music and rich multimedia, IT enabled innovations such as 24-hour book drop service, and groundbreaking concept libraries, like the self-service library, have all played a part in redefining the learning experience of Singaporeans. The NLB has become the de facto market leader of reading services in Singapore over and above bookshops, rental bookshops, media bookshops and so on."

STUDY QUESTIONS

1. How has the NLB used technology to increase the productivity and efficiency of its employees?

2. How has the NLB used technology to increase service quality to its customers?

3. Not everyone is comfortable with the use of technology. For example, older library visitors or visitors who are not comfortable reading or writing English (e.g. immigrants and visitors who received their education in another language). Give recommendations to NLB on ways they can make it easier for this group of visitors to use their self-service technologies, aside from what they are currently doing.

[1] © 2009 by Chai Kah Hin, Jochen Wirtz and Robert Johnston.

Chai Kah Hin is Assistant Professor of Industrial Systems Engineering at the National University of Singapore. Jochen Wirtz is Associate Professor of Marketing and Academic Director of the UCLA – NUS Executive MBA Program at the National University of Singapore. Robert Johnston is Professor at Warwick Business School.

The support and feedback of the management of the National Library Board in Singapore in the writing of this case is gratefully acknowledged and we thank the interviewees for their participation in this project and Johnson Paul and Sharon Foo for facilitating the research. The authors are grateful for the insightful feedback provided by Professor Christopher Lovelock on earlier versions of this case. Finally, we are thankful for the excellent research assistance provided by Teo Yi Wen, Department of Industrial and Systems Engineering at the National University of Singapore.

[2] Reprinted with permission © 2008. National Library Board Singapore

Dr Beckett's Dental Office[1]

Lauren Wright

A dentist seeks to differentiate her practice on the basis of quality. She constructs a new office and redesigns the practice to deliver high quality to her patients and to improve productivity through increased efficiency. However, it's not always easy to convince patients that her superior service justifies higher fees that are not always covered by insurance.

MANAGEMENT COMES TO DENTISTRY

"I just hope the quality differences are visible to our patients," mused Dr. Barbro Beckett as she surveyed the office that housed her well-established dental practice. She had recently moved to her current location from an office she felt was too cramped to allow her staff to work efficiently —a factor that was becoming increasingly important as the costs of providing dental care continued to rise. While Dr. Beckett realized that productivity gains were necessary, she did not want to compromise the quality of service her patients received.

The classes Dr. Beckett took in dental school taught her a lot about the technical side of dentistry but nothing about the business side. She received no formal training in the mechanics of running a business and understanding customer needs. In fact, professional guidelines discouraged marketing or advertising of any kind. That had not been a major problem 22 years earlier, when Dr. Beckett started her practice, for profit margins had been good then. But the dental care industry had changed dramatically. Costs rose as a result of labor laws, malpractice insurance, and the constant need to invest in new equipment and staff training as new technologies were introduced. Dr. Beckett's overhead was now between 70–80 percent of revenues before accounting for her wages or office rental.

At the same time as provider overhead was rising, there was a movement in the United States to reduce health care costs to insurance companies, employers and patients by offering "managed health care" through large Health Maintenance Organizations (HMOs). The HMOs set the prices for various services by putting an upper limit on the amount that their doctors and dentists could charge for various procedures. The advantage to patients was that their health insurance covered virtually all costs. But the price limitations meant that HMO doctors and dentists would not be able to offer certain services that might provide better quality care but were too expensive. Dr. Beckett had decided not to become an HMO provider because the reimbursement rate was only 80–85 percent of what she normally charged for treatment. She felt that she could not provide high-quality care to patients at these rates.

These changes presented some significant challenges to Dr. Beckett, who wanted to offer the highest level of dental care rather than being a low-cost provider. With the help of a consultant, she decided that her top priority was differentiating the practice on the basis of quality. She and her staff developed an internal mission statement that reflected this goal.

The mission statement (prominently displayed in the back office) read, in part: "It is our goal to provide superior dentistry in an efficient, profitable manner within the confines of a caring, quality environment."

Since higher quality care was more costly, Dr. Beckett's patients sometimes had to pay fees for costs that were not covered by their insurance policies. If the quality differences were not substantial, these patients might decide to switch to an HMO dentist or another lower-cost provider.

REDESIGNING THE SERVICE DELIVERY SYSTEM

The move to a new office gave Dr. Beckett a unique opportunity to rethink almost every aspect of her service. She wanted the work environment to reflect her own personality and values as well as providing a pleasant place for her staff to work.

Facilities and Equipment

Dr. Beckett first looked into the office spaces that were available in the Northern California town where she practiced. She did not find anything she liked, so she hired an architect from San Francisco to design a contemporary office building with lots of light and space. This increased the building costs by US$100,000 but Dr. Beckett felt that it would be a critical factor in differentiating her service.

Dr. Beckett's new office was Scandinavian in design (reflecting her Swedish heritage and attention to detail). The waiting room and reception area were filled with modern furniture in muted shades of brown, grey, green and purple. Live plants and flowers were abundant, and the walls were covered with art. Classical music played softly in the background. Patients could enjoy a cup of coffee or tea and browse through the large selection of current magazines while they waited for their appointments.

The treatment areas were both functional and appealing. There was a small conference room with toys for children and a VCR that was used to show patients, educational films about different dental procedures. Literature was available here to explain what patients needed to do to maximize the benefits of their treatment outcomes.

The chairs in the examining rooms were covered in leather and very comfortable. Each room had a large window that allowed patients to watch birds eating at the feeders that were filled each day. There were also attractive mobiles hanging from the ceiling to distract patients from the unfamiliar sounds and sensations they might be experiencing. Headphones were available with a wide selection of music.

The entire "back office" staff (including Dr. Beckett) wore uniforms in cheerful shades of pink, purple and blue that matched the office décor. All the technical equipment looked very modern and was spotlessly clean. State-of-the-art computerized machinery was used for some procedures. Dr. Beckett's dental degrees were prominently displayed in her office, along with certificates from various programs that she and her staff had attended to update their technical skills (Exhibit 1).

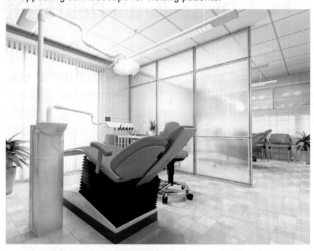

Exhibit 1: A current and state-of-the-art treatment room projects an appealing servicescape for visiting patients.

Service Personnel

There were eight employees in the dental practice, including Dr. Beckett (the only dentist). The seven staff members were separated by job function into "front office" and "back office" workers. Front office duties (covered by two employees) included receptionist and secretarial tasks and financial/budgeting work. The back office was divided into hygienists and chair side assistants.

The three chair side assistants helped the hygienists and Dr. Beckett with treatment procedures. They had specialized training for their jobs but did not need a college degree. The two hygienists handled routine exams and teeth cleaning plus some treatment procedures. In many dental offices, hygienists had a tendency to act like "prima donnas" because of their education (a bachelor's degree plus specialized training) and experience. According to Dr. Beckett, such an attitude could destroy any possibility of team work among the office staff. She felt very fortunate that her hygienists viewed themselves as part of a larger team that worked together to provide quality care to patients.

Dr. Beckett valued her friendship with staff members and also understood that they were a vital part of the service delivery. "Ninety percent of patients' perceptions of quality comes from their interactions with the front desk and the other employees —not from the staff's technical skills," she stated. When the dentist began to redesign her practice, she discussed her goals with the staff and involved them in the decision-making process. The changes meant new expectations and routines for most employees, and some were not willing to adapt. There was some staff turnover (mostly voluntary) as the new office procedures were implemented. The current group worked very well as a team.

Dr. Beckett and her staff met briefly each morning to discuss the day's schedule and patients. They also had longer meetings every other week to discuss more strategic issues and resolve any problems that might have developed. During these meetings, employees made suggestions about how to improve patient care. Some of the most successful staff suggestions include: "thank-you" cards to patients who referred other patients; follow-up calls to patients after major procedures; a "goodie box" for patients including toothbrush, toothpaste, mouthwash and floss; buckwheat pillows and blankets for patient comfort during long procedures; coffee and tea in the waiting area; and a photo album in the waiting area with pictures of staff and their families (Exhibit 2).

Exhibit 2: Service delivery is enhanced through improved customized interaction with patients both young and old.

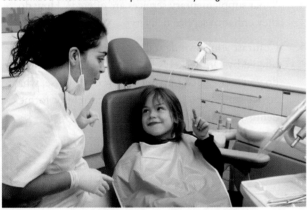

The expectations for staff performance (in terms of both technical competence and patient interactions) were very high. But Dr. Beckett provided her employees with many opportunities to update their skills by attending classes and workshops. She also rewarded their hard work by giving monthly bonuses if business had been good. Since she shared the financial data with her staff, they could see the difference in revenues if the schedule was slow or patients were dissatisfied. This provided an extra incentive to improve service delivery. The entire office also goes on trips together once a year (paid for by Dr. Beckett); spouses were welcome to participate but had to cover their own trip expenses. Past destinations for these excursions had included Hawaii and Washington, D.C.

Procedures and Patients

With the help of a consultant, all the office systems (including billing, ordering, lab work and patient treatment) were redesigned. One of the main goals was to standardize some of the routine procedures so that error was reduced and all patients would receive the same level of care. Specific times were allotted for each procedure and the staff worked very hard to see that these times were met. Office policy specified that patients should be kept waiting no longer than 20 minutes without being given the option to reschedule, and employees often called patients in advance if they knew there would be a delay. They also attempted to fill in cancellations to make sure office capacity is maximized. Staff members would substitute for each other when necessary or help with tasks that were not specifically in their job descriptions in order to make things run more smoothly.

Dr. Beckett's practice included about 2000 "active" patients (and many more who came infrequently.) They were mostly white collar workers with professional jobs (university employees, health care workers and managers/owners of local establishments.) She did no advertising — all of her new business came from positive word of mouth by current patients.

The dentist believed that referrals were a real advantage because new patients did not come in "cold." She did not have to sell herself because they had already been told about her service by friends or family. All new patients were required to have an initial exam so that Dr. Beckett could do a needs assessment and educate them about her service. She believed this was the first indication to patients that her practice was different from others they might have experienced. Patients might sometimes have to wait another 3–4 months for a routine cleaning and exam because the schedule was so busy, but they did not seem to mind.

THE BIGGEST CHALLENGE

"Redesigning the business was the easy part," Dr. Beckett sighed. "Demonstrating the high level of quality to patients is the hard job." She said this task was especially difficult since most people disliked going to the dentist or felt that it was an inconvenience and so came in with a negative attitude. Dr. Beckett tried to reinforce the idea that quality dental care depended on a positive long-term relationship between patients and the dental team. This philosophy was reflected in a section of the patient mission statement hanging in the waiting area: "We are a caring, professional dental team serving motivated, quality-oriented patients interested in keeping healthy smiles for a lifetime. Our goal is to offer a progressive and educational environment. Your concerns are our focus."

Exhibit 3: A team of closely-knit professionals working behind a clear, common mission statement, can help overcome the most negative pre-conceived notions about visiting the dentist.

Although Dr. Beckett enjoyed her work, she admitted it could be difficult to maintain a positive attitude. The job required precision and attention to detail, and the procedures were often painful for patients. She often felt as though she were "walking on eggshells" because she knew patients were anxious and uncomfortable, which made them more critical of her service delivery. It was not uncommon for patients to say negative things to Dr. Beckett even before treatment began (such as, "I really hate going to the dentist — it's not you, but I just don't want to be here!"). When this happened,

she reminded herself that she was providing quality service whether patients appreciated it or not. "The person will usually have to have the dental work done anyway," she remarked, "So I just do the best job I can and make them as comfortable as possible." Even though patients seldom expressed appreciation for her services, she hoped that she had made a positive difference in their health or appearance that would benefit them in the long run.

STUDY QUESTIONS

1. Which of the seven elements of the Services Marketing Mix are addressed in this case? Give examples of each "P" you identify.

2. Why do people dislike going to the dentist? Do you feel Dr. Beckett has addressed this problem effectively?

3. How do Dr. Beckett and her staff educate patients about the service they are receiving? What else could they do?

4. What supplementary services are offered? How do they enhance service delivery?

5. Contrast your own dental care experiences with those offered by Dr. Beckett's practice. What differences do you see? Based on your review of this case, what advice would you give (a) to your current or former dentist, and (b) to Dr. Beckett?

---

[1] © 2007 by Lauren K. Wright

Glossary

A

activity-based costing (ABC): an approach to costing based on identifying the activities being performed and then determining the resources that each consumes.

adequate service: minimum level of service that a customer will accept without being dissatisfied.

advertising: any paid form of non-personal communication by a marketer to inform, educate, or persuade members of target audiences.

arm's-length transactions: interactions between customers and service suppliers in which mail or telecommunications minimize the need to meet face to face.

attitude: a person's consistently favorable or unfavorable evaluations, feelings, and action tendencies toward an object or idea.

auction: a selling procedure managed by a specialist intermediary in which the price is set by allowing prospective purchasers to bid against each other for a product offered by a seller.

augmented product: core product (a good or a service) plus supplementary elements that add value for customers (*see also* **flower of service**).

B

backstage (or technical core): those aspects of service operations that are hidden from customers.

banner ads: small, rectangular boxes on web sites that contain text and perhaps a picture to support a brand.

benchmarking: comparing an organization's products and processes to those of competitors or leading firms in the same or other industries to find ways to improve performance, quality, and cost effectiveness.

benefit: an advantage or gain that customers obtain from the performance of a service or use of a physical good.

blog: a publicly accessible "web log" containing frequently updated pages in the form of journals, diaries, news listings, etc.; authors— known as bloggers— typically focus on specific topics.

blueprint: a visual map of the sequence of activities required for service delivery that specifies front-stage and backstage elements and the linkages between them.

boundary-spanning positions: jobs that straddle the boundary between the external environment, where customers are encountered, and the internal operations of the organization.

brand: a name, phrase, design, symbol, or some combination of these elements that identifies a company's services and differentiates it from competitors.

business model: means by which an organization generates income from sales and other sources through choice of pricing mechanisms and payors (e.g, user, advertiser or sponsor, other third parties), ideally sufficient to cover costs and create value for its owners. (*Note:* For nonprofits and public agencies, donations and designated tax revenues may be an integral part of the model.)

C

chain stores: two or more outlets under common ownership and control, and selling similar goods and services.

chase demand strategy: adjusting the level of capacity to meet the level of demand at any given time.

churn: loss of existing customer accounts and the need to replace them with new ones.

clicks and mortar: a strategy of offering service through both physical stores and virtual storefronts via web sites on the Internet.

competition-based pricing: setting prices relative to those charged by competitors.

competitive advantage: a firm's ability to perform in ways that competitors cannot or will not match.

complaint: a formal expression of dissatisfaction with any aspect of a service experience-.

complaint log: a detailed record of all customer complaints received by a service provider.

conjoint analysis: a research method for determining the utility values that consumers attach to varying levels of a product's attributes.

consumption: purchase and use of a service or good.

control chart: a chart that graphs quantitative changes in service performance on a specific variable relative to a predefined standard.

control model of management: an approach based on clearly defined roles, top-down control systems, a hierarchical organizational structure, and the assumption that management knows best.

core competency: a capability that is a source of competitive advantage.

corporate culture: shared beliefs, norms, experiences, and stories that characterize an organization.

corporate design: consistent application of distinctive colors, symbols, and lettering to give a firm an easily recognizable identity.

cost leader: a firm that bases its pricing strategy on achieving the lowest costs in its industry.

cost-based pricing: relating the price to be charged for a product to the costs associated with producing, delivering, and marketing it.

credence attributes: product characteristics that customers zmay not be able to evaluate even after purchase and consumption.

critical incident: a specific encounter between customer and service provider in which the outcome has proved especially satisfying or dissatisfying for one or both parties.

critical incident technique (CIT): a methodology for collecting, categorizing, and analyzing critical incidents that have occurred between customers and service providers.

CRM system: information technology (IT) systems and infrastructure that support the implementation and delivery of a customer-relationship management strategy.

customer contact personnel: service employees who interact directly with individual customers, either in person or through mail and telecommunications.

customer equity: total combined customer lifetime value (*see definition*) of the company's entire customer base.

customer interface: all points at which customers interact with a service organization.

customer lifetime value (CLV): net present value of the stream of future contributions or profits expected over each customer's purchases during his or her anticipated lifetime as a customer of a specific organization.

customer relationship management (CRM): overall process of building and maintaining profitable customer relationships by delivering superior customer value and satisfaction.

customer satisfaction: a short-term emotional reaction to a specific service performance.

customer training: training programs offered by service firms to teach customers about complex service products.

customization: tailoring service characteristics to meet each customer's specific needs and preferences.

cyberspace: a virtual reality without physical existence, in which electronic transactions or communications occur.

D

data mining: extracting useful information about individuals, trends, and segments from often massive amounts of customer data.

data warehouse: a comprehensive database containing customer information and transaction data.

database marketing: building, maintaining, and using customer databases and other databases for contacting, selling, cross-selling, up-selling, and building customer relationships.

defection: a customer's decision to transfer brand loyalty from a current service provider to a competitor.

delivery channels: physical and electronic means by which a service firm (sometimes assisted by intermediaries) delivers one or more product elements to its customers.

demand curve: A curve that shows the number of units the market will buy at different prices.

demand cycle: a period of time during which the level of demand for a sendee will increase and decrease in a somewhat predictable way before repeating itself.

demographic segmentation: dividing the market into groups based on demographic variables such as age, gender, family life cycle, family size, income, occupation, education, religion, or ethnic group.

desired service: the "wished for" level of service quality that a customer believes can and should be delivered.

discounting: a strategy of reducing the price of an item below the normal level.

dynamic pricing: a technique, employed primarily bye-tailers, to charge different customers different prices for the same products, based on information collected about their purchase history, preferences, and price sensitivity.

E

e-commerce: buying, selling, and other marketing processes supported by the Internet (*see also* **e-tailing**).

emotional labor: expressing socially appropriate (but sometimes false) emotions toward customers during service transactions.

empowerment: authorizing employees to find solutions to service problems and make appropriate decisions about responding to customer concerns without having to obtain a supervisor's approval.

enablement: providing employees with the skills, tools, and resources they need to use their own discretion confidently and effectively.

enhancing supplementary services: supplementary services that may add extra value for customers.

e-tailing: retailing through the Internet instead of through physical stores.

excess capacity: an organization's capacity to create service output that is not fully utilized.

excess demand: demand for a service at a given time that exceeds the organization's ability to meet customer needs.

expectations: internal standards that customers use to judge the quality of a service experience.

experience attributes: product performance features that customers can evaluate only during service delivery.

expert systems: interactive computer programs that mimic a human expert's reasoning to draw conclusions from data, solve problems, and give customized advice.

F

facilitating supplementary services: supplementary services that aid in the use of the core product or are required for service delivery.

fail point: a point in a process at which there is a significant risk of problems that can damage service quality (sometimes referred to humorously as an OTSU, short for "opportunity to screw up").

financial outlays: all monetary expenditures incurred by customers in purchasing and consuming a service.

fishbone diagram: a chart-based technique that relates specific service problems to different categories of underlying causes (also known as a cause-and-effect chart).

fixed costs: costs that do not vary with production or sales revenue.

flat-rate pricing: quoting a fixed price for a service in advance of delivery.

flowchart: a visual representation of the steps involved in delivering service to customers (*see also* **blueprint**).

flower of service: a visual framework for understanding the supplementary service elements that surround and add value to the product core (*see also* **augmented product**).

focus group: a group, typically consisting of six to eight people and carefully preselected on certain characteristics (e.g., demographics, psychographics, or product ownership), who are convened by researchers for in-depth, moderator-led discussion of specific topics.

franchise: A contractual association between a franchiser (typically a manufacturer, wholesaler, or service organization) and independent businesspeople (franchisees), who buy the right to own and operate one or more units in the franchise system.

frequency program (FPs): a program designed to reward customers who buy frequently and in substantial amounts.

front stage: those aspects of service operations and delivery that are visible or otherwise apparent to customers.

G

geographic segmentation: dividing a market into geographic units such as countries, regions, or cities.

goods: physical objects or devices that provide benefits for customers through ownership or use.

H

high-contact services: services that involve significant interaction among customers, service personnel, and equipment and facilities.

human resource management (HRM): coordination of tasks related to job design, employee recruitment, selection, training, and motivation; also includes planning and administering other employee-related activities.

I

image: a set of beliefs, ideas, and impressions held regarding an object.

impersonal communications: one-way communications directed at target audiences who are not in personal contact with the message source (including advertising, promotions, and public relations).

information processing: intangible actions directed at customers' assets.

information-based services: all services in which the principal value comes from the transmission of data to customers; also includes mental stimulus processing and information processing (*see definitions*).

in-process wait: a wait that occurs during service delivery.

inputs: all resources (labor, materials, energy, and capital) required to create service offerings.

intangibility: (*see* **mental intangibility** *and* **physical intangibility**).

intangible: something that is experienced and that cannot be touched or preserved.

integrated marketing communications (IMC): a concept under which an organization carefully integrates and coordinates its many communications channels to deliver a clear, consistent, and compelling message about the organization and its products.

internal communications: all forms of communication from management to employees within an organization.

internal customers: employees who receive services from an internal supplier (another employee or department) as a necessary input to performing their own jobs.

internal marketing: marketing activities directed internally to employees to train and motivate them and instill a customer focus.

internal services: service elements within any type of business that facilitate creation of, or add value to, its final output.

Internet: a large public web of computer networks that connects users from around the world to each other and to a vast information repository.

inventory: for *manufacturing*, physical output stockpiled after production for sale at a later date; for *services*, future output that has not yet been reserved in advance, such as the number of hotel rooms still available for sale on a given day.

involvement model of management: an approach based on the assumption that employees are capable of self-direction and, if properly trained, motivated, and informed, can make good decisions concerning service operations and delivery.

iTV: (interactive television) procedures that allow viewers to alter the viewing experience by controlling TV program delivery (e.g., TiVo, video on demand) and/or content.

J

jaycustomer: a customer who acts in a thoughtless or abusive way, causing problems for the firm, its employees, and other customers.

L

levels of customer contact: extent to which customers interact physically with the service organization.

low-contact services: services that require minimal or no direct contact between customers and the service organization.

loyalty: a customer's commitment to continue patronizing a specific firm over an extended period of time.

M

market focus: extent to which a firm serves few or many markets.

market segmentation: process of dividing a market into distinct groups within each of which all customers share relevant characteristics that distinguish them from customers in other segments, and respond in similar ways;to a given set of marketing efforts.

marketing communications mix: full set of communication tools (both paid and unpaid) available to marketers, including advertising, sales promotion, events, public relations and publicity, direct marketing, and personal selling.

marketing implementation: process that turns marketing plans into projects and ensures that such projects are executed in a way that accomplishes the plan's stated objectives.

marketing research: systematic design, collection, analysis, and reporting of customer and competitor data and findings relevant to a specific marketing situation facing an organization.

marketplace: a location in physical space or cyberspace (*see definition*) where suppliers and customers meet to do business.

mass customization: offering a service with some individualized product elements to a large number of customers at a relatively low price.

maximum capacity: upper limit to a firm's ability to meet customer demand at a particular time.

medium-contact services: services that involve only a limited amount of contact between customers and elements of the service organization.

membership relationship: a formalized relationship between the firm and a specified customer that may offer special benefits to both parties.

mental intangibility: difficulty for customers in visualizing an experience in advance of purchase and understanding the process and even the nature of the outcome (*see also* **physical intangibility**).

mental stimulus processing: intangible actions directed at people's minds.

mission statement: succinct description of what the organization does, its standards and values, whom it serves, and what it intends to accomplish.

molecular model: a framework that uses a chemical analogy to describe the structure of service offerings.

moment of truth: a point in service delivery at which customers interact with service employees or self-service equipment and the outcome may affect perceptions of service quality.

mystery shopping: a research technique that employs individuals posing as ordinary customers to obtain feedback on the service environment and customer-employee interactions.

N

needs: subconscious, deeply felt desires that often concern long-term existence and identity issues.

net value: the sum of all perceived benefits (gross value) minus the sum of all perceived outlays.

nonfinancial outlays: time expenditures, physical and mental effort, and unwanted sensory experiences associated with searching for, buying, and using a service.

non-monetary costs: (*see* **non-financial outlays**).

O

opportunity cost: potential value of income or other benefits foregone as a result of choosing one course of action instead of other alternatives.

optimum capacity: point beyond which a firm's efforts to serve additional customers will lead to a perceived decline in service quality.

organizational climate: employees' shared perceptions of the practices, procedures, and types of behaviors that are rewarded and supported in a particular setting.

organizational culture: „ shared values, beliefs, and work styles that are based on an understanding of what is important to the organization and why.

OTSU ("opportunity to screw up"): (*see* **fail point**).

outputs: final outcome of the service delivery process as perceived and valued by customers.

P

Pareto analysis: an analytical procedure to identify what proportion of problem events is caused by each of several different factors.

people: customers and employees who are involved in service production.

people processing: services that involve tangible actions to people's bodies.

perception: process by which individuals select, organize, and interpret information to form a meaningful picture of the world.

perceptual map: a visual illustration of how customers perceive competing services.

permission marketing: a marketing communication strategy that encourages customers to volunteer permission to a company to communicate with them through specified channels so they may learn more about its products and continue to receive useful information or something else of value to them.

personal communications: direct communications between marketers and individual customers that involve two-way dialog (including face-to-face conversations, phone calls, and email).

personal selling: two-way communications between service employees and customers designed to influence the purchase process directly.

physical effort: undesired consequences to a customer's body resulting from involvement in the service delivery process.

physical evidence: visual or other tangible clues that provide evidence of service quality.

physical intangibility: service elements that are not accessible to examination by any of the five senses; (*more narrowly*) elements that cannot be touched or preserved by customers.

place and time: management decisions about when, where, and how to deliver services to customers.

positioning: establishing a distinctive place in the minds of customers relative to the attributes possessed by or absent from competing products.

possession processing: tangible actions to goods and other physical possessions belonging to customers.

post-process wait: a wait that occurs after service delivery has been completed.

post-encounter stage: final stage in the service purchase process, in which customers evaluate the service experienced, form their satisfaction/dissatisfaction judgment with the service outcome, and establish future intentions.

predicted service: level of service quality a customer believes a firm will actually deliver.

pre-process wait: a wait before service delivery begins.

pre-purchase stage: first stage in the service purchase process, in which customers identify alternatives, weigh benefits and risks, and make a purchase decision.

price and other user outlays: expenditures of money, time, and effort that customers incur in purchasing and consuming services.

price bucket: an allocation of service capacity (e.g., seats) for sale at a particular price.

price bundling: charging a base price for a core service plus additional fees for optional supplementary elements.

price elasticity: extent to which a change in price leads to a corresponding change in demand in the opposite direction. (Demand is described as *price inelastic* when changes in price have little or no effect on demand.)

price leader: a firm that takes the initiative on price changes in its market area and is copied by others.

process: a particular method of operations or series of actions, typically involving steps that need to occur in a defined sequence.

product: the core output (either a service or a manufactured good) produced by a firm.

product attributes: all features (both tangible and intangible) of a good or service that can be evaluated by customers.

product elements: all components of the service performance that create value for customers.

productive capacity: amount of facilities, equipment, labor, infrastructure, and other assets available to a firm to create output for its customers.

productivity: how efficiently service inputs are transformed into outputs that add value for customers.

promotion and education: all communication activities and incentives designed to build customer preference for a specific service or service provider.

psychographic segmentation: dividing a market into different groups based on personality characteristics, social class, or lifestyle.

psychological burdens: undesired mental or emotional states experienced by customers as a result of the service delivery process.

public relations: efforts to stimulate positive interest in a company and its products by sending out news releases, holding press conferences, staging special events, and sponsoring newsworthy activities put on by third parties.

purchase process: the stages a customer goes through in choosing, consuming, and evaluating a service.

Q

quality: the degree to which a service satisfies customers by consistently meeting their needs, wants, and expectations.

queue: a line of people, vehicles, other physical objects, or intangible items waiting their turn to be served or processed.

queue configuration: the way in which a waiting line is organized.

R

rate fences: techniques for separating customers so that segments for whom the service offers high value are unable to take advantage of lower-priced offers.

reengineering: analysis and redesign of business processes to create dramatic performance improvements in such areas as cost, quality, speed, and customers' service experiences.

relationship marketing: activities aimed at developing long-term, cost-effective links between an organization and its customers for the mutual benefit of both parties.

repositioning: changing the position a firm holds in a consumer's mind relative to competing services.

retail displays: presentations in store windows and other locations of merchandise, service experiences, and benefits.

retail gravity model: a mathematical approach to retail site selection that involves calculating the geographic center of gravity for the target population and then locating a facility to optimize customers' ease of access.

return on quality: financial return obtained from investing in service quality improvements.

revenue management: a pricing and product design strategy based on charging different prices to different segments at different times to maximize the revenue that can be derived from a firm's available capacity during a specific time frame (also known as *yield management*).

role: a combination of social cues that guides behavior in a specific setting or context.

role congruence: extent to which both customers and employees act out their prescribed roles during a service encounter.

S

sales promotion: a short-term incentive offered to customers and intermediaries to stimulate faster or larger purchase.

satisfaction: a person's feelings of pleasure or disappointment resulting from a consumption experience when comparing a product's perceived performance or outcome in relation to his or her expectations.

script: a learned sequence of behaviors obtained through personal experience or communication with others.

search attributes: product characteristics that consumers can readily evaluate prior to purchase.

segment: a group of current or prospective customers who share common characteristics, needs, purchasing behavior, or consumption patterns.

sensory burdens: negative sensations experienced through a customer's five senses during the service delivery process.

service: an economic activity offered by one party to another, typically without transfer of ownership, creating value from rental of, or access to, goods, labor, professional skills, facilities, networks, or systems, singly or in combination.

service blueprint: (*see* **blueprint, flowchart**).

service concept: what the firm offers, to whom, and through what processes.

service delivery system: that part of the total service system during which final "assembly" of the elements takes place and the product is delivered to the customer; it includes the visible elements of the service operation.

service encounter: a period of time during which customers interact directly with a service.

service encounter stage: the second stage in the service purchase process, in which the required service is delivered through interactions between customers and the service provider.

service factory: a physical site where service operations take place.

service failure: a perception by customers that one or more specific aspects of service delivery have not met their expectations.

service focus: extent to which a firm offers few or many services.

service guarantee: a promise that if service delivery fails to meet predefined standards, the customer is entitled to one or more forms of compensation.

service marketing system: that part of the total service system in which the firm has any form of contact with its customers, from advertising to billing; it includes contacts made at the point of delivery.

service model: an integrative statement that specifies the nature of the service concept (what the firm offers, to whom, and through what processes), the service blueprint (how the concept is delivered to target customers), and the accompanying business model (how revenues will be generated sufficient to cover costs and ensure financial viability).

service operations system: that part of the total service system in which inputs are processed and the elements of the service product are created.

service preview: a demonstration of how a service works, to educate customers about the roles they are expected to perform in service delivery.

service quality: customers' long term, cognitive evaluations of a firm's service delivery.

service quality information system: an ongoing service research process that provides timely, useful data to managers about customer satisfaction, expectations, and perceptions of quality.

service recovery: systematic efforts by a firm after a service failure to correct a problem and retain a customer's goodwill.

service sector: the portion of a nation's economy represented by services of all kinds, including those offered by public and nonprofit organizations.

service-profit chain: a strategic framework that links employee satisfaction to performance on service attributes to customer satisfaction, then to customer retention, and finally to profits.

services marketing mix: (*see* **seven (7) Ps**).

servicescape: the design of any physical location where customers come to place orders and obtain service delivery.

SERVQUAL: a pair of standardized 22-item scales that measure customers' expectations and perceptions concerning five dimensions of service quality.

seven (7) Ps: seven strategic elements, each beginning with P, in the services marketing mix, representing the key ingredients required to create viable strategies for meeting customer needs profitably in a competitive marketplace.

standardization: reducing variation in service operations and delivery.

stickiness: a web site's ability to encourage repeat visits and purchases by providing users with easy navigation, problem-free execution of tasks, and keeping its audience engaged with interactive communication presented in an appealing fashion.

sustainable competitive advantage: a position in the marketplace that can't be taken away or minimized by competitors in the short run.

T

tangible: capable of being touched, held, or preserved in physical form over time.

target market: A part of the qualified available market with common needs or characteristics that a company decides to serve.

target segments: segments selected because their needs and other characteristics fit well with a specific firm's goals and capabilities.

time expenditures: time spent by customers during all aspects of the service delivery process.

three-stage model of service consumption: a framework depicting how consumers move from a prepur-chase stage (in which they recognize their needs, search for and evaluate alternative solutions, and make a decision), to a service encounter search (in which they obtain service delivery), and thence a post-encounter stage (in which they evaluate service performance against expectations).

third-party payments: Payments to cover all or part of the cost of a service or good made by a party other than the user (who may or may not have made the actual purchase decision).

total costs: The sum of the fixed and variable costs for any given level of production.

transaction: an event during which an exchange of value takes place between two parties.

transactional survey: a technique to measure customer satisfaction and perceptions of service quality while a specific service experience is still fresh in the customer's mind.

U

undesirable demand: requests for service that conflict with the organization's mission, priorities, or capabilities.

V

value chain: The series of departments within a firm or external partners and subcontractors that carry out value-creating activities to design, produce, market, deliver, and support a product or service offering.

value exchange: transfer of the benefits and solutions offered by a seller in return for financial and other value offered by a purchaser.

value proposition: a specified package of benefits and solutions that a company intends to offer and how it proposes to deliver them to customers, emphasizing key points of difference relative to competing alternatives.

value-based pricing: the practice of setting prices based on what customers are willing to pay for the value they believe they will receive.

variability: a lack of consistency in inputs and outputs during the service production process.

variable costs: costs that depend directly on the volume of production or service transactions.

viral marketing: using the Internet to create word-of-mouth effects to support marketing efforts.

W

wheel of loyalty: a systematic and integrated approach to targeting, acquiring, developing, and retaining a valuable customer base.

word-of-mouth: positive or negative comments about a service made by one individual (usually a current or former customer) to another.

Y

yield: the average revenue received per unit of capacity offered for sale.

yield management: (*see* revenue management).

Z

zone of tolerance: the range within which customers are willing to accept variations in service delivery.

BLANK

Credits

Chapter 1 — p. 4: Mary Lane/Dreamstime.com; p. 5: Used with permission by Bumrungrad International Hospital; p. 7: Joe Chang/Flickr; p.12: Used with permission by Randy Glasbergen; p. 13: Juha Huiskonen/iStockphoto; p. 16 Marin Conic/Dreamstime.com; p. 16: Dr. Heinz Linke/iStockphoto; p. 16: Sudheer Sakthan/Dreamstime.com; p. 17: Pavel Losevsky/Dreamstime.com; p. 18: Lisa F. Young/Dreamstime.com; p. 21: Inga Ivanova/iStockphoto; p. 22: Carl Durocher/Dreamstime.com; p. 23: Kirill Zdorov/Dreamstime.com; p. 24: Erwin Ps/iStockphoto.

Chapter 2 — p. 32: David Shankbone/Wikipedia; p. 33: Hua Zhuang/Dreamstime.com; p. 35: Courtesy of The Hertz Corporation; p. 35: Ben Blankenburg/iStockphoto; p. 36: Marcus Clackson/iStockphoto; p. 36: Used with permission by Randy Glasbergen; p. 38: Courtesy of HSMAI, All rights reserved; p. 38: Used with permission by MasterCard. © 1994-2008 MasterCard, All rights reserved; p. 38: Courtesy of McAfee Inc., All rights reserved; p. 39: Courtesy of Zurich Financial Services, © 2008 Zurich Financial Services; p. 39: © James Steidl; p. 39: 【B™】/Flickr; p. 41: Dave Weatherall/Flickr; p. 42: Courtesy of Singapore Airlines, © 2008 Singapore Airlines, All rights reserved; p. 43: Niderlander/Dreamstime.com; p. 44: Used with permission by JuanJ. This photo can be found at www.flickr.com/photos/juanj/808223504/sizes/sq/; p. 44: Stephen Coburn/Dreamstime.com; p. 45: Used with permission by Randy Glasbergen; p. 47: Ugur Bariskan/iStockphoto; p. 47: David Shankbone/Wikipedia; p. 48: Ron Chapple Studios/Dreamstime.com.

Chapter 3 — p. 56: Courtesy of Bright Horizons LLC, © 2008 Bright Horizons LLC, All rights reserved; p. 57: Pavel Losevsky/Dreamstime.com; p. 58: Courtesy of Synergy A+D, © 2006 Synergy A+D, All rights reserved; p. 59: Johnston, R. (1996). *Achieving focus in service organizations*, 16 (January), pp. 10–20, Reprinted by permission of The publisher (Taylor & Fracis Ltd, http://www.informaworld.com p. 59: Roza/Dreamstime.com; p. 60: Remus Eserblom/iStockphoto; p. 62: Courtesy of Contiki Holidays, © 2008 Contiki; p. 62: Brett Matthews/Wikipedia; p. 63: Scott Brown/Flickr; p. 64: Used with permission by CEVA Logistics. © 2006 CEVA Logistics Holdings; p. 65: Courtesy of Benji Lanyado/Flickr; p. 65: Used with permission by Randy Glasbergen; p. 66: Courtesy of Grant Thornton, © 2007 Grant Thornton International, All rights reserved; p. 68: Kutay Tanir/iStockphoto; p. 69: Courtesy of Cirque du Soleil/Éric Piché; p. 70: Rene Drouyer/Dreamstime.com; p. 74: Caribb/Flickr;

Chapter 4 — p. 84: Courtesy of Getty Images; p. 85: Reproduction rights obtained from www.CartoonStock.com; p. 86: Steve Cole/iStockphoto; p. 90: Courtesy of OpenTable, © 2008 OpenTable Inc., All rights reserved; p. 92: Edward Bock/iStockphoto; p. 94: David H. Lewis/iStockphoto; p. 96: Courtesy of Getty Images; p. 96: dra_schwartz/iStockphoto; p. 98: M Highsmith/Wikipedia; p. 98: BrokenSphere/Wikipedia; p. 101: Courtesy of Landry's Restaurants, © 2006 Landry's Restaurants Inc.; p. 102: Courtesy of Barnes and Noble, © 1997-2008 Barnesandnoble.com LLC; p. 103: Courtesy of YouTube, © 2008 YouTube LLC; p. 104: Adam Kazmierski/iStockphoto.

Chapter 5 — p. 110: Courtesy of www.wizzit.co.za; p. 111: Courtesy of www.wizzit.co.za; p. 113: Image reproduced by permission of Compass Group PLC; p. 115: Use with permission by Aggreko PLC; p. 116: Used with permission by Randy Glasbergen; p. 116: Courtesy of Karl Baron/Flickr; p. 117: Krzysztof Ziebinski/Flickr; p. 117: © Christopher H. Lovelock; p. 118: Roberto Ruiz (www.flickr.com/photos/belrobplace); p. 119: Courtesy of JC Buck/Flickr; p. 121: Used with permission by Randy Glasbergen; p. 122: Courtesy of Cisco Systems Inc.; p. 123: Used with permission by HSBC Bank PLC. © 2008 HSBC Bank PLC; p. 124: Used with permission by Yellow Pages. © 2008 YELLOWPAGES.COM LLC, All rights reserved; p. 126: Courtesy of Saks, © 2008 Saks Franchise Services Ltd, www.saks.co.uk; p. 128: Courtesy of Wolfgang Hammer/Flickr; p. 129: Courtesy of Sananko.

Chapter 6 — p. 134: Julia Fikse/Dreamstime.com; p. 135: Edgar Zessinthal/Flickr; p. 137: Yali Shi/Dreamstime.com; p. 138: Erwin Purnomosidi/Dreamstime.com; p. 140: Used with permission by Randy Glasbergen; p. 141: © King Features Syndicate; p. 142: Courtesy of Amazon.com, © 1996-2008 Amazon.com Inc.; p. 142: Courtesy of eBay, © 1995-2008 eBay Inc., All rights reserved; p. 143: Courtesy of priceline, ©1998-2008 priceline.com Inc., All rights reserved; p. 144: Ken Hurst/Dreamstime.com; p. 146: Ilka-Erika Szasz-Fabian/iStockphoto; p. 148: Used with permission by www.flightstats.com; p. 149: Xavier Marchant/Dreamstime.com; p. 150: Courtesy of Paul Duke/Flickr; p. 153: Wendell Franks/iStockphoto; p. 154: Scott Rothstein/Dreamstime.com; p. 156: Hermann Danzmayr/iStockphoto; p. 157: Nikolay Okhitin/Dreamstime.com; p. 157: iofoto/iStockphoto; p. 159: Mayumi Terao/iStockphoto; p. 160: Used with permission by Randy Glasbergen; p. 160: Andres Rodriguez/Dreamstime.com; p. 161: Webphotographeer/iStockphoto; p. 161: © 2008 JP Morgan Chase & Co; p. 162: Andre Blais/Dreamstime.com.

Chapter 7 — p. 168: Jeremiah Garcia/iStockphoto; p. 169: Courtesy of Westin Hotels & Resorts, ©2007 Starwood Hotels & Resorts Worldwide Inc.; p. 170: Courtesy of eBay, © 1995-2008 eBay Inc., All rights reserved; p. 173: Used with permission by the Julius Baer Group; p. 173: Used with permission by Accenture. ©1996-2008 Accenture, All rights reserved; p. 174: Courtesy of Stu Bertles/ Flickr; p. 174: Courtesy of Mastercard, © 1994-2008 MasterCard, All rights reserved; p. 179: Courtesy of Linden Lab, © 2008 Linden Research Inc.; p. 179: Courtesy of FedEx, © 1995-2008 FedEx, All rights reserved; p. 180: Used with permission by Randy Glasbergen; p. 181: Used with permission by Randy Glasbergen; p. 181: Sheldon Kralstein/iStockphoto; p. 182: Courtesy of Bénévoles Canada; p. 183: © 2005 pinstorm.com, All rights reserved; p. 185: Courtesy of Yale University Press, © 2008 Yale University Press; p. 186: Pablo Leonidas Chamorro; p. 188: Courtesy of Google, © 2008 Google; p. 190: Giorgio Martini/Wikipedia; p. 190: seo75/ Wikipedia; p. 190: Arpingstone/Wikipedia.

Chapter 8 — p. 198: Simon Gurney/Dreamstime.com; p. 199: Sengkang/Wikipedia; p. 201: Courtesy of BBC; p. 203: Juriah Mosin/Dreamstime.com, p. 203: Christian Bernfeld/Dreamstime.com; p. 205: Andy Hwang/iStockphoto; p. 205: Paul Vasarhelyi/ iStockphoto; p. 210: Dwphotos/Dreamstime.com; p. 210: Stacey Walker/iStockphoto; p. 211: Millan/Dreamstime.com; p. 213: Lisa F. Young/Dreamstime.com; p. 214: Courtesy of J. Bennett; p. 215: © China Ocean Shipping Company, All rights reserved; p. 217: Erwin Purnomosidi/Dreamstime.com; p. 217: Stephan Zabel/iStockphoto; p. 218: Jeffrey Smith/iStockphoto; p. 219: Used with permission by Randy Glasbergen; p. 220: Courtesy of KF/Wikipedia; p. 221: Ivonne Wierink/Dreamstime.com; p. 222: Max Melchior/Flickr.

Chapter 9 — p. 228: Courtesy of Arni Tryggvason/Flickr; p. 229: Used with permission by Mont Tremblant Ski Resort. © Mont Tremblant Ski Resort, Québec, Canada and Golf Le Diable; p. 231: Vladimir Piskunov/iStockphoto; p. 233: Roger Lim/iStockphoto; p. 233: Chuck Peterson; p. 234: Lisa F. Young/iStockphoto; p. 236: Christoph Moser, Cologne, Germany; p. 238: Karin Lau/ Dreamstime.com; p. 240: Radu Razvan/Dreamstime.com; p. 241: Pryzmat/Dreamstime.com; p. 241: Britta Kasholm-Tengve/ iStockphoto; p. 243: Used with permission by Randy Glasbergen; p. 245: Courtesy of Prime Time Table LLC.

Chapter 10 — p. 252-253: © 2008 FMGB Guggenheim Bilbao Museoa, Photo: Erika Ede, All rights reserved, Total or partial reproduction is prohibited; p. 254: Courtesy of Brian Sayler/Flickr; p. 255: Use with permission from Fairmont Hotels & Resorts; p. 255: Douglas Waldron; p. 258: "The Servicescape Model," reprinted with permission from the *Journal of Marketing*, published by the American Marketing Association, (Bitner, M.J.), (April/56) and (p. 57-71); p. 261: Courtesy of Dreamstime.com; p. 263: Courtesy of Dreamstime.com; p. 264: Courtesy of Jason Kuffer/Flickr; p. 264: Alton.arts/Wikipedia; p. 266: Courtesy of s.rejeki/Flickr; p. 266: Jean Bellon; p. 267: Courtesy of Dreamstime.com; p. 268: Chan Pak Kei/iStockphoto.

Chapter 11 — p. 276-277: Quavondo Nguyen/iStockphoto; p. 278: iofoto/iStockphoto; p. 279: claudiobaba/iStockphoto; p. 281: Matthew P. Gonzalez; p. 281: Used with permission by Randy Glasbergen; p. 282: Chris Schmidt/iStockphoto; p. 285: Courtesy of Global Legal Services Organisation, DLA Piper; p. 286: Used with permission by Randy Glasbergen; p. 287: Courtesy of shawiz/ Flickr; p. 288: Joselito Briones /iStockphoto; p. 289: one2c900d/Flickr; p. 290: Eliza Snow/iStockphoto; p. 291: Courtesy of Simonyfrontsjones/Flickr; p. 292: Courtesy of Wac/Wikipedia; p. 293: Courtesy of the United States Department of Defense; p. 294: Used with permission by Randy Glasbergen; p. 294: Courtesy of Singapore Airlines, © 2008 Singapore Airlines, All rights reserved.

Chapter 12 — p. 306: Courtesy of ForzaVale/Flickr; p. 307: Courtesy of iStockphoto; p. 312: Yuri Arcurs/Dreamstime.com; p. 314: Lisa F. Young/Dreamstime.com; p. 315: Courtesy of Vanguard, ©1995-2008 The Vanguard Group Inc., All rights reserved; p. 317: Courtesy of ING Group, © 2001-2008 ING Groep N.V., All rights reserved; p. 319: © Justin Lane/epa/Corbis; p. 322: Charles Gullung/zefa/Corbis; p. 323: Courtesy of Jamie Henthorn/Flickr; p. 325: Courtesy of AOL, © 2008 AOL LLC, All rights reserved; p. 328: Used with permission by David Wertheim; p. 330: Martin Allinger/Dreamstime.com; p. 331: Suprijono Suharjoto/Dreamstime. com.

Chapter 13 — p. 338: Courtesy of Matt Hintsa; p. 339: Courtesy of Atsushi Shibayama/Flickr; p. 339: Courtesy of JetBlue Airways; p. 340-341, 343, 347: Used with permission by Randy Glasbergen; p. 342: Robert Lerich/Dreamstime.com; p. 349: Used with permission by Mozy Inc.; p. 351: Used with permission by Hilton Hotels. © 2008 Hilton Hotels Corporation; p. 354: Tomasz Tulik/ Dreamstime.com; p. 357: Ben Blankenburg/iStockphoto; p. 358: Sean Locke/iStockphoto; p. 359: David H. Lewis/iStockphoto.

BLANK

Name Index

Pande, P. S., 400, 404
Pangarkar, N. 106, 108, 294, 302, 392
Paper Valley Hotel, 276
Parasuraman, A., 55, 335, 369, 370, 371, 373, 374, 376, 396, 403
Parkinson, S., 104, 106, 108
Patchell-Evans, David, 522
Payne, A., 327, 336, 337
PayPal, 92
Pearse, J., 250
Peninsula Academy, 264
Peppers, D., 192, 195, 336, 337, 408, 429
Peppiat, E., 250
Perry, David, 195
Personal Concierge International, 245
Peters, T. J., 422, 429
Pfeffer, J., 302
Phelps, Joseph E., 195
Pickens, M., 133
Pin, B. J., 55
Pinstorm, 182, 183
Pitta, D., 336
Pizza Hut, 98, 375
Plaza, Beatriz, 273
Pod Hotel, 65
Porter, M. E., 80
Prahlahad, C. K., 419, 429
Preble, J. F., 133
Prenshaw, P. J., 55
Priceline.com, 142, 149
PrimeTimeTables, 245
Procter and Gamble, 24, 62
Progressive Casualty Insurance Co., 51
Prudential, 173
Pullman, M. E., 273, 274

Q

Qantas Airlines, 183, 190, 320
Qbic, 65
Quan, X., 260
Quiring, K. N., 336

R

Rabkin, M. T., 213–214, 226, 423
Rainforest Café, 101
Rajendran, C., 404
Rajendran, G., 398
Raju, R., 398

Raman, Niranjan, 195
Rao, R. C., 167
Rao, V. R., 108
Rayport, L. F., 227
Red Hat, 185
Red Lobster (case), 502–503
Regency, 72, 73, 74, 75
Rego, L. L., 335
Reichheld, F. F., 195, 308, 309, 315, 335, 336
Reimer, A., 273
Reinartz, W. J., 335
Reñaca Resort, 118
Rentokil Initial, 59, 61
    RADAR, 61
Reppel, A. E., 336
Reynolds, D., 166
Reynolds, K. E., 55
Reynolds, K. L., 364
Riffaud, 245
Rigby, D. K., 336
Ringling Bros, 420
Ritz-Carlton Basics, 296
Ritz-Carlton Hotels Group, 288, 417
    Ritz-Carlton, 98, 296, 297, 350, 399
    Ritz-Carlton Gold Standards, 296
Riyadh Care Hospital, 291
Robson, S. K A., 274
Rodie, A. R., 226
Rogers, M., 336, 408, 429
Rohleder, T. R., 250
Roos, I., 336
Rosenbaum, M. S., 336
Rosencrance, L., 379
Rosenfeld, J., 31
Rossiter, J. R., 273
Roundtree, R. I., 226
Royal Bank of Canada, 190
Royal Flying Doctor Service, 113
Rubel, C., 108
Ruiz, F. J. M., 250
Rumford, Rodney L., 185
Russell, J. A., 273
Rust, R. T., 55, 316, 335, 384, 403
Rutgers University, 424
Ruyter, K. D., 302

S

Saks, 126, 133
Sakthivel, P. B., 398
Salentein Winery, 186
SAP, 182

Sarner, A., 335
SAS International Hotels, 180
Sasser, W. E, Jr., 133, 250, 308, 309, 409, 429
Scandinavian Airlines System, 44
Schefter, P., 335, 336
Schlesinger, L. L., 302
Schlesinger, L. A., 133, 408, 429
Schneider, B., 226, 302, 429
Schroeder, R., 404
Schwab, Charles, See also Charles, Schwab & Co., 316, 392
    Schwab's golf-rewards program, 184
Schwartz, T. A., 55, 226, 364
Schweikhart, S. B., 404
Schwepker, C. H., Jr., 302
Sealink British Ferries, 366
Second Life, 179, 185
Seddon, M., 250
Seiders, K., 133, 166
Sen, I., 335
Sergeant, A., 302
Severson, K., 245
Shane, S., 133
Shangri-La, 73, 74, 438, 439
Shankar, V., 336
Sharpe, A., 167
Shaw, Robert, 178
Shell, 190
Sher, P. J., 166
Sheraton, 74, 75, 120, 350
Shih, H. Y., 166
Shirks, A., 404
Shoemaker, S., 166
Shostack, G. L., 31, 55, 226
Shouldice Hospital (case), 492–501
Shultz, D. E., 99, 108
Siebel, 182
Siegel, Norman J., 41
Siguaw, J. A., 337, 404
Silverthorne, S., 185
Silvestro, R., 429
Simchi-Levi, D., 143
Simon, H., 150, 166
Singapore Airlines (SIA), 93, 281, 294, 378
    Singapore Airlines Raffles Class, 97
    Singapore Airline Suites, 42
Singapore General Hospital, 291
Singh, S., 335
Site59, 124
Skålén, P., 351, 364
Skogland, I.., 336
Smalley, K., 336

Whistler-Blackholm, 128
White, L., 364
Whiting, A., 133
Wiedmann, K. P., 336
Wielanga, D., 250
Wikipedia, 183, 185, 242
Willcox, S., 250
Williams, J. D., 189
Winklhofer, H., 133
Wirtz, J., 55, 108, 133, 166, 189,
    195, 226, 250, 271, 272, 273,
    274, 294, 302, 335, 355, 364,
    376, 392, 403, 437, 438, 453,
    475, 491, 525, 531, 534
WIZZIT Payments (Pty) Ltd
    (WIZZIT), 110, 111
Woo, K. S., 335
Wooden, J., 288, 302
Woods, Tiger, 173
Working Mother, 407
World Championship Indoor
    Windsurfing, 114

World Wide Web, 219
Wright, Lauren, 55, 537
Wujin, C., 364
Wynter, L., 166

X

Xerox Emirates, 291
Xia, L., 166

Y

Yahoo!, 142, 182, 183
Yale New Haven Children's Hospital, 41
Yanamandram, V., 364
Yankelovich, Partners, 178
Yates, JoAnne, 195
Yellow Pages, 124, 125
Yen, Chang-Hua, 31

Yotel Capsule Hotel, 65
Young "Sally" Kim, K., 155
Young, R. F., 46, 55
Young, S., 429
YouTube, 69, 103, 184, 185
Yum! Brands, 98

Z

Zahonik, Anthony, 384, 403
Zayre Corporation, 423
Zeithaml, V. A., 55, 164, 166, 226,
    316, 335, 355, 369, 370,
    371, 373, 374, 396, 403
Zemke, R., 348
Zimring, C., 260
Zuji, 124
Zurich, 39

Subject Index

BLANK